FINANCIAL INVESTIGATION and FORENSIC ACCOUNTING

Third Edition

FINANCIAL INVESTIGATION and FORENSIC ACCOUNTING

Third Edition

George A. Manning, Ph.D, CFE, EA

CRC Press
Taylor & Francis Group
Boca Raton London New York

CRC Press is an imprint of the
Taylor & Francis Group, an **informa** business

CRC Press
Taylor & Francis Group
6000 Broken Sound Parkway NW, Suite 300
Boca Raton, FL 33487-2742

First issued in paperback 2019

ISBN-13: 978-1-4398-2566-2 (hbk)
ISBN-13: 978-0-367-86434-7 (pbk)

Library of Congress Cataloging-in-Publication Data

Manning, George A.
  Financial investigation and forensic accounting / George A. Manning. -- 3rd ed.
    p. cm.
  Includes bibliographical references and index.
  ISBN 978-1-4398-2566-2 (hardcover : alk. paper)

  1. White collar crime investigation--United States. 2. Forensic accounting--United States. 3. Fraud investigation--United States. I. Title.
  HV8079.W47M35 2011   2010044043

Visit the Taylor & Francis Web site at
http://www.taylorandfrancis.com

and the CRC Press Web site at
http://www.crcpress.com

In loving memory of my wife, Lois E. Manning,
who passed away suddenly in 2002.
She was a very loving and devoted wife
and mother to our two children.

Table of Contents

Figures

Tables

Exhibits

Acknowledgment

My special thanks and appreciation to Cynthia Weeks for her assistance in research and writing this book. She spent many hours researching in the library and on the Internet, and performing secretarial duties.

About the Author

Dr. George A. Manning, PhD, CFE, EA, is retired from working as a fraud examiner, forensic accountant, and expert/summary witness for the Internal Revenue Service. He has a bachelor's degree in Business Administration from the University of Miami, Miami, FL, and holds MS and PhD degrees in Criminal Justice Administration from Lynn University, Boca Raton, FL. He is a Certified Fraud Examiner and is enrolled to practice before the Internal Revenue Service (Enrolled Agent). He has worked with various federal, state, and local law enforcement agencies. He has 22 years of experience in the fraud investigation and forensic accounting field. He currently does consulting work and works as an adjunct professor.

Economics of Crime

1

1.1 Introduction

Crime affects the economy in two primary ways. Microeconomic crime affects individuals and businesses. Macroeconomic crime affects local, national, and international economies. Individuals and businesses can easily understand the effect of crime in their everyday activities. However, most individuals and businesses have difficulty understanding the effect crime has upon the community, national, and international levels.

1.2 Cost Reality

The cost of crime on the economy in the United States is now at a staggering height. The outlook does not look any better. There is no real compensation for emotional and social harms done to members of a society by criminal acts. The average citizen would be shocked to know the actual costs. There are no consolidated figures as to the total cost of crime. However, if all the various costs were compiled into a consolidated figure, then they would surely be enormous. The cost of crime involves all of the following elements:

1. Law Enforcement. This encompasses the cost of training and maintaining a police department and all of its support staff, equipment, buildings, etc.
2. Crime Prevention. This involves all the community programs that try to help prevent crime. Some common programs are "Crime Stoppers," school programs, and other programs sponsored by local community tax dollars.
3. Drug Prevention and Rehabilitation. This involves both public and private financing. Both government and private organizations offer programs to prevent and rehabilitate drug and alcohol offenders. This costs money to both the taxpayers and the patients.
4. Incarceration. It costs taxpayers money to house, supervise, train, feed, clothe, and provide medical care for inmates in a jail or detention center.
5. Courts. The cost of operating and maintaining the court system costs the taxpayers tax dollars. It involves judges, court reporters, clerks, buildings, etc.
6. Prosecutors. The costs of employing prosecutors and their staffs, buildings, and all of the associated costs of operating and maintaining them are enormous, especially in large metropolitan areas.
7. Public Defenders. Many defendants are not able to afford defense attorneys; therefore, the taxpayers must foot the bill. This bill includes costs of defense attorneys, their staff, and all the costs of operating and maintaining them.

8. Hospitalization. Medical costs for criminals, victims, and those involved in the justice system are a significant item. With the increase in AIDS and other diseases, it has made this cost even more obvious.
9. Businesses. Businesses suffer losses when customers or employees steal from them. They have to raise prices or lay off employees because of thefts.
10. Insurance Companies. Individuals and businesses that have insurance file claims for losses that they suffer from crime. This, in turn, causes insurance companies to raise premiums to individuals and businesses.

The cost of crime can be very high. Some people say that some types of crimes do not cost society (e.g., illegal gambling and prostitution). You can see that it does cost society. Let us take an example of a simple case. A bookmaker takes bets from his bettors. It is illegal in his area. The bettors are not forced to place bets. They place wagers because they want to "place their money where their mouth is." Most bettors are middle class workers. The bookmaker pays off the winners and collects from the losers. When law enforcement makes an arrest after a considerable investigation, they must put the bookmaker in jail. The bookmaker usually posts bond or bail and is out after a short period of time. The book-maker claims poverty and must retain a public defender. The case goes to trial, and the bookmaker is found guilty. He is sentenced to 60 days in the county jail.

The cost to society in terms of money in this example is high. First, the bettors who placed the bets should not have placed bets since they were using their hard earned money that should have been used to pay their living expenses. It cost money to the taxpayers to pay the salaries and all supporting staff for the investigators to investigate the book-maker. In addition, it cost taxpayers' money to try the bookmaker in court. The judges and their staff have to draw salaries and pay for their expenses. It cost more taxpayers' money to house the bookmaker in jail. The taxpayer has to pay for food and medical costs while the bookmaker is in jail. Also, jailers and correction officers must be paid along with their benefits to guard the bookmaker while he is in jail. It costs taxpayers for the detention facilities. The public defender must be paid from public funds. One can see that it cost society in dollar terms, even though there is no violence. This example can apply to other "victimless" crimes, for example, traffic violations, prostitution, and other misdemeanors.

1.3 Microeconomics

This segment of economics deals with individuals and businesses. The primary effect is the direct loss of money or property by the victim. In most cases, the dollar amount of money or property can be determined after the commission of the crime. In other cases, this may not be true. There are a few crimes where the reputation of the victim is damaged. The victim usually suffers a loss. Any person or business can become a victim. The cost to the victim can be enormous or there can be no economic loss. The costs to the local community and the nation can be enormous when considering the total costs. The following examples of crimes show how victims can suffer a loss.

1.3.1 Arson

This crime can affect both the victim and the insurance company. If the victim has no casualty insurance coverage, then the business or individual will undoubtedly be put out of business or home if the owners do not have the capital to rebuild. If the victim has insurance, then the insurance company has to pay the claim. If the casualty is caused by the victim in order to collect insurance, then the insurance company can refuse to pay, and the victim will normally suffer the loss. In either case, one or the other, or both will realize a loss of property or money.

1.3.2 Bankruptcy Fraud

This crime affects the creditors of a business. They ship goods to a customer with the expectation of receiving payment on agreed terms. The customer diverts the goods elsewhere and does not make the payment. The creditor suffers a loss of not only the cost of the merchandise but also the gross profits. For small businesses, this can be devastating. They are usually not able to recover the losses. For larger businesses, they pass the loss on to other customers by raising their prices which could take weeks, months, or even years to recover.

1.3.3 Forgery and Uttering

This crime usually involves writing bad checks or cashing stolen checks. The amount of the loss is the amount of the check(s) involved. This crime also involves the criminal submitting false or forged documents to obtain a financial gain.

1.3.4 Larceny

Larceny is also called theft. It involves the criminal taking of property from a victim. The value of the property is the economic loss incurred by the victim.

1.3.5 Identity Theft

This crime involves using the identity of the victim to obtain financial gain. The criminal uses the victim's social security number and/or driver's license number to obtain credit. The criminal uses credit to obtain goods and services. The goods and services are not paid by the criminal. The creditors try to get the victim to pay the bills. Even though the victim does not have to pay the bills, it ruins the credit standing of the victim. In this case, the creditors suffer the economic loss.

1.3.6 Loan Sharking

The borrower pays interest at a very high rate. Usually, the interest is so high that the borrower can never get the principal reduced. As a result, the loan shark may use violence against the borrower which, in turn, results in the borrower getting further behind on his payments because of additional bills, for example, medical expenses. In the case of organized crime, the borrower may be forced to commit some other act, usually economic, which will either repay the lender or help the lender to get some economic advantage.

1.3.7　Credit Card Fraud

Most stolen credit cards are stolen before they reach the intended customer, although many credit card numbers are stolen by store cashiers or other store employees. In some cases, credit cards are counterfeited, sometimes using legitimate numbers. Stolen credit cards are used to purchase merchandise, which is fenced to an illegitimate vendor. They, in turn, sell the merchandise for cash. The card holder is not liable for the purchases if he reports the theft to the credit card company within 30 days. This requires the card holder to review his statements every month. After he discovers that his card is stolen, he is still out some money, usually $50 after the credit card company is notified. One organized crime group ships the goods overseas for resale. Credit card companies report that they lose multiple millions of dollars through credit card fraud. This is the primary reason for them charging high interest rates of 14% to 18% or even higher in some states.

1.3.8　Mail Order Operations

This crime occurs when a customer sends money in to a mail order house for the purchase of merchandise, and the mail order house does not send the merchandise, pocketing the money instead. This is called a "boiler room operation." Some states have required licensing of telemarketers. However, this has not prevented or deterred these operations. It has made it somewhat easier to track down corrupt telemarketers by law enforcement.

1.3.9　Medicare/Medicaid Fraud

This crime involves health professionals obtaining Medicare/Medicaid numbers from patients. The health professionals submit false claims to the government for goods and services not provided to the patient. This is fraud against the government.

1.3.10　Repair Fraud

This crime involves various types of repairmen who do not fix the item needing repair or charge for services not performed. The victim suffers a loss by the amount charged by the repairman.

1.3.11　Skimming/Embezzlement

Skimming involves the diversion of business receipts from the business, in effect stealing from the business and the government. The owner of the business is usually trying to hide money from either the tax collector or a partner. Embezzlement is the stealing of money from the employer. The economic loss is the amount of funds diverted or stolen.

1.3.12　Stock Manipulation

Stock manipulation is the transfer of stock between related entities or people in order to increase the market value. When the value is high, normally far above the market value, the stock is sold to other investors. Later, the value of the stock or bonds drops to the actual market values. The investor later suffers a loss measured by the cost less the amount realized when sold.

1.3.13   Swindling

This crime is often referred to as a "Con." The word "Con" is short for confidence. The criminal gains the confidence of a victim. When the "Con" man has a victim's confidence, then he/she will take money and/or property from the victim and disappear. The economic loss is determined by the amount of money and/or property lost by the victim.

1.3.14   Narcotics

The use of narcotics by consumers has devastating effects at both the micro- and macro-economic levels. This section deals with the microeconomic level. First, narcotic use diverts the consumer's funds for narcotics instead of the everyday living expenses. The narcotic user becomes addicted which drives the user to want to buy more and more. After a time, the narcotic user will use all his resources to purchase the illegal substance. "Crack cocaine" is one narcotic which will do this in a relatively short time. There is no such thing as a casual drug user. The narcotic user will eventually do anything to get funds to purchase more narcotics. The user's job performance drops and absenteeism increases. Eventually, the user will lose his job. In some instances, he will steal from his employer and may get caught. Narcotics users would rather pay for narcotics than pay their living expenses. When they lose their jobs, then they resort to borrowing and stealing from others.

The street pusher, who sells the narcotics to the consumer, is usually a user himself. If not, the pusher is trying to make money in order to get out of his economically depressed state. Street pushers have been found to be as young as 12 years old. In recent years, organized crime organizations like to have kids do their drug pushing because they do not serve time in jail or correctional centers. Secondly, they have an easy market for drugs because they can sell to elementary, middle, and high schools.

The drug kingpins reap the major profits from drug trafficking. They usually do not use or possess any drugs. They control and direct the shipments and distribution of drugs. A major part of the profits goes to the drug kingpin. This, in effect, causes the wealth of a community to become concentrated from the many to the few. In small communities, this can be readily evident by observing who the wealthy people are in the community and considering their occupation or business ventures. In metropolitan areas, this is not so evident because of the intermingling of wealthy people from both legal and illegal business ventures.

1.4   Macroeconomics

Macroeconomics involves the local community (city and/or county), regional, national, and international levels. Academia is interested in the economic aspects of crime. Law enforcement is also interested. Large metropolitan police departments monitor crime areas in order to move resources to combat it. Various federal agencies have economic or statistical units. These units keep track of various types of crimes.

1.5   Organized Crime

Organized criminal organizations operate at both the micro- and macroeconomic levels. Legally speaking, organized crime is defined as three or more individuals. Actually, they range from a handful to thousands of members. These individuals usually operate as a group. Their main goal is financial gain. In some organizations, power is another goal. Organized crime provides the biggest threat to local communities and the nation.

The magnitude of organized crime, as measured by its income, continues to be debated. James Cook, *Forbes Magazine* (1980), estimated that organized crime is a large and growing part of the national economy. He estimated that its income at the time was over $150 billion annually. Cook based his estimate on gross criminal income by types of activity taken from several original sources. However, Peter Reuter (1983) believed Cook's estimates were too high by a factor of 4. Cook asserted that organized crime was the second largest industry in the U.S. during 1979. The Wharton School of Economics conducted an independent study of the income of organized crime using new data sources on the number of persons engaged in organized criminal activities and on the average income of people involved with criminal organizations. The data were collected from law enforcement agencies and from a sample of 100 IRS tax cases involving members of criminal organizations. Wharton estimated that gross receipts ranged from a high of $106.2 billion to a low of $65.7 billion. It also estimated that net income ranged from a high of $75.3 to a low of $46.6 billion. Wharton indicates that organized crime is a major industry. Wharton's income estimated at $47 billion in 1986 equaled 1.13% of the U.S. gross national product. They estimated that organized crime employed at least 281,487 people as members and associates with the estimated number of crime-related jobs ranging to more than 520,000.

Manufacturing and mining operations are the only major industries which do not appear to be heavily infiltrated. A major concern with organized crime involvement in legitimate industries is that threats and intimidation may be used to limit competition and obtain excessive profits. The measurable result of such activities is higher prices. Taxes are not paid on much of the income generated by organized crime; implicitly, this results in higher taxes being imposed on the incomes of other citizens to make up for this loss in tax revenues. Based on the lower level estimate of organized crime income ($29.5 billion) and the assumption that taxes are not paid on 60% of this criminal income, it is estimated that personal taxes on other citizens were $6.5 billion higher than would be the case if all organized crime income were taxed.

Most studies often used about organized crime do not actually relate to organized crime. Most of the income estimates are for all types of criminal activity and include much more than organized crime. The other common characteristic of most studies is a focus on illegal activities, especially drugs and gambling. Less attention is paid to the other side of organized crime: its involvement in legitimate businesses and labor unions. As a result, part of the income of organized crime is not counted and part of its impact on society, through its infiltration of the legitimate economy, is missed. It is known that organized crime involvement in the legitimate economy is increasing. Previous studies were used and updated. In some cases, new data was obtained and used for the 1986 report to the President's Commission on Organized Crime.

1.6 Local Industries

In the local community, organized crime operates many businesses, legal and illegal. Organized crime likes to operate illegal activities in communities as follows:

- Prostitution
- Gambling
- Narcotics trafficking
- Trafficking in stolen goods
- Auto theft and repairs
- Extortion
- Illegal liquor making and/or distribution
- Trafficking in tobacco.

Local legal businesses where organized crime likes to operate are

- Construction
- Waste removal
- Garment industry
- Food processing, distribution, and retailing
- Hotels
- Bars
- Banking
- Business and personal services
- Legalized gambling
- Liquor retailing and wholesaling
- Entertainment
- Motor vehicle sales and repairs
- Real estate
- Other cash oriented businesses.

They like to operate these businesses for three reasons. First, they can launder their illegal profits through a legitimate business. Second, they can skim profits by various methods. Last, if organized crime can obtain a monopoly in the area, then they can get higher prices for their products and services. This results in greater profits.

1.6.1 Construction

Organized crime likes the construction industry, particularly in major metropolitan areas, because they can get profits through "ghost" employees, extortion, and control of materials. For contractors to get jobs, they must employ "ghost" (nonexistent) employees, pay kickbacks, and pay higher prices for raw materials. All of these costs are passed down to the consumer in the form of higher prices for goods and services, higher rents, higher taxes, and other costs.

1.6.2   Waste Removal

Organized crime affects the waste removal industry by either controlling labor and/or the dumping sites. Labor unions are a favorite target for organized crime since they can gain from exploiting labor. The labor is mostly uneducated; therefore, they are easy targets. Dumping sites are either owned by organized crime with excessive charges or are simply dumped at unsuspecting sites without the permission or knowledge of the property owners.

1.6.3   Motor Vehicle Sales and Repairs

Organized crime deals in motor vehicles in several ways. First, they steal vehicles and transport them to other states where they are sold to unsuspecting customers. Second, they like to use repair shops to sell parts from stolen cars that were previously obtained from "chop" shops. These parts are sold at "new" part prices.

1.6.4   Cash Businesses

Organized crime particularly targets cash businesses, for example, bars, restaurants, hotels, package stores, and convenience stores. First, they can easily launder their illegal profits. Second, they are susceptible to skimming and embezzlement. People who do not like to pay taxes particularly like cash businesses since records are not usually kept.

1.7   Data and Statistics

In the United States, crime statistics are compiled by the Federal Bureau of Investigation (FBI). The Uniform Crime Reporting (UCR) Program was conceived in 1929. In 1930, the FBI was tasked with collecting, publishing, and archiving those statistics. Today, the FBI publishes an annual statistical report called "Crime in the United States." The data is provided by more than 17,000 law enforcement agencies across the United States. It also publishes other annual reports, which address specialized facets of crime. The FBI also publishes specialized reports using the data from the UCR program. One of these specialized reports is "The Measurement of White Collar Crime Using Uniform Crime Reporting Data."

The UCR Annual Reports provide data as to:

- Murder and nonnegligent manslaughter
- Forcible rape
- Robbery
- Aggravated assault
- Burglary
- Larceny-theft
- Motor vehicle theft
- Arson

The UCR reports provide the number offenses in total, by state, and by age groups. The reports also provide data as to victims, number of arrestees, and cases closed. It must be kept in mind that the data provided are crimes reported to law enforcement. Many white collar crimes are not reported to law enforcement. Businesses who suffer losses from embezzlement sometimes do not report the crime. Instead they just fire the person. Individuals sometimes do not report offenses for various reasons.

1.7.1 National

Using the UCR reports, one can determine the economic loss. However, the economic loss is computed for the direct loss of property stolen. In general, the value of the property is determined by assigning fair market value to depreciated items and replacement costs to new or almost new items. However, credit cards and nonnegotiable instruments are submitted with no value associated with them. The economic costs of incarceration, trial, and imprisonment are not taken into consideration. For example, the economic loss due to embezzlement would be done by finding the number of embezzlements and the average value of funds taken. In 1999, the number of embezzlements was 21,356 reported. The average value was $9,254.75. The result is a loss of $197,644,441.00 (21,356 times $9,254.75) nationwide.

1.7.2 State

The UCR reports provide data by state. Using the data provided, one can extrapolate the loss by embezzlement at the state level. The results for Florida were $8,264,491.75 (893 times $9,254.75) statewide in 1999. In this illustration, the average loss for the state of Florida was not given so the national average was used. The highest crime state as reported by the UCR reports in 2002 was California, whereas Delaware had the smallest crime rate in 2002.

1.8 International Statistics

Most industrialized countries keep statistics on crime. The International Criminal Police Organization (INTERPOL) publishes annual International Crime Statistics. They maintain information on offenders, drug seizures, counterfeits, and stolen property. Their data comes from various national police agencies which are members of Interpol. At present, there are 166 member countries. The United Nations Office on Drugs and Crime publishes an annual report on drug production, trafficking, and consumption. Not all countries report. One reason is some countries do not keep statistics on crime and drugs.

1.8.1 International

Macroeconomics deals not only with national economic policies, but also with the international economic arena. This section discusses the international impact of organized crime. International organized crime is almost solely involved in narcotics trafficking; however, this is changing. Basic narcotic substances are produced in one country and exported to another country where they are sold for huge profits. A lot of the huge profits are returned to the country where the narcotic substances are produced. These profits are not only used to acquire wealth, but also to acquire power which can be almost as strong as the government itself.

1.9   Cocaine

Cocaine production has a great impact on South and Central American countries. Coca plants are grown, harvested, and sold to the drug lords who produce coca paste. They not only produce the coca paste but sometimes carry the production down to pure cocaine powder. The cocaine is shipped to other countries, principally the United States, where it is sold. The profits are then smuggled back to the country of origin where it is invested in the local economy.

1.9.1   Mexico

Mexico has become in recent years the largest supplier of cocaine and marijuana to the United States. The United States has complained to the Mexican Government that they are not doing enough to stop the drug trafficking and has even accused their law enforcement agencies of corruption. It was not until the brutal murder of Enrique Camarena, a U.S. DEA Agent, in February 1985, that the Mexican Government began getting some "heat." However, it was not until the murder of Excelsior columnist Manuel Buendia who was shot and killed that the Mexican Government began to take action. In June 1990, the Mexican Government finally acted, arresting the Chief of Domestic Intelligence, Jose Antonio Zorrilla Perez, and four other members of the National Security Directorate, a combination of the CIA and the FBI. Prosecutors charged that Zorrilla killed Buendia because the reporter learned Zorrilla was protecting top drug traffickers. The allegations of drug trafficking or protection involved a former Defense Minister, two brothers of the governor of Baja, California, and the cousin of a former president. In addition, they arrested a drug kingpin known as the godfather, Miguel Angel Felix Gallardo. It is well known that drug profits went not only to these officials, but to others who have not been identified. Mexico has provided a classic case that drug profits corrupt public officials at all levels.

1.9.2   Costa Rica

Even though Costa Rica is not a producer of cocaine, it does have means to be an attractive "money launderer" of cocaine profits. In addition, it serves as a transshipment point from South America to the United States. The United States warned Costa Rican officials of their position of being a "laundering alternative." A Costa Rican commission in 1988 concluded that drug traffickers influenced all three branches of the government. Former government officials were accused of links to drug traffickers and even some were charged and arrested. A drug trafficker, Roberto Fionna, was arrested who previously was able to get legal residence through his political connections.

1.9.3   Guatemala

Guatemala is a big producer of opium poppies (the raw material for heroin) and a transshipment point for cocaine bound for the United States. Mexican drug traffickers who were lining up with left-wing guerrillas to protect growers of poppies controlled large geographical areas. This resulted in the Guatemalan police's refusal to enter these areas. In recent years, Guatemala has become active in cocaine production, and corruption is increasing.

1.9.4   Honduras

Honduras is an important transshipment point for Colombian cocaine. It is also a growing center for money laundering. In 1989, Honduran authorities arrested Juan Ramon Matta Ballesteros, a cocaine kingpin, and expelled him to the United States. This has sparked anti-government and anti-American demonstrations. The corruption of public officials is not countrywide but has been limited to area or district level military officials.

1.9.5   Panama

Prior to the United States' invasion of Panama in December 1989, General Manuel Noriega was indicted by U.S. District Courts for drug trafficking and money laundering. Top Panamanian military officers were living far above their means. This source of wealth was from drug trafficking or money laundering. It was alleged that General Manuel Noriega had stashed $200 million in various bank accounts. It was discovered that when the Bank of Credit and Commerce International was seized by U.S. law enforcement agents in the United States, nearly half of the assets in the Panamanian branch belonged to General Noriega. The United States invaded Panama in December 1989. The findings have not been fully disclosed at this time; however, newspaper accounts have indicated that corruption was very widespread.

1.9.6   Bolivia

Hundreds of thousands of Bolivians are involved in growing, making, or distributing cocaine. Drugs account for $300 to $500 million of the nation's economy. The total exports total only $600 million from legal goods or services. Vast areas of Bolivia are not patrolled by the police so that traffickers are able to fly cocaine to Colombia or Brazil without any interference. Corruption is rampant. The right-wing government was installed by the military in 1980. They were backed by drug traffickers. The Bolivian Interior Minister at that time was under indictment in Miami on drug trafficking charges.

1.9.7   Brazil

Brazil is a vast country. Unguarded borders and underpaid police have resulted in alarming increases in shipments and processing operations. Colombian cartel bosses have for many years spent vacations there and began their work in the jungles as far back as 1984. The growing of coca is greatly increasing. It is expected that Brazil will become a major coca producer in the years ahead.

1.9.8   Ecuador

This country is a minor producer of coca. However, it is becoming an important center for dug trafficking and money laundering. Shipments to the United States and Europe from Ecuador have had cocaine hidden in various merchandise such as handicrafts, canned goods, and wood products. Officials have reported that Colombian drug traffickers launder from $200 to $400 million through Ecuador every year. Newspapers have expressed concern about the corruption of government officials by drug cartels. In one case, two judges signed an order for the release of a drug trafficker from jail. The judges fled when people made an outcry. One judge was captured with about $20,000 in cash. The other judge and drug trafficker are still at large.

1.9.9   Peru

The most potent coca plants are produced in Peru. Most of the coca plants are grown in the Huallaga Valley, which is northeast of Lima. This area is controlled by Colombian cocaine producers and distributors. In addition, the drug traffickers have formed alliances with the guerrillas, The Shining Path, to unite their effort to seize power in the area. They have become so violent that government officials are unable to appear in the region. It is estimated that there are at least one to two killings a day as a result of narcotics trafficking. Cocaine brings from $700 million to $1.2 billion every year to the Peruvian economy, while legal exports bring in $2.5 billion.

1.9.10   Colombia

This country has become the cocaine industry processing and exporting center. Most of the raw materials come from remote areas of Peru and Bolivia. There are two areas where major drug traffickers have formed cartels. One is located in Medellin and the other in Cali. The Medellin cartel has gained more prominence than the Cali cartel; however, they have been known to work together in many aspects. These cartels have gained such wealth, influence, and power that they have considerable control over the affairs of Colombia in both political and economic matters. After the killing of a presidential candidate in Colombia, the Colombian government pronounced war against the Colombian drug cartels. As the war against the drug cartels escalated, the Colombian government began to make raids and seizures of cartel members' property. One piece of property that was owned by Gonzalo Rodriguez Gacha covered one city block. The mansion was almost entirely constructed of marble and had gold fixtures in the bathrooms with toilet paper that was designed with nude women on each sheet. Even lesser men of authority had equivalent estates. Gacha was finally cornered and shot to death. The other cartel members fled to the jungles. The cartel members still control much of the economy and exercise political power. Yet, one can read on an almost daily basis that the Colombian government is still actively involved in a "war" with the drug cartels. It is believed that the cartel attacked the Justice Building and killed many of the country's top judges. Many bombings are attributed to the cartels. In essence, this is a country under siege.

1.9.11   Bahamas

The Bahamas is an ideal way station between South and Central America and the United States. It is estimated that over half of the cocaine shipments from South America go through the Bahamas. Corruption in high offices has surfaced for many years. One convicted drug trafficker testified in South Florida that he paid Prime Minister Pindling $100,000 per week. Former Prime Minister Lynden O. Pindling has been the subject of many federal grand jury investigations and official inquiries in the Bahamas; however, Pindling has never been charged in the United States, and corruption proceedings in the Bahamas are rare. Bahamian police have been cooperative in the anti-drug activities. Yet, many U.S. law enforcement officers confirm that the Bahamian police are being corrupted by drug traffickers. They take bribes from drug traffickers and at the same time inform on some of them.

1.9.12 Cuba

Castro prosecuted seven high ranking officials for helping the Medellin Cartel leader Pablo Escobar for shipping cocaine to Florida. Four of the conspirators were executed. This is the first time Castro acknowledged any official involvement in cocaine trafficking. In 1982, the U.S. Attorney in Miami indicted two members of the Central Committee of the Cuban Communist party for marijuana trafficking. A former Panamanian official testified before Congress that Castro mediated a dispute between General Manuel Noriega and the Medellin cocaine cartel.

1.9.13 Middle East

The Middle East is a source of morphine base for the Sicilian and U.S. Mafia. Most of this morphine base comes from Turkey, Lebanon, and Pakistan. The impact on the local economies of these countries is limited so far. It does pump currency into their economy. On the other hand, no reliable economic data are available. Other criminal activities in this area involve gun and weapon smuggling and sales, exploiting of foreign labor, smuggling of various consumer goods, and white slavery.

1.9.14 Sicily

Like Colombia, Sicily has become a country under siege by organized crime, the Sicilian La Cosa Nostra. The Sicilian Mafia had a governing commission, which was created by the American Mafia leader, "Lucky" Luciano. But unlike their American counterparts, they began to fight among themselves. The Corlenesse Family began to get the upper hand. One family head, Thomasa Buscetta, had to leave Sicily and flee to Brazil. The principal activity of the Sicilian Mafia was the control of the heroin trade. They imported the morphine base from Turkey and other Mideastern countries. They processed the morphine base into heroin using French chemists. The heroin was smuggled to the United States where it was sold on the street. The profits were enormous. The money was smuggled back to Sicily and Switzerland through Bermuda. The Sicilian Mafia began to control Sicily. Judges and police were killed; in fact, anyone who tried to investigate their activities were killed. They had control of the economy. With the capture and trial of Buscetta, Sicilian authorities began taking back control; yet, today the Sicilian authorities are still battling the Mafia using military tactics against their heroin trafficking activities.

1.9.15 Far East

There are various organized crime organizations in the Far East. In Japan, there is the "Yakuza." In China, there are the "Triads" with a long history expanding many centuries. In Indochina, there are various criminal organizations. One of the major producers of heroin is a place called the "Golden Triangle," which encompasses an area around Laos, Cambodia, and Burma. All Asian criminal organizations are involved in drug production and trafficking, extortion, protection rackets, armed robberies, burglaries, gambling, prostitution, and slavery. Prostitution has grown to massive proportions in Thailand in recent years with AIDS and other sexually transmitted diseases on the rise. In various parts of the countryside, these criminal groups control the local government or have become the local government as provincial lords.

1.10 Summary

The economic costs of crime affect both individuals and the community. It also affects national governments. In some instances, governments are controlled or manipulated by criminal organizations. Some national economies are dependent upon illegal activities, that is, drugs, in order to survive. One important factor to remember is that there is no victimless crime. Crime costs everyone either directly or indirectly.

Financial Crimes

2

2.1 General

There are many types of financial crimes. Some of these crimes can be solved in a short period of time while others take long periods of time. The time required directly relates to the complexity of the crime. Complex financial crimes consume a large amount of time to gather enough financial records to support a conviction. However, all financial crimes have one common factor, greed. Most people are honest and trustworthy when the temptation is not present. There are three factors that are present in financial crimes: something of value must be present, an opportunity to take something of value without being detected must be present, and there must be a perpetrator who is willing to commit the offense.

The most common financial crimes are shown below. The federal statutes are shown for those crimes that are federal offenses. Many financial crimes are not directly an offense at the federal level, but may become indirectly an offense. Some federal statutes place some state crimes under federal jurisdiction when the criminal crosses state line(s).

2.2 Arson

Arson is defined by law as the malicious and willful burning of another person's dwelling house or outhouse. The crime is not primarily concerned with the resulting property damage but rather with the danger to which the occupants of the dwelling were exposed by the criminal act. Dwelling has a broad definition, encompassing any building. Setting fire to timberlands, prairies, or grasslands is a statutory offense. The burning must be willful or malicious to be arson. A person who burns a dwelling while committing a felony, such as burglary, is guilty of arson regardless of the absence of any intent to set the fire or to destroy the house. It is essential to the crime of arson that there be an actual burning of some part of the property. Mere scorching, smoking, or discoloration of the building without any charring, destruction, or actual burning is not sufficient to be a crime of arson. Arson is considered a felony in all states. 18 USC 81 prohibits arson of any federal installation, structure, and personal property.

2.3 Bankruptcy Fraud

The prime characteristic of bankruptcy fraud is the hiding or nondisclosure of assets. This leaves little or no means of recovery by creditors. This is called "bust out." "Bust outs" have become more prevalent in recent years, especially in high inventory turnover businesses. This crime usually requires identification of inventory purchased, sold, and "carted" off. Inventory is usually shipped to the enterprise premises. Afterward, it is transported to another enterprise premise, which is controlled by the same principals. There, it is sold, and the profits are diverted to the principals. Normally, a corporate shield is in place to hide the principals involved in the scheme. Organized crime takes over a business not to keep it alive and healthy but to force the company into bankruptcy after making a quick cash profit. Individuals commit bankruptcy fraud by not disclosing or hiding assets from the trustee.

Bankruptcy fraud is primarily a federal crime under 18 USC 151 through 157. It prohibits any debtor from concealing assets, making false oaths or claims, or bribing any custodian, trustee, marshal, or other officers of the court charged with the control or custody of property (18 USC 152). It prohibits any person who knowingly or fraudulently appropriates any property to a person's own use, embezzles, spends, or transfers any property or secrets or destroys any document belonging to the estate of the debtor (18 USC 153). It is bankruptcy fraud if a person devises or schemes to defraud creditors (18 USC 157).

2.4 Bribery

This is a crime of offering and acceptance of money or favors for some kind of preferential treatment or to influence another party for such treatment whether in public service or private business. A problem in investigating bribery or kickbacks is the difficulty in tracing it back through books and records if they exist at all. If the payment is uncovered, a problem arises as to locating who actually received the payment. To constitute this crime, the thing of value must be given with the intent of influencing official conduct. The acceptance of a gift without corrupt prior intent is not bribery. The offense of bribery includes both the acts of offering or giving and the accepting or receiving, thereby rendering the giver as well as the receiver criminally liable. The offeror is guilty even if the bribe is refused. It is not required that the act for which the bribe was given be accomplished. Federal Statute 18 USC 201 prohibits anyone to directly or indirectly corruptly give, offer, or promise anything of value to any public official or person with the intent to:

1. Influence any official act.
2. Influence such public official to commit or aid in committing, or allow any fraud, or make opportunity for such commission on the United States.
3. Induce such public official or person to do or omit to do any action in violation of lawful duty.

2.5 Loan Sharking

Loan sharking is the lending of money at higher rates than the law allows. Many people get involved with loan sharks. Gamblers borrow in order to pay gambling losses; narcotics users borrow to purchase drugs; and businessmen borrow when legitimate credit channels are closed. Loan sharks menace both white and blue collar workers as well as small and large corporations. Employees have agreed to disclose corporate secrets, leave warehouses unlocked, steal securities, ship stolen goods, and pass along information about customers, which sets the business up for burglaries. Officers of both small and large corporations are forced to turn over control of their companies to organized crime.

Loan sharking is identified as Extortionate Credit Transactions under federal statutes as well as many state statutes (18 USC 891 through 894). The elements of extortionate credit transactions are:

1. The extension of credit would be unenforceable through civil judicial processes against the debtor.
2. The extension of credit was made at a rate of interest in excess of 45% per annum.
3. The extension of credit was collected or attempted to be collected by extortionate means.
4. The interest or similar charges exceeded $100.

Loan shark's funds come from organized crime lieutenants that charge rates of 5% to 6% per week. The lieutenant has to pay from 1% to 3% per week. Sometimes the rates to the public reach 20% weekly. This is called a 6 for 5 loan, which means for every $5 borrowed, $6 is required to be paid weekly. The loan shark is usually more interested in getting interest than principal. When the borrower defaults on the loan, the loan shark resorts to force against the borrower or his family so that a borrower hesitates to report his dilemma to the authorities.

2.6 Credit Card Fraud

Credit card fraud is a multimillion-dollar business, which hurts business and the public. Most credit card fraud is controlled by organized crime. The scheme is a classic pattern. Credit cards are stolen, fenced, and sent elsewhere. Generally, the credit cards are stolen before the credit cardholder is able to report its disappearance, or before the issuing company is able to warn its subscribers of the theft so that they can refuse to honor them. Credit cards are often obtained in the following ways:

1. Credit card is stolen in the delivery process.
2. Credit cards are stolen in the printing process or duplicated.
3. Credit cards are stolen when returned to the issuer when they are refused or were undeliverable.
4. Credit cards are sometimes stolen on the street like cash or checks.
5. Business employees deliberately "forget" to return credit cards to their customers.
6. Credit cards are counterfeited.
7. Credit card numbers are copied from legitimate customers and used to make purchases.

A person with intent to defraud the issuer or a person or organization providing money, goods, services or anything else of value, uses, for the purpose of obtaining money, goods, services, or anything of value, without the consent of the cardholder is committing credit card fraud. This is fraud by the customer. Credit card fraud is also committed by businesses. Any person who uses a credit card to defraud an issuer or cardholder to acquire money, goods, services, or anything of value is committing credit card fraud. Federal Statute 15 USC 1644 as well as many state statutes prohibits the fraudulent use of credit cards. The federal statute prohibits:

1. The use of credit cards by any person who knowingly uses or conspires to use any counterfeit, fictitious, altered, forged, lost, stolen, or fraudulently obtained credit cards to obtain money, goods, services, or anything of value aggregating $1000 or more.
2. The transportation, attempted or conspired, in interstate or foreign commerce of any counterfeit, fictitious, altered, forged, lost, stolen, or fraudulently obtained credit card knowing it to be same.
3. Anyone who knowingly receives, conceals, uses, or transports money, goods, services, or anything of value from the use of credit cards.
4. Anyone who knowingly furnishes money, property, services, or anything of value through the use of fraudulent credit cards.

The federal statute actually prohibits anyone who receives, gives, or transports goods, services, and other consideration through the use of fraudulent credit card use in addition to the fraudulent use of credit cards per 18 USC 1029.

2.7   Prostitution and Pandering

Prostitution is the selling of oneself or another for purposes of sexual intercourse, debauchery, or other immoral acts for monetary gain. A panderer is one who solicits clients for a prostitute, usually called a pimp. Their clients usually pay in cash, which is shared between the prostitute and the pimp. Organized crime is often involved. Credit cards have become acceptable. This is especially true in operations called escort services. Records are usually not maintained for very long. There are two types of prostitutes. Those called "street walkers" are one type, while "call girls" are the other type. "Street walkers" get this name because they walk along the street to solicit clients. "Call girls" use referrals from friends, associates, and pimps. Many call girls rely on repeat clients. Many prostitutes are used to steal from clients. Organized crime makes huge profits from prostitution.

Most states have statutes which prohibit prostitution and pandering. The Federal Statute (18 USC 2421) prohibits anyone who transports any individual in interstate or foreign commerce with the intent that such individual engages in prostitution or in any sexual activity. Section 2422 prohibits anyone to persuade, induce, entice, or coerce any individual to travel interstate to engage in prostitution or any sexual activity. Section 2423 prohibits the transportation of minors to travel interstate for prostitution or sexual activity. A minor is defined as anyone under 18 years of age.

2.8   Fencing

This involves the purchase of stolen goods by someone from a thief. In general, this involves organized crime figures stealing large quantities of goods, usually from hijacked trucks, ships, or planes, and then distributing and selling the merchandise.

1. Federal Statute 18 USC 2113(c) prohibits anyone who receives, possesses, conceals, stores, barters, sells, or disposes of any property, money, or anything of value which has been taken or stolen from a bank, credit union, or savings and loan association.

2. Federal Statute 18 USC 2114(b) prohibits anyone who receives, possesses, conceals, stores, barters, sells, or disposes of any property or money or anything of value which has been taken or stolen from the U.S. Postal Service.

The federal statutes are limited to the fencing of personal property that is stolen from government control or financial institutions.

2.9   Mail Order Operations

These operations involve fraudulent schemes of advertising products in the media such as magazines, newspapers, radio, or television. Customers send money to the mail order house. The mail order house keeps the money but does not ship the merchandise. This is called a "boiler room" operation. Sometimes, operators use high pressure telephone solicitors who call and persuade with statements like, "You'll miss out on this great deal if you don't buy now." Or they might say, "This deal is too good to pass up." The most common characteristic in this kind of fraud is that you cannot reach them later because the telephone is disconnected or the address is no longer valid. There are three basic federal statutes which address this type of fraud. They are:

1. 18 USC 2325 which prohibits anyone from conducting a plan, program, promotion, or campaign to induce someone to purchase goods or services or participate in a contest or sweepstakes through the use of the telephone.
2. 18 USC 1341 prohibits anyone to scheme or defraud anyone by obtaining property or any means of false or fraudulent pretenses, representations, or promises through the use of mail service by the postal service.
3. 18 USC 1343 prohibits anyone to scheme, defraud, or obtain money or property by means of false pretenses, representations, or promises through the use of wire, radio, or television communication in interstate or foreign commerce.

2.10   Pornography

This industry includes production, distribution, and sale of sex novels, magazines, photographs, stag films, and other sex-related items. Most of these items can be purchased in adult bookstores. Manuscripts are purchased from individuals for a minimal price and sent to a printing firm for large volume printing. In the case of video or films, the master negatives or videos are purchased from a producer and put into mass production. The books, videos, and films are sold to adult bookstores through shell corporations for legal insulation. Payments are not always paid to the printing and production firms once the books, videos, and films are delivered.

Organized crime usually does not directly own the retail adult bookstores. When they do own these stores, they hire employees to actually operate the stores for a salary. In some areas where adult bookstores are illegal, hard core material is generally sold "under the counter" and only to those customers who are not suspected to be law enforcement officers.

Another attraction of the adult bookstores is the peep show. This is a viewing machine where a customer can see a stag video or film. Each film or video is usually 12 minutes in length and the customer is required to drop a quarter for every twelve-minute segment. 18 USC 2251 prohibits any person to employ, use, persuade, induce, entice, or coerce any minor to engage in or transport any minor in interstate with the intent to have such minor engage in sexually explicit conduct for the purpose of producing any visual depiction of such conduct. 18 USC 2258 prohibits the importation of child pornography.

2.11   Gambling

Gambling attracts organized crime. Large gambling operations require a staff to run such an operation. Organized crime in large cities controls gambling operators. Gambling involves betting on sports events, lotteries, off track racing, large dice games, and illegal casinos. Most large gambling operations have a sophisticated organization that ranges from the operator who takes bets from customers through people who pick up money and betting slips, from people in charge of particular areas or districts, to the main office or bank. The profits move through channels so complex that even most people working for the organization do not know the identity of the leader. The uses of telephone systems have kept the bookmaker remote from the district or area management.

Independent bookmakers have joined organized crime operations for the following reasons:

1. Organized crime syndicates have resources for backing all bets so the independent operator does not hedge his bets or reinsure bets through a "layoff" operation.
2. Independent operators can handle more bettors.
3. Bookmakers does not need to work on the streets taking bets.
4. The bookmakers no longer handle many telephone bets, which could alert police.
5. The bookmakers have legal services and connections available to them.
6. The bookmaker has a territorial assignment which minimizes conflicts with other bookies.

18 USC 1955 prohibits anyone who conducts, finances, manages, supervises, directs, or owns all or part of an illegal gambling business. The gambling activities must also be illegal under state law or any political subdivision and involve five or more people. It does not apply to gambling activities, for example, bingo, lottery, or similar games of chance, by an exempt organization as defined by the Internal Revenue Code, Section 501(c) if no part of the gross receipts inures to the benefit of a private member or employee of the organization.

Bettors usually do not know the location of the betting operation, but the bookmaker advises the bettor of the telephone numbers at which bets can be placed. The bettor is later contacted by telephone for collection and payment. The bookie usually makes 10% before paying off winners, expenses, and commissions to runners and solicitors.

Projections of income should be based upon gambling records seized by law enforcement on the number of days of operations shown in the records. Bookmakers do not keep records for any great length of time, usually about one or two weeks. Gains from this activity will usually require an indirect method of proving income.

2.12   Skimming/Embezzlement

Skimming is the act of diverting business receipts to one's own personal use. Officers or owners of the business enterprise can only do this. Embezzlement is diverting funds or receipts of the business by an employee. Cash businesses are very susceptible to both skimming and embezzlement. Cash businesses include bars, nightclubs, grocery stores, laundry mats, coin operated machines, liquor stores, etc. In most cases, funds skimmed or embezzled usually cannot be traced from the business enterprise to the individuals. An indirect method of proving income is usually required. 18 USC 641 prohibits any person who embezzles, steals, purloins, or knowingly converts to his use or the use of another, without proper authority, who sells, conveys, or disposes of any record, voucher, money, or anything of value that belongs to the United States or any department or agency thereof.

2.13   Labor Racketeering

Labor unions provide many methods for illicit gains.

1. Kickbacks from employers for favorable contracts and labor peace are common, as is extortion.
2. The unions can provide a vehicle for embezzlement. Organized crime syndicates use excessive or fictitious salaries or expenses, nonworking associates, or personal work done by union officers or employees. Professional or legal services are used to benefit union officials or employees. Sometimes they make donations to organizations to benefit a union official or employee.
3. Welfare and pension funds provide vehicles for kickbacks from insurance agents and organized crime investments and loans.

The audit program and techniques are many when dealing with union racketeering. There are various federal statutes which deal with the various facets of labor racketeering. They are:

a. 18 USC 1027. This section prohibits a pension plan administrator from making false statements or concealing facts or information relating to pension plans that are covered by the Employee Retirement Income Security Act of 1974 as amended.
b. 18 USC 664. This section prohibits any person who embezzles, steals, or unlawfully or willfully abstracts or converts to his own use or the use of another any money, funds, securities, premiums, credit, property, or other assets of any employee welfare benefit plan or employee pension benefit plan.
c. 18 USC 1954. This section prohibits any administrator, officer, trustee, custodian, counsel, agent, or employee to offer, accept, or solicit any fee, kickback, commission, gift, loan, money, or anything of value with the intent to influence any action or decision with respect to employee pension or benefit plans. Also, it is unlawful for anyone to offer, solicit, kickback, give any commission, gift, loan, money, or anything of value to influence the action or decision of a plan administrator, trustee, etc.

2.14   Stock Fraud and Manipulation

Some criminals use stock and bond fraud schemes to make illicit gains. They use counterfeit stock certificates as collateral on loans. They set up dummy corporations to sell worthless stock in "boiler room" operations. A legitimate corporation can be taken over and sold back and forth between insiders so as to highly inflate the market price of the stock. Then the stock is sold at highly inflated prices, the company is abandoned, and the stock is allowed to drop to the correct market value. Stock and bond fraud is a complex and sophisticated area that requires an extremely detailed investigation and analysis. The investigation requires analysis of transactions before, during, and after the scheme to determine the trends.

The federal statutes that deal with securities fraud include:

a. 18 USC 513. This section prohibits anyone from making, uttering, or possessing counterfeit securities of any state, political subdivision, or organization.
b. 18 USC 2314. This section prohibits the transporting, transmitting, or transfer of securities when anyone knows that the securities have been stolen, converted, or taken by fraud.

2.15   Narcotics

The sale of narcotics functions like a well-organized large corporation. It involves numerous people from all levels. The large amount of profits and the international connections necessary for long term narcotic supplies can only be supplied by an organized crime organization. There are various types of narcotics which come from various parts of the world. Heroin comes from Turkey in the Middle East and the "Golden Triangle" in Southeast Asia. Cocaine comes from Central and South America. Synthetic drugs are made in the United States and Canada. Organizations involved in distribution are loosely knit for the most part and involve individuals of all walks of life. The profits from narcotics are enormous. Federal statutes, which address drug trafficking, are listed under Title 21 of the United States Code (USC). The principal sections are:

848. Continuing Criminal Enterprise is any person who occupies a position of organizer, supervisor, or any management position with five or more other people who engage in illegal drug manufacturing, distribution, and sale, and obtains substantial income or resources.
858. This section prohibits anyone who manufactures or transports any material, including chemicals that create a substantial risk to human life.
860. This section prohibits the manufacturing and/or sale of controlled substances in or near schools and colleges within 1000 feet.
952. This section prohibits the importation of controlled substances.

2.16   Racketeering

Racketeering, in the past, has been hard to define. In 1968 when the Omnibus Control and Safe Street Act was passed, it defined racketeering as any unlawful activity by members of a highly organized, disciplined association engaged in supplying illegal goods and services. In 1970, Congress passed the Racketeer Influenced and Corrupt Organization statute (RICO), which has become the centerpiece of federal and most state law proscribing organized criminal activity. A pattern of racketeering activity requires at least two acts of racketeering activity. Racketeering activity means almost any illegal act such as gambling, murder, kidnapping, robbery, drug trafficking, etc. It encompasses any individual, organization, corporation, union, or group of associated individuals. RICO was not used very much until the late 1970s and the early 1980s when many organized crime figures were indicted and convicted of racketeering. When the conviction rates soared, district and U.S. attorneys became more aggressive. Now, RICO indictments are becoming more common. However, convictions are not increasing as much as the indictments. The major reason is the lack of evidence, particularly in the form of financial data. The RICO act provides for the use of financial data in prosecutions and forfeitures. Section 1963 of Title 18 reads as follows:

> In lieu of a fine otherwise authorized by this section, a defendant who derives profits or other proceeds from an offense may be fined not more than twice the gross profits or other proceeds.
> (b) Property subject to criminal forfeiture under this section includes
>   (1) Real property including things growing on, affixed to, and found in land
>   (2) Tangible and intangible personal property, including rights, privileges, interests, claims, and securities

Clearly financial data is a major element in these criminal cases. In some instances, the gross profits are more than the net assets of the criminal or the criminal enterprise. In other cases, the fines or penalties are less than the gross profits of the illegal enterprise. This will put any criminal enterprise out of business if there is a conviction since forfeitures are based on gross profits instead of fines and penalties.

2.17 Continuing Criminal Enterprise

This is defined by federal statute under 21 USC 848. Many states have adopted variations of this statute as well. It defines continuing criminal enterprise as any person who commits three or more felonies with five or more other persons with respect to whom such person occupies a position of organizer, a supervisory position, or any other position of management and who obtains substantial assets or resources from these acts. This person is guilty of engaging in continuing criminal enterprise. The elements of this offense are:

1. A person has committed three or more felonies.
2. The person is in a supervisory capacity.
3. The person has five or more people working for him in some illegal capacity.
4. The person has acquired substantial assets or financial resources.

Title 21 USC 855 repeats the fines as stated in Title 18 USC 1963, that is "In lieu of a fine otherwise authorized by this section, a defendant who derives profits or other proceeds from an offense may be fined not more than twice the gross profits or other proceeds."

2.18　Nonprofit Organization Fraud

This type of fraud is primarily a tax fraud even though other types of fraud are also committed. In some cases, the victims do not know that they have been defrauded, while in other cases, the victim suffers both great financial and emotional losses. The Internal Revenue Service, as well as many state laws, allow various types of organizations to operate without paying taxes, obtaining permits and licenses, and exempt from various laws and regulations. Religious institutions, social clubs, paternal organizations, and various charities operate to help or benefit its members or the community in which it operates. These nonprofit organizations are very beneficial to members and the community; however, there are individuals who operate or control these organizations for their own benefit. It is illegal for individuals to operate these nonprofit organizations for their sole benefit. As a case in point, bingo operations are legal in most states when it benefits the nonprofit organization that is sponsoring it. However, some bingo operations are conducted for the sole benefit of operators, which is illegal. Social clubs operate bars and restaurants for the benefit of its club members. However, some social clubs operate for profit, which benefits the operators. After the terrorist attack on September 11, 2001, it was discovered that nonprofit organizations financed terrorist activities. The Patriot Act was passed in October 2001. It made financing terrorist organizations illegal under Section 2332d of USC 18.

2.19　Corrupt Churches

Churches and other religious organizations are exempt from federal and state taxes. These organizations do not pay property, sales, or income taxes. However, there are individuals and criminal organizations that like using a church "cover" to obtain profits and gains for their own benefit. There are three facets of an abusive church. First, the church appears to be an attractive group of motivated, high-principled Christians or other religious sect. They want to talk to you. They want you to be part of their church. The rank and file of its membership sees the second facet. It is a facet of discipline and authority. The word of the leader is law. No questioning is allowed. The leader is always demanding more from you: more commitment to the church or group, more obedience to the leader's directives, more financial sacrifices, more separation from friends and family, more adulation of the leader. Its inner core of leadership sees the third facet. It is a facet of excess. The leader, his immediate family, and his inner, favored group lead a life of open or secret extravagance. The signs of a corrupt church are:

1. The church is God's special, and perhaps only, true church on earth at this time. You may be called upon to make great sacrifices now, but they will be worth it, because not to join the church is to miss out on your chance to be in God's face or favor.
2. The human leader is the link to God. He is the most important person on earth. His interpretation of the Bible or similar religious literature is the only correct one. The leader never wants any criticism. He denounces any criticism as the product of a negative attitude.

3. The leadership attempts to control your personal life. The leader sets forth his own rules and regulations. You are told what to eat, wear, live, marry, divorce, raise your children, etc.

4. The member is no longer responsible for his/her self. The leader tells the member what is right and wrong. The member has no mind or conscience of his own. The member becomes confused by contradictory attitudes, and strives to subjugate himself to the church.

5. The church is the only reality. True spirituality and obedience to God are found only in this church. The rest of society is Satan's world of vanity and deceit. The member will find himself less able to function "in the world," but more at home "in the church." The member will move to church headquarters, live in church accommodations, work for a church-owned business, spend spare time in church activities, and be friends with only church members. The member's life is totally consumed by the church.

6. The church is isolated. They only want to build and maintain membership, improving its image in society, and gratifying the whims of the leadership. The church wants to keep its financial affairs secret. The church does all it can to avoid newspaper reporters so that they will not publish "gross lies and distortions."

7. The church is a prison. Once in the church, the member is a captive. If the member leaves the church, he leaves behind his financial security, home, job, and family.

This type of crime usually comes under the Federal Civil Rights Laws, which are listed in Sections 241 through 248 of Title 18, USC.

2.20 Burglary

Burglary is defined as the breaking and entering of a dwelling place or habitation of another with the intent to commit a felony therein. The statutory offense of burglary has included trains, automobiles, barns, business establishments, storehouses, public buildings, telephone coin boxes, and boats. It is the intent of the perpetrator in the breaking and entering to commit a felony. Without such intent, the mere breaking and entering may only be a civil trespass and not punishable as a crime. Breaking does not necessarily require physical damage to or any destruction of property. It is the breaking of the secure feeling rather than any physical violence to the property itself. It is breaking when an intruder unlocks a door, opens a window, removes screening, or a window pane. If a person has permission to enter a building and then commits a felony inside, he has not committed burglary, because there was no "breaking" in order to make entry. Constructive breaking is made when an entry has been obtained by trickery, fraud, threats, intimidation, or conspiracy. If entry is achieved as the result of a pretense of a business or social call, it may be deemed to be "breaking" for purposes of committing burglary. Burglary requires "entry" into the dwelling as well as breaking. Burglars steal property for the purpose of selling the property to unsuspecting customers. Pawnshops are an ideal place to sell stolen property. However, the burglar cannot sell too much stolen property without the pawn shop owner becoming suspicious. Organized crime groups set up businesses for the purpose of selling stolen property. There are various federal statutes which involve burglary. These burglary statutes basically involve property either belonging to the United States or are in possession of the United States. The more common federal statutes are:

1. 18 USC 2112. This prohibits anyone to rob or attempt to rob personal property belonging to the United States.
2. 18 USC 2113. This prohibits anyone from robbing banks and other financial institutions.
3. 18 USC 2114. This prohibits anyone from robbing any postal service employee.
4. 18 USC 2115. This prohibits anyone from robbing any postal facility.
5. 18 USC 2116. This prohibits anyone from robbing any car, steamboat, or vessel assigned to carry mail service.

2.21   Forgery and Uttering

Forgery is the false making or material alteration, with the intent to defraud, of any writing to the prejudice of another person's rights. The intent to defraud is the very essence of the crime of forgery. It is immaterial that the alteration or false writing in fact deceived no one. It is not necessary to show that any particular person was intended to be defrauded. A general intent to defraud is sufficient, and it is not limited to the possibility of obtaining money or other property. Forgery may be committed by writing in ink or pencil, by typewriter, printing, engraving, or even pasting one name over another name. It has been frequently held that every such crime must contain at least the following two elements.

1. The signature was not made by the hand of the person whose signature it purports to be, and
2. Another wrongfully made the signature.

It is not necessary that the entire instrument be fictitious, nor is it required that the forged document contain incorrect statements. The act of making a forged instrument in its entirety is distinct from the act of altering an instrument already made, although both acts are forgeries. A forgery can be committed even though the name alleged to be forged is in fact a fictitious one. Signing a fictitious name to a check with intent to defraud is forgery even where the check is made payable to cash. It is not necessary that the forged signature resemble the genuine one. Forgery may be committed by a person signing his own name, where it appears that his name is the same as that of another person and he intends his writing to be received as that of such other person and he intends his writing to be received as that of such other person. Generally, a mere immaterial change or alteration, which does not affect the legal liability of the parties concerned with the instrument involved, does not constitute a forgery.

Uttering is the offering of a forged instrument, knowing it to be such, with the intent to defraud. It is immaterial whether such offer is accepted or rejected. A defendant may be guilty of uttering a forged instrument even though he was not the actual forger. The offense is complete when one knowing it is forged, with the representation by work or action that it is genuine offers a false instrument. In this sense, the words utter and publish have frequently been held to be synonymous as used in forgery statutes. Specific instances of uttering or publishing have been held to include:

1. Exhibiting a forged license to teach as evidence of a right to receive compensation.
2. Depositing a forged check to one's own account.
3. Delivering a forged note to satisfy a debt.
4. Procuring the probate of a forged will.
5. Using a forged instrument in judicial proceedings.

The federal statutes, which deal with forgery and uttering, are:

1. 18 USC 472. Prohibits uttering counterfeit obligations or securities of the United States.
2. 18 USC 496. This section prohibits anyone from forging, counterfeiting, or falsely altering any writing made or required to be made in connection with the entry or withdrawal of imports or collection of customs duties.
3. 18 USC 473. This prohibits anyone from dealing in counterfeit obligations of the United States.
4. 18 USC 482. This prohibits any forgeries, counterfeits, or false alterations of any obligations or securities of foreign banks or corporations.
5. 18 USC 478. Prohibits any forgeries, or counterfeits any bond, certificate, obligation, or other security of any foreign government.
6. 18 USC 1542. Prohibits anyone who falsely makes, forges, counterfeits, mutilates, or alters any passport.
7. 18 USC 1546. Prohibits anyone who forges, counterfeits, alters, or falsely makes any immigrant or nonimmigrant visa, permit, border crossing card, alien registration receipt card, or other documents.
8. 18 USC 2314. Prohibits anyone who transports in interstate or foreign commerce any falsely made, forged, altered, or counterfeit securities, tax stamps, traveler's checks, or tools to be used in making, forging, or counterfeiting any securities.

2.22 Larceny

The crime of larceny is the wrongful taking and carrying away of personal property of another person without his consent and with the intent to deprive the owner thereof of such property permanently. Many states divide larceny into two grades, grand larceny and petit larceny. The distinction between the two is usually based solely on the value of the appropriated property. In some states, the crime of larceny is known as theft and stealing.

There is no separate offense for each article taken at the same time. Similarly, stealing property at the same time and from the same place belonging to different owners constitutes only one offense of larceny since there is but one act of taking. Where separate items of property are stolen from different owners at different times, of course, separate larcenies have taken place. In order to be a proper subject of larceny, the thing taken by a defendant must conform to the following conditions:

1. It must be capable of individual ownership.
2. It must be personal rather than real property.

3. It must be of some intrinsic value, although it is not necessary that it have any special, appreciable, or market value.
4. It must have corporeal existence, regardless of its value to the owner who has had it. If it is not capable of a physical taking, then it is not a subject of larceny.

Animus furandi, the intent to deprive the owner permanently of the property taken, is an essential element of larceny. In order to indicate such intent, it has generally been held that the item of personal property must be taken from the possession of the owner or possessor into the possession of the thief and be carried away by him. There is no larceny when a person takes property temporarily with the intent of returning it later to the owner. The intent must be to deprive the owner permanently of his property. In order to constitute robbery as distinguished from larceny, either force or fear must be used by the thief. There is a distinction between owning something and having it in one's possession. Ownership is legal title; possession is physical control. Ownership and possession are regarded as synonymous in the crime of larceny. A taking in jest or mischief is not deemed to be larceny, particularly when such taking is done openly in the presence of numerous witnesses. The federal statutes, which deal with embezzlement and theft, are listed in Title 18, Sections 641 through 668.

2.23   Robbery

Robbery is the unlawful taking of any property from the person or in the presence of another by the use of force or intimidation. The offenses of assault and larceny are deemed to be essential elements of the crime of robbery. Robbery is a felony. The elements of this crime include:

1. A felonious taking.
2. The use of actual or constructive force.
3. No consent by the victim.
4. Personal property of any value.
5. An intent by the perpetrator to deprive the owner permanently of his property.

A person is not guilty of robbery in forcibly taking his own property from the possession of another. It is not necessary to the crime of robbery that the property is taken from the actual owner. A robbery may be committed by a taking from the person having only care, custody, control, management, or possession of the personal property. It is vital to the crime of robbery that the taking of the property be accomplished by the use of force, fear, or intimidation. The degree of force or violence is immaterial if it is enough to compel a person to give up his property against his will.

The federal statutes that address robbery are:

1. 18 USC 1951. Interference with commerce by threats or violence.
2. 18 USC 2113. Robbery of banks and other financial institutions.
3. 18 USC 2119. Robbery of motor vehicles with the intent to cause death or serious bodily harm in interstate or foreign commerce.

2.24 Tax Evasion

The federal and state governments have laws that make it a felony for those who willfully attempt to evade or defeat any tax. The crime of willful tax evasion is completed when the false or fraudulent return is willfully and knowingly filed. Tax evasion must be proved by an affirmative act. The willful failure to collect or pay over tax is a felony. It, likewise, must be proved by an affirmative act. The net worth, nondeductible expenditure method is the one most used by the Internal Revenue Service and states with individual income tax laws. These methods have been approved by the Supreme Court. This method is explained in a later chapter. Although voluntary disclosures by taxpayers of intentional violation of tax laws prior to the initiation of an investigation does not ensure that the government will not recommend criminal prosecution. There is no requirement that returns be made under oath. The law merely requires that returns contain a declaration that they are made under the penalties of perjury. Perjury is considered a felony. Any person who willfully delivers or discloses any list, return, account, statement, or other document that is known to be fraudulent or to be false is committing a crime. The federal government classifies this as a misdemeanor; however, many states classify this as a felony. The taxpayer is responsible for the correctness of any return filed, even if he pays a preparer. If the preparer has willfully prepared a false return, then he/she can be criminally prosecuted.

1. 26 USC 7201 through 7216 deal with the various types of criminal tax law violations.

2.25 Bank Frauds

Bank frauds encompass both customers and employees of banks. Bank frauds relate to the passing of bad checks, fraudulent loans, and check kiting. Officers or employees usually embezzle funds from the bank through various schemes. Customers defraud banks by writing bad checks or presenting false documents to obtain funds. 18 USC 1344 defines bank fraud as anyone who knowingly executes, or attempts to execute, a scheme to defraud a financial institution. It involves obtaining any of the moneys, funds, credits, assets, securities, or other property owned by, or under the custody or control of, a financial institution by means of false or fraudulent pretenses, representations, or promises. The financial institution does not have to suffer a loss. A person only has to submit false documents.

2.26 Restraint of Trade

Restraint of trade is a violation by corporate decision makers on behalf of their organizations. The major federal statute involved is the Sherman Antitrust Act of 1890. It was designed to curb the threat to competitive, free enterprise economy posed by the spread of trusts and monopolies to combine or form monopolies. There are three principal methods of restraint of trade:

1. Consolidation, so as to obtain a monopoly position.
2. Price fixing to achieve price uniformity, and

3. Price discrimination, in which higher prices are charged to some customers and lower ones to others.

For those corporate decision makers, restraint of trade makes sense in that the less competition it has and the greater control over prices, the larger the profits. However, small and independent businesses will lose business and the public at large will face higher prices and loss of discretionary buying power. The most common violations are price fixing and price discrimination. Antitrust laws are usually prosecuted under 18 USC 1505.

2.27   Government Contract Fraud

There are many federal statutes that involve fraud against the government for products and services. They can be classified into the following categories:

1. Fraudulent billing for products and services.
2. Providing faulty or inferior products or services.
3. Providing "substituted" products.
4. Overcharging on government contracts.

2.28   Corporate Raiding

Corporate raiding involves individuals or organizations that take over business entities for the purpose of exploiting the business assets for gains. These corporate raids may be for the control of the industry or for personal gains. Generally, corporate raiding involves either violations of the Sherman Antitrust Act or a combination of other offenses, for example, embezzlement, pension fraud, bankruptcy fraud, or stock fraud or manipulation. 18 USC 1348 usually deals with securities fraud. Corporate raiders gain control of a company usually by committing unlawful control of a corporation by acquiring the controlling interest in its stocks.

2.29   Extortion

This crime involves the threat by an individual to another for money. It is usually committed by organized crime organizations in their areas where they operate, but they do not have control of the market on this type of crime. Many of the federal statues address extortion. 18 USC 871 through 880 address extortion by or to federal employees.

2.30   Coupon Fraud

This crime usually involves individuals who operate a business. The business operator collects various coupons and submits them to either a clearinghouse or to the company that issued them for refunds or rebates on products that "bogus" customers have submitted when they have purchased products from the business. This is primarily a state crime, but the federal statutes for mail fraud would normally apply in this type of case.

2.31 Money Laundering

Money laundering is a criminal offense under federal statute 18 USC 1956, 1957, and 1960. It has made it a crime for individuals or business entities to launder gains from illegal activities through various methods and schemes. Money laundering activities encompass:

1. Transporting money and other money instruments to and from offshore.
2. Purchasing various intangible and tangible properties with large sums of cash.
3. Depositing large sums of cash into various financial institutions.
4. Maintaining bank accounts offshore with large balances.
5. Transmitting funds on behalf of the public, whether offshore or within the country.
6. Any funds derived from illegal activities.

Title 31, Money and Finance, Sections 5311 through 5355, goes into money laundering and reporting by various financial institutions and businesses. Financial institutions are very broadly defined, including, but not limited to banks, credit unions, brokers, postal services, pawnbrokers, travel agencies, dealers in precious metals, stones, or jewels, casinos, etc. There are penalties for not properly reporting cash or cash equivalent transactions by almost anyone. A later chapter describes these reporting requirements, forms, and penalties. Another later chapter will provide money laundering investigative techniques.

2.32 Medicare and Medicaid Fraud

This crime involves various health care providers of submitting claims to the government programs for services and products that were either not provided or overcharging for those services or products. 18 USC 286 makes any conspiracy or claim against the government a crime. It states, "Whoever enters into any agreement, combination, or conspiracy to defraud the United States, or any department or agency thereof, by obtaining or aiding to obtain the payment or allowance of any false, fictitious, or fraudulent claim, shall be fined under this title or imprisoned not more than ten years, or both." Also, 18 USC 1347 prohibits any fraud against any health care benefit provider by any means. In other words, it is a crime to commit fraud against an insurance company.

2.33 Repair and Maintenance Fraud

Maintenance and repair attracts swindlers who prey on consumers because typical consumers find it necessary to maintain or repair things that they own but do not usually have the time, resources, or know-how to do themselves. The best opportunities for fraud in maintenance and repair are expensive products and those so sophisticated or specialized as to be beyond the technical expertise of most consumers. Automobiles, electrical appliances of every sort, and home maintenance items are the most susceptible. Home maintenance is especially common. 18 USC 286 is used to prosecute those elements that submit false, factitious, or fraudulent claims to the United States.

2.34   Computer Thefts

Computer crime is viewed more as a means of crime rather than a type of crime. As an instrument of crime the computer may be used to victimize individuals, one's own company, competitive companies, the government, the public at large, or even other countries. Computers are involved in the following ways:

1. Submitting false claims to employers or government agencies.
2. Embezzling funds from one's employer or financial institutions.
3. To manipulate stock and bond prices.
4. Deleting information that may be harmful if made known.
5. Deleting information that would interrupt business day-to-day activities.
6. Selling company's secrets or software.

18 USC 1030 deals with computer fraud and related activities. It prohibits:

1. Accessing government computers without authorization that require protection against unauthorized disclosure.
2. Intentionally accessing financial institution or card issuer records without authorization.
3. Accessing government computers of any department or agency without authorization.
4. Accessing a government computer to defraud the government.
5. Transmission of a program, information, code, or command to cause damage to a computer system, network, information, data, or program used in interstate commerce or communications.

2.35   Insider Trading

It is a crime under federal and state statutes for corporate officers or employees of companies who trade their stocks or bonds on the various exchanges when they have knowledge of their company's internal activities. The Securities Exchange Act of 1933 as amended prohibits this type of conduct. Indictments for insider trading are usually returned under both 18 USC 1341 and 15 USC 77(x).

2.36   Corporate Fraud

Corporate fraud involves crimes committed by organizations or to organizations in the following areas:

1. Stealing company secrets by employees for gain.
2. Stealing company secrets by corporate organizations often called corporate espionage.
3. Copyright and patent infringements.
4. The production, distribution, and sale of harmful food and drug products to the public.

It is not a federal crime for an employee or organization to steal secrets from a business organization, unless the theft deals with interstate or foreign commerce. (18 USC 2315)

Copyright fraud is a violation under 18 USC 2319. The production, distribution, and sale of harmful food and drug products to the public are governed by various sections of Title 21, USC. In 1906, Congress passed the Federal Food and Drug Act which was the first step in declaring it illegal to manufacture or introduce into the market any adulterated or misbranded food or drug. Congress further expanded this in 1938, when they passed the Food, Drug, and Cosmetic Act. This expanded to cover areas of cosmetics and other health devices.

2.37 Swindlers

Swindlers are confidence artists who rely on the principal of getting something for nothing. They do this through a system of persuasion. First, they must find a victim. Second, they gain the confidence of the victim. Third, they convince the victim to depart with something, usually their money, on some enterprise, and fourth, they get rid of the victim through consolation and not by fear. There are many hundreds of variations. It may take con artists only a short period of time to fleece a victim or it may take a long period of time. 18 USC 1341 prohibits swindlers from using the postal service to defraud or obtain money by means of false or fraudulent pretenses, representations, or promises. 18 USC 1343 prohibits swindlers from using wire, radio, or television to defraud or obtain money by means of false or fraudulent pretenses, representations, or promises.

2.38 Conspiracy

A person who agrees, combines, confederates, or conspires with another person to commit any criminal offense is committing a felony. Usually, the punishment for conspiracy is related to the type of crime that the person is conspiring to commit. The person does not have to commit the offense, but only agree or plan to commit the offense. The offense does not have to take place. The most commonly used federal conspiracy charges revolve around 18 USC 1962, 1951, and 241.

2.39 Principal

A principal is anyone who commits any criminal offense or aids, abets, counsels, hires, or otherwise procures such offense to be committed or attempted to be committed. The person does not actually or constructively have to be present at the time of the commission of such offense. (18 USC 2)

2.40 Accessory

A person can be an accessory either before the fact or after the fact. An accessory is anyone who gives an offender any aid, knowing that he had committed a felony. Normally, an accessory after the fact aids the criminal with intent to escape detection, arrest, or trial. The primary element is that the accessory has knowledge that a person committed an offense. (18 USC 3)

2.41 Kidnapping

Kidnapping means forcibly, secretly, or by threat confining, abducting, or imprisoning another person against his will and without lawful authority, with intent to:

1. Hold for ransom or reward or as a shield or hostage.
2. Commit or facilitate commission of any felony.
3. Inflict bodily harm upon or to terrorize the victim or another person.
4. Interfere with the performance of any governmental or political function.

Under federal statute (18 USC 1201 through 1204), kidnapping is a capital offense.

2.42 Theft

Theft is normally defined as any person who obtains or uses, or endeavors to obtain or to use, the property of another with intent to, either temporarily or permanently, deprive the owner. Many states have placed various degrees of theft from petit to grand theft, which is usually based upon the value of the property taken. In addition, many states address theft to particular types of theft. The most common are shoplifting, hijacking, trade secrets, utilities and cable theft, dealing in stolen property, mortgage or loan fraud, cheating, misleading advertising, and many others. (See the paragraphs on Larceny, Burglary, and Robbery.) Section 2311 through 2322, 18 USC, address theft of various kinds of property which cross state lines.

2.43 Identity Theft

Identity theft or fraud is all types of crimes when someone wrongfully obtains and uses another person's personal data in some way that involves fraud or deception. Typically, it is for economic gain. Personal data, especially Social Security number, bank account, credit card number, telephone calling card, and other valuable identifying data can be used to profit at the victim's expense. With enough identifying information about an individual, a criminal can take over an individual's identity to conduct a wide range of crimes. This would include false applications for loans and credit cards, fraudulent withdrawals from bank accounts, or obtaining other goods and services which the criminal probably would be denied if he used his real name. 18 USC 1028 makes it a crime to fraudulent obtain, possess, or use someone's identity.

2.44   Child Support

Many states have laws which make it a crime for a person to misuse child support payments, whether from another person or by any government agency. A person shall be deemed to have misapplied child support funds when such funds are spent for any purpose other than necessary and proper home, food, clothing, and the necessities of life, which expenditure results in depriving the child of the above named necessities. Some states require public welfare agencies to give notice of these provisions at least once to each payee of any public grant for the benefit of any child and shall report violations to the proper authorities.

The failure to pay legal child support obligations with respect to a child who resides in another state is a violation under 18 USC 228.

2.45   Counterfeiting

Counterfeiting is the act of imitating something genuine so as to defraud someone. Most people think of counterfeiting in terms of printing money or forging coins that are false. However, both federal and state statutes provide for criminal sanctions for imitating or publishing or tendering anything with the intent to utter and pass something as true. Counterfeiting can encompass money, contracts, merchandise, documents, licenses, certificates, or any document or property. Sections 470 through 513, 18 USC, deal with many kinds of counterfeiting under federal statutes. Also, 18 USC 2320 prohibits trafficking in counterfeit goods or services.

2.46   Bad Checks

Most states have statutes which prohibit anyone from giving checks, drafts, bills of exchange, debit card orders, and other orders on banks without first providing funds in or credit with the depositories on which the same are made or drawn to pay and satisfy the same. It usually includes any person who, by act or scheme, cashes or deposits any item in any bank or depository with intent to defraud. Bad checks, drafts, etc. are prohibited for purchasing goods and services with the intent to defraud any person, firm, or corporation.

The issuing of bad checks comes under the Bank Fraud Statute, 18 USC 1344.

2.47   False Statements

Federal Statute 18 USC 1001, as well as many state statutes, prohibit anyone from giving false information to any law enforcement or official in the performance of their duties. Title

18 USC 1001 read, "Whoever, in any manner within the jurisdiction of any department or agency of the United States and knowingly and willfully falsifies, conceals, or covers up by any trick, scheme, or device a material fact, or makes false, fictitious, or fraudulent statements or representations, or makes or uses any false writing or document knowing the same to contain any false, fictitious, or fraudulent statement or entry, shall be fined under this title or imprisoned not more than five years, or both."

2.48   Misprison of Felony

18 USC 4 defines a misprison of felony as "Whoever, having knowledge of the actual commission of a felony cognizable by a court of the United States, conceals and does not as soon as possible make known the same to some judge or other person in civil or military authority under the United States, shall be fined under this title or imprisoned not more than three years, or both." The key element in this offense is that one, having knowledge of an offense, must take an affirmative act of reporting the crime.

2.49   Summary

There are many federal statutes which cover a wide variety of crimes, most of which are financially related. States and possession of the United States have the same or similar laws. A fraud examiner must know the state or federal statute that is being violated in order to examine and gather evidence to support a conviction. The fraud examiner should study the appropriate statute and determine the elements of each offense, then he should see if the evidence supports each one of the elements required to sustain a conviction.

Offshore Activities 3

3.1 General

Organized crime organizations, as well as individuals, have taken their illegal gains to offshore countries. Legitimate businesses have been using offshore countries for many years to avoid taxes and preserve capital. These countries which offer various business services, especially to multinational corporations, are called "tax havens." International businessmen know that countries have different tax systems. This disparity may constitute tax havens in relation to a particular operation or situation as compared with the tax treatment given to the identical taxable event in another country's tax system. Hence, "tax haven" is a relative concept. As mentioned in our economic chapter, organized crime and individual illegal operations pay no taxes on their income; therefore, tax havens become very attractive vehicles for hiding their untaxed income from both tax authorities and law enforcement. Secrecy is an important element for criminals.

3.2 Characteristics

Tax havens have many common characteristics which make them ideal for both multinational businesses and criminal organizations. These characteristics are:

3.2.1 Taxes

Countries fall into one of five categories when it comes to tax systems:

1. Countries which impose virtually no direct taxes.
2. Countries which impose tax at relatively low rates.
3. Countries which impose tax only on domestic source income.
4. Countries whose tax treaties can be used as a conduit.
5. Countries granting special tax privileges.

Organized crime and white collar criminals, of course, prefer categories 1 and 2. The primary function is to eliminate the connecting factor between the taxing jurisdiction and the taxpayer or taxable event. The principal connecting factors for individuals are residence, domicile, and citizenship. For companies, the connecting factors are management and control, ownership, place of incorporation, and location of registered office. An important connecting factor is the center of economic interests and the presence of a permanent establishment. Therefore, organized crime and other criminals try to eliminate any connecting factors from the taxable events such as profits from narcotics trafficking, gambling, loansharking, etc., and the taxpayer.

3.2.2 Exchange Control

The exchange control system of a country is a body of statutory and administrative regulations that has an objective of control over a country's liquid resources abroad and the international movement of currency owned by its residents. Both organized crime and multinational companies seek countries which have little or no exchange controls. This affords them the ability to easily and quickly transfer funds without any interference.

3.2.3 Banking

Many international banking takes place offshore. Most of the world's banks have operations in tax havens. Tax haven countries have enacted various laws and set up regulatory agencies to control banking activities. Banks offer the same type of services in tax havens as they do in other countries; however, branch offices of international banks in tax havens have the ability to move funds swiftly and have better expertise in handling international transactions. Nonresident banks are only licensed to serve clients who are not tax haven residents.

3.2.4 Bank Secrecy

Secrecy is an important element in tax havens. The banker is required to keep the customer's affairs secret. In some tax havens, breaches of bank secrecy is a criminal violation; however, there are specific exemptions where the banker is discharged. Organized crime cherishes tax havens with bank secrecy laws. This gives them the ability to further hide the illegal gains.

3.2.5 Stability

Political and economic stability are important factors. Neither businessmen nor organized crime organizations want to do business with any country that is not politically and economically stable.

3.2.6 Communication

Communication is another factor in selecting a tax haven. Some tax havens are small islands, which have limited communication and transportation facilities. The Colombian cartels have used small islands as transshipment points. These transshipment points require good communication. The Colombian drug cartels have installed sophisticated communication equipment and facilities on small islands in the Caribbean. Organized crime requires good communication facilities so that illegal gains can be transferred by wire quickly and easily.

3.2.7 Corruption

International businessmen do not want to establish operations in a tax haven country in which public officials are corrupt. This would require them to make payoffs and kickbacks to public officials, which in turn reduces their profits. On the other hand, organized crime has the opposite view. They want to make payoffs and kickbacks so the public officials will "look the other way" and will not interfere with their operations. For organized crime, this is a small price of doing business.

3.3   Tax Haven Countries

The following countries are classified as tax havens because they seek business and promote themselves as tax havens. In addition, criminals and organized crime elements look to these countries for ways of money laundering and concealing their illegal gains.

3.3.1   Andorra

This principality is located in the heart of the Eastern Pyrenees, between France and Spain. It is a principality covering 468 km² in mountainous terrain. It lacks adequate transportation, since there is no airline and train service. Roads can be clogged for up to three hours. It has a president, who is elected by the General Counsel or Parliament. The Parliament members, called "Consellers General," are elected. There are no taxes on income, capital, and duties although they do have a property tax imposed by the local *Comu* (a parish) each year. The official language is Catalan, but French and Castilian are in daily use. English is understood in banks and public offices. The French franc and the Spanish peseta are both everyday currencies. There are no exchange controls or monetary authority. The telephone system is tied to both the Spanish and French systems, so it is possible to dial out through either country. Generally, the service is efficient and costs are similar to those of neighboring countries. The postal system is supplied by the French and Spanish postal services which provide their own stamps. They generally follow Roman law; however, in many instances they follow the Napoleonic code. The main industry is tourism, which sells duty free goods to its neighboring residents. There are three types of business entities that can be formed and operate in Andorra:

a. A Collective Society (SRC), essentially a partnership. There are no capital requirements. However, one partner must be a native Andorrian.
b. A Societat Anonima (SA), essentially a large corporation. There must be real capital investment of 5 million in pesetas or equivalent with no more than 10 shareholders.
c. A Societate De Responsibilitat Limitada (SL), essentially a small corporation. There must be real capital investment of 3 million pesetas or equivalent with no less than three shareholders.

A foreign national cannot own more than one-third interest in any Andorrian company. Foreign nationals use Andorrians as trustees or nominees. Bank accounts can be opened in any amount and in any currency. Breach of bank secrecy is a criminal offense. Every bank offers a numbered account facility.

3.3.2   Anguilla

Anguilla is a British Overseas Territory about 190 miles east of Puerto Rico. The Virgin Islands (British and American) are not far away. The island is 35 square miles with a population of about 10,000. Tourism is the biggest source of foreign exchange. The governor is appointed from London, while the four Ministers of Government are locally appointed among the elected members of the House of Assembly. It is a democracy with elections held every 5 years. The constitution of Anguilla with a bill of rights was created by the Order in Council of the British Privy Council. Anguilla's relationship with the European Union is governed by Britain's legislation and British agreements with her European partners. English is the language of Anguilla. The law is based on British common law, supplemented by local statutes enacted by the local House Assembly. There are no currency restrictions in Anguilla. Commercial banks accept deposits in U.S. dollars, pounds sterling, and Eastern Caribbean dollars, the local currency. There is a 2% tax on any purchase of foreign currency. There are no restrictions on bringing foreign currency in or out of Anguilla. Also, there is no income tax, withholding tax, asset tax, gift tax, profits tax, capital gains tax, distributions tax, value added tax, asset departure tax, inheritance tax, or estate duty tax. Professionals and banks in Anguilla are subject to the Confidential Relationships Ordinance (1981) which imposes a criminal penalty for breaches of confidence. Shareholders and directors of ordinary companies must be published to the Registrar of Companies annually, but the common use of nominee shareholders holding shares under a trust agreement provides an additional layer of secrecy. Attorneys and banks require full disclosure of clients' names and backgrounds, but will not disclose such information without a court order or similar obligation. Banks require the source of funds to be identified in case of significant deposits. Money laundering is not encouraged by banks or professional advisors in Anguilla. Under the Mutual Legal Assistance Ordinance (1990) the treaty between Britain and the United States has been extended to Anguilla. Corporations are established under either the Companies Ordinance, 1994, or the International Business Companies Ordinance (1994). A Limited Liability Company may be registered under the LLC Ordinance (1994). Its terms may be either perpetual or of limited duration, as provided by the LLC agreement. A public company is one which may be quoted on a stock exchange and is subject to stringent auditing and filing requirements. Limited partnerships in Anguilla are subject to the Limited Partnership Ordinance (1994). Partners may be individuals, corporations, or other partnerships. One general partner of a limited partnership must be an Anguillian company or resident. The name must end with LP. A trust is a relationship recognized by rules of equity under the Trust Ordinance (1994). There are rules for regulating spendthrift trusts, memoranda of wishes, purpose trusts, protectors, variation of terms, foreign trusts, and variant trusts. The rules against perpetuities are abolished. A trust may provide for beneficiaries to be added or excluded. If the settler and trustees are not resident in Anguilla, the trust is guaranteed to be exempt from taxes in Anguilla. There is one offshore bank and four banks having branches on the island. Anguilla has cable and wireless communications. There are airlines servicing Anguilla from San Juan, Puerto Rico, and St. Maarten.

3.3.3 Antigua and Barbuda

These two islands are east-southeast of Puerto Rico. Antigua is about 108 square miles and Barbuda is about 62 square miles. The two islands have a population of about 67,000. The islands have a tropical climate. English is the official language of the islands. It has a constitutional monarchy with the Queen of England as head and the English style Parliament. The governor general is appointed by the English crown. The prime minister and the Cabinet are appointed by the governor general. The Senate consists of a 17-member body appointed by the governor general. The House of Representatives are elected and serve 5-year terms.

It gained independence from England in 1981. The legal system is based on English common law. Tourism dominates the economy. The currency is the East Caribbean dollar. It has good communication on the island and internationally. There are 16 Internet providers on the island. It has paved roads, two good airports, and one seaport in Saint John's. It is known for its offshore financial center. The International Business Corporations (IBC) Act 1982 provides for the formation of a company on the islands. An IBC must have a minimum of one shareholder. There are low set-up and renewal costs. There are no requirements for filing or submitting accounting or audit reports. There are no minimum capital requirements. However, one must maintain a registered office and agent in the country. There is no agreement on exchange of information with other countries.

3.3.4   Aruba

Aruba is an island nation, situated approximately 12 miles off the coast of Venezuela in South America. Its capital is Oranjestad; its population totals about 65,000 inhabitants. Aruba is a small island measuring 19.6 miles long and 6 miles across at its widest point. Until January 1, 1986, Aruba together with Curacao and some small islands formed part of the federation which formed the country of the Netherlands Antilles. On that date, it acquired a separate status. Aruba has a parliamentary democracy with a governor representing the Queen of the Netherlands. The Parliament consists of 21 members that are elected by universal suffrage. The Aruba legal system of civil and penal law is a copy of the Dutch legal system; a system derived from Roman law. The basic laws are the Civil Code (Burgerlijk Wetboek) and the Commercial Code (Wetboek van Koophandel). Besides these two principal codes, there are numerous laws, regulations, and directives. As Aruba is part of the Kingdom of the Netherlands, all laws are in Dutch. The Arubian florin (or guilder) is divided into 100 cents. The Arubian florin is tied to the U.S. dollar at a rate of Af. 1.79. Papianmento is the native language; however, Dutch is the official language. Most professional advisors speak English fluently. Dutch, English, and Spanish are widely spoken. French and German are also spoken. Professionals have mostly had either Dutch or a North American education. Aruba is an associate member of the European Economic Community (EEC). Aruba has excellent communications on the island. Automatic international communication is possible with most countries in the world. Telegraphic communication services are provided by SETAR, a government-owned company. There is also a data communications system through which several data networks in the United States and Europe are accessible.

The country has excellent telephone, telex, and cable communications as well as daily connections by air with major cities in the United States, Latin America, and Europe. There are a number of reputable international and local banks to service the financial needs of the tax haven sector. There are also many law firms, accounting firms, and trust companies established in Aruba. With the termination in 1988 of its treaty base, the Aruban government passed legislation for zero tax offshore company facilities in Aruba. Aruba is an attractive tax haven in the Caribbean and Central America region because of political stability. All legal and natural persons, carrying on a business enterprise in Aruba, are subject to a number of obligations to provide the tax inspector's office with certain information. Numbered bank accounts are not permitted in Aruba. In order to open a bank account one normally has to prove one's identity, or, if the bank account is for a legal entity, a certificate of the Chamber of Commerce must be lodged.

There are two kinds of limited companies in Aruba: the Naamloze Vennootschap (NV) and the Aruba Vrijgestelde Vennootschap (AVV) or "Aruba Exempt Company." Prior to the introduction of the Aruba Exempt Company (AEC), all limited companies were NVs. There are many similarities between NV and AVV, but also fundamental differences. In general, it can be said that the Aruban zero tax company has a more modern corporate structure than the Aruban NV. The Aruban zero tax company provides an attractive vehicle for international tax planning because of the absence of taxes, relatively low cost of formation and maintenance, the flexibility of its corporate structure and the absence of red tape and regulatory restrictions. An Aruba Exempt Company may not conduct business activities in Aruba other than those which are necessary in connection with the maintenance of its office in Aruba. The company is also prohibited from conducting banking, insurance, or any other activity which would make it a creditor of a financial institution under Aruban law. This rule applies regardless of whether the activities are conducted in or outside Aruba. The required minimum capital is Afl. 10,000, which is approximately US$5600. The company must be registered in the Commercial Register and is open to the public. It contains the names and other personal data about the directors and legal representatives. There are no currency exchange controls for AEC companies or foreign nationals and companies.

3.3.5 Bahamas

The Bahamas are located off the Florida East Coast. The area consists of 700 islands, of which only about 40 are inhabited. The population is approximately 340,000. It is part of the British Commonwealth; however, they obtained their independence on July 10, 1973. There are no income, sales, capital, estate, or inheritance taxes. They have property taxes, which are assessed at 1% to 3% on nonresidents. Most of the Bahamas' revenue comes from custom duties. They have exchange control to conserve foreign currency resources of the Bahamas and assist in the balance of payments. Exchange controls on nonresidents are nonexistent. The Bahamas uses the Bahamian dollar, which is tied to the U.S. dollar. There are good transportation and communication to both the United States and Europe. There are many branch offices of international banks in both Nassau and Freeport. The Bahamas have strict bank secrecy laws. No banker can disclose a customer's affairs without an order from the Supreme Court of the Commonwealth of the Bahamas. The legal system is based on English common law and rules of equity. It has a parliamentary form of government consisting of the Senate and House Assembly. The Queen of England is the Head of State and is represented by the governor general. The governor general appoints the Senate and prime minister. A Bahamian company can be formed with minimum formalities. For companies wanting to do business in the Bahamas, there are various types of licenses that need to be obtained. International Business Companies Act of 2000 (IBC) has restrictions. IBCs cannot trade within the Bahamas or own real estate unless government permission is granted. They cannot undertake business in banking, insurance, investment schemes, trust management, trusteeship, or any other activity that would suggest an association with the banking or insurance industries. Also, it cannot sell its own shares or solicit funds from the public. For nonresidents, only a resident agent is required to be in the Bahamas. The officers and directors of a Bahamian company can hold meetings anywhere. Directors can be as few as one, but two is better. Nominees can be used as directors and shareholders. However, all directors' names and addresses are to be registered in the public register. The Bahamas is not a party to any double tax treaties since it has no direct taxation of income tax, capital gains tax, gift tax, or inheritance tax. There is no requirement to file audited accounts with authorities; however, a company is required to keep financial records which reflect the financial position of a company.

3.3.6 Barbados

This country is an island in the Caribbean chain. It was a British colony until 1966 at which time it gained its independence; however, it remains part of the British Commonwealth. Its official language is English. The Barbados dollar is tied to the U.S. dollar at the rate of US$1 = BDS$2. They have an Exchange Control Authority; however, it does not control companies operating in the offshore sector. Under the Offshore Banking Act, the affairs of nonresident customers are not to be disclosed. Share warrants are permitted. The names and addresses of beneficial owners of shares must be made to the Central Bank. The Central Bank keeps them confidential although it is not a criminal violation for government officials or employers to reveal such information. Barbados has a tax information exchange agreement with the United States. There are many international bank branches in Barbados. Transportation and communication from Barbados to the United States and Europe are good. There are regularly scheduled flights. Income tax is imposed on income, both individuals and corporations, on domestic income. Foreign income is not taxed, except on residents. There are no capital gains or inheritance taxes. Barbados also imposes withholding taxes on income derived within the country. Barbados has tax treaties with the United Kingdom, United States, Canada, Denmark, Norway, Sweden, and Switzerland. Barbados has a parliamentary form of government consisting of a Senate and House of Assembly. It follows the English common law and law of equities. The Companies Act allows for flexibility in forming, operating, and winding up or transferring the domicile of a company. Single shareholder and director companies are allowed. Board meetings can be held both within and outside Barbados. Shareholder anonymity can be achieved by:

a. Using nominees.
b. Using foreign trusts.
c. Using share warrants (a form of bearer stock).

3.3.7 Belize

Belize is located next to southern Mexico and Guatemala by the Caribbean Sea in Central America. English is the official language, but Spanish is also spoken. Belize has a population of about 266,000. Belize has a tropical climate and is hot and humid. It is a democracy. Belize gained its independence in September 1981. The legal system follows English law. The governor general and the prime minister are appointed by the Queen of England. The leader of the majority party is usually appointed prime minister. The Senate has 12 members appointed by the governor general. The House of Representatives are elected by the electorate. There are 29 members in the House of Representatives who serve 5-year terms. Tourism is the principal industry, followed by sugar cane, citrus, marine products, and bananas. There is good communication, internal and external. They have automatic systems for direct dialing, faxes, cellular telephones, and e-mail. They have two Internet service providers. They have both a seaport and an airport. The International Business

Company Act provides for privacy. Directors and shareholders of IBCs can remain anonymous and are not recorded other than the company's registered office, which may not be divulged to any authority. Shares may be issued in "bearer shares" and a company may have nominee directors. There are no restrictions on trade. Bank secrecy is enforced by law, and bank records cannot be made available to authorities in any jurisdiction. All normal banking services are available. A merchant can have credit card receipts credited to IBC's offshore account. In Belize, IBC's assets cannot be touched by any authority. In Belize, a trust can be set up for nominal costs, minimal formalities, and on short notice. The trust must be irrevocable to qualify as a true asset protection device. There is no requirement for accounting reports to any agency. Claims, judgments, liens, or bankruptcy proceedings from any country cannot be imposed on earnings or assets of irrevocable discretionary Belize trusts. Another vehicle is the Suisse-Belize International Investment Trust. It operates very similar to a mutual fund except with certain provisions. First, it is private, not public. Second, instead of shares it issues the bearer unit certificates. Since secrecy is paramount for this money, the certificates are not issued in name, but are the property of the bearer. This allows for transferability. To safeguard against stolen bearer unit certificates, the account number and a password are required to validate cashing in the certificate. The Suisse Belize Investment Trust operates under the Trust Act of Belize, 1992. There are no annual reporting requirements on this type of Offshore International Investment Trust. To protect the trust, a standard form must be filled out and notarized declaring that the funds to purchase the bearer unit are not from criminal or illegal activities.

3.3.8 Bermuda

This country is located in the middle of the Atlantic Ocean about half way between the United States and Europe. It is a self-governing colony of the British Commonwealth. Transportation and communication are very good to both the United States and Europe. The official language is English. Bermuda has exchange control authority on local residents. However, offshore companies and individuals can maintain bank accounts in the currency of the country that they choose. The government has restrictions on who can incorporate and do business there. There is no income, capital gains, or withholding taxes. Nominees can be used to safeguard real beneficial owners. There are many branches of international banks on the island. Bermuda has its own Monetary Authority and dollar, which can be converted into any currency of choice. The legal system is based on English common law. The Companies Act allows for the formation of "exempt" companies, which are corporations that do not operate on the island. These exempt companies are not taxed but must maintain an office in Bermuda. An auditor located on the island must audit the books every year. There must be at least three shareholders. The shareholders must be registered in company registers, which are open to the public. Nominees can be used as shareholders.

3.3.9 Cayman Islands

The Cayman Islands are located between Cuba and the Yucatan Peninsula. They are a British colony. The official language is English. Transportation and communication to the United States and Europe are very good. There is no income, capital gains, estate, or inheritance taxes. Income is derived from import duties. The currency is the Cayman dollar which is pegged to the U.S. dollar at CI$1 = US$1.20. There are many branches of international banks on the island. The Cayman Islands have bank secrecy laws. There are no currency exchange controls. There are criminal penalties on government officials and professionals who make unauthorized disclosure of a customer's accounts. The British government signed an agreement with the United States to prevent drug traffickers from enjoying benefits of the Cayman Islands laws in 1984. The law provides a mechanism for obtaining evidence in federal court proceedings through the Attorney General of the United States and the Caymans. The procedure must be strictly complied with and cannot be used in any other case or for any other purpose. There are no currency exchange controls. The Cayman Islands are politically and economically stable. The Islands have a substantial trade surplus with the outside world. Employment and standard of living are very high. The Islands have direct dial telephone, telecopier, cable, Internet, and telex links. The postal service is efficient with air courier services available to virtually all parts of the world. The Companies Act provides for "exempt" corporations. These are corporations that do not operate on the island. An exempt corporation must have one meeting a year on the island. It must also have at least one director. The company register is not open for public inspection. Nominee directors and shareholders can be used and are customary. Proper books are necessary to give a fair view of the company's affairs and to explain its transactions. An annual return is required by law, but it is not necessary that it be audited. Cayman trusts are governed by the trust law, 1976. A trust can be created by a resident of any country, and the settler does not have to be physically present on the islands. While the trustee should be located in the Caymans, it is not necessary to keep trust assets there. A stamp tax of US$50 is payable on a trust deed, but there is no requirement for public recording or registration. No statutory restrictions exist in Cayman regarding accumulation of income, but the common law rule against perpetuities applies, except in the case of exempt trusts. The trustee of an offshore trust should be a resident of the Cayman Islands. An ordinary trust usually assigns a bank or trust company to act as trustee. Neither the settler nor the beneficiaries have to be physically present within Cayman, and the trust's assets may be kept outside the islands. An exempt trust must pay an annual fee of US$120 each year, and the trustees must file with the Registrar such accounts, minutes, and information as the Registrar may require. Documents filed with the Registrar are open to inspection by the trustees or any other person authorized by the trust and by the Registrar, but they are not open to public inspection. An exempt trust may provide for perpetuity of up to 100 years, and during its subsistence the beneficiaries have no interest, vested or future; all rights of the beneficiaries are bested in the Registrar of Trusts, who is an official of the Cayman government. Switzerland, Panama, the Bahamas, and Caymans have well-established bank secrecy laws designed to prevent unauthorized disclosure of a client's financial affairs to outside authorities. The Caymans do not recognize tax evasion or avoidance as a crime and in 1979 they reinforced the Confidential Relationships (Preservation) Law with heavier penalties for disclosure. The Cayman Islands were the first to set up a Limited Duration Company. It is a corporation that is treated as a partnership for U.S. tax purposes, "enabling a flow-through" but without the complexity of the limited partnership structure.

3.3.10   Costa Rica

This country is located in Central America. The official language is Spanish, but English is used in commercial practice. The country has a democratic form of government and no military forces. The national currency is the colon. There is exchange control on the colon; however, there is no control of funds transferred into a Costa Rican account and maintained in a foreign currency account. The banks are required by law to maintain secrecy regarding the affairs of their customers. There are income, capital gains, and withholding taxes. Costa Rican law provides for foreigners to reside in Costa Rica, especially those on retirement income. The pensioned resident must reside in Costa Rica for at least six months per year. In addition, the pensioned resident can travel on a Costa Rican passport called a "Passport of Convenience." Organized crime figures like this characteristic because they can go directly to Costa Rica when things get "hot" in the United States. They in turn can travel to other countries using a Costa Rican passport instead of a United States passport. Costa Rican Law establishes five different legal capacities in which people can engage in business. These are:

a. Individual enterprise with limited liability, regarded as an individual.
b. Collective company, similar to partnership in common law countries.
c. The limited partnership, a partnership that has limited liability.
d. Stock corporation or chartered company, a corporation.

The stock corporation can be formed with two or more incorporators. A single person may be the only shareholder. A stock corporation can issue "bearer" shares of stock. This allows the shareholder who wants to keep his or her identity from being known and is ensured secrecy regarding the investment. The bearer stock must be paid in full; otherwise the shares must be registered with the Public Registry.

3.3.11 Cyprus

Cyprus has been an independent republic since 1960. It was previously a British colony. Cyprus is a member of the United Nations, British Commonwealth, and the Council of Europe. In 1974 part of the island was occupied by Turkish forces and is still occupied. This study does not relate to the area under Turkish occupation. The legal system is mainly based on English common law and equity. English case law is widely followed. The official language is Greek, but English is very widely spoken and used especially in court, government offices, and businesses. The economy after the Turkish invasion in 1974 has recovered and has surpassed its pre-1974 standard of living. Foreign investments are increasing, mainly in the industrial and tourist sectors. Political and economic stability is now rated as good. The Cyprus pound is divided into 100 cents; it is subject to fluctuation. Cyprus is not in the sterling area. There is very good air and sea communication. It has excellent telecommunications facilities with automatic connections with 69 countries and automatic telex communications with 148 countries. Cyprus is rated among the top five countries with excellent automatic telecommunications. A satellite earth station started operating in 1980. There are also marisat, facsimile, and datel services. Secrecy laws bind banks. Banks do not have numbered bank accounts. Cyprus has exchange control on residents, but it is not applicable for IBC companies. The geographical position, the climatic conditions, the availability of local skilled personnel, and the low cost of living make Cyprus a very suitable place from which to manage offshore activities, especially for the Middle East. Cyprus has Double Taxation Agreements with 18 countries, which includes the United States. Cyprus has an income tax on individuals and companies who operate on the island.

Income earned offshore is not taxable. There are exchange controls for local residents and companies who do business on Cyprus. All foreign incorporated companies are nonresident. Foreign companies who do not have business on Cyprus are free from exchange control. Only local lawyers with a minimum of two shareholders can form corporations. There can be two classes of stock. Bearer shares are prohibited. Shareholders names must be filed with the Registrar of Companies; however, nominees can be used. Cyprus has a network of double tax treaties which follows the OECD model. This is beneficial for trade with certain East European countries, including Russia.

3.3.12 Dominica

The Commonwealth of Dominica is a beautiful English speaking country, located in the Eastern Caribbean between the French Islands of Martinique and Guadeloupe. Dominica was named and first sited by Christopher Columbus in 1493 on his second voyage to the West Indies. Dominica is called the "nature island" of the Caribbean because its forest covers 60% of the country. It has 365 rivers and hot springs. The population stands at about 72,000. The country's infrastructure is good with excellent water, power, and communication. It has direct dial facilities worldwide via undersea fiber cable, and Internet and data transmission facilities. There are direct flights to Dominica from San Juan, Puerto Rico, Antigua, St. Luicia, and the French islands, with onward connections to North America and Europe. Dominica gained independence from Britain in 1978. A Westminster style of parliamentary democracy was adopted with elections every 5 years. The President is head of state, but the prime minister and his cabinet of ministers run the state. English is the official language. The legal system is based on English common law. Dominica passed the International Business Act in June 1996 and provides for the incorporation, operation, and regulation of IBCs. The Act provides for total confidentiality with civil and criminal penalties for any disclosure of information. There is no requirement for the disclosure of the beneficial owner to any authority. Bearer shares are allowed. There is no requirement to file audited financial statements with authorities. Online banking and trading accounts are available on the island. There are no exchange controls. The registry is closed, meaning directors and shareholders are kept totally secret. Shareholders' and directors' meetings can be held outside Dominica. Dominica is a member of the Eastern Caribbean Central Bank, which issues the Eastern Caribbean dollar. The EC dollar is fixed to the U.S. dollar at US$1.00 to EC$2.6882. The U.S. dollar is also legal tender on the island.

3.3.13 Gibraltar

Gibraltar is a British Crown Colony situated at the southern end of the Iberian Peninsula. The legal system is based on English law using both common law and Acts of Parliament. The official language is English, and all official documents are produced in English. The legal tender consists of currency notes of the Gibraltar government. United Kingdom currency is also legal tender. Gibraltar notes are not easily convertible outside Gibraltar. There are no currency exchange controls. There are no double taxation treaties and no provisions for exchange of information with any other country. There are excellent communication facilities and bank facilities. A corporation formed in Gibraltar can be exempted from submitting an annual account to the Commissioners of Income Tax but must apply for an exemption. The corporation can remain exempt so long as no one is a resident of Gibraltar or the United Kingdom. It can issue bearer shares of stock, but must be paid in full. Identity of a person or persons applying for exemption must be kept secret.

3.3.14   Guernsey

This is an island nation off the coast of England about 108 miles south of Southampton and about 40 miles from France. It is a British possession, but has its own legal system and government. Committees of the State generally administer public services and departments. Their law is customary law of the Duchy, which dates back to the Normandy customary law. The customary law of Normandy is nowadays significant in matters of succession and real property. In taxation and commercial legislation, English Acts are followed, especially, in matters of investor protection. The United Kingdom negotiated special terms upon accession to the Treaty of Rome within the framework of Article 227 of the Treaty as amended by the Treaty of Accession. The arrangements, which are set out in Protocol Number 3 of the Treaty of Accession, have the effect of retaining fiscal independence of Guernsey and freedom from the imposition of duties and levies, in particular value added tax. There is no requirement on Guernsey to adopt community fiscal, commercial, or economic policies. English is the official language; however, many laws have been enacted in French. Many law firms and staff are fluent in French and English. The currency is sterling, and both English and local notes are circulated freely. The economy of Guernsey is based on horticulture, tourism, finance, and light industry. Guernsey is dependent on communication. They have stable links with the United Kingdom, Jersey, and continental Europe. Telecommunications and postal services are cheaper than mainland services and are available at most professional offices and banks. There is no local legislation enacted relating to secrecy of information, but English common law, which imposes a duty on a bank and bank personnel to maintain secrecy, is applicable. Nominee and numbered account facilities are available. The Double Taxation Agreements with Jersey and the United Kingdom do provide for exchange of information but only to the revenue authority of those jurisdictions respectively. Guernsey has a low income tax of 20% on any income that is derived or remitted to Guernsey. A company or individual is liable for income taxes if he or she is a resident for a year or conducts a substantial part of business there. An individual is a resident if he spends more than 182 days in Guernsey. There are no exchange controls on the island. At least seven people must form a corporation. Their names, addresses, nationalities, and domiciles are filed with the law officer of the Crown in court only on Thursdays. Annual reports are required to be sent to the Greffier not later than January 31 of each year. These reports must identify shareholders and their respective holdings. Annual meetings must be held in Guernsey.

3.3.15   Hong Kong

Hong Kong is situated on the southeast coast of China, 90 miles southeast of Canton and 40 miles east of the Portuguese province of Macau. The total land area is 404 square miles. The estimated population in 1987 was about 5.6 million, of which 98% are Chinese. Great Britain and the People's Republic of China signed an agreement in 1984 which allowed Hong Kong to revert back to the control of China on July 1, 1997. This joint agreement provided for Hong Kong to remain a separate customs territory after June 30, 1997. Hong

Kong has experienced dynamic economic growth since the end of World War II. Hong Kong is the third largest financial center in the world, after New York and London. The Hong Kong government has a policy of nonintervention on the financial sectors. English common law and rules of equity apply in Hong Kong to the extent that they are applicable to local circumstances. English acts have force in Hong Kong by virtue of their own terms or by an order of the Legislative Council of Hong Kong. Chinese and English are the official languages of Hong Kong. Most important documents are published in both languages, and are required in many instances. There is no central bank in Hong Kong, but Hong Kong currency notes are issued by two commercial banks. On June 6, 1972, the Hong Kong government decided to quote the Hong Kong dollar in terms of the U.S. dollar. Hong Kong is not a tax haven per se, but an area with a low tax structure. There are no residence or nationality restrictions regarding the ownership of real estate in Hong Kong. There are no exchange controls or restrictions in force. Banks and their personnel maintain secrecy as a matter of custom and not by law. Hong Kong has not entered into any double taxation agreements with other countries. Transportation and communication are of the best in the world. There are regularly scheduled flights to and from Hong Kong to most of the major cities around the world. A corporation can be formed with no less than two subscribers. It can have different classes of stock. Nominees can be used to hide true identities of shareholders. There are no nationality or residency requirements, and it is not required to disclose beneficial interests. Annual returns must be filed with the Registrar of Companies, which must disclose the shareholders of the company. Minutes of shareholder meetings must be kept in Hong Kong and be open to inspection. Directors' meetings can be held anywhere in the world, and they are not open to inspection. At least two directors must be shareholders.

3.3.16   Isle of Man

The Isle of Man lies in the Irish Sea and forms part of the British Isles but not the United Kingdom. It is a possession of the British Crown but remains self-governing. The island is within the European Economic Community as far as free trade in agriculture and industrial products are concerned, but it is outside the community for all other aspects of the Treaty of Rome. There are scheduled flights to and from London, Manchester, Liverpool, Glasgow, and Blackball. There are also regularly scheduled ferries to Liverpool and Heysham. There are normal telephone and telex services available worldwide. The currency is the pound sterling, which the government issues through the Isle of Man Bank, Ltd. English, Scottish, and Manx notes are all in circulation. There are about 30 international banks, which have branches on the island. They offer a wide range of services. There is a Double Taxation Treaty of mutual disclosure with the United Kingdom. Bank secrecy is a matter of custom and not of law. There is an income tax on resident individuals and associations and nonresidents whose income is derived from the Isle of Man. There are no gift, estate, and capital gains and stamp duty (document tax) on the island. There are no exchange controls on the island. Two or more people can form a private corporation. The corporation must keep a register of all shareholders. For residents outside the Isle of Man, this register is called a "dominion register." All corporations must have two directors and also hold shares. Annual reports are required which must show the names, addresses of shareholders, and its registered office. A registered office must be located on the island.

3.3.17 Jersey

Jersey is the largest of the Channel Islands that is situated in the English Channel. It is 103 miles south of Southampton and 14 miles from the coast of France. The business center is in St. Helier. There is a busy passenger and cargo port at St. Helier providing services to England, France, and the other islands. There are frequent and regular air services to London, Paris, and other airports in the United Kingdom, France, and Ireland. Jersey has a long history of political and economic stability. The currency is the sterling. Jersey does not like the term "tax haven." It prefers to be known as a finance center and has the attitude of maintaining respectability and protection of investors dealing on the island. There are no exchange controls. There is no legislation on secrecy of information or bank secrecy, but bankers and professional advisors can use numbered bank accounts and nominees. There is a 20% income tax on resident individuals and businesses which has remained constant since 1940. English and French are the official languages. Most legal firms maintain principals and staff who are fluent in French and can translate French into English. There are many international banks on the island. Three or more people are required to form a corporation. At least nine shares must be issued and paid up. The share capital can be in any currency. There are no nationality or residence requirements for shareholders. However, a register of shareholders must be kept at the registered office and be available for public inspection. There is no requirement to disclose nominee holdings. Annual reports reflecting names and addresses of shareholders are required to be filed with the Company Registry.

3.3.18 Liberia

The Republic of Liberia was established in 1847 and has enjoyed independence and a stable free enterprise economy since its formation. The official language of commerce and government is English. The U.S. dollar is legal tender. There are no currency regulations or exchange controls. There are excellent transportation and communication facilities. Liberia has several of the most modern seaports in the world. There are no bank secrecy laws. Secrecy is a matter of custom and not law. Liberians are subject to the Liberian Internal Revenue Code. Liberia has a tax law that attracts incorporation of Liberian companies by foreign investors. Corporations that qualify are not required to file income tax returns. Liberian corporations do not incur income tax liability in Liberia if not more than 25% of the stock is owned by residents, and the company does not carry on operations in Liberia. Anyone can form a corporation in Liberia. A single person can form a corporation. It can issue "bearer" stock if fully paid. Only the registered agent must be present in Liberia. No annual reports are required to be filed with any government agency. Shareholders and directors meetings can be held any place in the world.

3.3.19 Liechtenstein

This country is located between Switzerland and Austria. It became an independent state in 1719 by the union of two Imperial Baronies of Vaduz and Schellenberg. It obtained full independence in 1806 when it joined the Confederation of the Rhine that was founded by Napoleon. After World War I, Liechtenstein favored Switzerland and drifted away from Austria with whom there was a customs union. Liechtenstein joined the Swiss customs arena, and the Swiss Franc became the country's official currency. The official language is German, but English is used in the economic sectors. It has a democratic form of government. It has taxes on income, property, estate, gift, motor vehicles, alcoholic beverages, etc. There are no currency exchange laws or regulations. It does permit bearer securities, bonds, and stock. They have bank secrecy laws. Bankers are forbidden to disclose customers' financial affairs. Transportation and communication are good. Peculiar to Liechtenstein is its law relating to associations of persons and the company without juridical personality, which is codified in the Laws on Persons and Companies (PGR Code). The PGR Code provides for a number of different kinds of corporate associations. The focal point of these legal forms, with their tax advantages, lies in holding companies and domiciliary enterprises. Holding companies and domiciliary enterprises are tax law concepts designating enterprises operating in Liechtenstein which are liable for capital and revenue taxes. These forms include

a. Companies limited by shares.
b. Private limited companies.
c. Establishments.
d. Trust enterprises.
e. Foundations.

The PGR code also provides for the limited partnership with a share capital, the company limited by quota shares, associations, cooperative associations, and others, and companies without juridical personality. The PGR code contains only a few mandatory provisions. The features of the holding company and domiciliary enterprise with their own juridical personality are:

a. The name and references to their legal form may be entered into public register in a foreign language.
b. One member of the board of directors must be a Liechtenstein citizen residing within the principality and also be a lawyer.
c. They are exempt from property, income, and revenue tax and subject to only capital tax, at a beneficial rate.
d. There must be a representative (registered agent) residing in the principality.

The establishment is an autonomous fund with its own juridical personality and for whose commitments only the resources of the undertaking are liable. It has no members or shareholders or participants of any other kind, and no capital distributed in share form, acknowledging only beneficiaries, that is, persons who draw economic advantage from it. The establishment is referred to as anstalt. The establishment may be authorized to issue its own shares in which case it comes closer to a corporation. The formers of an anstalt may be natural persons or juridical entities with residence in Liechtenstein or abroad. The founders must draw up and sign articles in written form which contain the following:

a. Company name including the designation anstalt.
b. The establishment's domicile, objects, and capital, and the powers of its supreme governing body.
c. The appointment of bodies for management and supervision.

d. The principles for preparing financial statements.
e. The form in which notices are published.

The objective of the anstalt must indicate whether the business will engage in commercial activities or investment or management of assets. The capital may be expressed in foreign currency, but must be at least Sw.Fr. 30,00 or equivalent. The bearer of the founder's rights constitutes the establishment of a supreme body. The supreme body can:

a. Appoint or dismiss the board of directors and auditors.
b. Determine the signing powers of management.
c. Approve the financial statements.
d. Change the Articles or by-laws.
e. Determine beneficiaries and their rights.
f. Appoint or dismiss the legal representative.

The establishment's beneficiaries are the people to whom the profit and benefit of the establishment accrue; this would include the people who are entitled to the income, the individual assets, and the eventual liquidation proceeds. Unless third parties are nominated as beneficiaries, the law assumes that the bearer of the founder's rights is the beneficiary.

3.3.20 Luxembourg

The Grand Duchy of Luxembourg is situated in Western Europe lying between Belgium, France, and Germany. The capital city, also called Luxembourg, is the government, business, and financial center. Transportation is good since they are in easy reach of all of Europe's road, rail, and air services. It is also linked directly to the northern European seaports through the Moselle River and the European canal system. Communication is also good with direct dialing with most of Europe and the United States. Luxembourg has developed a sophisticated banking sector. There are more than 115 international banks operating in Luxembourg. In recent years, Luxembourg has become a center for Euro-bond issues. Luxembourgish is the spoken language, and French, German, and English are widely used in official and business circles. French is used in administration while many laws still exist in German. The currency is the Luxembourg franc, currently on a par with the Belgium franc which is also legal tender in Luxembourg. Luxembourg has no central bank although the Luxembourg Monetary Institute has been created which is entitled to issue 20% of money in circulation and rediscount bills held by Luxembourg banks. The laws are based on the Code of Napoleon and the legal system has much in common with Belgium and France. It is common practice in Luxembourg for registered companies to issue bearer bonds or shares which can be held or deposited anywhere in the world. Bank secrecy with numbered accounts is normal and respected. It is governed by civil law. Luxembourg has double taxation treaties with fifteen countries under which information may be exchanged. The United States is one of those countries. Holding companies are the most commonly used in Luxembourg. The ordinary holding company pays no corporation, income, capital gains, wealth, withholding, or liquidation taxes. Exchange control regulations are in effect with the Central Bank in Brussels. Local banks are entrusted with the control of financial transactions based on the directives of the Central Bank in Brussels.

3.3.21 Malta

Malta is comprised of three islands south of Sicily in the Mediterranean Sea. The islands are approximately 122 square miles. It has mild and rainy winters and hot and dry summers. It has a population of about 400,000. Maltese are mainly descendants of ancient Carthaginians and Phoenicians with strong Italian roots. It is mostly a Roman Catholic country. English is the official language. It gained independence from Britain in 1964. Its legal system is based on English common law and Roman civil law. The president is elected by the House of Representatives for a 5-year term. The leader of the majority party is appointed prime minister. The representatives are elected for 5-year terms. Judges are appointed by the president on the advice of the prime minister. Malta is dependent on foreign trade. Tourism, electronics, shipbuilding and repair, and textiles are its major industries. It is currently contemplating entry into the European Union. It has good communication, both internal and external. There are two Internet service providers. Roads are good and paved. It has an excellent seaport and airport at Valletta. However, it is a minor transshipment point for hashish from North Africa to Western Europe. Malta is a host of many foreign banks, mostly from Europe and the Middle East. The two local banks are Bank of Valletta, Ltd. and Mid-Med Bank, Ltd. Major credit cards are honored on the islands. In 1996, a new form of company structure was introduced to cater for the growing demands of nonresidents who wished to establish their business or holding interest in Malta. The International Trading Company (ITC) is a normal onshore Maltese company with no distinction from other local companies. ITCs are taxed at the normal corporate tax rate of 35%. However, nonresident shareholders may benefit from partial refund of tax, potentially reducing the incidence of tax to 4.17%. An International Holding Company (IHC) is a company resident in Malta, formed with the objective of holding overseas investments and to distribute that income to nonresidents. Nonresident shareholders of IHCs qualify for a full refund of the Maltese tax paid by the company on profits and gains arising from participating holdings when such profits are distributed. Requirements for incorporation in Malta require a minimum capital of US$1500.00 with minimum paid up share capital of 20%. Nominee shareholders are permitted. Only one director is required. One general meeting each year is required. There are no exchange controls if the company is fully owned by nonresidents. Companies can do business in any currency. However, an annual return with audited financial statements is required. Malta has target online offshore betting operations. Maltese betting operations are carried out through an ITC setup for the purpose. Nonresident shareholders are taxed at 4.17%. Betting transactions are taxable at .5% on turnover. There are no license fees or applications fees. Betting licenses are granted to persons having the appropriate business ability to conduct betting successfully. Licenses are issued for 5 years and are renewable. A special law was enacted to allow for the setting up of trusts. The advantages of trusts in Malta are favorable taxation, confidentiality, control of assets, no probate, and investment income from trusts can be accumulated tax-free. Trusts must be in writing. Neither the settler nor beneficiaries can be a resident of Malta. The trust property shall not include immovable property situated in Malta. The trust instrument is a highly confidential document, and no person may be ordered to divulge to any authority including any court of any manner relating to a trust. The Professional Secrecy Act (1994) prohibits any lawyer, banker, stockbroker, and accountant from divulging any information about their clients unless there is international criminal activity (money laundering, drug dealing, etc.) involved.

3.3.22　Mauritius

Mauritius is a mountainous sub-tropical island in the Indian Ocean with an area of approximately 788 square miles. It lies about 800 km east of Madagascar. The capital is Port Luis. It has a tropical climate with warm, dry winters and hot, wet, humid summers. Mauritius has a population of 1,210,000 which is mostly Indonesian. Creole is the second largest group. English is the official language even though French, Creole, and Hindi is spoken. The British took possession of the islands in 1810. Mauritius gained independence in 1968 and became a member of the Commonwealth. The Queen was Head of State until March 12, 1992, when it became a Republic. The head of state is the president who is elected by the National Assembly and serves a 5-year term. The prime minister and cabinet are appointed by the president. The National Assembly is elected and members serve 5-year terms. The legal system is based on French civil law with elements of English common law in certain areas. Mauritius has developed to a middle income diversified economy with growing industrial, financial, and tourist sectors. Sugar cane is the major agricultural business. It has good telecommunication facilities including cellular phone service and two Internet service providers. It has good roads, one good seaport, and two good airports. There are two types of companies used for international tax planning: the International Company (IC) governed by the International Companies Act and the Offshore Company (OC) governed by the Mauritius Companies Act of 1984. Offshore banks and insurance companies cannot operate as ICs. OCs need not make annual returns but must file an audited profit and loss statement and balance sheet with the Offshore Authority. Every Mauritian company must have a registered office in Mauritius. The registered office must have accounting records and certain documents including a register of members, debenture holders, and officers. OCs must have a minimum of two individual shareholders, and/or they must hold annual general meetings. The meetings need not be held in Mauritius. Incorporation takes up to 14 days. The ICs cannot transact business in Mauritian rupees with Mauritian residents. It cannot be used for public, banking, insurance, or fund related activities or to access Mauritius double taxation agreements. An IC can be incorporated on the same day. The identities of the beneficial owner(s) need to be disclosed only to the management company. There are no filing requirements to file annual accounts and returns, or to hold directors and shareholder meetings. The IC is not resident in Mauritius and therefore not liable to tax. An OC can be converted to IC and vice versa. The Mauritius Offshore Trusts may be created by oral declaration or by writing. To be enforceable the declaration of trust must be registered with the Mauritius Offshore Business Activities Authority (MOBAA). There are no forced heirship rules. The perpetuity rule is 100 years from the date the trust came into existence. There is no disclosure of trustee's deliberations or the names of the settlers and the beneficiaries unless the latter is a Mauritian resident. Claims against the trust assets must be made within 2 years of settling of property into the trust. Under the Mauritius Finance Act 1996, nonresident trusts and nonresident beneficiaries will be exempt from tax and all filing requirements. Charitable trusts are exempt from taxation.

3.3.23　Montserrat

Montserrat is an island east of Puerto Rico and the United States Virgin Islands. The island is a dependent territory of the United Kingdom with an appointed governor by the British government. The island has a history of political stability. The legal system is based on the common law of England. The local and official language is English. The economy is based on agriculture, light industry, and tourism. Tax incentives are available for new business enterprises on the island. The Eastern Caribbean dollar is the official currency, although the U.S. dollar and the sterling are circulated. The EC$ is tied to the U.S. dollar and is fully convertible. The government has provided incentives for businesses to operate on the island. It offers incentives of tax holidays and duty free imports. The Confidential Information Ordinance (1985) provides heavy penalties for unauthorized revealing of information. Montserrat has double taxation treaties through the extension of some of the United Kingdom treaties with the governments of Canada, Denmark, Japan, New Zealand, Norway, Sweden, and Switzerland. Two local banks, Barclays and the Royal Bank of Canada, do not permit numbered accounts although there are no legal bars against them. Corporations can be formed under the provisions of the International Business Companies Ordinance (1985). It provides that only one subscriber is necessary. There are no restrictions on the transfer of shares, number of shareholders, or debentures. The Memorandum of Association must include the name of the company, which must contain "limited," registered office in Monserrat, purpose, authorized capital, and number of shares. A registered office must be maintained on the island. Annual reports must be filed with the Registrar of Companies for private companies, but none are required for International Business Companies. Bearer stock is allowed provided that it is paid in full. Annual meetings of shareholders and directors can be held anywhere in the world. All international business companies are specifically exempted from exchange control. Montserrat is part of the Eastern Caribbean Banking network. There are good transportation facilities, both air and sea. Communication facilities are also good.

Recently, a volcano has erupted on the island, which has sent many residents fleeing to neighboring islands. The British government has asked for the remaining residents to move off the island, since it is expected that the volcano will erupt again. This island may become deserted, which will leave its tax haven status in doubt. Currently, the government and business are still operating, but only at one end of the island not affected by the volcano.

3.3.24 Niue

Niue was formerly called Savage Island. The island is in the South Pacific, east of Tonga. Niue is dependent on New Zealand for financial support. It is only 100 square miles with a population of about 1800 people. It has no paved roads, only one airport, and no seaport. Ships have to anchor offshore. The economy is heavily dependent on New Zealand. The sale of postage stamps to foreign collectors is an important source of revenue. There are no exchange controls. English is spoken, but the indigenous language of Polynesian tongue is closely related to Tongan and Samoan. Niue provides a jurisdiction in an alternative time zone to the Caribbean as well as certain features embodied in the International Business Corporation Law, favorable to clients in Asia and the former Soviet Union. Niue offers total secrecy and anonymity. There are no requirements to disclose beneficial owners or to file annual returns and financial statements. Holding annual general meetings of shareholders or directors is not required. They offer full exemption from taxation arising on any business activity or transaction carried on outside of Niue. There are no minimum or maximum capital requirements. Companies may use different classes of shares at the owner's option. Another unique feature is the ability for the company name to be incorporated in

Chinese characters as well as Cyrillic script and other accepted language forms (with an English translation). Foreign companies may be redomiciled as Niue IBC's. There are a few names and suffixes available to indicate that it is a corporation: Limited, Ltd., Corporation, S.A., Incorporation, Inc., A/S, NV, BV, GmbH, Aktiengesellschaft, AG, etc. A problem for Niue is the loss of population to New Zealand. There are 20,000 Niueans living in New Zealand who believe Niue will have to surrender its independence and return to New Zealand since the island has no economy. Their tourism and tax haven revenues have not been able to support the island nation. New Zealand makes up for the shortfall in its budget.

3.3.25 Nauru

The smallest island nation, Nauru became an independent sovereign state on January 31, 1968, and subsequently became an associate member of the British Commonwealth. It is in the center of the Pacific Basin, being located about equidistant from Sydney, Australia, to the southwest and from Hawaii to the northeast. Nauru has close educational links with Australia. Nauru has a democratic government with elected Parliament and president. It has a well-developed and efficient civil service and judicial system. Air Nauru, the airline of Nauru, connects Nauru with Australia, Fiji, Hong Kong, Manila, Honolulu, and other Pacific Islands on a regular basis, usually twice a week. Nauru is well connected through a satellite in order to render telephone, cable, telex, and facsimile services to and from the principal cities of various countries, including the United States. The official currency of Nauru is the Australian dollar, which is freely convertible into different currencies. Nauru designed legislation with the intent to provide facilities for tax planners. It wants to help entrepreneurs, both new and existing, to generate and mobilize their resources for economic expansion. At the same time, it guards against fraud on creditors, investors, depositors, and shareholders. It offers full freedom for entrepreneurs to establish holding and trading companies but does not hesitate to terminate the corporate existence of those corporations which carry out fraudulent business within or outside Nauru. Corporations offer the following advantages:

   a. Minimum formation time (24 hours).
   b. Low formation costs.
   c. Minimum pre- and post-incorporation legal formalities.
   d. Low capitalization.
   e. Freedom to issue bearer shares.
   f. Complete secrecy of operations.
   g. Anonymity of promoters.

A resident secretary is required by statute. Shares must be stated in Australian currency. There are some exceptions. Annual reports are required to be filed with the Registrar. The reports only require the names of directors, secretaries, and the registered agent.

3.3.26 Netherlands Antilles

This country is located off the coast of Venzuela. It is dominated and controlled by the Netherlands. The Netherlands Antilles is also part of the European Economic Community.

These islands have their own island government. The official language is Dutch; however, English, German, French, and Spanish are used. The monetary unit is the Netherlands Antilles guilder. It is pegged to the U.S. dollar at $1.79 per 1 guilder. Identity of shareholders is not available for public inspection until all issued shares of stock have been fully paid up. Income tax is imposed only on income derived within the Netherlands Antilles. Currency exchange is only imposed on individuals and corporations doing business within the Netherlands Antilles. Transportation and communication are very good. The government does not mandate bank secrecy; however, it is bankers' custom to regard their customers' affairs as confidential. A Limited Liability Company (NV) is allowed to issue "bearer" shares, but they must be fully paid. Shareholder meetings must be held in the Netherlands Antilles, but proxy can represent them. It requires two or more people to incorporate. The managing director, "Directeur," must be a resident of the island. He serves as the registered agent. Financial reports are required to be filed with the Commercial Registry if the corporation has issued (1) bearer shares exceeding 50,000 guilders, (2) shares or bonds on a stock exchange, and (3) the corporation borrows from third parties. Auditors are required to audit the financial statements. Only auditors from the Netherlands Antilles can be used.

3.3.27 Nevis

This Caribbean Island lies east of Puerto Rico west of Montserrat. It is a democratic country that is part of the British Commonwealth. Britain is responsible for external affairs and defense. Nevis is part of the Federation of St. Kitts and Nevis. The Judicial Commonwealth of the Privy Council of Great Britain is the court of ultimate jurisdiction and consists of members from the House of Lords. The official language and language in use is English. Nevis is self-sufficient in food production but has a trade deficit. The government is seeking diversification through expansion of tourism, fisheries, light manufacturing, and offshore financial activities. The currency is the Eastern Caribbean Currency dollar (EC$). It is pegged to the U.S. dollar at EC$2.70 = US$1. The EC$ is not an internationally traded currency. The adoption of the Nevis Business Corporation Ordinance (1984) signified the government's commitment to become a modern tax haven. The Ordinance provided that they conduct no commercial business on the island. Corporations can be formed in 24 hours. The Government adopted the Confidential Relationships Act (1985) which is applicable to Office of the Registrar of Companies and professionals engaged in related services, financial and otherwise. There are no treaties respecting information exchange. Numbered bank accounts are not available through Nevis banks. Corporations formed under the Nevis Business Corporation Ordinance are not subject to exchange controls. Exchange controls on EC$ are in effect when exchanged for foreign currency. Transportation and communication are good. There are regularly scheduled flights to other major islands in the Caribbean Basin. Only two people are required to form a corporation. The Articles of Incorporation must show the names and addresses of the incorporators and the initial directors. "Bearer" stock is authorized, but must be paid in full. There must be three directors who can be of any nationality or domicile. There is no requirement to show the names of subsequent shareholders or directors. Shareholders and directors meetings can be held anywhere in the world. A registered agent is required to be a resident of the island. Most corporations use Corporate Services Company on Charlestown, Nevis, as the registered agent. No annual reports are required to be filed.

3.3.28   Panama

This country is located in Central America, north of Colombia. It has an area of approximately 76,900 km². The official language is Spanish, but English is spoken in urban areas and used in daily commerce. Transportation and communications are excellent. They are supposed to have a democratic form of government; however, they have had dictators during the past several decades. The United States military invaded Panama in December 1989 and removed General Manuel Noreiga. The currency of Panama is the balboa; however, since there is no balboa currency, the U.S. dollar is circulated and accepted as the medium of exchange. The judicial system follows English common law. Panama has income taxes, but they are imposed at the provincial level. Income derived outside Panama is not taxed. There are no currency exchange controls in Panama. There are no bank secrecy laws, but custom has its bankers to regard their customers' affairs as confidential. A corporation can be formed by as few as two people and be of any nationality or domicile. "Bearer" shares can be issued. The full names and addresses of directors must be recorded in the Public Registry Office. Every corporation must have a resident registered agent, which is generally some lawyer in Panama. There is no requirement for general or special meetings of shareholders or directors. The directors can be of any nationality or domicile. There must be three directors. They do not have to be shareholders.

3.3.29   Switzerland

This country is located in the heart of Europe. Switzerland has three official languages: German, French, and Italian. English is not used for official documents but is used in official correspondence. This is a democratic country. The currency is the Swiss franc. Transportation and communication to and from Switzerland is very excellent. The banks guard their customers' financial accounts. Switzerland has income, estate, capital gains, and inheritance taxes on residents. There are no currency exchange controls. The substantive law of Switzerland is codified. The Civil and Commercial Codes are applicable throughout Switzerland. While the law is based on federal and cantonal legislation, court decisions and precedents play an important role. Foreign nationals can open numbered bank accounts in most banks. Switzerland does have double taxation treaties with many countries including the United States. Three or more individuals or companies can form a Swiss corporation. Their nationality and residence do not matter. The corporation must have a minimum capital of Sw.Fr. 50,000 and paid up of Sw.Fr. 20,000. They can have either ordinary shares or preference shares. Both classes of stock can be bearer or registered shares. Shareholders can use nominees. Shareholder names are not allowed to be identified to third parties or fiscal authorities. Auditors in Switzerland must audit the financial statements. They can only release their results to directors and shareholders as a group. The registered agent must be a resident of Switzerland and his/her name is published in the Commercial Gazette.

3.3.30   Turks and Caicos Islands

The Turks and Caicos Islands lie about 100 miles north of Haiti and the Dominican Republic. They are a British Crown Colony under the jurisdiction of the British government. The British government appoints the governor. The legal system is based on British common law. Ultimate appeal is the Privy Council sitting in London. English is both the official and spoken language. The U.S. dollar is the official currency in the islands. The Turks and Caicos' government enacted the Companies Ordinance (1981) to establish the islands as a major offshore center. The government has a strong desire to attract offshore financial and business activity. The principal banks on the islands are Barclays Bank International and the Bank of Nova Scotia. There is no central bank. The economy is based primarily on tourism, offshore business, and fishing. There are good transportation and communication. There are regularly scheduled flights to the United States and other islands. Direct dial service is available on the islands. Bank secrecy is a matter of custom and not of law. The Turks and Caicos Islands have no income, capital gains, corporate, sales, property, withholding, payroll, inheritance, gift, or estate taxes. The islands get most of their revenue from import duties. The Turks and Caicos Islands enacted the Narcotic Drug Ordinance (1986) under which the Attorney General of the United States may certify to the Attorney General of the Turks and Caicos that certain documents and testimony are needed for Grand Jury investigation of narcotics offenses. The islands can compel both public and private sources to comply with requests. The islands do not want to become a haven for drug traffickers. An "exempt" company is one that does not operate on the islands. An exempt corporation can be formed with as few as one shareholder. The corporation can be formed without going to the islands. Annual reports are not required. It does not have to hold either shareholder or director meetings. A registered agent is required to be on the island. Identities of shareholders and directors are not shown in public records. Bearer shares can be issued.

3.3.31   Vanuatu

Vanuatu is an independent democratic republic. It was formally called the New Hebrides when it was part of the British Commonwealth. Vanuatu lies east of Australia. English and French are widely used together with Bislama. Bislama is the official language. The official currency is the Vatu which is linked to Special Drawing Rights (1 SDR = 110 VT). In 1985, 106 VT = $1.00 US. Exempt companies under Vanuatu law are secret companies and breach of that secrecy can entail fines and imprisonment. There are no taxes on income and capital; thus there are no double taxation treaties with other countries. Number accounts are not available in Vanuatu. It can take only three days to two weeks to set up a company. "Exempt" companies are not allowed to do business in Vanuatu. Every company is required to keep a register of members, directors, officers, and proper books of account on the island. Annual reports are required to be filed every year. For exempt companies, these records and reports are to be kept secret. It is against the law for any government official to disclose this information. An auditor and registrar are required for all companies to be on the island. Exempt companies are not required to have an auditor but must have a registrar. Shareholders' and directors' names of an exempt company are not available to the public. There are no income or capital gains taxes on the island. There are no exchange controls. Bank accounts can be kept in foreign currency.

3.3.32   British Virgin Islands

These islands lie just east of Puerto Rico in the Caribbean basin. They consist primarily of four islands: Tortola, Anegada, Virgin Gorda, and Jost Van Dyke. The main and largest city is Road Town. The official and common language is English. The British Virgin Islands are a part of the British Commonwealth. The British government appoints the governor. Its main industry is tourism. Transportation is good. There are regularly scheduled flights to Puerto Rico, Miami, and eastern Caribbean Islands. Communication is also good. There is direct dial telephone service to Puerto Rico and other countries. Sterling is the main currency; however, U.S. dollars are also accepted. There are no exchange controls. There is no central bank. There is no income, capital gains, gift, or estate taxes. The primary source of revenue is import duties. The government encourages foreign investment and capital. Banking and finance in the islands are the same as those in the Turks and Caicos Islands. The legal system is the same for the British Virgin Islands as it is for the Turks and Caicos Islands. An International Business Company is a corporation that does no business on the islands. A single individual can incorporate in the British Virgin Islands. Bearer stock is allowed but must be paid in full. Annual reports for exempt companies do not reflect names and addresses of shareholders or directors. A registered agent is required and is a resident of the islands. Shareholder and director meetings can be held anywhere in the world.

3.4   Mutual Legal Assistance Treaties

Mutual Legal Assistance in Criminal Matters Treaties (MLATs) are a relatively recent development. Their purpose is to obtain judicial assistance and to regularize and facilitate procedures. Treaty members designate a central authority, usually Justice Departments, for direct communication. The treaties include the power to summon witnesses, to compel the production of documents and other real evidence, to issue search warrants, and to serve process. Generally, the remedies offered are only available to prosecutors. The defense must usually proceed with the methods of obtaining evidence in criminal matters under the laws of the host country which usually involve letters regatory. The United States has entered into MLATs with some tax haven countries. These countries are Antigua/Barbuda, Bahamas, Barbados, Hong Kong, Luxembourg, Montserrat, Panama, St. Kitts-Nevis, and Switzerland. The treaty with the United Kingdom extends to the Cayman Islands, British Virgin Islands, and Anguilla. These MLAT treaties allow the governments to exchange information on criminal matters. However, most of the MLAT treaties do not allow the exchange of information involving tax evasion. In fact, evidence acquired under MLAT cannot be used in either criminal or civil tax matters. One purpose of these treaties was to overcome the bank secrecy laws. Those individuals or organizations involved in illegal activities within tax haven countries are becoming more transparent.

3.5   Financial Action Task Force

The Financial Action Task Force (FAFT) is an international organization of 31 nations. It was created in 1989 for the purpose of coordinating international money laundering efforts. The FAFT's most significant accomplishment has been the establishment of Financial Intelligence Units in 58 countries which share financial information without resorting to courts. It initially had blacklisted 19 countries with bank secrecy laws. Bank secrecy laws were an impediment to its efforts. FAFT issued a report in 2000 designating 15 countries as uncooperative. They threatened with unspecified action if the countries did not change their laws and begin sharing financial information. Some countries have complied with the mandate, some remain uncompliant, and some others have been added. One action taken by FAFT was to advise U.S. financial institutions against a particular tax haven country as a significant money laundering threat and transactions were to be scrutinized. This resulted in offshore banks losing U.S. correspondent relationships. The United Kingdom has taken a similar action.

3.6   Organization for Economic Cooperation and Development

The Organization for Economic Cooperation and Development (OECD) came into force in 1961 and is based in Paris. It was composed of most all industrialized nations. It also is the parent to FAFT. Since 1998, the OECD has promoted a global cooperative framework to offset harmful tax practices. Harmful tax practice is defined as meeting one of four criteria. First, there is no effective exchange of information. Second, there is a lack of transparency. Third, there are no substantial activities or ring fencing from domestic activities. Last, there is an offer of low, nonexistent, or nominal tax rates. The OECD's aim is to establish effective exchange of information and transparency for tax purposes. The OECD's council recommended, inter alia, the following enforcement strategies against tax havens:

1. Removing barriers of access to banking information by tax authorities.
2. Exchanging information at a greater level and more efficiently.
3. Strengthening coordinated enforcement regimes.
4. Increasing assistance in recovery of tax claims.
5. Strengthening foreign information reporting rules.

The OECD identified some potential defensive measures to be utilized against tax havens in their July 31, 2001 report. Some possible defensive measures are:

1. To disallow deductions, exemptions, credits, or other allowances related to transactions with uncooperative tax havens.
2. To require comprehensive information reporting rules.
3. To withhold taxes on certain payments to residents of uncooperative tax haven countries.
4. To abstain from any comprehensive income tax conventions with uncooperative tax havens.
5. To impose transactional charges or levies on certain transactions involving uncooperative tax haven countries.

In 2000, the OECD focused its attack on the issue of bank secrecy and the exchange of information in tax investigations. It initially targeted 41 jurisdictions as tax havens and threatened economic sanctions unless the countries pledged to cooperate on tax matters, including the elimination of tax secrecy. At first, most nations stood firm but one by one began to fold. The tax haven countries have accused the OECD of infringing on their sovereignty and have accused the OECD of tyranny. Tax haven countries fear the crackdown will hinder their efforts to develop new businesses. This is especially true for those tax haven countries whose economies are fragile, have resource constraints, infrastructure limitations, and are dependent on financial services. The OECD's overreach must be seen in the context of an increasingly centralized Europe. Europeans are being guided into a supranational European state with is heading toward central planning, homogenization of laws throughout the continent, heavy taxation, and inflation of the money supply. Even more, the United Nations is pushing for an international tax collection organization for global taxes and for an emigrant tax. In May 2001, the United States withdrew support for the OECD's initiative. The United States did not believe that any country or group of countries should interfere with another country's tax system. The United States did not support efforts to dictate to any country what its own tax rates or tax system should be and would not participate in any initiative to harmonize world tax systems. In June 2001, the OECD gave in to the U.S. demands and agreed to a less aggressive approach to combat tax evasion. The OECD agreed not to impose sanctions on tax havens that simply offer favorable tax breaks to foreign corporations and investors (ring fencing). The United States agreed to support its campaign to disclose account information of those suspected of tax evasion.

The OECD developed a Model Tax Standard with the cooperation of non-OECD countries. It was endorsed by the G20 Finance Ministers at their Berlin meeting in 2004. The UN Committee of Experts on International Cooperation in Tax Matters endorsed the Model Tax Standard at their October 2008 meeting. The Model Tax Standard requires exchange of information on request in all tax matters for the administration and enforcement of domestic tax law. The country requested should supply the information without regard to domestic tax interest or bank secrecy. Thirty-two countries have committed to the international tax standard but have not fully implemented, and four countries have not made any commitment.

3.7   Fraud Indicators

Fraud examiners will invariably come across offshore entities when examining organized crime elements with international connections. The fraud examiner should become familiar with the country of origin as well as the type of entity. An entity that is located in a "tax haven" country should be examined very closely. Indicators of fraudulent offshore entities are:

1. No Payments. The offshore entity either lends or invests funds in the United States. However, there are no interest or dividend payments going out.
2. Not U.S. Registered. The offshore entity is not licensed to do business in the United States. A check with the secretary of state or Bureau of Corporations of any particular state shows that the corporation or business entity is not registered or licensed to conduct business in the state. Failure for the foreign entity to register with the state bars any legal recourse or remedy.

    What company would loan or invest funds without having some legal recourse if the capital provided is not protected?
3. Failure to File Tax Returns. The offshore entity does not file federal or state tax returns. In general, income derived in the United States by foreign entities is taxable at both federal and state levels.
4. No Place of Business. The entity does not have any place of business in either the country of origin or the United States. This will clearly show that the offshore entity is a means of concealing ownership of illegal funds.

Finance, investment, insurance companies, and trusts are the most common type of entities used to launder illegal gains from illegal activities through offshore companies.

3.8 Outlook for Tax Havens

Tax haven countries have been a target of the industrialized world. Since 1998, the OECD nations have begun to target tax havens. Many tax havens are British protectorates. They are expected to comply with OECD dictates. For the remaining countries, OECD sanctions could destroy their tax haven businesses. The United States needs to be careful with tax havens in the Caribbean, since their economies need to be preserved. If the economies were to collapse, the drug cartels would take over. Tax havens will survive but in a different form. Tax havens will agree to information sharing with OECD countries, but only when there is an actual tax or criminal investigation. There will not be indiscriminate disclosure of identities and activities in using tax havens. There are some safeguards to protect the confidentiality of the information exchanged by treaty.

3.9 Summary

The fraud examiner should pay close attention to foreign individuals and entities that are located offshore. Attention is particularly necessary when foreign individuals and entities are located in "tax haven" countries that have bank secrecy laws or customs. Many tax haven countries have treaties whereby a prosecutor can obtain information. In some countries, records of legal entities are public and freely available. However, bank records are not available and will require some judicial proceeding to obtain them. Some of the tax haven countries cooperate with international law enforcement agencies, particularly in the drug trafficking area. Official requests can be made, but should go through the Department of State. The fraud examiner should study the country's legal system and find out what records are available and how to obtain them. Records that fall in the public domain can be obtained by a consular officer and certified by him/her for use in federal or state courts. Various federal law enforcement agencies, for example, Customs, FBI, and DEA, have liaison offices in many countries. These representatives can help obtain information for law enforcement. For instance, they can see if a foreign corporation has a going business in the country of origin. They can secure public information and interview witnesses. For local law enforcement agencies, these resources should be utilized. All tax haven countries that allow bearer stock and bonds require that they be paid in full before they are issued. When these bearer stock and bonds are found in the course of searches, these securities have the same value as money. Depending on the circumstances, these securities can be exchanged for cash.

Evidence

4

4.1 General

Forensic accountants must gather evidence to support an investigation of a financial crime. Too often this takes much time and effort to gather and compile. The objective of this chapter is to show the forensic accountant what evidence is admissible in both civil and criminal court proceedings. The Federal Rules of Evidence (FRE) are used in this chapter; therefore, forensic accountants should check with local prosecutors to ensure these rules are applicable to local courts.

4.2 Evidence

Evidence is all means by which an alleged matter of fact is established or disproved. A forensic accountant can obtain documents and statements which show that a bank account has increased substantially. This is an evidentiary fact from which an inference may be drawn relative to the ultimate or principal fact, namely, that the subject was involved in a profitable activity. Evidence is legally admissible in court under the rules of evidence because it tends to support or prove a fact. Evidence is distinguished from proof in that the latter is the result or effect of evidence.

Direct evidence is that which proves the existence of the principal or fact without any inference or presumption. It is direct when those who have actual knowledge of them by means of their senses swear to the very facts in dispute. It may take the form of admissions or confessions made in or out of court.

Circumstantial evidence is that which tends to prove the existence of the principal fact by inference. The courts recognize the use of circumstantial evidence as a legitimate means of proof. It involves proving several material facts, which, when considered in their relationship to each other, tend to establish the existence of the principal or ultimate fact. Violations involving willful intent are provided by circumstantial evidence. It is the only type of evidence generally available to show such elements of a crime as malice, intent, or motive, which exists only in the mind of the perpetrator of the act. Circumstantial evidence may be as convincing as direct evidence. Sometimes, a jury may find that it outweighs conflicting direct evidence.

Evidence also may be classified as oral, documentary, or real. Evidence may be presented orally through witnesses or by the submission of records or other physical objects. Oral testimony consists of statements made by living witnesses under oath. Documentary evidence consists of writings such as judicial and official records, contracts, deeds, and less formal writings such as letters, memorandums, and books and records of private persons or organizations. Maps, diagrams, and photographs are classified as documentary evidence.

Real or physical evidence relates to tangible objects or property that are admitted in court or inspected by a trier of facts, such as a knife or pistol. Evidence must be relevant, material, and competent in order for it to be admissible in court.

4.2.1 Relevancy

Relevancy relates evidence in some manner to the principal fact. It implies a traceable and significant connection. It is sufficient if it constitutes one link in a chain of evidence or if it relates to facts that would constitute circumstantial evidence that a fact in issue did or did not exist. Rule 401 defines relevant evidence as "evidence having any tendency to make the existence of any fact that is of consequence to the determination of the action more probable or less probable than it would be without the evidence." Rule 402 provides that all relevant evidence is admissible, except as otherwise provided by the Constitution of the United States, by an Act of Congress, or by other rules prescribed by the Supreme Court pursuant to statutory authority. Evidence that is not relevant is not admissible.

Investigators should obtain all facts that relate to the case. They should never omit any significant facts because of doubt regarding relevance. There are no set standards for relevancy because facts vary from case to case and judges have wide discretion in determining what evidence is relevant. Also, investigators should not omit evidence because of doubt as to its materiality or competency.

4.2.2 Materiality

Evidence is material if it is essential to the subject matter in dispute as to affect the outcome of a trial, or to help establish the guilt or innocence of the accused. This definition is included in the definition of relevancy.

4.2.3 Competency

Evidence must not only be relevant and persuasive but also legally admissible. Relevant evidence may be incompetent and hence inadmissible because it is hearsay or not the best evidence. Evidence, such as documents, is competent if it was obtained in a manner, in a form, and from a source proper under the law.

4.3 Limited Admissibility

Evidence may not be admissible for one purpose but does not preclude its use for another. A piece of evidence may not be admissible as independent proof of a principal fact and still may be admitted to corroborate another fact.

4.4 Hearsay

Hearsay has been defined as evidence which does not come from the personal knowledge of the witness but from what he has heard others say or from a document prepared by others. Hearsay is secondhand evidence and is not admissible in court. An investigator's testimony that payees of corporate checks were for personal expenses of the subject, an officer of the corporation, is inadmissible as hearsay (Greenberg Rule). The personal nature of the payments should be proven through the subject's own records or others as to his admission or testimony of the third parties.

Cross-examination is essential as a test of the truth of the facts offered. It provides an opportunity to test the credibility of the witness, his observations, memory, bias, prejudice, and possible errors. It subjects the witness to the penalties of perjury and may eliminate deliberate or unintentional misstatements of what he has been told.

4.5 Admissions and Confessions

An admission is not considered to be hearsay. An admission may be defined as a statement or act of a party which is offered in evidence against him. It also may be defined as a prior oral or written statement or act which is inconsistent with his position in the pleadings or at trial. Admissions can be used either as evidence of facts or to discredit a party as a witness. They can be used only as to facts, not as to matters of law, opinion, or hearsay. A confession is a statement of a person that he is guilty of a crime.

4.6 Exceptions to Hearsay Rule

The courts have made certain exceptions to the hearsay rule. The exceptions are based on two principal reasons: necessity for use and probability of trustworthiness. The necessity rule usually comes into being from the unavailability of the person who made the statement to appear or testify, and the court would thereby be deprived of evidence that is important in the decision of an issue. The evidence must also have the probability of truthfulness that will substitute for cross-examination. Evidence that meets the above standards is admissible as an exception to the hearsay rule. Other exceptions are as follows:

4.6.1 Business Records, Public Records, and Commercial Documents

Records containing entries made in the regular course of business, as well as marriage, baptismal, and similar certificates are admissible without testimony of the person who made the entries if some witness properly identifies them. Public records made by an officer in the performance of his duties are also admissible after proper authentication.

4.6.2 Expert and Opinion Testimony

Expert opinions are the conclusions of a person who has been qualified as an expert in his field; they are admitted to aid the jury in its deliberations. Opinions of laymen may also be admitted into evidence under certain circumstances (e.g., handwriting recognition and physical condition). A police officer may give his opinion concerning the speed of an automobile. The basis for permitting this is that the police officer has specialized experience beyond that of the ordinary person, which would qualify him to give his opinion in the matter.

4.6.3 Reputation

A defendant in a prosecution may offer witnesses to testify as to his good reputation in the community where he lives. Such evidence is competent because it may tend to generate a reasonable doubt of his guilt. The evidence should be restricted to the character trait in issue and should bear an analogy to the nature of the charge. For instance, if a witness for the defendant in a bribery case were asked on direct examination if he knew the defendant's general reputation for peacefulness, there would be an inconsistency to the nature of the charge. The witnesses must confine their testimony to general reputation and may not testify about their own knowledge or observation of the defendant or about his specific acts or courses of conduct. Once the defense has raised the issue of character, the prosecution may offer evidence of bad reputation in rebuttal of character testimony. Rule 405 provides that "on cross-examination inquiry is allowable into relevant specific instances of conduct."

4.6.4 Records of Documents Affecting an Interest in Property

If a document affecting an interest in property (e.g., deed) is recorded in a public record and an applicable statute authorizes the recording of documents of that kind in that office, the record of such document may be admissible as proof of the original recorded document and its execution and delivery by each person by whom it purports to have been executed (FRE 803(114)).

4.6.5 Mental and Physical Condition

Contemporaneous or spontaneous declarations of a person may be admissible to prove his mental or physical condition. While such statements carry more weight when made by a physician for purposes of treatment, they may be competent even if made to family members or to other persons. Thus, a trial court in a fraud case might admit a lay witness's testimony that he heard the defendant complain of severe headaches and inability to concentrate just before preparing his alleged false travel expense voucher.

4.6.6 Excited Utterance (also known as "Spontaneous Declaration")

This has been defined as a "statement relating to a startling event or condition made while the declarant was under the stress or excitement caused by the event or condition" (Rule 803.2). The trustworthiness of such statements lies in their spontaneity, for the occurrence must be startling enough to produce a spontaneous and unreflected utterance without time to contrive or to misrepresent.

Excited utterances may be made by participants or by bystanders, and a person who made or heard such statements may testify about them in court.

4.6.7 Recorded Recollection

If a witness once had knowledge regarding a memorandum or record but at the time he is called to testify has insufficient recollection to enable him to testify fully and accurately, the evidence may still be used in court. It must be shown, however, that the memorandum or record was made or adopted by the witness when the matter was fresh in his memory and reflects his knowledge correctly. If admitted, the memorandum or record may be read into evidence, but may not itself be received as an exhibit unless offered by an adverse party (Rule 303.5).

4.6.8 Absence of Entry

The FRE also provides for an exception to the hearsay rule with respect to evidence of the absence of an entry in records kept in the regular course of business and absence of a public record or entry if the matter was of a kind in which the business or public office ordinarily made and preserved a record. It must be shown that a diligent search of the records has been made, and the evidence may be ruled inadmissible if "the sources of the information or other circumstances indicate of trustworthiness" (Rules 308.7 and 308.10).

4.7 Hearsay Exceptions: Declarant Unavailable

The following exceptions to the hearsay rule relate to situations in which the declarant (the person who made the statements) is unavailable for the trial (e.g., if he has died, has disappeared, is mentally or physically incapacitated, is beyond the jurisdiction of the court, or is exempted by ruling of the court on the ground of privilege concerning the subject matter of his statement):

4.7.1 Former Testimony

This is testimony given by a witness at another hearing of the same or a different proceeding, or in a deposition taken in compliance with law in the course of the same or another proceeding, if the party against whom the testimony is now offered (in a criminal proceeding) had an opportunity and similar motive to develop the testimony by direct, cross, or redirect examination (Rule 804(b)(1)). Testimony and evidence in civil proceedings can be used later on in criminal proceedings.

4.7.2 Statement against Interest

This is a statement against interest that relates to an oral or written declaration by one who is not a party to the action and not available to testify. It must be shown that such statement was, at the time of its making, so far contrary to the declarant's pecuniary or proprietary interest or so far tended to make invalid a claim by him against another, that a reasonable person in his position would not have made the statement unless he believed it to be true. For example, in order to establish that a defendant paid off a large debt with currency on a certain date, the government may prove the payment through an entry in the personal diary of the deceased creditor. The diary could be identified by a relative of the deceased as having been found among his papers after his death (Rule 804(b)(3)). Some courts have extended this rule to include statements against penal interest.

4.7.3 Dying Declarations

Dying declarations are statements made by the victim of a homicide who believes that death is imminent. To be admissible, such statements must relate only to facts concerning the cause for and circumstances surrounding the homicide charged. They are admitted from the necessities of the case to prevent a failure of justice. Furthermore, the sense of impending death is presumed to remove all temptation of falsehood. The statements may be admitted only in the murder trial or under Rule 804(b)(2) in a civil proceeding.

4.8 Documentary Evidence

Documentary evidence is evidence consisting of writings and documents as distinguished from oral evidence.

4.8.1 Best Evidence Rule

The best evidence rule, which applies only to documentary evidence, is that the best proof of the contents of a document is the document itself. The best evidence rule, requiring production of the original document, is confined to cases where it is sought to prove the contents of the document. Production consists of either making the writing available to the court or opposing counsel. Facts about a document other than its contents are provable without its production. For example, the fact that a sales contract was made is a fact separate from the actual terms of the contract and may be proven by testimony alone.

The best evidence rule has applied essentially to documents. Modern techniques of storing data have made its expansion to include computers, photographic systems, and other new developments. In Rule 1001 writings and recordings are defined as letters, words or numbers, or their equivalent, set down by handwriting, typewriters, printing, photostating, photographing, magnetic impulse, mechanical or electronic recording, or other form of data compilation. The original of a writing or recording is defined as "the writing or recording itself or any counterpart intended to have the same effect by a person executing or issuing it."

Certain documents, such as leases, contracts, or even letters, which are executed "signed" in more than one copy are all considered originals, and any one of the copies may be produced as an original.

4.8.2 Application of Best Evidence Rule

When an original document is not produced, and its absence is satisfactorily explained, secondary evidence, which could consist of testimony of witnesses or a copy of writing, will be received to prove its contents. Unavailability of the original document is a question to be decided by the trial judge just as he decides all questions regarding admissibility of evidence.

The reason for the rule is to prevent fraud, mistake, or error. For example, the testimony of an investigator as to the contents of a sales invoice will be excluded unless it is shown that the invoice itself is unavailable. If the document is unavailable, the investigator's testimony is admissible, even though the person who prepared the invoice is available to testify. The best evidence rule will not be invoked to exclude oral testimony of one witness merely because another witness could give more conclusive testimony.

4.8.3 Secondary Evidence

All evidence that does not meet the best evidence rule is classified as secondary evidence and is a substitute for better evidence. Secondary evidence may be either the testimony of a witness or a copy of a document. There is no settled rule for which of these is a higher degree of secondary evidence. Secondary evidence of any nature may be admitted in court. There must be evidence of the present or former existence of an original document, it must be established that the original has been destroyed, the destruction must be provable by an eyewitness, and the party proving the document must have used all reasonable means to obtain the original; that is, he must have made such diligent search as was reasonable under the facts. Some cases have specifically set the rule that a search must be made in the place where the document was last known to be, or that inquiry must be made of the person who last had custody of it. In every case, the sufficiency of the search is a matter to be determined by the court. If a document is offered as secondary evidence, it must be shown to be a correct copy of the original to be admissible.

When the original document has been destroyed by the party attempting to prove its contents, secondary evidence of the contents will be admitted if the destruction was in the ordinary course of business or by mistake or even intentionally, provided it was not done for any fraudulent purpose.

With respect to an original document in the possession of an opponent, Rule 1004 provides that the original is not required and that other evidence of the contents is admissible if, at the time the original was under the control of the party against whom offered, he was put on notice by the pleadings or otherwise that the contents would be subject to proof at the hearing, and he does not produce the original at the hearing.

4.8.4 Admissibility of Specific Forms of Documentary Evidence

These include records of regularly conducted (business) activity. Rule 803(6) states, "A memorandum, report, record, or data compilation, in any form, of acts, events, conditions, opinions, or diagnoses, made at or near the time by, or from information transmitted by, a person with knowledge, if kept in the course of regularly conducted business activity, and if it was the regular practice of that business activity to make the memorandum, report, record, or data compilation, all as shown by the testimony of the custodian or other qualified witness, unless the source of information or the method or circumstances of preparation indicate lack of trustworthiness, is admissible." The term "business" as used in this paragraph includes business, institution, association, profession, occupation, and call of every kind, whether or not conducted for profit.

The above rule permits showing that an entry was made in a book maintained in the regular course of business without producing the particular person who made the entry and having him identify it. For example, in proving a sale, an employee of the customer may appear with the original purchase journal and cash disbursement book of the customer and testify that these were books of original entry showing purchases by the customer, even though the witness is not the person who made the entries.

4.8.4.1 Regular Course of Business

This rule relies on records made under circumstances showing no reason or motive to misrepresent the facts. As stated by the courts, "The rule contemplates that certain events are regularly recorded as 'routine reflections' of the day-to-day operations of the business so that the character of the records and their earmarks of reliability import trustworthiness." For example, the rule is applied to bank records under the theory that the accuracy of the records is essential to the very life of the bank's business.

The fact that a record has been kept in the regular course of business is not enough to make it admissible. The rules of competency and relevancy must still be applied. If a ledger is offered in evidence to prove entries posted from an available journal the journal itself, as the book of original entry, should be produced.

If it is the practice to photograph, photostat, or microfilm the business records mentioned above, such reproductions, when satisfactorily identified, are as admissible as the original. Also, enlargements of the original reproductions are admissible if the original reproductions are in existence and available for inspection under the direction of the court. This rule is particularly helpful in connection with bank records because of the common practice of microfilming ledger sheets, deposit tickets, and checks.

4.8.4.2 Photographs, Photostats, and Microfilmed Copies

Photographs, photostats, and microfilmed copies of writings not made in the regular course of business are considered secondary evidence of the contents, generally inadmissible if the original can be produced and no reason is given for failure to produce it. The same rule is usually applied where the original is already in evidence and no reason has been given for offering the copy. However, notes of the Advisory Committee regarding the Federal Rules of Evidence indicate an intent to liberalize the rule with respect to photostat copies to the extent that such copies may be admitted in evidence in absence of a showing of some reason for requiring the original (Rule 1003).

A photographic or photostat reproduction of a document may be admitted after evidence has been produced that the original cannot be obtained and that the reproduction is an exact and accurate copy. This principle has been followed where the original was in the hands of the defendant, and the government could compel its production. It has further been held that a photograph of a promissory note taken because the writing was becoming faded and illegible was admissible in place of the illegible original.

When photostats of documents are obtained during an investigation, they should be initialed on the back, after comparison with the original, by the one who made the photostat or by the investigator who obtained the document which was photostatted. The date of such comparison should be noted following the initial. The source of the original document should be set out on the reverse of the photostat or on an initialed attachment or memorandum relating to each photostat or group of photostats covered by the one memorandum. This procedure will ensure proper authentication at a trial.

4.8.4.3 Transcripts

Transcripts are copies of writings. They are admissible as secondary evidence. The investigator should ensure proper authentication for their admission in court when the original documents are not available. The investigator should compare the transcript with the original and certify it. The certification should show the date of transcripts, by whom, where, and the source. Each page should be identified to show that it forms part of the whole or is a partial.

4.8.4.4 *Charts, Schedules, and Summaries*

Charts, schedules, and summaries prepared by summary/expert witness can be placed in evidence if they are summaries of evidence previously admitted in court. Charts, summaries, and schedules have been permitted in the jury room to aid in the jury's deliberations. Schedules may be used to summarize specific business transactions, that is, the accumulated cost of a construction project after the introduction of the pertinent records and testimony. Prejudicial headings or titles should be avoided, for example, "false claims."

4.8.4.5 *Notes, Diaries, Workpapers, and Memorandums*

Notes, diaries, workpapers, and memorandums made by auditors and accountants are not considered evidence. Auditors and accountants can use them on the witness stand or prior to testifying as an aid to recollection or may be introduced into evidence by the adverse party if they constitute impeaching evidence. Any documents used by a witness are subject to inspection by opposing counsel.

4.9 Proving Specific Transactions

It is not sufficient to rely on documents and recorded entries. Documents and recorded entries are not facts but a written description of the event. Witnesses will have to testify about the transaction and authenticate the documents. This is called the Greenberg Rule. The investigator must interview the party of the transaction to insure the documents or entries substantiate the circumstances. The witness may have additional facts or documents relating to the transaction or other transactions. Vendors should be questioned as to all transactions and any other information. Sellers and agents should be questioned as to the details of the transactions for possible nominees and nonexistent parties. Complete documentation and witness interviews should be obtained for every transaction as much as possible.

4.10 Official Records

The provisions of the Federal Rules of Evidence and rules of criminal and civil procedure cover the admissibility of official public records and copies or transcripts thereof in federal proceedings.

4.10.1 Authentication of Official Records

Evidence must be authenticated in order to establish its reliability. It must be shown that a certain document actually is an official record of a particular state or local government. Document authenticity does not mean it will be admissible in court.

4.10.2   Admissibility of Official Records

The admissibility of official records and copies are provided by the Federal Rules of Evidence. Rule 1005 states, "the contents of an official record, or of a document authorized to be recorded or filed and actually recorded or filed, including data compilations in any form, if otherwise admissible, may be proven by copy, certified as correct in accordance with Rule 902 or testified to be correct by a witness who has compared it with the original. If a copy, which complies with the foregoing, cannot be obtained by the exercise of reasonable diligence, then other evidence of the contents may be given. Under this rule, there is no requirement that the original be introduced."

Rule 902 provides that extrinsic evidence of authenticity is not required for certain types of documents, including public documents under seal, certified copies of public records, newspapers and periodicals, trade inscriptions and the like, or labels purporting to have been affixed in the course of business and indicating ownership, control, or origin, and commercial paper and related documents to the extent provided by general commercial law. This does not mean that the documents will be admitted.

A method of authentication of copies of federal records is set forth in the Federal Rules of Civil Procedure, which is made applicable to criminal cases by Rule 27 of Federal Rules of Criminal Procedure. Authentication of a copy of a government record under these rules would consist of a certification by the officer having custody of the records and verification of the official status of the certifying officer by a federal district judge over the seal of the court.

4.11   State and Territorial Statutes and Proceedings

The admissibility of copies of legislative acts of any state, territory, or possession of the United States and of court records and judicial proceedings is provided for in the United States Code (28 USC 1738) as follows:

> Such acts, records and judicial proceedings or copies thereof, so authenticated, shall have the same full faith and credit in every court within the United States and its territories and possessions as they have by law or usage in the courts of such state, territory, or possession from which they are taken.

The procedures for authentication of the above records are recited in the same section of the code.

Nonjudicial records or books kept in any public office of any state, territory, or possession of the United States, or copies thereof, are made admissible by the United States Code and given full faith and credit upon proper authentication (28 USC 1739). Rules 901 and 902 provide procedures for authentication of the documents covered in this section.

4.12   Chain of Custody

"Chain of Custody" is an expression that is applied to consecutive custodians of the physical items or documents in its original condition. Documents or other items used in a crime are generally admissible in court. The judge must be satisfied that the writing or other items are in the same condition as when the crime was committed. The witnesses through whom the document or other item is sought to be introduced must be able to identify it as being in the same condition as when it was recovered. Investigators must identify and preserve in original condition all evidentiary matter that may be offered into evidence.

4.13   Identification of Seized Documentary Evidence

In order that a seized document be admissible as evidence, it is necessary to prove that it is the document that was seized and that it is in the same condition as it was when seized. Since several persons may handle it in the interval between the seizure and the trial of the case, it should be adequately marked at the time of seizure for later identification, and its custody must be shown from that time until it is introduced in court.

An investigator who seizes documents should at once identify them by some markings so that he can later testify that they are the documents seized and that they are in the same condition as they were when seized. The investigator should put his initials and the date of seizure of the back of each document or put the document into an envelope and write a description and any other identifying information on the face of the envelope and seal the envelope.

4.14   Constitutional Provisions

The principal constitutional limitations relating to investigative techniques are the Fourth, Fifth, and Sixth Amendments to the U.S. Constitution and similar provisions in the state constitutions.

4.14.1   The Fourth Amendment

The Fourth Amendment provides, "The right of the people to be secure in their persons, houses, papers and effects, against unreasonable searches and seizures, shall not be violated, and no warrants shall issue, but upon probable cause, supported by oath or affirmation, and particularly describing the place to be searched and the persons or things to be seized."

This protection is given to corporations as well as individuals.

4.14.2   The Fifth Amendment

The relevant part of the U.S. Constitution's Fifth Amendment provides that

> No person shall be compelled in any criminal case to be a witness against himself, nor shall he be deprived of life, liberty, or property without due process of law.

This privilege is given only to individuals, not to corporations.

4.14.3   The Sixth Amendment

The relevant part of the U.S. Constitution's Sixth Amendment states,

> In all criminal prosecutions the accused shall enjoy the right to have the assistance of counsel for his defense.

4.15   Statutory Provisions

Statutes can be passed permitting financial investigations if they are within constitutional guidelines. Challenges to financial investigations have been litigated primarily in federal courts, particularly tax related cases. Therefore, federal court decisions are based on the federal constitution and statutes, most of which deal with tax cases.

4.15.1   Court Decisions

U.S. Supreme Court decisions are based on the U.S. Constitution and are binding on state courts and officers. Federal court decisions relating to federal statutes are not directly binding on state officers, since they operate under state statutes. But state statutes must conform to federal statutes either directly or indirectly; so the rulings on similar provisions are quite relevant on how the state courts can interpret its statutes.

4.15.2   Access to Books and Records

Federal and many state statutes provide that certain auditors can examine a subject's books and records and summon subjects (including third party witnesses) to come before them to give testimony or bring records. The Fourth Amendment prohibits illegal search except for probable cause. The Fifth Amendment prohibits self-incrimination. If the federal and state auditors request these records in the normal course of their business, then this does not violate the Fourth or Fifth Amendment. If the subject voluntarily submits to the auditor's request, then this is not a violation of his Fourth or Fifth Amendment rights. However, if the auditor requests these records for a criminal investigator without the suspect's knowledge, then this is a violation of the suspect's Fourth Amendment rights (United States v Nicholas J. Tweel, 550 F2d 297).

Some courts and state statutes permit certain regulatory searches to be made without warrants, but these regulatory searches cannot be used in criminal cases.

4.16   Privileged Relationships

The rule on privileged communications is based on common law and the legislature's belief that it is necessary to maintain the confidentiality of certain communications. It applies only to those communications, which relate to a unique relationship. They must have been made in confidence and not in the presence of third parties, unless the speaker has a privileged relationship with the third party. Common law has granted the privilege to the following relationships:

1. Husband-Wife.
2. Attorney-Client.
3. Ordained Clergyman-Parishioner.
4. Physician-Patient.
5. Reporter-Source.
6. Accountant-Client (not recognized in federal courts).

Only the holder of a privilege or someone authorized by him can assert a privilege. The privilege can be waived if he fails to assert it, after having notice and an opportunity to assert it. He also waives it if he discloses a significant part of the communication or if the communication is made in the presence of a third party whose presence is not indispensable to the conversation. The presence of a secretary or an interpreter would not abolish the privilege.

The client holds the attorney-client privilege, not by the lawyer, and the privilege does not terminate at the client's death. The communication is protected only if its purpose was related to legal consultation. An exception is where the attorney was consulted for the purpose of aiding in the perpetration of a crime or fraud or for the giving of business advice.

4.17   Foreign Evidence

Evidence from foreign countries is admissible in federal courts. Some criminal elements operate on an international level. Therefore, it is important that foreign countries, when known, be asked for assistance and cooperation. In most cases, foreign governments will cooperate and give assistance as necessary. The United States has many mutual assistance, extradition, and tax treaties. As a general rule, only high tax countries have tax treaties with other high tax countries. Tax haven countries will not provide financial information in criminal or civil tax cases. Some tax haven countries will provide financial information in nontax criminal cases. However, the requesting country must certify that the evidence provided will not be used for tax purposes.

4.17.1   Foreign Public Documents

Foreign public documents are admissible in federal courts when properly attested and certified. Also, a secretary of an embassy or legation, consul general, consul, or consular agent of the United States may make a final certification. If reasonable opportunity has been given to all parties to investigate the authenticity and accuracy of official documents, the court may, for good cause shown, order that they be treated as presumptively authentic without final certification or permit them to be evidenced by an attested summary with or without final certification. Foreign public records are the most easily obtained since public access is readily obtained.

4.17.2   Foreign Documents

Title 18 USC 3491 provides that any book, paper, statement, writing, or other document, or any portion thereof, of whatever character and in whatever form, as well as any copy thereof equally with the original which is not in the United States shall, when certified, be admissible in evidence in any criminal action or proceeding in any court of the United States. This clearly shows that foreign documents, when property certified, are admissible in criminal cases.

4.17.3   Consular Officers Commission

U.S. Consular Officers are responsible for taking oral or written interrogatories of witnesses in foreign countries. They are also tasked with the authority of authenticating foreign documents that will be used in any criminal proceeding. The court shall make provisions for the selection of foreign counsel to represent each party to the criminal action. Selection of foreign counsel shall be made within ten days prior to taking testimony. Foreign counsel does not represent the United States. If the consular officer has an interest in the outcome of the criminal action or proceeding or has participated in the investigation or preparation of evidence, then the consular officer is disqualified from taking oral or written interrogatories (18 USC 3492).

4.17.4   Deposition on Foreign Documents

Title 18 USC 3493 provides that the consular officer shall caution and swear in testimony as to the whole truth. The witness testimony shall be reduced to writing by the consular officer or by some person under his personal supervision. Every foreign document shall be annexed to such testimony and subscribed by each witness for the purpose of establishing the genuineness of such document. The consular officer shall obtain an interpreter if needed.

4.17.5   Foreign Records

The rules for admission of foreign documents are about the same as domestic documents. Foreign records of regularly conducted activity, or a copy of such record, shall be admissible as evidence provided that such document is authenticated as being genuine.

4.17.6   Foreign Witnesses

If a person is held in custody in a foreign country which is needed in the United States in a criminal proceeding, the attorney general shall request the foreign country to temporarily transfer that person to the United States for the purpose of giving testimony. The person shall be returned to the foreign country when the task is finished. If a treaty or convention is in effect with the foreign country, then the terms of the treaty or convention shall be adhered.

4.18   Awareness

The forensic accountant should always be aware of the rules of evidence. Evidence obtained improperly is inadmissible and thus becomes worthless. The following checklist should help in verifying compliance with the rules of evidence:

1. Chain of Custody: Is a log maintained of evidence obtained and who has had access to the evidence?
2. Witnesses: Are interview memorandums, depositions, etc. maintained for each witness? Also, are name, addresses, and contact telephone numbers maintained for each witness?
3. Physical Evidence: Is physical evidence properly secured? Only copies of documents should be used for marking and not originals.
4. Diary: The fraud examiner should maintain a diary showing dates of interviews, when and where evidence was obtained, and a description of work performed.
5. Notes: All interview notes should be kept and not destroyed.
6. Expenses: All expenses should be documented. If informants are paid, then some type of receipt should be obtained. Informant can initial a diary entry or appointment book.

In the chapter discussing accounting and auditing techniques, there is a recommended witness list that can be maintained on a computer database. This witness list will help the forensic accountant keep track of witnesses and evidence. It can also help the prosecutor in planning and scheduling of witnesses for trial.

4.19 Summary

Both fraud examiners and law enforcement must have some knowledge of the rules that allow evidence into court. No prosecutor wants evidence that is not admissible. If inadmissible evidence is entered into court then the defendant has grounds on appeal to get his conviction thrown out. The Supreme Court, under its "exclusionary rule," will overturn convictions when inadmissible evidence is introduced in court. Evidence must be properly guarded and handled. Any defacing or alteration of evidence will make the evidence inadmissible. Evidence can only be obtained in a legal manner. Security procedures should be set up and followed in order to preserve evidence. Without evidence, there is no case. Evidence from any part of the world is admissible, provided that it is obtained in a proper and legal manner.

Net Worth Theory 5

5.1 General

The Internal Revenue Service (IRS) was the first to use the Net Worth Method. According to Section 61, Internal Revenue Code, all taxpayers are to report all taxable income. When taxpayers do not report all their taxable income, the IRS devised the Net Worth Method to determine the amount of unreported taxable income. The IRS acknowledges that this method is appropriate in cases where the taxpayer accumulates a vast amount of assets. It is not useful in cases where the taxpayer has little or no assets and spends all his income on "lavish" living. When Congress passed the Racketeer Influenced and Corrupt Organizations (RICO) Act in 1970, it expanded the use of the Net Worth Method to organized crime.

5.2 Tax Use

The Net Worth Method is preferred by the Justice Department and was used as far back as 1931 on Alfonso Capone (2 USTC 786) by the IRS. The Net Worth Method is not an accounting method, but is a method of proof by circumstantial or indirect evidence. The IRS attempts to establish an "opening net worth," which is defined as assets less liability. It then proves increases in the taxpayer's net worth for each succeeding year during the period under examination. The taxpayer's nondeductible personal expenditures less nontaxable income are added to each year's increase in net worth. This is compared to income reported. Any differences are considered to be unreported income. Figure 5.1 illustrates this theory.

5.3 RICO Use

The above theory relates to tax purposes. The use in RICO and other economic crime cases requires a different set of principals and a different presentation. The basic theory in RICO net worth is similar to the tax method. The basic objective is different. In a RICO net worth, the objective is to determine the amount of illegal income. Like the tax purpose net worth method, RICO net worth is defined as assets less liabilities. It proves increases in net worth for each succeeding year. The subject's personal expenditures are added to each succeeding year's increase in net worth. This gives the gross income. The legal income is subtracted to determine the amount of illegal income derived. Figure 5.2 illustrates this theory.

YEAR ONE	YEAR TWO
ASSETS	ASSETS
LESS: LIABILITIES	LESS: LIABILITIES
EQUALS NET WORTH	EQUALS NET WORTH
	LESS NET WORTH YEAR ONE
	EQUALS NET WORTH INCREASE
	ADD: NONDEDUCTIBLE EXPENDITURES
	LESS: NONTAXABLE INCOME
	EQUALS CORRECTED TAXABLE INCOME
	LESS: REPORTED TAXABLE INCOME
	EQUALS UNREPORTED TAXABLE INCOME

Figure 5.1 Tax net worth theory.

5.4   History

The first net worth case was *Alfonso Capone v. United States* (2 USTC 786). The U.S. Supreme Court heard the first net worth case in 1943 with United States v Johnson (43-1 USTC 9470). In the Johnson case, the Supreme Court approved its use as a potent weapon in establishing taxable income from undisclosed sources when all other efforts failed. Since then the net worth has been widened until now it is used in run of the mill cases, regardless of the tax deficiency involved. The Supreme Court has denied certiorari because the

YEAR ONE	YEAR TWO
ASSETS	ASSETS
LESS: LIABILITIES	LESS: LIABILITIES
EQUALS NET WORTH	EQUALS NET WORTH
	LESS: NET WORTH YEAR ONE
	EQUALS NET WORTH INCREASE
	ADD: PERSONAL EXPENSES
	EQUALS LEGAL INCOME
	LESS: LEGAL INCOME
	EQUALS ILLEGAL INCOME

Figure 5.2 RICO net worth theory.

cases involved were only questions of evidence and presented no important questions of law. The Court of Appeals had serious doubts regarding the implications of the net worth method. In 1954, the Supreme Court granted certiorari in four cases. One of these was *M. L. Holland v. United States* (54-2 USTC 9714). The High Court pointed out the dangers that must be kept in mind in order to assure adequate appraisal of facts in individual cases. These dangers include:

1. *Cash hoard.* A favorite defense is the existence of substantial cash on hand. The defense is that the cash is made up of many years of savings, which for various reasons were hidden and not expended until the prosecution period. Obviously, the government has great difficulty in refuting such a contention. However, this can be overcome when the emergence of hidden savings also uncovers a fraud on the taxpayer's creditors. Also, taxpayers frequently give lead to agents indicating specific sources of cash on hand. This forces the government to run down all such leads in the face of grave investigative difficulties; still a failure to do so might jeopardize the position of the taxpayer.

2. *Assumptions.* The method requires assumptions, among which is the equation of unexplained increases in net worth with unreported taxable income. It may be found that those gifts, inheritances, and loans account for newly acquired wealth. Base figures have a way of acquiring an existence of their own independent of the evidence which gave rise to them. Therefore, the jury needs the appropriate guarding instructions.

3. *Poor memory or business judgment.* The taxpayer may be honest yet is unable to recount his financial history. The Net Worth Method could tend to shift the burden of proof from the government to the taxpayer. The taxpayer would then be compelled to come forward with evidence, which could lend support to the government by showing loose business methods or apparent evasiveness.

4. *Books and records.* When the government uses the net worth method, and the books and records of the taxpayer appear correct at face value, an inference of willful tax evasion could be inferred which might be unjustified where the circumstances surrounding the deficiency are as consistent with innocent mistake as with willful violation. On the other hand, the very failure of the books to disclose a proven deficiency might include deliberate falsification.

5. *Taxpayer statements.* The prosecution, in many cases, relies on the taxpayers statements made to revenue agents in the course of their investigation. When revenue agents confront the taxpayer with an apparent deficiency, then he or she may be more concerned with a quick settlement than an honest search for the truth. The prosecution may pick and choose from the taxpayer's statements relying on the favorable portion and throwing aside that which does not bolster the taxpayer's position. An investigation must not only include inculpatory evidence, but also exculpatory evidence.

6. *Time periods.* The statute defines the offenses by individual years. While the government may be able to prove with reasonable accuracy an increase in net worth over a period of years, it often has great difficulty in relating that income sufficiently to any specific prosecution year. Unless the increase can be reasonably allocated to the appropriate tax year, the taxpayer may be convicted on counts of which he is innocent.

The Supreme Court also added that the trial courts should approach these cases in full realization that the taxpayer may be ensnared in a system which is hard for the defendant to refute. Charges should be especially clear and formal in instructions as to the nature of the net worth method, the assumptions on which it rests, and the inferences available to both sides.

The main thrust of the net worth method since the Holland case is that the net worth method can be used against the ordinary average citizen without criminal affiliations. It may also be used to show that the taxpayer books do not reflect true income or to corroborate specific adjustments in the agent's report. Revenue agents must make an effort to seek the truth rather than trying to get a quick settlement to close out the case.

Since the Holland case, there have been many court decisions which affect either the net worth presentation or the source of such item on the net worth. Some of the court decisions should be kept in mind when preparing a net worth statement. They are:

5.4.1   Burden of Proof

In Jacobs v United States (54-1 USTC 9704), the burden of proof rested with the taxpayer in rebutting a net worth method, especially when he did not keep required books and records.

5.4.2   Cash on Hand

In the W. Epstein (57-2 USTC 9797) case, the government used cash on hand figures which came from financial statements submitted by the taxpayer to his bank and reports to Dun and Bradstreet. On the other hand, the courts have ruled that the IRS may not determine that the taxpayer had no cash on hand at the beginning of a specified period merely because the taxpayer make no affirmative showing to the contrary (Thomas, 56-1 USTC 9449, and L. Fuller, 63-1 USTC 9248).

5.4.3   Family Group

In the William G. Lias (56-2 USTC 9817) case, the court approved a consolidated net worth of family members where the taxpayer had no permanent books and refused to furnish financial statements. From the combined taxable income, agents deducted income reported or adjusted for the other members of the family group and treated the balance as taxable income of the taxpayer.

5.4.4   Cost of Living

In the H. G. Leach (36 TCM 998) case, the court allowed cost of living data supplied by the Bureau of Labor Statistics, but adjustments were made to reflect the size of the taxpayer's family and their geographical location. This was a civil case; it cannot be used in a criminal case. It can be inferred that this data can be used in civil RICO cases as well. So far, it has not been tried.

5.4.5   Corroboration

In the Daniel Smith v United States (54-2 USTC 9715) case, the court determined that the government, in a criminal case, must corroborate a defendant's opening statement of net worth. The use of the taxpayer's tax returns which shows poor financial history prior to the prosecution period is considered corroboration of the defendant's opening net worth. However, in the *Greenberg v. United States* case (61-2 USTC 9727), a criminal case, the agent prepared a check spread and made the assumption that all expenditures were personal in nature. Further, no records or admissions of the defendant corroborated the agent's testimony, nor did any payee or other third party testify. This case pointed out that the use of check spreads or third parties, and not the agent's conclusions or assumptions, must corroborate any method used.

5.5   RICO Use

Congress, since the Holland case, has enacted new laws and amended others in order to fight organized crime and drug kingpins. The Comprehensive Crime Control Act of 1984 and the Anti-Drug Abuse Act of 1986 have now forced the use of the net worth method to be used in nontax cases. In civil cases, the net worth method is used to identify assets for seizure and forfeiture. In criminal cases, the net worth method is used to show the amount of financial benefit derived from some illegal activity. Under 18 USC 371, the prosecution can obtain a conviction under the conspiracy section to defraud the United States Government. In *Klein v. United States* (355 US 924), the conspiracy to defraud the United States by impeding, impairing, obstructing, and defeating the lawful functions of the Department of the Treasury in the collection of taxes was upheld. No proof of financial loss to the government was necessary.

U.S. attorneys, as well as state attorneys, whose states have adopted or copied U.S. Title 18 laws, have been obligated to rely on the net worth method in proving both their civil and criminal cases. 18 USC 1963(a)(b), RICO, provides the following:

> . . . In lieu of a fine otherwise authorized by this section, a defendant who derives profits or other proceeds from an offense may be fined not more than twice the gross profits or other proceeds.
> (b) Property subject to criminal forfeiture under this section includes:
>> (1) Real property including things growing on, affixed to, and found in land; and
>> (2) Tangible and intangible personal property, including rights, privileges, interests, claims, and securities.

The net worth method provides prosecutors the precise means of determining the illegal gains and at the same time, identifies the assets and expenditures. For prosecutors to get twice the gross profits, one must first determine the amount of the gross profit. The net worth method, from an accountant's point of view, provides a complete snapshot of a person's financial affairs over a specified period of time.

5.6   Continuing Criminal Enterprises

Congress, in addition to the RICO act, passed the Continuing Criminal Enterprise Act (CCE). This act was passed by Congress to combat drug trafficking. Title 21 USC 848 defines Continuing Criminal Enterprise as being any person, in concert of five or more people, who occupies a position of organizer and supervisory position who obtains substantial income or resources. The alternative fine is, "A defendant who derives profits or other proceeds from an offense may be fined not more than twice the gross profits or other proceeds" (21 USC 855). It is clear from this statute that prosecutors can use the net worth method of proving illegal gains and identifying assets for forfeiture.

5.7   Connection

In *United States v. J. C. Pate Jr.,* the Court of Appeals, 11 Circuit, made a ruling in a drug forfeiture case. To demonstrate the substantial connection between property and illegal drug transaction in forfeiture action, the government is not required to show the relationship between property and a specific drug transaction. However, the claimant can meet his burden of proof in civil forfeiture proceedings to establish by a preponderance of evidence that the property is not subject to forfeiture either by rebutting the government's evidence that property represents proceeds of illegal drug activity or by showing that the claimant is an innocent owner without knowledge of the property's connection with illegal drug activities. In order to establish probable cause for forfeiture under Section 881(a)(6), the government must show that "a substantial connection exists between the property to be forfeited and an illegal exchange of a controlled substance." The government's burden of demonstrating probable cause requires "less than prima facie proof but more than mere suspicion." The net worth method is considered one of the best methods of showing the relationship between illegal gains and the related asset acquisitions if properly prepared and documented.

5.8   When Use Is Required

The net worth method should be used in tax cases when one or more of the following conditions prevail:

a. Subject maintains no books and records.
b. Subject's books and records are not available.
c. Subject's books and records are inadequate.
d. Subject withholds books and records.

A taxpayer's keeping of accurate records does not prevent the use of the net worth method. The government can still use the method to either confirm or deny the taxpayer's declarations. It can be used in either organized crime or illegal activities or in general fraud cases. The net worth method can be used as a primary means of proving taxable income, or it can be used to corroborate or test the accuracy of reported taxable income.

The net worth method should be used in RICO cases when one or more of the following conditions prevail:

a. The target acquires large amount of assets.
b. The target spends beyond his means.

c. The target is a high-level drug trafficker where most, if not all, witnesses against him are drug distributors for him.

d. Illegal income needs to be determined in order to determine the forfeiture amount.

5.9   Theory

When the determination has been made to use the net worth method, then the questions of how to prepare and present items on the net worth schedule arise. The following guidelines are provided:

1. As a general rule for tax purposes, items on the net worth should be treated in the manner prescribed for tax purposes. Only cost figures should be used. Market values can be used, but only in extreme or unusual circumstances or if the tax law and regulations require it.

2. As a general rule for RICO purposes, the source and use of funds principle is to be applied. Only cost figures should be used. Market values cannot be used unless they relate, either directly or indirectly, to the source and use of funds. No phantom figures are to be used. Phantom figures are defined as accounting entries for amortization, depreciation, and depletion allowances. These figures do not reflect the use of funds and therefore should not be used.

5.9.1   Cash on Hand

You must anticipate this particular problem and show that the taxpayer had no large sum of cash for which he or she was not given credit. Consequently, it is important that you interview the taxpayer early in the investigation to tie down a maximum cash accumulation. You should attempt to obtain the following:

1. The maximum amount claimed to be on hand at the end of each year from the starting point through the present.
2. How it was accumulated (from what sources).
3. Where it was kept and in what denominations.
4. Who had knowledge of it.
5. Who counted it.
6. When and where it was spent.

All of the above information is necessary to establish the consistence and reliability of the taxpayer's statements. Usually no direct cash on hand evidence is available but statements made as to the sources, amount, and use of funds can be corroborated or refuted with circumstantial evidence.

Examples of evidence, which may tend to negate the existence of a cash hoard, include:

1. Written or oral admissions of the taxpayer to investigating officers concerning a small amount of cash on hand.
2. Financial statements prepared by the taxpayer showing a low net worth and/or cash on hand.

3. Compromises of overdue debts by the taxpayer.
4. Foreclosure proceedings against the taxpayer.
5. Collection actions against the taxpayer.
6. Tax returns (or no returns) are evidencing little or no income in prior years.
7. Loan records.
8. Consistent use of checking and savings accounts.

It may be possible to reconstruct the taxpayer's cash on hand from prior earning records. If cash on hand for an earlier period can be reasonably established, income earned from that period to the starting point could be used to establish a maximum available cash on hand.

The problem for cash on hand or cash hoard is the same for both RICO net worth purposes as it is for tax net worth purposes. However, for tax purposes, the agent is more likely to interview the taxpayer, while for RICO net worth purposes, the investigator will either not want to interview the target or will not be able to do so because of some legal or safety reason.

5.9.2   Cash in Banks

The main problem here can be whether to use the bank statement balances or use the book balances. Either can be used. However, if book balances are used then bank reconciliations must be provided as well. Whether book balances are used or bank balances are used, they must be consistently used. One cannot use book balances for one year and the bank balance in the next. Bank balances can be used from some bank accounts while book balances can be used for other bank accounts. Each bank account must use a consistent method.

5.9.3   Inventory

Taxpayers tend to understate their inventories by using various devices. Stealing or fencing stolen goods can make large profits. This is particularly true in business "bust outs" when a taxpayer purchases inventory on credit at one location and transports the inventory to another location where it is sold off, leaving the creditors holding the bag. A problem arises in correcting continuing understatements of inventory. The resulting increase in closing inventory in a closed year creates a deficiency that cannot be corrected due to statute of limitations. A possible remedy in this situation is IRC 481 regarding changes in method of accounting. The agent should verify inventory in stock. IRM 424(10) provides the minimum tests to be made. In using the RICO net worth method, it is unlikely that the investigator can verify inventory. The investigator might be able to verify inventory from surveillance photographs if surveillance was done. Otherwise, the investigator will have to use some other method of determining inventory, usually from witness testimony or by computation based upon a constant gross profit percentage.

5.9.4   Accounts/Loans Receivable

Normally, the investigator can confirm and verify receivables whether using RICO or tax net worth methods by third party contact. Problems arise in this area where related parties are involved, especially if they are subjects of the investigation, whether it be individuals, partnerships, or corporations. Remember, a receivable on the taxpayer's books must be a payable on the other, and the amounts must agree for both principal and interest.

5.9.5 Intercompany Transfers

Shareholders can invest in multiple corporations and partnerships. These corporations or partnerships can transfer funds or goods between each other. Whether it is for tax or RICO purposes, these transfers should be ignored as to the individual net worth. The additional investment in a particular corporation should be reflected on the individual net worth. Whatever the corporation or partnership does with the money is a matter of the entity. In the case of partnerships and Sub S corporations, basis reverts back to the original entity that received the funds from the individual.

5.9.6 Sole Proprietorship

The tax net worth only requires that the assets and liabilities be shown on the sole proprietor. The RICO net worth requires not only the assets and liabilities of the sole proprietorship but also the income and expenses. For RICO purposes, the problem lies in converting the sole proprietorship into a fund statement. Remember, all depreciation, amortization, and depletion expenses must be reversed out. Only cash expenses should be shown. If the sole proprietorship keeps its books on the accrual method, then the assets, liabilities, income, and expenses should be shown on the individual net worth after adjustments are made for the accountant's depreciation, amortization, and depletion deductions.

5.9.7 Exchanges

Individuals, at times, will pay for expenses of another person. In turn, the other person will pay the individual back. The reverse is that another person will give the individual funds to pay for expenses of the other person. There are two ways of showing this situation. First, the expenses can be shown as an expenditure, and the reimbursements can be shown as a source (nontaxable in the tax net worth method) of income. The last method is to show the receipts as a receivable, and any reimbursement shows a decrease in the receivable.

5.9.8 Securities

Subjects have a tendency to report to financial institutions the fair market value instead of the cost. For net worth purposes, only cost figures can be used. Another problem to face with securities is how the subject acquired the securities by means other than by direct purchase. The basis must be firmly established, and any doubts should be made in favor of the subject. Drug traffickers use commodities to launder their money. Commodities such as gold and platinum, and securities, such as bearer bonds, can be transported much easier than hauling around cash. Also they are easier to convert back into currency. This is where Currency Transaction Reports and IRS 8300's should be obtained, if possible, and examined for leads.

5.9.9 Personal Property

Actual cost figures must be used in reflecting personal property (e.g., cars, boats, furniture, jewelry) instead of fair market values. The cost of cars, boats, and airplanes can be determined from state and federal agencies, whereas the costs of other personal property cannot be unless the investigator discovers it from a canceled check or some other source by chance. Surveillance of the subject shopping at expensive stores will be very helpful. Also, the proceeds from disposition of nontraceable personal property are hard to trace unless the subject deposits a check into his bank account. The main thrust here is to fully document nontraceable personal property by third party confirmation. The county tax assessor's office maintains files for tangible personal property which is used in business operations. These tangible personal property tax returns show costs of personal property used in business operations.

5.9.10 Real Property

Real estate must be reported at cost instead of fair market value. However, real estate is probably the most easy to verify because these records are easily accessible at the county records department. In Florida, the state document stamps are charged by set rates upon the purchase price of the real property. In addition, the tax assessor is supposed to assess real property at two thirds of the market value. The problem with real property records is that sometimes they are difficult to read from microfilm, and if real property is transferred by quitclaim deed, no purchase price is reflected from the document stamps. Quitclaim deeds are usually between related parties.

5.9.11 Cash Value Insurance

The subject, sometimes, has life insurance, which has cash values (called whole life policies). The subject has access to these cash values and can withdraw by either borrowing or canceling the policy. The investigator will have to break down the premium between cash value and insurance expense for both RICO and tax net worth purposes. This information can readily be obtained from the insurance company.

5.9.12 Subchapter S Corporation

Subchapter S corporations are treated differently from Chapter C corporations for tax purposes. In Chapter C corporations, the investigator picks up his net cash investment in the corporation. In Sub S corporations, the investigator picks up not only the net cash investment but also makes allowances for any income and losses attributed to the subject from such entity, but never below zero (no negative basis). For RICO net worth purposes, the Sub S corporation is treated the same as for Chapter C corporations which is net cash investment in the corporation. This is definitely an item that will have a different effect from a RICO net worth and a tax net worth.

5.9.13 Partnership

Partnerships are treated similar to Subchapter S corporations. The investigator picks up his net cash investment plus makes allowances for the subject's share of income and losses.

However, the subject can have a negative basis, but only to the extent at which the taxpayer is at risk. Nonrecourse financing is considered not at risk and therefore cannot be used in having a negative basis. For RICO net worth purposes, only net cash investment is considered. This is another item that will have a different effect between the RICO and tax net worth.

5.9.14   Prepaid Insurance

The problem here is whether to reflect prepaid insurance, or any other expense for that matter, as an asset and show a write-off in subsequent periods or just reflect one lump sum expenditure. Since the subject can cancel the insurance before its expiration, prepaid insurance should be capitalized and later amortized based upon potential refund of premium for tax net worth purposes. However, for RICO net worth purposes, prepaid insurance should be expensed in the year incurred. Phantom costs, such as amortized costs, are not to be recorded in subsequent years on RICO net worth schedules.

5.9.15   Controlled Foreign Corporations (CFC)

For tax net worth purposes, the agent should pick up not only the net cash investment, but also the taxpayer's share of net income. For RICO net worth purposes, only the subject's net cash investment should be used. Another problem that arises in foreign corporations is the effect of foreign exchange rates. Gains and losses from foreign exchange rates will have to be reflected for both tax and RICO net worth computations. On RICO net worth schedules, gains are identified sources and losses are identified expenses.

5.9.16   Accounts Payable

Accounts payable is used for accrual taxpayers only. A problem can arise when payables are from related persons or entities which are not on the accrual basis. For RICO purposes, accounts payable is not used, since this would defy the FUND concept which RICO net worth is based upon. However, if the subject has a sole proprietorship with inventory and cost of sales, then accounts payable will have to be used on the RICO net worth schedule.

5.9.17   Credit Cards

In a net worth, credit card balances are shown as a liability, and the total charges are reflected in the personal expenditure section. One problem that could arise at year-end is when charges are made but do not show up until the subsequent period. There is sometimes a lag as long as two or three days or more. Also, the charges have to be confirmed and differentiated as to what is personal or business, especially for those credit cards that have a widespread use. Another method of presentation is where no liability is reflected on the net worth and only the payments are reflected to the credit card company as a personal expenditure. The agent still has the problem of distinguishing between business and personal use as well as expenses versus assets. Credit cards cannot be ignored because the funds spent can be enormous. The problem with credit cards is the same for both tax and RICO net worth purposes. Whether you use the total charges and ending liability presentation or the total payment expenditure presentation, you must be consistent with only one presentation. For RICO purposes, there is really no need to distinguish between business and personal charges since they are just expenditures. The agent, however, must distinguish between expense and asset.

5.9.18   Deferred Gains

This item comes about when the taxpayer reports sales on the installment method or is allowed to use the installment method to report a gain. For tax purposes, the agent will have to set up a deferred gain in the liability section of the net worth schedule and recognize the gain in subsequent periods based upon receipts. For RICO purposes, deferred gains are not recognized in subsequent periods. They are recognized in full when they are incurred.

5.9.19   Prepaid Interest

This item comes about from installment loan contracts. The installment loan is recorded by a bank with principal, interest, and other charges combined. Interest should be recognized the same way that a bank recognizes the interest income. It should be noted that when the installment method is paid off early, the bank uses a different method of rebating the interest (called the rule of 78) from the method used in computing the interest. The IRS issued a ruling that the rule of 78's cannot be used in computing interest expense by the taxpayer. For RICO purposes, prepaid interest is not capitalized and later amortized. Prepaid interest is expensed in the year incurred.

5.9.20   Contributions

Cash contributions are treated the same both for tax and RICO net worth purposes. In the case of noncash contributions, tax net worth computations reflect the fair market value, but not more than the original cost. For RICO net worth computations, only cost figures should be used.

5.9.21   Capital Gains and Losses

Capital gains and losses are treated differently for tax net worth purposes versus RICO net worth purposes. For tax purposes, losses are limited to $3000.00 per year. This will result in an asset called deferred capital losses. For capital gains prior to 1987, the gain will be recognized, but a portion of the gain called 1202 deduction will be shown as nontaxable income. RICO net worths must recognize the gains and losses in full during the period incurred.

5.9.22   IRA and Keogh Accounts

People are increasingly funding Individual Retirement Accounts and Keogh Plans for self-employed individuals. The contributions to these plans are tax deductible, and the interest and dividend income is tax-free. On tax net worth computations, these retirement plans should be reflected as an asset, and the interest and dividend income should be reflected as nontaxable income. On RICO net worth computations, these retirement plans should be reflected as an asset and the income appropriately recognized as identified income.

5.9.23 Personal Living Expenses

There are other expenses that should be considered in doing a net worth computation whether for tax or RICO purposes. These expenses should be identified as early as possible and records obtained. They are as follows:

1. Food and outside meals.
2. Home and other repairs.
3. Utilities, that is, electric, water, waste, etc.
4. Telephone, both the charges and payments as well as toll calls should be obtained. Toll calls can help tie the target to other individuals as well as offer leads for additional financial information.
5. Vacation and/or trips.
6. Alimony.
7. Child support.
8. Property taxes.
9. Medical expenses including health insurance.
10. Educational expenses.
11. Moving expenses.
12. Gifts.
13. Federal and state income taxes.
14. Personal bad debts.

5.9.24 Various Income Items

There are income items that should be kept in mind. Some items will have different affects on net worth computations from tax versus RICO purposes. RICO net worths will probably use income items that tax net worths will either not use or present differently. Some of these items are:

1. Tax exempt interest.
2. Social Security benefits.
3. Unemployment compensation.
4. Dividend exclusion.
5. Life insurance proceeds.
6. Inheritance.
7. Disability income.
8. Two wage earner deduction.
9. Educational assistance.
10. Military allowances.
11. Casualty insurance proceeds.

5.9.25 Civil versus Criminal

In tax cases, there usually are differences between the criminal case and the civil case. The primary reason is the civil agent is trying to establish a tax deficiency, while the criminal agent is trying to show intent to defraud the government. The criminal agent has to interview and have witnesses testify about various income and expenditure items. The civil agent does not have to obtain very many witnesses since deductions are the responsibility of the taxpayer and not the government. The following items will inevitably reflect differences between criminal and civil agent's reports:

1. Dividend versus reduction in capital investment in corporations.
2. Interest versus loan.
3. Personal expenditures. Civilly, the taxpayer must prove deductions; criminally, the government must prove deductions.
4. Basis of assets, that is, auto basis on trade-ins.

In RICO cases, the net worth computation is used for both criminal and civil purposes. There should be little or no differences. The only differences that might appear in RICO cases are items not admitted in criminal court because they were unknown at the time, just were not introduced, or the hearsay rules forbade their use in criminal proceedings but not in civil proceedings. Otherwise, there should be no difference in technical issues.

5.10 Defenses

Whenever using any indirect method to determine correct taxable income or to determine the amount of illegal gain from an illegal enterprise, the defendant will have various defenses. Some of the more common defenses are:

1. *Cash on hand.* This is the cash hoard story. The defendant claims to have accumulated wealth in years prior to the prosecution years.
2. *Loans.* The defendant testifies that the sudden wealth came from somebody or entity as loan proceeds. In some cases, the lender does not have the resources to make any loans to the defendant. This is common with loans from relatives, family members, and closely held corporations.
3. *Gifts.* The defendant claims to have received gifts from family members, relatives, or friends. The investigator should verify whether the donor has the resources to make such a gift to the defendant.
4. *Inheritance.* When the defendant claims inheritance(s) as a sudden source of wealth, the investigator should check probate court records. If the inheritance is very large, it could lead the defendant to possible estate tax fraud if no estate tax returns were filed, whether for federal or state purposes.
5. *Innocent Bystander.* The defendant could claim to be an innocent bystander where money was left in his or her possession while another person was on the run.
6. *Agent or Nominee.* Defendants like to deny ownership and place assets in nominees or alter egos. The investigators should determine whether the nominee or alter ego has the resources to acquire the assets. (The issue of nominees and alter egos are addressed in a later chapter.)
7. *Possession.* The defendant may claim that he or she is an agent for an anonymous person or is unaware the goods were in his or her possession.

8. *Jointly Held Assets.* The defendant may claim that the other party purchased the jointly held assets. The investigator should confirm that the other party purchased the jointly held asset. If the other party purchased it, then the asset should not be shown on the net worth schedule.
9. *Overstated inventories.* The defendant may claim that the inventory or other assets are overstated. The investigator should confirm with subject (if permitted), employees and records, or some covert means as available.
10. *Failure to account for other sources of funds.* The defendant may not be able to account for all sources of income. It is the duty of the investigator to check all possible sources of income.
11. *Commodities.* The subject claims the purchase of commodities (e.g., gold, silver, auto parts) that were accumulated prior to the prosecution years. The investigator has the difficult job of confirming this claim.

Remember, particularly in criminal cases, whether for tax or RICO, the burden of proof is placed on the government when a net worth method is used. In the Holland case, the Supreme Court said that the government is responsible to:

1. Establish the opening net worth with reasonable certainty. This includes verification of subject's admissions.
2. There must be significant signs that there is a likely source of taxable income and refute nontaxable sources for tax purposes. In RICO cases, it is evident that all sources of any legal income should be identified.
3. If the subject offers any leads of income, they must be investigated and accepted or refuted.

In RICO cases, the defendant will use the same defenses as in tax cases. The tendency in RICO cases is to try to introduce more legitimate income or disclaim ownership of various assets. Organized crime figures and high-level drug traffickers have the pattern of using nominees or agents to hide their assets and illegal income. The investigator in these situations has to determine if the agent or nominee has the ability to acquire assets or generate that kind of legal income.

5.11 Summary

The net worth method, whether for RICO or tax purposes, is a very powerful tool. It tends to place the burden upon the defendant to disprove once introduced into evidence. The examiner or investigator has a tedious job of locating, obtaining, analyzing, and preparing a net worth schedule. The examiner has to pay close attention to all the details presented in a net worth schedule. All the issues should be identified and resolved.

Expenditure Theory

6

6.1 General

The Internal Revenue Service (IRS) was also the first to use the Expenditure Method. The Expenditure Method is a derivation of the Net Worth Method, which has been used since the early 1940s. Like the Net Worth Method, the Expenditure Method is used to determine the amount of unreported taxable income. This method is appropriate in cases where the taxpayer does NOT accumulate assets, but spends all his income on "lavish" living. When the Racketeer Influenced and Corrupt Organizations (RICO) Act of 1970 was passed, the Expenditure Method was expanded to encompass organized crime figures.

6.2 Tax Use

The Expenditure Method is a method of proof by circumstantial or indirect evidence. The IRS establishes the total expenditures less total nontaxable sources to arrive at adjusted gross income. Exemptions and itemized deductions are subtracted to arrive at corrected taxable income. This is compared to the reported taxable income to arrive at any unreported taxable income. Figure 6.1 illustrates this theory.

6.3 RICO Use

Like the Net Worth Method, the Expenditure Method is used in RICO and other economic crime cases. In a RICO case, the basic objective is to determine the amount of illegal income. The RICO Method is defined as total expenditures less legal sources to derive at illegal income. The RICO Expenditure does this for each succeeding year. Figure 6.2 illustrates this theory.

6.4 History

The Expenditure Method came into use in the early 1940s. Since then, it has been used more frequently than the Net Worth Method. There are various reasons for this. First, it is more easily prepared. Second, it is easier to explain to a jury in a trial. The Expenditure Method has not been ruled upon directly by the U.S. Supreme Court. One reason is that the Expenditure Method is a derivation of the Net Worth Method. Any accountant can take a net worth computation and convert it to an expenditure computation and vice versa. The Supreme Court in its decisions in net worth cases has referred to the Net Worth and Expenditure Methods. This alone implies that the Supreme Court approves of the

		YEAR
TOTAL		EXPENDITURES
LESS:		TOTAL NONTAXABLE SOURCE
EQUALS:		ADJUSTED GROSS INCOME
LESS:		ITEMIZED/STANDARD DEDUCTION
LESS:		EXEMPTIONS
EQUALS:		CORRECTED TAXABLE INCOME
LESS:		REPORTED TAXABLE INCOME
EQUALS:		UNREPORTED TAXABLE INCOME

Figure 6.1 Tax expenditure theory.

Expenditure Method. As such, the rules which the Supreme Court outlined in net worth cases apply to expenditure cases.

The IRS has been using the Expenditure Method against the ordinary average citizen. It can be used to show that the taxpayer books do not reflect true income or to corroborate specific adjustments. Revenue Agents are sometimes using the Expenditure Method by using figures on the tax return even before beginning their examinations or contact with the taxpayer. Revenue agents call this Expenditure Method the "T" account. The "T" account method is actually the Expenditure Method in which sources of income are reflected on the left side of a spreadsheet. The expenditures are shown on the right side of the same spreadsheet. If the right side of the spreadsheet, the expenditure side, is greater than the left side, the income side, then the revenue agent will suspect that the taxpayer has unreported taxable income.

The Tax Court and some District Courts have, on occasion, disapproved the Expenditure Method. The primary reason is that the IRS failed to establish the amount of funds available at the beginning of the taxable years in question. Like the Net Worth Method, the prosecution has to show that the taxpayer does not have a cash hoard or other convertible assets prior to the prosecution years.

6.4.1   RICO Use

The Expenditure Method, like the Net Worth Method, can be used in the prosecution of organized crime figures and drug kingpins. The primary use in organized crime figures

		YEAR
TOTAL		EXPENDITURES
LESS:		LEGAL SOURCES
EQUALS:		ILLEGAL INCOME

Figure 6.2 RICO expenditure theory.

and drug kingpins is to show the amount of illegal income. When the illegal income is determined by the Expenditure Method, the prosecution can recommend the fine. Unlike the Net Worth Method, the Expenditure Method does not identify the assets which the defendant has accumulated. It only identifies the assets acquired in any specific year. It does not mean that the defendant still has those assets. The Expenditure Method can identify sales and disposition of assets but only in the year of disposition. Assets can be destroyed or abandoned, and the investigator may not learn of it right away. In addition, assets can be disposed of after the years under examination or investigation.

6.4.2   When Use Is Required

The Expenditure Method should be used in tax cases when one or more of the following conditions prevail:

  a. Taxpayer maintains no books and records
  b. Taxpayer's books and records are not available
  c. Taxpayer's books and records are inadequate
  d. Taxpayer withholds books and records
  e. Taxpayer has no visible or identifiable assets

The Expenditure Method should be used in RICO cases when one or more of the following conditions prevail:

  a. The target does not seem to acquire assets
  b. The target spends beyond his means, lavish living
  c. The target is a high level "kingpin" where most, if not all, witnesses against him are convicted criminals
  d. Illegal income needs to be determined in order to determine the fine or forfeiture amount

6.5   Theory

When the determination has been made to use the Expenditure Method, then the questions of how to prepare and present items on the Expenditure Method arises. The following guidelines are provided:

As a general rule for tax purposes, items on the expenditure schedule should be treated in the manner prescribed for tax purposes. Only cost figures should be used. Market values can be used, but only in extreme or unusual circumstances or if the tax law and regulations require it.

As a general rule for RICO purposes, the source and use of funds is to be applied. Only cost figures should be used. Market values cannot be used unless they relate, either directly or indirectly, to the source or use of funds. No phantom figures are to be used. Phantom figures are defined as accounting entries for amortization, depreciation, and depletion allowances. Also, earnings and profits from partnerships and corporations are not to be used. These figures do not reflect the use of funds and therefore should not be used.

The Expenditure Method treats assets and liabilities different from the treatment of assets and liabilities on the Net Worth Method. Assets and liabilities are shown on the expenditure method during the period that they are acquired or disposed of. Accumulated or ending balances are not shown on the Expenditure Method. Those items that are presented in a different manner are discussed below.

6.5.1   Cash on Hand

The Net Worth Method reports the amount of cash on hand at year-end. The Expenditure Method reports either the increase or decrease in cash on hand from one year to the next. However, the same rules apply as to the determination of cash on hand for each year under investigation as well as the prior year's. The cash hoard defense applies to the Expenditure Method as well as the Net Worth Method. If the subject has or claims cash hoard, then the cash hoard will decrease over the periods under investigation.

6.5.2   Cash in Bank

The Expenditure Method reports either the increase or decrease of cash in bank rather than the bank or book balances. Whether the book balances or bank balances are used, the use must be consistent. You cannot use book balance increases or decreases in one year and the bank balance in a subsequent year. This applies to both tax and RICO purposes. Increases and decreases in bank accounts can be used using the bank balances for one account and the book balances in another account.

6.5.3   Inventory

The Expenditure Method has the same presentation problems as the Net Worth Method. Except in the Expenditure Method, the inventory is stated by the increase or decrease in ending inventory balances. It is suggested that the investigator determine the inventory balance. Then, the investigator determines the increase or decrease by subtracting the beginning and ending inventory balances for the period.

6.5.4   Intercompany Transfers

Intercompany transfers should be ignored on the individual expenditure schedule. Only the initial investment should be accounted for on the individual expenditure schedule. What the corporation or partnership does with funds has no effect on the individual expenditure schedule.

6.5.5   Sole Proprietorships

The net changes in assets and liabilities should be reflected on the individual expenditure schedule whether the tax or RICO method is used. The income and expenses should be reflected on the RICO expenditure schedule. The examiner will have to make adjustments to eliminate any phantom figures (accountant's depreciation, amortization, and depletion allowances). The tax Expenditure Method does not reflect the income and expenses of a sole proprietorship since they relate to net income or loss to derive adjusted gross income.

6.5.6   Exchanges

Both the tax and RICO method should reflect exchanges identically. This means that payments to or on behalf of other people should be reflected as an expenditure. Any reimbursements should be reflected as a source of funds. For the tax method, this source of receipts should be reflected as a nontaxable source of income. Another method of reflecting exchanges is to show the net effect of exchanges. This applies to both tax and RICO methods. If the net effect is an expenditure, then this should be shown in the expenditure section. If the net effect is a source, then it should be shown as a source of funds. In RICO cases, this is a source of receipts.

6.5.7   Accounts/Loans Receivable

The Expenditure Method shows the increases or decreases in the accounts and loans receivable. It also does not show the year end balances. The investigator has the same problems in the Expenditure Method as in the Net Worth Method. The year-end balances must be confirmed before the differences can be determined. The related party issue in this area is the same as the Net Worth Method. The increase or decrease in loans and accounts receivable on the subject's books must correspond to the opposite increase or decrease on the related party books. The examiner must determine if related party loans are bona fided. The related party may not be able to make large loans.

6.5.8   Subchapter S Corporation

For tax purposes, the Expenditure Method accounts for the total earnings or losses plus any contributions less any withdrawals for the period. The Net Worth Method only shows the beginning and ending balances for the period. For RICO purposes, the Expenditure Method accounts for the net change during the period as to the subject's cash investment. Earnings and losses are not accounted for in this computation. Regular corporations are treated the same for both RICO and tax purposes. The net changes in cash investment for the period are reflected on the expenditure computation.

6.5.9   Partnership

For tax purposes, the Expenditure Method accounts for the total earnings or losses plus any contributions less any withdrawals for the period. Negative changes can be reflected for both RICO and tax purposes. However, for tax purposes, the negative changes will not be allowed if the taxpayer is not at risk on loans that the partnership has acquired.

6.5.10   Credit Cards

The net change in credit card balances is reflected on the Expenditure Method if the total charges are shown on the expenditure schedule. It is easier for both the examiner or investigator to reflect the net cash payments to the credit card companies than to reflect total charges and changes in credit card balances. For tax purposes, the payments for business expenses have to be separated from personal expenses. This can be extremely difficult. Interviews of witnesses or the subject will have to be done to determine the nature of the expenditures. The best evidence on credit card payments is to see how the taxpayer paid for the credit cards. If they come from his personal bank accounts, then it is obvious that they are personal expenses. If paid from a business account, then it implies that they are for business purposes. This can leave the investigator open for debate between both counsels. For RICO purposes, this is not an issue.

6.5.11   Other Assets

The net change in assets is reflected on the Expenditure Method whether tangible or intangible or real or personal property. In tax cases, the expenditure will reflect a decrease in intangible assets such as prepaid interest and insurance. In RICO cases, prepaid items are not recognized since they do not exist. Prepaid items on the RICO expenditure schedule are expensed in the year incurred.

6.5.12   Loans and Mortgages Payable

The Expenditure Method shows only the receipt of the funds borrowed (source of funds) during the period and the total payments (application of funds) made during the period. Loan proceeds should not be netted out with loan repayments. This can be confusing for the jury.

6.5.13   Income and Expenses

Income and personal living expenses are reflected the same way for expenditure computations as they are for net worth computations. They are considered to be actual disbursement of funds. This applies to both tax and RICO purposes. The Tax Expenditure Method recognizes only nontaxable sources of income. Expenses are recognized when paid for cash basis taxpayers and when incurred for taxpayers on the accrual method. The RICO Expenditure Method recognizes all personal income and expenses of the subject when received or paid. However, if the subject has a sole proprietorship that is on the accrual method of accounting, then the income and expenses should be recognized when incurred along with the changes in accounts payable.

6.5.14   Deferred Gains

Deferred gains are not recognized on the RICO Expenditure Method. Gains are recognized in full when incurred. For tax purposes, deferred gains are recognized by showing an acquired liability. Since this is an adjustment to arrive at adjusted gross income, it will be reflected on the expenditure schedule as a nontaxable source.

6.5.15   Depreciation, Amortization, and Depletion

Depreciation, amortization, and depletion are not recognized on the RICO expenditure schedule since these are accountant's figures that do not relate to the use of funds. In tax cases, depreciation, amortization, and depletion allowances are shown as an accumulated liability but not as a personal living expense. The Internal Revenue Code and regulations govern the amount that can be claimed.

6.5.16   Controlled Foreign Corporations (CFC)

For tax purposes, the investigator should pick up the net cash investment plus the taxpayer's income and loss for the period. For RICO purposes, only the subject's net cash investment for the period should be used. These net investment figures should be in U.S. currency. Any gains and losses should be reflected in other sections of the expenditure schedule. This applies to both tax and RICO purposes. However, for tax purposes, losses will be limited to the loss limitation rules.

6.5.17   IRA and Keogh Accounts

On tax expenditure schedules, Individual Retirement Accounts and Keogh plan contributions should show the amount of the contributions plus earnings for the period. Earnings for the period are reflected as a nontaxable source. For RICO purposes, the plan contributions are shown as an expenditure plus any earnings. However, the earnings for the period are reflected as a source of income.

6.5.18   Capital Gains and Losses

There are differences between the Tax Expenditure Method and the RICO Expenditure Method. For tax purposes, capital losses are not recognized on the expenditure computation, because they are adjustments to arrive at adjusted gross income. However, losses in excess of the amount allowed to be deducted during the period should be shown as an intangible asset. This intangible asset is reduced by the amount of loss allowed in subsequent years. For RICO expenditure purposes, both gains and losses are recognized for the period in the appropriate section, income or expense. In addition, the recovered costs are to be reflected in the source section. In RICO cases it is easier to show the gross proceeds from the sale of capital assets as a source and reflect the cost of the asset as an expenditure.

6.6   Civil versus Criminal

Like the Net Worth Methods, the Expenditure Methods have the same issues. Like the Net Worth Methods, the Expenditure Methods will have to solve the same issues in somewhat the same manner. In tax cases, there will be differences between a criminal and civil case. This is due primarily to the degree of proof required in criminal cases, which is greater than in civil cases. In tax civil cases, issues can become more technical than in criminal cases. In RICO cases, there should be little or no differences. Any difference usually relates to the admissibility during criminal proceedings or later discovery of additional items.

6.7   Defenses

The defenses for the Expenditure Method, whether tax or RICO, are the same as for the Net Worth Method. In criminal cases, the burden of proof is the responsibility of the government when the Expenditure Method is used. The cash hoard or conversion of old assets is the most used defense in the Expenditure Method. Any defense will have to be investigated and refuted. The Expenditure Method will have to use the same investigative techniques to refute any cash hoard or asset conversion as used in the Net Worth Method. Defense attorneys use the same defenses in both expenditure and net worth cases.

6.8 Summary

Like the Net Worth Method, the Expenditure Method is also a powerful tool. It also tends to place the burden on the defendant to disprove once introduced into evidence. The examiner or investigator has a tedious job of locating, obtaining, analyzing, and preparing an expenditure schedule. The examiner has to pay close attention to all the details presented in an expenditure schedule. All the issues must be identified and resolved. The principal difference between the expenditure and Net Worth Methods is the presentation of assets and liabilities. The Expenditure Method only reflects assets and liabilities that are obtained or disposed of during a period.

Scenario Case

7

7.1 Case

This case problem is designed to acquaint the reader on how to put together a net worth computation schedule, an expenditure computation schedule, and a tracing schedule for Title 26, U.S. Code (Income Tax) and for Title 18, U.S. Code (Racketeering). It is designed to show the theory and objective. It illustrates these objectives and addresses the most common problems and issues that forensic accountants will encounter.

This case is based on real-life incidents. The material for this case is divided into two parts for the purpose of showing the importance of both financial information and nonfinancial information and their interrelationships. The first section, Financial Data, will provide you with financial data for use in your various computational schedules. The second section, Intelligence, will provide you with information about the subject's activities and dealings. This section also has some financial information but is not generally admissible in court because the Federal Rules of Evidence disallow it.

This case scenario is used to prepare four schedules using the theory for both tax and Racketeer Influenced and Corrupt Organization (RICO) purposes. The following chapters will explain in detail and provide the schedules for the following:

1. Net worth schedule for tax purposes
2. Net worth schedule for RICO purposes
3. Expenditure schedule for tax purposes
4. Expenditure schedule for RICO purposes

The tax laws and regulations are the basis for computing a tax net worth or expenditure schedules. The objective is to determine the amount of unreported taxable income. The funds principal is the underlying guide in preparing the RICO net worth or expenditure schedules. No amortization, depreciation, or depletion allowances are allowed in a RICO net worth or expenditure schedule. The objective is to determine the amount of illegal income and identify forfeitable assets. The subsequent chapters show how these schedules should appear and the explanations as to how they were determined for each type of schedule.

7.2 Financial Data

7.2.1 Search Warrant Data

Investigators conducted an authorized search warrant on John Doe's residence on December 31, 19X3. During this search, the following items were discovered and seized:

1. Cash found in a floor safe, $50,000.
2. Two kilos of cocaine. The wholesale value at time of search warrant was $25,000 per kilo.
3. Bank statements in the name of John Doe from Barclays Bank of London, England. The statement transactions are given below in British pounds (BL). At the time of deposits, the exchange rate was US$1.00 = BL$2.00.

Date	Deposits ($)	Withdrawals ($)	Balance ($)	Interest ($)
1/28/X1	1,000,000		1,000,000	
2/10/X1	1,000,000		2,000,000	
3/15/X1	2,000,000		4,000,000	
3/30/X1			4,120,000	120,000
5/1/X1		2,000,000	2,120,000	
6/30/X1			2,203,600	83,600
7/2/X1	2,203,600		–	

4. Ten gold bullion bars were found at his residence in a hidden compartment in the kitchen cabinets. Market value at time of seizure was $20,000 per bar.

7.2.2 Public Records

During the investigation, the following data were discovered in County Public Records:

1. Public records show John Doe purchased his residence at 100 Alpha Street. The Warranty Deed shows purchase was on 1/30/X1. The document stamps paid on the purchase were $1500. Document stamps are based on $5.00 per thousand. A mortgage is recorded along with the Warranty Deed. The mortgage shows John Doe obtained a mortgage for $250,000. The mortgage states monthly payments of $1000 per month plus interest at 10% per annum are due commencing 3/1/X1. The mortgage is Panama Mortgage Company, a foreign corporation (Panama Republic).
2. On 5/8/X1, John Doe purchased an apartment building on 100 Bravo Street. The Warranty Deed shows document stamps paid were $20,000. Document stamps were paid on purchase price of $5.00 per thousand. A mortgage is recorded at the same time by Florida Mortgage Corp., a domestic corporation. The principal amount is $2,000,000. Monthly payments are $10,000 per month plus interest until the mortgage is paid commencing 6/1/X1. Interest rate is 10%.

7.2.3 Life Insurance

John Doe purchased a life insurance policy for $10,000 on 6/30/X1. The policy is for $1,000,000 with John Doe's mother as beneficiary. This is a whole-life policy. Doe paid 5 years at one time. The policy shows the cash value as follows based on annual installments of $2,000.

Date	Value ($)
19X1	–
19X2	2000
19X3	3000
19X4	5000

7.2.4 Home Improvements

John Doe purchased furniture and fixtures for his house. Receipts obtained show the following purchases from vendors:

Description	Amount ($)	Date
Furniture	50,000	2/2/X1
Cabinets	20,000	2/3/X1
Paintings	20,000	3/1/X1
Fixtures	10,000	4/1/X1
Pool and tennis court	100,000	7/1/X1
Appliances	20,000	9/1/X2
Electronic equipment	100,000	9/1/X2
Security system	50,000	2/1/X3

7.2.5 Corporations

A check with the State Bureau of Corporations shows that John Doe is owner of the following entities. All these entities were formed on 10/1/X1.

1. Lounge Doe, Inc.—a Florida corporation
2. Doe's Kwik Stop, Inc.—a Florida corporation
3. Real Property, Ltd.—a Florida partnership

7.2.6 Individual Tax Returns

The individual tax returns were obtained on John Doe. They show the following data:

Description	19X0 ($)	19X1 ($)	19X3 ($)
Wages	10,000	190,000	200,000
Sole proprietor			(250,000)
Doe Lounge dividend		100,000	
Doe's Kwik Stop, Inc.		(25,000)	175,000
Real Property Ltd.		(100,000)	(30,000)
Rental Property Schedule E		(70,000)	(30,000)
Adjusted gross	10,000	95,000	65,000
Deductions:			
Standard	3,000		

(continued)

Description	19X0 ($)	19X1 ($)	19X3 ($)
Mortgage interest		25,000	22,600
Property taxes		5,000	5,000
Exemptions	2,000	2,000	2,000
Taxable income	5,000	63,000	35,400
Tax liability	500	15,750	7,000
Refund in 19X1	500		
Refund in 19X2		79,250	
Withholding	1,000	95,000	150,000

John Doe filed a schedule C for his sole proprietorship with the returns that he filed. John Doe did not file his tax return for 19X2. This business sells women's clothes. Suzy Que runs the business after she leaves her bank job. John Doe does not manage the business and frequently checks the business operations. The tax return and financial statements provide the following information:

A. Balance Sheet Presentation

Balance Sheet	19X2 ($)	19X3 ($)
Cash in bank	20,000	10,000
Accounts receivable	10,000	20,000
Inventory	140,000	50,000
Business assets	150,000	150,000
Accumulated depreciation	(30,000)	(60,000)
Total	290,000	170,000
Accounts payable	–	50,000
Bank loan payable	100,000	80,000
Capital	700,000	800,000
Accumulated earnings	(560,000)	(760,000)
Total	290,000	170,000

B. Income Statement Presentation

Income	19X2 ($)	19X3 ($)
Sales	80,000	440,000
Beginning inventory	–	140,000
Purchases	180,000	130,000
Total inventory	180,000	270,000
Ending inventory	140,000	50,000
Cost of sales	40,000	220,000
Gross profit	40,000	220,000
Overhead Expenses		
Advertising	80,000	40,000
Depreciation	30,000	30,000
Interest	10,000	8,000
Insurance	50,000	50,000
Professional fees	25,000	25,000
Office expenses	30,000	10,000
Rent expense	50,000	50,000

(*continued*)

B. Income Statement Presentation

Income	19X2 ($)	19X3 ($)
Repairs	20,000	10,000
Supplies	30,000	10,000
Taxes	50,000	40,000
Utilities	40,000	40,000
Wages	120,000	150,000
Miscellaneous	15,000	7,000
Total	550,000	470,000
Net loss	510,000	250,000

The business has a part-time bookkeeper who maintains the books. The bookkeeper prepares all the various journals (cash receipts, disbursements, payables, receivables, and purchases). Mr. I. M. Balance, CPA, prepares the individual tax returns for John Doe. In addition, he does a certified audit of the sole proprietorship that is known as "Suzy's Women Clothes." The bookkeeper does the bank reconciliation, but they are reviewed by I. M. Balance, CPA.

C. Rental Income Schedule

Description	19X2 ($)	19X3 ($)
Rental receipts	200,000	450,000
Interest expense	120,000	180,000
Property taxes	20,000	40,000
Insurance	20,000	40,000
Maintenance	10,000	20,000
Depreciation	100,000	200,000
Total expenses	270,000	480,000
Net loss	70,000	30,000

Note: Depreciation is based on the straight-line method over 15 years.

7.2.6.1 Lounge Doe, Inc.

The corporate tax returns and financial statements were obtained. This is a calendar year corporation. The corporate records were also obtained and they substantiate the tax return figures.

A. Balance Sheet Presentation

Description	19X1 ($)	19X2 ($)	19X3 ($)
Cash	10,000	50,000	40,000
Inventory	500,000	400,000	300,000
Personal property	500,000	500,000	500,000
Real property	1,000,000	1,000,000	1,000,000
Accumulated depreciation	(50,000)	(200,000)	(350,000)
Land	500,000	500,000	500,000
Organization cost	1,000	900	800
Total assets	2,461,000	2,250,900	1,990,800
Accounts payable	1,000	50,000	40,000

(*continued*)

A. Balance Sheet Presentation

Description	19X1 ($)	19X2 ($)	19X3 ($)
Shareholder loan	2,435,000	2,435,000	2,134,900
Stock	5,000	5,000	5,000
Retained earnings	20,000	(239,100)	(189,100)
Total	2,461,000	2,250,900	1,990,800

B. Income Statement Presentation

Description	19X1 ($)	19X2 ($)	19X3 ($)
Income	1,070,100	891,000	1,400,100
Cash expenses	100,000	150,000	300,000
Depreciation	50,000	150,000	150,000
Amortized costs	100	100	100
Inventory:			
Beginning	–	500,000	400,000
Purchases	1,300,000	750,000	800,000
Ending	500,000	400,000	300,000
Cost of sales	800,000	850,000	900,000
Total costs	950,100	1,150,100	1,350,100
Net income (loss)	120,000	(259,100)	50,000

Examination of the corporate books and records reveal that the corporation purchased a fast boat for $100,000 on 11/1/X1. It is not used for business purposes.

7.2.6.2 Doe's Kwik Stop, Inc.

The corporate records were obtained for this corporation. The corporate tax return shows that Doe's Kwik Stop, Inc. is a Subchapter S corporation.

A. Balance Sheet Presentation

Description	19X1 ($)	19X2 ($)	19X3 ($)
Cash	20,000	20,000	310,100
Inventory	50,000	60,000	70,000
Personal property	500,000	500,000	500,000
Accumulated depreciation	50,000	200,000	350,000
Prepaid insurance	10,000	5,000	–
Organization cost	1,100	1,000	900
Total assets	531,100	386,000	531,000
Accounts payable	50,000	60,000	30,000
Shareholder loan	501,100	396,000	396,000
Stock	5,000	5,000	5,000
Retained earnings	(25,000)	(75,000)	100,000
Total	531,100	386,000	531,000

B. Income Statement Presentation

Description	19X1 ($)	19X2 ($)	19X3 ($)
Income	275,100	405,100	1,000,100
Cash expenses	100,000	150,000	400,000
Amortized insurance	–	5,000	5,000

(continued)

B.   Income Statement Presentation

Description	19X1 ($)	19X2 ($)	19X3 ($)
Amortized organization	100	100	100
Depreciation	50,000	150,000	150,000
Inventory:			
Beginning	–	50,000	60,000
Purchases	200,000	160,000	280,000
Ending	50,000	60,000	70,000
Cost of sales	150,000	150,000	270,000
Total expenses	300,100	455,100	825,100
Net income (loss)	(25,000)	(50,000)	175,000

7.2.6.3   Real Property, Ltd.

The partnership records were obtained. The partnership records are summarized below. John Doe has a 50% partnership interest and contributed equally.

A.   Balance Sheet Presentation

Description	19X1 ($)	19X2 ($)	19X3 ($)
Cash	10,000	10,000	30,000
Building	10,000,000	10,000,000	10,000,000
Accumulated depreciation	250,000	750,000	1,250,000
Land	2,000,000	2,000,000	2,000,000
Total assets	11,760,000	11,255,000	10,780,000
Mortgage	7,900,000	7,500,000	7,000,000
Capital	3,860,000	3,755,000	4,890,000
Total	11,760,000	11,255,000	10,780,000

B.   Capital Account Analysis

Description	19X1 ($)	19X2 ($)	19X3 ($)
Beginning	–	3,860,000	7,000,000
Contributions	4,060,000	–	85,000
Net loss	(200,000)	(105,000)	(60,000)
Ending balance	3,860,000	3,755,000	3,780,000

C.   Income Statement Presentation

Description	19X1 ($)	19X2 ($)	19X3 ($)
Rental income	330,000	1,285,000	1,300,000
Depreciation	250,000	500,000	500,000
Interest	200,000	750,000	700,000
Taxes	10,000	40,000	40,000
Insurance	20,000	50,000	60,000
Maintenance	50,000	50,000	60,000
Total expenses	530,000	1,390,000	1,360,000
Net loss	200,000	105,000	60,000

7.2.7 Bank Accounts

John Doe's bank accounts were obtained from First National Bank. The following is a summary of those accounts:

A. Checking Account				
Date	Deposits ($)	Withdrawals ($)	Balance ($)	Interest ($)
12/31/X1	5,010,000	5,000,000		10,000
12/31/X2	600,000	560,000		50,000
12/31/X3	200,000	150,000		100,000

B. Savings Account				
Date	Deposits ($)	Withdrawals ($)	Balance ($)	Interest ($)
12/31/X1	100,000	–	110,000	10,000
12/31/X2	400,000	–	550,000	40,000
12/31/X3	50,000	–	650,000	50,000

7.2.8 Credit Card

John Doe's credit card records were obtained. The following is a summary of this account:

Date	Charges ($)	Payments ($)	Balance ($)
12/31/X1	30,000	30,000	–
12/31/X2	100,000	70,000	30,000
12/31/X3	180,000	160,000	50,000

All charges were for personal living expenses for both himself and his girlfriend.

7.2.9 Living Expenses

Various vendor records were obtained as to John Doe's personal living expenses. They are summarized below.

Description	19X1 ($)	19X2 ($)	19X3 ($)
Utilities	10,000	10,000	20,000
Telephone	30,000	40,000	45,000
Insurance	5,000	10,000	10,000
Church donations	–	10,000	50,000

7.2.10 Automobiles

John Doe purchased a Mercedes Benz for $80,000 in 19X1. He put $30,000 down and financed the remainder with the First National Bank. In 19X2, John Doe purchased a Toyota for $18,000. He put $10,000 down and financed the remainder with the First National Bank. Records for both cars were obtained from the sellers. The following summarizes these transactions:

Description	19X1	19X2
Mercedes Benz	$80,000	
Toyota		$18,000
Financed amount	$50,000	$8,000
Finance charge	$10,000	$2,000
Monthly payments	$1,000	$200
Term	60 months	50 months
Paid during the year	$9,000	$1,200

7.2.11 Rental Property

Records were obtained for John Doe's rental property for 19X2. I. M. Balance, CPA, had these records in his possession. They are summarized below.

Description	19X2 ($)
Rental receipts	400,000
Interest expense	190,000
Property taxes	40,000
Insurance	40,000
Maintenance	20,000
Depreciation	200,000
Total expenses	490,000
Net loss	90,000

7.2.12 Individual Retirement Accounts

John Doe opened several Individual Retirement Accounts at First National Bank: one for Suzy Que and the other for himself. The bank records show the following:

A. For John Doe			
Year	Deposits ($)	Interest ($)	Balance ($)
19X2	2,000	200	2,200
19X3	2,000	400	4,600

B. For Suzy Que			
Year	Deposits ($)	Interest ($)	Balance ($)
19X2	2,000	200	2,200
19X3	2,000	400	4,600

7.2.13 Trusts

John Doe set up trust accounts for his parents, two brothers, and sister at First National Bank during 19X3.

Parents	$100,000
Brothers (2)	100,000 each
Sister	100,000

The trust funds for the brothers are paying for their college tuition and books.

7.2.14   Earnings

The Unemployment Bureau was contacted about the earnings of Suzy Que. They provided the following data:

Date	Bank ($)	Que's Clothes ($)	Total ($)
19X1	13,000	–	13,000
19X2	14,000	50,000	54,000
19X3	15,000	70,000	85,000

7.2.15   Securities

John Doe purchased 100 shares of ABC stock for $10,000 on 6/30/X2. Three months later, Doe sold the stock for $12,000. On 9/30/X2, Doe purchased 10 shares of XYZ stock for $12,000. Two months later, the XYZ stock was sold for $9,000.

7.2.16   Property Taxes

The county tax collector's office provided records on property taxes assessed and collected from John Doe on his personal residence at 100 Alpha Street. The records show that John Doe paid $5,000 in 19X1 and $5,000 in 19X3. John Doe is delinquent on his property tax bill for 19X2 of $5,000.

7.3   Intelligence

7.3.1   Background

John Doe is a 24-year-old young man. He dropped out of high school during his sophomore year. He held only menial jobs as a boat mechanic helper. He never married but dated many girls on a regular basis. Even though he had no formal training in boat mechanics, he became fairly good at fixing boat engines, especially diesel engines. He was born in Cuba and came to the United States with his parents, two brothers, and a sister. In high school, he smoked marijuana and sold it to fellow high school students. His father is a medical doctor who worked as a laboratory technician until he became certified in this country in 19X4. His mother also worked as a laboratory technician until she got certified as a registered nurse in 19X4. His two brothers, who are older, are attending college. One brother is studying to become a civil engineer, and the other is studying to become a dentist. Doe's sister is still in high school.

7.3.2   Commodities

Investigators observed John Doe on 6/30/X1 going to a jewelry store with a black attaché case. He stayed in the store for about 30 minutes and came out with his black attaché case. The investigators went into the store after Doe drove away. The store manager told the investigators that Doe purchased 10 bars of gold bullion for $100,000 in cash. The store owner was very reluctant to talk about this transaction.

7.3.3 Offshore Mortgage

Investigators in Panama did a check on Panama Mortgage Company. They discovered that the corporation was a registered corporation. The registered agent was a law firm. The law firm would not give any information about the corporation. The president and director of the corporation were shown on public records. When the investigators checked out the address of the president and director, they found only a vacant lot in Panama.

7.3.4 Offshore Bank

A formal request was issued to Scotland Yard, London, England, for bank records from Barclays Bank of London. The British authorities sent the records to the United States. An examination of these records shows that John Doe deposited cash in the British bank. The funds were later sent by wire transfer to the Panama National Bank in Panama. Banks in Panama will not give any banking information because of Bank Secrecy Laws.

7.3.5 Surveillance

During surveillance, it was observed that John Doe and Ramon Calderone were having dinner at the luxury club Tootie on 12/22/X0. Ramon Calderone is a well-known drug kingpin from Colombia. Calderone has been arrested five previous times, but the charges were dropped because the witnesses were found floating in the Miami River.

7.3.6 Corporate Check

Bureau of Corporations shows that Real Estate, Ltd., a partnership, has only two partners, John Doe and Ramon Calderone. Panama Mortgage Company has no registered agent in the United States. It is not even registered to do business in any state of the United States.

7.3.7 Girl Friend

John Doe met a girl, Suzy Que, on 2/28/X1 at the First National Bank, where she worked as a teller. She was seen regularly with John Doe at various nightclubs, sporting events, and shopping malls. Shortly after John Doe purchased the house on 100 Alpha Street, Suzy moved in with John. She drove her own car until John purchased the Toyota for her. She drove the Toyota exclusively. Suzy continued working at the First National Bank. Friends said that she used cocaine regularly after meeting John Doe. Suzy Que, in 19X2 and 19X3, operated the Suzy's Clothes business after she leaves her bank teller job and on weekends. Suzy hired and supervises employees. However, John Doe controlled all finances. John Doe was frequently seen at the business. When Suzy Que traveled with John Doe, Ms. Betsy Low, the bookkeeper, would manage the business. Betsy Low kept the books. She maintained all journals, ledgers, and prepared a trial balance each month. John Doe never told Suzy Que about his drug trafficking activities. She only assumed that John Doe was a legitimate businessman because of all of the business activities that John Doe controlled. She never overheard any conversations of John Doe's illegal activities.

7.3.8   Currency Transaction Reports

A check of currency transaction reports reveals that First National Bank filed no reports for John Doe or any of his businesses. Also, there were no payments to Panama Mortgage Company for the mortgage on the residence by either check, wire transfer, cashier's check, or money order.

7.3.9   Wiretap

During an authorized wiretap of Doe's residence during the last two months of 19X3, it was discovered that Doe was talking with Ramon Calderone in Colombia about a large shipment of cocaine by ship from Colombia to the Bahamas. Doe was to pick up the cocaine by his fast boat while the ship was docked in Freeport, Bahamas. Two weeks later, Doe and Suzy along with two other couples, not identified, got on the fast boat for the weekend. U.S. Customs intercepted the boat on the way back to the United States, but no drugs were found on the boat.

7.3.10   Telephone Records

The telephone toll records were obtained from the telephone company on John Doe's home telephone. These records cover the period of 1/1/X1 through 12/31/X3. They reflected the following data, including the subscriber's information, which was provided by the telephone company:

Telephone Number	No. of Calls	Subscriber	Country
809-XXX-XXX1	33	Residence[a]	Bahamas
809-XXX-XXX2	20	Barclays Bank	Cayman Islands
809-XXX-XXX3	18	Central Bank	Barbados
809-XXX-XXX4	6	Central Bank	Jamaica
809-XXX-XXX5	65	Central Bank	Bahamas
011-41-1-XXXXXA	2	Credit Swiss	Switzerland
011-44-1-XXXXXB	8	Barclays Bank	England
011-57-4-XXXXXC	24	R. Calderone	Colombia
011-507-XXXXXD	10	Panama Bank	Panama
011-599-8-XXXXXE	36	Panama Bank	Netherlands Antilles
011-34-3-XXXXXF	18	Residence[b]	Spain
011-34-3-XXXXXG	12	Central Bank	Spain

[a] Residence in the name of John Doe.
[b] Residence in the name of Ramon Calderone.

7.3.11   Bahama Banks

A request to the Bahamian authorities was made as to the property in the Bahamas and for banking information from the Central Bank. They provided the following:

1. The residence in the Bahamas was purchased on 7/1/X2 for US$100,000. It was a four-bedroom, three-bath house on Blue Lagoon Bay. The house is recorded in the

name of Suzy Que. There are no liens. The house has excellent dockage facilities along with a small guesthouse.

2. The Bahamian authorities obtained the following bank records along with other information regarding the bank account. The bank account at Central Bank is held under the name of Transshipment, Ltd. The corporate officers and directors are John Doe and Suzy Que. The corporation was formed on 6/1/X2 in Freeport, Grand Bahamas. The bank account is summarized as follows:

Date	Description	Deposits ($)	Checks ($)	Balance ($)
6/1/X2	Cash	2,000,000		2,000,000
6/30/X2	Cash	1,000,000		3,000,000
7/1/X2	Blue Lagoon Realty	110,000		2,890,000
7/10/X2	Calderone		1,500,000	1,390,000
10/1/X2	Cash	5,000,000		6,390,000
10/30/X2	Wire Calderone		2,000,000	4,390,000
3/1/X3	Cash	10,000,000		14,390,000
3/10/X3	Wire Calderone		6,000,000	8,390,000
3/31/X3	Cayman Islands		2,000,000	6,390,000
3/31/X3	Barbados		2,000,000	4,390,000
3/31/X3	Spain		1,000,000	3,390,000
3/31/X3	Switzerland		1,000,000	2,390,000
3/31/X3	Panama		500,000	1,890,000
3/31/X3	Aruba		370,000	1,520,000
3/31/X3	Bank charges		20,000	1,500,000
3/31/X3	Jamaica		1,000,000	500,000
10/1/X3	Cash	8,000,000		8,500,000
10/10/X3	Spain		4,500,000	4,000,000
12/1/X3	Panama		3,500,000	500,000

7.3.12 Barbados Banks

A request was made to the Barbados authorities as to the banking information from their Central Bank. The account is titled to John Doe. Suzy Que can also sign on the account. The authorities provided the following information:

Date	Description	Deposits ($)	Checks ($)	Balance ($)
3/31/X3	Bahamas	2,000,000		2,000,000
3/31/X3	Bank fees		10,000	1,990,000
12/31/X3	Interest	199,000		2,189,000

7.3.13 Spanish Banks

A formal request to the Spanish authorities was made for banking information from their Central Bank. Transshipment, Ltd. holds the account. The officer is John Doe. The authorities provided the following information:

Date	Description	Deposits ($)	Checks ($)	Balance ($)
3/31/X3	Bahamas	1,000,000		1,000,000
6/30/X3	Interest	100,000		1,100,000
6/30/X3	Bank charges		10,000	1,090,000

The Spanish authorities provided additional information. The Central Bank of Spain has an account for Ramon Calderone. In addition, Calderone owns a residence on the Coast at Costa del Sol. Calderone paid $2,000,000 for the residence, which has seven bedrooms, four baths, a three-car garage, swimming pool, and dock space for two yachts. The residence has two guest houses and servant quarters for eight servants.

7.3.14   Cayman Island Banks

A request to the Cayman Island authorities was made for banking information from Barclays Bank, plus any other information that they could provide. The account is titled under John Doe with Suzy Que as a signatory on the account. The authorities provided the following data:

Date	Description	Deposits ($)	Checks ($)	Balance ($)
3/31/X3	Bahamas	2,000,000		2,000,000
6/30/X3	Interest	200,000		2,200,000
6/30/X3	Bank charges		20,000	2,180,000
9/30/X3	Interest	210,000		2,390,000
9/30/X3	Bank charges		20,000	2,370,000
12/31/X3	Interest	230,000		2,600,000
12/31/X3	Bank charges		20,000	2,580,000

7.3.15   Swiss Banks

The Swiss authorities provided the following information in response to a formal request. The account is held under Transshipment, Ltd. John Doe is shown as president.

Date	Description	Deposits ($)	Checks ($)	Balance ($)
4/1/X3	Bahamas	1,000,000		1,000,000
12/10/X3	Panama	3,000,000		4,000,000
12/20/X3	Aruba		2,000,000	2,000,000
12/31/X3	Interest	100,000		2,100,000
12/31/X3	Bank fees		10,000	2,090,000

7.3.16   Aruba Banks

Authorities in Aruba provided the following data. The bank account is listed under Doe Holding NV. John Doe is shown as president, and Suzy Que is shown as treasurer and secretary.

Date	Description	Deposits ($)	Checks ($)	Balance ($)
4/4/X3	Bahamas	370,000		370,000
4/4/X3	Jamaica	100,000		470,000
4/10/X3	Schmidt Mgt. Co.		20,000	450,000
6/30/X3	Bank fees		10,000	440,000
12/20/X3	Switzerland	2,000,000		2,440,000
12/31/X3	Interest	150,000		2,590,000
12/31/X3	Schmidt Mgt. Co.		25,000	2,565,000

7.13.17   Jamaican Banks

The bank records from Jamaica were obtained. The account is only in John Doe's name. These records are shown in the following:

Date	Description	Deposits ($)	Checks ($)	Balance ($)
3/31/X3	Bahamas	1,000,000		1,000,000
4/3/X3	Aruba		100,000	900,000
4/3/X3	Boat Repair Shop		100,000	800,000
4/10/X3	Montego Hotel		20,000	780,000
4/10/X3	Gulf Oil		500	779,500
12/31/X3	Interest	7,500		787,000
12/31/X3	Bank fees		1,000	786,000

7.3.18   Accountant

I. M. Balance, CPA, prepares all the various tax returns for John Doe, including his corporations and partnerships. I. M. Balance did not suspect John Doe of being a drug trafficker or money launderer. John Doe periodically brings all of his various records to Mr. Balance, except for the sole proprietorship. Mr. Balance goes to "Suzy's Women's Clothes" store in order to perform his certified audit. He performs the entire audit tests and analysis that are required under Standard Audit Procedures. Mr. Balance had the records for John Doe's apartment building for 19X2. He had in his possession all the records required to complete John Doe's individual tax return for 19X2 but failed to complete this return. His excuse was that he had simply forgotten to prepare the individual tax return for 19X2. Investigators had no evidence that Mr. Balance helped John Doe in laundering his illegal profits. In fact, Mr. Balance believed that John Doe was a young and successful businessman who would adhere to his advice. Doe was friendly and personable to Mr. Balance. Doe would give small gifts to Mr. Balance at Christmas time.

RICO Net Worth Solution
8

8.1 General

The following solution and explanations relate to the scenario case problem as presented in chapter 7. The solution and explanations are based upon the Racketeer Influenced and Corrupt Organizations (RICO) net worth principals in this chapter.

8.2 Principals

The RICO net worth is based on the fund principal. Funds involve the use of cash, either directly or indirectly. As mentioned in Chapter 5, there is no amortization, depreciation, or depletion allowances allowed in a RICO net worth. Cash spent for asset purchases and expenses are recognized immediately. Cash spent to reduce liabilities and some income items are recognized indirectly. In the case of liabilities, the liability balance is shown instead of the payments for the liability. However, the payments can be determined by subtracting the ending balance from the beginning balance. In the case of some income such as wages, the gross wages are shown as income, and the various withholdings are shown as an expense.

8.3 Problem

The following net worth schedule shows how each item in the scenario problem is presented. In addition, an explanation of why it is presented in this manner is explained after the net worth schedule. The explanation section will refer to the line items on the net worth schedule.

8.4 RICO Net Worth Schedule

The next several pages present a RICO net worth schedule. The first section of the net worth schedule is entitled assets. These are items that can be forfeited in case of conviction or civil ruling. The next section is liabilities. These are claims on the assets by creditors. They have prior claims on these assets if secured. The liabilities are subtracted from the total assets. This will give the net worth of the subject. This net worth is compared to find the increase from one period to the next. The following section shows the business expenses from the sole proprietorship titled business expenses. The next section is personal expenses. This is the cost that the subject incurs in everyday living. The last section is legal income or identified income. This reflects the subject's legal sources of funds. When the personal expenses and the business expenses are added to the net worth increase less the legal income or identified income sources, the amount of unexplained income is derived. Under federal law, this is the amount of illegal income. The fine and forfeiture can be calculated at twice this amount.

8.4.1 Cash on Hand

In this case, cash on hand is based on the currency found at John Doe's residence during the execution of the search warrant (Table 8.1, line 1). There are tax cases that say that there must be cash-on-hand figures. Cash on hand must be established as much as possible. There are various methods to determine cash on hand. One method is to check on bank deposits shortly after year-end. Any cash deposits can be shown as cash on hand at year-end. Another method is to show the difference between cash deposits and checks to cash during the year. Another method is to use the cash-on-hand figure used on personal financial statements to creditors. If there is no cash on hand at year-end, then the investigator must present some evidence that the subject has no possible cash on hand.

8.4.2 Cocaine, 2 Kilos

In this situation, the market value of cocaine is used (Table 8.1, line 2). The main reason is that no receipts will be available. However, it is well known that the subject purchased the cocaine. There were no facilities discovered to indicate that the cocaine was manufactured there. This means that the subject had to purchase the cocaine. Because the suspect is a subject of a drug investigation, the suspect is in the business of reselling cocaine, thus he is a wholesaler. The Drug Enforcement Agency, as well as some local law enforcement agencies, keeps records of the market values of drugs on a weekly, monthly, and yearly basis by type of drug over long periods of time. During a trial, an expert who keeps statistics on drug market values will have to testify on this issue.

8.4.3 Bank Accounts

The bank balances are used in this schedule for the personal bank accounts, and the book balance is used for the business account (Table 8.1, lines 3, 4, and 5). The personal bank accounts require no need for a bank reconciliation schedule if only the expenses, asset purchases, and liability payments are based solely on checks that clear the bank during the year. Because there are two bank accounts, a year-end confirmation should be made to see if funds from one account are transferred to the other account or for asset purchases, liability payments, and personal expenses that will overlap years. This is not the case here. The business bank account is based on what is recorded in the books. A bank reconciliation will be needed for this bank account.

8.4.4 Accounts Receivable

The accounts receivable is an asset of John Doe. Sole proprietorship assets are assets of the individual because the sole proprietor has accepted title and personal liability (Table 8.1, line 6). In criminal cases, the fraud examiner will have to confirm these accounts receivables or else have the customer testify in court that the receivable is his/her personal liability.

Table 8.1   John Doe's RICO Net Worth Schedule (Title 18)

Description	19X0 ($)	19X1 ($)	19X2 ($)	19X3 ($)
		Assets		
1. Cash on hand	—	—	—	50,000
2. Cocaine, 2 kilos				50,000
3. First National Bank checking		10,000	50,000	100,000
4. First National Bank savings		110,000	550,000	650,000
5. Business cash in bank			20,000	10,000
6. Accounts receivable			10,000	20,000
7. Inventory			140,000	50,000
8. Business assets			150,000	150,000
9. Security system				50,000
10. Electronic equipment			100,000	100,000
11. Appliances			20,000	20,000
12. Fixtures		10,000	10,000	10,000
13. Furniture		50,000	50,000	50,000
14. Cabinets		20,000	20,000	20,000
15. Paintings		20,000	20,000	20,000
16. Pool and tennis court		100,000	100,000	100,000
17. 100 Alpha Street		300,000	300,000	300,000
18. 100 Bravo Street		4,000,000	4,000,000	4,000,000
19. Gold bullion, 10 bars		100,000	100,000	100,000
20. Lounge Doe, Inc.		2,440,000	2,440,000	2,440,000
21. Doe's Kwik Stop, Inc.		506,100	401,000	401,000
22. Real Property, Ltd.		2,030,000	2,030,000	2,072,500
23. Mercedes Benz		80,000	80,000	80,000
24. Toyota sedan			18,000	18,000
25. IRA—John Doe			2,200	4,600
26. IRA—Suzy Que			2,200	4,600
27. Bahamas residence			110,000	110,000
Total assets	—	9,779,100	10,723,400	10,980,700
		Liabilities		
28. FNB—Mercedes loan		51,000	39,000	27,000
29. FNB—Toyota loan			8,800	6,400
30. Credit card			30,000	50,000
31. Accounts payable				50,000
32. Florida Mortgage Co.		1,930,000	1,810,000	1,690,000
33. Business bank loan			100,000	80,000
Total liabilities	—	1,981,000	1,987,800	1,903,400
Net worth	—	7,795,100	8,735,600	9,077,300
Net worth increase		7,795,100	940,500	341,700
		Business Expenses		
34. Purchases			180,000	130,000
35. Inventory change			−140,000	90,000
36. Cost of sales			40,000	220,000

(*continued*)

Table 8.1   John Doe's RICO Net Worth Schedule (Title 18) (Continued)

Description	19X0 ($)	19X1 ($)	19X2 ($)	19X3 ($)
37. Advertising			80,000	40,000
38. Interest on loan			10,000	8,000
39. Insurance			50,000	50,000
40. Professional fees			25,000	25,000
41. Office expenses			30,000	10,000
42. Rent expense			50,000	50,000
43. Repairs			20,000	10,000
44. Supplies			30,000	10,000
45. Taxes and licenses			50,000	40,000
46. Utilities			40,000	40,000
47. Wages			120,000	150,000
48. Miscellaneous			15,000	7,000
Total business expenses			560,000	660,000
	Personal Expenses			
49. Florida Mortgage interest		200,000	188,000	176,000
50. Utilities		10,000	10,000	20,000
51. Telephone		30,000	40,000	45,000
52. Insurance		5,000	10,000	10,000
53. Life insurance		10,000		
54. Interest car loans		10,000	2,000	
55. Income tax withheld		95,000		150,000
56. Property taxes		5,000		5,000
57. Credit card charges		30,000	100,000	180,000
58. Church donations			10,000	50,000
59. Trust funds				400,000
60. Loss—XYZ stock			3,000	
Total personal expenses		395,000	363,000	1,036,000
Total expenses		395,000	923,000	1,696,000
	Legal Income			
61. Wages and salaries		190,000	—	200,000
62. Dividends		100,000		
63. Rental income		30,000	113,000	170,000
64. Gain—ABC stock			2,000	
65. IRA—interest Doe			200	400
66. IRA—interest Que			200	400
67. Tax refunds			500	79,250
68. Sale—XYZ stock			9,000	
69. Business income			80,000	440,000
Total legal income		320,500	283,650	810,800
Illegal/unidentified income		7,869,600	1,579,850	1,226,900

8.4.5 Inventory

Inventory of the sole proprietorship is an asset of John Doe because he has title and personal liability (Table 8.1, line 7). The key problem with inventory is determining the proper quantity and costs. It is preferred to use the sole proprietor's quantity and costs unless there is other evidence that would show something different. In this case, the sole proprietor's quantity and costs are used.

8.4.6 Business Assets

The business assets of the sole proprietorship are assets of John Doe because he has title and personal liability (Table 8.1, line 8). These assets are recorded at costs.

8.4.7 Security System

The purchase of this asset is recorded at the purchase price paid (Table 8.1, line 9).

8.4.8 Electronic Equipment

This asset is recorded at cost (Table 8.1, line 10).

8.4.9 Appliances

This asset is recorded at cost (Table 8.1, line 11).

8.4.10 Fixtures

This asset is recorded at cost (Table 8.1, line 12).

8.4.11 Furniture

This asset is recorded at cost (Table 8.1, line 13).

8.4.12 Cabinets

This asset is recorded at cost (Table 8.1, line 14).

8.4.13 Paintings

This asset is recorded at cost (Table 8.1, line 15).

8.4.14 Pool and Tennis Court

This asset is recorded at cost (Table 8.1, line 16). If the subject is making periodic payments for the construction of this asset, then a payment schedule will have to be obtained from the vendor to show the total costs. Remember that only the cost incurred for the period should be reflected on the schedule. Subsequent period costs will be added on as they are incurred.

8.4.15   100 Alpha Street

The purchase of the house is recorded at cost (Table 8.1, line 17). In this case, public records are used to determine the cost. However, the closing agent can be contacted for the closing statement, which can also be used. The Best Evidence Rule should be followed whenever possible.

8.4.16   100 Bravo Street

The purchase of this apartment is recorded at cost (Table 8.1, line 18). Public records are used to determine the cost. The closing statement, which will show the exact cost including any closing costs, can be obtained from the closing agent.

8.4.17   Gold Bullion, 10 Bars

The gold bullion is recorded at cost (Table 8.1, line 19). The market value is given at the time of seizure. If the cost was not known, then the market value would be used. Commodities, such as gold, are becoming more prevalent in money laundering. In this case, the market value is much higher than the original costs. The date of purchase is also known. If the date is not known, then the market value would be used but only for the period discovered. If the market value and year discovered are used, then the defense would have the burden of proof to show otherwise. If the defense does present such evidence, then the cost(s) and purchase date should be used.

8.4.18   Lounge Doe, Inc.

The net investment in this corporation is to be used (Table 8.1, line 20). This is normally a positive balance, but there are occasions when the net cash investment is negative. This can happen when the shareholder withdraws more out than the investment. Corporate assets belong to the corporation and not the shareholder. In this case, the corporation has a boat that is not used in the ordinary course of business. The boat might be used in illegal activities; if so, law enforcement can seize the boat. If the shareholder is caught in illegal activities, the shareholder's stock can be forfeited. The corporation then can be dissolved and the assets sold, or the corporation can be operated by a court appointed Trustee and later sold. Generally, the U.S. Marshal Service is responsible for seized assets.

8.4.19   Doe's Kwik Stop, Inc.

The net investment in this corporation is to be used (Table 8.1, line 21). Its tax status has nothing to do in a RICO computation. The net investment should take into consideration capital stock, additional paid in capital, and loans from shareholder. If the corporation has loans to shareholders, then they should be subtracted from the other investment accounts.

8.4.20   Real Property, Ltd.

This is a partnership in which the subject has a half interest (Table 8.1, line 22). Like corporations, the net investment is used for the partner's interest only. The other partner(s) interest is not considered. Partnership assets belong to the partnership. If the assets of the partnership can be identified to the partner under investigation, then they can be severed from the partnership. In this case, the partners have an undivided interest in the assets, real property; therefore it cannot be severed.

8.4.21   Mercedes Benz

This automobile is recorded at cost (Table 8.1, line 23). One problem that can arise with vehicles is trade-ins. The car dealer will allow a trade-in allowance for an old car against the purchase of a new car. This trade-in allowance will have to be accounted for. The cost of the old automobile should be subtracted from the trade-in allowance. This will give a profit or loss that will have to be recognized on the net worth schedule. The purchase price will be recognized in full for the new automobile. Even though there is no cash exchanging hands, funds have been used. This is a good example of the use of funds where cash is not used.

8.4.22   Toyota Sedan

This automobile is also recorded at cost (Table 8.1, line 24). Even though Suzy Que is driving the car, it is still charged to Doe because he paid for it. Even if the car is registered to Suzy Que's name, John Doe purchased it, so he should be charged for it. In essence, John Doe made a gift to Suzy Que. Another method of presentation is to show the car purchase as a gift in the expenditure section of the net worth schedule instead of an asset of John Doe.

8.4.23   IRA—John Doe and Suzy Que

Individual retirement accounts and Keogh plans should be shown as an asset (Table 8.1, lines 25 and 26). The earnings from these accounts should also be shown in the source of income schedule and added to the asset account.

8.4.24   Bahamas Residence

The cost of foreign real estate should be shown at cost (Table 8.1, line 27). If the property is acquired in anything other than U.S. dollars, any loss or gain on the conversion will also have to be recognized.

8.4.25   First National Bank—Car Loans

These are two bank installment loans (Table 8.1, lines 28 and 29). Installment loans are presented as a liability. Period balances are shown at the end of each period. When these liabilities are incurred, they include both the principal and interest. For RICO net worth purposes, the interest is charged off to expense in the year incurred.

8.4.26 Credit Card

Balances owed on credit cards can be shown as a liability at period end (Table 8.1, line 30). The charges are shown as an expense for the period. This is an example of where the use of funds is shown indirectly. The use of funds is reflected by subtracting the liability balance from the total charges for the period. If there is a beginning liability balance, it will have to be taken into account. Another method of recognizing credit card payments is to only show the payments as an expenditure and ignore the total charges and ending liability balances.

8.4.27 Accounts Payable

Liabilities of a sole proprietorship are personal liabilities because the proprietor is personally liable. Accounts payable are claims by vendors for the business purchases (Table 8.1, line 31). In criminal cases, the fraud examiner should confirm the accounts payable or else each vendor will have to testify as to their accounts receivable from the subject.

8.4.28 Florida Mortgage Corp.

Mortgage balances are shown at period end (Table 8.1, line 32). There is only one major issue to speak of in this area and that is proper recognition of year-end balances. The test of mortgage balances is to subtract the interest from the total payments. This gives the amount of principal payments that reduce the mortgage balance. The escrow payments, if any, must be subtracted from the mortgage payments before the computation for principal payments is done.

8.4.29 Accumulated Depreciation

Accumulated depreciation is not used in RICO net worth computations. It must be remembered that there is no depreciation, amortization, or depletion allowances allowed in RICO net worth computations.

8.4.30 Business Bank Loan

Loans made to a sole proprietorship are personal liabilities. John Doe acquired a bank loan to help finance his business. This is a personal liability and is presented the same way as other personal liabilities (Table 8.1, line 33).

8.4.31 Business Expenses

The business expenses that are paid or accrued (if on the accrual basis of account) are to be added to the increase in net worth. These are period expenses that must be recognized during the period incurred whether paid or accrued in this case (Table 8.1, lines 34, 37–48).

8.4.32 Inventory Changes

This account relates to the change in inventory (Table 8.1, line 35). If inventory goes up, then this account will have a negative amount to reduce purchases (as shown on line 34).

If inventory decreases as shown for 19X3, then this account will have an increase. These increases and decreases will directly relate to the changes in inventory balances (as shown on line 7). This inventory change account has two purposes. First, it accounts for the changes in inventory. Second, it explains the composition of the cost of sales. The combination of purchases and inventory changes make up the cost of sales account.

8.4.33   Cost of Sales

The cost of sales accounts for the sale of goods sold is comprised of purchases and changes in inventory (Table 8.1, line 36). This is an expenditure for each period.

8.4.34   Florida Mortgage Co.

As explained previously, this is the interest portion of the mortgage payments (Table 8.1, line 49). This is a period expense that must be recognized during the period incurred.

8.4.35   Utilities

This is a period expense that must be recognized during the period incurred (Table 8.1, line 50).

8.4.36   Telephone

This is a period expense that must be recognized during the period incurred (Table 8.1, line 51).

8.4.37   Insurance

This is a period expense that must be recognized during the period incurred (Table 8.1, line 52).

8.4.38   Life Insurance

This is a period expense that must be recognized during the period incurred (Table 8.1, line 53). This is a prepaid expense. Prepaid expenses are generally shown as an asset. For RICO purposes, this is recognized as an expense in the year paid. For forfeiture purposes, this is an asset that can be seized.

8.4.39   Interest

This is interest paid for the two installment loans (Table 8.1, line 54). This is the total interest for the life of the loans. For RICO purposes, the interest charged is recognized during the period incurred. In this case, the interest was incurred when the loan was obtained. Even though the interest is over a period of time beyond the current period, it is only recognized during the period incurred. It is not capitalized and amortized; instead, it is expensed in the year incurred.

8.4.40   Income Tax Withheld

This is a period expense that must be recognized during the period incurred (Table 8.1, line 55). Even though there is a refund in later years, the fact that the income tax is withheld makes it a period expense in the period incurred. Refunds will be recognized in the period received as an identified source of funds.

8.4.41   Property Taxes

This is period expense that must be recognized during the period incurred (Table 8.1, line 56). In this case, the tax return figures are used. This can be admissible in a court of law, but it is advisable to get the property taxes confirmed with the local tax collector.

8.4.42   Credit Card Charges

This is a period expense that must be recognized in the period incurred (Table 8.1, line 57). This is a situation where the actual charges are shown as an expense. In the case of a criminal trial, the vendors will each have to testify unless there is a stipulation to the charges made. Otherwise, the alternative solution is to show the payments made to the credit card company, which results in no credit card liability. The problem of distinguishing between business and personal use is not necessary in this case. If a corporation pays for part or all of the personal credit card balance, then these payments should be ignored.

8.4.43   Church Donations

This is a period expense that is recognized in the period incurred (Table 8.1, line 58).

8.4.44   Trust Funds

This is a period expense that is recognized in the period incurred (Table 8.1, line 59).

8.4.45   Loss—XYZ Stock

This is a period expense that is recognized in the period incurred (Table 8.1, line 60).

8.4.46   Wages and Salaries

This is a period income item (Table 8.1, line 61). Wages and salaries are reported at the gross amounts. The various withholding items are reported as a personal expense.

8.4.47   Dividends

This is period income that is reported for the period earned (Table 8.1, line 62).

8.4.48   Rental Income

This is period income that is reported for the period earned (Table 8.1, line 63). It must be noted that these figures reflect net cash flow. Depreciation is not reflected in this net income figure. For RICO purposes, the net income that is shown on a tax return or financial statement for rental property should be adjusted by adding back any amortized and depreciation expenses. The prosecutor may want the forensic accountant to present all of the income and expenses on the net worth schedule instead of net figures.

8.4.49 Gain—ABC Stock

Gains on the sale of capital assets, such as stock, bonds, commodities, and other properties, are reported on the RICO net worth schedule (Table 8.1, line 64). Gains are computed by subtracting the original costs from the gross proceeds received. This is an identified source of receipts.

8.4.50 Sales—XYZ Stock

The proceeds from the sale of capital assets, such as stocks, bonds, commodities, and other properties, are also reported on the RICO net worth schedule (Table 8.1, line 68), provided they are not reinvested into other assets. If they are reinvested into other assets, then the other assets will be reflected on the asset section of the net worth schedule. If they are not reinvested, then this is a source of funds that must be recognized in the source of funds section in the net worth schedule.

8.4.51 Tax Refunds

This is a source of funds for the period that must be recognized (Table 8.1, line 67). Many people file tax returns where income tax was withheld in the prior period but a refund is due because of overpayment of the tax liability. When the subject files a tax return, it is in essence a claim for the excess payment.

8.4.52 Interest

Earnings from savings is income for the period earned and becomes available (Table 8.1, lines 65 and 66). When interest is credited to the savings account, it is recognized in the source of funds section of the net worth schedule. Interest may be actually earned in a prior period, but if it is not credited to the account, then it is not recognized.

8.4.53 Business Income

Gross receipts from a sole proprietorship are income to the individual owner (Table 8.1, line 69). Gross receipts are income to the proprietor whether or not all of it is collected when the proprietor is using the accrual method of recognizing income. This is the case here. When accruing sales income, there is a related account called "Accounts Receivable." The accounts receivable is actually gross receipts that have not been collected. If any part of the accounts receivable are determined to be uncollectible, then they should be reduced to the collectible amount and a business expense created that is called "bad debts," which is the amount of uncollectible accounts receivable.

8.4.54   Illegal Income

After adding the net worth increases, personal and business expenses, and subtracting legal or identified income, illegal income or unidentified income is derived. In presenting this case to the jury, the words "unidentified income" should be used instead of "illegal income" because the Defense will object and be sustained on the grounds of leading the jury or invoking a verdict.

8.4.55   Offshore Evidence

The scenario problem shows many offshore transactions. You will note that these transactions are not used except for one exception. Many countries have bank secrecy laws that provide heavy criminal and civil penalties for any violations. However, certain types of records can be used if they are provided to the general public. In this case, the real property acquired in the Bahamas by John Doe is public record in the Bahamas. The U.S. Embassy or Consulate in the Bahamas can obtain certified copies of documents and present them in court. Many countries have various treaties with the United States. Tax treaties are not in existence with "tax haven" countries. However, there are many treaties with countries, including tax haven countries, that will provide information and assistance in criminal cases other than tax cases. For instance, Switzerland will provide financial information in a criminal case, for example, drug trafficking, but will not provide financial information in a criminal tax case. Swiss authorities, like many other tax haven countries, will require that the United States not use financial information for criminal tax cases even if obtained for other criminal charges. Introducing bank records or other nonpublic records from a foreign country has other problems. The principal problem is obtaining a witness from a foreign country to introduce records into court. Foreign nationals do not like to come to the United States and testify in a criminal case. Second, the government (federal or state) must bear the expense of bringing these foreign nationals to the United States. In some instances, foreign nationals want fees and expenses.

8.5   Offshore Records

In this scenario, it will be assumed that witnesses will be obtained to introduce evidence into court. John Doe, as well as Suzy Que, has financial transactions offshore in various countries. If offshore evidence is obtained and properly introduced into court, then the net worth schedule will be modified as shown in Table 8.2.

8.5.1   Transshipment, Ltd.

Transshipment, Ltd. is a Bahamian Corporation. It is registered in the Bahamas. It does no business in the United States. However, it has opened up bank accounts in Spain and Switzerland, as well as in the Bahamas. One can see that this is an entity that is used for laundering illegal income because it does not have the normal business expenses. First, it receives funds in cash that are used to pay for drug shipments. These funds are obviously smuggled out because there is no CMIR report (i.e., Report of International Transportation of Currency or Monetary Instruments). Calderone is a supplier of drugs. For trial purposes,

Table 8.2   RICO Net Worth Schedule Adjustment for Offshore Activities

Description	19X1 ($)	19X2 ($)	19X3 ($)
Illegal/unidentified income	7,869,600	1,579,850	1,226,900
Assets			
70. Transshipment, Ltd.			
71. Bahamian bank account		4,390,000	500,000
72. Spanish bank account			1,090,000
73. Swiss bank account			2,090,000
74. Barbados bank account			2,189,000
75. Cayman bank account			2,580,000
76. Jamaica bank account			786,000
77. Doe Holding NV			2,565,000
Total additional assets	—	4,390,000	11,800,000
Net worth increase	—	4,390,000	7,410,000
Expenses			
78. Barbados bank charges	—	—	10,000
79. Cayman bank charges			60,000
80. Jamaica bank charges			1,000
81. Jamaica travel expenses			120,500
82. Wires to Calderone		3,500,000	6,000,000
83. Spanish bank charges			10,000
84. Aruba bank charges			10,000
85. Bahamas bank charges			20,000
86. Schmidt Mgt. Co.			45,000
Total offshore expenses	—	3,500,000	6,276,500
Identified Income			
87. Interest Income—Cayman			640,000
88. Interest Income—Spain			100,000
89. Interest Income—Swiss			100,000
90. Interest Income—Aruba			150,000
91. Interest Income—Jamaica			7,500
Total identified income	—	—	997,500
Illegal/unidentified income	7,869,600	9,469,850	13,915,900

witnesses will have to be introduced who will confirm this fact. Witnesses are hard to come by because they are often found deceased. The profits are transferred to other countries, for example, Cayman Islands, Barbados, Aruba, Panama, Jamaica, and Switzerland. Transshipment, Ltd. has no financial statements or tax returns prepared. Therefore the only financial information about this corporation is the bank balances in the various bank accounts (Table 8.2, lines 70–73, 82, 83, 85, 88, and 89).

8.5.2   Barbados Bank Account

John Doe opened up a bank account in Barbados. He has put Suzy Que on the account by having her be a signatory on the account (Table 8.2, lines 74 and 78). This is a personal bank account that can be used on the net worth schedule. However, a witness from Barbados will have to testify in court that John Doe opened and maintained the account. It is easy to see that this bank account is used for money laundering. The only expenses in this account are bank charges. The only income is interest income.

8.5.3 Cayman Island Bank Account

John Doe opened a bank account in the Cayman Islands (Table 8.2, lines 75, 79, and 87). These funds came from the Bahamian bank account by wire transfer. In reality, this is an investment account because it is an interest-bearing account and no funds have been withdrawn except for service charges by the bank.

8.5.4 Jamaican Bank Account

John Doe opened a bank account in Jamaica. John Doe has used this account to pay for expenses (Table 8.2, line 76, 80, 81, and 91). It does not earn any interest, but, in fact, has paid for expenses while John Doe was in Jamaica. The vendors for those expenses would have to testify before they could be used on the net worth schedule.

8.5.5 Doe Holding NV

Aruba is part of the Netherlands Antilles. It comes under Dutch control. John Doe formed this corporation along with his girlfriend, Suzy Que. Doe Holding NV is basically an entity that is used to conceal his illicit income. The only expenses are bank charges and fees for maintaining this corporation. The only asset of this corporation is the bank account (Table 8.2, line 77, 84, 86, and 90).

Tax Net Worth Solution

9

9.1 General

The following solution and explanations relate to the scenario problem as presented in chapter 7. The solution and explanations are based on tax net worth principals.

9.2 Principals

The tax net worth is based on the federal income tax laws and regulations. The Federal Tax Code defines a few concepts. One concept is gross income. Gross income means income from whatever source unless specifically exempt. Adjusted gross income is another concept. It means gross income less specified deductions. Some of these deductions are individual retirement account contributions, Keogh plan contributions, alimony payments, and capital losses. Taxable income is another concept; it involves subtracting exemptions, itemized deductions, or standard deduction from adjusted gross income. The tax net worth schedule is based on these concepts. The first objective in a tax net worth is to establish corrected adjusted gross income, if the person filed an individual federal income tax return. After corrected adjusted gross income is determined, the corrected taxable income must be determined. Some itemized deductions have limitations based on adjusted gross income. Medical expense is one example of a deduction that has limitations on amount deductible based on adjusted gross income.

9.3 Problem

The following net worth schedule shows how each item in the scenario problem is presented. An explanation of why it is presented in the manner shown is explained after the net worth schedule. The explanation section will refer to the line item on the net worth schedule.

9.4 Tax Net Worth Schedule

The next several pages present a tax net worth schedule. The first section is assets. Assets are items that have future value and can be levied against if additional tax is due. The next section is liabilities. These are the claims by creditors against the assets. They have priority if secured. The liabilities are subtracted from the assets to derive the net worth. This is compared from one period to the next to derive increases. The next section is personal living expenses. This reflects the taxpayer's cost of living. The next section is nontaxable income.

This is income derived from sources that are not taxed. When the net worth increase is added to personal living expenses less nontaxable income, the adjusted gross income is derived. To arrive at taxable income, exemption(s) and itemized deductions or standard deduction is subtracted from adjusted gross income. This corrected taxable income is compared to reported taxable income for the net increase, if taxpayer filed a return.

9.4.1   Cash on Hand

Cash on hand is based on the currency found at John Doe's residence during the execution of a search warrant (Table 9.1, line 1). There are many tax cases that say that there must be cash-on-hand figures. Cash on hand must be established precisely whenever as possible. There are various methods to determine cash on hand. One method is to check on bank deposits shortly after year-end. Any cash deposits can be shown as cash on hand at year-end. Another method is to show the difference between cash deposits and checks to cash during the year. Yet another method is to use the cash-on-hand figures used on personal financial statements to creditors. If there is no cash on hand at year-end, then the investigator must present some evidence that the taxpayer has no possible cash on hand.

9.4.2   Cocaine, 2 Kilos

The market value of cocaine is used (Table 9.1, line 2) because no receipts will be available. There were no facilities discovered to indicate that the cocaine was manufactured there. This means that the taxpayer had to purchase the cocaine for resale. The Drug Enforcement Administration, as well as some local enforcement agencies, keeps records of the market values of drugs on a weekly, monthly, and yearly basis by type of drug over long periods of time. At trial, an expert who keeps statistics on drug market values will have to testify on this issue.

9.4.3   First National Bank Accounts

The bank balances are used in this case (Table 9.1, lines 3 and 4). This requires no need for a bank reconciliation schedule. Because there are two bank accounts, a year-end confirmation should be made to see if funds from one account are transferred to the other account, which will overlap years. This is not the case here.

9.4.4   Business Cash in Bank

This bank account is based on book balances (Table 9.1, line 5). The sole proprietorship is kept on the accrual method of accounting. When books are kept on the accrual method of accounting, the book balances are used. There are various reasons. First, there are books and records kept on each transaction, showing their appropriate time of occurrence. Second, timing differences are eliminated. If a loan is made to the bank, then the book balance of the loan will be recognized instead of the bank balance, which would be higher because they received the payment in the subsequent year. Book balances will reflect proper account balances throughout the business accounts. Third, bank reconciliations will normally be available to prove out the book balances of accounts. This not only applies to the bank account but also related accounts, for example, accounts receivable, accounts payable, loans, and capital accounts.

Table 9.1 John Doe's Tax Net Worth Schedule (Title 26)

Description	19X0 ($)	19X1 ($)	19X2 ($)	19X3 ($)
		Assets		
1. Cash on hand	—	—	—	50,000
2. Cocaine, 2 kilos				50,000
3. First National Bank (FNB) checking		10,000	50,000	100,000
4. FNB savings		110,000	550,000	650,000
5. Business checking			20,000	10,000
6. Accounts receivable			10,000	20,000
7. Inventory			140,000	50,000
8. Business assets			150,000	150,000
9. Security system				50,000
10. Electronic equipment			100,000	100,000
11. Appliances			20,000	20,000
12. Fixtures		10,000	10,000	10,000
13. Furniture		50,000	50,000	50,000
14. Cabinets		20,000	20,000	20,000
15. Paintings		20,000	20,000	20,000
16. Pool and tennis court		100,000	100,000	100,000
17. 100 Alpha Street		300,000	300,000	300,000
18. 100 Bravo Street		4,000,000	4,000,000	4,000,000
19. Gold bullion		100,000	100,000	100,000
20. Lounge Doe, Inc.		2,440,000	2,440,000	2,440,000
21. Doe's Kwik Stop, Inc.		481,100	326,000	501,000
22. Real Property, Ltd.		1,930,000	1,877,500	1,890,000
23. Mercedes Benz		80,000	80,000	80,000
24. Toyota sedan			18,000	18,000
25. IRA—Doe			2,200	4,600
26. IRA—Que			2,200	4,600
27. Bahamas residence			110,000	110,000
28. Prepaid interest		8,500	8,260	5,780
Total assets	—	9,659,600	10,504,160	10,903,980
		Liabilities		
29. FNB—Mercedes loan	—	51,000	39,0000	27,000
30. FNB—Toyota loan			8,800	6,400
31. Credit card			30,000	50,000
32. Accounts payable				50,000
33. Accumulated depreciation		100,000	330,000	560,000
34. Florida Mortgage Co.		1,930,000	1,810,000	1,690,000
35. Business bank loan			100,000	80,000
Total liabilities	—	2,081,000	2,317,800	2,463,400
Net worth	—	7,578,600	8,136,360	8,440,580
Net worth increase		7,578,600	607,760	254,220
		Personal Living Expenses		
36. Florida Mortgage interest		200,000	188,000	176,000
37. Utilities		10,000	10,000	20,000

(continued)

Table 9.1   John Doe's Tax Net Worth Schedule (Title 26) (Continued)

Description	19X0 ($)	19X1 ($)	19X2 ($)	19X3 ($)
38. Telephone		30,000	40,000	45,000
39. Insurance		5,000	10,000	10,000
40. Life insurance		10,000		
41. Interest—Mercedes loan		1,500	2,000	2,000
42. Interest—Toyota loan			240	480
43. Income tax withheld		95,000		150,000
44. Property taxes		5,000		5,000
45. Credit cards		30,000	100,000	180,000
46. Church donations			10,000	50,000
47. Trust funds				400,000
Total personal expenses		386,500	360,240	1,038,480
Nontaxable Income				
48. IRA interest—Doe			2,200	2,400
49. IRA interest—Que			2,200	2,400
50. Tax refunds		500	79,250	
Total nontaxable income		500	83,650	4,800
Adjusted gross income		7,964,600	884,350	1,287,900
Itemized deductions		206,500	200,240	233,480
Exemptions		2,000	2,000	2,000
Corrected taxable income		7,756,100	682,110	1,052,420
Reported taxable income		63,000	0	285,400
Increase		7,693,100	682,110	767,020

9.4.5   Accounts Receivable

Even though this is a business asset, it is an asset of the individual because assets of a sole proprietorship are individually owned (Table 9.1, line 6). Accounts receivable is amounts owed to the individual by customers of the sole proprietorship. This is an intangible asset of the individual, in this case, John Doe.

9.4.6   Inventory

This is an asset of the individual owner of the sole proprietorship (Table 9.1, line 7). This is an asset that is hard to prove out, especially if the business has many product lines. If the business takes inventory at year-end, then this inventory quantity and value should be used, especially if done by independent parties. If inventory is not taken, then the inventory value should be estimated as closely as possible to its costs. One method of doing this is the gross profit method, which uses a fairly constant cost of sales percentage based on either the business markups or industry average that will force out inventory values at year-end.

9.4.7   Business Assets

Business assets of a sole proprietorship are assets of the individual who owns the business (Table 9.1, line 8). These assets should be recorded at cost, especially when they are recorded on the books and records at cost, which is normal for keeping business books and records. This will have a contra asset account called "accumulated depreciation." This account will be addressed in a later paragraph.

9.4.8 Security System

The purchase of this asset is recorded at the purchase price (Table 9.1, line 9).

9.4.9 Electronic Equipment

This asset is recorded at cost (Table 9.1, line 10).

9.4.10 Appliances

This asset is recorded at cost (Table 9.1, line 11).

9.4.11 Fixtures

This asset is recorded at cost (Table 9.1, line 12).

9.4.12 Furniture

This asset is recorded at cost (Table 9.1, line 13).

9.4.13 Cabinets

This asset is recorded at cost (Table 9.1, line 14).

9.4.14 Paintings

This asset is recorded at cost (Table 9.1, line 15).

9.4.15 Pool and Tennis Court

This asset is recorded at cost (Table 9.1, line 16). If the taxpayer is making periodic payments for the construction of this asset, then a payment schedule will have to be obtained from the contractor to show the total costs. Remember that only the cost incurred during the period should be reflected on the schedule. Subsequent period costs will be added on as they are incurred.

9.4.16 100 Alpha Street

The purchase of the house is recorded at cost (Table 9.1, line 17). In this case, public records are used to determine the cost. However, the closing agent can be contacted for the closing statement, which can also be used. Remember that the Best Evidence Rule should be used when possible.

9.4.17   100 Bravo Street

The purchase of this apartment building is recorded at cost (Table 9.1, line 18). Public records are used to determine cost. The closing statement, which will show the cost including any closing costs, can be obtained from the closing agent.

9.4.18   Gold Bullion Bars

The 10 gold bars are recorded at cost (Table 9.1, line 19). The market value is given at the time of seizure. If the cost was not known, then the market value would be used. The market value is higher than the original cost in this case. If the market value and year discovered are used, then the defense would have the burden of proof to show otherwise. If the defense does present such evidence, then their costs and purchase date should be used.

9.4.19   Prepaid Interest

Installment loans have the characteristic of computing interest for the life of the loan and adding it to the principal balance. For tax purposes, the interest can only be recognized over the period of the loan (Table 9.1, line 28). This will result in a deferred expense account called "prepaid interest." It is shown in the asset section of the net worth schedule. Each subsequent year, a pro rata portion is written off to the personal expenditure section. In addition, it is shown again as an itemized deduction, if deductible.

9.4.20   Lounge Doe, Inc.

The net investment in this corporation is to be used (Table 9.1, line 20). This is normally a positive balance, but there are occasions when the net cash investment can be negative. This can happen when the shareholder withdraws more than his/her investment. Corporate assets belong to the corporation and not the shareholder. This corporation has a boat that is not used in the ordinary course of business. The boat might be used in illegal activities. However, the boat cannot be depreciated on the corporate books for tax purposes.

9.4.21   Doe's Kwik Stop, Inc.

This is a Sub S Corporation (Table 9.1, line 21). The net worth schedules not only use the shareholder's net cash investment but also must take into consideration any earnings or losses the corporation has during the period. The Sub S Corporation is not a taxable entity. Instead, the earnings and losses are passed on to the individual shareholders on a pro rata basis. The total net cash investment, earnings, and losses are shown on the net worth schedule but never below zero.

9.4.22   Real Property, Ltd.

This is a partnership in which the taxpayer has half interests (Table 9.1, line 22). Like the Sub S Corporation, partnerships are nontaxable entities. Any earnings or losses are passed through to the partner based on the partner's interest. The total net cash investment, earnings, and losses are shown on the net worth schedule. This can be negative only to the extent that the partner is at risk for his share of the liabilities.

9.4.23 Mercedes Benz

This automobile is recorded at cost (Table 9.1, line 23). One problem that can arise with vehicles is accounting for trade-ins. The car dealer will allow a trade-in allowance for an old car against the purchase of a new car. This trade-in allowance is used to reduce the purchase price. For tax purposes, the trade-in allowance is used to determine the gain or loss of the old car by subtracting the net basis (cost less any accumulated depreciation) from the trade-in allowance. The gain or loss on the old car will be subtracted (gains) or added (losses) to the cost of the new car. This is referred to as like kind exchanges.

9.4.24 Toyota Sedan

This automobile is also recorded at cost (Table 9.1, line 24). Even though Suzy Que is driving the car, it is still charged to Doe because he paid for it. Even if the car is registered in Suzy Que's name, if John Doe purchased it, then he should be charged for it. Another method of presenting the car purchase is a gift in the personal expenditure section of the net worth schedule instead of as an asset of John Doe.

9.4.25 IRA—John Doe and Suzy Que

Individual retirement accounts and Keogh plans should be shown as an asset (Table 9.1, lines 25 and 26). The earnings from IRA's and Keogh plans are nontaxable. One method of presentation is to show as an asset the total contributions and earnings. The earnings for the period will be reflected in the nontaxable source of income. The other method of presentation is to show as an asset the total accumulated contributions and to ignore the accumulated earnings. Either method is acceptable; however, the former is preferred because it shows the actual fund(s) in the account.

9.4.26 Bahamas Residence

The cost of foreign real estate should be shown at cost (Table 9.1, line 27). If the property is acquired in other than U.S. currency, then a conversion will have to be made to U.S. dollars. Any loss or gain on the conversion will also have to be recognized. Because this would be an adjustment to gross income, it would not be recognized on the tax net worth schedule.

9.4.27 First National Bank Auto Loans

There are two bank installment loans (Table 9.1, lines 29 and 30). Installment loans are presented as a liability. Period balances are shown at the end of each period. When these liabilities are incurred, they include both the principal and interest.

9.4.28   Credit Cards

Balances owed on credit cards can be shown as a liability at period end (Table 9.1, line 31). The charges are shown as a personal expenditure for the period. Another way of presenting credit cards is to only show the amount paid to the credit card company as a personal expenditure. Either method can be used, but they must be used consistently.

9.4.29   Accounts Payable

Accounts payables are liabilities of the sole proprietor (Table 9.1, line 32). Liabilities of a sole proprietor are liabilities of the individual because the individual is personally liable.

9.4.30   Florida Mortgage Co.

Mortgage balances are shown at period end (Table 9.1, line 34). The mortgage payments include principal and interest. In many cases, mortgage payments also include escrow payments to cover property taxes and insurance. If this is the case, a corresponding asset for escrow balances will have to be reflected on the net worth schedule.

9.4.31   Accumulated Depreciation

Accumulated depreciation balances have to be shown on the net worth schedule (Table 9.1, line 33). This is a liability on the grounds that this is a potential liability. The federal tax laws and regulations require the recovery of accumulated depreciation as ordinary taxable income to the extent of any gain recognized on the sale of the depreciable asset.

9.4.32   Business Bank Loan

Loans from financial institutions by a sole proprietor are individual loans (Table 9.1, line 35). The individual is personally liable for the business bank loan; therefore, it is a personal liability.

9.4.33   Florida Mortgage Co.

This is the interest portion of the mortgage payments (Table 9.1, line 36). This is shown as both a personal expenditure and an itemized deduction.

9.4.34   Utilities

This is a period expense that must be recognized during the period paid as a personal expenditure (Table 9.1, line 37).

9.4.35   Telephone

This is a period expense that must be recognized during the period paid as a personal expenditure (Table 9.1, line 38).

9.4.36 Insurance

This is a period expense that must be recognized during the period paid (Table 9.1, line 39). It also must be kept in mind that medical insurance premiums can also be deducted as an itemized deduction.

9.4.37 Life Insurance

Life insurance is normally a period expense (Table 9.1, line 40). However, in the case of whole-life policies that have surrender or cash values, life insurance policies should reflect the cash value as an asset and the noncash value as an expense. This solution has treated the whole-life policy as an expense.

9.4.38 Interest Amortized

This is the pro rata portion of the prepaid interest (Table 9.1, lines 41 and 42). This is shown as a current period expense. In addition, it can be used as an itemized deduction.

9.4.39 Income Tax Withheld

This is a period expense (Table 9.1, line 43). Even though this is a personal expenditure, there will not be any payments found for this expense in the taxpayer's possession. The employer pays this expense out of the taxpayer's gross wages and salaries. In addition to the income tax withholding, Federal Insurance Contributions Act (FICA) tax (Social Security contributions) is also withheld and should be reflected as a personal expense. The FICA tax was not presented in this problem.

9.4.40 Property Tax

This is a period expense (Table 9.1, line 44). Property taxes must be recognized only in the period when paid. Sometimes, taxpayers will pay their property taxes for 2 years in 1 year.

9.4.41 Credit Card Charges

This is a period expense (Table 9.1, line 45). This presentation shows the total charges made during the period. It does not show the payments to the credit card company. For trial purposes, the vendors who accepted the credit card charges will have to introduce these into court. The alternative method is to introduce the credit card record custodian as to the payments received from the taxpayer. A problem can arise if any of the charges made were for business expenses. If any charges were made for business expense, then they will have to be subtracted from the total charges or the total of the payments.

9.4.42 Church Donations

This is a period expense (Table 9.1, line 46). In addition to be shown on the personal expenditure section, it is also used as an itemized deduction.

9.4.43 Trust Funds

This is a period expense (Table 9.1, line 47). The key question in this situation is whether the trust is a viable instrument. Sometimes, trusts are set up to cover a taxpayer's own funds. If this is the case, then the trust fund should be shown as the taxpayer's asset.

9.4.44 Loss—XYZ Stock

This is a period expense. For tax purposes, losses on stock are not recognized because this is a capital asset. Losses on sale of capital assets are not recognized on the net worth computation. The main reason is that this is an adjustment to derive adjusted gross income. The purpose of the tax net worth schedule is to derive adjusted gross income, and not gross income. Therefore, it is not shown on the tax net worth schedule.

9.4.45 IRA Interest

The interest earned on individual retirement accounts and Keogh plans is not taxable (Table 9.1, line 48 and 49). As explained previously, if these accounts are shown in the asset section with both earnings and contributions, then the interest earned for the period will have to be shown as a nontaxable source of income.

9.4.46 Tax Refunds

Tax refunds are nontaxable sources (Table 9.1, line 50). This net worth schedule reflects the total taxes paid as a personal expenditure and refunds as a source of nontaxable income. However, it can be shown as net. It is better to show it separately in order to disclose both.

9.4.47 Itemized Deductions

Itemized deductions or the standard deduction are allowed to reduce adjusted gross income to derive at taxable income. The federal income tax code allows certain expenses to be deducted. The primary ones are medical expenses, interest expenses, charity contributions, certain taxes, and some other miscellaneous expenses. In this solution, itemized deductions are the total personal expenditures for interest (mortgage and amortized interest), church donations, and property taxes. Limitations on these deductions that are built in the Tax Code have been ignored in this problem. The itemized deductions are delineated in the following:

Description	19X1 ($)	19X2 ($)	19X3 ($)
Florida Mortgage interest	200,000	188,000	176,000
Interest—Mercedes	1,500	2,000	2,000
Interest—Toyota		240	480
Property taxes	5,000		5,000
Church donations		10,000	50,000
Total	206,500	100,240	233,480

9.4.48 Exemptions

Exemptions are an income tax concept. The amount of these exemptions varies from year to year. For the sake of simplicity, $2000 per exemption is used in this case.

9.5 Offshore Evidence

The scenario problem has many offshore assets and transactions. These assets and transactions cannot be used on the net worth schedule unless witnesses are available to introduce them into court. There are exceptions. One exception is the introduction of public records from a particular country. In this case, the Bahamas real property is public record and can be introduced into court. The U.S. Embassy or Consulate in the Bahamas can obtain certified copies of documents and present them into court records. Bank records cannot be introduced into court because many countries have bank secrecy laws, which provide heavy criminal and civil penalties for any violations. Also, many "tax haven" countries will not allow bank records for criminal or civil tax trials in the United States. Another problem of introducing nonpublic records is obtaining a witness from a foreign country. Foreign nationals do not like to come to the United States and testify in a criminal case. The government (federal and state) must bear the expense of bringing these foreign nationals to the United States.

9.6 Offshore Records

Now, it will be assumed that witnesses will be obtained to introduce evidence into court. John Doe and Suzy Que have assets and financial transactions in various countries. If the offshore evidence is properly obtained and introduced into court, then the net worth schedule will be modified as follows:

9.6.1 Bank Accounts

This is an asset of John Doe (Table 9.2, lines 54 through 56). Bank balances are used instead of book balances. These accounts are in three different countries, two of which are tax haven countries. In tax cases, tax haven officials, whether bank or government, will not cooperate in tax matters. However, these records can be used if found during a search. The Jamaican bank account was used to pay expenses while in that country. The other two accounts were used only to park illegal gains. In all probability, the government will not be able to seize these funds. The corporate bank accounts are also assets of John Doe.

9.6.2 Bank Charges

This is a period expense (Table 9.2, lines 58 through 60). Record custodians will have to introduce these records into trial court unless the defense will stipulate. This can be a problem if the foreign witnesses refuse to come. Another problem area is the conversion of foreign currency into U.S. currency. Bank charges on corporate accounts are not shown because this would be a corporate expense. However, they could be shown in this case

Table 9.2 John Doe's Tax Net Worth Adjustments for Offshore Activities (Title 26)

Description	19X1 ($)	19X2 ($)	19X3 ($)
	Assets		
Transshipment, Ltd.:			
51. Bahamian bank account	—	4,390,000	500,000
52. Spanish bank account			1,090,000
53. Swiss bank account			2,090,000
Personal Accounts:			
54. Barbados bank account			2,189,000
55. Cayman Island bank account			2,580,000
56. Jamaica bank account			786,000
57. Doe Holding NV bank account			2,565,000
Total additional assets	—	4,390,000	11,800,000
Net worth increase	—	4,390,000	7,410,000
	Expenses		
58. Barbados bank charges			10,000
59. Cayman bank charges			60,000
60. Jamaica bank charges			1,000
61. Jamaica travel expenses			120,500
Total expenses	—	—	191,500
Previous corrected income	7,756,100	682,110	1,052,420
Corrected taxable income	7,756,100	5,072,110	8,653,920
Reported taxable income	63,000	—	285,400
Increase	7,693,100	5,072,110	8,368,520

based on the fact that these corporations were only "shells." Assets of shell corporations are, in reality, assets of the individual that are being concealed by corporate identity.

9.6.3 Travel—Jamaica

This is a period expense (Table 9.2, line 61). This could be classified as either a vacation trip or a business trip. A vacation trip is a personal expense and should be reflected on the net worth schedule. If this is a business trip, then this is not reflected on the net worth schedule if it is part of a sole proprietorship. As an employee or officer of a corporation, it can be classified as a personal expense but later on can be deducted as an itemized deduction with limitations. However, if the business trip is to facilitate drug trafficking activities, then this is not an allowable business expense per the Federal Income Tax Code. Thus, it then becomes a personal expense.

9.6.4 Transshipment, Ltd. Bank Accounts

Transshipment, Ltd. is a Bahamian corporation. Because corporate books and records were not kept, the bank accounts are assets of the corporation, as well as the capital, which is the shareholder's equity. The corporation does not do any business; therefore, it is a shell corporation. Transshipment, Ltd. has bank accounts in three foreign countries (Table 9.2, lines 51–53).

9.6.5   Doe Holding NV

Aruba is part of the Netherlands Antilles, which is under Dutch control. Doe Holding NV is a Netherlands Antilles corporation that was formed by John Doe and Suzy Que. The only asset of this corporation is the bank account (Table 9.2, line 57). The corporation has no business activities. The funds are capital contributions by John Doe. This is a shell corporation.

RICO Expenditure Solution 10

10.1 General

The following solution and explanations that relate to the scenario problem as presented in a previous chapter. The solution and explanations are based on the Racketeer Influenced and Corrupt Organizations (RICO) expenditure principles.

10.2 Principles

The RICO expenditure method is based on the fund principle. Funds involve the use of cash either directly or indirectly. There are no amortization, depreciation, or depletion allowances on a RICO expenditure schedule. Unlike the RICO net worth method, the RICO expenditure method, by its nature, shows the use of funds more directly than indirectly. It is also easier to explain to a jury of laymen. One disadvantage of the expenditure method is that it does not list the accumulated assets and liabilities. Assets are only reflected when they are purchased. Liabilities are only shown when they are acquired. It also only shows the amount of payment on liabilities and not the balances.

10.3 Problem

The following expenditure schedule shows how each item in the scenario problem is presented. Following the expenditure schedule is an explanation of why the item is presented in this manner. The explanation section will refer to the line item on the expenditure schedule.

10.4 RICO Expenditure Schedule

Table 10.1 presents a RICO expenditure schedule. The first section deals with the expenditure side. The second section deals with the identified or legal source of income. The difference between the total expenditures and the total sources of identified receipts gives the amount of income derived from unidentified sources. Whether the expenditure method or the net worth method is used, the bottom line should be the same. An expenditure schedule can be converted to a net worth schedule and vice versa.

10.4.1 Cash on Hand

Cash on hand is based on the currency found at John Doe's residence during the execution of the search warrant (Table 10.1, line 1). Cash on hand should be established as much as possible for each period, and it should show the addition to or decrease of funds for the period, and not the ending balance.

10.4.2 Cocaine

The market value of cocaine is used in this solution (Table 10.1, line 2). This is a situation where market values are used. The primary reason is that receipts will not be available. It is well known that the subject purchased the cocaine. There were no facilities discovered that

Table 10.1   John Doe's RICO Net Worth Schedule (Title 18)

Description	19X1 ($)	19X2 ($)	19X3 ($)
	Assets		
1. Cash on hand	—	—	50,000
2. Cocaine, 2 kilos			50,000
3. Gold bullion, 10 bars	100,000		
4. First National Bank (FNB) checking	10,000	40,000	50,000
5. FNB savings	110,000	440,000	100,000
6. Business cash in bank		20,000	(10,000)
7. Accounts receivable		10,000	10,000
8. Inventory		140,000	(90,000)
9. Business assets		150,000	
10. 100 Alpha Street	300,000		
11. 100 Bravo Street	4,000,000		
12. Furniture	50,000		
13. Cabinets	20,000		
14. Paintings	20,000		
15. Fixtures	10,000		
16. Pool and tennis court	100,000		
17. Appliances		20,000	
18. Electronic equipment		100,000	
19. Security system			50,000
20. Lounge Doe, Inc.	2,440,000		
21. Doe's Kwik Stop, Inc.	506,100	(105,100)	
22. Real Property, Ltd.	2,030,000		42,500
23. Mercedes Benz	80,000		
24. Toyota sedan		18,000	
25. IRA—John Doe		2,200	2,400
26. IRA—Suzy Que		2,200	2,400
27. Residence—Bahamas		110,000	
Total asset purchases	9,776,100	947,300	257,300
	Liabilities		
28. Florida Mortgage Company	70,000	120,000	120,000
29. FNB—Mercedes loan	9000	12,000	12,000
30. FNB—Toyota loan		1,200	2,400
31. Business bank loan			20,000
Total liabilities	79,000	133,200	154,100

(*continued*)

Table 10.1   John Doe's RICO Net Worth Schedule (Title 18) (Continued)

Description	19X1 ($)	19X2 ($)	19X3 ($)
	Business Expenses - Inventory		
32. Inventory purchases		180,000	130,000
33. Inventory changes		(140,000)	90,000
Total business expenses - inventory	—	40,000	220,000
	Business Expenses - Overhead		
34. Advertising		80,000	40,000
35. Interest on bank loan		10,000	8,000
36. Insurance		50,000	50,000
37. Professional fees		25,000	25,000
38. Office expenses		30,000	10,000
39. Rent expense		50,000	50,000
40. Repairs		20,000	10,000
41. Supplies		30,000	10,000
42. Taxes		50,000	40,000
43. Utilities		40,000	40,000
44. Wages/salaries		120,000	150,000
45. Miscellaneous		15,000	7,000
Total business expenses - overhead	—	520,000	440,000
	Personal Expenses		
46. Florida Mortgage interest	200,000	188,000	176,000
47. Life insurance	10,000		
48. Income tax withheld	95,000		150,000
49. Property taxes	5,000		5,000
50. Credit card charges	30,000	70,000	160,000
51. Utilities	10,000	10,000	20,000
52. Telephone	30,000	40,000	45,000
53. Insurance	5,000	10,000	10,000
54. Church donations		10,000	50,000
55. Interest on loan—Mercedes	10,000		
56. Interest on loan—Toyota		2,000	
57. Trust funds			400,000
58. Loss—XYZ stock		3,000	
Total personal expenses	395,000	333,0000	1,016,000
	Identified Receipts		
59. Florida Mortgage interest	2,000,000		
60. Auto loans	60,000	10,000	
61. Accounts payable			50,000
62. Income tax refunds	500	79,250	
63. IRA interest—John Doe		200	400
64. IRA interest—Suzy Que		200	400
65. Dividends	100,000		
66. Wages/salaries	190,000		200,000
67. Rental income	30,000	113,000	170,000

(*continued*)

Table 10.1   John Doe's RICO Net Worth Schedule (Title 18) (Continued)

Description	19X1 ($)	19X2 ($)	19X3 ($)
68. Gain—ABC stock		2,000	
69. Sales—XYZ stock		9,000	
70. Business income		80,000	440,000
71. Business bank loan		100,000	
Total receipts	2,380,500	393,650	860,800
Illegal/unidentified income	7,869,600	1,579,850	1,226,900

show the cocaine was manufactured there. This implies or suggests that the subject purchased the cocaine. The Drug Enforcement Agency and other local law enforcement agencies keep statistics on the market values of drugs, both retail and wholesale, on a regularly periodic basis.

10.4.3   Gold Bullion

The 10 gold bars are recorded at cost (Table 10.1, line 3). The market value at the time of the search warrant is higher than the original cost. If the cost and date of purchase is not known, then the market value and time of discovery can be used. If market value is used, then the burden of proof is placed on the defense to establish cost and date of purchase.

10.4.4   Cash in Banks

Increases or decreases in bank balances are reflected in this schedule (Table 10.1, lines 4, 5, and 6). The increase or decrease in bank balances can be based on either the book changes or the bank changes. Whatever method is used, it must be used consistently for each bank account. It is suggested that a better way of presenting the changes in bank balances is to show the ending balance on the expenditure schedule and subtract the beginning balance. It shows the jury where and how the figures were obtained. Also, it helps confirm the change computations. In this case, the personal bank accounts use the bank balances while the business account is based on book balances. The business bank account is kept and reconciled on a monthly basis and is used as a basis for keeping the cash receipts and disbursement journals. Also, the sole proprietorship uses the accrual method of accounting, while the personal expenses and receipts are based on the cash method of accounting.

10.4.5   Accounts Receivable

Accounts receivable from a sole proprietorship is a personal asset of the individual owner (Table 10.1, line 7). The expenditure method requires only changes be reflected on the expenditure schedule. A suggested way of presenting the changes in accounts receivable balances is to show the ending balance on the expenditure schedule and subtract the beginning balance. It shows the jury from where and how the figures were obtained by relating them to the financial statements or tax returns that are introduced into evidence.

10.4.6 Inventory

Inventory from a sole proprietorship is a personal asset of the individual owner (Table 10.1, line 8). The expenditure method requires only changes be reflected on the expenditure schedule. This also can be presented by showing the ending balances less the beginning balances so the jury can find where the figures were derived.

10.4.7 Business Assets

The purchase of assets for use in the business of a sole proprietorship is assets of the individual owner (Table 10.1, line 9). Business assets are recorded at cost for the period purchased.

10.4.8 100 Alpha Street

The purchase of the house is recorded at cost (Table 10.1, line 10). In this case, public records are used to determine the cost. However, the closing statement from the closing agent, which would also show additional closing costs, can be used. The Best Evidence Rule requires the original document(s) to be produced instead of copies.

10.4.9 100 Bravo Street

The purchase of the apartment building is recorded at cost (Table 10.1, line 11). Public records are used to determine the cost. The closing statement from the closing agent, which would show additional closing costs charged, can be used.

10.4.10 Furniture

The furniture is recorded at cost for the period purchased (Table 10.1, line 12).

10.4.11 Cabinets

Cabinets are recorded at cost for the period purchased (Table 10.1, line 13).

10.4.12 Paintings

Paintings are recorded at cost for the period purchased (Table 10.1, line 14).

10.4.13 Fixtures

Fixtures are recorded at cost for the period purchased (Table 10.1, line 15).

10.4.14 Pool and Tennis Court

These assets recorded at cost for the period purchased (Table 10.1, line 16). If there were subsequent purchases or additional costs, these costs would be shown for the period incurred and not the accumulated balances.

10.4.15 Appliances

Appliances are recorded at cost for the period purchased (Table 10.1, line 17).

10.4.16 Electronic Equipment

These assets are recorded at cost for the period purchased (Table 10.1, line 18).

10.4.17 Security System

This asset is recorded at cost for the period purchased (Table 10.1, line 19).

10.4.18 Lounge Doe, Inc.

This investment is recorded at the net cash investment for the period (Table 10.1, line 20). This can be either a positive or negative change. A negative change means the subject withdrew more funds than what was invested into the corporation. The boat is a corporate asset and not the shareholder. Therefore, the boat is part of the investment in the corporation.

10.4.19 Doe's Kwik Stop, Inc.

Investment in this corporation is also recorded at the net cash investment for the period (Table 10.1, line 21). Its tax status has nothing to do with a RICO investigation. The net investment, like any other corporation, should take into consideration capital stock, additional paid in surplus, and loans from and to shareholder. If the corporation has made any loans during the period to the shareholder, then they should be subtracted from the other investment accounts.

10.4.20 Real Property, Ltd.

Investment into this partnership by the partner is recorded as the net cash investment (Table 10.1, line 22). The partner's shares of liabilities are not considered in this computation. The other partner's interest is not considered. Partnership assets belong to the partnership and not the partners. If the partner's assets can be identified separate from the other partners, then they can be severed for forfeiture purposes, but not for expenditure method purposes. In this case, the partners have an undivided interest in the assets, specifically real property. The partner's interest cannot be severed in this situation. Another problem arises when one partner either contributes or withdraws assets out of proportion of his partnership interest. These out-of-proportion contributions or withdrawals should be reflected in the expenditure schedule.

10.4.21 Mercedes Benz

This car is recorded at cost during the period purchased (Table 10.1, line 23). A problem can arise if another car was traded-in for this one. Like the net worth method, the trade-in allowance will have to be accounted for in the same manner as in the net worth computation. In essence, the gain or loss on the old car will increase or decrease the cost of the new car.

10.4.22 Toyota Sedan

This vehicle is also recorded at cost during the period purchased (Table 10.1, line 24). The car is charged to John Doe if he paid for it. This vehicle can be shown either as a gift or as an asset purchase.

10.4.23 Individual Retirement Accounts

Contributions to individual retirement accounts and Keogh plans should be shown for the period (Table 10.1, lines 25 and 26). These accounts will also have earnings for the period. There are two ways of presenting these accounts on the expenditure schedule. One is to show the contributions only and ignore the earnings altogether. The other way is to show the contributions plus the earnings. The earnings would be reflected as a source of income for the period.

10.4.24 Bahamas Residence

This asset should be shown at cost for the period acquired (Table 10.1, line 27). One problem involved in this case is the possible conversion from a foreign currency to U.S. currency. Any gain or loss on the conversion will have to be recognized. In this case, the Bahamas accepts U.S. currency as well as their own currency in their everyday economy. Thus, no conversion is necessary in this case.

10.4.25 Florida Mortgage Co.

The proceeds from a mortgage should be shown on the expenditure schedule as a source of funds (Table 10.1, line 28). The payments to the mortgage company should be shown as an application of funds. Mortgage payments usually include principal and interest. Many times, escrow payments are included to cover property taxes and insurance. A breakdown of these payments will have to be made as to both principal and interest. If escrow payments are included in the mortgage payments, then a breakdown of escrow payments will have to be made. The breakdown of the mortgage payments can be done on a supporting schedule. Any closing costs should be expensed for the period.

10.4.26 Installment Loans

The proceeds from installment loans should be shown as a source of funds for the period obtained (Table 10.1, lines 29 and 30). The payments to these installment loans should be reflected as an application of funds. A problem arises when the bank adds the interest to the principal balance. The interest is for the whole period of the loan, which normally extends beyond the current period. In this situation, the interest is recognized at the same period the loan proceeds are recognized. This interest is not capitalized and later amortized. It is expensed in the period the loan was incurred.

10.4.27   Business Bank Loan

Payments on a loan are classified as expenditure of funds (Table 10.1, line 31). This is a business loan from his sole proprietorship. Loans from a sole proprietorship are personal loans because the sole proprietor is solely liable for the loan.

10.4.28   Purchases

The purchases of inventory for a sole proprietorship are expenditure by the individual owner (Table 10.1, line 32). These expenditures are classified as personal expenditures even though they are for resale in a business. Assets of a sole proprietorship, whether used personally or for resale, belong to the individual.

10.4.29   Inventory Change

This account is used to show the changes in inventory as it affects the cost of sales (Table 10.1, line 33). The total purchases plus or minus the changes in inventory composes the total cost of sales of inventory that is sold. When inventory increases, the inventory change account decreases because part of the purchases has not been sold. When the inventory decreases, the inventory change account increases because part of the inventory has been sold in addition to the purchases that have been made during the period.

10.4.30   Business Expenses

The expenses of operating a sole proprietorship are considered personal expenditures (Table 10.1, lines 34 through 45). When the sole proprietorship uses the accrual method of accounting, all business expenses are recognized when incurred whether or not they have been paid. Any outstanding liabilities will be recognized as a source of funds. This will offset the expenses that are not paid.

10.4.31   Mortgage Interest

This is the interest portion of the mortgage payments to Florida Mortgage Company (Table 10.1, line 46) that was paid during the period.

10.4.32   Life Insurance

This is an expense during the period incurred (Table 10.1, line 47). This expenditure is recognized during the period paid. It is not amortized over the period for which the premium covers.

10.4.33   Tax Withholdings

This is a period expenditure (Table 10.1, line 48). Even though a refund is made in later years, withholding is recognized during the period incurred. The employer pays withholding during the year from the employee's salaries and wages. Thus, it is a personal expenditure even though it was not paid directly by the employee.

10.4.34 Property Taxes

This is an expense for the periods involved (Table 10.1, line 49). It should be kept in mind that expenditures are recognized during the period paid and not when incurred.

10.4.35 Credit Card Charges

This is an expense for the periods involved (Table 10.1, line 50). This case shows only the amount of funds paid to the credit card company and not the charges made against it. The expenditure method normally uses the payments to the credit card company instead of the charges. However, the expenditure method can use credit card charges, but this is offset in the source of funds by the change in the liability to the credit card companies.

10.4.36 Utilities

These are also expenses for the period involved (Table 10.1, line 51).

10.4.37 Telephone

This is an expense for the period incurred (Table 10.1, line 52).

10.4.38 Insurance

This is also an expense for the periods involved (Table 10.1, line 53).

10.4.39 Church Donations

These represent an expenditure for the period involved (Table 10.1, line 54).

10.4.40 Installment Loan Interest

This is an expense for the period incurred (Table 10.1, lines 55 and 56). It is not capitalized and amortized over the term of the loan. It is expensed during the year the loans were incurred. The interest relates to an installment loan where the bank charges interest for the term of the loan and adds it to the principal borrowed.

10.4.41 Trust Funds

Trust funds are an expenditure for the period involved (Table 10.1, line 57). Trust(s) should be examined closely because there may be funds set aside for the contributor. In this case, the trust funds are set aside for the benefit of the subject's relatives and not the subject.

10.4.42 Stock Losses

Stock losses are an expense for the period (Table 10.1, line 58). Losses on the sale of assets are recognized as an expenditure during the period the loss was incurred.

10.4.43   Accounts Payable

Accounts payable is a personal liability of the sole proprietor (Table 10.1, line 61). The purpose of this account is to offset the purchases of goods and services that have not been paid. This remaining liability is actually a source of funds for goods and services that are not paid for the sole proprietorship. The sole proprietor is the subject of investigation. The expenditure schedule should show the change in the liability and not the balance.

10.4.44   Income Tax Refunds

Income tax refunds are a source of funds during the period received (Table 10.1, line 62).

10.4.45   Interest

This is a source of funds for the period when credited to the accounts (Table 10.1, lines 63 and 64). Also, the earnings should show up as an application to the contributions made for the period.

10.4.46   Dividends

Corporate distributions, called dividends, should be recognized during the period received (Table 10.1, line 65).

10.4.47   Wages/Salaries

Earnings from employment should be recognized when received or reported for the period received or declared (Table 10.1, line 66). Any withholding should be recorded as an expenditure for the period paid or reported.

10.4.48   Rental Income

Earnings from rental income are solely based on the net funds either received or paid for the period (Table 10.1, line 67). Any "phantom" figures are to be removed from the earnings or losses shown on the appropriate financial statements. Rental income should be shown only as the net cash flow from earnings. Any asset payments or liability reductions will be reflected on the expenditure schedule for those respective line items.

10.4.49   Stock Gains

Gains from the sale of capital assets will be shown on the expenditure schedule as a source of funds (Table 10.1, line 68), even if the gains are reinvested into other capital assets.

10.4.50   Stock Sales

The sale of XYZ stock are the proceeds that recover the original cost (Table 10.1, line 69). Any gains or losses will be recognized separately. If the proceeds from the sales were reinvested into other capital assets, then this recovery of cost would not be recognized as a source of funds. The application side would show the purchase of other assets.

10.4.51   Business Income

This is the gross receipts of the sale of goods and services from a sole proprietorship (Table 10.1, line 70). Income from a sole proprietorship is income to the individual. This sole proprietorship's income is based on the accrual method of accounting. As shown above, the sole proprietor has accounts receivable. Accounts receivable is the amount of gross receipts at year-end that has not been collected.

10.5   Offshore Evidence

The scenario problem shows many offshore assets and financial transactions. Offshore transactions are generally not admissible in court. However, there are some exceptions. Public records in foreign countries are admissible when properly certified. The Bahamas residence in this case is one example. Land transfer records are open to the public in the Bahamas, as well as many other countries. Bank records are not public and in many countries, improper disclosure can result in criminal and civil actions. Some "tax haven" countries bank records are not allowed in criminal or civil tax cases; however, by treaty agreements, other countries will provide bank records in other criminal cases (e.g., racketeering, drug trafficking, and other criminal activities). One major problem in admitting foreign, nonpublic records is obtaining witnesses to introduce them into court. Government budgets may not allow the travel expenses of the witnesses. Many foreign nationals do not like to testify in court, especially if they feel that they can be charged for aiding and abetting.

10.6   Offshore Records

It is now assumed that witnesses will be obtained to introduce evidence into court. This offshore evidence, as you will see, has a material effect on the expenditure method. The RICO expenditure schedule would be modified as shown in Table 10.2.

10.6.1   Assets

The assets consist primarily of changes in the various offshore bank accounts (Table 10.2, lines 70 through 77). In 19X3, the bank account in the Bahamas under the alter ego of Transshipment, Ltd. had a decrease in the account. This is a source of funds, therefore, the negative amount. The other accounts, whether under a corporate name or individual, show an increase in the accounts, thus an application of funds.

10.6.2   Expenses

This section records the disbursements made from the various bank accounts that have been identified (Table 10.2, lines 78 through 86). Mr. Calderone received a large part of the

Table 10.2 John Doe's RICO Expenditure Schedule (Title 18)

Description	19X1 ($)	19X2 ($)	19X3 ($)
Illegal/unidentified income	7,869,600	1,579,850	1,226,900
Assets			
70. Transshipment, Ltd.			
71. Bahamian bank account		4,390,000	(3,890,000)
72. Spanish bank account			1,090,000
73. Swiss bank account			2,090,000
74. Barbados bank account			2,189,000
75. Cayman bank account			2,580,000
76. Jamaica bank account			786,000
77. Doe Holding NV			2,565,000
Total assets	—	4,390,000	7,410,000
Expenses			
78. Barbados bank charges			10,000
79. Cayman bank charges			60,000
80. Jamaica bank charges			1,000
81. Jamaica travel expenses			120,500
82. Wires to Calderone	—	3,500,000	6,000,000
83. Spanish bank charges			10,000
84. Aruba bank charges			10,000
85. Bahamas bank charges			20,000
86. Schmidt Management Company			45,000
Total offshore expenses	—	3,500,000	6,276,500
Identified Income			
87. Interest income—Cayman			640,000
88. Interest income—Spain			100,000
89. Interest income—Swiss			100,000
90. Interest income—Aruba			150,000
91. Interest income—Jamaica			7,500
Total identified offshore income	—	—	997,500
Legal/unidentified income	7,869,600	9,469,850	13,915,900

funds by wire transfer. These payments are probably for drug purchases. Wire transfers are a quick and easy way of disbursing funds. Some charges are for bank fees. Doe had some personal expenses because he paid for a hotel and other expenses in Jamaica. The payments to Schmidt Management Company are for the formation of Doe Holding NV, a foreign corporation. If this were an active corporation, these expenses would be capitalized on the corporate books. It would not be considered a personal expenditure. Expenditures on a "shell" corporation are considered personal expenses.

10.6.3 Income

The identified income from offshore activities is from interest income from his savings accounts (Table 10.2, lines 87 through 91). Those accounts held under corporate names are identified as Mr. Doe's personal income because those offshore corporations are only shells. Shell corporations are just a way of hiding income from authorities.

Tax Expenditure Solution $\quad$ 11

11.1 General

The following solution and explanation relate to the scenario problem as presented in a previous chapter. The solution and explanations are based on the tax expenditure principles.

11.2 Principles

The tax expenditure method is based on the federal income tax laws and regulations. The federal tax code defines a few concepts. One concept is gross income. Gross income means income from whatever source unless specifically exempt. Adjusted gross income is another concept. It means gross income less specified deductions. Some of these deductions are individual retirement account contributions, Keogh plan contributions, alimony payments, and a few others. Taxable income is another concept; it involves subtracting exemptions, itemized deductions, or standard deductions from adjusted gross income. These principles are the same for both the net worth method and the expenditure method. The first objective in a tax expenditure method is to establish adjusted gross income or corrected adjusted gross income if the taxpayer filed a tax return. After adjusted gross income is determined, taxable income or corrected taxable income must be determined. Some itemized deductions have limitations that are based on adjusted gross income. Medical expenses are an example of a category of deductions that has limitations on the amount deductible based on adjusted gross income. Whether the user is applying the net worth method or the expenditure method, the bottom line should be the same as is shown in these examples.

11.3 Problem

Table 11.1 shows how each item in the scenario problem is presented. An explanation of why it is presented in the manner shown is provided after the expenditure schedule. The explanation section will refer to the line items on the expenditure schedule.

11.4 Tax Expenditure Schedule

The expenditure schedule is shown in Table 11.1. Each line item is numbered. After the tax expenditure schedule, an explanation of each line item is presented. The first section shows all the expenditures by the taxpayer. The second section shows all nontaxable sources of income or receipts. Adjusted gross income is determined by subtracting nontaxable income from the total expenditures. From adjusted gross income, exemptions and

Table 11.1   John Doe's Tax Expenditure Schedule (Title 26)

Description	19X1 ($)	19X2 ($)	19X3 ($)
	Expenditures		
1. Cash on hand	—	—	50,000
2. Cocaine, 2 kilos			50,000
3. Gold bullion			100,000
4. First National Bank (FNB) checking	10,000	40,000	50,000
5. FNB savings	110,000	440,000	100,000
6. Business bank account		20,000	(10,000)
7. Accounts receivable		10,000	(10,000)
8. Inventory		140,000	(90,000)
9. Business assets		150,000	
10. 100 Alpha Street	300,000		
11. 100 Bravo Street	4,000,000		
12. Furniture	50,000		
13. Cabinets	20,000		
14. Paintings	20,000		
15. Fixtures	10,000		
16. Pool and tennis court	100,000		
17. Appliances		20,000	
18. Electronic equipment		100,000	
19. Security system			50,000
20. Lounge Doe, Inc.	2,440,000		
21. Doe Kwik Stop, Inc.	481,000	(155,000)	175,000
22. Real Property, Ltd.	1,930,000	(52,500)	12,500
23. Mercedes Benz	80,000		
24. Toyota Sedan		18,000	
25. IRA—Doe		2,200	2,400
26. IRA—Que		2,200	2,400
27. Bahamas residence		110,000	
28. Florida Mortgage Company	70,000	120,000	120,000
29. Mercedes Benz loan	9,000	12,000	12,000
30. Toyota Sedan loan		1,200	2,400
31. Prepaid interest	8,500	1,760	
32. Florida Mortgage interest	200,000	188,000	176,000
33. Business bank loan			20,000
34. Life insurance	10,000		
35. Income tax withheld	95,000		150,000
36. Property tax	5,000		5,000
37. Credit card payments	30,000	70,000	160,000
38. Utilities	10,000	10,000	20,000
39. Telephone	30,000	40,000	45,000
40. Insurance	5,000	10,000	10,000

(continued)

Table 11.1 John Doe's Tax Expenditure Schedule (Title 26) (Continued)

Description	19X1 ($)	19X2 ($)	19X3 ($)
41. Church donations		10,000	50,000
42. Interest on loan—Mercedes	1,500	2,000	2,000
43. Interest on loan—Toyota		240	480
44. Trust funds			400,000
45. ABC stock purchase			
Total expenditures	10,125,100	1,310,000	1,575,180
	Nontaxable Sources		
46. Florida Mortgage Company	2,000,000		
47. Mercedes Benz	60,000		
48. Toyota sedan loan		10,000	
49. Business bank loan		100,000	
50. Accounts payable			50,000
51. Income tax refunds	500	79,250	
52. IRA—Doe		2,200	2,400
53. IRA—Que		2,200	2,400
54. Depreciation	100,000	230,000	230,000
55. Prepaid interest		2,000	2,480
Total nontaxable sources	2,160,500	425,650	287,280
Adjusted gross income	7,964,600	884,350	1,287,900
Itemized deductions	206,500	200,240	233,480
Exemptions	2,000	2,000	2,000
Corrected taxable income	7,756,100	682,110	1,052,420
Reported taxable income	63,000	—	285,400
Increase	7,693,100	682,110	767,020

itemized deductions or standard deduction is subtracted to arrive at corrected taxable income (if taxpayer previously filed). This is compared to what the taxpayer reported for possible increases. The explanations refer to the line item on the expenditure schedule and the paragraph in the scenario problem.

11.4.1 Cash on Hand

Cash on hand is based on the currency found at John Doe's residence during the execution of the search warrant (Table 11.1, line 1). Cash on hand should be established as much as possible for each period, and it should show the addition to or the use of funds for the period, and not the ending balance.

11.4.2 Cocaine, 2 Kilos

Market value of cocaine is used in this solution (Table 11.1, line 2). This is a situation where market values are used. The primary reason is that receipts will not be available. It is well known that the taxpayer purchased the cocaine. There were no facilities discovered that the cocaine was manufactured there. This implies or suggests that the taxpayer purchased the cocaine. The Drug Enforcement Agency and other local law enforcement agencies keep statistics on the market value of drugs on a regularly periodic basis.

11.4.3   Gold Bullion

The 10 gold bars are recorded at cost (Table 11.1, line 3). The market value at time of the search warrant is higher than the original cost. If the cost and date of purchase is not known, then the market value and time of discovery can be used. If market value is used, then the burden of proof is placed on the defense to establish cost and date of purchase. The defense is not going to do this because it would be an admission by the defendant.

11.4.4   First National Bank Accounts

Increases or decreases in bank balances are reflected in this section (Table 11.1, lines 4 and 5). The increase or decrease in bank balances can be based on either the book changes or the bank balance changes. Whatever method is used, it must be used consistently. It is suggested that a better way of presenting the changes in bank balances is to show the ending balances on the expenditure schedule and subtract the beginning balance. It shows the jury from where and how the figures were obtained. Also, it helps confirm the change computations.

11.4.5   Business Cash in Bank

This bank account is based on change in book balances (Table 11.1, line 6). The sole proprietorship keeps its books on the accrual method of accounting. The accrual method of accounting recognizes income and expenses when incurred and not when received or paid. The changes in book balances are used because, first, books and records are kept of each transaction, which shows their appropriate time of occurrence. Second, timing differences are eliminated. Third, bank reconciliations will normally be available to prove out the book balances of accounts. In this case, the changes in bank balances increase during one year and decrease the subsequent year.

11.4.6   Accounts Receivable

Assets of a sole proprietorship are assets of the individual since he has title and personal liability (Table 11.1, line 7). The expenditure method recognizes the net changes in these assets. Accounts receivable is an intangible asset that accounts for funds owed by customers to the sole proprietor, John Doe.

11.4.7   Inventory

Inventory is an asset of the sole proprietor, John Doe (Table 11.1, line 8). He has title and personal liability for inventory. The expenditure method recognizes only the net changes during the period. In this case, inventory increased for the first year and decreased the following year.

11.4.8 Business Assets

These assets are property of John Doe, the sole proprietor because he has title (Table 11.1, line 9). The expenditure method only recognizes acquisitions and dispositions during the period.

11.4.9 100 Alpha Street

The purchase of the house is recorded at cost (Table 11.1, line 10). In this case, public records are used to determine the cost. However, the closing statement from the closing agent, which would also show additional closing costs, can be used.

11.4.10 100 Bravo Street

The purchase of the apartment building is recorded at cost (Table 11.1, line 11). Public records are used to determine the cost. The closing statement, which would show additional closing costs charged by the escrow agent, can be used.

11.4.11 Furniture

The furniture is recorded at cost for the period purchased (Table 11.1, line 12).

11.4.12 Cabinets

Cabinets are recorded at cost for the period purchased (Table 11.1, line 13).

11.4.13 Paintings

Paintings are recorded at cost for the period acquired (Table 11.1, line 14).

11.4.14 Fixtures

Fixtures are also recorded at cost for the period purchased (Table 11.1, line 15).

11.4.15 Pool and Tennis Court

These assets are recorded at cost for the period purchased (Table 11.1, line 16). If there were subsequent purchases or additional costs, these costs would be shown for the period incurred, and not when the contract was signed. Only period costs should be shown and not accumulated balance.

11.4.16 Appliances

Appliances are recorded at cost for the period acquired (Table 11.1, line 17).

11.4.17 Electronic Equipment

These assets are recorded at cost for the period purchased (Table 11.1, line 18).

11.4.18   Security System

This asset is also recorded at cost for the period acquired (Table 11.1, line 19).

11.4.19   ABC Stock Purchase

This intangible asset is recorded at cost for the period purchased. The cost is reflected on the expenditure schedule. However, this asset was sold during the period. Any gain or loss will not be recognized on the expenditure schedule because this is an adjustment to arrive at adjusted gross income.

11.4.20   Lounge Doe, Inc.

This investment is recorded at the net cash investment for the period (Table 11.1, line 20). This can be either a positive or negative change. A negative change means the taxpayer withdrew more funds than what was invested into the corporation during the period. The boat is a corporate asset and not the shareholder. The corporation is taxed on its income and not the shareholder. The net investment should take into consideration capital stock, additional paid in surplus, and loans from shareholder. If the corporation has made any loans to the shareholder, then they should be subtracted from the other investment accounts.

11.4.21   Doe's Kwik Stop, Inc.

This is a Sub S corporation (Table 11.1, line 21). Like taxable corporations, the expenditure schedule should reflect the net cash investment from all accounts, but in addition, the earnings and losses for the period. Sub S corporations are not taxed, but the earnings and losses are passed on to the shareholders. It should also be noted that Sub S corporations cannot have a negative balance. Losses on Sub S corporations are limited to the shareholder's investment.

11.4.22   Real Property, Ltd.

Investment into this partnership by the partner is recorded at the net cash investment plus any earnings less any losses for the period (Table 11.1, line 22). The other partner's interest is not considered. Partnership assets belong to the partnership and not the partners. If the partner's assets can be identified separately from the others, then they can be severed. The partnership is not a taxable entity. The partner can have a negative basis provided that the partner is at risk for his share of the partnership liabilities. The expenditure method only recognizes the changes in the partnership investment for the period and not year-end balances.

11.4.23   Mercedes Benz

This car is recorded at cost during the period purchased (Table 11.1, line 23). A problem can arise if another car was traded in for this one. Like the net worth method, the trade-in allowance will have to be accounted for in the same manner. In essence, the gain or loss on the old car will increase or decrease the cost of the new car.

11.4.24   Toyota Sedan

This vehicle is also recorded at cost during the period purchased (Table 11.1, line 24). The car is charged to John Doe because he paid for it. This vehicle can be shown either as a gift or as an asset purchase. Because the car is financed and John Doe is probably making the payments, this vehicle should be shown as an asset.

11.4.25   IRA Accounts

Contributions to individual retirement accounts and Keogh plans should be shown for the period (Table 11.1, lines 25 and 26). These accounts will also have earnings for the period. Contributions to these plans are an adjustment to arrive at adjusted gross income. The earnings are nontaxable until withdrawn. Therefore, there are two ways to present these items. One is to completely ignore them altogether. The issue in this case would be that the taxpayers have an asset that they can access. The other way of presenting this issue is to show the contributions and earnings, and later back out the earnings and contributions as a nontaxable source.

11.4.26   Bahamas Residence

This asset should be shown at cost for the period acquired (Table 11.1, line 27). One issue involved in this case is the possible conversion from a foreign currency to U.S. currency. Any gain or loss on the conversion is not recognized because this would be an adjustment to arrive at adjusted gross income.

11.4.27   Florida Mortgage Co.

The proceeds from a mortgage should be shown on the expenditure schedule as a nontaxable source of funds (Table 11.1, line 28). The payments to the mortgage company should be shown as an application of funds. Mortgage payments usually include principal and interest. Many times, escrow payments are included to cover property taxes and insurance. A breakdown of these payments will have to be made as to both principal and interest. If escrow payments are included in the mortgage payments, then a breakdown of the escrow payments will have to be made as to changes in the escrow balance, property taxes, and insurance paid for the period.

11.4.28   Automobile Loans

The proceeds from installment loans should be shown as a source of funds for the period obtained (Table 11.1, lines 29 and 30). The payments to these installment loans should be reflected as an application of funds. A problem arises where the bank adds the interest to the principal balance. The interest is for the whole period of the loan, which normally extends beyond the period. In this situation, the interest is shown as an expenditure. The interest is amortized over the period of the loan and is later shown as an itemized deduction. For the initial year that the loan was obtained, the prepaid interest is divided up between current year's expense and the unamortized expense.

11.4.29   Prepaid Interest

This is the unamortized portion of the interest charged by the bank on installment loans (Table 11.1, line 31). This interest is amortized over subsequent periods. It is shown as an expense and later as an itemized deduction, if deductible.

11.4.30   Mortgage Interest

This is the interest portion of the mortgage payments to Florida Mortgage Company (Table 11.1, line 32) that was paid during the period. This same amount will also be shown on the itemized deduction schedule.

11.4.31   Life Insurance

This is an expense for the period incurred (Table 11.1, line 34). It is not amortized over the period for which the premium was incurred. If this were a medical insurance premium, then an itemized deduction would be made in subsequent years, subject to limitations. Prepaid medical insurance should be treated the same way as prepaid interest on installment loans.

11.4.32   Income Tax Withheld

This is a period expenditure (Table 11.1, line 35). Even though a refund is made in later years, withholding is recognized during the period withheld.

11.4.33   Property Tax

This is an expense for the period involved (Table 11.1, line 36). In addition, this expenditure is also an itemized deduction.

11.4.34   Credit Card Charges

These are expenses for the periods involved (Table 11.1, line 37). This case shows only the amount of funds paid to the credit card company and not the charges made against it. The expenditure method uses the payments to the credit card company instead of the charges. If the credit card has charges for business expenses, then payments for these expenses will have to be subtracted from the payments.

11.4.35   Utilities

Utilities are expenses for the periods involved (Table 11.1, line 38).

11.4.36   Telephone

This is also an expense for the periods involved (Table 11.1, line 39).

11.4.37 Insurance

This is an expense for the periods involved (Table 11.1, line 40).

11.4.38 Church Donations

This is an expense for the periods involved (Table 11.1, line 41). In addition, these are itemized deductions that are subject to limitations.

11.4.39 Installment Loan Interest

This is an expenditure for the period (Table 11.1, lines 42 and 43). This is the portion of interest charged by the bank that is expensed for the period. It also is used as itemized deductions. In subsequent periods, the interest is shown as an expense and as a possible itemized deduction. Another way of presenting the future amortized interest and itemized deduction is not to show it at all.

11.4.40 Trust Funds

Trust funds are expenses for the periods involved (Table 11.1, line 44). Trusts should be examined closely because they may be funds that the contributor can obtain access.

11.4.41 XYZ Stock Loss

Losses on the sale of capital assets, such as stock in this case, are an adjustment to arrive at adjusted gross income. Therefore losses are ignored in this case.

11.4.42 Mortgage Proceeds

The mortgage proceeds from Florida Mortgage Company are a nontaxable source of funds (Table 11.1, line 45). The gross proceeds should be recognized as a source of funds. Any closing costs should be expensed or added to the cost of the real property.

11.4.43 Automobile Loans

The installment loans for the purchase of automobiles are shown as a nontaxable source of funds (Table 11.1, lines 46 and 47). Installment loans should be shown with both principal and interest charged for the term of the loans. The interest for the loan term will offset the initial loan balance with a charge to prepaid interest. For subsequent years, the prepaid interest will be amortized as an expenditure for the period. Installment loan payments are shown on the expenditure side of the expenditure schedule.

11.4.44 Business Bank Loan

John Doe, the sole proprietor, borrowed funds from the bank (Table 11.1, line 48). Even though this is a business loan, John Doe is personally liable. This is a nontaxable source of funds that should be recognized when received.

11.4.45   Accounts Payable

Accounts payable of a sole proprietorship are liabilities of the individual (Table 11.1, line 49). The individual is personally liable for business payables of sole proprietorship. The expenditure method recognizes the net changes in this account for the period.

11.4.46   Income Tax Refunds

Income tax refunds are a source of funds during the period received (Table 11.1, line 50). This should be shown as a nontaxable source.

11.4.47   IRA Accounts

As explained earlier in Section 11.4.25, if this is to be shown as an expenditure for the period, then it has to be offset by a nontaxable source of funds. The purpose is to arrive at adjusted gross income (Table 11.1, lines 51 and 52). When preparing an individual tax return, this is an adjustment to gross income in order to arrive at adjusted gross income.

11.4.48   Depreciation

This is considered a nontaxable source of funds for the period (Table 11.1, line 53). This does not deal with the source of funds. It is considered a phantom figure for RICO purposes. For tax purposes, it is considered a source of funds on the grounds that this is a potential liability. The federal laws and regulations require the recovery of depreciation as ordinary taxable income to the extent of any gain recognized on the sale of the depreciable asset. Depreciation, amortization, and depletion charges for the current period is recognized, not the accumulated balances.

11.4.49   Prepaid Interest Reduction

Installment loans have been recorded with prepaid interest for the term of the loan (Table 11.1, line 54). The tax expenditure method requires this prepaid interest to be capitalized and amortized over the term of the loan. During subsequent years, the prepaid interest account will be reduced by the amount of interest recognized for the period. This reduction of the prepaid interest account is a source of funds and becomes an expense for the period. The expense was recognized above (Table 11.1, lines 42 and 43).

11.4.50   Itemized Deductions

Itemized or the standard deduction is allowed to reduce adjusted gross income to derive at taxable income. The federal income tax code allows certain expenses to be deducted. The primary ones are medical expenses, interest expenses, certain taxes, charity donations, and other miscellaneous expenses. In this solution, itemized deductions are the total of personal expenditures for interest (mortgage and amortized interest), church donations, and property taxes. Limitations on these deductions that are built into the tax code have been ignored in this problem. The itemized deductions are identified in Table 11.2.

Table 11.2 John Doe's Itemized Deductions

Description	19X1 ($)	19X2 ($)	19X3 ($)
Interest—Florida Mortgage	200,000	188,000	176,000
Interest—Mercedes	1,500	2,000	2,000
Interest—Toyota		240	280
Property taxes	5,000		5,000
Church donations		10,000	50,000
Total	206,500	200,240	233,480

11.4.51 Exemptions

Exemptions are an income tax concept. The amount of these exemptions varies from year to year. For the sake of simplicity, $2,000 per exemption is used in this case.

11.4.52 Offshore Evidence

This scenario problem shows many offshore assets and financial transactions. Offshore transactions are generally not admissible in court. However, there are some exceptions. Public records in foreign countries are admissible when properly certified. The Bahamas residence in this case is one example. Land transfer records are open to the public in the Bahamas, as well as in many other countries. Bank records are usually not public and in many countries improper disclosure can result in criminal and civil actions. Some "tax haven" countries bank records are not allowed in criminal or civil tax cases. One major problem in admitting foreign nonpublic records is obtaining a witness to introduce them into court. Government budgets may not allow the travel expenses of the witness. Many foreign nationals do not like to testify in court, especially, if they feel that they can be charged for aiding and abetting.

11.4.53 Offshore Records

Now, it will be assumed that witnesses will be obtained to introduce evidence into court. This offshore evidence, as you will see, has a material effect on the tax expenditure method. The tax expenditure schedule will be modified as shown in Table 11.3.

11.4.54 Doe Holding NV

The net cash investment in this foreign corporation for the period is reflected on the expenditure schedule (Table 11.3, line 58). The fees paid to Schmidt Management Company are for the creation of this corporation. Thus, this is a corporate expenditure. The expenditure method shows the net cash investment for the period. Like any offshore transaction, it must be shown in U.S. currency and any gain or loss on the conversion must also be recognized. The tax expenditure schedule does not recognize any gains or losses on currency exchange because this is an adjustment to arrive at adjusted gross income.

Table 11.3   John Doe's Tax Expenditure Schedule (Title 26)

Description	19X1 ($)	19X2 ($)	19X3 ($)
Previous corrected income	7,756,100	682,110	1,052,420
	Expenditures		
56. Bahamian bank account		4,390,000	(3,890,000)
57. Spanish bank account			1,090,000
58. Swiss bank account			2,090,000
59. Aruba bank account			2,565,000
60. Barbados bank account			2,189,000
61. Cayman Island bank account			2,580,000
62. Jamaica bank account			786,000
63. Barbados bank account			10,000
64. Cayman bank charges			60,000
65. Jamaica bank charges			1,000
66. Jamaica travel expenses			120,500
Corrected taxable income	7,756,100	5,072,110	8,653,920
Reported taxable income	63,000	—	285,400
Increase	7,693,100	5,072,110	8,368,520

11.4.55   Offshore Bank Charges

These expenses are recognized during the period paid (Table 11.3, lines 62 through 64). The main issue in these expenditures is the conversion of foreign currency to U.S. currency. This problem does not address this issue.

11.4.56   Jamaica Travel

This is an expenditure for the period (Table 11.3, line 65). Expenditures are recognized only during the period paid.

11.4.57   Transshipment, Ltd.

This is a Bahamian corporation. Its only assets and capital is the bank accounts set up by the sole shareholder (Table 11.3, lines 55 through 57). The Spanish and Swiss banks were interest-bearing accounts because they were credited with interest income. This income is an adjustment to arrive at adjusted gross income. Therefore, it is ignored. Because some expenditures cannot be specifically identified, other than those that are transferred to other bank accounts, only the changes in the bank balances are used. The Bahamian bank account shows payments going to Calderone, who is a known drug trafficker; however, he cannot be used as a witness. The reason should be obvious. He would not testify without self-incrimination.

11.4.58   Foreign Bank Accounts

Changes in bank balances are recognized as sources or expenditures of assets, principally cash (Table 11.3, lines 59 through 61). If the bank account balances go up, as it does here, this is an application of funds. If the bank account balances go down, then it is a source of funds.

Organized Crime

12

12.1 Definition

Both the judicial and legislature have had disputes in defining organized crime. In 1967, the Administration of Justice defined organized crime as "a society that seeks to operate outside the control of the American people and their government. It involves thousands of criminals, working within structures as large as those of any corporation." The McClellan Committee, following highly publicized investigations, increased public awareness of organized crime as a pervasive social force and prompted federal legislative action. However, they did not sufficiently emphasize the importance and roles of groups other than the La Cosa Nostra in American organized crime. In 1968, Congress passed into law the first major organized crime bill, The Omnibus Crime Control and Safe Streets Act. This act defined organized crime as the unlawful activities of the members of a highly organized, disciplined association engaged in supplying illegal goods and services, including but not limited to gambling, prostitution, loan-sharking, narcotics, labor racketeering, and other unlawful activities. In 1970, Congress passed the Racketeer Influenced and Corrupt Organizations Statute (RICO), which has become the centerpiece of federal law proscribing organized criminal activity. RICO defines racketeering activity as any act or threat involving murder, kidnapping, gambling, arson, robbery, bribery, extortion, or dealing in narcotic or dangerous drugs, and other denominated crime. A pattern of racketeering requires at least two acts of racketeering activity.

Organized crime is the collective result of the commitment, knowledge, and actions of three components: the criminal groups each of which have at their core persons tied by racial, linguistic, ethnic, or other bonds; the protectors, persons who protect the group's interests; and specialist support, persons who knowingly render services on an ad hoc basis to enhance the group's interests.

12.2 Criminal Group

The criminal group is a continuing, structured collection of persons who utilize criminality, violence, and a willingness to corrupt in order to gain and maintain power and profit. The characteristics of the criminal group are: continuity, structure, criminality, violence, membership based on a common denominator, a willingness to corrupt, and a power/profit goal.

The criminal group carries out its purpose over a period of time. The group operates beyond the lifetime of individual members and is structured to survive changes in leadership. At different times, activities are focused, organized, and controlled in various ways. Group members work to ensure that the group continues and their interests are subordinate to those of the group.

The criminal group is structured as a collection of hierarchically arranged inter-dependent offices devoted to the accomplishment of a particular function. It can be highly structured or fluid. It is distinguishable and ordered in ranks based on power and authority.

Membership is the core in a criminal group that is restricted and based on a common trait, such as ethnicity, race, criminal background, or common interest. Potential members of a criminal group are closely scrutinized and required to prove their worth and loyalty to the criminal group. Membership in most instances requires a lifetime commitment to the group. The rules of membership include secrecy, a willingness to commit any act for the group, and intent to protect the group. In return for loyalty, the criminal group member receives benefits from the group, including protection, a certain prestige, an opportunity for economic gain, and, perhaps most importantly, a sense of belonging.

12.2.1 Criminality

Organized crime is aimed at the pursuit of profit along well-defined terms. The criminal group relies on continuing criminal activity to generate income. Some groups engage in a range of illegal activities, while others limit to one central activity. Some criminal groups are involved in legitimate business activities in order to skim or launder profits and increase its power.

12.2.2 Violence

Violence and the threat of violence are an integral part of the criminal group. Both are used to control and protect against both members of the group who violate their commitment and those outside the group to protect it and maximize its power. Members are expected to commit, condone, or authorize violent acts.

12.2.3 Power/Profit Goal

Members of a criminal group are united in that they work for the group's power and ultimately its profit. Political power is achieved through the corruption of officials. The group's structure and the fear it instills through the use of violence manifest power. The criminal group maintains power through its association with the criminal protectors, which defend the group and its profits.

12.2.4 Protectors

The protectors are a complement of corrupt public officials, attorneys, and businessmen who individually or collectively protect the criminal group through abuses of status and/or privilege and violation of law. Protectors includes lawyers, judges, politicians, financial advisors, financial institutions, and business in the United States and worldwide. As a result, the criminal group is insulated from both civil and criminal government actions. Protectors are members of organized crime. The success of organized crime is dependent on this buffer, which helps to protect the criminal group from civil and criminal action.

12.2.5 Specialist Support

The criminal group and protectors rely on skilled individuals or specialists to assist in the attainment of group goals. These individuals do not share a continuing commitment to the group's goals. Nonetheless, they are considered part of organized crime.

12.3 Groups

There will be little lasting benefit in disabling the La Cosa Nostra if other groups successfully claim its abandoned criminal franchises. If progress is to be made, the perspective of organized crime must be on not only the current groups but also the possible successors and the protectors of organized crime.

12.3.1 La Cosa Nostra

The La Cosa Nostra ("This Thing of Ours") has been the largest, most extensive, and most influential crime group in this country for more than a half century. Today, it must share some of the criminal enterprises that it once thoroughly dominated with newer crime groups. The La Cosa Nostra (LCN) undertakings range from heroin trafficking to storefront numbers operations and from extortion by violence to sophisticated infiltration of legitimate businesses. The LCN is so formally organized, so broadly established, and so effective that it can demand a portion of the proceeds of other crime groups.

12.3.1.1 Background and Structure

The basic territorial unit with the La Cosa Nostra is the family, which is known as a borgata. The name does not imply any blood relationship. The LCN families total about 1700 members, with a concentration in the northeastern United States. About one-half of the strength is in the five New York families. The number of formal members represents only a small portion of the criminal network by which the organization survives and prospers.

Nearly all the LCN families around the country fall under the authority of the "National Commission," established by Salvatore "Lucky" Luciano in 1931. The exception is the New Orleans family, the longest established LCN group, which is independent of the commission in most matters. The Commission traditionally has consisted of the bosses or acting bosses from the five New York families and bosses from several of the more important families around the country. Besides the five New York bosses, the LCN Commission currently includes bosses from Buffalo, Chicago, Detroit, and Philadelphia.

The national commission regulates joint ventures between families, intervenes in family disputes, approves the initiation of new members, and controls relations between the U.S. and Sicilian branches of La Cosa Nostra. In 1964, electronic surveillance by the Federal Bureau of Investigations (FBI) recorded a conversation in which Sam DeCavalcante, boss of the New Jersey family, discussed the commission's intervention in a leadership struggle within New York's Joseph Profaci family. While the commission has precedence in issues that affect the overall conduct of LCN and its families, lesser rights are still reserved for the individual families, such as what they do, who they kill, and who they do business with, as explained by informant James Fratianno, a former member of the Los Angeles LCN group.

Not all LCN families have equal power. Those in the west are less formally organized, and their leadership is less easily identified. Law enforcement has speculated that power within LCN is gravitating to Chicago. The five New York families influence activities as far west as Chicago, while the midwestern and western families are believed to report to the boss of the Chicago LCN family. Angelo Lonardo, a former Cleveland underboss, has testified that Chicago dominates over midwestern families, while the Cleveland LCN family reports to New York. Ken Eto, a former associate of the Chicago family, has stated that the Cleveland family is subordinate to the Genovese family in New York.

The structure of a La Cosa Nostra family typically consists of the following positions:

Boss. He is head of the family. He does not participate in the day-to-day activities of the organization but is supposed to receive a cut from every income source. He usually has his own legitimate and illegitimate businesses.

Underboss. He assists the boss. Usually, he is being groomed to succeed the boss, but succession is not automatic. There is only one underboss per family.

Consiglieri. Literally, this means "counselor." The consiglieri assists the boss but has no leadership authority. He is generally an older, experienced member who can advise family members. There usually is only one per family.

Capo. Caporegima, or captain, supervises the family's day-to-day criminal operations and represents the family among the soldiers, whom they oversee. A Capo gains his position by proving his ability as an "earner," that is, one who earns a great deal of profit for the family. They may have their own legitimate and illegal ventures and retain part of the income paid by their soldiers before passing it on to the leadership. The number of capos in a family depends on the size of the family.

Soldier. This is the basic rank in the family. Sometimes the soldier is known as a "wise guy," "button," or a "made man," which refers to any formal member of the LCN, one who has undergone the initiation ritual. To be "made," a man must be of Italian ancestry.

Associates. This is an informal position, yet one that is crucial to the family. An associate need not be of Italian descent. He is someone whose skills or position make him of value to the organization. Some associates are used as soldiers, while others are more distantly connected. The FBI has estimated for every formal member of the LCN, there are 10 criminal associates who cooperate with members and share their enterprise.

Protectors. Among any family's associates is a support network of "protectors." These are corrupt public officials, bankers, lawyers, accountants, and other professionals who protect the criminal group from governmental action, both civil and criminal. Angelo Lonardo has described the role of Milton Rockman, who acted as a conduit for cash skimmed from Las Vegas casinos for several midwest families, "We all belonged to the same organization. He always took care of the labor movement and financial movement; he was a member of the organization, but he was not a member of the family."

La Cosa Nostra structure usually insulates the boss from the crimes committed by soldiers in his family. Often he receives money derived from illegal enterprises that he did not organize and about which he has no real knowledge.

12.3.1.2 Activities

The true nature of La Cosa Nostra is derived from the lowest and the uppermost elements of its overall structure. The existence of the commission, the highest level of authority, makes the American LCN an organized crime group in every sense of the definition, a cartel with national oversight, and it is the soldier who makes the organization such a truly predatory creation.

The soldier is Italian and male. Typically, he already has a background in burglary and robbery before he is considered for membership. Except in unusual circumstances, a candidate for membership cooperates with family members in some criminal tasks as part of a testing process; he may be asked to participate in a murder, at least as an accomplice. Before he is accepted as a member, his name will be circulated around the family. In New York, other family bosses will review the name. Associates with contacts in law enforcement do part of the screening.

To be a "made" member of the LCN requires a sponsor. This is no casual relationship, because the sponsor's life may be in jeopardy if the initiate later turns "sour." The candidate vows that the organization will be foremost in this life and acknowledges that only death will release him from the oath. One immediate effect of his new status is that among other members, he will now be referred to as "a friend of ours," while associates and outsiders are referred to as "a friend of mine" when one member introduces them to another.

Martin Light, an attorney close to the LCN who was serving a sentence for a drug conviction, testified on January 29, 1986, and stated that prospective members are watched from childhood on, judged on their toughness and ability, and on their respect for superiors. Their willingness to "do the right thing" may be to share criminal profits with family leaders, to risk a jail term for refusal to testify before a grand jury, or to plead guilty to a crime actually committed by more important figures in the family. It is to follow unquestioningly the self-perpetuating practices of a most secret and exclusive criminal society. Rank in the LCN is strictly observed. Dealings between families always involve members of equal rank; an underboss will deal only with his counterpart in another organization. Within a given family, bosses deal exclusively with his consiglier and underboss, from whom the captain gets his orders. Each captain has a "crew" of several soldiers who are affiliated with him for life; each soldier has a crew of several soldiers who are affiliated with him for life; and each soldier has a crew of nonmember associates, some of whom may be Italian, prospects for initiation some day. Thus several buffers are created between the lowest and the topmost levels of the family.

The soldier is the lowest-ranking formal member of the organization, but he commands respect and fear on the street. Light testified that Gregory Scarpa, a soldier of the Colombo family, would not allow anyone to do anything without getting his permission, even down to double parking.

Even as the captains and the family leadership reap the fruits of the soldier's aggressiveness and respect, they are also engaged in large-scale crime that requires the full influence and capital of the family. Even a partial recounting of LCN criminal activities is a virtual catalogue of organized crime: drug trafficking, illegal gambling, extortion, theft, fraud, prostitution, loan sharking, labor racketeering, embezzlement, money laundering, bribery, bombing, hijacking, kidnapping, auto theft, arson, kickbacks, burglary, smuggling, and forgery are all common.

There are regional differences. In the northeast, labor racketeering and infiltration of the construction trades are among the LCN primary activities, while firearms trafficking is common in the north central region. The Bruno family in Philadelphia seems to be more heavily involved than other families in trafficking of methamphetamines. Forgery and arson are prominent in the southern and western regions.

Intelligence reports that gambling is the largest source of income for the Midwestern LCN groups; these reports are supported by the recent trail of family leaders from Chicago, Kansas City, Milwaukee, and Cleveland in the Argent Corporation skimming case; in the conviction of Carl Deluna and others in a similar 1983 skimming case involving the Tropicana Casino in Las Vegas; in the 1985 bookmaking convictions of Caesar DeVarco and others in Chicago; and in the guilty pleas entered by Kansas City LCN figures Anthony and Carlo Civella on gambling charges in 1984. Chicago also is considered one of the few cities where prostitution is controlled by the LCN.

The New Orleans family of Carlos Marcello generates most of its income by infiltrating legitimate businesses, and it gains most of its power through political influence. New Orleans serves as an example for other LCN families, which in recent years have infiltrated legitimate businesses, including liquor and food purveyors, restaurants, construction, banking, vending, jewelry, meat packing, sanitation and toxic waste disposal, import/export, tobacco, and laundry, among many others.

12.3.1.3 Prosecutions and Their Effect

During the 1980s, the leadership in 17 of 24 La Cosa Nostra families has been indicted or convicted. In 1984, organized crime indictments totaled 2194, involving predominately LCN members and associates. One of the most valuable tools for prosecutors has been the Racketeer Influenced Corrupt Organizations Act (RICO), signed into law in 1970, which recognizes the true institutional nature of organized crime.

Professor Howard Abadinsky believes that the arrest of a single capo or even a boss does not disrupt the entire organization because family power is decentralized. He further adds that imprisonments may serve as the equivalent of forced retirement, allowing younger members to move into authority. The FBI, from their investigations, has seen this trend.

Ronald Goldstock, former head of the New York Organized Crime Task Force, sees the families move from active crime into financing crime by others, such as importing heroin or backing numbers operations. This has become more prevalent in recent years owing to the large number of LCN prosecutions. Law enforcement intelligence has found the LCN is helping the Triads, the Columbian drug cartels, and the Russian mobs.

Working law enforcement has a different view. The imprisonment of LCN bosses has brought to power a generation of inexperienced leaders who have not been fully groomed for responsibility and who do not subscribe to the old customs of loyalty and secrecy, producing an organization that is more vicious, less skillful at crime, and less bound by honor and heritage than their predecessors. Financial ties are more easily broken than obligations of honor and loyalty. Numerous cases against LCN figures have hinged on the testimony of their former colleagues. Because of the convictions of LCN bosses and other high-level figures, the LCN has been recruiting members and killers from Sicily. Also, they have been sending soldiers to Sicily to learn the Mafia code of honor.

12.3.1.4 Sicilian Faction

An important new development is the disclosure of an element of the Sicilian La Cosa Nostra that is operating in the United States. Its existence was revealed almost simultaneously during a 1984 investigation of a heroin smuggling ring known as the "Pizza Connection," which involved Sicilian La Cosa Nostra crime boss Gaetano Badalamente, and by the testimony of Tommaso Buscetta, a high-level Sicilian LCN figure, who has become a witness for prosecutors in Italy and the United States. It has been held that Sicilian members were bound to the American LCN families. It is now apparent that while Sicilian and American groups may cooperate in some crime, there is, in fact, an independent Sicilian organization in the United States.

The LCN in Italy has undergone several periods of severe repression, including a purge by Mussolini in the 1920s. American groups became safe havens for Sicilian members during these periods of difficulty. During the 1920s, formative Sicilian members fled to the United States. Among them were Joseph Bonanno, Carlo Gambino, Stefano Maggadino, and Joseph Profaci, men who were among the leadership of U.S. organized crime during the next 40 years.

There appears to have been a short break in relations between the two groups around 1950. In 1957, American LCN leaders Lucky Luciano, Joe Bananno, Carmine Galante, and Frank Garofalo met in Palermo with Sicilian leaders, including Tommaso Buscetta and Gaetano Badalamente. One of the products of that meeting was the formation of a Sicilian Commission, similar to the one instituted by Luciano in 1931. Unlike the U.S. Commission, the first Sicilian Commission included soldiers, not bosses, and it dissolved in 1962.

In the early 1960s, the Italian LCN again came under intense pressure from police as a result of murderous factional conflict. Scores of LCN members in Italy were arrested and tried. LCN members fled to the United States, Canada, and South America. Law enforcement experts naturally assumed that the new arrivals would be absorbed into existing families. However, these expatriates remained loyal to their original families in Sicily and formed the nucleus of an independent LCN group in the United States.

Sicilian leaders established a second national commission, this one headed by Badalamente, Stefano Bontade, and Salvatore Reina. Around the end of 1977, Badalamente was expelled from his seat under pressure from the faction based in the Corleone area and went into exile, fearing for his life. Friction between the Corleonese group and Badalamente's organization resulted in what has become known in Italy as La Grande Guerra, The Great War. More than 500 LCN members and associates died in this conflict between 1980 and 1983, as Badalamente attempted to regain his position. Eventually, the Corleone faction prevailed with Michele Greco as head of the Commission. The Corleone faction has held exclusive rights in the Sicilian LCN to drug trafficking since 1981. Under the Corleonesi, the heroin industry in Sicily was taken from individual LCN members and supervised by family bosses. An elaborate smuggling network supplied morphine base from Afghanistan, Pakistan, and Iran to Sicilian processing laboratories, from which it was shipped via Spain or Switzerland, most often, to the United States and the Sicilian LCN faction in place there.

Michele Greco went into hiding in 1982 when Italian police made mass arrests of LCN figures following a series of murders of judges, prosecutors, and police. In 1984, Greco was sentenced in absentia to life imprisonment for the assassination of Palermo Judge Rocco Chinnici. On February 20, 1986, Greco was arrested at a farmhouse near Palermo and was bound over for trial with 467 suspected LCN members. Tommaso Buscetta became an informant for prosecutors in Italy and the United States after two of his sons, a son-in-law, two brothers, and two nephews died in La Grande Guerra. He was a key witness against Greco and the others.

12.3.1.5 Sicilian Operations in the United States

The number of Sicilian LCN members in this country is not known. However, they are believed to be concentrated mainly in the northeastern United States. They apparently operate without geographical restrictions. There has been little friction between U.S. families and Sicilian members in this country, which suggests that working agreements are in effect. In the Pizza Connection case, it has been documented that Sicilian members supplied heroin to an American LCN faction headed by Salvatore Catalano, capo of the Bonanno family. Since the early 1970s, the Sicilians have been one of the principal suppliers of Southeast Asia heroin in this country. They moved into the trade after the end of the French Connection, through which American LCN interest controlled the flow of Turkish heroin into this country. In 1977, authorities of the United States, France, and Italy began assembling evidence of the Sicilian network. In 1980, Italian police discovered two laboratories in Palermo capable of processing up to 50 kg of heroin per week.

The Sicilian LCN in the United States has generated enormous amounts of cash that must be laundered through its drug trafficking operations. Members have bought into businesses in which illicit proceeds may be hidden along with the legitimate cash flow. The Sicilians have used investment schemes involving commodity futures and a courier system for transporting bulk currency out of the United States to banks in the Bahamas and Bermuda, which then transfer the funds to commercial accounts overseas. Sicilian members have also purchased large amounts of real estate. The property can be resold for its true value and the proceeds are considered legitimate.

12.3.2 Outlaw Motorcycle Gangs

When they first appeared, outlaw motorcycle gangs were a disenchanted anomaly within the general contentment of the postwar U.S. groups of young men, newly returned soldiers, who formed motorcycle clubs and rejected normal civilian lifestyles. In the next few years their behavior was boisterous and rebellious. Today, there are 800 to 900 outlaw motorcycle gangs, ranging in size and sophistication from loosely organized single chapters to gangs with dozens of chapters in the United States and foreign countries. During the 1970s, at least five outlaw motorcycle gangs, Hell's Angels, the Outlaws, the Bandidos, the Pagans, and the Mongols, evolved into fully organized crime groups. Together, their member chapters reach across the continental United States and into Europe and Australia. They engage in almost every conceivable crime, including murder, extortion, and drug trafficking schemes. They have been known to cooperate with LCN figures.

In addition to these five gangs, a few other outlaw motorcycle groups are active in the United States. They include the Sons of Silence (midwest and Great Lakes region); The Vagos (Los Angeles and Mexico); the Peacemakers (southeastern United States); and the Dirty Dozen (Arizona and the southwest). However, none of these groups is thought to have achieved the status of true organized crime groups. In recent years, motorcycle gangs have established ties with Mexican drug organizations. The Mongols have allied themselves with the Bandidos, Outlaws, Sons of Silence, and Pagans against the Hell's Angeles. The Sons of Silence have five chapters in Germany.

12.3.2.1 Background

Today's outlaw motorcycle gangs are secretive and closely knit groups, and they are selective about their membership. The gangs usually require that a member introduce a prospective recruit to the group. During a probationary period the recruit's loyalty and willingness to commit crime is tested.

The symbol of membership in an outlaw motorcycle gang is its "colors," usually a sleeveless denim or leather jacket with embroidered patches sewn on the back. The patches display a gang logo, sometimes slogans, or initials. There may be "rockers" that identify the name of the gang member's most prized possession. They represent the foremost commitment of his life, his commitment to the gang and its criminal lifestyle.

Part of that lifestyle, common to most outlaw motorcycle gangs, is the member's outrageous treatment of the women who associate with them. Women are held to be less important than the gang itself and the gang member's motorcycle. In some cases, women are used to generate income through prostitution and topless dancing, as well as for the transportation of drugs and weapons. Some gangs regard women as "club property," available for the gratification of all the members. Others are considered the property of individual members.

Members of outlaw motorcycle gangs refer to themselves as "one percenters" in reference to the estimate by the American Motorcycle Association that outlaw motorcyclists comprised less than 1% of the motorcycling population.

12.3.2.2 Membership

No firm figures of gang membership exist. The estimated membership is 8450 in the five gangs as follows:

Motorcycle Gang	Membership
Hell's Angels	2500 (worldwide)
Outlaws	1700 (worldwide)
Bandidos	2500 (worldwide)
Pagans	900
Mongols	850

Every gang has a coterie of associates, followers, and aspiring members. Some associates may include their conspirators in the manufacture and distribution of chemical drugs such as methamphetamines. It is estimated that there are 10 "hangers on" for every full member. In 1985, the FBI listed 16 major crimes typical of outlaw motorcycle gangs; these include illegal drugs, murder, extortion, kidnapping, arson, robbery, bombings, and receiving stolen property.

12.3.2.3 Structure

The leadership hierarchy of an outlaw motorcycle gang chapter generally consists of a president, vice president, secretary-treasurer, and sergeant of arms, usually elected for specific terms. However, informal leaders also emerge and often exercise more control than the elected officers. Chapters usually are gathered into regional groups that support the national organization. The national organization is frequently headed by a "mother club," which may be either an original chapter or a national ruling body in which each member supervises several chapters. The national president may be the actual leader or simply a spokesman for the gang.

The Hell's Angels' ties to La Cosa Nostra are well established. Informants have corroborated reports that members of the Cleveland chapter were involved in contract killings and drug trafficking for the Licavoli LCN family. Associations between members of the Hell's Angels and the Genovese crime family have been identified. In Troy, New York, Hell's Angels members are known to have a relationship with an associate of the Buffalino LCN family.

As is true of most organized crime groups, the Hell's Angels must launder their illicit income before it can be used legitimately. When income exceeds the immediate needs of the members, it is invested. The West Coast faction has been especially active in buying legitimate businesses, including motorcycle and automobile services, catering operations, bars and restaurants, antique stores, landscaping operations, and machine shops. The faction has recently acquired large parcels of acreage in the California "gold country," a foothill area of the Sierra Nevada Mountains, east of Sacramento. The gang's only discernible weakness is that its members are easily identified by their colors. However, some members are abandoning their outlaw image, wearing business suits and driving luxury cars, in essence, becoming outlaw motorcycle gangs without motorcycles. The gang's strengths are many. It is institutionally wary of authority and uses sophisticated methods to protect itself from surveillance. Some clubhouses are fortified with elaborate electronic and physical security systems. Gang members do extensive background checks on prospective members, often using female associates who have been placed in positions with government services and law enforcement agencies to assist them.

12.3.2.4 *The Outlaws*

Founded in the late 1950s in the Chicago area, the Outlaws are an international group with chapters in Canada and Australia. The group's territory, which is divided into four or five regional areas, each with a president, runs mainly though the midwestern United States. Outlaw territory includes Michigan, Illinois, western New York, Ohio, western Pennsylvania, and parts of Oklahoma, Arkansas, and Kentucky, and it reaches into North Carolina, Georgia, and Florida. The Outlaws are intense rivals of the Hell's Angels in those areas where the two gang's territories overlap. Like the Hell's Angels, the individual chapters of the Outlaws are independent and may cooperate with one another where that may be mutually beneficial. The Outlaws are considered less criminally sophisticated than some chapters of the Hell's Angels, but they are perhaps even more violent.

The Outlaws are heavily involved in the production and distribution of methamphetamines. The group's strength in the midwestern border states has allowed it to smuggle "Canadian Blue" valium into the United States, while its chapters in Florida have made use of cocaine and marijuana smuggling outlets from South America.

The Outlaws have a record of involving their women associates in crime. Their general treatment of those women, who are typically regarded as gang property, borders on slavery. Women are used in drug transactions to insulate members from arrest and are put to work as masseuses, prostitutes, and topless dancers in bars controlled by the gang. Some women are said to have been sold from one member to another. Besides trafficking in illegal drugs, the Outlaws are known to be involved in extortion, armed robbery, rape, mail fraud, auto theft, and witness intimidation. Their reputation for violence is strong. The Outlaws have had at least some contact with the LCN families. Clarence Michael Smith, a member of the Tampa, Florida, chapter, was convicted of the murder of Robert Collins in New Orleans. Collins had testified against a nephew of Carlos Marcello, the LCN boss in New Orleans.

12.3.2.5 *Bandidos*

The Hell's Angels and the Outlaws were already well-established gangs when Donald Chambers organized the Bandidos, also known as "the Bandido Nation," in 1966 in Houston, Texas. The Bandidos are about a decade behind the Hell's Angels in their development but are quickly catching up. The mother chapter is in Corpus Christi, although the powerbase is believed to be in Rapid City, South Dakota. Its territories reach throughout the southwest, through the Rocky Mountain region, and into Washington State. It has strength in Louisiana, Arkansas, and Mississippi.

The Bandidos are involved in a wide variety of crimes. A former female associate said that the Outlaws in Florida began supplying cocaine to the Bandidos as early as 1978. Many have been arrested for offenses involving dynamite and explosives. Massage parlors and escort services are among their favorite business enterprises.

Since 1979, the Bandidos have undergone several changes in leadership. The founding president, Donald Chambers, was convicted of a double murder and began serving a life term in 1979. Ronald Hodge succeeded him but stepped down in 1982. Leadership then passed to Alvin Frakes, who died of cancer, and the presidency may have reverted to Hodge.

12.3.2.6 *Pagans*

The Pagans have no international connections. They are considered second only to the Hell's Angels in criminal sophistication, and the strength of their internal structure is unmatched by any of the other three major gangs. Its territory is mainly in the mid-Atlantic region. The original chapter was formed in Prince George's County, Maryland, in 1959. Since then, the mother chapter was moved to Marcus Hook, Pennsylvania, and then to its current location of Suffolk County, New York.

The Pagans' mother chapter is unique among outlaw gangs because it functions like a board of directors or a ruling council. Each member of the mother chapter is responsible for a certain geographic area and has authority over chapters in that area, a system similar to the La Cosa Nostra's National Commission.

12.3.2.7 *Sons of Silence*

The Sons of Silence has between 250 and 275 members in 30 chapters in 12 states. This club also has five chapters in Germany. This motorcycle gang is implicated in various criminal activities, for example, murder, assault, drug trafficking, intimidation, extortion, prostitution operations, money laundering, weapons trafficking, and theft of motorcycles and parts.

12.3.2.8 *Mongols*

The Mongols are extremely violent, posing an extremely criminal threat to the Pacific and southwestern regions of the United States. Mongols members transport and distribute cocaine, marijuana, and methamphetamine and frequently commit violent crimes to defend their territory and uphold its reputation. The Mongols have 70 chapters nationwide with most members in California. Many members are former street gang members with a long history of using violence to settle grievances. The Mongols have allied themselves with other motorcycle gangs and maintain ties to Hispanic street gangs in Los Angeles.

12.3.3 Street Gangs

Many gangs started up during the 1970s; however, some gangs began in the late 1950s and early 1960s. There are an estimated 1 million members in gangs today, and they are growing. Gang membership can range from around a dozen to thousands. There are estimated to be about 28,000 gangs in the United States. Most gangs are localized in particular neighborhoods; however, some gangs have developed into regional and national size. Gang members range from 16 to 24 years old. In recent years, members have been recruited as young as 12 years old. Most gangs were formed in the major cities, for example, Los Angeles, California; Chicago, Illinois; and New York City, New York. In the 1970s, gangs began to expand into neighboring communities. In the 1980s, gangs migrated into suburban areas. In the 1990s, gangs expanded into rural areas. Membership in gangs has increased because gangs are recruiting members from middle schools and high schools. The most vulnerable are children from single family homes. Also, high school dropouts are used to recruit new members and sell drugs. Street gangs are composed along the same racial and ethnic identities. Hispanics street gangs can be composed of individuals from many countries, but they all have Hispanic heritage. Asian street gangs can be composed of nationalities from Japan, Korea, China, or from Southeast Asia. Most gang violence takes place between different racial groups. The organizational structure for small street gangs consists of a leader with followers. The larger gangs will have a leader with one or more lieutenants. The larger gangs will have cells in which the cell leader will not know the leaders above him.

There are 16 regional and national street gangs. They are:

1. 18th Street (National). It was formed in the Rampart neighborhood of Los Angeles, California. Most of the gang members are Mexican migrants who migrated to Los Angeles in the late 1960s. Originally, these Mexican migrants were not allowed to join other native-born Mexican American gangs. The 18th Street gang grew by expanding its membership to other nationalities and races. It was the first multiracial, multiethnic gang in Los Angeles. It is a loosely associated sets or cliques that are lead by an influential member. Membership is estimated at 30,000 to 50,000. In California, this gang is made up mostly of illegal aliens from Mexico and Central America. This gang is active in 44 cities in 20 states. Its main source of income is street-level distribution of cocaine and marijuana. It also does some heroin and methamphetamine. Gang members also commit assaults, auto theft, carjacking, drive-by shootings, extortion, homicide, identification fraud, and robbery.
2. Almighty Latin King and Queen Nation (National). The Latin Kings were formed by predominantly Mexican and Puerto Rican males in the 1960s. It was originally formed for overcoming racial prejudice but evolved into a criminal enterprise. It was formed by two factions coming together, King Motherland of Chicago and Bloodline of New York. All members refer to themselves as Latin Kings. Latin Kings of the Motherland refer to themselves as Almighty Latin King Nation (ALKN), whose membership is estimated to be 20,000 to 35,000. They have more than 160 structured chapters operating in 158 cities and 31 states. The Latin Kings of the Bloodline also refer to themselves as Almighty Latin King and Queen Nation (ALKQN). Their membership is estimated to be 2200 to 7500. They operate in 15 cities in 5 states. The Bloodline was founded by Luis Felipe in the New York State prison system. The Bloodline chapters do not report to the Chicago

leadership hierarchy. The gang's primary source of income is street-level distribution of cocaine, heroin, and marijuana. The Latin Kings portray themselves as a community organization while still involved in assault, burglary, homicide, identity theft, and money laundering.

3. Asian Boyz (National). This is one of the largest Asian street gangs operating in 28 cities in 14 states. Members are primarily Vietnamese and Cambodian males. They are estimated to have 1300 to 2000 members in 28 cities and 14 states. They are involved in producing, transporting, and distributing methamphetamine and marijuana. They are also involved in assault, burglary, drive-by shootings, and homicide.

4. Black P. Stone Nation (National). This organization is one of the largest and most violent of street gangs. It has seven highly structured street gangs with single leadership and a common culture. It is composed of African American males from Chicago, Illinois. The main source of income is from street-level distribution of cocaine, heroin, marijuana, and some methamphetamine. Members are also involved in assault, auto theft, burglary, carjacking, drive-by shootings, extortion, homicide, and robbery.

5. Bloods (National). The Bloods is an association of structured and unstructured gangs who have developed into a single gang culture. The original Bloods were formed in the early 1970s to provide protection from the Crips street gang in Los Angeles, California. Bloods membership is estimated at 7000 to 35,000 members nationwide. Most members are African American males in 123 cities and 33 states. The main source of income is from transporting and distributing cocaine and marijuana. They are also involved in assault, auto theft, burglary, carjacking, drive-by shootings, extortion, homicide, identity theft, and robbery.

6. Crips (National). Crips are a collection of structured and unstructured gangs who have adopted a single gang culture. Bloods membership is estimated to be 30,000 to 35,000, operating in 221 cities in 41 states. The main source of income is street-level distribution of cocaine, marijuana, and PCP. They are also involved in assault, auto theft, burglary, and homicide.

7. Florencia 13 (Regional). Florencia 13 (F13 or FX13) originated in Los Angeles, California, in the early 1960s. Membership is estimated to be about 3000 members, who operate in California, Arkansas, Missouri, New Mexico, and Utah. Florencia 13 is subordinate to the Mexican Mafia prison gang and claims affiliation with Surenos. The primary source of income is trafficking in cocaine and methamphetamine, which is supplied by sources in Mexico. Gang members also produce large quantities of methamphetamine in southern California for distribution. They are also involved in assault, drive-by shootings, and homicide.

8. Fresno Bulldogs (Regional). This gang originated in Fresno, California, in the late 1960s. They are the largest Hispanic gang operating in central California with membership estimated at 5000 to 6000. Gang members associate with Nuestra Familia members, particularly when trafficking drugs. Street-level distribution of methamphetamine, marijuana, and heroin is the primary source of income. Members are also involved in assault, burglary, homicide, and robbery.

9. Gangster Disciples (National). This organization was formed in Chicago, Illinois, and is structured like a corporation. It is lead by the chairman of the board. Membership is estimated at 25,000 to 50,000; most members are African Americans

from the Chicago area. The gang is active in 110 cities in 31 states. Street-level distribution of cocaine, marijuana, and heroin is their main source of income. It is also involved in assault, auto theft, firearms violations, fraud, homicide, operating prostitution rings, and money laundering.

10. Latin Disciples (Regional). Latin Disciples, also known as Maniac Latin Disciples and Young Latino Organization, originated in Chicago, Illinois, in the late 1960s. It is made up of 10 structured and unstructured factions with membership estimates of 1500 to 2000. Most members are Puerto Rican males. The gang is most active in the Great Lakes and southwestern regions of the United States. Street-level distribution of cocaine, heroin, marijuana, and PCP is their main source of income. They are involved in assault, auto theft, carjacking, drive-by shootings, home invasion, homicide, money laundering, and weapons trafficking.

11. Mara Salvatrucha (National). Mara Salvatrucha, also known as MS-13, is one of the largest Hispanic street gangs in the United States. It is a loosely affiliated group known as cliques; however, law enforcement officials have seen an increased in coordination of criminal activity among the cliques in Atlanta, Georgia; Dallas, Texas; Los Angeles, California; Washington, D.C.; and New York City, New York. The gang is estimated at 30,000 to 50,000 members and associates worldwide with only 8000 to 10,000 residing in the United States. Members smuggle cocaine and marijuana into the United States and distribute it throughout the country. They are involved in assault, drive-by shootings, homicide, identity theft, prostitution operations, robbery, and weapons trafficking. They have cells in El Salvador and Mexico who maintain ties with drug trafficking organizations. MS-13 originated in Los Angeles in the 1980s. During the 1980s, many Salvadorans fled the civil war in their country. MS-13's early membership is reported to have former guerrillas and Salvadoran government soldiers whose combat experience contributed to the gang's notoriety as one of the more brutal and violent Hispanic gangs. MS-13 has a propensity for indiscriminate violence, intimidation, and coercion that transcends borders.

12. Surenos and Nortenos (National). These gangs were formed in the California Prison System. Gang members who were sentenced to prison formed their own gangs in prison based on their prior location. Those from northern California were known as Nortenos, meaning northerners. Those from southern California were known as Surenos, meaning southerners. The Nortenos came from agricultural areas and were considered weak, while the Sorenos came from cities in the south. The Nortenos were affiliated with the Nuestra Familia, while the Sorenos were affiliated with the Mexican Mafia. The Fresno Bulldogs remained independent of the Nortenos and Sorenos. The Sorenos main source of income comes from retail level distribution of cocaine, heroin, marijuana, and methamphetamine within the prison system and extortion of other drug distributors in the community. The Sorenos were involved in assault, carjacking, home invasion, homicide, and robbery. Some members had ties with the Mexican drug organizations and brokered deals for the Mexican Mafia and for themselves. The Nortenos income comes from retail level distribution of cocaine, heroin, marijuana, methamphetamine, and PCP and extortion of other drug distributors on the streets. They were also involved in assault, carjacking, home invasion, homicide, and robbery.

13. Tango Blast (Regional). Tango Blast is one of the largest prison/street gangs operating in Texas. This organization was formed in the late 1990s while members were

incarcerated in federal, state, and local prisons for protection against other prison gangs such as the Aryan Brotherhood, Texas Syndicate, and Mexican Mafia. Tango Blast originally had four city chapters: Houston, Texas; Dallas, Texas; Fort Worth, Texas; and Austin, Texas. They were also known as the Puro Tango Blast or the Four Horsemen. New chapters were established in El Paso, San Antonio, Corpus Christi, and the Rio Grande Valley. It is estimated that about 14,000 members have been incarcerated in Texas. Leaders are elected to represent the gang in prisons and to lead street gang cells.

14. Tiny Rascal Gangsters (National). The Tiny Rascal Gangsters is one of the largest and violent Asian street gangs in the United States. It is composed of at least 60 cells, referred to as sets. Members and associates are estimated to be 5000 to 10,000 members. They are active in the southwest, Pacific, and New England regions of the United States. The primary source of income is street-level distribution of cocaine, marijuana, and methamphetamine. They are also involved in assault, drive-by shootings, extortion, home invasion, homicide, robbery, and theft.

15. United Blood Nation (Regional). This organization is often confused with the Bloods; however, they are a different organization. United Blood Nation was started in 1993 at the George Mochen Detention Center as protection from the Latin Kings and Netas. United Blood Nation is a loose confederation of street gangs composed mostly of African Americans. Membership is estimated to be between 7000 and 15,000 along the U.S. eastern corridor. Income is derived from street-level distribution of cocaine, heroin, and marijuana. It is also involved in robbery, auto theft, arson, carjacking, credit card fraud, extortion, homicide, identity theft, intimidation, prostitution operations, and weapons distribution.

16. Vice Lord Nation (National). This organization is based in Chicago, Illinois. It has structured gangs in 74 cities in 28 states in the Great Lakes region. It is led by a national board. Membership is estimated to be between 30,000 and 35,000, and it is composed of African American males. Their income is from street-level distribution of cocaine, heroin, and marijuana. They are also engaged in assault, burglary, homicide, identity theft, and money laundering.

12.3.3.1 Criminal Activities

Street gangs are responsible for a significant portion of crime in communities. Gang members are responsible for as much as 80% of the crime in some areas. Violence is common between street gangs. The violence erupts mainly over control of drug territory. Gang members also engage in a host of other crimes. The most common are auto theft, assault, alien smuggling, burglary, drive-by shootings, extortion, firearms offenses, home invasion robberies, homicide, identity theft, insurance fraud, operating prostitution rings, and weapons trafficking. Local street gangs are usually involved in retail drug trafficking, while national and regional street gangs are involved in many criminal enterprises. Regional and national street gangs have established ties to drug trafficking organizations in Mexico, Central America, and Canada. Regional and national street gangs have cells in foreign countries who maintain ties to drug trafficking organizations and other criminal organizations. Mexican drug cartels use regional and national street gangs to sell drugs in the United States and to launder their proceeds back to Mexico. Mexican drug cartels use street gangs to support their activities by smuggling and by providing transportation and security. The

Mexican drug cartels also act as mediators between street gangs. Neighborhood street gangs account for most gang activity. However, national and regional gangs commit more organized crime activity and continue to expand their networks.

12.3.3.2 Finance

Street gangs earn their income from retail level drug sales. The proceeds are used to pay their living expenses, make consumer purchases, or purchase luxury goods. Regional and national street gangs launder their criminal proceeds through front companies and real estate investment. Street gangs use front companies such as clothing stores, hair salons, and music recording and production companies. Some gang members use mortgage fraud schemes or purchase real estate as investments. They commingle rental payments with drug proceeds. In Chicago, street gangs use straw purchasers and unscrupulous mortgage brokers and appraisers to purchase properties at minimal cost and sell them at a higher value to a third party. They also default on loans, which defrauds banks or mortgage companies. The networks used to smuggle drugs into the United States are also used to smuggle currency back to Mexico.

12.3.3.3 Female Involvement

Street gangs are composed mostly of males, but females also join gangs. In recent years, females are joining gangs at a much higher rate than males. Many street gangs use females as prostitutes. They are often used as couriers of drugs or money. Female gang members do not attract the attention of law enforcement like males do. They do not wear gang symbols such as tattoos and particular color clothing.

12.3.4 Prison Gangs

In the past 20 years, some groups in United States prisons have evolved into self-perpetuating criminal gangs. Several operate both in and out of prison and have taken one of the characteristics of true organized crime associations. Prison gangs engage in narcotics and weapons trafficking, extortion, robbery, and murder. Members released from prison remain in the gang, often providing support and enforcement for the organization inside.

The Department of Justice has identified 114 different gangs, not all of which are formally organized. A close examination of the 114 gangs yielded 5 that appear to meet the criteria of an organized crime group: the Mexican Mafia, La Nuestra Familia, the Aryan Brotherhood, the Black Guerrilla Family, and the Texas Syndicate. All five operate in more than one state. In all five, either murder or the drawing of blood is a prerequisite for membership.

12.3.4.1 Mexican Mafia

In 1957, members of the Mexican American youth gang were incarcerated at the Deuel Vocational Institute in Tracy, California. They banded together, at first for self-protection but soon began to control illicit activities such as homosexual prostitution, gambling, and narcotics. They called themselves the Mexican Mafia out of admiration for La Cosa Nostra. They are also known as La Eme (Spanish for the letter M). The group spread throughout California and into the federal prison system because of gang member transfers. The group recruited heavily from among the most dangerous and violent Mexican-American prisoners. A general and a few "godfathers" direct the activities of captains, lieutenants, and "soldados." Prospects must be sponsored for membership and must be approved by vote of other members. They are required to kill without question; this gives the gang a continuous pool of potential contract killers.

Since 1968, the Mexican Mafia has been in a constant feud with La Nuestra Familia, another Mexican American gang whose members are primarily from rural areas of central California. The feud began when La Nuestra Familia ("Our Family") attempted to take over heroin trafficking inside the California prison system. By 1972, 30 prisoners had died in prison as a result of the feud.

The Mexican Mafia's allies in the feud have been the white supremacist prison group, the Aryan Brotherhood, with whom they cooperate in prison contract killings, as well as in robberies and illicit drug transactions on the outside. The Mexican Mafia is most active in the Pacific and southwestern United States. Its power base is in California. The gang's income sources are from drug distribution both inside and outside the prison. Some members have direct links to Mexican drug trafficking organizations and broker deals for themselves and other criminal groups. They also control some gambling operations.

12.3.4.2 Mexikanemi
The Mexikanemi prison gang, also known as Texas Mexican Mafia or Emi, was formed in the 1980s within the Texas Department of Corrections. The gang is highly structured and is estimated to have about 2000 members, most of whom are Mexican nationals or Mexican American males who were living in Texas. Gang members operate mostly in Texas but are found in the southwestern states. They traffic in large quantities of drugs from Mexico into the United States. Most of their drugs are from the Jaime Herrera-Herrera organization, Osiel Cardenas-Guillen, and the Vicente Carrillo-Fuentes Mexican drug cartels. They also maintain a relationship with the Los Zeta, a Mexican paramilitary organization, who is employed by the Cardenas-Guillen drug cartel.

12.3.4.3 La Nuestra Familia
Originally formed in 1967 as a Latin cultural organization in Soledad prison, La Nuestra Familia began to sell protection to others that had been victimized by Mexican Mafia. Soon the group moved into the extortion rackets that their rivals had monopolized. In 1975, the gang began establishing "regiments" outside prison, using Fresno County, California, as a home base.

The gang's organizational structure consists of a single general with supreme power, captains, lieutenants, and soldados. Rank is usually achieved by the number of "hits" in which a member is involved.

La Nuestra Familia is allied closely with the Black Guerrilla Family.

12.3.4.4 Aryan Brotherhood
San Quentin prison in California was the origin of the group first known as "the Diamond Tooth Gang," now the Aryan Brotherhood, a white, Nazi-oriented gang dominated by members and associates of outlaw motorcycle gangs. The Aryan Brotherhood (sometimes known as the A-B's) has branches in prisons around the country but seems most active in state prisons in California, Arizona, Wisconsin, and Idaho, and throughout the federal prison system. It is primarily active in the Pacific and southwestern regions. Its main source of income is from drug trafficking both inside and outside the prison system. It is involved in murder for hire. It has links to the Mexican Mafia, but this link has weakened in recent years.

The Aryan Brotherhood's typical crimes include robberies and extortion of inmate's families outside prison, as well as offenses commonly associated within the walls: extortion, protection schemes, and crimes of intimidation and violence. A commission and a governing council rule the group; members advance in the ranks through acts of violence.

12.3.4.5 Black Guerrilla Family

George Jackson, a former member of the Black Panther party, founded the Black Guerrilla Family in San Quentin Prison in 1966. It is the most politically oriented of the five major prison gangs, and often follows a Maoist philosophy.

The goal of the gang is cultural unity and the protection of black prison inmates. Many members formerly belonged to the Black Liberation Army, the underground organization responsible for the October 1981 robbery of a Brinks armored truck, during which a guard and two New York police officers were killed. New recruits for the prison organization frequently have belonged to black street gangs. They join the prison gang to share its criminal profits, which has led to a split between a political faction and the moneymaking faction.

The gang's ruling structure consists of a single leader (known as a chairman or supreme commander), a central committee, and a very loose ranking of soldiers. The gang is organized along paramilitary lines. It has a national charter, code of ethics, and oath of allegiance. It operates mostly in California and Maryland. The gang has between 100 and 300 members who are African American males. Their primary source of income is from drug trafficking. They get most of their drugs from the Nuestra Familia or from local Mexican drug organizations. They are also involved in auto theft, burglary, drive-by shootings, and homicide.

12.3.4.6 The Texas Syndicate

A third major Mexican American prison gang is the Texas Syndicate. It was formed in California's Folsom prison in 1974. Its founders were all from Texas. They banded together for mutual protection and soon became known for their swift retaliation against any opposition. As gang members were released from California, they returned to their home state. Many were soon re-arrested and imprisoned in Texas. Today, the Texas Syndicate is the largest gang in that state's prison system.

The gang is active in drug trafficking, contract murders, assaults, and intimidation within the prison. Members take a life oath and are more secretive than most prison gangs. Under the leader is a chain of command similar to that of most prison gangs. The Texas Syndicate is known to be exceptionally violent, frequently assaulting or killing nonmembers and prison staff. They have no working relationship with other prison gangs.

12.3.5 Chinese Organized Crime

Secret Chinese criminal societies known as Triads were originally formed as resistance groups to the Ching Dynasty, which ruled China from the early 17th century until 1912. Triads flourished in Hong Kong and Taiwan through the 1950s and 1960s, controlling many important police posts in Hong Kong until the early 1970s.

Now members of Triads in Hong Kong and Taiwan are living in the United States. They have formed Triad-like crime groups in major American cities and are active in drug trafficking, illegal gambling, and loan sharking, among other sophisticated criminal offenses. They operate through youth gangs, under the direction of established Chinese businessmen and community leaders. They cooperate with LCN families and maintain close ties to criminal associates in Hong Kong, Taiwan, Thailand, and the People's Republic of China.

12.3.5.1 History and Background

With the end of the Chiang Dynasty, Dr. Sun Yat Sen, who had been a Triad member, called for the disbanding of the secret societies in 1912. Many nationalists heeded Sun's appeal; some moved into government posts. Criminal elements filled the vacated positions in the Triads.

While General Chiang Kai Shek, also a former Triad member, enlisted a number of the groups in his fight against communism, all Triads were politically oriented. Many took advantage of lawless conditions in China to expand their organized criminal activities, and some Triads made open agreements with Japanese occupational forces in order to continue their illegal enterprises.

Many Triad members fled China in 1949 after the collapse of the Nationalist government. A large group followed Chiang to Taiwan; others sought refuge in Hong Kong, reinforcing an already strong Triad presence in that British Colony. When Kuomingtang and nationalist armies retreated to Burma and Thailand, they established an important foothold in the Golden Triangle and began to supply the Hong Kong Triads with opium and heroin. That connection continues today. The drugs are now shipped out of Hong Kong to the United States, Canada, Australia, and northern Europe.

Triad members in Hong Kong developed extortion rackets, illegal gambling, drug trafficking, prostitution, loan sharking, and other criminal trades. Despite frequent and bloody territorial battles, they thrived almost unhindered after compromising and corrupting police and local officials. During an anticorruption drive in 1970, five former sergeants in the Hong Kong police, known as the "Five Dragons," fled the country, carrying as much as $1 million each. One of the associates of the Five Dragons was Eddie Chan, now a businessman in New York's Chinatown and a leader of the On Leong Tong there.

Triads based in Taiwan were allowed to continue operating on the condition that they support the anti-Communist stand of General Chiang and his exile government. Thus Taiwan based Triads and their affiliates in other countries are known as "right hand" groups, a political reference. They have been involved in political intelligence gathering and, at least once in this country, in the assassination of political opponents.

"Left Hand" Triads, many based in Hong Kong, maintain working relationships within the People's Republic of China. For example, the Kung Lok Triad, a Hong Kong group, has ties to officials of the People's Republic of China.

After more than 200 years of underground existence, the Triads developed an intricate secret structure, with arcane designations and ceremonies, many of which survive today. Various offices in the organization are identified by numbers, each beginning with the digit 4, which is a reference to the ancient Chinese belief that the world is surrounded by four seas. The leader of a Triad group is given number 489. Second-tier leaders, each with specific duties, are known by the number 432 and (messenger or liaison) and 438 (incense master or recruiter). Lower ranking officers are designated as 426 (organizer or enforcer) or 415 (an expert on administration and finance). Ordinary members are given the number 49. Initiation rituals include the beheading of a chicken (intimating the fate of a member who betrays the group), the mingling of blood by members and initiates, and the recitation of 36 loyal oaths. The Los Angeles Police Department found a Code of Ethics during one of their investigations. This Code of Ethics was translated to read as follows:

Member's Code of Ethics

1. Harmony with the people is the first priority. We have to establish good social and personal connections so as not to create enemies.
2. We have to seek special favors and help form uncommitted gang members by emphasizing our relationships with outside people.
3. Gambling is our main financial source.
4. Do not take it upon yourself to start things and make decisions you are not authorized to make.
5. Everyone has their assigned responsibility. Do not create confusion.
6. We must not divulge our plans and affairs to outsiders (e.g., wives, girlfriends).
7. We have to be united with all our brothers and obey elder brother's orders.
8. All money earned outside the group must be turned over to the group. You must not keep any of it for yourself.
9. When targeting wealthy prospects do not act hastily. Furthermore, do not harass or threaten them.
10. If anything unexpected happens, do not abandon your brothers. If arrested, shoulder all responsibility and blame. Do not involve your brothers.

12.3.5.2 Triad Groups and Tongs

As early as the nineteenth century, Chinese immigrants in America had formed benevolent associations known as "Tongs," a term that loosely means "meeting hall." Today many Tongs are national organizations with chapters in cities that have large Chinese communities. Tongs function as business associations, ethnic societies, and centers of local politics.

However, there is a sinister aspect of many Tongs. Several of the largest and most respected are used as fronts for vicious Chinese organized crime groups that prey mainly on Chinese immigrants and Chinese Americans. Tong members direct gang enterprises that include extortion, illegal gambling, narcotics trafficking, robbery, and protection schemes for prostitution and pornography. Among the prominent Tongs associated with Chinese organized crime are the On Leong Tong, headquartered in New York; the Hip Sing, also New York based; and the Hop Sing, with headquarters and operations on the west coast.

The Tong members who supervise Chinese criminal groups frequently are Triad members with Triad designations. The 426 is the street level leader of the gang. Gang members are Chinese males in their late teens and twenties. They are often chosen specifically for their youth and malleability and on the further assumption that the justice system is lenient with young offenders whose criminal records, in this country, are negligible or nonexistent.

A secret commission witness identified as 426, designating his position as captain and enforcer in a Chinese crime gang in the United States, described in a deposition how, as a teenager, he had been inducted into a Triad group while in Hong Kong. He told how he left Hong Kong to avoid prosecution and came to North America where he eventually joined a Triad chapter. Later, he was active in a New York group that included Triad members among its leadership. The gang functioned as a criminal arm of a major national Tong and was involved in narcotics, extortion, and murder, often drawing on its ties with a Triad group in Hong Kong. He described international collaboration between branches of Triad groups on such matters as intimidation of witnesses, assassinations, and the importation of heroin from sources in the Golden Triangle, sometimes through mainland China.

12.3.5.3 *Chinese Crime Groups in New York*

Chan Tse-Chiu, also known as Eddie Chan, is president of the On Leong Tong in New York. He has been president of the national organization, which has chapters throughout the United States. Currently, he is its honorary national president. Chan is also a former Hong Kong police sergeant, who served in the post during the era of the Five Dragons. According to several sources, he is also the supervisor of a street gang known as the Ghost Shadows, a national crime group with chapters in several cities and with intimate ties to the On Leong Tong.

In New York and elsewhere, the Ghost Shadows engage in narcotics trafficking, loan sharking, illegal gambling, and extortion rackets. At one time the gang was led by Nicky Louie, whose influence in the group was such that he attempted to wrest control from Eddie Chan. Loyalists from Ghost Shadow groups in Boston, Massachusetts, and Chicago, Illinois, sided with the Louie faction in the gang war that resulted when Chan ordered the murder of his rival. Eventually, Louie and his coterie fled to Chicago. Eight assassins from the Chan faction of the New York Ghost Shadows were dispatched to Chicago. A car they used was eventually traced back to the rental account of On Leong Tong officials in Chicago. Louie was critically wounded in an ambush at On Leon headquarters in Chicago. He survived, but his driver was killed.

As part of a negotiated settlement, Nicky Louie was allowed to retire. Eddie Chan and the On Leong Tong retained control of the Ghost Shadows and their criminal enterprises.

The other major association in New York's Chinatown is the Hip Sing Tong, located on Pell Street. Its leader is 75-year-old Feilo Chat, known as Benny Ong, "Uncle Seven," or "Uncle Benny." Ong is an immigrant and gang member who served 17 years for a homicide and was released in 1952. He was among the most visible members of the Chinese community in New York with significant business holdings throughout Manhattan.

The criminal arm of the Hip Sing Tong is the Flying Dragons, whose activities include extortion, illegal gambling, and narcotics trafficking. A truce with the On Leong Tong in the 1960s secured Hip Sing's hold on Pell Street and the nearby area.

Another Chinese gang is the Fuk Ching. They are regarded as one of the most powerful and have transnational operations. They are extensively involved in human smuggling and kidnapping. They have dominance in the Fujian Province. This is where they get their source of migrants to smuggle to the United States and Canada. It is this human smuggling that has caught law enforcement attention on both the east and west coast of the United States and Canada. Ships with loads of illegal immigrants have been seized in recent years.

Most Chinese business owners comply with gang extortion demands because compliance is easier and less risky than resistance. Gang affiliation with a Tong gives them a degree of acceptability in the neighborhoods. Chinese who live in the neighborhoods are fully aware of the gangs. Chinese businessmen would prefer tougher gang punishment, the reinstitution of the death penalty, and the deportation of chronic Chinese criminals. They want more Chinese police officers in the neighborhoods. Chinese gangs are not involved in political terrorism either abroad or at home. In the United States, they have not been able to corrupt police or judges.

12.3.5.4 Violence Among Chinese Crime Groups

In New York, rivalries among newer groups have resulted in three massacres of associations in the early 1980s. On December 23, 1983, members of the White Tiger's group were ambushed at a bar. Eleven people, most of them White Tiger's recruits, were killed or wounded. On September 4, 1977, at the Golden Dragon restaurant in San Francisco's Chinatown, five innocent people were murdered. The restaurant was a favorite of the gang, known as the Hop Sing Boys. They killed five people and seriously wounded 11 others. None of the victims were gang members, because the Wah Ching and the Hop Sing Boys had fled when they noticed the gunmen approaching.

In addition to New York, Chicago, and San Francisco, Chinese organized crime groups have a strong presence in Monterey Park, California; Boston, Massachusetts; and many other U.S. cities.

12.3.5.5 The Hong Kong Summit

During the early 1980s, the principal leaders of Chinese organized crime in North America, or their representatives, met in Hong Kong to discuss a possible détente between major rival groups. Those in attendance included Kis Jai (Peter Chin), leader of the New York Ghost Shadows under Eddie Chan; Vincent Jew, west coast leader of the Wah Ching; Danny Mo (Danny Mo Sui Chen), the operational leader of the Kung Lok Triad in Canada; and Stephen Tse, leader of the Ping On gang from Boston, who is also believed to be a former associate of the 14K Triad in Hong Kong.

The meeting resulted in recognition of territories and an agreement to assist one another when necessary. The participants "burned the yellow paper," a ritual that symbolizes brotherhood and the start of a new venture. Later, the principals formed a joint venture, the Oriental Arts Promotion Company, by which they have attempted to monopolize the U.S. bookings of Chinese-speaking entertainers from Hong Kong and Taiwan.

In 1998, a federal grand jury charged 21 gang members for drug trafficking and money laundering after a 13-month investigation called Operation Hardtac. Arrests were made in New York; Philadelphia, Pennsylvania; Atlanta, Georgia; and Hong Kong. The Chinese gang was controlled by Weng Keek Hoo. He was previously deported to Hong Kong. The Chinese gang imported heroin from Southeast Asia to Vancouver, Canada. The drugs went to Toronto, Canada, before being smuggled into the United States.

12.3.5.6 Canada: The Kung Lok Triad

The international scope of the Chinese crime gangs is evident in the Canadian chapter of the Hong Kong based Triad, Kung Lok. This group undertakes the standard range of crimes against Chinese Canadians and is considered active in Toronto, Montreal, Ottawa, Vancouver, Hamilton, and other metropolitan areas. The Kung Lok is a more traditional Triad establishment. Its members in Canada undergo the same ritual initiation as those in Hong Kong.

There is constant traffic of Kung Lok members among Canada, the United States, and various Caribbean locations, particularly Santo Domingo. In the early 1980s, Kung Lok established an illegal gambling house on Division Street in New York through agreement with the Hip Song and the On Leong. Lau Wing Kui, deported leader of Kung Lok in Canada, owns an interest in at least one casino in Santo Domingo and has interests in several other Hong Kong gambling establishments. It is believed that the Kung Lok members carry large sums of cash out of Canada to be laundered at the Santo Domingo casino before the money is brought to the United States. Kung Lok has members in the United Kingdom and Europe who act on orders of the Hong Kong leadership, giving them a worldwide capability to intimidate witnesses, directly or through threats against the witness's family in any area where Kung Lok members operate.

12.3.6   Vietnamese Gangs

In the first 8 years after the communist victory in Vietnam, about 650,000 Indochinese immigrated to the United States. Among them were criminals with backgrounds in drug trafficking, extortion, and prostitution. Many criminals assumed the identities of deceased Vietnamese who had no arrest records.

Small bands of these criminal refugees formed in resettlement camps. Later, they formed gangs in Vietnamese communities around the United States. There are seven cities in California with active Vietnamese gangs, four gangs in Texas, three in Louisiana, two in Alabama, and one in each of the following states: Washington, Colorado, Florida, Massachusetts, New York, Pennsylvania, Oregon, Virginia, and Hawaii.

In some cases, the groups are little more than street gangs. Others conduct sophisticated criminal schemes, extortion, gambling, and drug trafficking that require organization and discipline. Police report that there is at least informal communication between gangs. Also, they are extremely mobile. There is evidence of networking among gangs, for example, Vietnamese fugitives in California finding sanctuary in New Orleans. Vietnamese gangs are known to cooperate with other Asian crime groups.

Generally, Vietnamese gangs confine themselves to communities of other Vietnamese who are particularly susceptible to extortion. The immigrant victims are reluctant to testify because they do not believe police will protect them from retribution.

12.3.7   Japanese Organized Crime

With membership as high as 110,000 in as many as 2500 associated gangs, the Japanese Yakuza may be the largest organized criminal group in the world. The Yakuza originated in 16th and 17th century Japan, where feudal lords maintained stables of Samurai warriors. Stronger national government in Japan subsequently made many regional warriors superfluous, and they allied themselves both with the ruling Shogunate and with dissident villages. Eventually, the vagabond warriors became known as "Yakuza," a gambling term for numbers that are worthless or losers, 8 9 3. The name evolved into an expression for "outlaw," with a connotation of respect based on fear. Through the next three centuries, the status of the Yakuza fluctuated, depending on the strength of the national government.

Immediately after World War II, immense social and economic changes in Japan meant opportunity for organized crime, particularly in black markets. The Yakuza prospered, adding pornography, narcotics, and systematic racketeering to their illicit enterprises, while expanding into entertainment, sports, labor unions, and corporate affairs. Their enforcement tactics became brutal; police and media in Japan referred to Yakuza as "Boryokudan," or "violent gang." Many street gangs associated with the Yakuza began to mimic American outlaw motorcycle gangs. Others imitated the dress and style of Prohibition-era gangsters, as interpreted by U.S. moviemakers.

Japanese police designate seven major groups of Yakuza. The largest is "Yamaguchi Gumi," with an estimated membership of 10,000, which has a hierarchical structure resembling that of the LCN family in this country. There is a single "Kaicho" (chairman), who has advisors without command authority. "Wakato" control several deputies, and beneath them are lieutenants who manage numerous soldiers or "wakai shu."

The other six major groups, with more elaborate structures, are confederations of smaller gangs that have combined to increase their power. These alliances control criminal activities in assigned territories. The most powerful and the most important rival of Yamaguchi Gumi is the alliance known as "Sumiyoshi Rengo," with an estimated strength of 8000 to 15,000 members.

Whatever the internal arrangement of the organization, a Yakuza member's status is determined by his efficiency as an earner, who passes profits to his higher ups. The more elevated his position, the more money he receives from below, although his obligations remain to those still above him. It is a highly competitive system calculated to maintain pressures for production; Yakuza members, particularly those in the lower echelons, are encouraged to find new enterprises with which to satisfy the constant demand from above. Loyalty to superiors is considered paramount. A Yakuza member who has angered his supervisor may apologize by amputating a finger or finger joint from his own hand, then presenting it to the offended party as a gesture of sincerity.

The Yakuza groups are active in drug trafficking, primarily smuggling amphetamines, from the United States into Japan. They also supply a lucrative Japanese market for firearms, which are strictly regulated in that nation. A handgun that sells for $100 to $200 here may be worth $1000 in Japan, and a single round of ammunition might sell for $12 to $15.

Yakuza enforcers are sometimes used by the boards of large corporations in Japan to keep order at open stockholder meetings, a practice known as "sokaiya." Strong-arm gang members discourage potentially embarrassing questions by stockholders. Also, the reverse occurs when a minority faction, perhaps affiliated with Yakuza interests, wishes to intimidate the board or majority. Physical violence is not uncommon.

12.3.7.1 *Yakuza in the United States*

The Yakuza, meaning the number 8 9 3, has been mainly involved in obtaining contraband for shipment to Japan. However, recent intelligence has shown that they are involved with factions of the LCN in east coast gambling operations catering to wealthy Japanese businessmen. On the west coast, they are involved in illegal gambling and prostitution. For at least 20 years, the Yakuza members have invested illegally earned profits in U.S. businesses. Recently, Yakuza interests have increased in legitimate businesses, massage parlors, and pornography. Three Yakuza groups, the Yamaguchi Gumi, Sumiyoshi Rengo, and Toa Taui Jigyo Kumiai, are currently active in southern California. In recent years, the Yakuza has bought shares of major corporations and has started the function of sokaiya, corporate intimidation. Also, the Yakuza has infiltrated legitimate businesses. In so doing, they have employed business practices that American companies cannot do because of fear of being prosecuted for anti-trust violations or illegal business practices. However, the Yakuza have been getting away with this because prosecutors have not developed their case to the extent necessary to obtain a conviction.

12.3.7.2 *Asian Characteristics*

Asians, citizens and criminals, have some common characteristics that a fraud examiner should be aware of as follows:

Authority. Asians do not view law enforcement as servants of the community. In Asia, law enforcement was set up to protect rulers and their parties and not protect and serve the community. Asian citizens are reluctant to report crimes when they become victims. This is due to no belief in or understanding of the criminal justice system as well as fear of retaliation by the criminals. Many Asians feel that the American justice system does not impose punishment to fit the crime.

Asset hiding. Asians have created their own underground currency by trading in commodities. They invest their cash into gold and precious stones, particularly diamonds, rubies, and jade. They prefer to keep their valuables in their homes or businesses rather than use banking services. They invest heavily into "taels" because they can be easily hid and exchanged. (A tael is a standard Chinese measurement that measures 3¾ by 1½ inches and weighs one troy ounce. It is 24 carat, and gold prices determine its market value.) Asian immigrants will invest in taels until they have enough to acquire their own business. Asians will launder their illegal profits by investing in legitimate businesses. This underground currency helps them avoid paper trails and evade taxes. Asian immigrants will work "under the table" and even collect public subsistence while accumulating their wealth.

Credit unions. Asians have organized together to form an informal "credit union." These self-help programs consist of 10 to 20 people who are mostly women. They are organized for definite periods and have regularly scheduled meetings. Members are required to invest specific amounts of money at each meeting. When cash holdings are ample, members bid for the cash. The highest bidder receives the funds. The bidder must repay the loan back with interest over a specific time. This allows the funds to be available to another member. These informal credit unions have no official recognition and usually involve large amounts of cash. They can also lend themselves to the organizer to rig bids or abscond with the cash. Asian credit unions are known by the following names:

Hui	Vietnamese
Gae	Korean
Cho Wui	Chinese
Tana-Moshi	Japanese

Corruption. Most Asians believe that all government officials have a price. "Payoffs" in Asian countries are very common. It is a way of life and is considered to be an additional tax by Asian businessmen. Payments begin small and build up from there. It starts out as free lunches and builds up to cash payments out of the cash register. Any government official who accepts any gifts will soon learn that the Asian businessman has announced in the community that he has a "friend downtown" who can cut through "red tape" or can provide protection.

Warning: Government officials should never accept any gifts or gratuities from any Asians, not even a cup of coffee or tea.

12.3.7.3 *Asian Crime Trends*

There are some obvious trends with Asian criminal enterprises. First, they cooperate with other ethnic and racial heritage lines. It is known that they cooperate with various families of the LCN in New York, Chicago, and Philadelphia. They are becoming more structured in a hierarchical fashion so they can be competitive. There operations have become more globalized. They are engaging in more white-collar crimes and are comingling their illegal activities with legitimate business ventures. They are becoming more mobile and can adapt easily to change. Many Asians are becoming multilingual and have financial capabilities. In some cases, they have commercialized their criminal activities by being viewed as business firms of various sizes, from small operations to large corporations.

12.3.8   Cuban Organized Crime

Since 1959, more than 1 million Cuban refugees have arrived in the United States. Most have come seeking political freedom and the opportunity to build productive lives. However, from the first wave of refugees in 1959 to the latest, a criminal minority of Cubans has found ground for illegal enterprises that are as ambitious and sophisticated as any before seen in this country.

There have been three periods of mass Cuban immigration to the United States: first, immediately before and after the fall of the Batista regime until Fidel Castro halted emigration in 1959; second, between 1965 and 1972 during the Camarioca boatlift "freedom flotilla," prompting the Family Reunification Program under which more than 250,000 Cubans migrated to the United States; and third, between April 21 and November 10, 1980, during a boatlift from Mariel Harbor, bringing nearly 125,000 new Cuban refugees to the United States. By far the greatest concentration of criminals was in the Mariel Harbor exodus, with nearly 2% of those arriving in the United States having been classified as prostitutes, criminals, drug addicts, or vagrants. Because of this minority, the term "Marielito" has come to imply a criminal or undesirable; it refers specifically to the career criminals who left Cuba during the 1980 boatlift.

There are differences between the criminals who immigrated in the first two waves and those who came in the 1980 Mariel boatlift. Criminal syndicates founded by the earlier arrivals tend to be more extensive, more highly structured, and more closely associated with other criminal groups, especially the La Cosa Nostra, than those of the Marielitos. While the established groups have partly built their criminal fortunes on less violent crimes, mainly on forms of gambling, the newcomers have shown a propensity for killings, kidnapping, and street crime. The differences may partly be attributed to the fact that for more than 20 years, while early arrivals were busy establishing themselves, the later arrivals were in primitive prisons and hospitals and in a brutal underworld subculture. There is evidence that the established Cuban syndicates have begun using Marielitos in their criminal enterprises, so these distinctions may soon become less clear. Nevertheless, the present differences between them are great enough so that the two groups are treated separately in this chapter.

There are two established groups in the United States known as the La Compania and the Corporation. The La Compania is involved in drug trafficking and gambling. Illegal gambling, particularly bolita or policy lotteries, are widely accepted by Cubans. While La Cosa Nostra controls most lotteries and bookmaking in Cuban communities, many of those operations have come under the control of the Cuban groups.

The most prominent emerging Cuban gambling cartel is The Corporation, headed by Jose Miguel Battle. This group's annual profit was estimated to be between $45 and $100 million in 1984. Battle, known as Jose Miguel Vargas, Miguel Blasquez, Rafael Franco Tesona, "Don Miguel," and "El Gordon" was a soldier in Batista's army and a Havana policeman until the fall of the Batista regime. After Cuba collapsed, Battle fled to Miami and joined the Brigade 2506, the Bay of Pigs landing group. After the failed invasion, Battle returned to Miami and found the first Cuban-controlled gambling organization. The group grew through police and political corruption.

In the late 1960s, Battle moved his operations to New York City, Union City with the help of Joseph Zicarelli and Santo Trafficante. He began to take over existing operations there by violent means.

By the early 1970s, Battle's group collected bets from most of the Hispanic bodegas and bars in New York and New Jersey. Zicarelli and James Napoli, soldiers of the Genovese crime family, help negotiate a settlement where Battle agreed to pay a percentage of his earnings to the La Cosa Nostra and lay off some of his betting action. The Corporation's records shows that the group grosses in excess of $2 million on a weekly basis. Battle and the Corporation have amassed assets valued at several hundred million dollars. The Corporation owns or controls Union Management and Mortgage Company, the Union Finance Company, the Union Financial Research Company, Inc., Union Travel and Tours, and El Zapotal Realty, Inc., all of which are in south Florida.

During the 1970s, Battle was convicted on RICO gambling charges. He fled to Madrid, Spain after receiving an 18-month sentence. He served 13 months after he was arrested trying to reenter the United States by way of Costa Rica. Battle received prison sentences totaling 34 years for a concealed weapon charge and murder of a former associate, Ernest Torres.

In 1982, Battle and several key associates, including Abraham Rydz, moved to Florida. Battle, his wife, son, and Rydz bought various real estate properties totaling $1,115,000 on which they paid $805,000 in cash. On April 8, 1983, New York Port Authority Police found $439,000 cash in luggage belonging to Rydz and Battle's son, Jose Battle Jr., after the two men resisted search of their carry-on baggage while boarding a flight to Miami. On December 3, 1984, British Customs authorities at Heathrow Airport in London detained several associates of the Corporation, including Humberto Davila Torres, whose itinerary included stops in the Bahamas, Switzerland, and Spain, with a return to Miami; among them they possessed $450,000 in U.S. currency. In all, cash seizures from members of the groups have totaled about $43 million.

The enormous cash flow is laundered through a complex web of influence in mortgage and lending companies. The Capitol National Bank in Manhattan received huge deposits of the Corporation's gambling receipts. The bank was also the largest redeemer of food stamps from the north New Jersey bars.

A task force in June 1985 arrested 16 people, including 11 present or former Puerto Rican bank officials. Operation Greenback, Puerto Rico uncovered a scheme by members of the Corporation to launder hidden income by the purchase of winning tickets in the legal Puerto Rican lottery. Members of the Corporation would privately buy the winning ticket from the owner, paying a premium price in "dirty" cash from the gambling operation. A $125,000 ticket, for example, would be bought for $150,000. The money then would be deposited without being traced to the source.

The La Compania was formed in the early 1960s. Its primary purpose was to import cocaine, heroin, and marijuana. The group is estimated to have about 125 members with a connecting group in Los Angeles. The La Compania has branches in New York, Las Vegas, Texas, Arizona, New Jersey, and Tijuana, Mexico. After more than 20 years, the Cuban group has produced large amounts of capital that is invested in businesses, real estate, and banks.

12.3.9 Marielito Crime Gangs

The Mariel boatlift had its genesis on April 1, 1980, when a small band of Cubans in a city bus attempted to gain political asylum by crashing the gates of the Peruvian Embassy. One Cuban guard at the gate accidentally killed another guard while trying to stop the bus. Fidel Castro was enraged and publicly announced the removal of all guards from the gates. Within days, more than 10,000 people had crowded into the embassy grounds, requesting political asylum. Eventually, Castro allowed them to be flown out of the country. This group and the majority of those who followed later included primarily decent and working class people who genuinely sought liberty. Castro proclaimed the refugees to be the scum of Cuban society. When the exodus continued, he tried to prove his description by forcibly including convicts, hard core criminals, prostitutes, and the mentally ill among those who left by boat from Mariel.

The career criminals who came to the United States during the Mariel boatlift are commonly known as "Marielitos." Some have formed crime gangs, including large drug trafficking rings and some formally organized groups with operations in several different cities. They have cooperated with longer-established Cuban crime groups as collectors and enforcers in drug or gambling operations. Gangs of Marielitos have assisted Colombian drug smuggling organizations, and at least once, the LCN family has used a Marielito as a hired killer.

There has been an unprecedented wave of violent crime among Cubans since their arrival in this country. Increased homicide rates in several locales are directly attributable to Mariel criminals. Homicide rates in Hialeah, Florida increased from 12 to 43 from 1980 to 1981; most of these incidents involved Marielitos.

Marielitos are involved in robbery, burglary, rape, counterfeiting, bookmaking, auto theft, shoplifting, extortion, and prostitution but are mostly involved in cocaine trafficking along with murders.

The profile of the Mariel career criminal is specific and unique. He is generally male, in his thirties, poorly educated, superstitious, with a good physique and poor personal hygiene. Many are former military conscripts who have seen service in Angola or Central America; thus, there is a good chance that the Marielito is familiar with automatic weapons and knowledgeable in guerrilla warfare. Commonly, the Marielito's body is marked with scars, which he often reveres as emblems of battle. Some are self-inflicted or the result of religious rituals.

More than 90% of the convicted Mariel refugees had a tattoo somewhere on their bodies. In Cuban society, tattoos are a sign of disgrace. Mariel tattoos are often intricate, displaying patron saints, names, words, or arcane symbols. A display of five dots on the web of the hand, between the thumb and forefinger, identifies a pickpocket or delinquent.

The Marielitos are members of Afro Cuban religious cults, which explains the aberrant behavior. The cult is called "Santeria," which is imbued with qualities of Christian saints and various African deities. Its antithesis is the practice of Palo Mayombe. Criminals honor the god of hunting, Ochosi, who is believed to guarantee freedom from incarceration, which leads them to take risks or perform acts they would normally avoid.

Another Afro Cuban sect is the Abaqua cult with origins in Cuban prisons. It is considered as much a fraternal order as a religious society. Members wear an arrow-shaped tattoo in the web of the hand.

In 5 years, the Marielitos formed two large gangs. The Abaqua Cult and the Mariel Bandidos are both located in the Washington, D.C. area and have memberships as high as 500 to 1000. Other groups are located in Las Vegas, New York, and Los Angeles. Intermediate size groups have appeared in other states, primarily dealing in illicit narcotics. They form small, loosely structured, highly mobile gangs that disband after the criminal task has been completed. Its members then drift to other cities. Investigation has been difficult because the gangs are so fluid and difficult to identify. The new gangs have earned a share in drug trafficking. They are crude in their approach, but established crime groups may supply the necessary sophistication.

12.3.10   Colombian Drug Cartels

About 75% of the cocaine consumed in the United States comes from Colombia. There are at least 20 Colombian drug rings. These rings are centered on two major cities, Medellin and Cali. Most of the drug rings are centered on Medellin, which is the second largest city in Colombia. Their members and workers handle every phase of production from manufacture, distribution, finance, and security. Each function is separate from the other; thus the loss of one member or group does not threaten the entire group. The rings can quickly adapt to outside pressure while continuing to pursue the goal of maximum production for maximum profit. The ring's influence is broad. They use foreign banks and tax havens in the Caribbean and Europe. Colombian traffickers are ruthless in pursuit of profit and use violence to protect their enterprises. The cocaine trade in South America is in a state of flux. The Medellin cartel has been hit hard by aggressive enforcement and interdiction strategy and is in a state of disarray and confusion. Some smaller traffickers have collapsed or moved their operations to neighboring countries. Concentration of resources by the Colombian government on the Medellin cartel, however, has allowed other groups to consolidate and to grab a larger share of the market. It is estimated that the Cali cartel has taken over 70% to 80% of the Medellin cartel's business. The Colombian government has indicted many bankers and lawyers in recent years for money laundering cartel profits. The best known case is Banco de Occident, which is based in the western city of Cali, where the bank was indicted for laundering millions for the late drug kingpin Gonzalo Rodriguez Gacha. The U.S. Drug Enforcement Agency (DEA) found Gacha's bank records in an oil drum. Fabio Ochoa and his sons have been indicted in the United States. Ochoa, after the Colombian government indictments, built his own jail. He stayed in the jail for awhile then escaped. Later, he was cornered by the Colombian police and was killed. Ochoa was considered to be one of the wealthiest men in the world. He lived a very lavish lifestyle. The Colombian government found that Ochoa has his own army of mercenaries, who were trained by former Israeli military. Prior to the Colombian government crackdown with the United States aid, the drug lords in Medellin controlled most of the countryside. It is believed that the communist rebels in the country tried to blackmail the drug lords by kidnapping family members. This backfired on them. The drug lords had more wealth and firepower. This later resulted in the communist rebels and the drug lords forming an alliance. The Colombian drug lords have expanded their operations to other surrounding countries. They have established sophisticated communication and transportation networks from South America to the United States and Europe.

The Colombian police with cooperation of U.S. authorities have arrested or killed top level Medellin drug lords. With the demise of the Medellin drug lords, the Cali cartels have taken over some of the Medellin operations. The top man in the Cali cartel is Gilberto Rodriguez Orejuela, nicknamed "The chess player." In the DEA investigation, Operation Green Ice, the Cali drug cartels were involved with the Sicilian Mafia. The Italian National Police found the Cali drug cartels were shipping cocaine to Sicilian Mafia for distribution through Italy and Europe. Seven top ranking financial managers for the Cali cartel were lured to the United States, Costa Rica, and Italy where they were arrested. The Colombian National Police raided the financial offices of the leader of the Cali cartel, Gilberto Rodriguez Orejuela.

12.3.11 Mexican Drug Cartels

The Mexicans saw the rise of the Colombian drug cartels and the money they were generating from drug trafficking. They wanted a piece of the action as well. They started getting into drug trafficking in the 1970s. At first, they were smuggling the drugs to the United States for the Colombians. In the late 1980s, the Mexican transporters were given 35% to 50% of each cocaine shipment. Eventually, they began to raise marijuana, cocaine, and heroin and transport it to the United States. This has led to the organizations becoming involved in both the manufacture and distribution. Mexico is currently the number one supplier of marijuana to the United States. Currently, it is estimated that 70% of the illegal drugs comes from or through Mexico. The organizations that control drug production and shipment and related money laundering and criminal activities are powerful. The drug organizations are well organized and possess substantial financial resources. They have corrupted police, the military, lawyers, and judges in Mexico.

Like Sicily, the Mexican government has been under siege by drug trafficking organizations. They have murdered law enforcement officials, lawyers, politicians, and innocent citizens. Most drug violence is centered on retaliatory killings of individual drug traffickers. They are known for kidnapping victims and later murdering them. Their remains are dumped along roadsides or isolated desert areas. Mexican drug traffickers are known for heinous acts of torture, including severe beatings, burnings, and severing body parts. Most of the violence has centered in the states of Baja, California, Nuevo Leon, Tamaulipas, and Sinaloa. This is due to production in the area as well as being a transportation corridor by rival groups through the area. The Mexican press reported 249 violent deaths in Tijuana, Baja California in 2002. Since then, the violent deaths have increased into the thousands. President Calderon sent 5000 Mexican Army troops to Ciudad Juarez in early 2009 after a battle between Tijuana and Sinaloa cartels in Tijuana killed 17 people. A grenade attack occurred in Morelia, killing eight civilians and injuring more than 100 in September 2008. Since then, President Calderon has increased the Army presence to 45,000 troops. This increase in Mexican troops has fostered a war between the Mexican government and the drug cartels. With the decline of the Colombian cartels, the Mexican cartels have become more powerful. The DEA reports the Mexican drug cartels are more sophisticated and dangerous than any organized criminal group in the United States. This is primarily due to the cartels use of grenade launders, automatic weapons, body armor, and sometimes Kevlar helmets. The Mexican cartels are using multiple youth gangs for retail sales, while they limit their activities to production and distribution. The Mexican cartels work with multiple gangs and claim not to take sides in gang conflicts. In some cases, they get gangs to cooperate with each other.

The Mexican drug cartels are also involved in the smuggling of arms into Mexico from the United States, Guatemala, and by sea. Most of the high-powered weapons come from

Central America and Asia. These weapons were acquired from leftover supplies from wars in Central America and Asia. Some weapons came from the United States, either by use of straw buyers or thief's from U.S. military bases. It is estimated that only about 17% of the weapons come from the United States, according to federal law enforcement. However, the media believes about 90% of the weapons comes from the United States. The Mexican authorities found only 32% of the weapons had serial numbers. Serial numbers are only required in the United States. This means the other 68% of the weapons seized by Mexican authorities had come from somewhere other than the United States.

The Mexican cartels are also involved in kidnappings. Mexico City has become the kidnapping capital of the world. The second largest city for kidnappings is Phoenix, Arizona. Most of the kidnappings in the United States involve drugs. Kidnappings in Mexico City involve both drugs and ransom. Wealthy people have become the target for kidnappings in Mexico City, but the other cities in Mexico are not immune.

The most prominent Mexican drug trafficking organizations are:

1. *Arellano-Felix Organization.* This is one of the most powerful drug trafficking organizations in Mexico. It operates mostly in Tijuana and between San Diego and Los Angeles, California. This cartel is known as the Tijuana cartel. Its enforcer, Ramon Arellano-Felix, died on February 10, 2002. The chief of operations, Benjamin Arellano-Felix, was arrested on March 9, 2002, and sentenced to 22 years in prison. In August 2006, Francisco Javier Arellano Felix was captured in the Sea of Cortes by U.S. authorities. He pleaded guilty to running a criminal enterprise and was sentenced to life imprisonment without the possibility of parole. Another brother, Francisco Rafael Arellano Felix, was extradited to the United States in 2006. He subsequently pleaded guilty to distribution of cocaine. He was sentenced to 6 years in federal prison. The Tijuana organization still continues to operate. The current leader of the cartel is not known. This cartel controls drugs from Tijuana and San Diego.

2. *Vicente Carrillo-Fuentes Organization.* This cartel is known as the Juarez cartel. Since the death of Amado Carrillo-Fuentes in July 1997, the organization has remained intact with key lieutenants retaining control of specific geographical areas. The most notable member is Vicente Carrillo Fuentes. The lieutenants are Amado's brother, Vicente Carrillo-Fuentes, Jan Jose Esparragosa-Moreno, and Ismael Zambada-Garcia. They cooperate together in moving cocaine to major U.S. cities. The cartel controls the drugs across the border at El Paso, Texas. Arturo Hernandez was acquitted of being a leader of Juarez cartel's hit men and spies in 2007 by a Mexican court.

3. *Armando Valencia Organization.* Armando Valencia-Cornelio is a key figure in the interrelationship between major Mexican and Colombian drug trafficking organizations. This organization is known as the Valencia cartel. The organization is based in Guadalajara, Jalisco, and the State of Michoacan. The Valencia Organization was receiving 20 tons of cocaine on a monthly basis. These shipments were transported to the west coast of Mexico from the north coast of Colombia via maritime vessels and subsequently moved to the United States. On August 15, 2003, Armando Valencia-Cornelio and seven of his associates were arrested in Mexico at a restaurant near Guadalajara. They are facing charges in both Mexico and Miami, Florida.

4. *Miguel Caro-Quintero Organization.* This organization is based in Caborca, the state of Sonora. Rafael Caro-Quintero was head of this organization. The head of this drug trafficking organization was arrested in 1985 for his involvement in the murder of DEA Special Agent Enrique Camarena. Miguel Angel Caro-Quintero took the leadership of the organization until his arrest in December 2001. The brothers, Jorge and Genaro Caro-Quintero, and sister, Maria Del Carmen Caro-Quintero, assumed control.

5. *Osiel Cardenas-Guillen.* Osiel Cardenas-Guillen was a major marijuana and cocaine trafficker of the Gulf cartel. It operates in the state of Tamaulipas, which is near Brownsville, Texas. Osiel Cardenas-Buillen was arrested on March 14, 2003. His former boss Juan Garcia-Abrego is currently incarcerated. Cardenas-Guillen is responsible for the attempted assault and abduction of DEA and FBI agents in Matamoros, Tamaulipas. Despite his incarceration, his organization remains active in drug trafficking. The Gulf cartel has branched out into migrant smuggling. It is believed by U.S. authorities that the Gulf cartel is using migrant smuggling to divert attention to their drug smuggling. The Gulf cartel is very violent. They are believed to be behind many shootings in the area. Cardenas created his own paramilitary organization, called the Zetas.

6. *Joaquin "El Chapo" Guzman.* The Guzman organization is known as the Sinaloa cartel. It is based in the northwestern state of Sinaloa. The head of the cartel is Joaquin "El Chapo" Guzman. Guzman is a fugitive who escaped from Mexican prison in 2001. Hector Palma Salazar is a cartel leader who was extradited to the United States in January 2007 to face charges in California for drug trafficking. He was sentenced to 16 years in February 2008. Sandra "Queen of the Pacific" Avila Beltran was arrested by Mexican authorities for drug trafficking in October 2007. Peruvian authorities believe the Sinaloa cartel is the largest purchaser of Peruvian cocaine, most of which goes to Europe. They have arrested five Sinaloa cartel members in Peru. The Sinaloa cartel has ties to the Colombian cocaine traffickers. In recent years, the Sinaloa cartel and the Gulf cartel have been battling for control. The Sinaloa cartel is also involved in migrant trafficking. They control most of the smuggling routes into Arizona. The Sinaloa cartel has cooperated with the Juarez cartel.

Several major drug traffickers were arrested in 2002 and 2003. Mexican authorities have arrested Arturo Guzman-Loera, the brother of Joaquin Guzman-Loera (aka El Chapo) in January 2002. In March 2002, Benjamin Arellano-Felix was arrested in Puebla, Mexico. Miguel Herrera-Barraza (aka El Tarzan) was also arrested in March 2002. In May 2002, the Mexican military apprehended Jesus Albino Quintero-Meraz, a top lieutenant of the Gulf cartel.

Bulk currency shipments continue to be the most prevalent method to move trafficking proceeds to Mexico. U.S. currency is concealed and transported by courier or cargo, either overland or by air. The money usually travels in the same vehicle or airplane that originally transported the drugs. Another common method of money laundering is drug proceeds being sent to Mexico through U.S.-based money service businesses. Money transmitters have operated with little or no controls. On August 18, 1999, the Financial Crimes Enforcement Network (FinCen) published regulations requiring money service businesses to comply with currency transaction reporting under the Bank Secrecy Act. So far, this has not deterred money transmitters from laundering drug money. It has helped law enforcement to identify the money launderers.

Alien smuggling from Mexico to the United States is a $300-million-a-year business. It is second only to drug trafficking. In fact, some drug cartels are also involved in alien smuggling. The Mexican intelligence service claims there are about 100 Mexican alien smuggling rings linked to a half-dozen networks. The networks have operatives located throughout the South and Central America. Some networks are connected to East Asian, Russian, and Ukrainian organized crime groups. These networks use cell phones with hard-to-trace numbers as well as digital equipment. The smugglers observe the Mexican–U.S. border and communicate the deployments of Border Patrol and its monitoring equipment. This has led to a technology war between the network operatives and the U.S. Border Patrol. In the United States, smuggling rings operate networks of drop houses where illegal immigrants are kept until they arrive at their destinations or until relatives pay off the balance of their fees.

Some of the major illegal alien smuggling organizations are:

1. *The Peralta-Rodriguez Organization.* This organization is run by the Peralta-Rodriguez family. This organization has been in business since the early 1980s. It reached its height in the 1990s when they were smuggling up to 1000 immigrants per week into the United States. They were charging between $800 and $1200 per person. The FBI found the group to be highly sophisticated, employing a substantial network of recruiters, escorts, drivers, transportation, and lodging providers as well as document forgery specialists. They also had a supply of high-quality cellular phones and a fleet of vans and cars. The organization paid for houses and hotel rooms throughout southern California for shelter. In 2000, the FBI arrested 60 operatives in the United States. The leaders, Vincente and Jose Ismael Peralta, have remained at large; however, the organization continues to function at a reduced level of activity.
2. *The Los Tello Organization.* The Los Tello Organization is based in Tijuana and competes with the Peralta-Rodriguez family for the U.S. southwest border illegal alien trade. The group leader, El Tello, is a long-time alien smuggler. He recruits illegal border crossers at the Municipal Market in Tijuana. El Tello smuggles illegal aliens across the U.S. border near El Hongo and La Hechicera.
3. *The Castillo Organization.* The Castillo Organization is based in Honduras. It is believed to be the largest multinational illegal alien ring in the Western Hemisphere. They specialize in overland smuggling from Central and South America through Mexico and into the United States. Jose Leon Castillo, a Honduran national, led the organization until he was arrested in Guatemala and deported to the United States in October 2000. Also, 12 Castillo operatives were arrested in 2000 as part of the multinational Operation Forerunner.
4. *The Martinez Teran Organization.* The Martinez Teran organization operates along the entire Western Hemisphere. It is suspected of having partnership with Asian smuggling rings. The organization's leader is Carlos Martinez Teran (aka El Yato). He has been in custody since January 2000. Teran's wife and mother-in-law were arrested in April 2000 for escorting 75 Central Americans through the state of Oaxaca to the United States. However, the organization still functions through the organization lieutenants who remain at large.

5. *The Castorena-San German Organization.* This organization is based in Guadalajara and was led by Castorena-San German. He is also known as "Don Alfonso." The Castorena-San German organization produces a vast network of forged documents and distributes them to Hispanic illegal aliens across the United States. Forged documents have been found in 55 U.S. cities and 32 states according to the Immigration and Naturalization Service (INS). Castorena and his associates have built a counterfeiting empire by counterfeiting documents. They produce very high quality documents. San German had operations in Chicago and Los Angeles. Juan San German, Castorena operations chief, was arrested in 1998 along with 10 accomplices. In 1998, the INS seized 31,000 counterfeit documents in Chicago's Little Village neighborhood. The Castorena-San German organization used the assistance of street gangs: Latin Kings in Chicago and the 18th Street gang in Las Vegas and Los Angeles. San German pleaded guilty and was sentenced to 6½ years in federal prison in January 2000.

6. *The Iglesias Rebollo Organization/Titanium Group.* This organization operates a prostitution and human trafficking ring in women from Central Europe, Central America, and South America. The Titanium Group partnerships with Russian and Ukrainian mafias to traffic women from Hungary for sexual exploitation. The organization is led by Alejandro Iglesias Rebollo. He became a fugitive when his nightclub, the Lobohombo, burned down in 2000 and 22 people were killed. He opened a new night club in Mexico City in 2002.

7. *The Salman Saleh/Chen/Lin Organization.* This is an international alien smuggling ring and document forgery ring that specializes in smuggling Chinese nationals into the United States through Ecuador and Mexico. Chinese nationals or their families pay smuggling fees ranging from $20,000 to $30,000 before departing China. The organization counterfeited INS documents in order to legitimize the alien's presence. The leader of the ring in Mexico, Saleh Ahmad Salman, is serving a 20-year prison term for human smuggling.

8. *The Heredia Organization "Airport cartel."* This organization operates at Tijuana's International airport. Guillermo Isiordia Heredia and members of his family lead the organization. The Heredia organization escorts illegal migrants through the Tijuana airport. It is also known to smuggle illegal immigrants from Central and South America, Europe, Asia, and Africa into the United States. The illegal immigrants are boarded onto commercial passenger buses and transported to Nogales, Sonora. The immigrants then cross into the United States through tunnels. They are then transported to Tucson and Los Angeles.

9. *The El Libanes Boughader Organization.* This organization operates out of Tijuana and was headed by Salim Boughader Mucharrafille, a Mexican of Lebanese decent. Boughader was arrested in December 2002. He worked with two other Mexicans, Patricia Serrano Valdez and Jose Guillermo Alvarez Duenas. They transported Middle Eastern immigrants across established smuggling routes through the San Ysidro Port of Entry and the mountains in East County. The ring charged migrants $2500 for the border crossing as part of their journey. U.S. law enforcement is concerned with the potential terrorists taking advantage of this route.

10. *"The Smuggler M" Organization.* This organization smuggles immigrants from Egyptian and other Middle Eastern countries into the United States. Two members of this ring, Adel R. Nasr and Gamal Abdalgalil Nasr, were arrested in May

2002. The indictment in the case claims the two brothers worked with an Egyptian national based in Guatemala City identified only as "Smuggler M."

As early as 1992, the Russian criminal organizations have set up shops in Mexico. Russian crime groups have been identified in Mexico. Some of these are Poldolskaya, Mazukinskaya, Tambovskaya, Solntsevskaya, and Izamailovskaya. There are other criminal groups from Chechnya, Georgia, Armenia, Lithuania, Poland, Croatia, Serbia, Hungary, Albania, and Rumania. Most Russian mobsters hang around resorts, hotels, or residences of Mexican drug lords. The Russian Mafias have supplied the Mexican drug cartels with weapons, grenade launchers, and small submersibles in exchange for cocaine, heroin, and other drugs. The DEA reports that 300 AK-47s and ammunition were sold to Carillo Fuentes in Costa Rica. Four Russian mobsters were turned back after they landed in Mexico City. They were Aleksandr Zakharov, Nicolay Novikov, Yevgeniy Sazhayev, and Vladimir Titov. In 2001, Mexican authorities seized 19 tons of cocaine from two fishing boats manned by Russian and Ukrainian crewmen. In March 2001, U.S. authorities seized 7 tons of cocaine hidden on the ship *Forever My Friend*. It was manned by a crew of eight Russians and Ukrainians. In May 2001, the coast guard towed a ship, *Zvezda Maru*, into San Diego, California, with 12 tons of cocaine on board. The ship had 12 Russians and Ukrainians on board. This has led the DEA to determine that the Arellano-Felix organization has ties to the Russian Mafia.

A Ukrainian crime group has used Mexico as a staging area to smuggle Ukrainian women into the United States for prostitution. Valery Komisaruk and Tetyana Komisaruk operated a safe house near the California border. The ring charged up to $7500 per person. This generated thousands of dollars. The immigrants were instructed on how to cross the border. Serhiy Mezherytsky, a Ukrainian immigrant, provided boats and cars for smuggling of illegal immigrants. He also cooperated with Mexican guides in smuggling immigrants into the United States. Mezherytsky lives in West Hollywood, California.

The Mexican authorities believe other organized crime groups are setting up shop in Mexico. These include Japanese, Chinese, and Korean Mafias. They are involved in human smuggling. In 1999, the Mexican authorities caught 400 Chinese immigrants being offloaded in the Ensenada area. The alien smugglers had to pay tolls to the Arellano Felix drug cartel. In 2002, the Mexican authorities clamped down on a Korean counterfeit ring. The authorities raided 24 locations and seized 180 tons of counterfeit merchandise that was manufactured in China and Taiwan. Forty-three Koreans were arrested including the ringleaders, Kookh Kim Sung and Hol and Hyo Sun Park.

The U.S. State Department has issued warnings about travel to Mexico. Some American tourists have been murdered or kidnapped for ransom. The U.S. Department of Justice issued a report on January 22, 2009, which said the Mexican drug cartels are the greatest threat to the United States. The Mexican groups often work with urban gangs and outlaw motorcycle groups inside the United States.

12.3.12 Irish Organized Crime

The Irish syndicate lost much of their territory and influence to Sicilian groups during Prohibition. However, they are still active in New York and Philadelphia by accommodation with the La Cosa Nostra.

Irish organized crime is in the hands of three groups. Jimmy Bolger, a reputed killer, bank robber, and drug trafficker controls one. The second is the McLaughlin gang. The third is headed by Howard Winter, who is involved in drug trafficking, hijacking, loan sharking, and contract murder on behalf of the Angiulo branch of the Patriarca LCN family in New England.

The three gangs have divided Boston into territories. The Winter gang controls the docks and Local 25 of the International Brotherhood of Teamsters. The Irish share their income with the Angiulo group in North Boston.

In New York, the Irish gang is known as the Westies. The group is lead by James Coonan. Like Boston, the New York gang is closely connected with LCN interests. Their overall impact on New York is insignificant; however, its influence is considerable in the entertainment industry.

12.3.13   Russian Organized Crime

There have been three waves of Russian immigration to the United States. It has been speculated that the Soviet Union attempted to empty their prisons and rid their undesirables from 1971 and 1980 as Castro did in 1980.

The first indication of Russian organized crime is when a gang from the Odessa region began to perpetrate a con game against other Russians living throughout the United States. The group became known as the "Potato Bag Gang" because victims who believed they had bought a sack of gold coins actually received a bag of potatoes.

Russian crime figures have been operating along both the east and west of the United States as well as in some cities, including Cleveland, Chicago, New Orleans, and St. Louis. They are involved in extortion, prostitution, insurance and medical fraud, auto theft, counterfeiting, credit card forgery, narcotics trafficking, fuel tax fraud, money laundering, and murder. On April 21, 1994, CIA Director James Woolsey told the Senate, "Organized crime is so rampant in Russia that it threatens Boris Yeltsin's presidency and raises concern that syndicates will obtain and smuggle Russian nuclear weapons to terrorists or foreign agents." The former Attorney General, Janet Reno, named Russian organized crime groups in the United States as a priority target for the U.S. Department of Justice. The Brighton Beach area of New York City became the hub for Russian organized crime in this country starting in the mid 1970s. The Russian criminals developed a working relationship with the LCN, which allowed them to establish fuel tax fraud schemes in certain areas of New York. The LCN forced the Russian criminals to pay a large portion of their proceeds as a "tax" to operate. Organized crime groups in Russia are not nearly as structured as those in the United States. A crime boss, called a "pakhan," controls four criminal cells through an intermediary called a "brigadier." The boss has two spies who watch over the action of the brigadier to ensure loyalty. At the bottom are criminal cells. These criminal cells specialize in various types of criminal activity such as drugs, prostitution, and "enforcers." This structure allows the leadership at the top to be insulated from the street operators. Street operators are not privy to the identity of the leadership. Strategy and planning is done at the top in order to minimize the risk of detection.

There is a traditional code of conduct within this style of organized crime in Russia, called "Vory v Zakone," or thieves in law. In this society, the thieves live and obey the "Vorovskoy Zakon," or thieves' code. The members are bound by 18 codes, and if they are broken, the transgression is punishable by death.

The Thieves' Code

A thief is bound by the Code to:

1. Forsake his relatives, mother, father, brothers, and sisters.
2. Not have a family of his own, no wife, no children; this does not preclude him from having a lover.
3. Never, under any circumstances work, no matter how much difficulty this brings.
4. Help other thieves.
5. Keep secret information about the whereabouts of accomplices.
6. In unavoidable situations to take the blame for someone else's crime; this buys the other person time of freedom.
7. Demand a convocation of inquiry for the purpose of resolving disputes in the event of a conflict between oneself and other thieves or between thieves.
8. If necessary, participate in such inquiries.
9. Carry out the punishment of the offending thief as decided by the convocation.
10. Not resist carrying out the decision of punishing the offending thief who is found guilty, with punishment determined by the convocation.
11. Have good command of the thieves' jargon, "Fehnay."
12. Not gamble without being able to cover losses.
13. Teach the trade to young beginners.
14. Have, if possible, informants from the rank and file of thieves.
15. Not lose your reasoning ability when using alcohol.
16. Have nothing to do with the authorities, not participate in public activities, nor join any community organizations.
17. Not take weapons from the hands of authorities; not serve in the military.
18. Make good on promises given to other thieves.

Intelligence indicates that most Russian organized crime groups are loosely organized and do not have elaborate levels of structure. They operate primarily as networks. Russian organized crime groups in the United States communicate and operate with their counterparts in Russia. In 1992, the Russian crime lords sent Vyacheslav Kirillovich Ivankov to the United States for the purpose of bringing them into the fold. Ivankov arrived in New York City on March 8, 1992. In a very short time, he expanded operations and made contacts with other Russian "thieves." Ivankov paid $15,000 to have an aging singer marry him so he could get a green card. They got a divorce in the Dominican Republic after he got his green card. In 1995, Roustam Sadykov, a Russian Banker, asked Ivankov to collect money from Summit International. Ivankov and two of his henchmen kidnapped the two bankers, Volkov and Voloshin. They were made to sign a note for $3.5 million. Unknown to Ivankov, the FBI had wired the two bankers. On June 8, 1995, Ivankov was arrested. He was later tried and sentenced to the Manhattan Correctional Center. While there, he was found with heroin in his cell and later transferred to Allenwood Federal Penitentiary.

On the FBI's most wanted list, a Semion Mogilevich is wanted for a fraud scheme to defraud investors in YBM Magnex International, Inc. (YBM), a public company incorporated in Canada. YBM Magnex is based in Newtown, Pennsylvania. Investors lost more than $150 million through a scheme of inflating stock values by preparing bogus financial books and records, lying to Securities and Exchange Commission officials, and offering bribes to accountants. A federal indictment was issued on April 24, 2003 in the eastern district of Philadelphia, Pennsylvania. Mogilevich and two accomplices, Igor L'Vovich Fisherman and Anatoli Tsoura, are charged with 45 counts of racketeering, securities fraud, wire fraud, mail fraud, and money laundering. Mogilevich is a 52-year-old Ukrainian. He holds an economics degree from the University of Lvov and is known as "Brainy Don." He has strong leadership qualities, acute financial skills, and has talented and highly educated associates. His use of technology has made him impervious to prosecution. It is believed that Mogilevich paid off a Russian judge to secure Vyacheslav Ivankov's early release from a Siberian prison.

It has also been discovered that the Russian Mafia is involved in drugs in south Florida. Ludwig Fainberg, known as Tarzan, ran Porky's Strip Club in Hialeah, Florida. Tarzan was born in Odessa, Russia, in 1958. In 1980, Tarzan fled Moscow to Brighton Beach, New York. In 1990, Tarzan moved to Florida after some of his associates were murdered. He opened Porky's with the help of William Seidle, who was connected to the LCN. Later, he linked up with Colombian drug cartels through Juan Almeida and Fernando Birbragher. Birbragher had close ties to the Cali drug cartel and was a friend of Pablo Escobar. Tarzan brokered the sale of six MI8 Russian helicopters in 1993. In 1996, Tarzan made a deal to acquire a Piranha class submarine from the Russian Navy for $5.5 million. The deal did not go through because Tarzan was arrested by the DEA on January 21, 1997. Tarzan pleaded guilty to racketeering charges, including conspiracy to sell heroin, cocaine, a submarine, and other charges. On October 14, 1999, Tarzan was deported to Israel with only $1500 in his pocket. He served only 33 months in prison.

The Russian mobsters are described as intelligent, professional criminals. Many have master's and doctorate degrees. Extortion appears to be the most frequent crime in the Russian communities during the 1970s, 1980s, and early 1990s. The Russian immigrant community is also a target of insurance fraud and con games. There are reports that Russian gangs in New York are linked to the Genovese family. Police have found the Russian gangs have to pay tax to the Genovese family to operate fuel scams. Police suspect that Evsei Agron was murdered by LCN because of a territorial conflict. Russian communities in this country are closed and suspicious of police.

12.3.14 Canadian Organized Crime

There are three major factions in Canadian organized crime that are active around the border region. In addition, members of Canadian crime groups have begun to concentrate in south Florida in an apparent expansion of both the scope and the base of their criminal enterprises.

The Vincent Cotroni crime family was identified during the 1960s and is an affiliate of the Bonanno LCN family in New York. Two Cotroni members from Montreal were convicted on drug conspiracy involving associates of Carmine Galante, a Bonanno capo. Today, the Cotroni group is headed by Santos "Frank" Cotroni and is engaged in drug trafficking.

Nine brothers control the French Canadian Dubois gang in Quebec Province. Four brothers are currently in prison. In 1985, Jean Paul Dubois headed the gang. Its main activity is drug trafficking.

Johnny McGuire, a one-time labor racketeer, has been called "The Canadian Jimmy Hoffa." Today the crime group, headed by McGuire, works its own rackets and cooperates with other groups in smuggling drugs, guns, and stolen cars into Canada.

In 1963, Pasquale Cuntrera, boss of the Siciliana family, left Italy. He went to Caracas, Venezuela, where in 1964, he established, with the approval of the Cupola, the base of the Siciliana family. The most known members of the Siciliana family living in Canada are Nicolo Rizzuto, Vito Rizzuto, Paolo Renda, Giuseppe Lopresti, and Agostino Cuntrera. The Rizzutos have very close ties with the Gambino, Bonanno, and DeCavalcante families in the United States. The year 1973 marked the beginning of the feud for control of criminal activities in Canada between the Cotroni and Rizzuto families. Nicolo Rizzuto achieved his goal by killing Paolo Violi, underboss of the Cotroni family, and Francesco and Rocco Violi, the Paolo's brothers. In 1984, Nicolo Rizzuto took control of all criminal activities in Canada after the death of Vincenzo Cotroni. In 1988, Nicolo Rizzuto was convicted in Caracas, Venezuela, for cocaine trafficking. His son, Vito Rizzuto, became the boss of the family. The Rizzuto crime family controls most of the gambling operations in Canada. Gambling consist of bookmaking, video poker machines, and casino operations. The Rizzuto crime family is also involved in narcotics, extortion, corruption, and money laundering.

Canadian organized crime groups have considerable presence in Florida, finding their customers and victims among both Floridians and the nearly 1 million Canadians who visit Florida. They engage in drug trafficking, loan sharking, bookmaking, and smuggling stolen automobiles.

In Florida, Canadian gangs are close to points of supply for cocaine. The trade in handguns smuggled to Canada is also lucrative, because weapons are readily available in Florida. Canadian crime groups have heavily invested in Florida business and real estate, particularly beachfront property. In some cases, they obtained the property after intimidating legitimate buyers. Since 1982, there have been a number of bombings involving eight pizza parlors in south Florida. Two Gambino family members who had been trying to open pizza restaurants in what apparently was Canadian-claimed territory were apparently murdered and found dead in the trunk of their car in Dade County, Florida.

12.3.15 Jamaican Posse

The Jamaican Posse is a growing group of bold and dangerous individuals who traffic in large quantities of firearms and narcotics. There are about 40 posses operating in the United States, Great Britain, Canada, and the Caribbean with an estimated 10,000 members. These illegal activities are increasing along with the propensity for violence. They are attributed to be responsible for more than 1000 homicides nationwide. About 1976, two large violent groups emerged on the island of Jamaica: The Raetown Boys and the Dunkirk Boys. The Raetown Boys consisted of people from Raetown, Jamaica, most of who became known as the "Untouchables." They were loyal to the People's National Party. They later became known as the Shower Posse. The Dunkirk Boys became known as the Spangler Posse. They were aligned to the Jamaica Labor Party. The largest posse is the Shower Posse. The second largest posse is the Spangler Posse. They distribute drugs on a wholesale and street level in many large cities in the United States. Most of the Jamaican posses believe in a doctrine called Rastafarian. The original thrust was for improvement of conditions in Jamaica and eventual migration of black people back to Africa, specifically Ethiopia. The most universal beliefs are:

- Jah is the living God.
- Ethiopia is the black man's home.

- Repatriation is the way of redemption for black men.
- The ways of the white man are evil.

Other doctrines that are not universally adhered to on an individual basis are:

- Eating pork is forbidden.
- The "herb" marijuana or ganja is a gift of God, who enjoined us to smoke it.
- Beards and long hair are enjoined on men; it is a sin to shave or cut the hair.
- Alcohol is forbidden, together with gambling.

When they recognize Emperor Selassie as God, they make a vow or pledge accepting the laws and decrees of conformance. Not all Rastafarians are criminals and not all Jamaicans are Rastafarians.

The Jamaican posses have a proclivity for violence seldom seen in other organized crime groups. They have little regard for public safety or human life. The posse's violence can be directed at members of their own groups, rival groups, or others who may interfere with their drug territories. Age and sex present no barrier to their acts of violence. They have killed women, children, friends, and relatives. The Jamaican Posse members have the following general traits:

- Usually well armed with high-powered weapons
- Will confront and kill police
- Use extensive surveillance methods
- Have disregard for innocent bystanders
- Use extensive aliases and false identification
- Use females to transport narcotics and weapons and to make weapon purchases

In recent years, the Jamaican posses have begun establishing working relationships with other organized crime groups. The LCN are working with the Jamaican posses, along with the Colombian cartels. Posse members have been known to steal credentials of police officers, federal agents, military officers, and intelligence officers. They have developed their own slang based on the existing elements of the English language. The Rastafarian language comes with a whole new vocabulary of "I" words, which express their individualism. The word "myself" is "I self" and "ourselves" is "I n I self." This new language is used to:

- Prepare cover stories
- Identify true believers
- Plan criminal acts
- Give appearance that individual does not know English

Jamaicans are highly mobile with tremendous access to false identification. Weapons are a mark of manhood. High-quality weapons are a status symbol. In some posses, assaults or murders are used as membership requirements.

Jamaicans lack many of the sophisticated money laundering methods. Most posses prefer to avoid direct use of traditional financial institutions. They smuggle most of their proceeds out of the United States. They use wire transfer companies by structuring their transactions. Higglers are street merchants in Jamaica. Higglers travel to the United States and purchase merchandise for resale in Jamaica using posse funds. The goods are sold in Jamaica, and the money is given to the posses. The Jamaicans use friends, relatives, and other straw purchasers to hide the true ownership of property. They like to use women's names in leasing cars, apartments, and obtaining other items. They have in recent years obtained small businesses, mostly cash sales operations (e.g., restaurants, grocery stores, nightclubs, record stores, boutiques, and garages).

12.3.16 Israeli Mafia

During the 1980s, the Israeli Mafia was discovered operating in the United States. They are involved primarily in narcotics trafficking. They use business fronts to launder their profits. Most Israeli Mafia members were born in a Middle East country and immigrated to Israel, where vast cultural and language difficulties were experienced. Most of the criminal elements were born in an Arab country, within a poor economic situation. Many were not able to assimilate into the Israeli culture. The Israeli National Police arrested and incarcerated many for criminal activity. Many of the Israelis left Israel for other countries in order to pursue a lifestyle of criminality. It should be noted that if the criminals remained in Israel, their prospect for financial success would be limited because Israel and its populace are not financially prosperous. In the United States, the Israeli Mafia is loosely knit. They have ties to the heroin trade in the Middle East and Southeast Asia and to the cocaine trade with ties to Colombia, Peru, Brazil, and Mexico. Besides drug trafficking, the Israeli Mafia is involved in other criminal activities such as extortion, fencing stolen property, and various kinds of fraud. They use the following methods of disguise:

1. They use one another's addresses on official documents, particularly driver's licenses and vehicle registrations. The true resident would deny any knowledge of anyone listed on any document.
2. The inclusion or omission of the Hebrew word "Ben" in their last name. This word means "son of."
3. The Hebrew alphabet is phonetic, and there is usually only one way of spelling a word or name. When translating a Hebrew name into the Roman alphabet, mistakes, whether intentional or unintentional, can occur in the spelling. The phonetic word of Levy can be translated into Levey, Levi, Levie, Leve, Leive, etc. These variations of spelling can provide numerous legitimate documents that can be used for identification purposes.

In the past, Israeli members maintained a low profile and a pretentious lifestyle. They met in small social clubs and drove old vehicles. Recently, members are driving luxury vehicles, are smartly attired, wearing expensive jewelry, and frequenting luxury cabarets.

12.3.17 Gypsies/Travelers

The gypsies are people from Eastern Europe. They have distinct coloring and body structure. The travelers are people from Ireland and the British Isles who have Caucasian coloring and cast. Both groups are involved in the same type of criminal activity of home invasions, shoplifting, store diversions, fortune telling, and jewelry store operations. The gypsies are dark skinned, with black or brown eyes, black hair, and they are short and stocky. They like to wear colorful clothing. The gypsies are small in number in the United States and seem to remain on the lower economic scale. The travelers, however, have become much more prosperous. They are scattered throughout the United States, but the larger clans are concentrated in or around North Augusta and Defilade, South Carolina. Other clans are located near Memphis, Tennessee, and Ft. Worth, Texas. Their numbers are estimated to be about 6000 individuals. The travelers live in a closed society. They do not socialize with nontravelers and discourage marriage outside the clan. Travelers get together about four times a year. At all other times, they are traveling and engaging in fraud and criminal activities. Men are the primary workers and head of the family. The travelers prefer to operate in rural areas. The European gypsies prefer to work urban areas because they can blend in with many cultural groups, targets of opportunity are more available, and they can get assistance from other gypsy groups. The gypsies and travelers like to seek the elderly because they:

- May live alone
- Are easily intimidated
- Make poor witnesses because of failing eyesight and memory capability
- Keep large sums of cash money in their homes
- Cannot physically make home repairs or improvements

Both the travelers and the gypsies are mostly involved in consumer fraud. Their primary operations center on:

1. *Painting.* The basic element here is giving an exaggerated estimate for the job using cheap grade of paint, poor quality due to thinning, and poor workmanship.
2. *Roof repair.* They use poor materials and workmanship. In addition, they will drive their victim to the bank to get cash for a discount.
3. *Home repairs/service.* They will pose as termite or building inspectors to advise people of bad conditions. They offer to do the repairs for an exaggerated fee. When the work is done, the quality is poor or the work was not even done. This is also used to get into people's homes for the purpose of canvassing and stealing valuables and money.
4. *Auto body repairs.* Travelers look for dented automobiles. When found, they offer to repair it for a low fee. After repairs are done, they will attempt to inflate the price.
5. *Selling tools.* The travelers like to sell cheap tools at inflated prices at flea markets, highway intersections, and even door to door.
6. *Social security/health scam.* Here, two travelers pose as social security workers or health department workers. They offer to give a free physical to the victim. While one traveler is keeping the victim's attention, the other traveler is stealing money and valuables from the house.
7. *Recreational vehicle sales.* The traveler purchases poorly constructed RV's. They sell these vehicles at two to three times their cost. These RV's are not inspected or approved by many states that have established standards of construction and safety requirements.

The principal characteristics of the travelers are:

1. *Workers.* The men do most of the work.
2. *Vehicles used.* The travelers use late model pickup trucks. There are no business names or advertising shown on the trucks.
3. *Housing on the road.* The travelers usually stay in family-oriented motels, campgrounds, and trailer parks.
4. *Group size.* They usually travel in groups of 3 to 5 vehicles with 10 to 15 people.
5. *Travel.* Travelers spend 40% to 70% of their time engaged in nomadic activity.
6. *Identification.* Travelers will have many sets of identification from different states. Identification should be checked with vehicle registration.

12.3.18   Haitians

The Haitians are not highly organized. They operate in gang fashion. For the most part, they are not highly educated. Many are illegal aliens in the United States. Even though they are not highly educated and are loosely organized, they are becoming very effective as being an organized crime group. In south Florida and elsewhere, they are successful in robberies, home invasions, and thefts. Since Haiti is a poor country, criminal groups have specialized in stealing bicycles, mopeds, small motorcycles, and economy automobiles. They steal these items and ship them back to Haiti for resale. The U.S. Customs, in the late 1980s, boarded a ship leaving Miami with a destination of Port-u-Prince, Haiti. On the ship, there were 20,000 bicycles. They found that all of the bicycles were stolen. For the Haitian gang, these bicycles were pure profit. Their intent was to ship the stolen bicycles to Haiti, where they would be sold. The disturbing aspect of the Haitians is that they are increasing their sophistication. This is because of their association with the Jamaican Posses and other criminal organizations. The Haitians are mostly Negroes, uneducated, and speak Creole. Because most cannot speak English very well, they have become limited in what they can do.

12.3.19   Nigerians

The Nigerian criminal elements operate out of three clans. Two clans are Christians, while the other is Muslim. The Nigerians are highly educated. Many have master's and doctor's degrees. Nigeria was a British Crown Colony until 1960 when it obtained its independence. Nigerians speak English with a British accent. This makes it easier for them to obtain employment and assimilate into American society. The Nigerians are principally involved in drug trafficking and various fraud schemes. The Nigerians have cost the credit card companies millions of dollars in losses. They apply to credit card companies using people's names with good credit standing. The cards are sent to an address different from the true person. They use the card to the maximum credit limit. The goods are then sent to Nigeria for resale. The address where the card is sent is only rented for a short time, usually 3 to 5 months. The Nigerians move to another rented dwelling. They use false identification or other people's identification, which was obtained in business establishments that require identification or the use of credit cards. Sometimes, reading local newspapers to find prominent people's names. Nigerians are involved in many fraud schemes. They get low income housing when they do not qualify. They are involved in food stamp fraud and other government programs. Nigerians are also involved in narcotics trafficking, principally, heroin, which is imported from Africa and the Middle East. They can be violent but generally are not, except in their drug trafficking operations. One unique characteristic of Nigerians is that they will deny any wrong doing even when caught "red-handed." They never admit to any crime.

12.3.20 Palestinians

The Palestinians are involved in fraud and weapons smuggling. They like to use convenience stores for fronts. They are involved in cashing checks for high fees and paying cash for food stamps at half the face value. Most of their business establishments are located in economically depressed areas. Profits are used to obtain various kinds of weapons for shipment to the Middle East. The Palestinians sponsor other Palestinians into this country. The new arrivals are set up in a convenience store. They repay their sponsor from their profits. They keep two sets of books, one for the sponsor, which is kept correctly, and the other set for government reporting purposes. The second set of books does not show all their income. It does not show the payments to the sponsor or the skimmed receipts. Weapons are purchased or stolen and shipped to the Middle East. There, they are sold to various terrorist groups. They will cooperate with the Israeli Mafia, if profits are available.

12.4 Organized Crime Patterns

Organized crime groups have a pattern of four stages of development. These stages are as follows.

12.4.1 Tactical Crimes

Most criminals start their career at this stage. It's labeled tactical because local law enforcement will have to use tactical methods of detecting. The most common crimes in this category are:

- Arson
- Assault
- Bribery
- Burglary
- Corruption
- Extortion
- Hijacking
- Murder
- Robbery

12.4.2 Illegal Business Activities

When criminal groups become more organized with a leadership structure, they move into more illegal enterprises. The most common criminal enterprises are:

- Counterfeiting
- Frauds

- Gambling
- Illegal alcohol
- Loan sharking
- Narcotics
- Prostitution
- Protection rackets
- Smuggling
- Stolen property

12.4.3   Legitimate Business

When criminal groups have developed a good organizational structure, they turn to legitimate business to disguise their profits and to appear respectable in the community. At the same time, they must obtain a business that lends itself to hiding their illegal profits without attracting attention to law enforcement and tax authorities. The most common businesses used by organized criminal groups are:

- Auto agencies
- Factoring
- Food products
- Garment manufacturing
- Juke boxes and video machines
- Liquor distributors and sales
- Night clubs and bars
- Trade unions and associations
- Trucking
- Vending machines
- Waste collections

12.4.4   Big Business

Sophisticated criminal groups retain lawyers and accountants when they get involved in medium and large businesses. They do this mostly to obtain respectability in the community and to launder their illegal gains. The most common businesses are:

- Banking
- Construction
- Credit cards
- Entertainment
- Hotel and motels
- Insurance
- Labor
- Mortgages
- Real estate
- Securities

The fraud examiner will be involved in the last three stages. Each stage will require different investigative and audit techniques. Stage two requires more investigative techniques than audit techniques, while stage four requires many more audit techniques than investigative techniques. The more complex the enterprise, the more time required to uncover the fraud.

12.5 Summary

There are 18 criminal organizations based on race or ethnicity. Some groups are very sophisticated with a structured hierarchy, while others operate in gangs with a single leader. Organized crime organizations operate primarily in large metropolitan areas. They are rarely found in rural areas. Criminals usually do not have any outward signs of being a criminal. However, in some organized crime organizations, the membership can be easily determined by how they dress, their body tattoos, how they speak, or their demeanor. The financial investigator should become familiar with criminal organizations. He/she should know their methods of operation and their organizational structure. A case cannot be made without knowing the organization structure and how the funds flow through the organization. Money laundering and racketeering charges are the most common charges for criminal organizations. For criminal organizations involved in drug trafficking, continuing criminal enterprise charges are most common along with money laundering.

Trial Preparation and Testimony 13

13.1 Definition

The purpose of this book is to prepare a forensic accountant to present accounting data in a court of law. Sooner or later, a forensic accountant will have to prepare and testify in a court of law. The basic function of a forensic accountant is to present accounting data that are admissible in a court of law. "Forensic" means anything that is admissible in a court of law or open to public debate.

13.2 Trials and Hearings

The forensic accountant will have to testify in a legal proceeding, whether for the prosecution or defense in a criminal case or the plaintiff or respondent in a civil case. The complexity of any case will depend on the issues raised. Some cases will only require a small amount of time to study and testify, while others will require many hours of study and testifying. In any case, the forensic accountant's testimony will provide the basis for the judge's rulings. The forensic accountant will normally be called to testify in the following types of legal proceedings.

13.2.1 Criminal Trials

In criminal trials, normally, the forensic accountant will testify about the defendant's net worth and expenditures, whether for the prosecution or defense. This will require a lot of time to study and testify in court. Other cases involve the tracing of funds and assets.

13.2.2 Civil Trials

In civil trials, normally, the forensic accountant will testify about the plaintiff or respondent's financial status. Most cases usually involve income tax litigation or divorce asset division and/or ability to make alimony and/or child support payments. The time required will depend on the complexity of the case.

13.2.3 Hearings

The forensic accountant will testify before a judge. No jury will be present. In criminal cases, the testimony will be aimed at the defendant's financial position or his/her financial affairs. A bond hearing is a common example of this kind of hearing. In civil cases, the forensic accountant will testify about the plaintiff or respondent's financial condition or ability to pay a claim.

13.2.4 Deposition

The forensic accountant will give testimony about some issue that involves litigation between two parties. There is no judge or jury present.

13.2.5 Sworn Statement

In the case of a deposition, the forensic accountant will give a sworn statement about a particular issue(s). There is no judge or jury present. This is a one-sided situation. The sworn statement is given in response to questions and answers asked by an attorney for his/her client or the government.

13.3 Preparing to Testify

As soon as you find that you will be testifying, you should begin preparing for the witness chair. Regardless of your role, you should take the following steps:

1. Discuss with the attorney what is expected, how your testimony is to be used, and when you will be expected to testify.
2. Review all available documents pertaining to the issue(s) being litigated.
3. Discuss your testimony with the attorney, ask what line of questioning will be used to develop the case, and get a general idea of how you will respond to those questions.
4. Consider what the opposing counsel's approach will be and the areas they will most likely probe during cross-examination.

13.4 Expert/Summary Witness

An expert witness is a person skilled in some art, science, profession, or business, or who has experience or knowledge in relation to matters that are not commonly known to the ordinary person. (See Federal Rules of Evidence, Rule 702, 28 U.S. Code Annotated.) The ordinary witness testifies to facts, that is, what one has seen, heard, or otherwise observed. The expert witness expresses an opinion or answers hypothetical questions based on facts presumably in the record. It should be kept in mind that the expert witness testimony is entirely within the province of the jury to determine the weight given to such opinions. The jurors are not bound by the opinion of experts.

13.5 Duties and Responsibilities

The forensic accountant has various responsibilities and duties that he/she must perform during a judicial proceeding. They are as follows:

1. In criminal cases, review the Prosecution Memorandum.
2. In criminal cases, review the indictment (if the case was presented to a grand jury) or the information (if the charges were filed by the federal or state prosecutor) that sets forth the specific allegations of the criminal act.

3. Review the anticipated evidence available to prove or disprove the indictment or information in criminal cases or support or deny the plaintiff or respondent position in a civil case.

4. Check the mathematical accuracy of the accounting data that are to be presented in court, whether criminal or civil.

5. Advise the attorney of the potential accounting or technical problems.

6. Determine the clearest manner to present your testimony in terms that the jury of lay persons will understand.

7. Prepare tentative summary computations based on the evidence that is expected to be admitted.

8. Supply to the attorney who you are assisting, a written a statement of your qualifications as a forensic accountant, and/or a current resume.

9. Testify only to those matters that are admitted by the court into evidence, either as testimony or documents or by stipulation.

10. Take notes about evidence that is admitted and prepare a list of documentary exhibits of both sides, whether criminal or civil case.

11. Alert the attorney about any evidence that has been overlooked. It is important that all evidence necessary to support your testimony has been admitted.

12. Allow enough time to check your computations and review witness testimony. You should be sure to make copies of those computations for the jury, court, and counsel. This helps the jury to understand your testimony. Some judges will not allow jury members to have copies of exhibits, while others will.

13.5.1 The Do's

To be a good witness, there are things that you should do or observe. They are:

1. Speak up so that the jury, judge, stenographer, opposing counsel, and all other parties in the case can hear you.

2. Define technical terms and put them into a simple language so the jury, judge, and counsel can understand them.

3. In testifying, refer to the exhibit number or some other identification. When indicating or pointing to an object in the exhibit, you should describe what you are referring to so that the court stenographer can make an accurate and complete record of your testimony.

4. Take enough time in answering questions to gather your thoughts and give an accurate and brief answer. If you are asked to give an opinion and feel that you have not enough facts or enough time to form an intelligent expert opinion, so inform the court. The jury is impressed with such frankness on the part of the witness.

5. Always have adequate notes available so that you can testify about all of the details.

6. Walk to the witness stand with even steps.

7. When taking the oath, hold your right hand high with fingers straight and look at the officer administering the oath. When the officer finishes the oath, you should answer "I do" in a loud voice so that all in the courtroom can hear. Do not act timid.

8. Think before you speak.
9. When one of the lawyers calls "Objection" or the court interrupts, stop your answer immediately and wait until the court gives its ruling.
10. Be fair and frank.
11. If you make a mistake, or a slight contradiction, admit it and correct it. Do not tie yourself up in knots trying to cover up some slip of speech or memory.
12. Keep your temper! Be firm, but flexible.
13. If you cannot answer "yes" or "no," say so.
14. If you do not know or cannot remember, say so.
15. Avoid mannerisms of speech.
16. Listen closely when the attorney asks you, "Do you want this jury to understand…?" If you do not want the jury to understand it that way, make clear what you want them to understand.
17. Never try to be a "smart" witness.
18. Express yourself well, using simple technical language that the jury, judge, and attorneys can understand.
19. Be brief. Just answer the question and stop.
20. During the recess, stand aloof from everyone except the attorney who retained you to testify. Do not carry on any conversation with other witnesses or parties to the controversy.
21. Wait until the entire question is asked before answering.
22. On cross-examination, do not look at your attorney.
23. Keep your hands away from your mouth or face.
24. Be serious and businesslike during recesses and on the witness stand.
25. Stay away from opposing counsel, defendant or plaintiff, and his/her witnesses.
26. Be available and answer promptly when called to testify.

13.5.2   The Don'ts

The following items are things that you should not do:

1. Do not discuss the case in the corridors.
2. Do not chew gum.
3. Do not memorize any of your testimony.
4. Do not nod or shake your head to indicate yes or no.
5. Do not make any public display of elation or disappointment over the outcome of the case after the verdict has been rendered.
6. Do not volunteer any information.
7. Do not show any emotion about proceedings, such as disbelief or astonishment.
8. Do not allow yourself to get caught in the trap of a defense counsel asking you to answer a question by either "yes" or "no." Some questions cannot be answered this way and you should so state to the court and jury and ask for permission to explain your answer.
9. Do not get caught by snares such as "Did you ever discuss this with anyone?" Of course you did and, if asked, name the people, the lawyers, and the parties to the suit.
10. Avoid "horseplay" in corridors. Do not be noisy.

Cross-examination will be your most difficult time on the witness stand. Opposing counsel will attempt to confuse you, discredit you, and destroy the value of your testimony.

13.6 Trial Presentation

In presenting financial information in a trial, whether civil or criminal, the following steps should be followed in order to get the maximum effect:

1. Before trial, set up net worth or other schedules with all items expected to go to trial listed. Do not list any references until the items have been admitted into evidence. This serves as a control to ensure that everything that must be entered is entered.
2. As a summary witness, before going on the stand, take a recess of four hours, more or less, to go over all items on the schedule(s) to be presented.
3. In trial, try to get the attorney to present his/her witnesses in the following order:
   a. Custodian of records
   b. Case investigators
   c. Likely source of income witnesses
   d. Summary witness

This serves to help the summary witness in several ways.

First, it gets all documentary evidence in first whereby the summary witness can have time to double-check his/her computations and review the evidence.

Second, it impresses the jury of the defendant having been involved in illegal activities and the financial effect of these activities.

13.7 Summary

The basic rules for the forensic accountant and investigator are to truthfully testify in court. His/her demeanor should be professional. Fostering cooperation with the attorney can be greatly beneficial. Communication between the attorney and other forensic accountants or investigators can enlighten you as well as those around you on the case. The forensic accountant and investigators should expect to work long hours during the trial. Most of the work is done outside the courtroom and not in it. The forensic accountant should be very familiar with the case. If not, the forensic accountant should study the case files at least a week before the trial begins. The forensic accountant or investigator may not go to trial on the case for many months or years after he/she worked the case. In those instances, the forensic accountant and investigator must refamiliarize themselves with the case.

Accounting and Audit Techniques

14

14.1 General

The forensic accountant must identify what accounting techniques and audit programs to use and when to use them. The criminal elements will use whatever means to cover up their acts. Organized crime organizations use teams of lawyers and accountants to "legitimatize" their illegal income. Such use of professionals requires sophisticated accounting techniques to uncover their schemes. This, in turn, requires more time, funding, and personnel. Individuals can also develop fraudulent schemes of a high degree of sophistication. This chapter identifies the more common accounting techniques and audit programs that the forensic accountant can use to uncover the fraudulent schemes used by criminals.

14.2 Net Worth and Expenditure Methods

In previous chapters, the net worth and expenditure methods have been discussed in detail as to how to prepare and present in a court of law. The forensic accountant should also know when to use them. These methods are very powerful tools in both civil and criminal cases. They are most appropriate when the subject's lifestyle appears to be much higher than known or probable sources of income. An extreme example would be a person who lives in a $100,000 house and drives an expensive automobile but works at a fast-food restaurant making income close to the minimum wage or is not working at all. These methods are particularly applicable to organized crime figures, narcotics traffickers, and other racketeering activities. In these cases, most of the witnesses against the leaders are usually convicted criminals. The best defense is to attack the credibility of these witnesses. At times, the defense wins a not guilty verdict when there is not corroboration. The net worth and expenditure methods help corroborate witness's testimony by showing the income they paid the leaders and how the leaders disposed of the funds.

14.3 Tracing

This accounting technique involves the flow of funds. It shows the flow of funds from either bank to bank, entity to entity, person to person, or a combination of each. This technique can be used in organized crime cases or on individuals. Its primary purpose is to identify illegal funds and trace them to the beneficiary in criminal or civil cases. In civil cases, its purpose is to trace funds from a source to the end receiver. Table 14.1 illustrates a tracing schedule. It should be noted that the sources initially identified are greater than what the end beneficiary receives. The courts have ruled that the exact amount is not necessary to establish but that the end receiver received funds from an illegal source over an established

Table 14.1 John Doe's Tracing Schedule

Date	Description	Bahamas Transshipment, Ltd. In	Bahamas Transshipment, Ltd. Out	Cayman Islands Transshipment, Ltd. In	Cayman Islands Transshipment, Ltd. Out	Barbados John Doe In	Barbados John Doe Out
6/1/X2	Cash	$2,000,000					
6/30/X2	Cash	1,000,000					
7/1/X2	Blue Lagoon Realty		110,000 (Bahamas residence)				
10/1/X2	Cash	5,000,000					
3/1/X3	Cash	10,000,000					
3/31/X3	TRF Cayman Islands		2,000,000	2,000,000			
3/31/X3	TRF Barbados		2,000,000			2,000,000	

Date	Description	Spain Transshipment, Ltd. In	Spain Transshipment, Ltd. Out	Switzerland Transshipment, Ltd. In	Switzerland Transshipment, Ltd. Out
3/31/X3	TRF Spain	1,000,000	1,000,000		
3/31/X3	TRF Switzerland	1,000,000		1,000,000	
12/10/X3	TRF Switzerland	3,000,000		3,000,000	
12/10/X3	TRF Switzerland to Aruba				2,000,000

Date	Description	Aruba Doe Holding NV In	Aruba Doe Holding NV Out	Jamaica John Doe In	Jamaica John Doe Out
3/31/X3	TRF Aruba	370,000	370,000		
4/04/X3	TRF Jamaica	1,000,000		1,000,000	
4/4/X3	TRF Aruba	100,000	100,000		
4/3/X3	Boat Repair Shop				100,000
4/10/X3	Montego Bay Hotel				20,000
4/10/X3	Gulf Oil				500
10/1/X3	Cash	8,000,000			
12/20/X3	TRF Switzerland		2,000,000		

Date	Description	Panama In	Panama Out
3/31/X3	TRF Panama	500,000	500,000
12/1/X3	TRF Panama	3,500,000	3,500,000
	Total	$26,000,000	$14,480,000
	Balance	$11,520,000	

time period. This accounting technique is very useful in money laundering cases, regardless of the illegal activity. This tracing schedule uses the scenario problem, intelligence section.

It should be noted that the Bahamas account was used to purchase real estate in the Bahamas; however, the offsetting (IN) is not shown. This is because it did not go to another bank account.

Also, the transfer from the Transshipment, Ltd. bank account in Switzerland goes to the Doe Holdings bank account in Aruba. This example shows the subject making another step in transferring funds before it reaches its final destination. Funds can go through many bank accounts and entities before reaching its final destination.

14.4   Check Spreads

This is an accounting method that should be used when the subject uses checking accounts. In a forensic accounting situation, the use of check spreads is different from the normal accounting practices. The forensic accountant must have the following information in performing a check spread:

1. *Date.* The date of the check must be recorded. The date that the check cleared the bank is not necessary. The main purpose is to determine the intent of the subject, which would be the date that the subject dated the check.
2. *Payee.* The name of the payee must be shown. This identifies the person or entity that is supposed to receive the funds.
3. *Check number.* The check number identifies the instrument that is paying the payee. It is useful in that it can identify the specific payment made. It shows in numerical order the payments made to any individual or entity. It serves as a good reference to identify specific transactions.
4. *Amount.* This shows the amount of funds used or given to an individual or entity. This serves as evidence in showing the cost of a purchase whether as asset, expense, or a reduction in a liability.
5. *Bank from.* The purpose of this is to show what bank account this expenditure was made from. The subject could have more than one bank account and usually does. This identifies which bank account that the subject is using. This can be the specific bank account number or by using a code that identifies what bank account, which is listed elsewhere.
6. *Bank to.* This should show the bank account where the check was deposited. In other words, the ultimate payee's bank account. This can show the specific bank account number or use a code that identifies the bank account. This field is mostly used for payments made to other bank accounts which are entities that are controlled by the subject.
7. *First endorsement.* The first person or entity that endorses the check should be shown. It is possible and sometimes common that the person who the check is made payable to is not the person or entity who receives the check. The check could be made payable to a "John Smith," but the check goes into an account called "ABC Corporation" with John Smith's signature. Also, someone who is not John Smith could cash the check. Therefore, the person or entity that endorses the check can be very important.

8. *Second endorsement.* The payee or first person receiving the check may give it to a second person that will endorse the check. Attention should be focused on the second endorsement. This may be a kickback or diversion of funds. The ultimate receiver of the funds should be fully identified as to any relationships with the company or person providing the funds.

9. *Account.* The purpose of this field is to group similar transactions. It can be used to group transactions for a particular type of expenditure or to group for a particular purpose. Account means purpose. For trial presentation, the forensic account may use "Purpose" as the heading so the jury of lay people can understand it.

10. *Note.* This field is used to show any memos or notes shown on the check. It also can be used to record any peculiar item on the check such as different amounts between the figure amount and the written amount.

11. *First signatory.* This field should show the person who is the primary signatory on the check. This can be important in determining who has control over the bank account.

12. *Second signatory.* This field should show the second person who has cosignatory authority over the checking account. This person has some degree of control over the bank account.

If the investigator or analyst records this on a computer using a database, then various printouts can be produced. The above fields can sort the check spread. This will show patterns of activities. Check spreads also can offer more leads that will need to be further investigated. Also, they provide data that will be used for the net worth or expenditure schedules.

14.5 Deposit Spreads

This is an accounting method that should be used when the subject uses checking accounts. The previous section deals with the disbursements from the checking account. This section deals with the receipts into the checking account. The use of deposit spreads is different from other normal accounting practices. The forensic accountant should have the following information in a deposit spread:

1. *Date.* The date of the deposit is recorded here. The date shows the time period when the funds are received by the bank.

2. *Source.* The source shows from whom the funds were received. For cash deposits, the source would not be known unless the subject kept other records to show who paid the funds to the subject.

3. *Amount.* This shows the amount of funds received by the individual or entity. This amount should only show on the deposited item and not the total.

4. *Bank.* The purpose here is to show into what bank account the deposit was made. The subject could have more than one bank account and usually does. This identifies which bank account that the subject made the deposit into. This can be the specific bank account number or a code that identifies what bank account, which is listed elsewhere.

5. *Account.* The purpose of this field is to group similar transactions. It can be used to group transactions for a particular type of deposit or for a specific purpose. Account means purpose.

6. *Reference.* This field should list the number of the item deposited, usually the check number of the check or draft being deposited.

7. *Number of items.* Many times deposits contain more than one deposited item. Each item in the deposit should be recorded separately. In order to connect all items in the deposit, this field will give the total items in the deposit. The date will be the same for each item in the deposit.

8. *Note.* This field should be used as a memo. The memo can record what was noted on the deposited item or it can be used to record strange things about the item.

If the investigator or analyst uses a computer, then various printouts can be produced. The above fields can sort the deposit spread. Sorting deposited items by any of the above fields will disclose patterns and offer more leads that will need to be investigated. Also, they provide data that will be used in the net worth or expenditure schedules.

14.6 Credit Card Spreads

The credit card spreads should be used when the subject uses credit cards frequently. Credit cards are being used more and more these days. Some criminals use stolen credit cards to make purchases, which are later fenced. Other criminals use credit cards legally. In either case, credit card transactions should be analyzed. They are also important in that they show where a subject has been geographically. The fraud examiner should prepare a credit card spread by using the following fields.

1. *Date.* The date should be the date of the transactions and not the date the credit card transactions were processed.

2. *Vendor.* The vendor is the company that sold the merchandise or provided the service to the credit card holder. They may be a valuable witness in trial, especially if it is a large transaction.

3. *Credit card number.* This field should show the credit card account number or a code that will identify the specific credit card account on a separate listing.

4. *Amount.* This field shows the amount of the charge.

5. *Reference number.* The reference number should be the charge slip number. This is found on either the credit card statement or the charge slip.

6. *Signer.* This should record the person who actually signed the charge slip. There are occasions when more than one person can sign on a credit card. Sometimes there is no signature but a statement stating "on file." This is common on mail orders. For criminal cases, the on file slip should be obtained from the vendor to confirm that the subject signed for the purchase.

7. *Account.* The purpose of this field is to group similar transactions. It can be used to group transactions either by type or purpose.

8. *Note.* This field is used to record any unusual characteristics of the transactions.

Access to a computer can be very helpful. The above fields can sort the credit card data. This will show patterns in transactions and can offer leads that can be followed up. Credit card transactions are useful in showing the subject's whereabouts over time if they frequently use the credit cards. The data from credit card transactions can be used on the net worth and expenditure schedules.

14.7   Gross Profit Analysis

An accounting method that is useful in cases of money laundering or skimming operations is the gross profit analysis. The subject will acquire a legitimate business. Normally, these businesses will be one that takes in cash. In a skimming operation, the subject will withdraw money from the business. The funds will not reach the business bank account but are diverted to personal use. In a money laundering operation, illegal funds will be added to legitimate funds and put through the business bank account. The amount of funds that are either skimmed out or added in can be determined by finding out the cost of merchandise purchased and the normal sales price or mark up. The following steps should be used to determine the amount of funds either skimmed out or laundered through the business:

1. The normal markups or sales prices should be determined. If there is more than one product with different markups, then each product markups will have to be determined.
2. The next step is to determine the amount of merchandise purchased for each period under investigation. Product lines should be separated according to the different markup rates.
3. The markup rates for each product is applied to product costs. This will give the gross proceeds that should be generated from the sales of the products.
4. After the gross sales have been determined for all products for the period, a comparison is made to the funds deposited into the business bank account(s). If the sales figures are higher than the bank deposits, then the difference indicates the amount of funds skimmed out of the business. If the sales figures were lower than the bank deposits, then this would indicate the amount of funds laundered through this business.

	PRODUCT A	PRODUCT B	PRODUCT C
	Cost of sales	Cost of sales	Cost of sales
Divide:	C/S rate	C/S rate	C/S rate
Equals:	Gross sales	Gross sales	Gross sales
Less:	Deposits	Deposits	Deposits
Equals:	Skimmed/ laundered income	Skimmed/ laundered income	Skimmed/ laundered income

Figure 14.1 Gross profit analysis schedule.

A suggested gross profit schedule is presented in Figure 14.1.

The cost of sales rate is the percentage of cost of goods sold to the sales price for those goods. The gross profit method is used in bookmaking cases. It is called the "commission" or the "vig" method. It is explained later.

14.8 Witness List

The use of either the net worth or expenditure methods in either criminal or civil cases will require many witnesses, most of whom will be records custodians. It is common to have anywhere from 100 to 200 record custodians in an average case. Keeping track of these witnesses can be very wielding. It is suggested that a computer database be used with the following fields:

1. *Name.* The full name of the individual.
2. *Firm.* The name of the company where the individual works as the records custodian. In case one individual is unable to testify, another person in the company can replace the initial individual.
3. *Street.* Street address and not a mailbox number.
4. *City.* The municipality of where the firm is located.
5. *State.* The state where the company is located.
6. *Home telephone.* This might be necessary if the records custodian is on vacation.
7. *Business telephone.* The telephone number of the company where the records custodian can be reached or their replacement if needed.
8. *Witness number.* The number as assigned by the attorney handling the case.
9. *Exhibit number.* The number assigned by the attorney handling the case.
10. *Exhibit description.* A brief description of what the documents are in the case.

The computer can sort these data by any of the fields mentioned. It normally takes a records custodian about 15 minutes to testify and introduce the documents. It is better for opposing counsels to stipulate rather than subpoena records custodians. If the records custodian has to be subpoenaed, then these data can be used not only to contact the witnesses but also to help in scheduling them for the appropriate court date and time.

14.9 Bank Deposit Method

Another indirect method of determining income, whether tax or RICO, is called the bank deposit method. In tax cases, this is referred to as the bank deposit expenditure method, which more aptly applies. The IRS and state tax authorities have used this method for many years. It has not been used in RICO cases, primarily because it is not known by many fraud examiners or investigators. Also, it requires that the subject use bank accounts to a great extent. This method is very useful for a subject who operates only one business and the only source of income seems to come from only one source. The subject's business is a cash type business, where receipts are received in cash.

14.9.1 Theory

Where a subject has income from an undisclosed source, the use of the bank deposit method is justified. Under the bank deposit method, the subject's gross receipts are determined by adding total bank deposits, business expenses paid in cash, capital items purchased in cash, personal expenses paid in cash, and cash accumulations not deposited in any bank account. For tax purposes, this is compared to his/her gross income reported on the tax returns. For RICO purposes, this is compared to his/her identified income. The difference is the amount of unreported taxable income or illegal income. When this method is employed, each item of income and expense must be examined as to the source of funds and their subsequent use. This method is similar to the expenditure method as discussed in a previous chapter.

14.9.2 Schedule

To illustrate this method in more detail, the following schedule is in Figure 14.2.

Figure 14.2 should be compared with the total identified income for RICO purposes and the total gross income reported on the tax return for tax purposes. The difference will be either illegal income or unreported taxable income for the purpose used. The schedule accounts in Figure 14.2 are for both cash basis as well as the accrual basis.

14.10 Telephone

The fraud examiner should be aware of telephone calls. Telephone calls will help identify personal contacts and associates of the subject. Also, it identifies one of the subject's expenses. If the subject is a heavy telephone user, then this could be a major expenditure. This is particularly true with bookmakers who rely on the telephone for their business. Law enforcement will sometimes use a court-authorized wire tap or pen register. A pen register is a listing of telephone numbers that are only either received or made by the subject. The fraud examiner will have to establish a database that will identify telephone contacts. This database should contain at least the following fields:

1. *Date.* This is the date the call is received or sent.
2. *Caller.* This field should identify the person who is making the call. It could be either the subject or another person.
3. *Receiver.* This field should identify the person who receives the call. This could be the subject or another person.
4. *Sender number.* This field should identify the telephone number of the person receiving the call. This could be the subject or another person.
5. *Receiver number.* This field should identify the telephone number of the person receiving the call. This could be the subject or another person.
6. *Time.* This field should show the time the call is either received or made.
7. *Length.* This field should show the length of the call in minutes as a minimum.

1. Total deposits:

a. Business checking:	$ _____
b. Personal checking:	_____
c. Savings account(s):	_____
Total deposits	$ _____

2. Plus: Cash expenditures:

a. Business expenses	$ _____
b. Personal expenses	_____
c. Capital purchases	_____
Total cash expenditures	$ _____

3. Less: Total checks written:

	a. Bank balances 1/1/XX	$ _____
	b. Total deposits for year	_____
Less:	c. Bank balances 12/31/XX	(_____)
	Total cash expenditures	$ _____
	Total receipts	$ _____

4. Less: Nonincome items:

a. Transfers	$ _____
b. Redeposits	_____
c. Loans	_____
d. Gifts	_____
Total nonincome items	$ _____
Total income receipts	$ _____

5. Accrual adjustments:

a. Accounts receivable—add increase	$ _____
b. Accounts receivable—less decrease	_____
c. Accounts payable—less increase	_____
d. Accounts payable—add decrease	_____
Total accrual adjustment	$ _____

6. Total income $ _____

Figure 14.2 Bank deposit method.

Telephone calls usually will not identify assets or expenses, but they can identify the leads to assets or expenses. Either the telephone company or a cross-reference guide can identify telephone subscribers. The subscribers can later be interviewed as to their relationships with the subject. It will be hard for the subject to disclaim knowing a person who is called frequently by the subject.

14.11   Flowcharts

There are many kinds of flowcharts that the fraud examiner can use. In many cases, the fraud examiner will probably use many kinds of flowcharts in the same case. The flowcharts most commonly used by fraud examiners are as follows:

1. *Organizational.* The flowchart identifies the chain of command or lines of authority. In organized criminal organizations, this is an important tool to be used during the investigation and in court as evidence. An example of this is shown in Figure 14.3.
2. *Chronological.* A chronology of events that shows people, transactions, dates, and events can be very useful. Its primary purpose is to identify a pattern. After a pattern is established, the fraud examiner or investigator can project future events. The best tool in this case is to use a calendar showing the particular events.
3. *Matrix.* A matrix is a grid that shows relationships between a number of entities. This is most commonly used with telephone numbers and physical contacts (e.g., meetings). An example of this is shown in Figure 14.4.
4. *Operational.* This flowchart depicted in Figure 14.5 shows the flow of operations. This kind of flowcharting is used by public accountants and various governmental auditors to examine internal controls. Its purpose is to illustrate the flow of documents through various departments within an organization. Internal controls are compromised when an individual or department has too much involvement in the processing of a receipt of income or payment of an expense.

14.12   Commission/Percentage Method

The percentage method of computing income is used primarily in sports bookmaking cases. Its primary objective is to determine income (gross receipts) earned from operations. It is generally referred to as the vig method (vigorish). For cases involving only football and

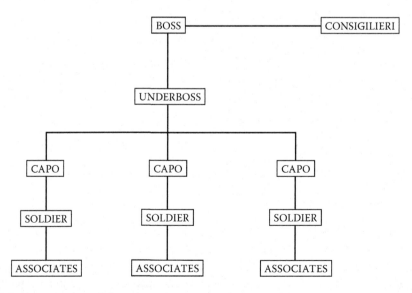

Figure 14.3 Organizational flowchart.

	1	2	3	4	5	
	6	7	8	9	1	
	2	8	9	1	2	
	-	-	-	-	-	
	6	7	8	9	5	
	4	3	2	1	5	
	6	7	8	9	1	
	2	3	4	5	6	TOTAL
162-6462	X	1	3	3	8	15
278-7373	3	X	1	5	8	17
389-8284	5	3	X	2	2	12
491-9195	8	2	6	X	1	17
512-5516	1	8	2	10	X	21
TOTAL	17	14	11	20	18	82

Figure 14.4 Telephone matrix.

basketball, this percentage method is often called the 4.54 method because the percentage is 4.5454%. It is determined by the following example. Let us say that Miami and Atlanta are playing. The bookmaker takes bets equally on both sides (balance his/her books).

	Miami	Atlanta
Total wagers placed	$10,000	$10,000
Add the vigorish/juice rate	1,000	1,000
Total amount at risk by the bettors	$11,000	$11,000

Regardless of who wins or loses, the bookmaker will collect $11,000 from losers and payout $10,000 to winners. He therefore has a $1,000 gross profit (commission). This $1,000 is divided by $22,000 (total wagers of $11,000 + $11,000) at risk by bettors equals 4.5454%.

In the case of baseball and hockey bets, the bets are based on odds, which will require a different computation. If the bookmaker is using a 10-cent line, the 5% of the total base bets will approximate the gross profit. Base bet as used here refers to the stated bet without regards to the odds. For example, if the Los Angeles Dodgers play the Atlanta Braves and the line is 160 Los Angeles, then the stated wager of $100 on Los Angeles means that the bettor is risking $160 against the bookmaker's $100. The $100 is the base bet. The odds are normally based on a 5:6 ratio.

14.13 When to Use

The forensic accountant should use as many of these accounting techniques as possible, whether or not they are used in a trial. The check and deposit spreads are the basic tools

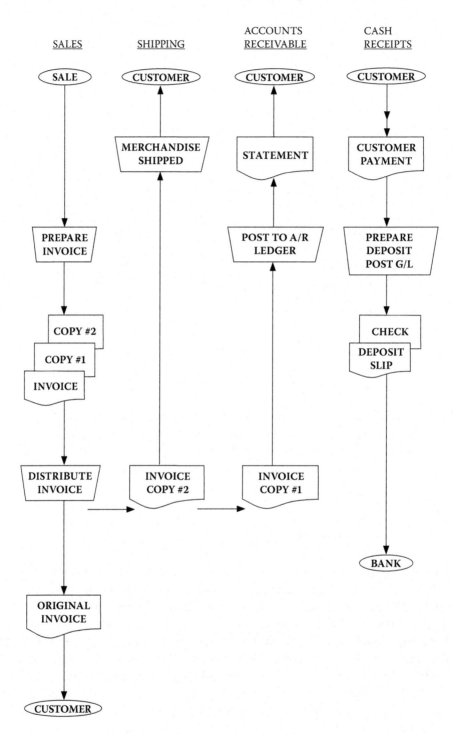

Figure 14.5 Operational flowchart.

of any forensic accountant or fraud examiner. They are the starting points of an examination and the building blocks to reach the final summary. The credit card spread is another building block in those cases where the subject uses them. These accounting techniques also provide leads to other financial information and establish connections with other people and entities. The subject's connections are a key to any fraud case. They are the building blocks for indirect methods, for example, net worth and expenditure schedules.

14.14 Summary

The forensic accountant has many tools that he/she can use. The use of those tools depends on the circumstances of each case. Some of the tools may not be needed. If the subject has no bank accounts, then the check and deposit spreads would not be necessary. These tools consist of:

1. Tracing schedule
2. Check spread
3. Deposit spread
4. Credit card spread
5. Gross profit analysis
6. Witness list
7. Bank deposit method
8. Telephone matrix
9. Organization chart
10. Operational flowchart
11. Commission/percentage method (use for bookmakers only)

Sources of Information   15

15.1 Introduction

The investigator has the monumental task of obtaining the information needed to put a case together, whether criminal or civil. The subject of the investigation will not usually provide financial information and documents. This is particularly true in criminal cases. Therefore, the investigator has to turn to third parties to obtain the financial information necessary to put their cases together. Some investigators, especially novice ones, do not know where to go to find financial information and documents. It can be surprising that financial information, in many cases, can be obtained fairly easily; however, in other cases, financial information cannot be obtained. It is imperative for the investigator to know where he/she can get the financial information needed to put the case together.

15.2 Objective

The objective of this chapter is to help the investigator identify the third parties from which he/she can obtain the financial information and/or documents to put his/her case together. Some sources will give the information with an oral or written request, while others require a subpoena. Yet, there are some sources that cannot give out information or documents unless authorized by a court of law. It is therefore necessary for the investigator to know what the sources require to obtain financial information and/or documents from them. Appendix B provides a list of Internet sites that an investigator can use to obtain information.

15.3 Codes

In the following paragraphs, each source has a code that will identify who may obtain the information and/or documents. These codes are identified below, along with their explanation.

1. *GP—General public.* This information is available to the general public. This means anyone can obtain this information. An example of this is county public records, which shows ownership of real property, mortgages, liens, judgments, tax liens, and many other items.
2. *LE—Law enforcement.* This information is available only to law enforcement agencies.
3. *CO—Court order.* This information can only be obtained by court order from either a state or federal court.

4. *LP—Limited public access.* This information is available only to members of the organization. An example of this is credit reporting agencies and financial institutions.

15.4   Federal Departments

This section covers the various federal agencies and departments that can supply information for the investigator's case.

Description	Code	Information Available
Department of Defense	LE	Personnel records for civilian and military personnel, e.g., pay, training, service locations
Defense Investigative Service	LE	Background investigations, security clearances
Department of Energy	LE	Background investigations, personnel records
U.S. Attorney	LE/CO	Prosecution of federal violations, indictments from grand juries, trial and hearing records; court orders are required for grand jury records
U.S. Border Patrol	LE	Information related to investigations of aliens and smuggling and apprehension of illegal aliens
Drug Enforcement Agency	LE	Information on drug criminals; monitors sales of legal and illegal drugs; drug company data
Federal Bureau of Investigation	LE	Information on investigations of federal laws in their jurisdiction; also, various records, e.g., fingerprints, U.S. property
U.S. Immigration and Naturalization Service	LE	Registered and unregistered aliens in United States; some financial information
Office of International Affairs	LE	Information to obtain formal requests to foreign governments for information through diplomatic channels
U.S. Marshal Service	LE	Investigations and arrests relating to bond defaults, escapes, parole, and probation
U.S. Department of Labor	LE	Investigations on labor violations, labor unions, and pension plans
Federal Probation Office	LE	Information on current federal probationers and parolees
U.S. Postal Service	LE	Investigations on postal law violations, mail fraud, and mailing obscene material
U.S. Department of State	LE	Passport information, visa fraud, terrorism, diplomatic motor vehicle registrations
U.S. Coast Guard	LP	Maintains vessel documentation over 5 net tons used in commercial operations; investigate high seas crimes
Federal Aviation Administration	LP	Maintains aircraft title history, aircraft owners, pilot, and aircraft information
Bureau of Alcohol, Tobacco, and Firearms	LE	Information on violations of firearms, explosive, bombs, liquor; files on firearm dealers
U.S. Customs Service	LE	Information on customs violations, smuggling activity, theft of shipments, CMIR data bank
Internal Revenue Service	CO	Information on tax law violations; various tax returns and reports

(continued)

Description	Code	Information Available
U.S. Secret Service	LE	Information on counterfeiting, forgery, altering government checks, currency, and bonds
Treasurer of the United States	LE	Photostats of government checks
Interstate Commerce Commission	LE	Information on individuals and companies engaged in interstate commerce
Securities and Exchange Commission	PL	Securities violations files, corporate officer and directors; quarterly bulletins; certified financial statements of corporations
Federal Courts	GP	Detailed records of civil and criminal cases; also claims, bankruptcy, and tax cases

15.5   State Agencies and Departments

This section covers agencies and departments within the state government that can provide information for an investigator's case. It must be kept in mind that each state does not title their particular agency or department the same as another state. This section uses the State of Florida as its model. Therefore, the investigator in another state will have to compare the State of Florida with their comparable state agency or department.

Description	Code	Information Available
Department of Agriculture and Consumer Services	LE	Issues permits and inspects amusement rides, fairs, expositions, carnivals, bazaars, and celebrations
Division of Animal Industry	LE	Investigation and enforcement of livestock, livestock and farm equipment thefts, livestock movement
Division of Consumer Services	GP	Receives inquiries and complaints against businesses
Division of Forestry	LE	Investigate fire and theft of forest and timber
Division of Public Assistance	LP	Investigate fraud by recipients and state employees of welfare programs
Medicaid Fraud Control Unit	GP	Investigate fraud provided by nursing homes, hospitals, pharmacies, etc.
Division of Banking	GP	Information on charter and regulation of state financial institutions
Division of Finance and Insurance	GP	Information on licensing, regulation of mortgage brokers, finance companies, money orders, traveler's checks, home improvements offering financing
Division of Securities	GP	Information on security dealers, agents, and advisors. Has national index of agents and dealers; corporate application
Division of Alcoholic Beverages and Tobacco	LP	Information on beverage and cigarette wholesalers, cigarette wholesalers, retailers
Bureau of Land Sales	GP	Maintains registration records on developers
Division of Pari-Mutuel Wagering	GP	Information on track employee concessions, owners of racing animals
Division of Corrections Bureau of Admission and Release	LE	Information on current and former prisoners, parole, and probation people

(continued)

Description	Code	Information Available
Department of Education	LP	Investigates violations of ethics and law of people holding teaching certificates
Department of Environment Regulation	LE	Information of all companies involved in hazardous materials
Game and Fresh Water Fish	LE	Information on wildlife law violations
Department of Health and Rehabilitative Services	LE	Information on state mental hospitals and patients
Child Support Enforcement	LE	Information on parents who stop child support
License and Certification	GP	License all health care facilities, day care centers, abortion clinics; investigates state law violations
Office of Vital Statistics	GP	Maintains records of birth, death, marriage, and divorce
Division of Drivers	LE	Maintains driver's licenses and driving record data; has photo of drivers in some states
Bureau of Records and Training	LP	Maintains copies of all accident reports in state
Division of Motor Vehicles Bureau of Licensing and Enforcement	LP	Maintains licenses on manufacturers, importers, distributors of all motor distributors of all vehicles including mobile homes
Bureau of Title and Lien Services	LP	Maintains records of titles, liens, and owners
Department of Insurance and Treasurer	LP	Maintains information on insurance agents, adjusters, bail bondsmen
Division of Consumer Services	GP	Maintains records of complaints, fines, legal actions on unethical business practices
Bureau of Insurer Company Regulation	LP	Maintains information on insurance companies and officers
Division of Insurance Fraud	LE	Investigates fraudulent claims activities involving companies, agents, and adjusters
Division of State Fire	LP	License dealers, users, and manufacturers of explosives; investigates arson, fires, and explosives
Department of Labor and Employment Security	GP	Information on public and private labor organizations in state
Department of Law Enforcement	LE	Investigates and maintains records on criminals; trends intelligence. Supplies services for local law enforcement
State Medical Examiner	LE	Investigates and determines cause of death
Florida Intelligence Center	LE	Maintains intelligence on criminals; supports local law enforcement
Attorney General	LP	Handles investigations of consumer complaints
Department of Lottery	LP	Information on retail applications and lottery winners of $600 or more
Department of Natural Resources, Florida Marine Patrol	LE	Investigates salt water violations, interdiction of narcotics smuggling on waters
Bureau of License and Motor Registration	LP	Maintains boat titles and data
Licenses and Permits Section	LP	Maintains and issues licenses for seafood dealers, dredge fill permits, commercial fishermen, and trolling permits
Division of Recreations and Parks	LE	Maintains records of state law violations on state lands
Parole Commission	LE	Information on parole status, release dates, and conditions
Department of Professional Regulation	LP	Maintains information on occupations regulated by boards

(*continued*)

Description	Code	Information Available
Professional Boards	LP	Accountancy; acupuncture; architecture and interior design; auctioneers; barbers; chiropractic construction industry; cosmetology; electrical contractors; geologists; funeral directors; hearing aids; landscape architects; land surveyors; massage; medical (physicians); nursing homes; occupational therapists; opticianary; optometry; osteopathic; pharmacy; physical therapy; pilots; professional engineers; podiatry; psychological services; real estate; respiratory therapists; veterinary medicine
Department of Revenue	LE/CO	State tax returns and information (subpoena only)
Department of State Divisions of Corporations	GP	Information on corporations (profit and nonprofit)
Division of Elections Bureau of Election Records	GP	Information forms filed by state public officials and some state employees
Department of Transportation, Bureau of Weights	LE	Information on trucking violations and their drivers
Aerial Surveys Section	GP	Provide aerial photos of the entire state

15.6   County and Municipal Agencies

This section covers departments and agencies within the county and municipal governments, which can provide information for an investigator's case. Not every county or municipality has the same departments and agencies. Some counties and municipalities have departments and agencies that others do not have. Also, they do not title their departments and agencies the same. This is true even in the same state. Therefore, the investigator will have to inquire in each county or municipality about their particular departments.

Description	Code	Available Information
Aviation Department	GP	Information on airline companies and license to operate
Building and Zoning	GP	License and permit applications, names of contractors, and identify owner and place of construction
Clerks of the Circuit and County Courts	GP	Court records on both criminal and civil cases
Library	GP	Various reference material and copies of old books, magazines, and newspapers
Environmental Services	GP	Licenses and other data on hazardous waste
Utilities	GP	Billings and payments of various utilities, e.g., water, waste, electric, and gas
Sheriff's Officer or Police Department	LE	Arrests, accidents, gun permits, towed or repossessed autos, traffic violations
Licenses	GP	Various licenses, e.g., fishing, hunting, marriage, occupational, dog and cat
Health Department	GP	License, inspections, and other data on businesses
Voter Registration	GP	Data on people registered to vote; political affiliations
State/District Attorney	LE	Detailed information on criminals and criminal activities

(continued)

Description	Code	Available Information
Public Records	GP	Gives detailed information on real estate, mortgages, liens, judgments, and various other items
Tax Assessor/Collector	GP	Records of personal and real property tax assessments and collections
Schools	LP	Maintains records of students; sometimes medical and other personal information
Social or Welfare Services	LP	Maintains records of recipients of welfare and other social programs
Personnel Departments	LP	Maintains records on employees
Purchasing and Procurement	LP	Maintains records on vendors, contracts, and others

15.7 Business Records

Businesses maintain records that can help in supplying data for a financial case. In most cases, it is one of the important sources of obtaining financial information. The following is a general listing of the types of businesses that can supply financial data.

Description	Code	Available Information
Abstract and Title Companies	GP	Provide records of real estate transactions, title policies, escrow files, maps, and plates
Bonding Companies	LP	Investigative and other records on persons or firms; financial statements, identity of person on bond
Credit Reporting Agencies	LP	Maintains data on people's loan history, bank accounts, employment, insurance, and other credit actions
Department Stores	LP	Maintains credit files and charge account records
Detective Agencies	LP	Investigative files, evidence and identifying information on clients and other parties
Fraternal, Veterans, Labor, Social, Political Organizations	LP	Membership, dues, location, and history of members
Hospitals	LP	Payments, entry and release dates
Hotels and Motels	LP	Identity of guests, phone calls, credit cards, payments, forwarding address, and date
Insurance	LP	Applications, assets being insured, ledger cards, dividends, cash values, claims refunds, and cancellations
National Credit Card Companies	LP	Applications, charge uses and payments, e.g., services
Telephone Companies	LP	Local directories, toll calls charges, and payments list of numbers called and calling numbers
Transportation	LP	Passenger list, fares paid, destinations, departure and arrival times and dates
Public Utility Company	LP	Charges and payments, service address, hookup and disconnect dates
Automobile Dealers and Manufacturers	LP	Franchise agreements, dealer's financial records, car sales, trade-ins, and service records

(continued)

Description	Code	Available Information
Brokerage Companies	LP	Monthly statements, amount and date of buy and sell of securities, market values, and types of security and accounts
Banks and other financial institutions	LP	Name, address, occupation, source of deposits and expenditures, signatures, wire transfers, safe deposit box, and letters of credit

15.8   Reference Materials

There are other sources of information that can be obtained by just going to the local library. It can give financial information as well as biographical profiles. The following references give some of the more common references that can be used in helping to develop a case.

Description	Code	Available Information
Moody's Industrial Manual	GP	Salary and wages by industry and region
Dun and Brad Street Reference Book	GP	Financial and other information about various public companies
Encyclopedia of Associations	GP	Names, addresses, and types of organizations
Funk and Scott Index of Corporations and Industries	GP	Names, addresses, stock issues, and summary financial data
F & S International Index	GP	Data about companies located offshore
Moody's Bank and Finance Manual	GP	Data about various financial institutions
Moody's Industrial Manual	GP	Data about various manufacturers in the United States
Standard & Poor's Register of Corporations, Directors, Executives	GP	Data about various publicly held companies; biographical summaries of officers and directors
Thomas Register of American Manufacturers	GP	Data about various U.S. manufacturing companies
Better Business Bureau	GP	Maintains complaints against a business and owners
Newspapers and magazines	GP	Provide index to their issues by topic and names

15.9   International

Evidence from foreign countries is admissible in federal courts when it is properly authenticated. Title 18 USC 3494 provides the procedures necessary to certify foreign documents for admission in federal criminal cases. Title 18 USC 3492 provides that testimony of foreign witnesses may be taken by oral or written interrogatories. Many law enforcement officers and prosecutors, federal and state, think that records from foreign countries are not obtainable. This is not true in every case. Some countries have various records more available than do others. This section identifies those records that are available by country. It must be kept in mind that there are federal procedures that must be followed in obtaining foreign evidence in criminal cases. Treaties sometimes provide procedures that must be followed such as in Japan. Direct contact is forbidden. Also, proper certification must be obtained and the chain of custody properly maintained in criminal cases. Another problem in obtaining foreign evidence is whether the records are centralized or decentralized. Centralized records mean that these records are located in one location. Decentralized records mean that they are located at various locations. The type of records are shown below that are public and identify whether they are centralized (CEN) or decentralized (DEC).

Country	Location	Type of Record
Anguilla	CEN	Court records
	CEN	Wills
	CEN	Commercial register
	CEN	Corporation charter
	CEN	Land transfer records
	CEN	Birth records
	CEN	Death records
	CEN	Marriage records
	CEN	Company records
	CEN	Company bylaws
	CEN	Company financial statements
Antigua	CEN	Court records
	CEN	Wills
	CEN	Patents
	CEN	Trademarks
	CEN	Copyrights
	CEN	Corporation charter
	CEN	Land transfer records
	CEN	Birth records
	CEN	Death records
	CEN	Marriage records
	CEN	Other public records
	CEN	Company bylaws
Argentina	CEN	Court records
	CEN	Patents
	CEN	Trademarks
	CEN	Copyrights
	CEN	Commercial register
	CEN	Corporation charter
	CEN	Land transfer records
	CEN	Birth records
	CEN	Death records
	CEN	Marriage records
	CEN	Public company records
	CEN	Company bylaws
	CEN	Public company financial statements
Australia	DEC	Court records
	DEC	Wills
	CEN	Patents

(continued)

Country	Location	Type of Record
	CEN	Trademarks
	DEC	Commercial register
	DEC	Corporation charter
	DEC	Land transfer records
	DEC	Company records
	DEC	Company bylaws
	DEC	Company financial statements
Austria	CEN	Patents
	CEN	Trademarks
	CEN	Copyrights
	DEC	Commercial register
	DEC	Corporation charter
	DEC	Land transfer records
	DEC	Birth records
	DEC	Death records
	DEC	Marriage records
	CEN	Company financial statements
	DEC	Company bylaws
	DEC	Alien registration (U.S. only)
Bahamas	CEN	Court records
	CEN	Wills, patents, trademarks, and copyrights
	CEN	Corporation charter
	CEN	Land transfer records
	CEN	Birth, death, and marriage records
	CEN	Company records and bylaws
Bahrain	CEN	Court records
	CEN	Corporate charter
	CEN	Commercial register
	CEN	Land transfer records
	CEN	Birth, death, and marriage records
	CEN	Bank and credit information
	CEN	Other public records
	CEN	Alien registration (U.S. only)
Bangladesh	DEC	Court records
	CEN	Patents and trademarks
	CEN	Commercial register
	CEN	Corporate charter
	CEN	Land transfer records
	CEN	Birth and marriage records
	CEN	Company bylaws and financial statements
Barbados	CEN	Court records
	CEN	Wills, patents, trademarks, and copyright records
	CEN	Corporation charter

(continued)

Country	Location	Type of Record
	CEN	Land transfer records
	CEN	Birth, death, and marriage records
	CEN	Other public records
	CEN	Company bylaws
Belgium	DEC	Court records
	CEN	Patents and trademarks
	CEN	Commercial register
	DEC	Corporation charter
	DEC	Land transfer records
	DEC	Company bylaws, records, and financial statements
Belize	CEN	Court records
	CEN	Patents and trademarks
	CEN	Commercial register
	CEN	Corporation charter
	CEN	Land transfer records
	CEN	Company bylaws
Bermuda	CEN	Court records
	CEN	Wills, patents, trademarks, and copyrights
	CEN	Corporation charter
	CEN	Land transfer records
	CEN	Birth, death, and marriage records
	CEN	Credit information
	DEC	Other public records
	CEN	Company records
Bolivia	DEC	Court records
	CEN	Patents and trademarks
	DEC	Copyrights
	CEN	Commercial register
	CEN	Corporation charter
	CEN	Land transfer records
	CEN	Birth, death, and marriage records
	CEN	Public company records
	CEN	Public company bylaws, and financial statements
Brazil	DEC	Court records
	CEN	Patents, trademarks, copyrights
	DEC	Commercial register
	DEC	Corporation charter
	DEC	Land transfer records
	DEC	Birth, death, and marriage records
	CEN	Public company bylaws and financial statements
British Virgin Islands	CEN	Court records

(continued)

Country	Location	Type of Record
	CEN	Wills, patents, trademarks, and copyrights
	CEN	Corporation charter
	CEN	Birth, death, and marriage records
	CEN	Other public records
	CEN	Company bylaws
Brunei	CEN	Court records
	CEN	Patents, trademarks, and copyrights
	CEN	Commercial register
	CEN	Corporation charter
	CEN	Land transfer records
	DEC	Birth, death, and marriage records
	CEN	Company bylaws and financial statements
Burma	DEC	Court records
	DEC	Wills
	CEN	Patents, trademarks, copyright
	CEN	Commercial register
	CEN	Corporation charter
	DEC	Land transfer records
	DEC	Birth, death, and marriage records
	CEN	Alien registration (U.S. only)
	CEN	Company records, bylaws, and financial statements
Canada	DEC	Court records
	DEC	Wills
	CEN	Patents
	DEC	Commercial register
	DEC	Corporation charter
	DEC	Land transfer records
	DEC	Company bylaws
Cayman Islands	CEN	Court records
	CEN	Wills, patents, trademarks, and copyrights
	CEN	Land transfer records
	CEN	Birth, death, and marriage records
	DEC	Other public records
Channel Islands—Jersey	CEN	Court records
	CEN	Wills, patents, trademarks
	CEN	Commercial register
	CEN	Corporation charter
	CEN	Land transfer records
	CEN	Birth, death, and marriage records
	CEN	Company records and bylaws
Channel Islands—Guernsey	CEN	Court records
	CEN	Wills and trademarks

(continued)

Country	Location	Type of Record
	CEN	Commercial register
	CEN	Corporation charter
	CEN	Land transfer records
	CEN	Birth, death, and marriage records
	CEN	Company records and bylaws
Channel Islands—Alderney	CEN	Court records
	CEN	Wills
	CEN	Corporation charter
	CEN	Land transfer records
	CEN	Birth, death, and marriage records
	CEN	Company records and bylaws
Chile	CEN	Court records
	CEN	Wills, patents, trademarks, and copyrights
	CEN	Corporation charter
	CEN	Commercial register
	CEN	Land transfer records
	DEC	Birth, death, and marriage records
	CEN	Credit information
	CEN	Public company records, bylaws, and financial statements
Colombia	DEC	Court records
	DEC	Wills
	CEN	Patents, trademarks, and copyrights
	DEC	Commercial register
	DEC	Corporation charter
	DEC	Land transfer records
	DEC	Birth, death, and marriage records
	DEC	Credit information
	DEC	Other public records
	DEC	Alien registration (U.S. only)
	DEC	Company records, bylaws, and financial statements
Cook Island	CEN	Court records
	CEN	Land transfer records
	CEN	Birth, death, and marriage records
	CEN	Alien registration (U.S. only)
	CEN	Company records and bylaws
Costa Rica	CEN	Court records
	CEN	Wills, patents, trademarks, and copyrights
	CEN	Commercial register
	CEN	Corporation charter
	CEN	Land transfer records
	CEN	Birth, death, and marriage records
	CEN	Credit information

(continued)

Country	Location	Type of Record
	CEN	Company bylaws
	CEN	Alien registration (U.S. only)
Cyprus	CEN	Patents and trademarks
	CEN	Corporation charter
	CEN	Birth, death, and marriage records
	CEN	Other public records
	CEN	Company records
	CEN	Company bylaws and financial statements
Denmark	DEC	Court records
	CEN	Patents, trademarks, and copyrights
	CEN	Commercial register
	CEN	Corporation charter
	DEC	Land transfer records
	DEC	Birth, death, and marriage records
Dominican Republic	CEN	Corporation charter
	CEN	Land transfer records
	CEN	Birth, death, and marriage records
	CEN	Other public records
Egypt	CEN	Patents, trademarks, and copyrights
	CEN	Commercial register
	CEN	Corporation charter
	CEN	Land transfer records
	CEN	Birth, death, and marriage records
	CEN	Other public records
	CEN	Company bylaws and financial statements
Fiji	CEN	Court record
	CEN	Wills, patents, trademarks, and copyrights
	CEN	Commercial register
	CEN	Corporation charter
	CEN	Land transfer records
	CEN	Company bylaws
Finland	DEC	Court records (limitations)
	DEC	Wills
	CEN	Patents and trademarks
	CEN	Commercial register
	DEC	Corporation charter
	DEC	Land transfer records
	CEN	Company bylaws and financial statements
France	CEN	Patents, trademarks, and copyrights
	CEN	Commercial register
	CEN	Corporation charter

(*continued*)

Country	Location	Type of Record
	CEN	Company bylaws and financial statements
Germany	DEC	Court records
	CEN	Patents and trademarks
	DEC	Commercial register
	DEC	Corporation charter
	DEC	Land transfer records
	DEC	Credit information
	CEN	Other public information
	DEC	Company bylaws and financial statements
Gibraltar	CEN	Court records
	CEN	Wills, trademarks, and copyrights
	CEN	Commercial register
	CEN	Corporation charter
	CEN	Land transfer records
	CEN	Birth, death, and marriage records
	CEN	Company bylaws and records
Greece	DEC	Court records
	DEC	Wills, patents, and trademarks
	CEN	Copyrights
	DEC	Land transfer records
	DEC	Birth, death, and marriage records
	DEC	Company bylaws and financial statements
Grenada	CEN	Court records
	CEN	Wills, patents, trademarks, and copyrights
	CEN	Corporation charter
	CEN	Land transfer records
	CEN	Birth, death, and marriage records
	CEN	Other public records
	CEN	Company bylaws
Guatemala	CEN	Corporation charter
	CEN	Land transfer records
	CEN	Birth, death, and marriage records
	CEN	Credit information (limited)
	CEN	Other public records
	CEN	Company records and bylaws
Haiti	DEC	Court records
	CEN	Patents, trademarks, and copyrights
	CEN	Corporation charter
	CEN	Land transfer records
	CEN	Birth, death, and marriage records
	CEN	Company records and bylaws
Honduras	CEN	Court records (limitations)

(continued)

Country	Location	Type of Record
	CEN	Wills, patents, trademarks, and copyrights
	CEN	Commercial paper
	CEN	Corporation charter
	CEN	Land transfer records
	CEN	Birth, death, and marriage records
	CEN	Other public records
	CEN	Company records and bylaws
Hong Kong	DEC	Court records
	CEN	Wills, patents, trademarks, and copyrights
	DEC	Commercial register
	DEC	Corporation charter
	CEN	Land transfer records
	DEC	Birth, death, and marriage records
	CEN	Credit information
	DEC	Other public records
	DEC	Company bylaws
Iceland	DEC	Court records
	CEN	Patents and trademarks
	CEN	Commercial register
	CEN	Corporation charter
	CEN	Land transfer records
India	CEN	Patents, trademarks, and copyrights
	CEN	Commercial register
	DEC	Corporation charter
	CEN	Birth and death records
	CEN	Other public records
	CEN	Company bylaws
Indonesia	DEC	Court records
	CEN	Wills, patents, trademarks, and copyrights
	CEN	Commercial register
	DEC	Land transfer records
	DEC	Birth, death, and marriage records
	DEC	Other public records
Ireland	CEN	Wills, patents, trademarks, and copyrights
	CEN	Commercial register
	CEN	Corporation charter
	CEN	Land transfer records
	CEN	Birth, death, and marriage records
	CEN	Other public records
	CEN	Company records, bylaws, and financial statements
Isle of Man	CEN	Court records

(continued)

Country	Location	Type of Record
	CEN	Commercial register
	CEN	Corporation charter
	CEN	Land transfer records
	DEC	Birth, death, and marriage records
	CEN	Company records and bylaws
Israel	DEC	Court records
	DEC	Wills
	CEN	Patents, trademarks, and copyrights
	CEN	Commercial register
	CEN	Corporation charter
	DEC	Land transfer records
	CEN	Company records, bylaws, and financial statements
Italy	DEC	Court records
	DEC	Wills
	CEN	Patents, trademarks, and copyrights
	DEC	Commercial register
	DEC	Corporation charter
	DEC	Land transfer records
	DEC	Birth, death, and marriage records
	DEC	Company records, bylaws, and financial statements
	DEC	Bankruptcy judgments
	DEC	Movie production records
Jamaica	CEN	Court records
	CEN	Patents and trademarks
	CEN	Commercial register
	CEN	Corporation charter
	CEN	Land transfer records
	CEN	Birth, death, and marriage records
	CEN	Company records, bylaws, and financial statements
Japan	CEN	Court records
	CEN	Patents, trademarks, and copyrights
	DEC	Commercial register
	CEN	Corporation charter
	DEC	Land transfer records
	DEC	Birth records
	CEN	Company bylaws and financial statements
Jordan	CEN	Patents, trademarks, and copyrights
	CEN	Commercial register
	CEN	Corporation charter
	CEN	Land transfer records
	CEN	Birth, death, and marriage records
Kenya	DEC	Court records

(*continued*)

Country	Location	Type of Record
	CEN	Patents, trademarks, and copyrights
	CEN	Commercial register
	CEN	Corporate charter
	CEN	Land transfer records
	DEC	Birth, death, and marriage records
Korea	DEC	
	DEC	Commercial register
	DEC	Corporation charter
	DEC	Birth, death, and marriage records
	CEN	Company bylaws and financial statements
Kuwait	CEN	Wills, copyrights
	CEN	Commercial register
	CEN	Corporation charter
	CEN	Land transfer records
	CEN	Birth, death, and marriage records
	CEN	Company records and bylaws
Lebanon	CEN	Land transfer records
	CEN	Birth, death, and marriage records
	CEN	Company records, bylaws, and financial statements
Liberia	DEC	Court records
	CEN	Wills
	DEC	Patents, trademarks, and copyrights
	DEC	Commercial register
	CEN	Corporation charter
	DEC	Land transfer records
	DEC	Marriage records
Liechtenstein	CEN	Patents, trademarks, and copyrights
	CEN	Commercial register
	CEN	Birth, death, and marriage records
	CEN	Other public records
Luxembourg	CEN	Patents, trademarks, and copyrights
	CEN	Commercial register
	CEN	Corporation charter
	DEC	Land transfer records
	DEC	Birth, death, and marriage records
	CEN	Other public records
	CEN	Company records, bylaws, and financial statements
Malaysia	CEN	Patents, trademarks, and copyrights
	CEN	Commercial register
	CEN	Corporation charter
	CEN	Land transfer records
	CEN	Birth, death, and marriage records
	CEN	Company records and bylaws

(*continued*)

Country	Location	Type of Record
Malta	CEN	Court records
	CEN	Patents, trademarks, and copyrights
	CEN	Commercial register
	CEN	Land transfer records
	CEN	Birth, death, and marriage records
Mexico	CEN	Patents, trademarks, and copyrights
	CEN	Commercial register
	CEN	Corporation charter
	DEC	Land transfer records
	CEN	Birth, death, and marriage records
	CEN	Company records
Monaco	CEN	Patents and trademarks
	CEN	Commercial register
	CEN	Corporation charter
	CEN	Land transfer records
	CEN	Company bylaws
Nauru	CEN	Wills, patents, and trademarks
	CEN	Land transfer records
	CEN	Birth, death, and marriage records
Nepal	DEC	Court records
	CEN	Commercial register
	CEN	Corporation charter
	CEN	Company records
Netherlands	CEN	Patents, trademarks, and copyrights
	CEN	Commercial register
	CEN	Corporation charter
	CEN	Land transfer records
	DEC	Birth, death, and marriage records
	DEC	Company bylaws and financial statements
Netherlands Antilles	CEN	Court records
	CEN	Wills, patents, trademarks, and copyrights
	CEN	Corporation charter
	CEN	Land transfer records
	CEN	Birth, death, and marriage records
	CEN	Other public records
	CEN	Company records and bylaws
New Zealand	DEC	Court records
	DEC	Wills, patents, and trademarks
	DEC	Commercial register
	DEC	Corporation charter
	DEC	Land transfer records
	DEC	Credit information
	DEC	Company records, bylaws, and financial statements

(*continued*)

Country	Location	Type of Record
Norway	DEC	Court records
	CEN	Patents and trademarks
	DEC	Commercial register
	DEC	Corporation charter
	DEC	Land transfer records
	CEN	Birth, death, and marriage records
	CEN	Register of ships
	DEC	Register of chattel, fishing vessels, and aircraft
Oman	CEN	Commercial register
	CEN	Bank information
Pakistan	CEN	Patents, trademarks, and copyrights
	DEC	Corporation charter
	DEC	Land transfer records
	CEN	Credit information
	DEC	Other public records
	CEN	Company records
	DEC	Company bylaws and financial statements
Panama	CEN	Court records
	CEN	Wills, patents, trademarks, and copyrights
	CEN	Corporate charter
	CEN	Land transfer records
	CEN	Birth, death, and marriage records
	DEC	Other public records
	CEN	Company bylaws
Paraguay	CEN	Court records
	CEN	Wills, patents, trademarks, and copyrights
	CEN	Commercial register
	CEN	Corporation charter
	CEN	Land transfer records
	CEN	Birth, death, and marriage records
	CEN	Company records, bylaws, and financial statements
Peru	DEC	Court records
	CEN	Wills, patents, trademarks, and copyrights
	CEN	Commercial register
	DEC	Corporation charter
	DEC	Land transfer records
	DEC	Birth, death, and marriage records
	CEN	Public company records, bylaws, and financial statements
Philippines	CEN	Patents, trademarks, and copyrights
	CEN	Commercial register

(continued)

Country	Location	Type of Record
	CEN	Corporation charter
	DEC	Land transfer records
	CEN	Company bylaws
Poland	CEN	Patents and trademarks
	DEC	Commercial register
Qatar	CEN	Commercial register
Romania	CEN	Patents and trademarks
	DEC	Land transfer records
St. Kitts–Nevis	CEN	Court records
	CEN	Wills, patents, trademarks, and copyrights
	CEN	Corporation charter
	CEN	Land transfer records
	CEN	Birth, death, and marriage records
	CEN	Other public records
	CEN	Company bylaws and financial statements
St. Vincent	CEN	Court records
	CEN	Wills, patents, trademarks, and copyrights
	CEN	Corporation charter
	CEN	Land transfer records
	CEN	Birth, death, and marriage records
	CEN	Other public records
	CEN	Company bylaws
Western Samoa	CEN	Court records
	CEN	Wills, patents, and trademarks
	CEN	Commercial register
	CEN	Corporation charter
	CEN	Land transfer records
	CEN	Birth, death, and marriage records
	CEN	Alien registration (U.S. only)
	CEN	Company records and bylaws
Saudi Arabia	CEN	Trademarks and copyrights
	CEN	Commercial register
	CEN	Corporation charter
	CEN	Company bylaws
Singapore	CEN	Court records
	CEN	Wills, patents, trademarks, and copyrights
	CEN	Commercial register
	CEN	Corporation charter
	CEN	Land transfer records
	CEN	Birth, death, and marriage records
	CEN	Company records and bylaws
Solomon Islands	CEN	Court records

(continued)

Country	Location	Type of Record
	CEN	Wills, patents, and trademarks
	CEN	Commercial register
	CEN	Corporation charter
	CEN	Land transfer records
	CEN	Birth, death, and marriage records
	CEN	Company bylaws and financial statements
South Africa	CEN	Court records
	CEN	Wills, patents, trademarks, and copyrights
	CEN	Commercial register
	CEN	Corporation charter
	CEN	Land transfer records
	CEN	Birth, death, and marriage records
Spain	DEC	Patents, trademarks, and copyrights
	DEC	Commercial register
	DEC	Corporation charter
	DEC	Land transfer records
	DEC	Birth, death, and marriage records
	DEC	Company bylaws
Sri Lanka	CEN	Patents, trademarks, and copyrights
	CEN	Commercial register
	CEN	Corporation charter
	DEC	Land transfer records
	DEC	Other public records
	CEN	Company records and bylaws
Sudan	CEN	Court records
	CEN	Commercial register
	CEN	Corporation charter
	CEN	Land transfer records
	CEN	Marriage
	CEN	Credit information
	CEN	Company bylaws
Sweden	DEC	Court records
	CEN	Patents and trademarks
	CEN	Commercial register
	CEN	Corporation charter
	DEC	Land transfer records
	DEC	Birth, death, and marriage records
	CEN	Company bylaws and financial statements
Switzerland	CEN	Patents, trademarks, and copyrights
	CEN	Commercial register
	CEN	Corporation charter
	CEN	Land transfer records
	CEN	Birth, death, and marriage records

(*continued*)

Country	Location	Type of Record
	DEC	Credit information
	CEN	Other public records
Syria	CEN	Commercial register
	CEN	Corporation charter
	CEN	Land transfer records
	CEN	Birth, death, and marriage records
	CEN	Company records, bylaws, and financial statements
Thailand	DEC	Court records
	DEC	Patents, trademarks, and copyrights
	DEC	Commercial register
	DEC	Corporation charter
	DEC	Land transfer records
	DEC	Birth, death, and marriage records
	DEC	Company records, bylaws, and financial statements
Trinidad and Tobago	CEN	Court records
	CEN	Patents, trademarks, and copyrights
	CEN	Corporation charter
	CEN	Land transfer records
	CEN	Birth, death, and marriage records
	DEC	Other public records
	CEN	Public company records
Tunisia	CEN	Court records
	CEN	Trademarks and copyrights
	DEC	Commercial register
	DEC	Corporation charter
	DEC	Land transfer records
	DEC	Birth, death, and marriage records
	DEC	Company bylaws
Turkey	CEN	Patents and trademarks
	CEN	Commercial register
	CEN	Land transfer records
Turks and Caicos Islands	CEN	Court records
	CEN	Corporation charter
	CEN	Land transfer records
	CEN	Birth, death, and marriage records
	CEN	Other public records
	CEN	Company records and bylaws
United Kingdom	DEC	Court records
	CEN	Patents and trademarks
	CEN	Commercial register
	CEN	Corporation charter
	CEN	Birth, death, and marriage records
	CEN	Other public records
	CEN	Company bylaws

(continued)

Country	Location	Type of Record
Uruguay	CEN	Court records
	CEN	Wills, patents, trademarks, and copyrights
	CEN	Commercial register
	CEN	Corporation charter
	CEN	Land transfer records
	CEN	Birth, death, and marriage records
	CEN	Company records, bylaws, and financial statements
Vanuatu	DEC	Court records
	CEN	Patents, trademarks, and copyrights
	CEN	Land transfer records
	DEC	Birth, death, and marriage records
Venezuela	CEN	Patents, trademarks, and copyrights
	CEN	Commercial register
	CEN	Corporation charter
	CEN	Land transfer records
	CEN	Birth, death, and marriage records
	CEN	Company bylaws
Yugoslavia	CEN	Patents and trademarks
	DEC	Commercial register
	DEC	Land transfer records
	DEC	Birth, death, and marriage records

15.10 Definitions

The terms shown above have different meanings from one country to another. Commercial register can mean nothing more than the name and address of a company in some countries, while it could mean a whole biographical sketch in other countries. Company records have different meanings from one country to another. Company financial statements imply complete financial statements are available. This may not be the case in every country. Some countries only require selected financial information, for example, inventory, sales, and net profit. Tax return information is not available unless a treaty is in effect. Banking information is not public record in any country. In some countries, banking information is prohibited by law to be disclosed to any party or governmental body.

15.11 Summary

For the investigator, knowing where to find financial information is very important. This is particularly true during the initial phase of developing a case. During the initial phase the investigator should get as much information as possible. A lot of information can be obtained from various public sources that can determine if the investigator has a possible subject or case. From that point, the investigator can concentrate on the most possible subject by obtaining more information from more difficult sources. Some sources of information are easy to get by just simply asking, while others may require administrative subpoenas or court orders. Remember the more information obtained, the better. Sometimes, only one or two pieces of information can make a case.

Wagering and Gambling 16

16.1 Introduction

Gambling, in its various forms, is illegal in most states. In many cases, organized crime organizations control illegal gambling. Gambling has become more complicated in the fact that many states have instituted state lotteries in order to obtain additional revenue without raising taxes. However, organized crime organizations have tied their operations to various state lotteries. In this chapter, the most common gambling activities are discussed. Their terminology and record keeping will be discussed in detail. The gambling activities that will be addressed are:

1. *Sports bookmaking.* This section explains the terminology and how sports bookmaking operates. Baseball, basketball, football, and hockey are the primary sports involved in sports bookmaking.
2. *Lotteries.* These are number games, policy, and similar types of wagering. The operator of the lottery pays a prize if the selected number(s) appear or are published in a manner understood by the parties. The state-operated lotteries require participants to pay a certain amount for selected numbers. If the numbers are chosen, then the participants win a percentage of the "pot." In illegal lotteries, which are sometimes called "bolito," prizes are paid in terms of $400 to $600 to $1.
3. *Bingo.* Bingo halls are illegal in most states; however, they are legal in many states where they are operated by and for the benefit of charitable organizations.
4. *Track betting (pari-mutuel wagering).* Many states have various racetracks where betting on a race or sporting event is legal. Races usually encompass dogs and horses, while Jai Alai is a sporting event.

16.2 Sports Bookmaking

This form of gambling that involves placing bets on sport events, principally baseball, basketball, football, and hockey. Professional and collegiate teams are subjects of bettors. This form of gambling is based on credit of the bettor. The bettor calls the bookmaker, who is commonly called the "bookie" and places his/her bet. If he/she loses, then he/she pays the bookie the amount of the bet plus a commission, usually 10%, at a collection site. If he/she wins, then he/she collects the amount of his/her bet at the same collection site. The collection site is designated in advance.

16.2.1   Elements

The elements of a bookmaking case are as follows.

1. *In the business.* The person is engaged in the business of wagering when evidence is located on the premises. This is easily established when law enforcement conducts surveillances, wiretaps, search warrants, etc. In some states, the mere fact that gambling paraphernalia is present puts the person in the business of gambling or wagering.
2. *Volume.* The volume of wagers means the size of the gross receipts. Records are normally destroyed after a week because settlement takes place once a week. The bookie destroys all records except for the amount outstanding on open accounts.
3. *Period of operation.* The period of the operation relates to the length of time the operation was conducted. This could range from weeks to years. Direct evidence may not be available but rather a preponderance of the evidence may be sufficient to establish the length of time.

16.2.2   Federal Law

Federal law prohibits illegal gambling under Title 18, section 1955. The Internal Revenue Code, under section 4401, imposes an excise tax on certain gambling activities. This excise tax is usually 2% of the gross wagers including vigorish. Federal law provides:

1. Whoever conducts, finances, manages, supervises, directs, or owns all or part of an illegal gambling business shall be fined not more than $20,000 or imprisoned not more than 5 years, or both.
2. Illegal gambling business means a gambling business that:
   a. Is a violation of the law of a state or political subdivision in which it is conducted.
   b. Involves five or more persons who conduct, finance, manage, supervise, direct, or own all or part of such business.
   c. Has been or remains in substantially continuous operation for a period in excess of 30 days or has gross revenue of $2000 in any single day.
3. If five or more persons conduct, finance, manage, supervise, direct, or own all or part of a gambling business, and such business operates for two or more successive days, then for the purposes of obtaining warrants for arrests, interceptions, and other searches and seizures, and probable cause that the business receives gross revenue in excess of $2000 in any single day shall be deemed to have been established.
4. This section shall not apply to any bingo game, lottery, or similar game of chance conducted by an organization exempt from tax under paragraph (3) of subsection (c) of section 501 of the Internal Revenue Code of 1954, as amended, if no part of the gross receipts derived from such activity inures to the benefit of any private shareholder, member, or employee of such organization except as reimbursement for actual expenses incurred by him in the conduct of such activity.

16.2.3 Terminology

The following list of commonly used sports bookmaking terms should represent a useful reference guide for use in wagering investigations. It identifies and explains bookmaker's language.

1. *Dime bet.* A wager of $1000.
2. *Dollar bet.* A wager of $100.
3. *Fifty-cent bet.* A wager of $50.
4. *Four dollar bet.* A wager of $400.
5. *Quarter bet.* This may be a bet of $25 or at times $2500. The bettor's betting pattern or checkup can be used to establish which applies.
6. *Nickel bet.* A wager of $500.
7. *Bettor balance sheet.* A list of amounts owed to and due from bettors. Usually amounts owed from bettors are designated by a minus sign (−) and amounts payable to bettors are designated by a plus sign (+).
8. *Bettor list.* This is the bookmaker's list of bettors, which include name, number, one or more telephone numbers, and address. The bettor list can be used as a witness list, if necessary.
9. *Bettor number.* The number assigned to a bettor for identification.
10. *Bookmaker or bookie.* This is the person who for his/her own account accepts wagers on sporting events and charges vigorish on the bettor's losses. He/she may also have others who accept wagers for him.
11. *Busted out.* This refers to a bettor who is "bankrupt." In other words, he/she is unable to pay off.
12. *Buy half a point.* A wager placed on which the bettor purchases an extra half-point advantage over the normal line by laying 6 to 5 odds.
13. *Check a figure or checkup.* The function of comparing the bettor's computation of the amount owed to or from the bettor with the amount computed by the bookie. If the amount stated by the bettor agrees with the bookie's figure, then there is no problem.
14. *Checkup sheet.* Another term used for bettor balance sheet.
15. *Cheese bet.* A combination bet on the straight line and the over-under line on a given game. The Braves and Dolphins are playing. Assume that the Braves are a three-point favorite, or −3, and the over-under line is 30, there are four combinations that make up a cheese bet: (1) the Braves +3, over 30; (2) the Braves +3, under 30; (3) the Dolphins −3, under 30; and (4) the Dolphins −3, over 30. A winning $100 wager would return $300 to the bettor. The bettor would usually have at risk $110 or $120, depending on the bookie with which he/she bet.
16. *Dog.* The team expected to lose a sporting event.
17. *Favorite.* The team expected to win a sporting event.
18. *Half-time bet.* A wager placed during the period between the first and second half of a game. Normally, a bettor must lay 6 to 5 odds on such bets. Most bookies limit half-time lines for betting to games carried on local television.
19. *In a circle.* This refers to a "homemade" or uncertain line on which the size bet the bookmaker will accept is restricted. In some cases, it refers to buying a half-point.

20. *Juice.* This is another term for vigorish, which is the commission charged to losers.
21. *Lay off.* This is a wager placed from one bookmaker to another bookmaker to reduce the bookmaker's amount of risk on a given game. If the bookmaker receives bets of $10,000 on team A of a sports event and $1500 on team B, then the bookmaker will place a bet of $8500 on team B with another bookmaker to balance his/her books.
22. *Line.* A number of points given to place two opposing team on equal footing. Adjustments may be made to influence betting on one team over the other. In baseball, hockey, and boxing, the line is expressed in terms of odds. If the odds are expressed as 8 to 5 in favor of team A, then the bookmaker dealing a "ten percent" line will require the bettor to place $165 against his/her $100 should the bettor place a bet on team A. A bettor wishing to bet the "Dog," team B, will place $100 at risk against the bookmaker's $155. A bookmaker dealing a "twenty cent" line will require $170 against his/her $100 on the favorite and place $150 at risk against the bettor's $100 on wagers placed on the Dog.
23. *Line sheet.* A schedule of sporting events to be played with the line and changes in the line penned in.
24. *Markup.* This is the same as vigorish or juice.
25. *Middled.* This is a situation where a drastic change has been made in the line and the final score is such that it falls between two different lines used on the same game and bettors have placed bets that win on each of two teams.
26. *Mule.* This is a bettor that has lost. He/she has incurred a betting liability and refuses to pay.
27. *Off the board.* A game, for various reasons, that a bookie will not accept wagers on. Therefore, the bookie takes it "off the board."
28. *Over-under bet.* A wager placed on either over or under the total points expected to be scored in a given game. Some bookies treat a score that is exactly the same as the over-under line as a loss on part of the bettor. Some bookies will treat a score that is exactly the same as the over-under line as a push and the bettor loses.
29. *Parlay bet.* This is a combination bet on a series of teams at the normal line. All teams must win. A winner parlay bet returns to the bettor more than the amount he/she has at risk but less than the true odds. The true odds of a three-team parlay winning are more than 8 to 1. The amount a bettor will win on a winning $100 three-team parlay bet is usually around $500 to $600. Normally, the more teams bet in a parlay bet, the greater the percentage disadvantage to the bettor.
30. *Percentage.* This is the same as vigorish or juice.
31. *Phone man.* An employee or owner/bookmaker who provides betting lines and accepts wagers over the telephone in a bookmaking operation. A phone man is often times referred to as a bookmaker or bookie.
32. *Pick or pick it.* A game that is considered a toss-up. Both teams have an equal chance on a bet at pick. No points are given.
33. *Post.* These are notations of the approximate amount of wagers received on each team of a given name. Such notations are primarily made for the purpose of attempting to avoid accepting substantially more in wagers on one team over the other. The bookmaker can change the line and make wagers less desirable and

become more desirable for the other team. However, care must be exercised to avoid making a large change. A large change could place the bookmaker in a position to "get middled."

34. *Push*. A tie bet based on the line. A bettor bets on team A at +3. The final score is 21 on team A and 18 on team B. When the score is adjusted for the line, the effective score is 21 on team A and 21 on team B or a tie. No one wins.

35. *Settle*. The act of paying or receiving amounts won or lost.

36. *Settlement sheet*. The same as the bettor balance sheet.

37. *Sharp*. A knowledgeable bettor.

38. *Square*. A novice bettor.

39. *Straight bet*. A bet placed on a single team at the normal line.

40. *Tax*. This is the same as vigorish or juice.

41. *Taxable bet*. Total amount at risk including any charge or fee incident to the placing of a wager.

42. *Teaser bet*. A combination bet on a series of teams with extra points added to the line depending on the number of teams in the teaser bet. Usually, 6 points (half points are rounded in favor of the bookie) are added to the normal line of each team on a two-team teaser, 10 points to a three-team teaser, 12 points to a four-team teaser, etc. Some bookies may vary from this pattern and permit a total number of additional points to be spread among the teams as desired by the bettor.

43. *The book*. This usually refers to the physical location from which the bookmaker is operating.

44. *To the game*. A wager placed by a bettor on a baseball game with regard to whether the scheduled pitcher starts the game.

45. *To the pitcher*. A wager placed by a bettor on a baseball game predicted on the scheduled or a certain pitcher starting the game.

46. *Vigorish*. This is the bookmaker's markup to provide a profit margin. Normally, the markup is 10%; that is, if a bettor places a wager of $100 and loses, he/she must pay $110. If he/she wins, he/she wins $100. Half-time bets are normally at 6 to 5 odds or 20%. Some bookmakers will permit a bettor to place a wager on a game with an extra half-point advantage, if the bettor will lay 6 to 5 odds. Sometimes, the bookmaker will require 6 to 5 odds. In the case of baseball, if the bookmaker is dealing a 10-cent line, there will be a $10 spread between the amount a bettor must place at risk on a stated bet of $100, if he/she bets on the favorite team, than what he/she can expect to receive if he/she bets on the underdog. If the true odds on a game between team A and team B is 8 to 5 in favor of team B. If a bettor places a stated bet of $100 on team B, he/she must pay $165 to the bookmaker if he/she loses; he/she will receive $100 if he/she wins. Conversely, if the bettor places a stated bet of $100 on team A and wins, he/she will win only $155; he/she must pay $100 if he/she loses. The spread on a 20-cent line would be $20 on a stated bet of $100. The bookmaker would state the line at team B minus 65 or team A minus 165. At times when the odds reach approximately 2 to 1, runs may be given rather than the foregoing.

47. *With a hook*. The adding of half a point to the line, for example, "3 with a hook" means 3½.

16.2.4 Teams

Sports betting encompasses professional and collegiate teams. The sports most commonly used for wagering are baseball, basketball, football, and hockey. The following paragraphs list the teams and its hometown by sport.

16.2.4.1 *Professional Baseball*

Professional baseball teams are grouped into two leagues: American and National. The two leagues with the teams are listed below:

A. American League

Team Name	Location
Baltimore Orioles	Baltimore, Md.
Boston Red Sox	Boston, Mass.
California Angels	Anaheim, Calif.
Chicago White Sox	Chicago, Ill.
Cleveland Indians	Cleveland, Ohio
Detroit Tigers	Detroit, Mich.
Kansas City Royals	Kansas City, Mo.
Milwaukee Brewers	Milwaukee, Wis.
Minnesota Twins	Minneapolis, Minn.
New York Yankees	Bronx, N.Y.
Oakland A's	Oakland, Calif.
Seattle Mariners	Seattle, Wash.
Texas Rangers	Arlington, Tex.
Tampa Bay Devil Rays	Tampa, Fla.
Toronto Blue Jays	Toronto, Ontario

B. National League

Team	Location
Arizona Diamondbacks	Phoenix, Ariz.
Atlanta Braves	Atlanta, Ga.
Chicago Cubs	Chicago, Ill.
Cincinnati Reds	Cincinnati, Ohio
Colorado Rockies	Denver, Colo.
Florida Marlins	Miami, Fla.
Houston Astros	Houston, Tex.
Los Angeles Dodgers	Los Angeles, Calif.
Milwaukee Brewers	Milwaukee, Wis.
Montreal Expos	Montreal, Quebec
New York Mets	Flushing, N.Y.
Philadelphia Phillies	Philadelphia, Pa.
Pittsburgh Pirates	Pittsburgh, Pa.
St. Louis Cardinals	St. Louis, Mo.
San Diego Padres	San Diego, Calif.
San Francisco Giants	San Francisco, Calif.

16.2.4.2 *Professional Basketball*
Professional basketball only has one league, the National Basketball League. Their teams are as follows:

Team	Location
Atlanta Hawks	Atlanta, Ga.
Boston Celtics	Boston, Mass.
Chicago Bulls	Chicago, Ill.
Charlotte Hornets	Charlotte, N.C.
Cleveland Cavaliers	Richfield, Ohio
Dallas Mavericks	Dallas, Tex.
Denver Nuggets	Denver, Colo.
Detroit Pistons	Pontiac, Mich.
Golden State Warriors	Oakland, Calif.
Houston Rockets	Houston, Tex.
Indiana Pacers	Indianapolis, Ind.
Kansas City Kings	Kansas City, Mo.
Los Angeles Clippers	Los Angeles, Calif.
Los Angeles Lakers	Inglewood, Calif.
Miami Heat	Miami, Fla.
Milwaukee Bucks	Milwaukee, Wis.
Minnesota Timberwolves	St. Paul, Minn.
New Jersey Nets	E. Rutherford, N.J.
New York Knickerbockers	New York, N.Y.
Orlando Magic	Orlando, Fla.
Philadelphia 76ers	Philadelphia, Pa.
Phoenix Suns	Phoenix, Ariz.
Portland Trail Blazers	Portland, Ore.
Sacramento Kings	Sacramento, Calif.
San Antonio Spurs	San Antonio, Tex.
Seattle Super Sonics	Seattle, Wash.
Toronto Raptors	Toronto, Canada
Utah Jazz	Salt Lake City, Utah
Vancouver Grizzlies	Vancouver, Canada
Washington Wizards	Landover, Md.

16.2.4.3 *Professional Football*
There are two major professional football leagues: National Football League and the Canadian Football League. The two leagues along with their teams are listed below.

A. National Football League	
Team	Location
Arizona Cardinals	Phoenix, Ariz.
Atlanta Falcons	Suwanee, Ga.
Baltimore Ravens	Baltimore, Md.

(continued)

A. National Football League

Team	Location
Buffalo Bills	Orchard Park, N.Y.
Carolina Panthers	Charlotte, N.C.
Chicago Bears	Chicago, Ill.
Cincinnati Bengals	Cincinnati, Ohio
Cleveland Browns	Cleveland, Ohio
Dallas Cowboys	Dallas, Tex.
Detroit Lions	Pontiac, Mich.
Green Bay Packers	Green Bay, Wis.
Indianapolis Colts	Indianapolis, Ind.
Jacksonville Jaguars	Jacksonville, Fla.
Kansas City Chiefs	Kansas City, Mo.
Los Angeles Rams	Anaheim, Calif.
Miami Dolphins	Miami, Fla.
Minnesota Vikings	Eden Prairie, Minn.
Nashville Predators	Nashville, Tenn.
New England Patriots	Foxboro, Mass.
New Orleans Saints	New Orleans, La.
New York Giants	E. Rutherford, N.Y.
New York Jets	New York, N.Y.
Oakland Raiders	Oakland, Calif.
Philadelphia Eagles	Philadelphia, Pa.
Pittsburgh Steelers	Pittsburgh, Pa.
St. Louis Rams	St. Louis, Mo.
San Diego Chargers	San Diego, Calif.
San Francisco 49ers	Redwood City, Calif.
Seattle Seahawks	Kirkland, Wash.
Tampa Bay Buccaneers	Tampa, Fla.
Washington Redskins	Washington, D.C.

B. Canadian Football League

Team	Location
B C Lions Football Club	Surrey, B.C.
Calgary Stampeders	Calgary, Alberta
Edmonton Eskimos	Edmonton, Alberta
Hamilton Tiger-Cats	Hamilton, Ontario
Montreal Alouettes	Montreal, Quebec
Ottawa Rough Riders	Ottawa, Ontario
Saskatchewan Roughriders	Regina, Saskatchewan
Toronto Argonauts	Toronto, Ontario
Winnipeg Blue Bombers	Winnipeg, Manitoba

16.2.4.4 Professional Hockey

There is only one hockey league, the National Hockey League. Their teams are as follows:

Team	Location
Anaheim Mighty Ducks	Anaheim, Calif.
Boston Bruins	Boston, Mass.
Buffalo Sabres	Buffalo, N.Y.
Carolina Hurricanes	Charlotte, N.C.
Calgary Flames	Calgary, Alberta
Chicago Black Hawks	Chicago, Ill.
Colorado Avalanche	Denver, Colo.
Dallas Stars	Dallas, Tex.
Detroit Red Wings	Detroit, Mich.
Edmonton Oilers	Edmonton, Alberta
Florida Panthers	Sunrise, Fla.
Hartford Whalers	Hartford, Conn.
Los Angeles Kings	Inglewood, Calif.
Minnesota North Stars	Bloomington, Minn.
Montreal Canadiens	Montreal, Quebec
Nashville Predators	Nashville, Tenn.
New Jersey Devils	E. Rutherford, N.J.
New York Islanders	Uniondale, N.Y.
New York Rangers	New York, N.Y.
Ottawa Senators	Ottawa, Canada
Philadelphia Flyers	Philadelphia, Pa.
Phoenix Coyotes	Phoenix, Ariz.
Pittsburgh Penguins	Pittsburgh, Pa.
Quebec Nordiques	Charlesbourg, Quebec
San Jose Sharks	San Jose, Calif.
St. Louis Blues	St. Louis, Mo.
Tampa Bay Lighting	Tampa, Fla.
Toronto Maple Leafs	Toronto, Ontario
Vancouver Canucks	Vancouver, B.C.
Washington Capitals	Landover, Md.

16.2.4.5 Collegiate Football

Many colleges have football teams. The colleges and universities are members of the National Collegiate Athletic Association (NCAA). The NCAA makes the rules for collegiate football. The college teams that are mostly used by bookmakers are the universities or colleges listed below:

Team	University/College
Air Force Falcons	Air Force Academy
Akron	Akron State College
Alabama	University of Alabama
Albright	Albright University
Arizona	University of Arizona
Arizona State	Arizona State University
Arkansas	University of Arkansas
Army	U.S. Military Academy
Auburn	Auburn University
Ball State	Ball State College
Baylor	Baylor University
Bethune-Cookman	Beth-Cookman College
Boston College	Boston College
Brigham Young	Brigham Young University
Brown	Brown University
Cal.	California University
Central Florida	University of Central Florida
Carroll	Carroll College
University of Chicago	University of Chicago
University of Cincinnati	University of Cincinnati
Citadel	Citadel Military Academy
Clemson	Clemson University
Colgate	Colgate College
Colorado	University of Colorado
Colorado State	Colorado State University
Columbia	Columbia University
Cornell	Cornell University
Dartmouth	Dartmouth College
Duke	Duke University
East Carolina	University of E. Carolina
Florida A&M	Florida A&M University
Florida Atlantic University	Florida Atlantic University
Florida Gators	University of Florida
Florida Seminoles	Florida State University
Fresno	Fresno University
Fullerton	Fullerton State College
Washington	George Washington University
Georgia Tech	Georgia Institute of Technology
Georgia	University of Georgia
Harvard	Harvard University
Hawaii	University of Hawaii
Holy Cross	Holy Cross University
Houston	University of Texas
Illinois	University of Illinois
Indiana	University of Indiana
Iowa	University of Iowa

(*continued*)

Team	University/College
Iowa State	Iowa State University
Kansas	University of Kansas
Kansas State	Kansas State University
Kent State	Kent State University
Kentucky	University of Kentucky
Wake Forest	Wake Forest College
Lafayette	Lafayette College
Lehigh	Lehigh College
Louisiana	Louisiana State University
Louisville	Louisville University
LA Tech	Louisiana Institute of Technology
Maryland	University of Maryland
Memphis State	Memphis State University
MIT	Massachusetts Institute of Technology
Miami Hurricanes	University of Miami, Florida
Miami	University of Miami, Ohio
Michigan	University of Michigan
Michigan State	Michigan State University
Minnesota	University of Minnesota
Mississippi	University of Mississippi
Old Miss	Mississippi State University
Missouri	University of Missouri
Navy	U.S. Naval Academy
Nebraska	University of Nebraska
Nevada	University of Nevada
New Mexico	University of New Mexico
North Carolina	University of North Carolina
North Carolina State	North Carolina State University
Northwestern	Northwestern University
Notre Dame	Notre Dame University
Ohio	University of Ohio
Ohio State	Ohio State University
Oklahoma	University of Oklahoma
Oklahoma State	Oklahoma State University
Oregon	University of Oregon
Oregon State	Oregon State University
Penn State	Pennsylvania State University
Penn	University of Pennsylvania
Pitt	University of Pittsburgh
Princeton	Princeton University
Purdue	Purdue University
Rice	Rice University
Rutgers	Rutgers University
Methodist	Southern Methodist University
San Diego State	San Diego State University
San Jose State	San Jose State University

(continued)

Team	University/College
South Carolina	South Carolina University
Southern Cal	University of Southern California
Southwest Louisiana	Southwest Louisiana University
Stanford	Stanford University
Syracuse	Syracuse University
Temple	Temple University
Tennessee	University of Tennessee
Texas	University of Texas, Austin
Texas–El Paso	University of Texas, El Paso
Texas Tech	Texas Institute of Technology
Toledo	University of Ohio, Toledo
Tulane	Tulane University
Tulsa	Tulsa University
Utah State	Utah State University
Vanderbilt	Vanderbilt University
VMI	Virginia Military Academy
UCLA	University of California, Los Angeles
Las Vegas	University of Nevada, Las Vegas
Utah	University of Utah
Virginia	University of Virginia
Virginia Tech	Virginia Institute of Technology
Wake Forest	Wake Forest University
Washington	University of Washington
Washington State	Washington State University
Wesleyan	Wesleyan University
West Virginia	West Virginia University
Western Michigan	Western Michigan University
Wisconsin	University of Wisconsin
Wyoming	University of Wyoming
Yale	Yale University

16.2.4.6 Betting on Baseball

Baseball is more complicated for a person to learn. In baseball, there are two lines: the money line and the western line. There are also totals, or over and under, on each game. The money line is also called "the pitcher's line" because the price of the favorite depends on who is pitching or it is also called the "dime line" because there is a "10 dollar" difference between the favorite price and the underdog price. When a player bets the money line, the pitcher must pitch, both of them or there is no action (or no bet). The only time a bettor receiving the money line has a bet is on the occasion that one of the two pitchers on the list does not pitch when the bettor states before the bet that he/she wants action on the plays. Action means if a pitcher did not go then he/she would have a bet at an adjusted price according to the strength of the new pitcher. The following chart illustrates all possible money lines and what the bet would be on the favorite and the underdog in terms of $100.

Possible Money Line		Bet	Win
Favorite	−110	110-	100 on favorite
Underdog	Even	100-	100 on underdog
Favorite	−115	115	100 on favorite
Underdog	+105	100	105 on underdog
Favorite	−120	120	100 on favorite
Underdog	+110	100	110 on underdog
Favorite	−125	125	100 on favorite
Underdog	+115	100	115 on underdog
Favorite	−130	130	100 on favorite
Underdog	+120	100	120 on underdog
Favorite	−135	135	100 on favorite
Underdog	+125	100	125 on underdog
Favorite	−140	140	100 on favorite
Underdog	+130	100	130 on underdog
Favorite	−145	145	100 on favorite
Underdog	+135	100	135 on underdog
Favorite	−150	150	100 on favorite
Underdog	+140	100	140 on underdog
Favorite	−155	155	100 on favorite
Underdog	+145	100	145 on underdog
Favorite	−160	160	100 on favorite
Underdog	+150	100	150 on underdog
Favorite	−165	165	100 on favorite
Underdog	+155	100	155 on underdog
Favorite	−170	170	100 on favorite
Underdog	+160	100	160 on underdog
Favorite	−175	175	100 on favorite
Underdog	+165	100	165 on underdog
Favorite	−180	180	100 on favorite
Underdog	+170	100	170 on underdog

(continued)

Possible Money Line		Bet	Win
Favorite	−185	185	100 on favorite
Underdog	+175	100	175 on underdog
Favorite	−190	190	100 on favorite
Underdog	+180	100	180 on underdog
Favorite	−200	200	100 on favorite
Underdog	+185	100	185 on underdog
Favorite	−210*	210	100 on favorite
Underdog	+190	100	190 on underdog
Favorite	−220	220	100 on favorite
Underdog	+200	100	200 on underdog
Favorite	−230	230	100 on favorite
Underdog	+210	100	210 on underdog
Favorite	−240	240	100 on favorite
Underdog	+220	100	220 on underdog
Favorite	−250	250	100 on favorite
Underdog	+230	100	230 on underdog
Favorite	−260	260	100 on favorite
Underdog	+240	100	240 on underdog

*You should note that on 210 or more this becomes a $20 difference instead of $10. This is done so that the bookmaker's vigorish/juice stays the same rate. When there is no favorite or pick, then both teams are the same or shown as Favorite 105 and Underdog 100. Also, note that the favorite always uses the minus sign, while the underdog uses the plus sign.

You can understand how baseball betting works by going through an example. A sports line service provides the line on the Mets versus Cincinnati as:

Mets – 160
Cincinnati

The Mets are the favorite because you have the price and the minus (–) sign by their name. The Mets are minus 160. This means that for every $100 a person wants to win on the Mets, then the bettor must risk $160. If the bettor bets on the Mets for $100 and loses, then he/she owes the bookmaker $160. If he/she wins, then the bookmaker owes him $100. The bookmaker's bettor sheet would show:

Team	Vigorish	Bet	Win
Mets	−60	160	100

The team column tells what team the bettor is placing his/her bet on to win. The vigorish column tells the bookmaker what amount of vigorish/juice that he/she is expected to win. The bet column is the amount wagered by the bettor. This is the full amount the bettor will have to pay the bookmaker if he/she loses. The win column shows the amount that the bookmaker will owe the bettor if the bettor wins.

Using the same line and teams, the bettor places a wager on the underdog, Cincinnati. The underdog is always $100 less than the favorite or +150. Here the bettor is risking $100 to make $150. The bookmaker's bettor sheet would show:

Team	Vigorish	Bet	Win
Cincinnati	+50	100	150

Now, let us go through another example but with a different bet amount. The bettor wants to place a wager on the Mets for 300. The bookmaker's bettor sheet would show:

Team	Vigorish	Bet	Win
Mets	−60	480	300

This requires computation on the part of the bookmaker. The calculation is based on the line of 160 to 100. So the bettor wants 300. This corresponds to $100 \times 3 = 300$. The bet would be $160 \times 3 = 480$. The bettor risks 480 to win 300. This rule also applies to the other team. If the bettor wants to place 300 on Cincinnati because they are the underdog, the computation changes as follows:

Team	Vigorish	Bet	Win
Cincinnati	+50	300	450

The win column will show the amount the bettor would win. It is computed by $150 \times 3 = \$450$. The bet column is based on the ratio of $100 \times 3 = \$300$.

The basic rule, from the examples above, is that it is impossible to win more on a favorite than you are betting. It is impossible to bet more on an underdog than the bettor can win.

A parlay is picking two or more teams to win their games. A parlay is for a set amount that the bettor wants. If the bettor wins, the bookmaker must figure it out by the prices (vigorish or juice). In a parlay, all teams must win; otherwise, the bettor loses.

The following examples illustrate a parlay.

The lines for two games are:

Mets   −160
Cincinnati   150
Los Angeles −120
Miami   110

The bettor places a wager of $200 parlay on the Mets and Miami. The bookmaker's bettor sheet would show the following:

Team	Vigorish	Bet	Win
Mets	−60		
Miami	+10	200	Parlay

You should notice that the Mets is a favorite, while Miami is the underdog. Remember all teams in a parlay must win before the bettor can win. If one team loses and the other wins, the bettor loses. In this example, if both teams win, then the bettor wins the following by the rules shown above.

Team	Vigorish	Bet	Win
Mets	−60	320	200
Miami	+10	200	220
Total			420

If one or both of the teams loses, then the bettor has to pay the bookmaker the following:

Team	Vigorish	Bet	Win
Mets	−60	320	200
Miami	+10	220	240
Total		540	

A "round robin" is a group of two-team parlays written in a shorter and easier way. A round robin must have at least three teams. The three-team round robin is the same as three two-team parlays. To illustrate a round robin and a three two-team parlay, the following example is given.

The line is given below on three games.

Mets	−160	Los Angeles	−120	Boston	−140
Cincinnati	150	Miami	110	Braves	130

The round robin must have at least three teams. The bettor calls the bookmaker and places a 200 round robin wager as follows:

Team	Vigorish	Bet	Win
Mets	−60		
Miami	+10		
Boston	−40	200 Round robin	

Note that two teams are favorites, while one team is an underdog. In a three two-team parlay, it would appear on the bookmaker's bettor sheet as follows:

Team	Vigorish	Bet	Win
Mets	−60		
Miami	+10	200 Parlay	
Mets	−60		
Boston	−40	200 Parlay	
Miami	+10		
Boston	−40	200 Parlay	

For the bettor to win, all teams must also win. Any team loses, then the bettor loses. In a round robin, the bettor would win the amount shown below when all teams win.

Team	Vigorish	Bet	Win
Mets	−60	320	200
Miami	+10	200	220
Boston	−40	280	200
Total			620

If the bettor loses, the bookmaker would collect the following:

Team	Vigorish	Bet
Mets	−60	320
Miami	+10	200
Boston	−40	280
Total		720

Bettors will also make wagers based on points either over or under the line. When points are placed on either over or under the line, then the bets change to only three possible combinations. They are:

120-100
110-100
100-100 or even money

These three combinations are called flat, over, or under. These are defined as:

1. *Flat* (F). When the total line is flat, the bettor goes either over (o) or under (u), he/she must lay 110 to win 100. Flat has no favorite.
2. *Over* (O). When the total line is favored over (o), the bettor must bet 120-100, because the over (o) is the bookmaker's favorite; if he/she goes under (u) then the bet is 100-100, because the bettor is going against the bookmaker's favorite.
3. *Under* (U). When the total line is favored under (u), the bettor wagers under, then he/she must lay 120-100, because the under is the favorite. If the bettor wagers over he/she lays 100-100 because the bettor is going against the favorite.

Using an example to illustrate, let's assume the same example as quoted before. The line is:

Mets   −160
Cincinnati   150

The bettor wants the Mets at over the eighth for $200. The bookmaker's sheet would show:

Team	O/U	Bet	Win
Mets	O 8	240	200

This shows that the bettor must pay $120 if he/she loses or he/she wins $100. Now, let's assume that the bettor wagers the Mets under the eighth for $200. The bookmaker's sheet should reflect:

Team	O/U	Bet	Win
Mets	U 8	200	200

In this instance, the favorite is the Mets. Therefore, the odds are 100-100 or even money. Now, let's assume that the bookmaker has no favorite. This is called a flat. In other words, there is no favorite or underdog. In a nonfavorite situation, the odds are always 110-100. The bettor calls and wagers 8 points under for 200. The bookmaker's tally sheet will show:

Team	O/U	Bet	Win
Mets	U 8	220	200

If the bettor wins, then he/she receives $200. If the bettor loses, then he/she pays $220.

The points, both over and under, can have ½ points. Many bookmakers use the minus sign (−) to represent a half point, sometimes called half run. For example, 7− = seven and a half runs.

The bettor calls up and wants to put 7− on the Mets for $300. The line is:

Mets	−160	7 − u
Cincinnati	150	

The bettor in this illustration wants 7½ points under on the Mets for $300. The bookmaker's tally sheet should show:

Team	Bet	WIN
Mets u 7−	360	300

In this illustration, the bettor must lay 120-100 because the team is the bookmaker's favorite.

When the bettor places bets in a parlay or round robin using points and half points (runs), then the bookmaker's tally sheet would probably look like this using $100:

Line		Team	Bet	Win
Mets	−160	Mets u 8 U	120	100
Cincinnati	150			
Los Angeles	−120	Miami o 7− F	110	100
Miami	110			
Boston	−140	Boston u 6 O	100	100
Braves	130			

The line is shown here as reference; otherwise, it would not be reflected on the bookmaker's sheet. In the above example, the Mets is given as eight runs for under. This is the bookmaker's favorite. In the Miami o 7− F, the bookmaker has no favorite or underdog. In the Boston u 6 O, the bettor is betting opposite the bookmaker. This is called an even bet. The rule of thumb is: when the bettor places bets in favor of the bookmaker's choice, then this is a favorite bet. When the bettor places a bet in opposite of the bookmaker's choice, then this is an even bet. When the bettor places a bet that is neither a favorite nor underdog to the bookmaker, then this is a flat.

When the bookmaker does not know who is pitching in a game, then the bookmaker will have four prices or odds. The bookmaker's sheet would read like the following example.

Team	Pitcher	Odds	Odds	Odds	Odds
SF Giants	Swan, Reuschel	PS-S	−8	G-S	G-R
Braves	P. Smith, Glavine	20	R-PS	35	15

The price is on the line that is the bookmaker's favorite. Above or below the price (odds) are the pitchers. When a bettor calls, the bookmaker would say Braves P. Smith is −20 over Swan, but Giants Reuschel is −8 over P. Smith, and Braves Glavine is 35 over Swan and −15 over Reuschel.

If the bettor does not care who pitches and places a bet, using the odds above, for $1000 on the SF Giants, then the bookmaker's tally sheet would show the following breakdown.

Team	Price	Pitcher	Bet	Win
Giants	+10	PS-S	1000	1100
	−08	R-PS	1080	1000
	+25	G-S	1000	1250
	+05	G-R	1000	1050

If the bettor places a bet on a Braves double header (two games by the same teams) with no pitcher identified, then the bookmakers tally sheet would show the following:

Team	Price	Pitcher	Bet	Win
Braves	−20	PS-S	1200	1000
	−02	R-PS	1020	1000
	−35	G-S	1350	1000
	−15	G-R	1150	1000

This bet would apply to both games.

Using the same teams and odds, the bettor places a bet on the Giants Reuschel but does not care who pitches against him, for $100. The bookmaker's tally sheet would reflect:

Team	Price	Pitcher	Bet	Win
Giants	−08	PS	108	100
	+05			

The bettor could change his/her odds or price on game 2 of a double hitter. The bettor bets on the Braves for $200. The tally sheet would show:

Team	Price	Pitcher	Bet	Win
Braves	−20	PS-S	240	200
	−02	R-PS	204	200
	−35	G-S	270	200
	−15	G-R	230	200

The bettor wants the Braves if Swan pitches for $1000. Swan is the Giants pitcher. The tally sheet would show:

Team	Price	Pitcher	Bet	Win
Braves	−20	PS	1200	1000
(Swan)	−35	G	1350	1000

This section has given a summary of how baseball sports betting works.

16.2.4.7 Football

Football only involves a point spread and a total. All bets are 110 to 100 odds. The only time a football bet is not 110-100 is when a player buys a half point or plays a gimmick. Like baseball, football has favorites and underdogs. Minus (−) points is always the bookmaker's favorite; plus (+) points is always the underdog, and a pick or even game has no favorite. The point spread can also have half points. The bookmaker gives the bettor the favorite team, the point spread (expressed in minus points), and the total. For example:

Phoenix	5 and 41
49ers	3 and 39

For every $100 a bettor places to win a football game, he/she must risk $110 or 10%. The 10% is called juice or vigorish, which the bookmaker earns. The bookmaker's tally sheet will always have as a minimum the bettor's number, team, point spread, and the amount of the bet. Example:

Team	Points	Bet
Buffalo	−30	500 Favorite
Dolphins	+3	400 Underdog

A parlay is picking two or more teams to win. A parlay is a set amount. How much the bettor wins depends on how many teams he/she puts in the parlay. The bettor must win all picks in order for the parlay to win. One loser will cause the whole parlay to lose. The bettor tells the bookmaker that he/she wants $100 parlay on the 49ers and Miami. The tally sheet would read:

Team	Points	Bet
49ers	−3	
Miami	+4	100 P

The bettor would win $260 or $100 × 2.6 = $260.

The bettor can use not only points but total as well. Example:

Team	Points	Bet
Rams	−6	
Denver	o 41	1000 P

The bettor would win $2600 or $1000 × 2.6 = $2600. This is based on the odds of 13-5 or amount times 2.6.

The odds are set by the bookmaker for parlays and round robin bets. These are normally as follows, but the bookmaker can change them.

Team	Odds	
2	13-5	or amount times 2.6
3	6-1	or amount times 6
4	10-1	or amount times 10
5	15-1	or amount times 15

In a three-team parlay, the bettor wants the Rams, Denver, and Dolphins under for $300. The tally sheet would read:

Team	Points	Bet
Rams	−2	
Denver	u 39	
Dolphins	−5	300 P

The bettor would win $1800 or $300 × 6 = $1800. The odds are 10-1.

A round robin is a group of two-team parlays playing three games. The bettor wants $100 round robin on the Rams, Denver, and the Dolphins for $100. The tally sheet reads:

Team	Points	Bet
Rams	+6	
Denver	+2	
Dolphins	+5	100 RR

Notice that the bettor is betting on the underdog. A round robin would be the same as writing three parlays as follows:

Team	Points	Bet
Rams	+6	
Denver	+2	100 P
Rams	+6	
Dolphins	+5	100 P
Denver	+2	
Dolphins	+5	100 P

A round robin has:

> three-team round robin has 3 two-team parlays
> four-team round robin has 6 two-team parlays
> five-team round robin has 10 two-team parlays

The only time a football bet is not 110-100 odds is when a bettor wants to buy ½ point in his/her favor, then it will cost the bettor 120-100 odds.

If the bettor is betting a favorite and wants ½ point, then this ½ point spread will be lower by ½ point.

Team	Points	Bet	Win
Denver	−2	120	100

If the bettor is betting on an underdog and wants to purchase ½ point, the spread will go up by ½ point.

Team	Points	Bet	Win
Dolphins	+2−	240	200

This bet is figured out by taking the amount times 1.2 equals 240.

A bettor can also buy ½ points on totals. There are two combination which are called over and under.

> Over (o) – When the total line is favored over (o), the bettor must bet 120 to 100 because the over (o) is the bookmaker's favorite.
> Under (u) – When the total line is favored under (u), then he must lay 120 to 100 because the under (u) is against the bookmaker.
> o is just like buying a favorite.
> u is just like buying on a dog.

Denver is 40. The bettor wants to buy ½ point and go over for 300. The bettor gets the total at 39−.

Team	Points	Bet	Win
Denver	o 39−	360	300

The bettor wants to buy ½ point and go under for 500. The total goes up to 40–.

Team	Points	Bet	Win
Denver	u 40–	600	500

Note that the only time the 120-100 odds on buying a ½ point change is when a customer is buying off a round robin. It then costs the bettor 125-100 or the amount times 1.25.

Note that the bettor can buy a full point; however, it will cost him/her 140-100 or the amount times 1.4.

Teaser bets are only used in the sport of football. Most bookmakers use the following chart. Bookmakers get many teaser bets.

No. of Team	6 Points	6– Points	7 Points
2	100-100	110-100	120-100
3	100-180	100-160	100-150
4	100-300	100-250	100-200
5	100-450	100-400	100-350

There are 12 possible combinations for a teaser using the above chart. The breakdown is as follows:

Team and Points	Odds
2 teamer 6	100-100
2 teamer 6–	110-100
2 teamer 7	120-100
3 teamer 6	100-180
3 teamer 6–	100-160
3 teamer 7	100-150
4 teamer 6	100-300
4 teamer 6–	100-250
4 teamer 7	100-200
5 teamer 6	100-450
5 teamer 6–	100-400
5 teamer 7	100-350

Teasers are gimmicks that offer to give the bettor another betting choice in which the bookmaker allows the bettor to add points to the bettor's team's point spread for a certain price. The bettor wants a two-team teaser for 6 points for 100 on Denver at –3 and the Dolphins at +5.

Team	Points	Teaser Points	Points Used
Denver	–3	6	+3
Dolphins	+5	6	+11

The bettor wants a two-team teaser, 7 points for 400 using Denver and the Dolphins. The points are Denver –3– and the Dolphins –3.

In this case, the bettor is using points of +3– on Denver and +4 on the Dolphins. The bookmaker's tally sheet would read as follows:

Team	Points	Bet	Win
Denver	+3–	480	400
Dolphins	+4	480	400 T

In a three-team teaser, the bookmaker's tally sheet would read as follows:

Team	Points	Bet	Win
Denver	+2–		
Dolphins	–1/2		
Dallas	+2	200	360

16.2.5 Basketball

Basketball is identical to football. If the fraud examiner knows football, then he/she will know basketball because the rules are the same. The point spread is the line that is rated to equal betting action on each team of a game. A total is based on an average of total points scored. Like football, basketball odds are 110-100.

16.3 Lottery

Lottery is a game of chance where bettors place bets on numbers that are randomly selected from some identified, independent source. In some areas, this form of betting is called "Bolito." In essence, the bettor picks a two- or three-digit number at random and places a bet of anywhere from $1 or more with a writer. If the bettor's number is selected, then the bettor wins anywhere from $30 to $600, depending on the digits and betting volume.

16.3.1 Terminology

Lottery operators and bettors have their own terminology. These terms are defined as follows:

1. *Add back*. An outstanding previous week's balance from a writer or ribbon. This amount is added back to the net of the current week's summary.
2. *Bag man* or *pick-up man*. A person who picks up monies generated from lottery activity from ribbons and/or writers or carries out funds needed to cover hits.
3. *Banker*. One who directs, finances, controls, and receives the final profit from a lottery.
4. *Box bet*. A wager placed on any permutation of a given three-digit number. Normally, such wagers are divisible by 3 and/or 6. For example, a 48-cent box bet on number 123 is the equivalent of an 8-cent bet on the numbers 123, 132, 213, 231, 321, and 312.

5. *Call sheets.* A list of writers and/or ribbons, the time or times they are to be called for their lottery and their telephone number or numbers.
6. *Combination bet.* A six-way number, or a box number. Sometimes it is a three-way number. Different terms are used in various locals.
7. *Cut number.* A number on which the payout rate is reduced. Cut numbers can be used to discourage betting on a number or series of numbers.
8. *High money.* Gross wagers prior to being reduced by a given commission.
9. *Highs.* A list of numbers on which wagers exceeding "X" dollars have been accepted.
10. *Hit.* A wager placed on the winning number.
11. *Layoff.* A bet placed by one lottery bank to another lottery bank to reduce the risk of substantial loss should a number on which a bank has a substantial number of betting hits. For example, lottery A has a total of $100 on number 601. At a payout rate of 400 to 1, if number 601 was the winning lottery number, payouts on that number would total $40,000. A lottery, especially a smaller lottery, may not wish to carry this potential loss and may place a bet itself with another lottery. For example, a $50 layoff would reduce the potential payout to $20,000.
12. *Low money.* This is gross wagers after being reduced by a given commission. For example, a writer receives $100 in gross wagers and is to receive a $25 commission. High money would be $100 and low money would be $75.
13. *Numbers lottery bet.* This is a wager placed on a series of numbers, usually two- or three-digit numbers, the winning number of which is determined by a relatively random set of events.
14. *Office or telephone relay station.* This is a location from which a person accumulates such items as wagers, hits, outstanding balances due from or to the writers, and other financial records of a lottery.
15. *Overlook.* This is a bet placed on a winning on a prior lottery day that was overlooked, that is, the lottery operation had to go back to records for the prior lottery day to ascertain if the bettor had placed a bet on the winning number and they failed to pay.
16. *Ribbon.* This is a person who supervises or receives wagers from writers and forwards such wagers. A ribbon may be a writer also. A ribbon may also be an adding machine tape.
17. *Six-way number.* This is any three-digit number from 000 through 999 in which none of the numbers are the same. There are six permutations of these numbers. For example, the numbers 1, 2, and 3 can be arranged as 123, 132, 231, 213, 321, and 312.
18. *Stock and bonds lottery.* This is a three-digit lottery in which the winning number is determined from the published results of trading on the New York Stock Exchange. Wagers can be placed on any one of 1000 numbers from 000 through 999. The first two digits of the winning number are determined from the hundred thousand and the ten thousand dollar digits of the total bond sales on a given day and the third digit being determined from the ten thousand digit of units traded on the New York Stock Exchange.
19. *Straight or triple number.* This is any three-digit number from 000 through 999 in which all three digits are the same.
20. *Three-way number.* This is any three-digit number from 000 through 999 in which two of the three digits are the same. There are three permutations of these numbers. For example, the numbers 1, 1, and 2 can be arranged 112, 121, and 211.

21. *Two-digit lottery.* This is any lottery on which wagers on two-digit numbers 00 through 99 are accepted. The winning number may be derived from any one of several random sources. For example, the winning number for the "Wednesday, Puerto Rico" is published in the *Pittsburgh Courier.* "The Saturday Dog" is determined from the results of pari-mutuel payoffs on certain races at a given dog track. The "Sunday Nighthouse" is determined by a drawing from a bag containing 100 numbered bolita balls, etc.

22. *Wall number.* This is a wager on a lottery number that is to be repeated for an extended period of time. For example, on a week wall bet, the wager would be repeated each day of a given week. A wall bet may be placed for 2 days or may extend through an indefinite period of time. This term varies by locality. For example, in the mid-Atlantic region, it is referred to as "keep in."

16.3.2   Lottery Operations

Figure 16.1 shows the structure of a lottery organization.

1. *Banker.* The banker is the person who directs, finances, controls, and receives the final profit. In many cases, the banker does not participate in the day-to-day operations. He/she relies on his/her office manager to handle the day-to-day operations. The banker usually receives 10% of the gross receipts as his/her profits from the operations. If the banker does not have an office manager, then he/she will participate actively in the day-to-day operations. In this case, the banker's commission will be 20% to 30%.

2. *Office manager.* The office manager accumulates the wagers, hits, and outstanding balances due from or to the writers, and other financial records of the lottery. He/she provides the cut-off time for writers to call in their final bets. This prevents writers from including winning numbers in the tally. The office manager will have collectors who collect from ribbons and writers and make payouts. The office manager directs and controls the collectors.

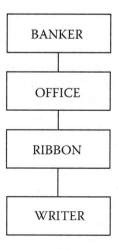

Figure 16.1 Lottery organization chart.

3. *Writer.* The writer takes the bets and money from the bettors. He/she reports to the office manager about the total bets placed and funds collected. The writer pays the collector the money owed to the banker less his/her commission. If the writer has to pay a winning number and does not have the funds to do so, then the collector will provide the funds from the office manager. Writers in large operations are known as "ribbon." The writers usually earn a commission of 25%. In large operations, the ribbon may have writers under them to which they pay a commission, usually 5% to 7%.

16.3.3   Lottery Examples

The following examples illustrate both two- and three-digit lotteries. An explanation follows the illustration.

1. *Two-digit lottery.* The following is an illustration of a two-digit lottery that a ribbon/writer has taken from his/her bettors:

Bettor	Number	Bet
Bill	12	$1
Chuck	78/	1
Dan	44	1
198	67	1
134	23/	1*

Bill placed a wager of $1 on number 12. Chuck placed a bet of $1 on number 78. This a box bet because Chuck wants number 78 and 87. Dan placed a bet of $1 on 44. This is a straight number because both digits are the same. Bettor 198 has placed a straight bet on 67 for $1. The bettor is not identified by name but by a number assigned to the bettor. Bettor 134 placed a box bet on number 23 for $1. The box numbers are 23 and 32. Bettor 134 is a winner and will receive $30 to $40 on a $1 bet. If this was not a box bet, then the bettor would receive $40 to $60. The writer will usually circle the number that is the winner on his/her tally sheet and trace the number back to his/her bettor's sheet.

The writer will summarize his/her bets for the ribbon or office manager as illustrated below:

Number	Bets
00	130
01	450
02	300
03	180
04	250
//	//
23*	210
//	//
98	100
99	50
Total	$18,500

In this case, the winning number is 23 and 32 for box bets. The total amount of wagers placed on this number is $210. The writer collected a total of $18,500 from all bettors. If the payout is $30 and $40 to one, then the writer would have the following accounting:

Gross bettor income	$18,500.00
Payouts:	
110 @ $30	3,300.00
200 @ $40	8,000.00
Commission earned (25%)	4,625.00
Net due office manager	$2,575.00

The 110 @ $30 is for box bettors, while 200 @ $40 is for straight bettors. It should be noted that some two-digit lottery operations do not allow box bets.

2. *Three-digit lottery.* The following illustrations show how a three-digit lottery operates at the ribbon/writer level.

Bettor	Number	Bet
Bill	235	$1
Chuck	111	1
148/	121	1
160/	365	1

Bill has placed a straight bet on number 235 for $1. Chuck has placed a bet of $1 on 111, which is a triple number where all three digits are the same. Bettor 148 placed a box bet on number 121 for $1. This is a three-way number because two of the three digits are the same. In a box bet, the bettor would win on number 121, 112, and 211. Bettor 160 placed a box bet on number 365 for $1. This is a six-way number. There are six permutations of this number that are 365, 635, 563, 356, and 653.

The ribbon/writer would summarize his/her bets for the office manager as follows:

Number	Bets
111	230
121	120
235/*	210
300	200
310/	280
365	180
465	312
535	295
678	286
//	//
879/	195
978	233
Total	$98,000

The winning number is 235. Bettors who made straight or box bets would win on this number. If the bettor placed a box bet on 235, 253, 532, 523, 325, and 352 would win. The bettor who made a straight bet, 235, would usually win $400 to $1, while those who bet on a box would normally win $300 to $1. The box bets are called cut numbers because they payout less than a straight bet.

The ribbon/writer would account for his/her business activity as follows:

Gross bets collected	$98,000
Payouts:	
$400 @ 90	36,000
$300 @ 120	36,000
Commission (20%)	19,600
Net due office manager	$ 6,400

In this scenario, the writer/ribbon collected $98,000 in gross bets. The writer had to payout $36,000 to straight bettors, those who bet three- or six-way numbers. The payout to box bettors was $36,000. The writer/ribbon gets a commission of $19,600 because his/her commission is 20%. The balance of $6400 goes to the officer manager or banker.

The ribbon/writer can estimate his/her average payouts as follows:

$$\frac{\left(\$400 \times \text{No. of winners}\right) + \left(\$300 \times \text{No. of winners}\right)}{1000} = \text{Average payout}$$

or

$$\frac{(\$400 \times 90) + (\$300 \times 120)}{1000} = \frac{(36,000) + (36,000)}{1000}$$

or

$$\frac{(72,000)}{1000} = 720 \text{ to } 1$$

16.4 Bingo

Bingo is a game of chance where the bettor matches random numbers between 0 and 75 in groups of 15 on a random selected card where it forms a straight line that is either vertical, horizontal, or diagonal. The bingo card has five random numbers going across and five down the card, totaling 25 numbers. Usually, the center box has no number; it is called a free space. The word "Bingo" denotes the group of numbers 0 through 75 as follows:

Letter	Numbers
B	0–15
I	16–30
N	31–45
G	46–60
O	61–75

When the random selected numbers form a straight line, whether vertical, horizontal, or diagonal, the winner calls out "Bingo." The winner receives funds of either a fixed amount

B	I	N	G	O
1	19	40	49	**71**
4	22	31	**50**	73
12	17	**FS**	53	69
10	**18**	42	47	66
6	29	39	58	75

Figure 16.2 Winning bingo card.

or a percentage of the gross receipts that are received by the "house." An example of a winning bingo card is as follows:

The house calls these numbers that is a winner for one player: 6, 18, 50, and 71. The center box has no number and is considered a free space (FS) (see Figure 16.2).

16.4.1   Tax Exempt

Many nonprofit organizations hold bingo games in order to raise funds. Neither the federal nor state governments tax these profits. Legitimate charities use the profits for their needs. However, organized crime and other criminal groups use bingo halls for personal profit. Many states allow bingo halls and parlors for charity. However, it is unlawful to operate bingo halls for personal profit. Criminal groups sometimes get around this "loophole" by giving charities funds ranging from $200 and up per week. The profits are skimmed from the operations after expenses have been paid.

16.4.2   Variations

There are three basic variations of playing bingo games. These types of bingo games are paper, grind, and lightning. Besides the normal way of getting numbers in a straight row, players must play games that get numbers that form various patterns, for example, X, H, O, 8, 7, E, F, etc., or "black-out" or "coverall" in which every block must be covered. Also, there are bingo games that have "highlighted" numbers that must be called before the player wins. There usually is no pattern for the highlighted or predetermined numbers.

16.4.2.1   Paper Bingo

In paper bingo, bingo cards are printed on disposable paper. They come in various sizes. One bingo card can be printed on a small sheet or multiple bingo cards, called "faces," on a single sheet. Multiple sheets are often put together to form a package that is sold to customers so that they can play multiple games. Players also purchase ink dabbers for use in playing bingo games. The ink dabbers are used to mark called numbers on the bingo faces. The players throw away the sheets after a winner has been called and use another sheet for the next game. In most cases, more than one game can be played on a single sheet. Bingo halls purchase these sheets from suppliers who produce these sheets in various sizes. The suppliers have a standard method of billing and identifying the bingo supplies. As an example, a bingo hall receives the following bill for bingo supplies (Figure 16.3):

Description	Quantity	Total Costs
3 on V padded (1-9000) olive	1 case	$11.50
3 on V padded (9-18000) purple	2 cases	36.00
6 on 5 up (1-9000) BN,GY,BK,PL,RD	1 set	84.15
12 on 5 up (1-9000) BN,GY,BK,PL,RD	5 sets	420.75
12 on 10 up (9-18000)	1 set	153.00
SBL,SOR,SGN,SYW,SPK,BL,OR,GN,YW,PK		
15 on 20 up (6001-9000) double	5 sets	292.00
SBL,SOR,SGN,SYW,SPK,BL,OR,GN,YW,PK		
18 on 20 up (18001-27000)	2 sets	306.00
SBL,SOR,SGN,SYW,SPK,BL,OR,GN,YW,PK		

Figure 16.3 Sample bingo paper invoice.

This example shows that a bingo hall purchased seven different products. The meanings of these products are explained below:

1. *3 on V padded.* There are three faces on a single sheet. The V means vertical. The faces are arranged from top to bottom. Padded means that they are all single sheets. The 1-9000 means that there are 9000 faces in a case. The sheets are all olive in color.
2. *3 on V padded.* There are three vertical faces on a single sheet. The 9-18000 means there are 9000 faces in a case with a series ranging from 90001 to 18000. The color is purple.
3. *6 on 5 up.* There are six faces on a sheet with three down and two across. The 5 up means that there are five sheets in the set. A player can play five bingo games. The series ranges from 1 to 9000. Each sheet in the set has a different color. This allows the bingo operators to make each player use the same color.
4. *12 on 5 up.* There are 12 faces on a sheet with three down and four across. The 5 up means that there are 5 sheets in the set with different colors.
5. *12 on 10 up.* There are 12 faces on a sheet with three down and four across. The 10 up means that there are 10 sheets in the set with different colors.
6. *15 on 20 up.* Here there are 15 faces on a sheet with three down and five across. The 20 up means that there are 20 sheets in the set with different colors.
7. *18 on 20 up.* This set has 18 faces on a sheet with three down and six across. The 20 up means that there are 20 sheets in the set with different colors.

Bingo operators and suppliers use the following guide to determine the number of faces per set and booklet and the number of booklets in an order.

Faces = Ups times series
Booklets = Series divided by on
Faces per book = Ups times on

16.4.2.1.1 Paper Bingo Terminology   Bingo operators and suppliers define the following terms:

1. *Series.* The number of faces contained in a single set. This is usually 9000. In large sets, it is 3000. The total series is 1 to 63,000.
2. *Face.* The individual bingo card containing 24 numbers plus a consecutively numbered center free space.
3. *On.* The number of bingo faces per sheet.
4. *Cut.* The direction a sheet of faces will be cut from a master sheet. A cut may be square, horizontal, or vertical.
5. *Up.* The number of sheets in a booklet.
6. *Off-cut.* Faces that cannot be cut from the master sheet in the desired "on." If the master sheet is a 24 on vertical and the order is a 9 on sheet, the result will be two 9 on cuts that equal 18 faces and an off-cut of six faces, which totals 24 faces from the 24 on vertical sheet.

16.4.2.1.2 Bingo Paper Sales   Bingo halls that sell paper usually do so in various size packages. The prices of each package vary according to size. The package sizes can be composed of only one bingo product or a combination of bingo products. For internal control or fraud examination, the gross sales can be determined by use of the gross profit method of determining income. This can be done by computing the number of bingo products sold times the sales price. This will give the amount of the gross proceeds that were collected. The gross profit can be determined by taking the gross proceeds and subtracting the direct costs. The direct cost is the cost of the bingo products and the prize money paid out. To illustrate the computation of gross income, the following example is given.

A bingo hall sells the following packs to customers:

A - 3 on V	Cost $20.00	Prize $50.00
12 on 10 up		
B - 6 on 2 up	Cost $35.00	Prize $75.00
12 on 10 up		
C - 3 on V 2 up	Cost $50.00	Prize $100.00
15 on 10 up		

The 12 on 10 up is the common product for packs A and B. It has a series of 1-9000. The number of booklets in a series is 9000/10 = 900 booklets. The 15 on 10 up is the main product for Pack C. It has a series of 1-9000. The number of booklets in this series is 9000/10 = 900 booklets.

Inventory shows 100 booklets of 12 on 10 up was sold and 20 booklets of 15 on 10 up was sold. The gross receipts are computed as shown below.

12 on 10 up ($20 + $35 = $55/2 = 22.50 × 100)	$2250.00
15 on 10 up ($50 × 20 =)	1000.00
Total sales	$3250.00

The 3 on V and 6 on 2 up are excluded from the computation because they are part of the packages sold. However, the cost of these products should be part of the cost of sales.

16.4.2.1.3 Prize Payouts The principal cost of sales is the prize money that is paid out. Using the above example, the cost of sales is computed as follows:

Prize ($50 + $75 + $100 = $225/3 =)	$75.00
The number of games in the session	×12
Total prize payouts	$900.00

The cost of the paper sold is computed on a prorated basis.

12 on 10 up (100/900 × $153.00 =)	$17.00
15 on 10 up (20/900 × $180.00 =)	4.00
Cost of packages sold	$21.00

It should be observed that the 3 on V and the 6 on 2 up should be added to the computation above. It is omitted in this case because the amount sold and on hand is not given.

The gross profit from this bingo hall session is computed as follows:

Gross proceeds from sales	$3250
Prize payouts	900
Cost of paper bingo sheets	21
Total cost of sales	921
Gross profit	$2329

16.4.2.2 Grind Bingo

Grind bingo uses reusable bingo cards. Grind bingo games usually is played faster than the paper bingo. Grind bingo has one or more color cards. The card colors determine both the price for the cards and the prize payouts. Example:

Blue cards cost 50 cents each but pay out $10.
Brown cards cost 75 cents each but pay out $20.
Red cards cost $1 each but pay out $25.
Gold cards cost $2 each but pay out $200.

The player obtains a bag of chips. When a number is called, the player puts a chip on the number called. When bingo is called, the winner receives the prize money for that game based on the type of card that the player purchased. The player places money in front for the operator to collect before the game begins. The money placed in front is dependent on the color and the number cards the player is using, for example, $.50 for blue cards, $.75 for brown cards, etc.

16.4.2.2.1 Grind Bingo Income Grind bingo income is determined simply by multiplying the average number of players times the average number of games per day times the average income per game. The key element to determine gross income is to know the following:

1. The average players during each session.
2. The number of games being played during the session. This usually averages about 20 to 26 games per hour.
3. The amount of funds collected from the floor based on the average type (colors) of cards being played.

This type of bingo is more labor intensive because it requires each set of tables to have a "floor" person to collect the coins. However, the floor person has to turn in a tally sheet and the coins to the manager after each game or session. This type of bingo is often called "ten cent bingo." Grind bingo callers must call the letter and the number, for example, B five, I twenty, and N thirty-three. These types of bingo halls are generally found in lower income neighborhoods because the costs seem low to play. In actuality, it costs the players almost the same as paper bingo.

16.4.2.3 Lightning Bingo

Lightning bingo is about the same as grind bingo, except that it uses cards that have some highlighted numbers. Players use reusable cards and play with coins. The players must get the highlighted numbers to win. The caller does not call out the letters, only the numbers. It is called "lightning bingo" because the games only last about 10 to 15 seconds a game. Gross proceeds for lightning bingo are computed the same way as for grind bingo. In many states, this form of bingo is illegal because it does not call out letters and is classified as a numbers racket.

16.5 Track Betting

Pari-mutuel wagering is gambling at various types of racetracks or sporting events. The racetracks usually involved are dogs, cars, and horse races. Jai Alai is the most common sport for pari-mutuel wagering. Many states have legalized pari-mutuel wagering on either racing or sporting events or both. Like other types of gambling activities, pari-mutuel wagering has its own terminology. Pari-mutuel means each player is competing against another player, not against the track.

16.5.1 Terminology

Understanding the terms of pari-mutuel wagering will help the examiner to understand the mechanics of pari-mutuel wagering. The following are the most common terms used:

1. *Across the board.* Three equal wagers placed on one animal to win, to place, and to show.
2. *Breakage.* The difference between true mutuel odds and lesser, rounded amounts given to winning players. Breakage usually is divided between track and state.
3. *Boxing.* The bettor selects any number of animals (three or more) in a race. If the selections finish one, two, or three in any order, the bettor wins. In a Quinella box, if any two selections finish one or two in any order, the bettor wins.
4. *Chalk.* A term that refers to the favorite in a race.
5. *Closing odds.* The odds displayed on the tote board after wagering closes.
6. *Coupled.* Two or more animals belonging to the same owner.
7. *Daily double.* A wager where the bettor must select the winners of two consecutive races, usually the first and second races, prior to the first race.
8. *Daily triple.* A wager where the bettor must select the winners of three consecutive races.

9. *Entry.* Two or more animals in a race owned by the same person(s) or trained by the same trainer. These are termed an "entry" and coupled as a single betting unit; a bet on one coupled horse is a bet on all horses it is coupled with.

10. *Exacta.* A wager that a bettor wins when he/she selects the first and second place finishers in a race in exact order.

11. *Field.* An animal grouped with other animals as a single betting interest in races where the number of starters exceeds the number of betting interests the track's tote system can handle; a bet on one field animal is a bet on all animals in the mutuel field.

12. *Handicapping.* Studying race histories to select the best wagering options.

13. *Handle.* The total amount wagered on a race or on a day's races.

14. *Hedging.* The art of covering the original bet by placing an additional wager to cover the potential loss of the first. An example would be buying a $2 place or show ticket to insure a $2 win bet.

15. *In the money.* Finishing first, second, or third.

16. *Minus pool.* In pari-mutuel betting, a situation in which so much money is bet on an animal (usually to show) that the pool is insufficient after the take and breakage to pay holders of winning tickets the legal minimum odds of 1 to 10 or 20. The track is required to make up the difference from its own funds.

17. *Morning line.* The track handicapper's estimate of the probable odds for each animal at post time.

18. *Mutuel field.* A grouping of animals as a single betting interest in races where the number of starters exceeds the number of betting interests the track's tote system can handle; a bet on one field animal is a bet on all mutuel field animals.

19. *Odds on.* Odds that are less than even money ($1 to $1).

20. *Off the board.* Failure to finish first, second, or third (in the money).

21. *On the nose.* A bet that an animal will win.

22. *Overlay.* An under-bet animal (not favored to win) and therefore a good value.

23. *Parlay.* A wagering format that allows each player to compete against the other players rather than against the track.

24. *Perfecta.* To win this wager, the animals must finish first and second in the exact order of finish.

25. *Pick-3.* A bettor wins when he/she selects the winners of three consecutive races on one ticket that he/she must buy before the first of the three races begins.

26. *Pick-6.* A bettor wins when he/she selects the winners of six consecutive races on one ticket that he/she must buy before the first of the six races begins. If no one correctly picks all six winners, half the pot will be paid to patrons correctly picking the most winners, and the other half will "carry over" to the Pick-6 pool on the next racing day.

27. *Place.* A bettor wins when his/her selection finishes first or second.

28. *Pool.* The total amount of money wagered on any one type of bet (win pool, show pool, exacta pool, etc.).

29. *Quinella.* A bettor wins when he/she selects two animals finishing first and second in a race, regardless of order.

30. *Show.* A bettor wins when his/her selection finishes first or second or third.

31. *Superfecta.* A bettor wins when his/her selection finishes first, second, third, and fourth in the exact order of finish.

32. *Takeout.* The percentage of betting pools taken out by the state and the race track, with the track putting its share of the takeout toward race purses and expenses. It also means the withholding on winning tickets over $5000, which is turned over to the Internal Revenue Service.

33. *Totalisator (tote).* The system of computers and electronic components tied to the pari-mutuel ticket issuing machines that calculates the odds to $1 and computes the various winning payoffs.

34. *Tote board.* An electronic board in the infield displaying approximate odds, amounts bet, track condition, post time, time of day, result of race, inquiry or objection sign if a foul is claimed, running time, and payoff prices.

35. *Trifecta (triple).* A wager in which the winning bettor picks the first three finishers of a race in exact order.

36. *Wheel.* To make an exotic wager (e.g., exacta or daily double) using a single "key" animal with the balance of the field (in the case of an exacta) or all the animals in the other race (in the case of a daily double).

37. *Win.* A bettor wins when his/her selection finishes first.

16.5.2   Odds and Payoff

The following chart is the odds on dogs or horses and the payoff to winners based on a $2 bet.

Odds	Payoff	Odds	Payoff	Odds	Payoff
1-5	$2.40	9-5	$5.60	8-1	$18.00
2-5	2.80	2-1	6.00	9-1	20.00
1-2	3.00	5-2	7.00	10-1	22.00
3-5	3.20	3-1	8.00	12-1	26.00
4-5	3.60	7-2	9.00	15-1	32.00
1-1	4.00	4-1	10.00	20-1	42.00
6-5	4.40	9-2	11.00	30-1	62.00
7-5	4.80	5-1	12.00	40-1	82.00
3-2	5.00	6-1	14.00	50-1	102.00
8-5	5.20	7-1	16.00	99-1	200.00

16.5.3   Ten Percenting

Ten percenting is illegal at both the federal level and in most states. Ten percenting is a scheme where the true winner of a bet sells his/her winning ticket to another person for a 10% fee, thus the term "ten percenting." The true winner of the winning ticket does not want the track to file a W-2G with the Internal Revenue Service. If the winning ticket pays off over $5000, then the track is required to withhold 28% from the winnings. A ten percenter takes the winning ticket to the track teller. He/she fills out the W-2G and collects the winnings. He/she keeps 10% of the winnings and gives the balance to the true winner. In the case of winning tickets that require income tax withholding, the ten percenter gives the true winner the balance of the winnings after the income tax withholding and his/her 10%

has been deducted. The Internal Revenue Service only requires W-2G's to be filed when the winnings exceed $1000. The ten percenter collects loosing tickets off the track floor. He/she gathers enough loosing tickets to offset the winnings. If there is income tax withholding, then the ten percenter files his/her income tax return to claim a tax refund of all or most of the amounts withheld. He/she also takes deductions for losing tickets. Most if not all losing tickets were obtained by people throwing away their losing tickets. In essence, the ten percenter is committing tax fraud.

16.5.3.1 *Indicators*

There are many indicators that show a person may be ten percenting at the tracks. These indicators are:

1. A very large amount of winnings from any particular track that requires the filing of W-2G's.
2. A very large amount of winnings from any particular track with only "take out" (withholding of income tax) W-2G's.
3. The bettor presents losing tickets that show two or more tickets with the same date and time. Some tracks use systems that do not show the times on the tickets; however, the tracks can provide data about when the tickets were purchased.
4. The bettor presents losing tickets from different tracks that were purchased on the same date but the time of purchase is minutes apart. The tracks are miles apart, meaning that it is impossible to go from one track to the other within the time frame.
5. The bettor presents losing tickets from the same teller. The teller history for that day shows a series of tickets being purchased in sequence in which none are winning tickets. The bettor does not have all of the sequential tickets that were purchased in a series (multiple tickets purchased at once).
6. The bettor has a full-time job but presents tickets that show he/she was at the track all day when, in fact, he/she was on his/her job.
7. The bettor provides losing tickets in such quantity that it is impossible to purchase in any one day.
8. The bettor's losing tickets do not show any constant pattern. Bettors usually have a pattern of betting.
9. The bettor has no other sources of income but W-2G's.
10. The bettor does not complete the W-2G correctly or completes it falsely. Ten percenters sometimes use false social security numbers, or false names, or both. Sometimes they use other people's names and social security numbers.
11. The bettor has a lot of winnings from one track but has large losses from another track.
12. The bettor has a criminal past of illegal gambling. Criminals that are involved in gambling activities go from one form of gambling to another when they hear or feel that law enforcement is looking into a particular type of illegal gambling.
13. A cash flow schedule of the winning and losing tickets is prepared. If the bettor does not have any other sources of funds, then any negative cash balances clearly indicates that the bettor is a ten percenter. No one can have negative cash on hand.

More than one of these indicators should be present before an examiner considers the bettor a ten percenter. If many of these indicators are present, then the bettor is a ten percenter. However, for item 13, this clearly shows that the bettor is a ten percenter because no one can have negative cash on hand.

16.5.3.2 Violation

For federal purposes as well as in many states, ten percenting is illegal. It is illegal in that taxes are not properly reported. The true winner is not paying the income taxes on his/her winnings, both federal and state. The ten percenter is not paying taxes on the winnings either. The ten percenter who signs the W-2G signs the form under penalties of perjury. This is also a felony of making a false statement. The signer of the W-2G is also declaring "and that no other person is entitled to any part of these payments." In essence, the ten percenter is committing two felony counts, that is, tax evasion and making a false statement. Each signed W-2G is a separate felony count.

16.6   Gambling

Many people gamble in various ways. Some of the common methods, both legal and illegal based on circumstances, were discussed in this chapter. Some gamblers, as described in the movies, play various kinds of card games. Card games are basically illegal in most states if it involves betting, but because most card games are privately held, law enforcement does not get involved unless something brings it to their attention, for example, extortion, murder, organized crime, and loan sharking. Many states now have lotteries. Those states use the profits from lotteries to help finance education, roads, and other types of services. Private lottery operations are illegal in all states. Bingo is legal in most states, provided that it benefits charitable organizations. Organized crime groups get involved in illegal gambling. In some areas, they control illegal gambling operations. Anyone who tries to set up a gambling operation in an area controlled by organized crime can find themselves at odds to say the least. Illegal gambling offers organized crime groups the ability to skim huge profits.

16.7   Summary

Illegal gambling is one occupation where organized crime is involved. In fact, there are individuals who get involved in illegal gambling. Individuals usually start out by taking a bet with friends, and it mushrooms into a large business venture. Criminal organizations usually set up operations when they find an area prone to such activity. The investigator needs to know how the various games operate in order to prepare a case. Police departments will get a tip of illegal gambling. When they do, they will usually start with getting an undercover officer to make bets and identify the principals. This will lead to getting wiretaps and making trash pickups. The final phase is executing search and arrest warrants. Before going to trial, the investigator will have to analyze and summarize the gambling information for trial. It is therefore important for the financial investigator to understand how the various gaming methods work.

Fraud Prevention for Consumers

17

17.1 Introduction

There are many precautions that the consumer can take to prevent fraud. There is an old cliché that goes "an ounce of prevention is worth a pound of cure." This is particularly true in the area of crime. If consumers take the appropriate steps and procedures to prevent fraud, then their losses can be nonexistent or minimal. In many cases, fraud can be prevented by making appropriate inquiries, while more investigative procedures are required in other cases. It should be stressed here that all precautions that can be taken do not guarantee that consumers will not become victims; however, it will reduce the chances of becoming a victim. Regardless of all precautions taken, there are many "con" artists who can "take your shoes while you are standing in them." Therefore, the procedures and precautions taken to prevent fraud do not guarantee anyone from being a fraud victim. It is also not true that all people or businesses are in the business of committing fraud.

17.2 Consumers

Consumers are vulnerable to many kinds of fraud schemes. These fraud schemes range from small car repairs to large investment schemes. Statistics show that the elderly, women, and minorities are victimized the most. However, in recent years, practically everyone is vulnerable to fraud schemes. Even well-educated and knowledgeable people have become victims. There are con men out there who can almost literally "steal your shoes while you are standing in them." These people are very personable and friendly. This chapter describes the more common fraud schemes that consumers will face. It should be remembered that the "consumer should beware." One advertiser said an "educated consumer is the best consumer"; however, it can also be said that "an educated consumer has the best defense against becoming a fraud victim."

17.3 Auto Purchases

There are auto dealerships that operate both unethically and fraudulently. An auto dealer will advertise a particular vehicle for a certain price. When the consumer goes to look at this particular vehicle, the salesman says that it is out of stock. He will try to direct the consumer to another model that usually costs more. Using high-pressure sales tactics, the salesman will get the consumer to purchase the more expensive car. This is true for both new and used car dealerships. If you have decided on a particular vehicle that you want, then you should make inquiries about when this model will become available. If the model will not become available anytime soon, then you should walk out and ignore any salesman's "deals." In the case of a used car dealership, you should ask the salesman if a mechanic of your own choosing could inspect and test the car. If the salesman denies your request, then you should not waste your time in looking at the car. Most likely, the vehicle is a lemon. If the salesman approves your request, then retain a mechanic who will check out the vehicle, and follow his/her advice whether to purchase or not. If you are going to finance the vehicle, it is recommended that you arrange for your own financing in advance. Most finance companies, banks, etc., will approve vehicle loans up to certain dollar amounts. The car dealerships have made arrangements with particular finance companies in which they will get a "rebate." These financing arrangements will charge higher interest rates on the vehicle loans so that they can cover the rebates. These arrangements are not illegal in most states. You will be better off if you can arrange for your own financing. Many banks and credit unions can approve your loan for a vehicle before purchasing. You have the advantage of knowing your interest rate, terms, and amount before you make the purchase.

Most people will have an old vehicle to trade in for the newer one. You should check with the bank or credit union as to the wholesale and retail value of your old car. The local library generally will have reference material that will provide the wholesale and retail value. Some reference material will also provide for the trade-in value of your old vehicle. It is best to find the best deal from the dealer before discussing the trade-in allowance.

New vehicles will have initial warranty coverage. Many dealerships will offer extended service contracts. You should read the contract carefully to determine what repairs are covered and the extent of coverage. When buying a used vehicle, you should ask about any warranties the dealer might provide. You should get the warranty in writing. The value of the service contract is determined by the cost of repairs. Will the service contract cover any future repairs? If not, then the service contract is not worth very much. If there is a disclaimer, then there is no warranty. A disclaimer will tell the buyer to buy the vehicle in "as is" condition. You have no legal protection.

You should ask if the vehicle has been in an accident. There are dealers who acquire accident vehicles, fix them up, and resell them. You should never buy a vehicle that has been in an accident. These types of vehicles have a high degree of needed repair work and are usually unsafe to drive.

The cost of a vehicle includes more than the purchase price. An unreliable vehicle will cost you more in frequent repairs plus the aggravation and lost time from work. Financing terms also affect the total cost.

Consumers who purchase vehicles over the Internet should also be aware of fraud. The Internet Crime Complaint Center (IC3.gov) advises consumers not to purchase vehicles outside of the United States. The U.S. buyer is required to send money by wire transfer. The money cannot be recovered, and the buyer does not receive the vehicle. Auto shoppers are cautioned about "second chance auctions" and other schemes in which the seller of a vehicle e-mails a potential buyer to inform the buyer that the high bidder on the auction defaulted and the vehicle can be purchased by the buyer at their previous bid or at a discount.

17.4 Auto Leasing

A lease is nothing more than a long-term rental agreement. You are paying for the right to use the vehicle. You do not own it. The title is retained by the leasing company. However, you are responsible for the repairs and maintenance of the vehicle. You are also responsible for the insurance that will require higher premiums and higher coverage. The capitalized cost, called "cap cost," is reduced by the amount of cash or trade equity at the start of the lease. The money factor, or interest rate, ranges from 0.0021 to 0.0046. The interest rate can be determined by multiplying the money factor by 2400. The money factor can be negotiable. You should not lease a vehicle on the first visit. Most leasing companies limit the annual mileage, usually between 10,000 and 12,000 miles per year. For any mileage over the limit, the leasing company will charge an extra mileage rate. The extra mileage charge can be very high. Leasing a vehicle may be cheaper than buying a new vehicle; however, if you do a lot of driving, it may be more costly. You must read the leasing agreement thoroughly. Leasing agents make most of their money from selling the vehicle after the lease is up. Many dealerships will sometimes try to have a consumer lease a vehicle instead of buying because of the expected profit. Lease agreements will usually be from 1 to 3 years. Leasing vehicles is usually better for traveling salesmen or self-employed individuals because of tax write-offs. They are usually not good for commuting. For most consumers, leasing a vehicle is not advisable.

17.5 Business Investment

Many people are losing their jobs because of economic conditions, "downsizing" of companies, and a whole host of other reasons. Many people are looking to acquire or start their own business. The problem of starting your own business is having the necessary capital and knowledge to do so. Many investors will turn to a business broker who can offer a wide range of existing businesses that are for sale. The broker may be legitimate, but the prospective business may not be. Business owners will try to inflate the books to show higher sales and profits in order to entice someone to buy when, in fact, the business is operating at a loss. Some owners will go so far to say that they are taking out funds that are not recorded on the books. They will even brag about it. This is an indication of fraud, both on federal and state taxes and to the prospective buyer. An established business is a better investment than to start from scratch; however, an established business could be a worse investment than starting from scratch. This is particularly true if the buyer does not know what to look out for or how to evaluate the prospective business. The following guidelines are provided.

17.5.1 Financial Statements

The prospective buyer should obtain financial statements for not only the current year but also the past 4 years as a minimum. In addition, tax returns should be obtained for the past 3 years. These financial statements and tax returns should be analyzed to see what are the trends and conditions of the business. Questions should be asked, for example, "Are sales increasing each year?"; "Are assets remaining steady or increasing?"; "Is inventory increasing with sales?" Further auditing procedures are explained in another chapter. If the buyer does not know how to analyze and audit the statements, then an accountant should be retained to do so. His/her fees will cost much less than the possible loss the buyer could have in acquiring a bad business.

17.5.2 Bank Statements

The prospective buyer should obtain the bank statements for at least the past 2 years along with the current year. The deposits should be compared to the gross receipts reported on the tax returns and the financial statements. Explanations should be sought out for any large differences; especially when inventory, liabilities, and assets do not increase.

17.5.3 Observation

The prospective buyer should visit the business location on various occasions. The purpose is to see what the customer traffic is in the business and if the assets and inventory exist as purported on the financial statements.

17.5.4 Purchase Price

The seller will always ask more than the business is worth. For businesses that have been in existence for many years, the owner will have a personal attachment and concern for whoever takes over. Therefore, they will want much more than what the business is worth. As a prospective buyer, you will want to acquire the business at a reasonable price. As a general guideline, the prospective buyer should acquire the business based on the following formula.

To determine the net worth of the business:

- Add to the net worth the accumulated depreciation and amortization.
- Add any shareholder loans (this item shows up as an outside liability).

This gives the total equity by the owner.

- Add the yearly officer salaries and bonuses.
- Add the yearly profits based on the time frame in which you plan to finance part of the purchase.

This gives the purchase price that the prospective buyer should pay for the business.

The profits can be considered the goodwill of the business. If the business is acquired solely for cash, then goodwill can be paid based on the net profits of the business. However, goodwill should not be paid for more than 5 years of profits. If there are no profits, then there is no goodwill.

From the seller's point of view, the business owner should not expect that he/she could get more than what the above formula shows. However, the seller will have to evaluate the buyer when he/she is going to take a note or payment plan for part of the purchase price. The seller will have to evaluate the prospective purchaser in the following ways:

1. *Payment of note.* Can the business pay off the note without any hardship on the buyer? If the formula described above is followed, then the business can pay off the note. It should be noted that the prospective buyer's only source of income would be the business.
2. *Buyer.* The buyer should be investigated if a note is part of the purchase price. The following questions should be answered:

    a. Does the prospective buyer have any expertise in this type of business? If not, how much time will the prospective buyer require for training? Some training is required to give the prospective buyer some knowledge of the operations. They will have to know the vendors and their policies, banking relationships, employees, regular customers, and the policies and procedures the business has been following.

    b. What is the character and integrity of the prospective buyer? References should be checked. County records should be checked for any criminal or civil actions. You should be aware of references with answering machines. Also, previous employers should be contacted about job performance and character.

    c. What is the credit rating of the prospective buyer? A credit report should be obtained from the credit bureau. It will show promptly the prospective buyer's record of paying off debts. If the prospective buyer has a record of delinquent payments, then you can expect the same.

17.6 Accountant Fraud

Many people go to accountants for various purposes. Among those purposes are to prepare their tax returns, accounting advice and services, management advice, and audits for their business. However, there are some accountants who are unscrupulous. In tax return preparation, they will decrease income or increase deductions or both. The taxpayer gets a large refund. When the Internal Revenue Service or other taxing authority audits the taxpayer, they have to repay the shortage along with penalties and interest. The penalties and interest can double or even triple the original tax liability. Only Certified Public Accountants (CPA) and Enrolled Agents (EA) are allowed to represent taxpayers before the Internal Revenue Service and most other taxing authorities. These individuals have the appropriate training and experience. There are many individuals and companies that prepare tax returns that are not qualified to represent taxpayers. There are some national chains that have offices across the country. Some of these national chains offer 6-week courses to train their tax preparers. When these tax preparers complete the course, they think that they have become tax "experts." This becomes ironic in that it takes nearly 6 months to train revenue agents in the Federal Tax Code and Regulations. The major problem with "nonlicensed" accountants is that they become negligent because of incompetence, while "licensed" tax preparers, who have the appropriate training and education, prepare fraudulent tax returns to obtain higher fees. The taxpayer thinks that the accountant is very good because he/she is getting a refund larger than usual. The taxpayer should consider the following factors when having their tax returns completed.

17.6.1 Fees

The charges for services should be known before engaging the accountant. Fees are charged either by the number of forms to be completed or by the time required to complete the returns.

17.6.2　License

If the taxpayer has a complex return, then a CPA or EA should be retained because they have the training and experience. Also, they can represent the taxpayer in an audit. Higher income and complex tax returns tend to be audited more than simple returns.

17.6.3　Check Return

The taxpayer should review his/her own return before signing and sending off. Remember that the taxpayer provided the information to the preparer; therefore, the taxpayer should compare the information provided to the information on the return to see if they match. The taxpayer should keep in mind that he/she is responsible for the accuracy of the return, not the accountant.

People who have their own business retain an accountant for various services, principally, preparing various federal and state tax returns, periodic financial statements, and management advice. The greater use of the services leads to greater contact, reliance, and trust on the accountant. However, the accountant may be a crook. There are many cases where the accountant has absconded with client's funds. The following precautions should be followed to prevent this:

1. The accountant should never be a signatory on any bank account.
2. All tax returns should be signed and mailed in by the taxpayer and not by the accountant.
3. The accountant should not have any custodial control over any personal or business assets.
4. Investments proposed by the accountant should be reviewed by someone else, for example, a certified financial planner. Accountants are trained to evaluate past performance, not future expectations. Financial planners are trained to evaluate investments for future returns.
5. The accountant should not be retained as trustee for any estate or trust. However, the accountant should be used to prepare tax returns and financial statements. This serves as a way to oversee the affairs of a trustee.

17.7　Adoption Fraud

There are couples who set their hearts on adopting a child. However, there are unscrupulous people who are out to defraud people through fraudulent adoption schemes. This not only defrauds couples of their money, but it also puts deep emotional pain on the adopting couple. To avoid the pain and expense, couples should do the following:

- Do your homework. Most states require adopting agencies and facilitators to be licensed. The prospective couple should contact their state licensing agencies for legitimate adopting agencies and facilitators.
- Do not rely on the Internet for research. They should always meet with the agency personnel.

- Obtain documentation and references.
- Be skeptical of agencies or individuals who say they have shortcuts. There are no shortcuts in adopting procedures.
- Interview the birthmother or hire your own social worker to interview the birthmother.
- Check the U.S. Department of State for international adoptions procedures. They can provide more information. Every country has various rules and regulations for foreigners adopting children in their country. These rules and regulations should be obtained and studied closely.

17.8   Advance Loan Fees

Consumers with bad credit or no credit sometimes seek loans from banks, savings and loan associations, credit unions, and other financial institutions. These financial institutions will not make loans to those with poor or no credit standing. Many companies advertise in newspapers, television, and magazines that will guarantee their ability to get loans for people regardless of their credit. Many advance loan fee brokers are nothing more than a scam. Legitimate credit grantors will not guarantee you a loan. Financial institutions cannot risk qualifying you for a loan without researching your credit history and determining your ability to repay the loan with interest. The swindler has no ability to secure a loan for you. He/she either steals your fee and disappears or remains in the area to bilk other unsuspecting victims while stalling you with various excuses why your loan has not been funded. Swindlers usually get a 5% fee in advance. Some danger signs of fraud are:

- You provide information over the phone.
- The lender can decide within hours after receiving the information.
- The lender claims the payment of the fee will "lock you into the loan."
- The lender wants you to send the money on the same day or have you overnight the payment by an overnight mail company.

Many states have passed legislation prohibiting loan brokers from charging advance loan fees. You can check with the state department of banking and finance or the state attorney general's office for information about complaints or legal actions pending against a company. They can also advise whether it is legal in their state.

The following guidelines will help the consumer avoid being victimized by an advance fee swindler.

- Know who you are doing business with. The consumer should obtain the name of the loan representative and the name, address, and telephone number of the company.
- Do not accept the promoter's claim of guaranteed loan services at face value.
- Insist on being told the name of the lending institution that supposedly will fund your loan.
- Verify with the supposed lender all oral and written representations made by the promoter regarding support from that lender.

- Ask for names, addresses, and phone numbers of other customers of the promoter, and contact them to see if they got their loans.
- Consider consulting an attorney or accountant for advice.

You should ask yourself why the promoter can obtain a loan for you from a legitimate lender when you yourself have been turned down for a loan, perhaps many times.

17.9   Affinity Fraud

Affinity fraud is conducted as a Ponzi scheme. Affinity relates to specific ethnic, religious, native language, or social club. Just because a person claims affinity with a specific class or group of people does not mean they are legitimate. Any investment offer by a person who has affinity with you should be checked out before making an investment. Steps to avoid becoming a victim are:

- Beware of promises of great financial rewards and no risk.
- Always request information in writing, detailing the risks and procedures to get your money out.
- Do not be pushed into a quick decision.
- Beware of testimonials that cannot be verified.
- Ask what state or federal agencies the firm is regulated by and with whom it is registered.

17.10   Art Fraud

Some people like to buy valuable art only to find that it is a counterfeit print. It is only worth a few dollars. The most frequent counterfeit art work is Salvador Dali, Pablo Picasso, Marc Chagall, and Joan Miro. Consumers will usually get advertising by mail and mail in a response. A telemarketer will later call. The telemarketer will use high-pressure selling techniques. They will usually claim:

- It is a great investment with unrealistic investment returns.
- The artist is close to death, which will increase the value of the art work.
- A Certificate of Authenticity will be provided.

Consumer should know some art galleries and auctions sell counterfeit or worthless art. Only an art expert can tell the difference between a valuable piece of art and a fake. Before purchasing original art, the consumer should have an independent art appraiser appraise the art work. The consumer should obtain as much specific information about the art as possible before purchasing it. A legitimate business will not push you into a purchase without you having an opportunity to have it independently appraised.

The consumer should find out about the company. What are the company's past successes and failures? The state attorney general's office or the Federal Trade Commission can provide information about complaints and lawsuits.

17.11 Attorney Fraud

Fraud that is committed by attorneys usually falls into two areas. The first area is over-charging the client for his/her services. The second area is a violation of trust where the attorney outright steals from the client. Some unscrupulous attorneys, in conjunction with doctors, operate an "ambulance chasing" scam. In personal injury cases, lawyers are paid on contingent fees. This means the lawyer and the client agree that the fee will be based on a percentage of the settlement or court award in the case. If no settlement or court award is made, the lawyer will not be paid. This type of law practice requires a high volume of cases to insure a steady cash flow. Lawyers running personal injury "mills" are not anxious to engage in litigation. They rely on the insurance company's desire to settle quickly, real-izing the expense a company must absorb by going to court to fight a claim. The lawyer will entice accident victims to cooperate by promising a big "payday" from the insurance company. The big payday often never arrives for the victim because medical fees, runner fees, and contingency fees may be deducted before the victim gets his/her share. Some ambulance-chasing lawyers blatantly rip-off their clients by forging the signature of the victim on the insurance company check. Even if the victims discover their lawyers cheated them, they are reluctant to report the fraud because they too conspired to defraud the insurance company. The consumer therefore should take the following measures in deal-ing with personal injury cases:

1. Consult his/her own doctor as to the extent of the injuries before consulting a lawyer.
2. Obtain a complete statement as to all the charges and evaluate their reason-ableness.
3. Discuss and obtain a copy of the engagement contract from the attorney.
4. Instead of using one the lawyer recommends, use his/her own doctor. It is almost certain that the doctor's fees by the lawyer-recommended doctor would be above those normally charged by others.
5. Check with their local or state consumer affairs departments as to any com-plaints or disciplinary actions against the lawyer. County public records should be searched for any lawsuits against the lawyer. Large number of complaints or lawsuits is an indication of an unscrupulous attorney.
6. Avoid ambulance-chasing lawyers, who use people called "runners" to obtain busi-ness. The runners will approach victims soon after the accident, sometimes while at the scene. They will give a lawyer's business card and urge the victim to call a certain attorney. They also promise big paydays. This is a clear sign of an attorney who the consumer will want to avoid.

The second area of fraudulent lawyers is the position of trust. The client is relying on the attorney to handle certain financial matters. The attorney, in handling these financial mat-ters, embezzles the funds of the client. This happens a lot in areas of real estate sales, pro-bating an estate, and performing trustee duties. This can be either very blatant or very clandestine. Few attorneys actually take their clients funds and flee; however, many attor-neys will pad expenses, overcharge fees, and inflate bills. The client should review these expenses before taking the final settlement.

17.12 Auto Repair Fraud

Every consumer will need to have their vehicle fixed at some point. Auto repair fraud is the most common fraud and ranks number one in consumer complaints. Before having your vehicle fixed, the consumer should ask friends and coworkers for repair shops they trust. This should be done before you need your vehicle repaired. Also, it avoids the pressure of a last minute choice. The consumer should make inquiries about:

- Does the auto repair shop honor the existing warranty on your vehicle? If it does not, then you may be paying for parts and labor covered by the manufacturer's or extended warranty.
- Does the auto repair shop have the experience in working on your type of vehicle?
- The consumer should be given a written estimate as to the parts needed and the amount of labor required. The auto repair shop should contact the consumer before exceeding the estimate by at least 10%.
- When the work is finished, the bad parts should be given to the consumer, then the consumer can evaluate the necessity for the part.
- When feasible, the consumer should get estimates from various repair shops.
- When the work is completed, the consumer should get a detailed invoice of the work done and an itemized description of the parts and labor charges as well as any guarantees.
- Check with local or state consumer agencies for any complaints and lawsuits.

Some states require auto repair shops to be licensed with the state. If they are required to be licensed in your state, then ask to see their registration. The licensing agency can also provide consumers with information about any complaints or lawsuits.

17.13 Auto Title Loans

In recent years, new companies have started offering title loans. A title loan is a way of borrowing money using your vehicle as collateral. On the basis of the vehicle's value, the lender determines how much money they can loan. These title loan companies are legal in some states and illegal in others. Very few states regulate these title loan companies. The following are characteristics of title loans:

- Title loans are very expensive. The finance charge on a $500 title loan can run up to 25% per month or 300% for a year. In addition to finance charges, many title loan companies charge additional fees of around $25.
- Title loan lenders will loan up to 55% of the value of the vehicle. Some states may put a cap of $2500 or $5000. Many title loan lenders make loans from $100 to $500.
- Title loan companies quote interest in monthly rates. Many times the title loan lender provides little information to the consumer. Some title loan lenders add insurance that drives up the cost of the loan.
- If the borrower defaults on the title loan, it can result in repossession of the vehicle. Consumers can still owe money even after the cars are sold to repay the loan.

Consumers should steer clear of title loan companies. The cost of these types of loans is very expensive. In some states, the finance charge is much higher than what even credit card companies charge on credit card balances.

Before the consumer signs the loan agreement, they should check for the amount of the loan, the interest rate, and term of the loan. The loan agreement should explain what will happen if you do not repay the loan with interest. In other words, they can repossess the vehicle and resale it. They can keep the proceeds up to the amount owed along with reasonable expenses to cover repossession and resale costs. The lender must notify you in writing if he/she intends to repossess your vehicle and you will have a chance to arrange to hand it over instead of having a repossession agent come and get it. The lender should give you the time and place of the sale and give you an accounting of what is owed. The consumer should ask what their policies and procedures are in notifying you in advance of a repossession or sale.

17.14 Bankers

Bankers can be thieves in various ways. First, they can embezzle funds from the bank using various schemes. Second, they can overcharge for their services. One way to steal from customers is to provide encoded deposit slips for their own account instead of the customer's account. Many banks have tried to prevent this by not having deposit slips displayed in the lobby. However, some customers will not have any deposit slips and will ask to obtain them from their banker. The banker then gives them some with an encoded account number not belonging to the customer. The customer makes a deposit, but the funds go to the banker. When a customer makes a deposit using "counter" deposit slips, he/she should check the encoded number on the bottom to see if it matches their account number on their checks.

Bankers also overcharge for obtaining a bank loan. In the case of car and boat loans, they will inflate the expenses of obtaining an appraisal for the used car or boat. In recent years, this has been a common practice in granting home equity loans. Also, bankers charge high rates of interest or large "points" for customers obtaining home equity loans. Points are bank fees for processing loan applications, principally, real estate loans. Customers should be aware of points exceeding 4%. Home mortgages should not be more than 3 points over the prime rate. The prime rate is what banks charge their preferred customers. This is published daily in most newspapers across the country.

With the advent of automatic teller machines (ATMs), unscrupulous bankers have been able to embezzle funds from customer accounts. The banker can get personal identification numbers (PIN) if the bank's internal controls are deficient. Also, they can obtain duplicate cards, allegedly by customer request. The banker, with duplicate ATM cards and PIN numbers, can access the customer's account and withdraw funds. To prevent this, the customer should review and reconcile his/her bank statements every month; otherwise, these withdrawals by the banker will go undetected.

17.15 Credit Cards

With the widespread use of credit cards, credit card fraud has become an easy source of income for criminals. Some bank credit cards, for example, VISA and MasterCard, can be used at ATM machines for cash withdrawals. However, most credit card thieves will not have access to PIN numbers. Credit card thieves are usually organized and have more than one person involved. Some credit cards are stolen from the mail at some point before the customer can receive it. Other thieves obtain the credit card or the numbers where the customer has made a purchase. The thieves use the customer's number or credit card to make additional purchases. The goods purchased are fenced to a store or through a store that they control or hooked at a pawnshop. Some business establishments will make additional charges on customer's credit cards for services or purchases not rendered. The counterfeiting of credit cards is becoming more prevalent. For the credit card holder, the following precautions should be followed:

1. If you have applied for a credit card, the credit card company will notify you of approval and approximately when the credit card will be sent. If you have not received the credit card by the time frame specified, then you should make inquiries about it.
2. When making purchases, you should always obtain a copy of the charge slip and any carbon paper used. You never rely on the business establishment to destroy the carbon paper. The carbon paper shows your account number and expiration date, which can be used to make purchases.
3. When making purchases, you should ensure that you get your credit card returned to you.
4. You should always review your statements as to the charges made, and ask yourself, "Did I make this charge?" Even if you are not sure, you should make inquiries to the credit card company. You should save your card receipts and compare them with your billing statements. Report promptly and in writing any questionable charges to the card issuer.
5. You should notify the credit card company if you get a statement for a credit card that you do not have. Also, it is advisable to notify your local police about this.
6. Never pay a fee when applying for a credit card. There are "boiler room" operators who advertise that they can obtain a credit card whether you have bad credit or no credit. For them to get a customer a credit card, they require that the applicant submit an application and a processing fee of anywhere from $100 and up. In some states, this processing fee is illegal. The applicant will find that he/she will not get a credit card and that they are out the fee.
7. You should sign your new cards as soon as they arrive.
8. You should carry your cards separately from your wallet. Also, you should keep a record of your card numbers, their expiration dates, and the phone number and address of each company in a secure place.
9. Avoid signing a blank receipt, whenever possible. Draw a line through blank spaces above the total when you sign card receipts.
10. You should obtain and destroy all carbons and incorrect receipts.
11. You should notify card companies in advance of a change of address.
12. You should never lend your card to anyone.
13. You should never leave cards or receipts lying around.
14. You should never put your card number on a postcard or on the outside of an envelope.

15. You should never give your number over the phone unless you are initiating a transaction with a company you know is reputable. If you have questions about the company, then check with your local consumer protection office or Better Business Bureau before ordering.

17.16   Contractors

Many people either want to build their dream house or remodel their current house. This involves building a house from the ground up or adding a room addition, reroofing, installing new windows and doors, or remodeling a room. Many people will buy new homes that were built by a land developer in a planned community. The contractors who commit fraud do so by either overcharging or by using inferior materials, and usually both. Consumers generally will call a contractor listed in the yellow pages of the telephone directory or maybe solicited over the telephone. Telephone solicitors are more prone to being scam artists. Also, their prices are usually much higher. Land developers will build a model for customers to inspect before their house is built. The model will usually be built to local building codes and with high-grade material; however, their house will be built using inferior materials and poor workmanship. There are danger signs that the consumer should be aware of in order to prevent being a victim. These are:

1. *Advertisements.* The consumer should check the listing in the telephone directory. The consumer should obtain business cards and contract proposals. Many states require a contractor license number on all advertisements.
2. *Down payment.* The consumer should never make a large down payment. Down payments should never be more than 25% of the total contract price. If the contract is financed, the down payment should never be more than what the finance company or bank requires.
3. *Partial payment.* In case of large jobs or building an entire house, partial payments should equal the amount of costs incurred by the contractor.
4. *Permits.* The contractor should always get the permits required. No one else should get them. If the consumer obtains the permits, then it leaves the consumer liable for anything that goes wrong, including an injury to an employee. Small jobs do not always require a permit, but you should contact your local building department for specific requirements. The contractor should post the permit before starting the job. Most states require building permits to be posted before the job is started.
5. *Proposal and contract.* The consumer should always get a proposal and contract in writing. No written agreement means no legal recourse.
6. *Insurance.* The contractor in most states is required to have insurance. Consumers should obtain a copy of their insurance binder before the work begins.
7. *Payments.* The consumer should always pay by check and not cash. The check should always be payable to the company and not the individual.
8. *Licenses.* The contractor should have both an occupational and a state contractor's license.

9. *References.* The contractor should be willing to provide references about his/her reputation, abilities, experience, and knowledge. Consumers should see previous work done and ask previous customers their likes and dislikes.

10. *License boards.* The consumer should call the state licensing boards to determine if they are actually licensed. There are some unlicensed contractors who use other contractor's license numbers.

11. *"Bird-dogging."* In the case of large remodeling jobs or house construction, the consumer should retain a person who knows the construction industry and who will act as an inspector during the course of the construction. The "inspector" should report only to the consumer.

12. *Bids.* The consumer should always get three bids for any contracting job. He/she should be sure that the contractors are bidding for the same job for comparison purposes. A bid for apples cannot be compared to a bid for oranges. Also, the consumer should never pay for a bid.

13. *Identification.* The consumer should ask for and get identification of the contractor or principals of the company. This should be done at the time of signing the contract. This will be helpful to law enforcement if the contractor skips town before the job is finished.

14. *Complaints.* The consumer should file complaints with local and state regulators and/or consumer affairs offices. They can act quickly in remedying your situation if notified early. Some state regulators have police powers; thus, they can take appropriate action on your behalf.

17.17   Doctors

There are unscrupulous doctors who commit fraud in various ways. One common way is overbilling for services to insurance companies. This is particularly true in auto, Medicare or Medicaid, and workman's compensation claims. Another way is charging for tests that were not performed either to the insurance company or to the individual. Still another is selling prescription drugs that are not needed by the patient.

The patient should take the following steps to help prevent overcharges:

1. The patient should check the local physician referral service for a recommended doctor.

2. After the patient has located a physician, the patient should check public records for any lawsuits. This should show any malpractice and financial lawsuits.

3. The patient should ask for a fee schedule before seeing the doctor.

4. The patient should inspect his/her bill for services. If there are charges for services that the patient feels were not performed, then inquiries should be made with the doctor.

5. When a doctor bills the insurance company for services, the patient should review the bill upon receipt and notify the insurance company of any possible overcharges. Remember inflated or nonperformed services mean higher insurance premiums because the insurance company has to pay higher claims.

These rules not only apply to doctors but also dentists, chiropractors, opticians, and other health care professionals. Hospital bills should definitely be examined because many hospitals will overcharge for services for people with health insurance to make up the losses for nonpaying patients.

Patients who purchase prescription drugs when there is no need put the doctor and patient at risk of being detected by law enforcement for drug possession and/or drug trafficking.

17.18 Insurance

Although most agents are reputable, some unscrupulous insurance agents may pocket premiums or use high-pressure tactics to gain a large commission. The signs of an unscrupulous agent are:

1. The agency employs a large number of support staff and has only one licensed agent (who is frequently absent).
2. The insured are those that are uneducated, young, or otherwise high-risk drivers and are the main victims.
3. The agent only accepts premium payments in cash or money orders.
4. No policy is received or provided.

Three of the more common agent schemes are described here.

17.18.1 Pocketing

In pocketing schemes, the agent issues a binder indicating the customer is insured against specific losses but never forwards the customer's premium payments to the insurance company.

17.8.2 Sliding

The term "sliding" means the art of including additional coverage with those requested by the consumer. The extra charges are hidden in the total premium. Because the consumer does not know about the extra charges, claims against that coverage are practically nonexistent, and the profits for the agent are astounding. Because many consumers do not read their insurance policies, the crime may go undetected. Coverages that are easy to slide include motor club memberships, accidental death, and travel accident policies, which carry premiums of less than $100 per year. The indicators of sliding are:

1. The "breakdown of coverage" provided by the agent lists coverage in addition to those requested.
2. Insurance applications and other forms are quickly shuffled in front of the consumer, and a signature is required on each.
3. The agent offers a package deal, which includes accidental death, travel accident, or motor coverage.

17.18.3   Twisting

Twisting is nothing more than the replacement of existing policies for new ones, where the primary reason for doing so is to profit the agent. Commissions are higher on first year sales; therefore, the consumer will pay more in premiums for less coverage. The signs of twisting are:

1. The agent suggests the policy that is less than 1 year is replaced with a new and "better" one.
2. When the consumer declines replacement coverage, the agent employs high-pressure tactics.

Insurance companies, either unknown by the agent or with the agent's cooperation, offer policies to consumers with the intent of not providing coverage. Most states have insurance regulatory agencies, some with enforcement authority. These insurance companies usually sell their products through boiler room operations or direct mail. Their advertisement will usually show premiums below the industry average for the area. All types of insurance are affected, for example, auto, life, health, and business. The consumer should take the following precautions:

1. Check with the state insurance commission to determine whether the insurance company is registered or licensed. Never purchase a policy with an unlicensed insurance company.
2. Consult an insurance advisory service, for example, Best. These advisory services evaluate the insurance company as to its product lines, premiums, and claims. It also rates insurance companies from bad to good based on their financial conditions and stability. The consumer should check these insurance advisory services as to the company's financial condition and compare the premium rates with other insurance companies. Most libraries have these advisory services, usually in their reference section.

17.19   Stockbrokers

Unscrupulous stockbrokers perpetrate fraud by either selling worthless securities or buying and selling their clients securities. Stockbrokers get commission on both sales and purchases of securities. Securities consist of stock, bonds, and mutual funds. Commodity brokers, like stockbrokers, buy and sell various kinds of commodities for their clients. They also get commission on both sales and purchases. The fraud schemes used by both stock and commodity brokers are as follows:

17.19.1   Client Accounts

Some investors will allow their stockbroker, also their commodity broker, to buy and sell securities for them. This is not a good practice for the investor to allow. This gives the broker a blank check. The broker will sell and purchase securities for the investor. Most of the time, the sales will result in losses. The broker will get a commission on both sales and purchases. The investor will finally learn that his/her investment has been depleted. When an investor opens up a margin account, they automatically allow the broker to liquidate their account when they fall below the margin requirements. Margin refers to the amount of funds required to be deposited with the broker. The Federal Reserve Board of Governors sets the margin requirements and changes them from time to time. The Securities and Exchange Commission is responsible for investigation and enforcement. These margin requirements are set at a percentage of the purchase price of securities. Unscrupulous brokers will sell securities or commodities to earn a commission and tell the investor that he/she fell below the margin requirements. These brokers do not notify or give the investor time to meet the margin requirements. The investor should take the following preventive measures:

1. Do not allow the broker to buy and sell without consulting the investor.
2. Advise the broker to contact the investor when the margin requirements have to be met when the investor is using margin accounts.
3. Investors should keep track of the market prices of their securities. A brokerage statement, which is provided each month, gives the market values of their securities. The investor should review these brokerage statements very closely.
4. The investor should check with the Securities and Exchange Commission to determine whether the broker is licensed. Brokers must be licensed with the Securities and Exchange Commission as well as state authorities.
5. The investor should ask for and check out references of the broker about his/her character, integrity, and professional abilities.
6. The investor should check public records as to any lawsuits or criminal actions against the broker.

17.19.2   Worthless Securities

Unscrupulous brokers, both stock and commodities, will sell worthless or phony securities to investors. In the 1980s, there were many corporate mergers. For one corporation to buy out another corporation, the purchasing corporation had to issue bonds. These bonds came to be called "junk" bonds since personal or real property did not secure them. The interest rate was very high, sometimes as high as 18% or more. The issuer found that they could not pay the interest on the bonds since the profits were not high enough to cover the interest expense. The issuing corporation had to declare bankruptcy. This led to the bondholders losing their investment. Some brokers will sell securities to investors knowing that they are on the verge of bankruptcy or in bankruptcy. Some brokers will even sell false or stolen securities to investors. These are some instances of fraud by brokers. Another area of stock and commodity fraud is selling securities at artificial inflated prices that the broker has created. This requires collusion or control between two or more investment companies. The stock or commodities are traded between cooperating members. This drives the stock value up on the over-the-counter securities market. It is then sold to the public. These securities can be either registered or nonregistered. This results in large profits by boosting the value of its shares to artificially high levels. Organized crime engages in the purchase, promotion, and sale of numerous securities. These sales are made through various boiler room operations that are controlled by these individuals. Even though stock and commodity fraud and manipulation are complex and sophisticated, there are steps that can be taken to prevent becoming a victim. They are:

1. The investor should never purchase securities from telephone solicitors. Invariably, these are false securities.
2. The investor should examine registration statements that are available to the public. Title 15 USC 77(f) requires registration of securities with the SEC if they are sold by mail or in interstate commerce. Section 77(g) and (aa) prescribe the contents of registration statements.
3. The investor should always obtain a prospectus. The law specifically prescribes the contents and timing of prospectuses. The investor should read these prospectuses and evaluate the risk of purchasing these securities.
4. Bonds should be purchased on the basis of the current interest rates. Bonds showing high rates of returns should be either avoided or investigated further. Further investigation should encompass the collateral of the bonds, the ability of the issuer to redeem the bonds, and the market value of the collateral at a minimum.
5. The stock market quotes should be reviewed over the past 2 or more years for any security or commodity. The investor needs to evaluate the trend for this security or commodity. If there is an upward swing in market value during a short period of time, usually less than a year, then the investor should try to determine the reason. If the security or commodity did not have increased earnings or dividends, then this is a danger sign of stock manipulation and should not be purchased.
6. The investor should find out if the issuer of the stock or bond is in bankruptcy or reorganization under the Federal Bankruptcy law. This can be determined by either calling another investment firm or consulting any of the investment services at a local library.
7. There are investment advisory services (e.g., Standard & Poor's and Moody's) that publish information about the company or commodity. This information encompasses earnings, dividends, market values and trends, assets, net worth, and management profiles. In addition, they have a rating system that evaluates the security or commodity from bad to good investment potential. The investor should consult these investment advisory services.

17.20 Auto Warranty Scam

Some auto owners may get postcards, letters, or even e-mails about extended warranties. The notices appear to come from your auto dealer or the car manufacturer. They usually appear with a warning, like: "Final Notice: Expiring Auto Warranty." These warranty notices can come before or after the manufacturer warranty has expired. In some cases, auto owners have received warranty notices when their vehicles have more than 50,000 miles or even 100,000 miles. The manufacturer warranty is usually 36,000 miles or 36 months and power train coverage is usually longer. Some manufacturers do have warranties up to 100,000. The consumer should check the warranty documents for their vehicle as to how many miles and years the manufacturer warranty covers. The manufacturer will offer extended warranties. However, these offers are usually made at the dealership when your vehicle is in for service. Auto manufacturer warranties are typically better than those offered by third parties. However, many extended warranty offers are by scrupulous companies who are only out for your money. Some dealers may tell you extended warranties are required by the bank. Lenders do not require it.

- If the consumer receives a warranty notice from a third party, just throw it away.
- If the consumer receives a call about extending warranties, just hang up.

17.21   Avoiding Mortgage Foreclosure

If you fall behind on your mortgage payments, then you should contact your mortgage company. The mortgage company can discuss various options with you. They are willing to work with the borrower during times of financial trouble. Lenders prefer to have you keep your home. You should be honest them.

You should learn about their mortgage rights and foreclosure laws in their state. You should review your mortgage documents to determine what your lender can do if you cannot make your payments. You may also want to attend a foreclosure prevention information session. Local information sessions are available at http://www.hud.gov. They provide resources about foreclosure prevention for homeowners. You can also get information from HOPE NOW. They have a 24-hour hotline that provides counseling assistance services. 1-888-995-HOPE. You can also obtain a list of U.S. Department of Housing and Urban Development (HUD) approved counseling services by going to www.hud.gov.

There are several options that the lender or housing counselor can provide:

- *Reinstatement.* The lender may let you pay the total amount that you are behind in a lump sum payment by a specific date. This is usually done when you can show funds will become available at a specific time in the future. Examples of this are bonus, tax refund, or some other source. You should be aware of late fees and other costs associated with reinstatement plans.
- *Forbearance.* The lender may offer a temporary suspension of your mortgage payments while you get back on your feet. This usually involves a repayment plan to pay off missed or reduced mortgage payments.
- *Repayment plan.* This is an agreement that gives the borrower a fixed amount of time to repay the delinquent amount by combining a portion with your regular monthly payment. By the end of the repayment plan, the borrower has gradually paid back the delinquent amount of the mortgage payments.
- *Loan modification.* This is a written agreement between you and the mortgage company that permanently changes one or more of the original terms of your note in order to make the payments more affordable.

If you and the mortgage company agree on your inability to keep your home, there are still more options to avoid foreclosure. Foreclosure fraud usually will occur when the mortgage company wants to seize your house and sell it to a willing buyer. An indicator is when the mortgage company commences foreclosure proceedings in less than 90 days.

Another indicator would be a high valued home with a low mortgage balance or an adjust-able rate mortgage. There are cases where mortgages are given to people whose homes were previously paid off. The mortgage company induces the owner the take out a mortgage that is loaded with various fees. The owner is unable to pay the mortgage payments and foreclosure begins.

17.22   Bad Check Scams

The bad check scam involves receiving a bad check that looks realistic. The victim does not discover it until after depositing the check and wiring money back to the crook. This is a popular scam perpetrated by people from Nigeria. The victim receives an e-mail making promises of having funds in a foreign country, mostly Nigeria or England. They maybe offer a prize, job, or overpayment for something you are selling. In any case, if someone is offering to send you a check and have you wire some amount back, it's a scam. Victims rarely, if ever, get their money back from a foreign country.

17.23   Boat Purchases

Boat dealers operate in the same manner as auto dealers. The rules that apply for autos, as explained earlier, also apply for boat dealers. For large used boats, banks require a "hull" appraisal and certification by an appraiser. The prospective buyer should make various inquiries with appraisers about area fees for such hull certifications. In some cases, the banks inflate the appraiser's fee. The consumer may want to hire their own appraiser instead of using the bank or finance company.

A boat dealer may advertise a particular boat for a certain price. When the consumer goes to look at that boat, the salesman like the vehicle dealer says the boat is out of stock. The salesman will try to direct the consumer to another model, which usually costs more. Using high-pressure sales tactics, the salesman may get the consumer to purchase the higher priced boat. This is true for both new and used boats. If you want a particular model boat, then you should inquire about when that particular model boat will become available. If the model boat will not become available anytime soon, then you should walk out and ignore the salesman's deals.

If you are purchasing a used boat, then get your own boat mechanic to inspect the boat. If the boat salesman refuses to let the boat be inspected by your boat mechanic, then do not purchase the boat. It is probably a lemon. If the salesman will allow your boat mechanic to inspect the boat, then follow your boat mechanic's advice.

Most finance companies and banks will approve a boat purchase up to a certain amount. It is recommended that you arrange for your own financing in advance. Like car dealerships, boat dealers have made arrangements with particular finance companies where they also get a "rebate." These financing arrangements will charge higher interest rates on the boat loans so they can cover the rebates. Many banks and credit unions can approve your loan for a boat before purchasing.

Some people may have an old boat to trade in for a newer one. You should check with the bank or credit union about the wholesale and retail value of the old boat. The local library generally will have reference material that will provide the trade-in value of your old boat.

New boats have initial warranty coverage. Many boat dealers will offer extended warranty contracts. You should read the contract carefully to determine what repairs are covered and the extent of the coverage. When buying a boat, the consumer should ask about any warranties the dealer might provide and what the manufacturer warranty covers. The warranty should be in writing. The value of the service contract is determined by the expected costs of repairs. Will the service contract cover any future repairs? If not, then the service contract is not worth the money. If there is a disclaimer, then there is no warranty.

Consumers who purchase boats over the Internet should be aware of fraud. The Internet Crime Complaint Center (IC3.gov) advises consumers not to purchase boats outside the United States. Funds sent to foreign countries usually cannot be recovered. Boat dealers, like car dealers, should be cautious about "second chance auctions" and other schemes that the seller of a boat e-mails to a potential buyer to inform them that the high bidder on the auction defaulted and the boat can be purchased by the buyer at their previous bid or at a discount.

17.24 Boat Repair Fraud

Every consumer will have to have their boat repaired at some point in time. Before having your boat fixed, ask friends and coworkers about repair shops they trust. This should be done before you need to have your boat repaired. The consumer should make inquiries:

- Does the boat repair shop honor existing warranties on your boat? If it does not, then you may be paying for parts and labor covered by the manufacturer's or extended warranty.
- Does the boat repair shop have the experience in working on your type of boat?
- The consumer should get a written estimate as to the parts needed and the amount of labor required. The boat repair shop should contact the consumer before exceeding the estimate amount by 10%.
- When the work is finished, the bad parts should be given to the consumer and the consumer can evaluate the necessity of the part.
- When feasible, the consumer should get estimates from various boat repair shops.
- When the work is completed, the consumer should get a detailed invoice of the work done and an itemized description of the parts and labor charges as well as any guarantees.
- Check with local or state consumer agencies for any complaints or lawsuits.

Some states require boat repair shops to be licensed with the state. If they are required to be licensed in your state, then ask to see their registration. The licensing agency can also provide consumers with information about any complaints or lawsuits.

17.25 Builder Bailout Schemes

Builders employ schemes that will offset losses and circumvent potential bankruptcy. Builder bailout schemes are common in any distressed real estate market. They typically consist of excessive incentives to buyers that are not disclosed on the mortgage documents. The typical bailout builder will inflate the sales price. He will offer no down payment. The mortgage company provides a mortgage to the buyer for less than the sales price assuming the borrower put down a good down payment. In reality, the mortgage company is financing 100% of the purchase price. The builder forgives the down payment and keeps the profits. If the mortgage is foreclosed, then the lender has no equity in the home and must pay foreclosure expenses. Also, the builder will close up shop. The buyer will not be able to get any repair work done, even though the builder will guarantee his/her work.

A buyer should be cautious of buying from a builder, especially during slow economic times. The buyer should:

- Check to see how other homes in the development were sold during better economic times.
- Check the property appraiser office for values of homes in the development or surrounding area.
- Check local real estate advertisements for values of new homes in the area.
- The buyer should pay a down payment but not put all of the down payment up front. The buyer should submit their down payment in full at closing. In reality, your down payment is your equity in the home.
- The payments should include principal, interest, taxes, and insurance.
- The buyer should have no monthly payments exceeding 25% of their take home pay.
- It would be wise for the buyer to obtain an independent property appraiser to value the property.
- The buyer should obtain his/her own building inspector to inspect the property for any defects before closing.
- Check the builder out. Is the builder licensed in the state? Check the principals of the contractor. Do they live in the county? If not, find out where they live and why.

17.26   Burglary

Burglary is the removal of some assets from a house, usually while the occupants are away. The thieves break into the house and remove items. Sometimes they are only interested in particular items, for example, jewelry and electronic equipment, but at other times, they may remove as much as they can. Many large cities are subject to high burglary rates. Drug users often commit burglary in order to sustain their habits. There usually is evidence of a break-in, for example, windows or doors pried open. This causes both a financial loss and emotional distress to the victims. To guard against burglary, the home occupant should:

- Have doors that are locked by a "dead bolt." The windows should always be locked.
- In many areas, the occupant should have an alarm system that can contact local law enforcement when a break-in occurs.

- Do not let mail or newspapers accumulate if away. The post office can hold your mail until you return. Newspaper delivery should stopped until the occupant returns home. Burglars look for signs of homes not occupied. You want to remove any signs that would indicate you are not home.
- You may want neighbors to watch your place while you are away.
- Keep an inventory of all valuables and appliances. You should keep the model and serial numbers of all appliances.
- Have insurance on all valuables, furniture, and appliances. It can help recover most of your losses from burglaries. Insurance companies will usually want photographs of the contents being insured, particularly of large valuables.

If you become a victim of a burglary, then you should contact local law enforcement immediately. You should provide a list of all items taken from the house along with the model and serial numbers to local law enforcement. If you have insurance, then you need to file a claim with your insurance company.

17.27 Carpet Cleaners

Many consumers will want to have their carpets cleaned in their home. Many consumers will turn to carpet cleaning companies instead of doing it themselves. Generally, carpet cleaning companies can do a better job than a consumer. The problem lies in overcharging for the service and damaging carpet and/or furniture. When getting a quote, the consumer should ask:

- What is the price of the service and what is included?
- What type of machines will be used (shampoo or something else)?
- Will the company move furniture or go around?
- How much time will it take to do the cleaning?
- What are the company warranties?
- Will the company compensate for any damages?
- Always get a written contract that spells out the specific services and costs.

The consumer should get more than one estimate. You should ask for references and contact those references as to their performance. The consumer should check with the local or state consumer affairs for any complaints or lawsuits. If the company wants to do a demonstration, be sure it is done in an inconspicuous place. Do not give your credit card number or bank account number to the company until it is time to pay for the cleaning. It would be wise to have a witness around when they are doing the job.

If you are a victim of a cleaning service, then file a complaint with the local or state consumer protection agency. You should provide:

- Copy of the contract
- Copy of payment (check or cash receipt)
- Picture of the damage

17.28   Caskets and Burial Vaults

When a loved one dies, there are demanding, quick, and costly decisions to make. Even worse, it is at a time when a consumer is under distress. You should consult a friend or your clergy for help or advice. They can more objectively evaluate merchandise and services.

17.28.1   Caskets

A casket or coffin is usually the most expensive funeral item. A casket is not required for a direct cremation. Caskets vary in price and style. They can be made of metal, wood, fiberglass, or plastic. Their prices can range from $1000 up to $50,000, and on some occasions even more.

17.28.2   Burial Vaults and Grave Liners

Cemeteries require a burial vault or a grave liner to enclose the casket in a grave. The vault or liner is used to prevent the ground from caving in as the casket deteriorates. Burial vaults are considerably more expensive than liners.

17.28.3   Burial Plots

Family will have to buy the plot of ground to place the burial vault. The price of plots can be expensive as well. Many funeral homes have grave sites, while others do not. You should shop around for the best price. Many funeral homes offer funeral services where family and friends can view the deceased. This is an additional expense. Funeral homes charge rental for the time and space for the funeral services.

17.28.4   Headstones and Plaques

When a loved one is buried in a burial plot, the consumer will want a headstone or plaque on the grave site. The price of headstones and plaques vary in cost. Plaques are cheaper than headstones.

17.28.5   Funeral Summary

As one can see above, funerals can cost a lot of money. The Social Security Administration only pays $255 for burial. However, it can cost from $6000 and up. Veterans can get a grave plaque at no charge.

There are companies who offer prearranged funerals. If so, the consumer should inquire about all types of merchandise and services available. You should also scrutinize any claims made by the funeral home or manufacturers of funeral products. Federal law requires funeral homes to provide detailed price information over the telephone, if requested. You should also obtain a written agreement/contract.

Some funeral homes overcharge for products and services. Therefore, it is advisable to shop around. Another problem in recent years is cemeteries selling the same burial plot to different people. A case in Florida found two or three bodies buried in the same plot.

The Funeral Service Consumer Assistance Program in Des Plaines, Illinois can assist consumers and funeral directors in resolving disagreements about funeral service contracts. Their number is 1-800-662-7666. You can contact the Federal Trade Commission to learn about Funeral Rules. *Funerals: A Consumer Guide*, Public Reference, FTC, Washington, DC 20580. Also, the American Association of Retired Persons (AARP) publishes, *Funeral Goods and Services* and *Pre-paying Your Funeral*. You can get free copies by writing to AARP Fulfillment, 601 E Street NW, Washington, DC 20049.

If the consumer believes they are a victim of funeral fraud, then they should file a complaint with the state attorney general's office and provide:

- Copy of funeral agreements
- Copy of payments (check and cash receipts)
- Name of salesman and the funeral home including address and telephone number
- A statement that describes the problem

17.29   Chain Letters

A chain letter is a get-rich-quick scheme. A typical chain letter includes names and address of several individuals with whom you may or may not know. You are instructed to send a certain amount of money, usually $5, to the person at the top of the list. The name at the top of the list is deleted and your name is placed at the bottom. The person is then instructed to forward multiple copies of the letter to a few more individuals who will do the same thing. Eventually, your name will move to the top of the list and you will receive lots of money.

There is a problem with chain letters. They are illegal if they ask for anything of value. Chain letters are a form of gambling, and sending them through the mail or delivering them in person or by computer is prohibited by 18 USC 1302. Chain letters that ask for minor items of value is not illegal. Chain letters are a bad investment. They do not work because they are mathematically impossible. Chain letters are aimed at getting money. Selling a product does not ensure legality. Some chain letters may claim the letters are approved by the U.S. Postal Service. The U.S. Postal Service or Postal Inspectors do not give approval to any chain letter.

If the consumer receives a chain letter, then they should turn it over to the local postmaster or Postal Inspector's office. On a transmittal letter, the consumer should write "I received this in the mail and believe it may be illegal."

17.30   Charges for Services the Government Provides for Free

There are a variety of scams that involve solicitations for services that the government provides for free. The company's solicitation often involves a name resembling a government agency. If you receive such a solicitation, then call the government agency that maintains the information being sold by the promoter and ask if it is available for free from that agency. Some common schemes are:

- *Child support collection scheme.* A company advertises assistance in collecting child support payments. Anyone needing such assistance should contact their local state/district attorney's office, which monitors and enforces child support payments.
- *Schemes involving social security.* The Social Security Administration provides services that involve obtaining social security numbers for newborn children, obtaining statements of personal earnings and benefit estimates, and notifying of name changes for new brides.
- *Unclaimed income tax refund.* Solicitors tell consumers of income tax refund checks being held. The solicitor requires a fee for collecting the income tax refund check. The consumer can contact the Internal Revenue Service directly, and they will reissue the income tax refund. There is no fee by the Internal Revenue Service.
- *Unclaimed funds scheme.* The solicitor promises to assist consumers to obtain unclaimed funds held by state or other agencies. The solicitor promises to assist the consumer in finding the funds for a fee. The solicitor does the search. Some promoters get a list from agencies holding the funds and contact the person on the lists. For a "finders' fee" the promoter offers to get the money for them. Unclaimed funds held by the state or agency are available to consumers at no cost directly from the state or agency holding the funds.
- *Property tax exemption scheme.* The promoter advertises assistance to homeowners in obtaining property tax exemptions. Such tax exemptions are available from the local county tax assessor's office at no cost to the homeowner upon completion of a simple form.

If the consumer has become a victim of one of the above schemes, then it should be reported to the appropriate agency. If the solicitation was done by mail, then the consumer should report it to the local U.S. Postal Inspector's office. The consumer should provide:

- Copy of the check for payment of the fee
- Copy of the solicitation letter

17.31 Charity Fraud

Charity organizations solicit charity contributions throughout the year, especially during the holiday seasons. Consumers usually receive mail or telephone calls soliciting donations from various charity organizations. Many charities are legitimate organizations, for example, the American Red Cross, the Salvation Army, and the American Cancer Society. However, there are solicitors who just want money for themselves.

To guard against this, the following guidelines will help.

- If you are unfamiliar with the charity, ask for an annual report and financial statement. If the organization is not willing to provide these reports, then the consumer should be suspicious and not contribute.
- Make checks payable to the organization and never to an individual.

- Be suspicious of solicitors who say they will accept only cash. Con artists want cash so there will be no paper trail.
- Check out the organization before contributing. This can be done by accessing Publication 78 on the Internal Revenue Service Web site or the Bureau's Wise Giving Alliance Web site.
- Ask what percentage of the donation will support the cause described in the solicitation.
- Call the charity to find out if it's aware of the solicitation and has authorized the use of its name.
- Do not provide any credit card or bank information until you have reviewed all information from the charity.
- Obtain a receipt showing the amount of the contribution and stating that it is tax deductible.
- Do not pay in cash. For security and tax record purposes, it's best to pay by check made payable to the charity and not the solicitor.

If you have been a victim of charity fraud, then report it to the local postal inspector's officer if the solicitation was done by mail and the state attorney general's office.

17.32   Check Overpayment Scam

This type of scam targets consumers who are selling cars or other valuable items through classified ads or online auction sites. The seller gets stuck with a big loss when the scam artist passes off bad cashier checks, corporate checks, or personal checks. The buyer offers to pay for the item with a check that has an amount larger than the item being sold. The difference is given back to the buyer. The bad check is returned by the bank to the seller after the seller has given the item to the buyer and accepted the bad check. The seller generally is unable to find the buyer in order to make the check good. The seller should follow the following tips:

- Know who you are dealing with. Independently confirm the buyer's name, address, and telephone number.
- Never accept a check for more than your selling price.
- Never agree to wire back funds to a buyer. A legitimate buyer will not pressure you to do so.
- Resist pressure to "act now." If the buyer's offer is good now, then it should be good when the check clears.
- If you accept payment by check, the seller should ask for a check on a local bank or a branch of a local bank. The seller can visit the bank branch to determine if the check is legitimate.
- You may want to consider an alternative method of payment such as an escrow service or online payment service. If the buyer wants to use a service you have not heard of, be sure to check it out. The seller should check the Web site or call the customer service hotline. If the seller does not feel comfortable with the service, do not use it.

If you have become a victim of an overpayment check scam, then you should file a complaint with the Federal Trade Commission and your local law enforcement agency. You should provide:

- Copy of the bad check
- Check consumer sent or a copy of the wire transfer

17.33   Cosigning a Loan

Cosigning a loan for someone can be costly. Parents usually have to cosign a loan for their children when buying their first vehicle. This is done to establish credit for their children. However, friends and acquaintances may ask a person to cosign a loan for them. Under 16 CFR 444.3, creditors are required to give a cosigner a notice explaining their obligations. A cosigner is obligated to pay the debt in full if the signer defaults on making payments. The cosigner is also obligated to pay late fees and collection costs. A creditor can collect from the cosigner without first trying to collect from the debtor. The creditor can file a lawsuit, garnish wages, etc., from the cosigner. It also affects the cosigner's credit record. In nearly all cases, the cosigner has to repay the debt of the borrower. Financial institutions know the borrower cannot repay a loan. This is why they want a cosigner.

The only legal remedy for a cosigner is to try to collect from the borrower or file a lawsuit against the borrower. Most cosigners never collect from the borrower.

17.34   Cosmetic Surgery

Many people are getting cosmetic surgery with the hopes of looking better. There is a growing demand. Now, many doctors are now advertising their ability to surgically correct those undesirable areas of one's anatomy. Most surgeons are qualified to do cosmetic surgery. However, because of inexperience and insufficiently trained doctors, many doctors are attracted to cosmetic surgery because of the dollars spent by consumers each year.

You should ask your family doctor for names of qualified surgeons. You can also call your local hospital for referrals. The state licensing board can provide a list of surgeons who specialize in cosmetic surgery. You should consult with two or more surgeons who specialize in the procedure you want. This will involve considerable investment in both time and money (consulting fees). You could be scarred for life if the procedure is not performed properly.

You should ask the doctor as many questions as possible about the procedures. You should get answers to the following questions:

- What are the doctor's hospital privileges?
- How many operations has the doctor performed?
- How safe is the procedure?
- What are the possible risks, complications, and side effects?
- Review each step of the procedure, including before, during, and after stages of operation.
- Who will administer the anesthesia?

- Who will handle post-op?
- Where will the surgery take place?
- How much will the procedure cost, including hospital charges, anesthesia charges, follow-up care, and any other incidentals?
- Will the doctor provide a list of patient referrals?

Medical insurance usually will not cover the costs of elective cosmetic surgery. Many physicians will require payment in advance. If the physician is going to do the operation in his/her office, you should check to see if the facility has passed an inspection.

The Food and Drug Administration (FDA) can provide further information about breast implants, collagen injections, and liquid silicone injections by writing to them at FDA, HFE-88, 5600 Fishers Lane, Rockville, MD 20857. You should make complaints to the local health care administration.

17.35   Credit Counseling and Debt Management

Some consumers who are living from paycheck to paycheck will turn to credit counselors. Many credit counseling organizations are nonprofit and work with consumers to solve their financial problems. Being nonprofit does not mean the organization the services offer are free. Most credit counseling companies will charge for services. Also, it does not mean the services are legitimate. Some credit counselors charge high fees, some of which are hidden. Some will ask for voluntary contributions that will cause the consumer more debt. Most services by credit counselors are offered through local offices, the Internet, or by telephone. Consumers can find in-person credit counselors on universities, military bases, credit unions, and housing authorities. Your financial institution or local consumer protection agency can provide information and referrals.

Legitimate credit counseling organizations can advise you on managing your money and debts, help develop a budget, and offer free educational materials and workshops. Their counselors are certified and trained in the areas of consumer credit, money, debt management, and budgeting. Credit counselors will discuss your entire financial situation and help you develop a personalized plan to solve your money problems. The first session will usually last an hour or more. They will also offer a follow-up session. Legitimate credit counseling agencies will send you free information about itself and the services it provides without requiring you to provide any information. If a firm does not provide free information, then consider it an illegitimate firm. The consumer should check out the potential credit counseling firm with the state attorney general or their local consumer protection agency for any complaints or lawsuits.

When dealing with a credit counseling organization, the consumer should ask the following:

1. What are your services? The consumer should look for organizations that offer a wide range of services. Avoid organizations that push a debt management plan (DMP) as your only option before they spend time in analyzing your financial situation.
2. Do you offer information? Are educational materials available for free? Avoid organizations that charge for information.

3. Does the organization develop a plan for avoiding problems in the future?
4. What are your fees? Are there setup and/or monthly fees? Get price quotes in writing.
5. What if I cannot afford the fees? If you cannot afford the fees, then look elsewhere.
6. Is the organization licensed for your services in your state?
7. Is there a formal agreement or contract? Get all promises in writing. Read the contract very carefully.
8. What are the counselor's qualifications? Are they accredited or certified by an outside organization? If so, by whom? If not, how are they trained? Use organizations that are trained by a nonaffiliated party.
9. What guarantees does the consumer get to ensure their personal data are kept confidential and secure? This is very important because it could become a target of identity thieves.
10. How are the employees compensated? If they are paid more for signing up consumers or if you make contributions to the organization, then the consumer should go elsewhere.

If the consumer's financial problem stems from too much debt or inability to repay debts, then the credit counselor may recommend enrollment in a debt management plan (DMP). DMPs are not for everyone. DMPs are not credit counseling. A DMP should only be considered after the credit counselor has reviewed your financial situation and offered you customized advice on managing your money. Even if a DMP is appropriate, a legitimate credit counselor will still help you create a budget and teach you money management skills.

A DMP requires money to be deposited with the credit counseling organization. The credit counseling organization uses the deposits to pay the client's unsecured debts, for example, credit card bills, student loans, and medical bills. This is done according to a payment schedule that the counselor has developed with you and your creditors. Creditors may have agreed to lower interest rates and waive certain fees. A successful DMP requires you to make regular, timely payments, and could take 48 months or more to complete. The consumer should ask the credit counselor to estimate how long it will take to complete the plan. The consumer will be asked not to apply or use any additional credit while participating in the plan. You should ask the credit counselor the following questions:

- Is a DMP the only option?
- Will you provide ongoing budgeting advice, even if I am not enrolled in a DMP?
- How will you ensure all creditors will be paid by the applicable due dates and in the correct billing cycle? If you are enrolled in a DMP, the creditors should be paid before the due dates and within the correct cycle.
- How is the amount of my payments determined?
- What if the amount is more than I can afford? If you cannot afford it, do not sign up for a DMP.
- How often can I get a status report? You should get regular, detailed statements each month.
- If the credit counselor can get lower interest rates and waive fees, then verify this with creditors.

- What debts are not included in a DMP? This is important because you will have to pay those bills on your own.
- Do I make any payments to my creditors before the creditors accept the proposed payment plan? Some creditors require payment to the credit counselor before accepting the consumer into a DMP. If the credit counselor says this is so, then call the creditor to verify the information.
- How will enrolling in a DMP affect my credit? Accurate negative information may stay on your credit report for up to 7 years. You should be cautious of any credit counselor saying that they can remove accurate negative information from your credit report.
- Can a credit counselor "re-age" negative information from past delinquencies? No. Negative information from past delinquencies or late payments will remain on your credit report.

The consumer should contact their creditors and confirm acceptance of any proposed plan before sending any payments to the credit counseling agency for the DMP. The consumer should ensure the credit counseling organization payment schedule allows debts to be paid before they are due each month. The consumer should call the creditors on the first of every month to ensure the agency has paid them on time.

Debt negotiation programs. The purpose of debt negotiation companies is to reduce or eliminate debt by negotiations with creditors. This can be risky and will have a long-term effect on the consumer's credit report and their ability to get credit. Many states have laws regarding debt negotiation companies and the services they provide. These companies may be nonprofit. They claim to reduce the debt balances by 10 to 50% of the balance owed. These firms also claim that this as an alternative to bankruptcy and that their services will have no impact on the consumer's ability to get credit in the future. Further, they claim that negative information can be removed from the credit report when the debt negotiation program is completed. They sometimes tell consumers to stop making payments to creditors. Instead, the consumer sends payments to the debt negotiation company. The company promises to hold the consumer's funds in a trust account and pay the creditors on the consumer's behalf. There is no guarantee the services they offer are legitimate. There is no guarantee the creditor will accept partial payment of a legitimate debt. When the consumer stops making payments on credit cards, late fees and interest are usually added to the debt each month. If the consumer exceeds the credit limit, additional fees and charges are added to the debt each month. This can cause the original debt to double or triple. Even more, debt negotiation companies charge the consumer substantial fees for their services, including a fee to establish the account, a monthly service fee, and a final fee of a percentage of the money the consumer has supposedly saved. Creditors have no obligation to negotiate the amount a consumer owes; however, they have an obligation to provide accurate information to the credit-reporting agencies. Creditors have the right to sue the consumer for the money they owe. In some cases, the creditors can win a lawsuit that will give them the right to garnish the consumer's wages or put a lien on his/her home. The Internal Revenue Service considers any amount of forgiven debt to be taxable income.

Consumers should steer clear of companies that:

- Guarantee they can remove unsecured debt.
- Promise that unsecured debts can be paid off with pennies on the dollar.
- Claim that using their system will let you avoid bankruptcy.

- Require substantial monthly service fees.
- Demand payment of a percentage of savings.
- Tell you to stop making payments to or communicating with your creditors.
- Require you to make monthly payments to them, rather than to your creditor.
- Claim that creditors never sue consumers for nonpayment of unsecured debt.
- Promise that using their system will have no negative impact on your credit report.
- Claim that they can remove accurate negative information from your credit report.

The consumer should check with the state attorney general's office, local consumer protection agency, and the Better Business Bureau. They can provide the consumer with information about complaints and lawsuits. Also, the consumer should ask the attorney general whether the company is required to be licensed to work in your state. If so, ask whether they are licensed.

17.36   Credit Repair Scams

When a consumer reads ads like the following:

"Credit problems? No problem."
"We can erase your bad credit 100% guaranteed."
"We can remove bankruptcies, judgments, liens, and bad loans from your credit file. Forever!"
"Create a new credit identity—Legally!"

Then the consumer should not believe any of these claims. Credit repair companies typically charge from $50 and up but do little or nothing before vanishing. Accurate information that is within 7 years of the reporting period or 10 years if the information relates to bankruptcy cannot be erased from a credit report. The only information that can be changed are items that are actually wrong or are beyond the 7- or 10-year reporting date. If you have a poor credit history, time is the only thing that will heal your credit report.

One credit repair scam is "hiding" bad credit by establishing a new credit identity. This is done by obtaining an Employer Identification Number (EIN) from the Internal Revenue Service and using it instead of your social security number when applying for credit. You may also be required to use a different mailing address. This practice, known as file segregation, is a federal crime.

In fact, the consumer can help themselves in building a better credit record. First, the consumer should have a copy of their credit report from all three credit bureaus. Second, the consumer should review the credit report for any mistakes or outdated information. There should be no data older than 7 years. Third, if there are mistakes, the consumer should request a dispute form. Last, the dispute form should be completed and supported with documentation and sent to the credit bureau.

The consumer should also know:

- Bankruptcy information is reported for 10 years.
- Lawsuit or judgment against them can be reported for 7 years or until the statute of limitation runs out, whichever is longer.

- Information reported because of a job application with a salary of more than $75 has no time limit.
- Information reported because of an application for life insurance or credit for over $150,000 has no time limit.

The consumer should contact local consumer agencies in the county where the company is located or the state attorney general's office to determine if there are any complaints or legal actions pending against the company. You can also contact Consumer Response Center, Federal Trade Commission, Washington, DC 20580; phone 202-326-2222. If you are the victim of such a scam, then file a complaint with the local or state consumer protection agency.

17.37 Dance Studios

Dance studios can offer entertainment in the form of dance lessons. They can be fun and offer companionship. However, they can be very costly if not monitored. The first step in selecting a dance studio is to check them out with state or local agencies. You can call the state attorney general's office, the Federal Trade Commission, or the Better Business Bureau. You should check for any complaints or lawsuits against the company.

The next step is to know your rights. The contract should provide:

- Provisions for services to be rendered in the future
- Rights for "cooling off"
- Cancellation rights
- Refund rights
- Studio bond requirements
- All promises in writing
- Prepayment protections
- Refund policy, if long-term contract

As a consumer, you should not sign an incomplete or uncompleted contract. If they use "relay salesmanship" or consecutive sales talks by more than one representative, then this is a red flag. The consumer should beware of falsely represented dance lessons that will enable you to achieve a given standard of dancing proficiency. The best rule is: "Start small and be cautious." Try it out first to see if you like it.

If the consumer is a victim of fraud, then file a complaint with the state consumer protection agency and provide:

- Copy of contract
- Copy of payments (check and/or cash receipts)

17.38 Dating Fraud

There are many dating Web sites on the Internet. Many single people are turning to these Web sites to find companionship. Most of these Web sites are legitimate, but some of the people, both male and female, are con artists who are out to find someone to scam. The dating Web sites solicit biographies from mostly females, though males are also listed on sites. These biographies are then listed on a Web page. Some sites try to match people up with similar interests and personalities. They charge a fee for this service, either to one party or both. These Web sites do not investigate the background of either party. Therefore, it allows con artists a wide field of people to contact and to defraud.

The danger signs of a con artist who wants to defraud the lonely person are:

- The con artist overwhelms you with praise, charm, attention, and flattery. They will almost immediately claim "I love you." A lonely person is the ideal target for this kind of attention.
- Con artists exaggerate or fabricate their credentials. They start by providing detailed resumes. Some resumes may seem unbelievable. They generally are. They will usually claim to be well off or a person of important status. The single person should make note of names, places, and accomplishments. They should be checked out.
- Con artists will honor commitments at first in order to gain trust. Later, they begin not keeping their commitments.
- Con artists are after your money. They may start by asking for loans after a few weeks or months. Normal people will not ask for loans during the dating process. At first, the con artist may repay the loan but eventually will stop repaying loans.
- Con artists want answers right away. The con artist wants your money before you can think or check out the plan.
- Con artists do not want you to have much contact with other people who may question his/her motives. They particularly do not want you to associate with family or close friends. Family and friends are a threat to a con artist.

The con artist looks for people who have the following characteristics and traits:

- Lonely
- Feelings of insecurity
- Trusting
- Successful, either has a lot of assets or a high paying job
- Honest
- Committed to their word

If you have any combination of the above, then you are a potential target. When providing a résumé for a dating Web site, you should:

- Never identify your income.
- Never specifically identify your job, for example, doctor, lawyer, dentists, engineer, teacher, or accountant. Professionals are prime targets.
- Never identify your specific education, for example, Medical Doctor, Juris Doctorate, or Bachelor's or Master's degree in engineering, nursing, teaching or accounting. The person should only say Bachelor's, Master's or Doctorate without giving specifics.

- Never meet for the first few weeks or months at your home until you can get comfortable with the person. You should only meet where other people are around, for example, restaurants, theaters, movie house, populated parks, and beaches.
- Never give your place of employment, for example, Doctor's Hospital, John Doe law firm, or accounting firm. Instead, use law or accounting office, etc.

On the first few dates, a person should obtain as much information about the person. The first thing a person should do is check the other person out before getting too involved. There are various sources available. There are a lot of places on the Internet that can provide information. Public and court records are a very good source. A person should call current or/and past employers. If a person talks about their military experience, then it is a strong fraud indicator. Military veterans rarely talk about their experiences. In many instances, it is very hard for them to do so. However, you can contact the National Personnel Records Center in St. Louis, Missouri. You can do this by downloading a form and then mailing or faxing it. The cover letter should request records under the FOIA and ask for all available releasable information. If the person was never in the military, then you will receive a reply saying the center has no record of him/her.

If you have been defrauded by a con artist, then you need to supply as much information about the individual as possible. You should contact your local police or sheriff's department. Also, you should provide local law enforcement:

- Copy of cancelled check, front and back
- Copies of credit card statements showing unauthorized charges
- Any pictures of the individual while dating

It should be noted that very few con artists involved in dating fraud are prosecuted. There are several reasons. First, the victim is embarrassed because they should have known better because of age and education. Last, the victim does not always have the evidence.

17.39   Debt Collections

A debt collector can contact a consumer if the consumer is behind in their payments to the creditor. Contact can be made by mail, telephone, telegram, fax, or in person. However, the collector may not communicate with the consumer or his/her family with such a frequency that it becomes harassing. The debt collector cannot contact the consumer at work if the employer disapproves. The debt collector may not contact the consumer at unreasonable times or places such as before 8:00 A.M. or after 9:00 P.M. unless the consumer agrees.

A debt collector must send written notice within 5 days after the first contact. The notice should tell the consumer the amount of money owed, who the creditor is, and what action to take if the consumer believes he/she is not liable. The consumer can stop the collector from contacting him/her by writing a letter to the agency telling them to stop. After the agency gets the letter, they may not contact the consumer unless the creditor intends to take some specific action.

If the consumer does not believe they owe the debt, then they should write to the collection agency within 30 days after receiving notice. However, if the agency sent proof of the debt, for example, copy of the bill, then they can contact again.

A debt collector cannot harass or abuse any person. They are not allowed to make threats of violence against a person, property, or reputation; use obscene or profane language; or advertise the debt. The debt collector cannot make false statements. They cannot seize, garnish, attach wages, or sell the consumer's property unless the creditor intends to do so and has a legal right to do so.

The consumer can contact the state attorney general's office or the Federal Trade Commission to determine whether a debt collection agency is properly registered. The consumer can also file a complaint with the state attorney general's office. A consumer can file a suit if the collection agency is violating state or federal law. If the consumer prevails, he/she may be awarded actual damages, attorney's fees, and costs.

17.40   Diploma Mills

For people to get a college degree, they must attend a college or university. This requires substantial sums of money, time, and effort. However, there are ads on the Internet, e-mails, and correspondence that offer degrees without any classroom work, whether attending classes or through the Internet. These companies offer degrees or certificates for a flat fee and require little or no course work. These degrees are based solely on life experiences. Most employers, government agencies, and educational institutions consider this lying if not fraud. If a person uses this so-called "degree" in applying for a job or promotion, the consumer risks getting fired and in the case of government jobs, being prosecuted.

The consumer should never respond to any advertisement, e-mail, or correspondence about getting a college degree or certificate unless they are going to attend a college or university. The consumer should report such contacts to the state attorney's office and the state department of education.

17.41   Disaster Cleanup

Various parts of the country suffer from floods. Floods can cause damage to homes. There is mud and water damage throughout the house. The homeowners need to have a cleaning company come in to clean up the mud and water. Some homes may be damaged beyond repair, requiring the home to be torn down and rebuilt. In other cases, the house can be cleaned up. This requires the services of a cleaning and restoration firm. Consumers should understand water-soaked carpet can be saved. The carpet padding needs to be thrown away. Soaked carpet needs to be professionally sanitized at a cleaning firm's facilities. This ensures disease-causing bacteria is eliminated. Floors and walls also need to be sanitized thoroughly. In selecting a restoration firm, the consumer should follow these tips:

- Make sure that the restoration contract includes a description of all the work to be performed, including the quality and quantity of materials to be used.
- Get at least two quotes.
- Do not rush into a contract without reading the details.
- Ensure all warranties and promises are listed in the contract.
- Keep all receipts, contracts, and payment records.
- Obtain references.

- Review all documents before any payments are made.
- Do not pay the full contract price up front. It is best to withhold at least 10% until the job is done.
- Check for licenses. Most states require a license for companies who do clean up after a disaster.
- Be suspicious of any door-to-door workers. Door-to-door workers may use scare tactics such as allegedly unsafe structural conditions. Homeowners should check to see if the company's name is on the worker's vehicle. Check the telephone directory to see if the company or person is listed along with a street address.

If the consumer has become a victim, then they should file a complaint with the state attorney's office and/or the state consumer protection agency. The consumer should provide:

- Copy of payments made
- Copy of contracts
- Name of company and individuals, address, and identifying information

17.42   Distributorship and Franchise Fraud

Distributorship and franchises can be profitable forms of business enterprise. Successful franchises can be great opportunities to people who are willing to invest large amount of funds and give the time to operate such businesses. However, there are con artists who seek investment opportunities to inexperienced investors. These con artists promise the world but deliver nothing. These con artists create their own investment opportunities.

The danger signs of promoters of fraudulent franchises and distributorships are:

- *Promises unrealistic profits.* The investor should be wary of huge profits, usually ranging from 40% and higher. The investor should get as much financial information as possible about the franchise or distributorship and have their accountant analyze it for feasibility.
- *Promises of guaranteed earnings in a protected market area.* Most bona fide business opportunities will usually not make such promises of guaranteed income. Also, the investor should check around the area for similar franchises and distributorships.
- *Guaranteed money back refund.* If the investor is not completely satisfied with the investment, then the investor can be refunded his/her investment so long as the investor has operated according to the instructions provided by the promoter. The promoter determines what the operating instructions mean. The investor is often judged not to have met the criteria, thus no refund.
- *Be wary of the promoter.* If the promoter is more interested in selling the franchise or distributorship and not the marketing of a product or service, then the distributorship/franchise is fake.
- *Be wary of the promoter.* If the promoter does not encourage or allow contact with other investors, then the investor should turn away from the investment.
- Check with the state consumer affairs branch of the state attorney general's office for information about the promoter.

- Check local newspapers and magazines for promoter's advertisement. They can provide information about the promoter and the franchise/distributorship.
- Check for any complaints with the state attorney's office and the Better Business Bureau.

17.43 Infomercials

Many people see television shows that are basically advertising a particular product. They often feature celebrities, but they are regular television shows. Infomercials are a type of television commercial. They look like real television shows because they have guests, a regular host, and sometimes an audience. Many people believe they are legitimate and unbiased shows. In reality, they are simply paid advertisements with compensated actors endorsing products or services. A consumer can spot an infomercial and should be aware of the following:

- Look for commercials during the show promoting the same product discussed in the show.
- Infomercials often feature a toll free number or ordering information on the screen during the program. They are trying to sell a product. They want you to know how to order their product.
- Federal Communications Commission rules require a sponsor of a paid program to disclose who is paying for the program either at the beginning or end of the infomercial. The consumer should look for an announcement that shows it is a commercial broadcast.
- Infomercials can sell a wide variety of products.
- Infomercials often feature endorsements by celebrities.
- Be wary of programs that endorse one product as better than all others.
- If the consumer orders, he/she should order by credit card for extra protection. If the product is not received or was returned, then the consumer should file a complaint with the credit card company.
- The product being marketed on the infomercial may be a good product, but the show promoting it is nothing more than an elaborate commercial.

If a person is a victim of purchasing a product from a television commercial, then the person should file a complaint with the state attorney's office, the Federal Trade Commission, and the local postal inspector if the product was received by U.S. mail. The best way is to file a complaint with your credit card company for removal of the credit card charge. The following evidence will help your case:

- Copy of credit card statement showing purchase
- The date and time the infomercial was aired on television

17.44 Internet E-Mail Fraud

Junk e-mail has become a big nuisance for the Internet user. The Federal Trade Commission (FTC) has found bulk e-mail offers to be scams. They are already known to rip off billions of dollars from consumers. According to a study done by the FTC, the 12 most likely scams in your e-mail boxes are:

- *Business opportunities.* E-mail business opportunities claim to make you $150 a day or more. Also, they say the business does not involve selling, meetings, or personal contact. Many of these Web sites ask the consumer to leave their name and telephone number. Later, you receive a call from a salesman who gives a sales pitch. Many of these are illegal pyramid schemes disguised as legitimate opportunities to earn money.
- *Bulk e-mail.* Bulk e-mail solicitations offer to sell you lists of e-mail addresses or software that will automatically send e-mail messages to millions of customers. Still others offer to send bulk e-mail solicitations on your behalf. They claim to make a lot of money by using this marketing method. First, sending bulk e-mail violates the service terms of most Internet service providers. Next, some states have laws regulating the sending of unsolicited commercial e-mail, which would violate sending bulk e-mail. Very few legitimate businesses engage in bulk e-mail for fear of offending potential customers.
- *Chain letters.* Customers may be asked to send a small amount of money (e.g., $5 to $20) to five or more names on a list. They want you to replace one of the names with your own and forward the revised message via bulk e-mail. The letter may claim to be legal because a lawyer has reviewed it or it refers to sections of law that supposedly legitimizes the scheme. Chain letters, in any form, are almost always illegal, and nearly all people who participate in them lose their money.
- *Work-at-home schemes.* Envelope-stuffing and craft assembly work promises to pay $2 for each brochure you fold and seal in an envelope or assemble a craft that takes many hours to a day with equipment the consumer has to buy. In envelope stuffing, the consumer has to pay a fee and get instructions on how to send the same envelope-stuffing ad in their own bulk e-mailings. In craft assembly work, after paying the initial investment and putting in time on the crafts, the consumer is likely to find promoters will refuse to pay because of substandard work.
- *Health and diet scams.* Pills that let you lose weight without exercising or changing your diet, herbal formulas that liquefy your fat cells so that they are absorbed by your body, and cures for impotence and hair loss are among the scams flooding e-mail boxes. Gimmicks do not work. Successful weight loss requires a reduction in calories and an increase in exercise. When words like scientific breakthrough, miraculous cure, or secret formula are used, the consumer should be wary. The e-mail may also use terms like available from only one source or for a limited time. The consumer should not buy any of these products. To do so is to be throwing your money away.
- *Effortless income.* There are get-rich schemes that offer unlimited profits in trading money on world currency markets, newsletters describing various easy money opportunities, and secrets to making $1000 or more in one day. These are schemes that fit into the realm of "If it sounds too good to be true, it probably is."
- *Free goods.* Some e-mail messages offer free computers, electronic items, and long-distance phone cards. The scheme is to pay a fee to join a club and sign up additional members to earn the free good. Most of these types of e-mails are pyramid schemes.

- *Investment opportunities.* If anyone promises high rates of return with no risk, then do not believe it. Many investment opportunities are Ponzi schemes, in which early investors are paid off with money contributed by later investors. These schemes will generally operate for a short time and then close down. Ponzi schemes eventually will collapse because there is not enough money coming in to continue simulating earnings.
- *Cable descrambler kits.* Cable descrambler kits are used to allow consumers to receive cable without paying any subscription fee. In some cases, the scrambler does not work. If it does work, the consumer is stealing cable service. If the person is caught, he/she has committed a felony and could serve prison time.
- *Guaranteed loans or credit easy terms.* Some e-mails promise home equity loans or unsecured credit cards, regardless of your credit history. Home equity loans usually turn out to be a useless list of lenders who will turn you down if you do not meet their qualifications. The promised credit cards never come.
- *Credit repair.* Some people offer credit repair services. They promise to delete any accurate information from your credit file so you can qualify for a credit card, auto loan, home mortgage, or job. If you follow their advice by lying on a loan or credit application or misrepresenting your social security number under false pretenses, then you will be committing fraud. Only paying your debt repayment on time will improve your bad credit.
- *Vacation prize promotions.* Some promoters send e-mail or mail in congratulating you on winning a vacation to an attractive place. Most unsolicited commercial e-mail goes out to thousands of people. More often these prize vacations book you in substandard conditions. If you want better accommodations, then the consumer must pay additional funds. It is also hard to schedule the vacation time that the consumer wants. Many timeshares offer vacation accommodations, but the consumer must attend a 1- to 2-hour presentation. Also, they have to pay for any upgrade in accommodations.

In all of the above cases, the consumer can file a complaint with the state consumer protection agency or the Federal Trade Commission in Washington, DC.

17.45   Internet Shopping

The Internet is becoming the fastest growing marketplace of goods and services. The Internet makes shopping easy and convenient. Just because shopping sites are on the Internet does not make them legitimate. However, the consumer should be cautious as with any person or telephone purchase. Before a person considers buying on the Internet, he/she should consider the following:

- Ask if the company can send you a catalog.
- Ask what the refund or exchange policy is before buying.
- Only use a secure browser that can encrypt or scramble credit card numbers, bank account numbers, or other personal data.
- Never give your social security number or date of birth. There is no reason for a company to have such information. Also, it is an indicator of possible identity theft.

- Always print out a copy of your order and confirmation number for your records.
- Never give out any passwords or PINs.
- Stay with well-known companies.
- A professional looking Web site does not mean the company is legitimate.

Remember that if it sounds too good to be true, it probably is.

17.46 Inheritance Scam

Many people would like to receive an inheritance from a long lost relative or friend. It does happen, but very rarely. If you receive a notification in the mail from an estate locator who claims an unclaimed inheritance for you, beware. They are sometimes known as "research specialists," but they did not find you by doing research. Thousands of individuals receive the inheritance notification. The recipients are charged a fee, anywhere from $30 and up for an estate report that supposedly explains where the inheritance is located and how it can be claimed. The chances are almost zero of getting an actual inheritance. In rare cases, the amount claimed is less than the fee charged. The consumer should:

- Check with relatives about any recent deaths in the family.
- Check with the local Better Business Bureau, state attorney general's office, or the postal inspection service.
- Remember legitimate law firms, executors of wills, and others who have been named to distribute estate funds to rightful heirs do not charge fees to find out about your share of the estate.

17.47 Invention Promotion Firms

If a person has developed an idea for a product and wishes to get it manufactured and marketed, then he/she can go to a promotion firm. However, some promotional firms do little more than promote their own interests by taking your money and giving you nothing in return. In order to limit your exposure, the inventor should:

- Ask questions about the firm's success and rejection rates. Success rates show the number of clients who made more money from their invention than they paid to the firm. The inventor should not do business with the promotional firms who refuse to disclose this information.
- Be wary of firms that make claims but refuse to back those claims up.
- Ask for the total costs for the services before paying any money. The inventor should be wary of large upfront fees.
- Before making any commitments, investigate the promotional company. He/she should contact the Better Business Bureau, state consumer protection agencies, the Federal Trade Commission, and the state attorney general's office for any complaints or legal actions.
- The invention promotion firm should review and evaluate your invention. However, if it refuses to disclose details about its criteria, system of review, or the

qualifications of company evaluators, then the inventor should not engage the firm any further.

- Require the firm to check existing invention patents similar to his/her own.
- Beware of high-pressure sales tactics.
- Closely examine the contract. The inventor should ensure the contract contains all agreed upon terms in writing. If necessary, the inventor should have the contract reviewed by an attorney.
- Most importantly, no reputable firm will guarantee the inventor's invention success.

17.48 Investment Fraud

Investment frauds are often called "Ponzi schemes" or "pyramid schemes." They are often marketed by telemarketers who use high-pressure and sophisticated selling techniques. They give the appearance of legitimacy by having a plush office with staff members present. They provide glossy brochures describing the investment. These investment schemes usually require substantial amounts of money. Senior citizens are one of their main targets because they have substantial savings. High income people are another target. These types of fraud offer investors high rates of return. In fact, the return rates are much higher than what the market shows. The investor will never see their funds again. The investor may get interest as promised, but the interest received is usually from funds of subsequent investors. The interest payments are a ploy to allay any suspicions the investor may have.

If one answers "yes" to any of the following questions, then one may be dealing with a swindler who wants you to put money into a fraudulent investment:

- Does the salesperson make it sound as if you cannot lose?
- Are you promised an unusually high rate of return or interest on your capital?
- Are you pressured to make a decision immediately or within a short period of time because new investment units are selling fast?
- Does the salesman have any successful experience in the investment area he/she is promoting?

The investor should be suspicious when:

- Promises of high rate of return.
- Promises of little or no risk.
- Know the person you are dealing with.
- Check the person and company out. The potential investor should call the Better Business Bureau, local postal inspector's office, and the state/district attorney of your state.

If you become a victim of an investment scam, then you need to provide the following evidence:

- Copies of cancelled checks
- Any investment brochures provided

- Name, address, and telephone of the person and company who sold the investment to you
- Copy of any investment application(s)

17.49   Job Listing and Job Search Firms

People who are out of work and in need of employment are easy targets for unscrupulous job listing and job search firms. Some job firms ask you to call a "900" telephone number exchange. This can cost from $10 and up and offer little or no information. Some job search firms have "800" numbers for you to call about availability of overseas jobs. Before signing up with a job listing or job search firm, the consumer should consider the following:

- Employment agencies cannot guarantee you a job. They can only help you find a job. If an employment firm guarantees you a job with specific salary and benefits, then the job probably does not exist.
- Job search firms will make promises for menial jobs with excess salaries and benefits that are usually not true. You should also check out the country where the overseas job is located. Overseas menial jobs that are in foreign countries are usually in remote places where there are no facilities, for example, housing and medical facilities. These jobs can be in very hot deserts or steamy tropical jungles or cold, barren, snowy climates. In such inhospitable places, the employer will usually provide housing, food, relocation expenses, etc. If the menial jobs are not in such inhospitable places, then ask why the company is not hiring local people, especially in countries with high unemployment.
- Legitimate companies are required to disclose charges up front. You should be aware of a company who asks for fees in advance of getting a job. Most reputable employment agencies only charge a fee after you have been placed. In many cases, the new employer will often pay for all or most of the fee.
- You should find out how long the job agency has been in business. Also, ask about their success rate. If the agency has not been in business long, then be wary.
- You should check with the state attorney general's office for any complaints or legal actions against the company.

If you have become a victim of a job search firm, then you should file a complaint with the state attorney general's office. If the U.S. mail system was used in any way, then report your experience with the local postal inspector's office.

17.50   Job Searches Online

With the advent of the Internet, many job seekers are turning to it to find jobs. Finding jobs on the Internet is easier, but it lends itself to fraud, particularly identity theft. Some indicators of fraudulent online job sites are:

- The employer has grammatical and spelling errors in their e-mails. Scammers from overseas do not have a good grasp of the English language. This results in poor grammar and spelling of common words.

- A job seeker may receive an e-mail that claims a problem with their account. These e-mails usually will direct the job seeker to a hyperlink for installation of new software. These are phishing e-mails that are designed to convince you to go to another Web site that will install malware or viruses on your computer.
- The prospective employer asks for extensive information over the Internet. You should never provide social security numbers or bank account numbers. The prospective employer does not do any interviews. All contacts are done over the Internet by e-mails.
- The prospective employer offers an opportunity to become rich without leaving home. You should not answer any such advertisement without first meeting the employer in person. Some companies do allow people to work at home, and they will furnish the new employee with all the computer equipment and software. If the job seeker gets e-mail promising work at home without first meeting the employer, then this is a scam.
- The prospective employer requires an upfront fee for something. Any prospective employer does not require upfront fees. This is an indicator of fraud.
- The prospective employer offers an unrealistic high salary and benefits for little or no experience. This would indicate there is something unusual about the job or is fraudulent. High salary jobs for little or no experience are usually associated with jobs in remote areas, for example, deserts or tropical jungles.
- The job requires you to cash a check and wire a portion of the money to another person or entity. The check is fake or bad and you will be out the money wired back to the scammer.

If you become a victim of a scammer, then file a complaint with the state attorney general's office or the Federal Trade Commission. You should provide the following evidence:

- Copy of the cancelled check(s) or wire transfers
- Copy of all e-mails from and to the prospective employer

17.51 Jury Duty Fraud

There are scam artists who either telephone people or use e-mails to contact people about jury duty. The scam artist advises a person of being selected for jury duty. The individual is asked to verify names and provide social security numbers, credit card numbers, and/ or bank account numbers. If the request is denied, then the person is threatened with fines. The judicial system does not contact people by telephone or e-mail nor do they ask for social security numbers, dates of birth, or bank and credit card numbers. This is an attempt to steal your identity. To prevent this, just hang up. If contacted by e-mail, print out the e-mail and refer it to the Federal Bureau of Investigations (FBI).

If you have given out your personal information, then you should monitor your bank and credit card accounts. Whether you are a victim or not, you should refer this matter to your local FBI office.

17.52   Land Flip Fraud

Land flipping involves increasing the market value of property by selling it to related parties or straw buyers. This is done in a relatively short period of time. Related parties can be either individuals or companies. The final buyer of the property has purchased property much higher than the real market value. The straw buyer will take out a mortgage for the property and later on take out a home equity loan. The straw buyer walks away with the funds from the home equity loan, leaving the lenders high and dry.

The buyer should research the following:

- Check out public records for how many sales took place in the past 5 years.
- Check with the county property appraiser about the value of the property over the past few years.
- If the property was sold and resold more than 3 times during the past 5 years, then see who purchased the property.
- If corporations purchased the property, then check with the secretary of state to determine who the officers and directors of the corporations are. In most cases, when corporations sell property, the corporations have the same directors and officers.

If the property was foreclosed on, then it will be auctioned off at the courthouse steps. If, during the application process, an appraiser values the property at its true value, then the mortgage company or broker will advise you and probably turn down the loan.

17.53   Land Sales Scams

Some consumers believe purchasing land is a safe investment. This is not always true. Consumers may realize that their dream has turned into a nightmare. Real estate like any other investment has risks. Some scam artists like to sell worthless lots and/or pay advance fees for the sale of your lot. Any promises of a great investment should arouse one's suspicions. The consumer should view with skepticism any slick brochures about booming communities. The consumer should take the following steps before purchasing land:

- View the property. You should never buy land over the phone, by mail, or e-mail. You should talk to the residents who live in the area.
- Find out about all the fees, such as real estate taxes and community assessment fees.
- Check with real estate agents in the area to find out the market value of the property. You should ask how it would take to sell the property if need be.
- Check with the county planning office to learn of plans for the land or property near the area that would affect the land value. It is important to know if an airport or dump is scheduled to be built nearby in the future.
- If the land is undeveloped, find out who will be responsible for the costs of building roads, utilities, and sewers.
- Find out how long the company has been in business.
- Check public records. They can provide you with a lot of information about the property.

- Check with the county tax assessors office. This can give you information about the tax bills and land value according the county appraisers.
- If the company is selling or leasing more than 100 lots through interstate commerce, then they must register with HUD. The developer must provide a copy of the disclosure statement called a "Property Report" to you before a contract is signed.
- Never pay an advance fee to companies for selling your property.
- Get any and all verbal promises and guarantees in writing.

The Interstate Land Sales Full Disclosure Act (15 USC 1701–1720) requires full disclosure of all material facts in the sale or lease of certain undeveloped land through the U.S. mail or interstate commerce. The developers must provide each purchaser or renter with a property report containing certain information before signing of any contract or agreement for the sale or lease of the land.

The consumer should file any complaints with the state attorney general's office. Also, the consumer should file a complaint with the Department of Housing and Urban Development's national office of Interstate Land Registration at 451 7th Street SW, Washington, DC 20410. Under the law, you have the right to cancel your sales agreement within 7 days of the signing if you have already seen the property. You also have the right to cancel the agreement within 2 years if you have not seen the property report before signing the agreement.

If you are the victim of a land sale scheme, then provide:

- Copy of cancelled check(s)
- Copy of sales contract
- Copy of sales brochures
- Name, address, and telephone numbers of person and company
- Any other documents relating to the property, for example, tax bills, title insurance

17.54 Lawn Service Contracts

Lawn service companies provide maintenance activities such as mowing, edging, watering, fertilizing, seeding, pruning, and feeding of trees and shrubs. Some companies want long-term contracts. Before signing one, you should check the company out.

- Ask neighbors who they use for lawn care services. They can tell you which companies have done either a good job or a bad job.
- Check with the Better Business Bureau about any complaints or legal actions.
- Verify if the company is insured to cover accidents while the work is being performed.
- Read your contract thoroughly for any extra charges. Also, you should state the terms of service and costs of renewal. Ask about guarantees.
- Ask about any specific or real problems before you agree to any agreement. Every lawn is different; even your neighbor's lawn is different from yours.

- If pesticides are going to be used, find out what specific problems are being addressed. If pesticides are used, find out what you need to do during the chemical treatment. Should you close doors and windows? Should you bring in lawn furniture and children's toys and keep pets inside? How long should one stay off treated areas? Some states require people or companies to register with the state when using pesticides. You should check with your state about licensed pest control companies.

You should file complaints with the state attorney general's office and provide:

- Copy of the contract
- Copy of payments
- Picture of lawn service results
- Name and address of salesman and company including address and telephone number

17.55   Lost Pet Scam

A pet owner may lose their pet, whether a dog, cat, or other animal. The pet may have wondered away or got loose from their leash or cage. However, there are unscrupulous people who prey on pet owners who lost their pets. To prevent becoming a victim, the pet owner should:

- Never put the pet's name in the ad or poster.
- Only put a partial description of your pet in the ad. This gives the pet finder an opportunity to describe your pet over the phone.
- Do not put your home address in the ad or poster. The pet finder should provide the street or the vicinity in which the pet was lost.
- Do not meet in a public location to obtain your pet. The scammer is out to get your money and does not have your pet. The person wants the reward and leaves without providing the pet.
- Someone calls from long distance claiming to have your pet, but the person wants you to pay for shipping. The scam artist, usually claiming to be a trucker, never had your pet and will only keep your money.

A victim of a pet reward scam should file a complaint with local law enforcement. If funds were sent out of state, then a complaint should be filed with local Federal Bureau of Investigation office.

17.56   Lottery Fraud

Lottery fraud is increasing in states that conduct a state lottery. Most of these frauds are in the form of advanced fee fraud. The victim usually receives notification by mail or e-mail advising them of winning a large prize. The winners have a short time to claim the winnings. The target is able to choose whether to receive the money by wire transfer, by opening a new bank account, or by meeting a claim representative to pick up the money directly. The victim is also requested to provide various forms of identification. The target is asked to pay several fees that are required to transfer the money. These fees might include licensing fees, registration fees, and various forms of taxes and attorney's fees. Advance fees might be required to open new bank accounts into which the money is to be transferred. All may seem plausible to unsuspecting victims and are required to be paid in cash before the winnings can be released. In all cases, the notes were found to be counterfeit.

In another version, the victim is approached by a person who claims to have won the lottery. He shows the victim the ticket and a newspaper with the winning numbers. In most cases, the winning ticket is a forgery or is not the winning ticket for the particular day of the lottery. The victim is told to go to his/her bank and withdraw funds usually about 10% or higher. The fraudster gets the money and disappears and the victim has a worthless ticket.

To avoid becoming a victim:

- Do not rely on any message regarding lottery winnings.
- Do not send or give any money.
- Do not send or hand over any identification documents, not even copies. This may result in identity thief.
- Never surrender details about your bank accounts or credit cards.

If you have already been contacted or have paid the advance fee, then you should:

1. Save all received and sent e-mail and text messages.
2. Save all documents about the transactions and remittances.
3. Never agree to meet the criminals in person in order to receive the prize. You will not receive any money, and you may be putting yourself in danger.
4. Contact your local police immediately and follow their advice.

17.57 Medicare Fraud

There are some medical providers who want to abuse and defraud the Medicare system. Medicare fraud costs the government millions of dollars. It also results in higher premiums for the consumer. In short, Medicare fraud is the false billing for goods and services rendered. Medicare fraud schemes are:

- Billing for another insurer for services or items not received.
- Billing for services or equipment that is different from what the consumer got.
- The use of another person's Medicare card to get medical care, supplies, or equipment.
- Billing Medicare for home medical equipment after it has been returned.

Consumers should be suspicious when a provider says that:

- The tests are free, but they need your Medicare number. The tests are not free because Medicare has to pay the full amount of the test.
- Medicare wants you to have the item or service. Medicare does not make decisions as to what you need.
- They know how to get Medicare to pay for it. This indicates a false billing by the provider.
- The more tests provided, the cheaper it is. Medicare does not provide discounts for multiple tests.
- The equipment or service is free; it will not cost you anything. Medicare pays for all prescribed equipment and services.

Consumers should also be suspicious when:

- The provider charges for copayments on clinical laboratory tests and on Medicare-covered preventive services, for example, PAP smears, prostate (PSA) tests, or flu and pneumonia shots.
- The provider routinely waives copayments on any services without checking your ability to pay. Note that some Medicare services require no copayments as mentioned above.
- Advertise "free" consultations to people on Medicare.
- People who claim to represent Medicare. Medicare has no representatives to call on people.
- Beware of people who use pressure or scare tactics to sell you high priced medical services or diagnostic tests.
- Bill Medicare for services you did not receive. The consumer should check their statement for any services or goods not provided.
- Beware of people who use telemarketing and door-to-door sales as marketing tools.

To guard against being a victim of fraud, you should:

- Never give out your Medicare Health Insurance Claim Number to anyone except your physician or other Medicare provider, for example, hospital, clinic, and drug store.
- Never allow anyone to review your medical records except appropriate medical professionals.
- Never ask your physician to provide a service that you do not need.
- Do not accept services that are represented as being free.
- If offered a free testing or screening, do not provide your Medicare card number.
- Be cautious of any provider who says they are endorsed by the federal government or by Medicare. Medicare does not make endorsements of any kind.
- Avoid any health care provider who says that the item or service is not covered by Medicare but that they know how to bill Medicare for payment.
- Review your Medicare payment notice for any errors. The Medicare bill shows what was billed, what was paid, and what you owe. Report any items that you did not receive.

Medicare can provide a list of providers in your area. They provide for physicians, hospitals and clinics, equipment suppliers, nursing homes, and dialysis facilities. This information can be obtained online at www.medicare.gov.

If you suspect that you are a victim of fraud, then call or write to Medicare. Your complaint should show the following:

- The provider's name and any identifying number you may have
- The item or service you are questioning
- The date on which the item or service was supposedly furnished
- The amount approved and paid by Medicare
- The date of the Medicare Summary Notice
- The name and Medicare number of the person who supposedly received the item or service
- The reason you believe Medicare should not have paid
- Any other information that you have that leads you to believe that the item or service should not have been paid by Medicare

The Office of Inspector General maintains a hotline that offers a confidential means for reporting fraud claims.

By phone: 1-800-447-8477
By fax: 1-800-223-8164 (limit of 10 pages)
By e-mail: HHSTips@oig.hhs.gov
By mail: Office of the Inspector General
                 HHS TIPS Hotline
                 P.O. Box 23489
                 Washington, DC 20026

17.58   Medicare Drug Coverage

Medicare Part D provides coverage for drugs. It was passed into law in 2005 by President Bush. Since then, there have been many scam artists who have misled and defrauded people. To prevent becoming a victim, you should know the following:

- Legitimate plans will only ask for your social security number at time of actual enrollment. Do not give your social security number unless you are actually enrolling in Medicare Part D.
- Do not give any bank account information unless you are enrolling and arranging automatic payments for your drug coverage.
- The Social Security Administration will never call and ask for your social security number or bank account information unless your application is not correct.
- It is illegal for any company or organization to come to your door or send you unsolicited e-mails.
- It is illegal for anyone to join a drug plan in order to get a prize or gift.
- You should be skeptical about any promotional materials claiming to come from the government.

- You should make sure the plan you are considering is approved by Medicare. Approved plans will have a seal on their materials with "Medicare Rx" in large letters and "Prescription Drug Coverage" in smaller letters under it.

The Office of Inspector General maintains a hotline that offers a confidential means for reporting fraud claims.

By phone: 1-800-447-8477
By fax: 1-800-223-8164 (limit of 10 pages)
By e-mail: HHSTips@oig.hhs.gov
By mail: Office of the Inspector General
           HHS TIPS Hotline
           P.O. Box 23489
           Washington, DC 20026

17.59   Medical Identity Theft

Medical identity theft is basically the same as Medicare or Medicaid theft, except that it is against an insurance company. A scam artist obtains personal identification, for example, social security number, date of birth, and health insurance policy number. A scam artist who needs medical attention but has no insurance or does not qualify for Medicare can use another person's identity including their insurance policy number. All insurance policies have deductibles and copayments. The doctors and hospitals will start billing the owner of the insurance policy for these deductibles and copayments. The victim starts getting bills for services not performed on him/her. The hospital and doctors will not allow review of their files because of federal privacy laws. Many doctors are starting to take pictures of their patients and placing them in their files. Scammers obtain patient identities by being a mole in a legitimate medical practice, going through trash outside medical offices, or soliciting a victim's personal data under the guise of selling health products. In a few states, scammers use phony doctors to lure seniors into free clinics in order to get insurance and personal information. To protect yourself, you should:

- Obtain copies of your medical file or ask for an accounting of disclosures that shows who accessed your records.
- Review all correspondence from medical insurers, including those "This is Not a Bill" statements. Look for any treatment you did not receive.
- Once a year, ask insurers for a list of all payment made in your name.
- Monitor your credit report with credit reporting bureaus (Equifax, Experian, and TransUnion) for reports of medical debts.

If you suspect medical identity theft, then you should report it to your state attorney general's office. In case of Medicare or Medicaid fraud, you should call the regional office for Medicare or Medicaid.

17.60 Missing Person Fraud Scheme

The missing person fraud scheme is unusual and preys on people whose loved ones have disappeared. The scam involves telling the family for money where their missing members are located. Families with missing members should be cautious about anyone who demands money for information leading to the whereabouts of those missing members. When such information is for sale, the consumer should immediately contact law enforcement authorities. Law enforcement authorities can validate such claims about the whereabouts of a missing person.

If you have been a victim of a fraudulent missing person scheme in which the U.S. mail was used, or if you received a suspicious solicitation in the mail that offers to provide information about a missing family member or friends for a fee, then report your experience to the local postal inspector.

17.61 Mortgage Fraud

Mortgage fraud is defined as the intentional misstatement, misrepresentation, or omission by an applicant or other interested parties, relied on by the lender or underwriter to provide funding for the purchase, or to insure a mortgage loan. Mortgage fraud usually involves misstatement of assets. The real estate values are inflated. The borrower's income may be false or inflated. Mortgage fraud in the United States has increased from 35,617 in 2006 to 46,717 in 2007. The filings of Suspicious Activity Reports (SARs) indicate a dollar loss of $813 million. SARs are filed with the Financial Crimes Enforcement Network. The top 10 mortgage fraud states were Florida, Georgia, Michigan, California, Illinois, Ohio, Texas, New York, Colorado, and Minnesota as reported by the FBI. The most reported occupations of mortgage fraud were accountants, mortgage brokers, and lenders. When properties are sold at inflated prices, properties surrounding the neighborhoods also become inflated. When properties foreclose as a result of mortgage fraud, neighborhoods deteriorate and surrounding properties depreciate.

Subprime mortgage loans are designed for people with blemished or limited credit histories and lower incomes. Subprime loans usually carry a higher interest rate. Most subprime loans have adjustable rates. The interest rate is adjusted higher in later years. The higher interest rate causes the mortgage payments to greatly increase. This causes borrowers payment shock and the possibility of default. When properties depreciated and demand decreased, the owners could not sell their homes to satisfy the debt.

Alt-A loans are designed for prime quality borrowers and in many instances do not require documentation. This makes them ideal for fraud. The loss rate of Alt-A loans was more than 3 times higher than nonprime loans. Losses from Alt-A loans were caused by income misrepresentation, employment fraud, straw buyers, investor-related fraud, and occupancy frauds.

Overall, the mortgage industry eased credit for home buyers. Also, the government encouraged lower income people to buy homes and the government encouraged financial institutions to lend money. The government-based organizations, Fannie Mae and Freddie Mac, guarantee most of these mortgages. Mortgage brokers and lenders charged points in making these loans. These points generated huge profits for mortgage brokers and lenders.

When the borrower could not make the payments, then the home was foreclosed and the lending institution was reimbursed by Fannie Mae or Freddie Mac.

People should be aware of mortgage fraud. To protect yourself from mortgage fraud, you should:

- Apply for a mortgage that you can afford. The mortgage payments should be no more than 25% of your take home pay in a month. This includes principal, interest, taxes, and insurance (PITI).
- The interest rate should be a fixed rate over the term of the loan.
- The mortgage should not be longer than 30 years. It is preferable to limit the term to 15 or 20 years. Homes require a lot of repairs and maintenance when they get older. It would be advisable to have the home mortgage paid off before the major repairs become due.
- There should be no prepayment penalties.
- Make a down payment of at least 5%. It is better to make a larger down payment, for example, 20%.
- Do not buy a home in an area where there is a large number of homes for sale. This indicates a problem in the area. The problem could be anything. It could be due to too many foreclosures, pollution in the area, air traffic overhead, or high taxes or insurance premiums, or high crime. The potential buyer should speak to residents in the area.
- Check the sale prices in the area. This can be done in a number of ways. One way is to check the property appraisal records in the county. Review the advertising of home sales in the area.

Mortgage fraud should be reported to the Federal Bureau of Investigation. They should be provided with:

- Copy of mortgage documents
- Copy of payments
- Names of salesman and company including address and telephone number

17.62 Moving Expense Fraud

Some moving companies engage in unscrupulous practices that can result in high costs or poor service. When dealing with a moving company, you should:

- Get three written estimates. An estimate is either binding or nonbinding. A binding estimate locks the moving company into a set price. The nonbinding estimate allows the moving company to charge based on the weight of your shipment. This will not be known until the truck is fully loaded. A binding estimate is advantageous because the consumer has no surprises at the end of the move.
- Ask about the type and extent of liability coverage the mover carries. A mover without adequate coverage for the workers could put you at risk. If a worker is injured, the worker can look to you for coverage. You should demand to see written

proof of insurance coverage. You may also need extra insurance to cover expensive items during the move.

- If you do your own packing, do a complete job. Many complaints arise after you unpack and find damaged goods. If the mover does the packing, then you should be sure what the charges are for this service. Custom packing can be expensive.
- Research the moving company. Find out about past successes and failures. Call the Better Business Bureau or the state or local government consumer agencies. You can also call the state attorney general's office and the Federal Trade Commission about any complaints or legal actions.

17.63 Multilevel Marketing

Multilevel marketing plans require a person to sell a product and enlist several other people to sell the same product. They promise you a profit on the products you sell and a cut on the products sold by the people you enlist. Before committing yourself to a multilevel marketing plan, you should:

- Research the company. What are its successes and failures? You should contact the Better Business Bureau and state and local consumer agencies about any complaints and legal actions. You can also call the state attorney general's office and the Federal Trade Commission.
- You should find out if the company belongs to any trade associations, for example, Direct Selling Association, which is located in Washington, DC. You should get names, addresses, and telephone numbers of people who have joined the plan and ask them about how long they have participated in the plan and what their experiences have been. You should be sure to ask about their average monthly sales and commissions. You should be wary of any person who claims enormous profits in a short time period. They may have been set up to make such exaggerated representations lure you into parting from your money.
- You should find out about any safeguards. Will the company buy back unsold merchandise from you? Are you are obligated to establish a certain volume of retail sales before being able to move up the network distribution? If the company focuses primarily on the recruitment of new members, it is an indicator of an illegal pyramid scheme.
- Be wary if anyone in the company says that they do not have to do anything to make lots of money. You have to work in order to make any money by selling and recruiting new distributors.
- Determine the saturation levels in your area of distribution. Legitimate companies do not have too many distributors in one area.
- If you decide to become a member of the multilevel marketing plan, then start with a small investment and build gradually. You should beware of companies that pressure you to invest large amounts of money up front.

If you are a victim of multilevel marketing, then you should report it to the local or state consumer protection agency and/or the state attorney general's office. You should provide:

- Copy of brochure
- Copy of payment
- Copy of any contract

17.64   Negative Option Marketing Plans

Consumers sometimes sign up for book or record clubs. These companies offer free or reduced prices for records or books. If you join the club, then you are required to purchase a minimum number of records or books. Before sending you a record or book, the company will send notice stating you will be billed automatically for a product unless you affirmatively decline by sending a reply card or calling the company. If the consumer does not send the reply card or call the company, then the consumer will receive the merchandise. In addition, the consumer is liable for payment.

Under the Federal Negative Option Rule, sellers must clearly and conspicuously disclose certain information.

- How many selections you must buy
- How and when you may cancel your membership
- How to notify the seller when you do not choose an item
- How postage and handling is charged
- How often you will receive the announcements

You should consider the overall cost when joining these clubs. You should keep a copy of the seller's promotional materials and the contract. You should fully understand the return deadline to the seller to cancel a selection. Otherwise, you will be bound to keep and pay for the item.

17.65   Nigerian 419

The Nigerian advance fee fraud has recently reached epidemic proportions. They promise big profits in helping them by moving large sums of money out of their country. They can give convincing sob stories and eloquent language with unequivocal promises of money. These advance fee solicitations are scams that play the consumer for a fool.

- The con artist offers to transfer millions of dollars into your bank account in exchange for a small fee. They claim to be Nigerian officials, business people, or some former government official. If you respond to the offer, then you will get official looking documents. They normally ask you to provide bank account numbers and some money to cover transaction or transfer costs and sometimes attorney's fees.
- In some cases, they ask people to travel to Nigeria or a border country to complete the transaction. They sometimes produce dyed or stamped money to verify their claims. In other cases, they feign unexpected situations and request more money to be sent. In the end, there are no profits and the person becomes a victim.

You should not respond to these letters or e-mail. They are a scam. Under no circumstances should you give any personal information, for example, bank account numbers or personal information. The U.S. Department of State advises citizens not to go to these places. People who have gone have been beaten, threatened, and in some cases, murdered.

If you receive an offer via e-mail from someone claiming to need your help getting money out of Nigeria or any other country, then you should forward it to the Federal Trade Commission at spam@uce.gov. If you have lost money to one of these scams, then you should contact your local Secret Service field office.

17.66 Odometer Fraud

If you know the mileage on a vehicle, then this will give you an idea of the condition of a used vehicle. If the odometer has been turned back, then mechanical problems could arise if they go unchecked or unrepaired. Because odometer readings have become so important, federal law and some states make tampering with odometers illegal. Disconnecting or turning back an odometer, even when towing, is illegal. It is also against the law to sell a vehicle without providing written statement that discloses the actual mileage at time of transfer.

If you are concerned about the odometer, you should:

- Look for oil-change stickers, service record, or warranty cards that would reflect the vehicle mileage.
- Ask to see the odometer statement received by the person who is selling the vehicle in order to verify the mileage when the vehicle was previously purchased.
- If buying from a dealer, contact the previous owner about the mileage and condition of the vehicle.

Some states department of motor vehicles and insurance companies can provide the mileage on vehicles.

You should report any odometer tampering to the state department of motor vehicles. You should provide:

- Name of salesman and company selling the vehicle including address and telephone number
- The current odometer reading
- Statement about the situation

17.67 Oil and Gas Investment Fraud

This type of investment requires a large amount of money to invest. Some oil and gas deals are done by "boiler rooms" or fly-by-night operations that consist of nothing more than a bare office space and dozens of desks with telephones. These con artists make repeated unsolicited calls and employ high-pressure sales tactics. They offer limited partnership interests to prospective investors who usually live outside the state where the well is located and outside the state where the calls are made. This limits the chances for an investor visiting the site of the well or the company headquarters.

If you receive an unsolicited call, the following are indicators of a swindler:

- The oil well investment "cannot miss."
- There is very little risk involved.
- The promoter has hit oil or gas on every other well previously drilled.
- A lot of oil or gas has been found in an adjacent field.
- A large reputable oil company is already operating near the company's leased property or is planning to do so.
- A decision must be made immediately to invest in order to assure the purchase of one of the few interests remaining to be sold.
- The deal is only available to a few lucky and specially chosen investors.
- The salesman has personally invested in the venture himself.
- A tip from a reputable geologist has given the company a unique opportunity to make its venture a success.

If you become a victim of such a scam, then you should contact the state/district attorney's office, the state consumer protection agency, or the local postal inspector's office. You should provide them with:

- Copy of cancelled checks
- Copy of any brochures
- Copy of K-1 schedules received after the year-end
- Copy of any applications
- Name, address, and telephone numbers of the person and company with whom you dealt

17.68   Overpayment Scam

In this scam, the scam artist targets people with large ticket items for sale. The scam artist gives the seller a check or money order for the purchase price, sometimes for a greater amount. The scam artist takes the merchandise. In the meantime, the check or money order is found to be worthless, and the seller is out both the money and his/her merchandise.

To avoid being a target, you should:

- Know the person with whom you are dealing. Independently confirm the buyer's name, address, and telephone number.
- The seller should never accept more than the purchase price of the item.
- If possible, only accept cash. If you do accept a check for payment, then do not turn the merchandise over until the check has cleared.
- Only accept checks on a local bank.
- If the buyer is in a rush and wants you to act now, then decline the sale. If the buyer's offer is good now, then it will be good later.

If you become a victim, report it to the local police and the state attorney general's office. You should provide:

- Copy of the check
- Identity of the person who presented you with the check, for example, name, address, and telephone number

17.69   Payday Lenders

Payday loans are usually short-term loans for small amounts. These types of loans can drown a borrower into debt. These loans are call "cash advance loans." For example, a typical borrower obtains a loan for $300. The borrower has to pay back $325. If the borrower cannot pay it, then the loans is extended with more fees. This is called "loan flip." When all is done, the original $300 can cost the borrower over $700. Payday lenders like to target Social Security recipients and other government-subsidized people. Another facet of the payday lenders is that they arrange prospective borrower's to direct deposit into the lender's bank account. Another twist, particularly because Social Security payments are prohibited from being sent directly to lenders, the payday lender will have the direct deposits made into accounts that they control. The best prevention is not to borrow from a payday lender. The consumer should never sign over access to their bank account to a payday lender. Unfortunately, payday lenders are legal in many states. Therefore, the consumer has no recourse.

17.70   Phishing

Phishing is a term used by Internet scammers who imitate legitimate companies in e-mails to entice people to share user information, for example, user names, passwords, and bank or credit card account numbers. The scammers set up Web sites similar to legitimate companies. They send out e-mails to consumers with the hope of enticing people to their scam. They often request the consumer to update or validate their billing information in order to keep their account active. If the consumer provides the information, then the scammer can use this information to order goods and services and obtain credit. In other words, the scammer uses this information to commit fraud or theft, particularly identity theft.

There are ways to prevent from falling into these scams.

- If you receive an e-mail that warns you about your account with the company, then the consumer should not respond to the e-mail, but call the company using a telephone number that is not from the e-mail. Responsible companies do not request sensitive information by e-mail.
- Do not e-mail personal or financial information.
- Regularly log on to their online accounts.
- Only communicate through a secure connection. Avoid filling out forms in e-mail messages that ask for personal financial information.
- Review your bank statement and credit card statements as soon as you receive them. If the statement is late by more than several days, then the consumer should

call the bank or credit card company to confirm your billing address and account balances.

- Always use a secure server when submitting credit card information The server is secure if it shows https:// and not http://. The gold padlock on the Web browser bar indicates that the Web site is secure, but it may not be. The absence of the gold padlock and the https:// indicates that the Web site is not secure.
- Never enter personal information in a pop-up screen.
- Update your Web browser with security patches. Microsoft Explorer browser can provide download patches by going to www.microsoft.com/security/ for certain phishing schemes.
- If you have replied to a possible fraudulent e-mail, then contact your bank and credit card company.

You should report suspicious activity to the FTC by sending the actual spam to spam@uce.gov. If you have become a victim, then file a complaint with the state attorney general's office. You can also report phishing to the Internet Crime Complaint Center at ic3.gov.

17.71 Pharming

Pharming is a form of Phishing. Pharming is a virus or malicious program that is secretly planted in a consumer's computer. It hijacks the computer's Web browser. When a consumer types in an address to a legitimate Web site, it takes them to a fake version of the site and the consumer may not realize it. Any personal information provided to the phony site is stolen and fraudulently used. The consumer should go to phishing section for steps in prevention and reporting fraud.

17.72 Prison Pen Pal Money Order Scam

Singles sometimes search the Internet for romance with prisoners. Some of the prisoners are genuine, while others are not. The dishonest prisoners put ads on the Internet to bilk suspecting singles. When prisoners ask singles to cash money orders, they are misusing money orders to bilk singles. Male prisoners will ask the woman to cash one or more postal money orders in order to pay for attorney fees or court fines. The male prisoner gets these money orders from an outside accomplice who purchases them for a dollar and sends them to the male prisoner. The male prisoner will change the amount on the money order to $500 or $700. Afterward, the male prisoner sends the bogus money order to the woman on the outside for her to cash and send the money to the accomplice. After the male prisoner has the funds in the hands of the accomplice, the woman then receives a "Dear Jane or John" letter, stating the relationship is over. In the meantime, the woman is out the money for the money orders that she cashed.

Women prisoners are more open. They ask for the single male to just send funds directly to her. She will use the funds to get personal care items and refreshments, but if she gets a large amount of funds, then she will use them to get favors from fellow prisoners. In essence, she is helping other prisoners as well. She will send a "Dear John" letter just before she is released calling the relationship over.

The U.S. Postal Service routinely compares all its cashed postal money orders with the original money order receipts. All altered postal money order will ultimately be discovered. Under the law, a person who cashes, or deposits and then withdraws, an altered money order is responsible for its total value, or the altered value. The altered value is the difference between the amount deposited or cashed and the amount purchased.

If a woman prisoner starts asking for more and more funds, then the single male should become suspicious. Prisons accept the practice of women receiving small amounts of money from family and friends, but large amounts will usually trigger a response from the prison officials about sending large amounts of funds, especially, if the funds range $500 or more in a month.

Some states have Web sites where a prisoner's profile can be viewed by the public. They are usually found in the state department of corrections Web site. It is advisable to check out the prisoner, whether male or female, before making contact with them. Many prisoners put false information on correspondence Web sites. There are Web sites that can find information about a prisoner for a small fee.

If you have received a money order from a prisoner, then you should immediately contact the local postal inspector. If you have become a victim of a prisoner money order, then you should contact the state attorney's office and/or the local postal inspector.

17.73   Postal Job Scams

Many people have seen advertisements in their local newspaper about companies offering jobs with the U.S. Postal Service. The U.S. Postal Service is one of the largest employers in the country. It has many benefits of good pay, retirement, and health benefits. The starting salary for the U.S. Postal Service is around $25 an hour. The U.S. Postal Service has both full time and part time jobs available. The Postal Service requires a preemployment examination.

Many promoters of postal service jobs require payment for information with dubious value. Also, they may promise training for the postal service examination. This will usually require additional expenses for purchasing books, study guides, and other training materials. The promoter may want you to think that you are talking to a postal service employee. Some promoters may claim they can place you in a postal job. This is false.

The best rule of thumb is not to reply to any advertisement about U.S. Postal Service jobs. If you are seeking a postal service job, then call or go to the local post office for information and applications. Also, you can go online at http://www.usps.com for employment information. You can also apply online.

Victims of postal job scams should report it to the local postal inspector.

17.74   Price Gouging after a Disaster

Victims of natural disasters, like hurricanes, floods, earthquakes, and tornados, are targets by scam artists. They like to prey on the misery of others. Some states have laws that ban unconscionable prices in the sale or rental of essential supplies and commodities. These items include lumber, ice, water, generators, chemicals, and other necessary goods and services.

Homeowners want quick repair of their homes after a natural disaster; however, be aware of contractors who knock on your door and offer to fix your windows or roofs. If someone is selling generators or chainsaws on the corner, then you should be wary because the items might not work or they may be stolen. Someone who knocks on your door and offers to fix your roof may not been around after he/she collects a deposit or full payment.

Before signing a contract with a contractor, you should:

- Obtain more than one estimate.
- Check on the qualifications and credentials on anyone working on your home.
- Check with the county occupational license bureau and state professional regulation division to determine if the contractor is licensed.
- Check with county and state professional regulation division about any complaints or pending legal actions.
- Ensure that the contractor has a county or city permit to do the work.
- Never pay for the whole job up front. Payments should be broken down to stages of work completed.
- When the work is completed, obtain releases of liens and final contractor's affidavit. Also, get the county or city final inspection report.

You should report price gouging to the state consumer protection agency and provide:

- Copy of receipt
- Name of salesperson and company including address and telephone number
- Provide cost of same product and services in the area

17.75   Precious Metal Investment

Many people lose billions of dollars by investing in precious metals. Consumers get telephone calls or e-mails asking them to invest in precious metals such as gold, silver, and platinum. These calls are conducted by high-pressure salesmen. The "dirt-pile scam" is one where the investor purchases a quantity of unprocessed dirt from a mine. The mine is "guaranteed" to contain enough precious metal to make a profit. In reality, the mine contains little or no precious metal, and the investment is worthless. Consumers should be wary of such investments. A legitimate company will allow the consumer time to review their literature. The consumer should:

- Never invest on the spot.
- Research the company who is selling the investment.
- Never borrow funds to invest.
- Do not be fooled by fancy brochures, so-called experts, or claims of secret formulas for extracting precious metals.
- Call the Bureau of Mines in the state where the mine is located for information about the mineral content in the area to be mined.
- Remember if it sounds too good to be true, it probably is.

You can file complaints with the securities office of the state where the mine is located. Also, you should file a complaint with the state attorney general's office.

17.76   Pump and Dump

This is a scheme by security brokers who sell securities to consumers at inflated prices. They do this by selling between two brokers. Each time the broker trades the stock at a higher price. Eventually, the balloon breaks when the broker sells the stock shares to an unsuspected investor(s). After the investor(s) purchases the securities, the securities fall in value. These types of securities are usually traded on the NASDAQ "pink sheets." These schemes frequently appear in e-mail solicitations or U.S. mail. The best way to prevent this kind of fraud is not to buy any securities offered by security brokers via e-mail or U.S. mail. The investor should:

- Check the trading history of the securities. The investor should determine what made the security increase in value. Was it due to earnings? If not, then what made it increase? Securities decline when a company has losses.
- Get opinions of other security dealers about the security. The investor should check if these securities are shown on the pink sheets.
- Securities traded at more than 10 times earnings should be avoided.

If you are a victim of a "pump and dump" scheme, then file a complaint with the state securities regulation agency. You should provide:

- Confirm slips of all trades
- Name of the security agent and the security firm name and address
- Copies of all correspondence including e-mail from the broker

17.77   Pyramid Schemes

Many Americans have lost thousands and even millions of dollars in pyramid schemes. Pyramid schemes are similar to chain letters. Pyramid schemes require people to make investments. The investment funds are used to pay people at the top from the people who later invest into the scheme. There is no tangible investment of any kind. It generally works like this. A promoter gets an investor to invest $1000. The promoter gets $500 and the balance goes to the first investor. The next person invests $1000. The promoter gets $500 and the balance goes to the first investor of $250 and the second investor gets $250. The first investors will get paid off with a profit, while the late investors will lose their investment. This scheme requires new levels of investors in order to pay the upper levels. When the promoter cannot get any more investors, then the scheme collapses and the lower level investors lose their investment. The scheme also requires more investors at each level down the pyramid. The first level may have two investors. The second level may have eight investors. The third level may have 32 investors, and so on. The number of subsequent investors usually increases exponentially. Mathematically, the pyramid scheme cannot work. It depends on an unlimited supply of investors, which is impossible.

Some pyramid promoters disguise their scheme as a multilevel marketing method. Multilevel marketing is legitimate. Multilevel marketing uses a network of independent distributors to sell consumer products. The distributor makes money from sales he/she makes along with a percentage of the sales from independent distributors. However, the pyramid promoter does not require people to sell products but only invest. In many cases, the new distributors are pushed to purchase large amounts of inventory when they sign up. Also, the products purchased are cheap and of low quality. There may not be a market for the product. The danger signs of a fraudulent multilevel marketing scheme are:

- The promoter requires a large investment. Legitimate multilevel marketing companies do not require a large investment. They want to make it easy and inexpensive to get started. Pyramid promoters want the money up front. They often want money up front for entry fees, training fees, computer services, and inventory.
- The investor may be stuck with a large inventory. Legitimate companies will buy back unsold products if you decide to quit the business. Some states and the Direct Selling Association (DSA) Code of Ethics require buy backs for at least 90% of your original cost.
- Products must be able to be sold to consumers. Legitimate multilevel marketing depends on selling to the consumer. Pyramid schemes are not concerned with selling products to consumers. They make their profits from selling to the investor. If the investor cannot find a market for the product, then he/she is stuck with unsellable products.
- The promoter wants a signed contract quickly before the investor can have promoter sales claims be investigated or obtain legal advice.
- The promoter promises extraordinary high or guaranteed profits.
- Profits can be achieved easily. The investor does not have to do much work in selling.
- There are a lot of initial fees. They can range from hundreds to thousands of dollars.
- The promoter does not give any disclosure documents or any time frame in which the investor can withdraw.
- The investor should be aware of statements like, "get in on the ground floor." This implies people who come in later will be defrauded.

Investors should obtain as much information as possible before investing in a multilevel marketing scheme.

- The investor should ask as many questions as possible. The investors should ask questions about:
  a. The company and its officers.
  b. The product cost, market value, source of supply, and the market in our area.
  c. The total costs involved.
  d. The company's buy back policy of inventory.
  e. What are the average earnings?
- Obtain copies of all company literature.
- Contact other people who have experience with the company and its products.
- Verify all information.

- Check with the Direct Selling Association about the company and its products. They are located at 1667 K Street NW, suite 1100, Washington, DC 20006-1660; phone: 202-452-8866; fax: 202-452-9010.
- Check with the local Better Business Bureau, Chamber of Commerce, state attorney's office, and the Federal Trade Commission about the company and its products.

If you have become a victim of a pyramid scheme, then you should file a complaint with:

- Local law enforcement
- State attorney's office
- Federal Trade Commission

The investor should provide the following evidence:

- Copy of check payments
- All documents about the company and its products
- Copies of contracts made with the company
- Identity of the promoter and company

17.78   Rare Coin Investment Schemes

Many consumers fall victim to rare coin investment schemes. Like precious gems and other commodities, telemarketers tell people how the dollar is weak and rare coins will grow in value. Not many consumers make a profit on investing in rare coins or other commodities. The main reason for losses is due to lack of information about the investment.

Before investing in rare coins, you should:

- Research about numismatic (coin) and investing publications. You should talk to respected coin dealers in your area or go to a numismatic show. Also, you can write to the American Numismatic Association at 818 N. Cascade Avenue, Colorado Springs, CO 80903; phone 719-632-2646. You should learn about the quality and grading of rare coins. The uninformed investor can lose a fortune.
- Deal with a reputable company. You can call the state attorney general's office or the Federal Trade Commission about a company. You should find out how long a company has been in business and whether there are any complaints or legal actions.
- Be skeptical of anyone guaranteeing value rare coins. Value of coins can be affected by the market. The condition of the coin will affect the value. You should find out about the retail value, wholesale value, and the liquidation value.
- Do not buy if the salesperson uses high-pressure sales tactics. If the salesperson says "We only have a few good items left" or "the offer expires tomorrow," then you should not invest.
- If you plan to sell rare coins, then you may find it hard to sell quickly. If the market is down, you may get less than your cost. Also, investors usually buy coins at retail

and sell at wholesale. This requires the investor to hold rare coins for at least 10 years before they can make a profit.

- Check the commodities market in a local newspaper. This can give an indication of how the market is doing in precious metals (e.g., gold, silver, and platinum).
- The U.S. Mint sells gold, silver, and platinum. You can go to their Web site at www .usmint.gov and find out what the selling values of their coins are.

If you become a victim, you should file a complaint with the state attorney general's office in the state where the company is located.

17.79   Real Estate Brokers

You may want to use a real estate broker to buy or sell your home, villa, or condominium. In many states, a real estate broker must obtain a real estate license. Before obtaining a real estate broker, you should ask:

- What are the current prices for a similar home?
- What would be an appropriate price to ask for my home?
- What is your commission? Will the commission remain the same if I find a buyer?
- How long do you estimate it will take to sell my home?
- What steps will you take to advertise my home?
- Will you place my home on the Multiple Listing Service (MLS)?
- Will you provide the names of former clients so that I can call them for a reference?
- Will you arrange for an "Open House"?

There are two types of contracts that engage a real estate broker.

- *Exclusive contract.* This type of contract gives the real estate broker the exclusive right to sell your property. This gives the real estate broker the right to a commission even if you sell the property yourself. Most brokers use this type of contract. However, you can have a "reserve clause," which would allow you to sell your home without paying a commission.
- *Exclusive agency.* If you sell your home yourself, then you will not have to pay a commission. If you enter into this type of contract, then you may not get the highest level of service. All contracts have a beginning and ending date. Most contracts go from 6 months to 1 year. If the broker does not sell your home during the contract period, then you should go to another broker after the contract expires.

In most cases, the broker represents the seller; therefore they are looking after the interest of the seller. Buyers should not disclose their top offer to the broker. There are some brokers who represent the buyer, but there may be a fee for this service. Foremost, the buyer and seller should understand their rights and obligations under the contract.

Most broker fraud takes place by taking the buyer's money or deposit. If the buyer is going to put a large amount or the total purchase price, then the buyer should only put a small deposit down with the broker to bind the deal. The balance should be done at closing with a closing agent.

If you have any problems with a broker or salesperson, then you should file a complaint with the state Real Estate Board or the state attorney general's office. The state Real Estate Board can provide information about any disciplinary actions against the broker or salesperson.

17.80   Recovery Rooms

There are scam artists who offer for a fee to recover money lost in some previous scam. They charge a fee in advance with the promise of recovering lost funds. Scam artists buy and sell names of people who lost money to previous scams. These are called "sucker lists." People who have lost money in a scam are vulnerable to additional scams. The best and only way to recover funds from a scam artist is to file a civil law suit or through a criminal restitution. The victim should never:

- Give out their social security number
- Give out bank account information
- Give out credit card account information

17.81   Reverse Mortgage Scams

In recent years, reverse mortgages have become available to senior citizens who are 62 and older. These are home loans that allow homeowners to borrow against the home equity without repaying the money until the home is sold or the borrower passes away or moves permanently. When the home is sold, lenders receive their principal plus interest. The remaining value of the home goes to the homeowner or their survivors.

Unfortunately, there are predatory lenders, unscrupulous loan agents, and dishonest brokers who target senior citizens. Deceptive practices and high-pressure sales tactics are being used to take advantage of senior citizens. Borrowers are often being steered into inappropriate loans and annuities by sales agents and insurance brokers who are often working together. Homeowners who take out reverse mortgages can receive payments in a lump sum or on an occasional basis as a line of credit.

The Department of Housing and Urban Development has approved counseling agencies that are available for free or at a minimal cost to provide information, counseling, and free referral lists of HUD-approved lenders. HUD does not recommend using an estate planning service or any service that charges a fee just for referring a borrower to a lender. This information can be obtained by calling 1-800-569-4287 or by going to their Web site at www.hud.gov/buying/rvrsmort.cfm.

17.82   Scholarship Scams

Many college-bound children need scholarships in order to pay for their college education. Many parents do not have the funds to support college tuition, books, and room and board. Parents and their children search for scholarships. Unfortunately, parents and children fall prey to scholarship and financial aid scams. There are unscrupulous companies who use high-pressure sales pitches at seminars. They require up-front payments or else parents and students risk losing out. Some scam companies guarantee scholarships for students. Some students have been selected as finalists for awards that require an up-front fee. Students should be aware of and look for fraud indicators. The fraud indicators are:

- "The scholarship is guaranteed or your money back."
- "You cannot get this information anywhere else."
- "I just need your credit card or bank account number to hold this scholarship."
- "We'll do all the work."
- "The scholarship will cost some money."
- "You've been selected" by a "national foundation" to receive a scholarship or "You're a finalist" in a contest you never entered.

If you attend a seminar on financial aid or scholarships, then you should:

- Take your time. Do not rush into paying at the seminar.
- Avoid high-pressure sales pitches that require you to buy now or risk losing out.
- Investigate the organization who is offering to help. Talk to a guidance counselor or financial aid advisor before spending any money.
- Be wary of success stories or testimonials of extraordinary success. Ask for three local families who have used the services in the past year.
- Be cautious about representatives who are reluctant to answer questions or give evasive answers to your questions.
- Ask how much money is charged for the service, what will be done for you, and inquire about refund policies.
- Never give them your social security number, credit card number, or bank account number over the telephone or on the Internet unless you made the contact.
- Get everything in writing.
- Read the fine print before signing anything.
- Do not pay a fee for Free Application for Federal Student Aid (FAFSA). The FAFSA provides applications for free and online at www.fafsa.ed.gov.
- Shred receipts and documents with personal information if they are no longer needed.

There are companies who can provide students with access to lists of scholarships in exchange for an advance fee. Some companies charge a fee to compare a student's profile with a database of scholarship opportunities for which a student may qualify. Legitimate companies never guarantee or promise scholarships or grants.

If you have become a victim of a scholarship scam, then you should file a complaint with the Federal Trade Commission and your state attorney's office. You should provide:

- Copies of payments
- All brochures and marketing material
- Copies of contracts
- Copies of applications

17.83   Service Contracts

When a consumer buys a vehicle or major appliance, they are usually offered a service contract. For many people, such a service can give peace of mind if something goes wrong. Service contracts are offered by new car dealers as well as used car dealers. The service contracts can range from $50 and go up to thousands of dollars. Before buying a service contract, the consumer should consider the following:

- What does the contract cover? Warranties usually cover the product over a certain period of time. The service contract in most products covers the same product as does the warranty. However, the service contract usually covers the product past the warranty period. The service contracts cost extra and are sold separately.
- What is covered by the service contract? Service contracts usually only cover certain parts of the product or specific repairs. The consumer should read the contract and determine what the contract covers. If an item is not mentioned, then it is not covered by the service contract.
- What does the service contract cover versus the warranty? The consumer should compare the service contract with the warranty to find out if the service contract is worth the additional expense.
- Is the product likely to need repairs? If the consumer feels the product will not need any repairs in the near future, then the consumer may find the cost of the service contract is not worth the investment.
- Where is the service available? A service contract may only be offered by the local retailer or dealer; therefore, it may not be valid at any other retailer or dealer.
- Who is responsible for the contract? Before buying the service contract, the consumer should check to see if the company is reputable. This can be done by checking with the Better Business Bureau or the state consumer protection agency.

In some states, service contracts are regulated by the state insurance department. You can file a complaint with them; otherwise, you can also file a complaint with the Federal Trade Commission. In either case, you should provide:

- Copy of the service contract
- Copy of payments made
- Name, address, and telephone number of company and salesman

17.84   Shopping by Mail, Phone, or Internet

It is convenient for consumers to shop by mail, telephone, or the Internet. Most retailers who sell by mail, telephone, or Internet are legitimate; however, there are some retailers who bilk billions of dollars from consumers. Before ordering, the consumer should check with the Better Business Bureau or the state or local consumer protection agency. The consumer should always find out about the company's refund and return policies. By law, the company is required to ship your order within 30 days or within the time period stated in its ads. If unable to ship your merchandise within the specific time period, then the company must give you a choice of agreeing to the delay or allow you to cancel your order and provide a prompt refund.

If the consumer pays by credit card, then he/she can dispute the error on your monthly statement. The dispute must be in writing within 60 days and withhold the payment for the disputed amount. The consumer is still responsible for other charges not in dispute along with finance charges. The billing error can be a charge for the wrong amount, for returned defective merchandise, or the merchandise was not received. The credit card company must acknowledge your complaint within 30 days after receipt in writing. They are also to resolve the dispute within two billing cycles but no more than 90 days after receiving your letter.

You can remove your name from direct mail or telephone lists. Your name can be removed from direct mailing lists by sending your name and address to: DMA Mail Preference Service, P.O. Box 9008, Farmingdale, NY 11735-9008. To remove your name from the national marketers list of telephone numbers, you should write to DMA Telephone Preference Service, P.O. Box 9014, Farmingdale, NY 11735-9014. If you have been defrauded, then you can file a complaint with the state consumer protection agency.

17.85 Short Sale Scheme

The perpetrator of a short sale scheme uses a straw buyer to purchase property. The straw buyer secures a mortgage for 100% of the property value. The straw buyer obtains a home equity loan or refinances the mortgage to obtain additional funds for repairs or improvements. The perpetrator pockets the additional funds. Repairs or improvement are not made. Mortgage payments are not made so the mortgage goes into foreclosure. The perpetrator approaches the lender prior to foreclosure and offers to pay less for the home than would otherwise be received in a competitive foreclosure sale. The lender agrees to the short sale while not knowing the mortgage payments were deliberately not made to create a short sale situation. The perpetrator sells the property at actual value for a profit or has the property artificially inflated to conduct an illegal property flip.

If you believe someone is committing a short sale, then call the FBI.

17.86 Smoking Cures

More smokers are setting goals of quitting. Smokers who want to quite may receive mail or e-mail about products that will help them quit smoking. It is best to consult with one's doctor on how to quit and methods of smoking cessation. However, there are some scam artists who will sell products that will not help anyone quit smoking. Some fraud indicators of smoking cessation programs are:

- Some programs offer hypnosis as a method of smoking cessation. There is no guarantee such a program works. The consumer should be wary of guarantees and high costs of such programs.
- Some unscrupulous companies offer a stop smoking patch. Many doctors will prescribe a patch. They can only be obtained by doctor's prescription. However, unscrupulous promoters will sell patches that are nothing more than a stick-on label. They have no medical value and can only remind the user not to smoke.

- Pills and similar programs are ineffective. Scam artists play on the smoker's desire for a cure that is fast and leaves no cravings. Only doctor's can prescribe pills for smoking cessation.
- Any promises of a miracle cure are too good to be true.

If you have become a victim, then you should file a complaint with the state attorney's office and the federal trade commission. You should provide them with the following:

- Copies of payments for the products
- Any correspondence or e-mail from the con artist
- If asked, sample of the products

17.87   Social Security Fraud

Social Security fraud is a form of identity theft. It involves a criminal applying for social security in your name and using your social security number. The claim is for either retirement benefits or for disability payments. The crook has to know your age eligibility in order to make a false claim for social security benefits. If the crook is claiming disability, then there will be a doctor involved in the scheme. Also, an attorney will probably be involved. However, there is a phishing scheme that steals a person's identity. A con artist might send an e-mail that contains the following, "Note: We now need you to update your personal information. If this is not completed by a certain date, we will be forced to suspend your account indefinitely." When the individual is directed to a phony Web site, the individual is asked to register for a password and confirm their identity by providing social security number, bank account information, and credit card information. People should:

- Never respond to any e-mail from Social Security Administration unless it has ssa.gov at the end of the sender.
- Know that the Social Security Administration does not ask for personal information over the telephone or Internet.
- Know that the Social Security Administration will advise the person of any problem via U.S. mail.

If you are a victim of social security fraud, then you should contact the Inspector General's Office of the Social Security Administration.

17.88   Spam

Spam is the term used for unsolicited commercial e-mail. Not all spam is illegal, but there is spam that is fraudulent, false, or deceptive. Spam is illegal if:

- It contains false or misleading information in the subject line;
- It contains a false header (falsified or missing routing information or otherwise obscures the path of the e-mail from the sender); or

- It contains false or deceptive information in the e-mail body designed to cause damage, for example, a virus.

If you are getting a lot of spam, then you can protect yourself:

- *Do not respond to spam.* If you respond, even if asking to be removed from the mailing list, then it can increase the amount of spam e-mail because the spammers know your address is active.
- *Look out for phishers.* Some spammers use phishing to steal personal information. Phishing is a term used for those who imitate legitimate companies. Spammers use your information to steal your identity, hijack bank accounts, and use your credit rating.
- *Avoid displaying your e-mail address in public.* Spammers look for any e-mail address that is displayed in public.
- *Read and understand Web forms.* You should read and understand the whole Web site form before you transmit personal information. You should check the privacy policy to see if it allows the business to sell your address.
- *Internet service provider.* You can contact your Internet service provider and complain about receiving spam. Internet providers are now empowered to sue spammers under the federal CAN-SPAM Act.
- *Use an e-mail filter.* The consumer should consider using spam filters. Consumers can purchase software that filters out many spam messages or offensive materials. Many Internet providers have spam filters. This may cost extra.
- *Contact net directories.* You can contact WhoWhere.com, 411.com, and Switchboard.com and request them to remove your name, e-mail address, and other personal information from their databases.
- *Delete your member profile.* Some Internet providers provide member profiles. Spammers use these e-mail addresses and profiles.
- *Avoid posting e-mail addresses.* You should avoid posting e-mail addresses in chat rooms, newsgroups, or on auction and sales sites. People who use chat rooms usually receive spam.
- *Use two e-mail addresses.* You may wish to use two e-mail addresses, one for newsgroups and chat room and the other for personal messages only.
- *Unique e-mail addresses.* Using a unique e-mail address can affect spam. Spammers use dictionary attacks to sort through possible name combinations. It is preferable to use letters and numbers in an e-mail account.

The consumer should file complaints with their state attorney general's office, the Internet Crime Complaint Center at ic3.gov. The consumer should forward phishing e-mail to reportphishing@antiphishing.com. Also, the consumer should forward abusive e-mail to the Federal Trade Commission at uce@ftc.gov.

17.89   Store E-Mail Scam

People are now getting e-mail from stores, for example, Walmart, Sears, and JC Penney. These e-mails ask individuals to provide their credit or debit card account information in order to receive a gift certificate of $50 or more. The e-mail also asks the recipient to complete a satisfaction survey of the store. After the survey is completed, the e-mail asks for the person's account information. The best prevention is not to respond to these e-mails and just delete them. This is a form of identity theft.

If you have become a victim, then follow the steps under Identity Theft.

17.90   Subprime Mortgage Fraud

Subprime lending is a term used to apply to making loans to borrowers with little credit, poor credit, or no credit. Subprime borrowers can be someone with reduced repayment capacity as determined by their credit score or debt-to-income ratios.

Subprime borrowers will have one or more of the following characteristics:

- Two or more 30-day delinquencies in the past 12 months or one or more 60-day delinquencies in the past 24 months
- A judgment, foreclosure, repossession, or charge off in the past 24 months
- A bankruptcy in the past 5 years
- A relatively high default probability with a credit score of 660 or below, or some other bureau score with default probability likelihood
- A debt service to income ratio of 50% or greater or limited ability to cover family living expenses after deducting total monthly debt service from monthly income

Subprime mortgage banknotes are not sold in the primary market. The secondary market provides for liquidity in the mortgage lending area. Mortgages are bundled into securities that are sold by investors. The secondary market provides a supply of money for mortgages.

Some people claim subprime lending is predatory lending because they lend to borrowers who could not meet the terms of their loans. This leads to default and foreclosures. There are three types of subprime mortgages:

1. Interest-only mortgages. Allows the borrowers to pay only interest for a period of time (usually 5 to 10 years).
2. Pick a payment loans. Borrowers choose their monthly payment, such as a full payment in some distance future, interest-only payment, or a minimum payment.
3. 2/28 Adjustable rate mortgage. The borrowers are qualified at a fixed rate for 2 years. Beginning the third year, the rate of interest changes and fluctuates over the remaining 28 years. Normally, the rates can move two percentage points beginning the third year and adjust every 6 months or every year. In short, the interest rate can double anywhere from 5 to 10 years. In many cases, the adjustable rate mortgage contains prepayment penalties.

Mortgage fraud has become more rampant in recent years and has caused many homes to go into foreclosure. Some examples of mortgage fraud are:

- Mortgage representatives have gotten people to take out a mortgage when their home has been paid off years before. Almost all have been put in adjustable rate mortgages. In addition, these people have low income or are retired. The mortgage payment would consume most of their retirement income, especially if the interest rate increases along with the monthly payment.

- Mortgage brokers and real estate agents have gotten people to buy homes that they would be unable to afford if the interest rate goes up substantially.
- Mortgage brokers have financed 100% of the purchase price for real estate investors. When the rental income and their personal income cannot meet the mortgage payment, then the real estate investor will try to sell the home. If the real estate investor cannot sell the home, then the home goes into foreclosure. Many real estate investors usually get an interest-only mortgage for a few years with the hope of selling the home for a profit.

The home buyers should:

- Never obtain an interest-only loan for a few years and later on make regular payments. Real estate takes longer to appreciate than other investments.
- Never obtain an adjustable rate mortgage. This clearly invites higher rate of interest in the future along with higher mortgage payments.
- Obtain a mortgage where the rate is fixed over the term of the mortgage. This can be 15 to 30 years. Many mortgage companies require an escrow for property taxes and insurance. When obtaining a mortgage, one should view the total cost of principle, interest, taxes, and insurance.
- The borrower should always put a down payment on the home. This can provide the owner with some equity in the home as well as reduce the monthly payment. If the home value declines because of the economy, the mortgage company may ask you to lower the principle on the mortgage in order to be in line with current market values.
- Never obtain a mortgage with a prepayment penalty.
- Try to put extra money toward principle each month. By doing so, it will reduce the term of the mortgage. Just putting $20 a month toward the principle each month will reduce the term by 2 years on a 30-year mortgage. Remember you will be paying 2 to 3 times the original mortgage over the term of the mortgage.

If you have entered into a subprime mortgage, then you should try to refinance for a lower fixed interest rate. If you cannot get the mortgage rewritten, then put the property up for sale before the payments become too expensive. You have no recourse when you take out a subprime mortgage, especially, with an adjustable rate mortgage.

17.91   Sweepstakes

Many people receive a letter or phone call that tells them that they won a fantastic prize. They should be extremely cautious because this is usually a scam of getting people to purchase some product. The likelihood of winning anything of value is very slim or mostly nil. These are usually a marketing scheme for inducing people to purchase a company's product.

Legitimate sweepstakes do not require you to pay anything in order to get the prize. If the consumer is told about paying money up front for taxes, then this is a scam. Taxes are withheld from cash prizes by legitimate companies and the Internal Revenue Service is advised of the prize by filing a 1099 form for both cash and prizes. If terms like "shipping and handling charges" or "processing fee" are being used, then this is an indicator that the offer is not legitimate. Legitimate companies pay the cost of delivery for the prizes.

The consumer should question and demand detailed descriptions of the prizes being offered. Often the representative uses terms that are deceiving. The consumer should be skeptical when the representative uses terms like "regulation," "model," "precious." They try to deceive the consumer of size, quality, and value of the product. Therefore, the consumer should ask questions about the size, quality, and value of the product. If the company makes claims of being sponsored or approved by a governmental agency, the consumer should be suspicious immediately. If the mailing or telephone solicitation requires an immediate response without any time to investigate, then this is a strong indicator of deception.

Legitimate sweepstake companies have no need for your credit card or for any kind of payment. So, if the company asks for a credit card number, this is a strong indicator of fraud.

The consumer should investigate the company. If the company is using a mail drop or post office box, then this is an indicator of a fraudulent company. You can also check with the National Fraud Information Center at 1-800-876-7060. Other places to find out about a company are the Better Business Bureau and state and local consumer protection agencies.

The Deceptive Mail Prevention and Enforcement Act was signed by President Clinton on December 12, 1999, and took effect 120 days after that date. The law requires mailings to clearly display:

- Rules and order form stating that no purchase is necessary to enter contest
- States that a purchase does not improve chances of winning
- The terms and conditions of the sweepstakes promotion, including rules and entry procedures
- The sponsor or mailer of the promotion and principal place of business or other contact address of the sponsor or mailer
- Estimated odds of winning each prize, the quantity, estimated retail value, and nature of each prize, and the schedule of any payments made over time

It imposes requirements for mail related to skill contest mailings, which must disclose:

- Number of rounds, cost to enter each round, whether subsequent rounds will be more difficult, and the maximum cost to enter all rounds
- Percentage of entrants who may solve correctly the skill contest
- The identity of the judges and the method used in judging
- The date the winner will be determined, as well as quantity and estimated value of each prize

The law imposes new federal standards on facsimile checks sent in any mailing. The checks must include a statement on the check itself that it is nonnegotiable and has no cash value.

The law prohibits mailings that imply a connection to, approval of, or endorsement by the federal government through the misleading use of a seal, insignia, reference to the Postmaster General, citation to a federal statute, trade or brand name, or any other term or symbol, unless the mailings carry two disclaimers. The law requires companies sending sweepstakes or skill contests to establish a system and include in their mailings a telephone number or address, which consumers could use to be removed from the mailing lists of such companies.

The consumer should report any company asking for money for winning a prize. The report should be made to the state attorney general's office and the Federal Trade Commission in Washington, DC. Also, the U.S. Postal Inspection Service is responsible for investigating cases of fraud where the U.S. mail is used as part of the scheme.

17.92   Tax Evasion Schemes

The Internal Revenue Service is cautioning the public about tax schemes that create sham trusts or tax shelters to evade federal taxes. Promoters promise taxpayers substantial tax reduction and asset protection.

A trust is a form of ownership that separates responsibility and control of assets from the benefits of ownership. The duties, powers, and responsibilities of the parties in a trust are determined by state statute. Promoters of abuse trust arrangements usually promise greatly reduced tax liabilities without any change in the taxpayer's overall control. They promise:

- Reduction or elimination of income subject to tax
- Deductions for personal expenses paid by the trust
- Deductions of an owner's personal expenses paid by the trust
- Depreciation deductions of an owner's personal residence and furnishings
- Stepped-up basis for property transferred to the trust
- Reduction or elimination of self-employment taxes
- Reduction or elimination of gift and estate taxes

All income a trust receives, whether from foreign or domestic sources, is taxable to the trust, the beneficiary, or the taxpayer. In abusive schemes, expenses are charged against the trust income. After the deduction of these expenses, the remaining income is distributed to other trusts, the beneficiary, or the taxpayer. The purpose of the deduction is to decrease the amount of income reported to the Internal Revenue Service.

Taxpayers should avoid these abusive trust arrangements. They will not produce any tax benefits as claimed by the promoters. Also, the Internal Revenue Service is actively examining these types of trust arrangements. Taxpayers and promoters are subject to civil and/or criminal penalties.

Tax shelters are schemes that reduce taxable income and tax liabilities by deductions from taxable income. In many cases, the taxpayer finances the purchase of an asset by nonrecourse financing. The income from the asset operations are used to pay down the nonrecourse note. Promoters make promises of write-offs (deductions) as high as 10 to 1 debt to equity ratio. The taxpayer purchases an asset, for example, a movie, master recording, ranch or farm, rental real estate, charter boat or aircraft, and computer software development. When the deductions have expired, the asset is either sold off or abandoned. Any gain from the sale is ordinary income. If the taxpayer has not paid off the nonrecourse note, then the note becomes ordinary income at time of abandonment. Many taxpayers have found their tax liability to greatly increase by thousands of dollars when the abandonment takes place.

The Internal Revenue Service is also actively pursuing tax shelters. The taxpayers and the promoters face stiff civil and/or criminal penalties.

If taxpayers have any questions about trusts or tax shelters, then they should call 1-866-775-7474 or send e-mail at irs.tax.shelter.hotline@irs.gov.

The Internal Revenue Service has issued warnings on e-mail and telephone scams. These scams are asking for personal information that is used in identity theft. There are seven specific scams.

1. *Rebate phone call.* Consumers receive a phone call about eligibility of receiving a rebate for filing his/her tax return. The caller claims to be an IRS employee. The caller needs the taxpayer's bank account number for the direct deposit of the rebate. If the consumer refuses, then he/she is told that they will not get the rebate. The caller uses the bank information to get funds from the consumer's bank account.

2. *Refund e-mail.* In this case, the sender falsely claims the consumer is eligible for a tax refund at a specific amount. It instructs the consumer to click on a link in the e-mail to access a refund claim form. The form asks the recipient to enter personal information. The fraudster uses the information to gain access to the taxpayer's bank account and/or credit card account.

3. *Audit e-mail.* The e-mail notifies the taxpayer that their return is being audited. The e-mail provides a link to a form for the taxpayer to fill out. The form asks for personal information that the scam artist can use to access bank accounts and/or credit card accounts.

4. *Changes to tax law e-mail.* This bogus e-mail is usually addressed to businesses and accountants. It instructs them to download tax law changes. The link downloads malware onto the recipient's computer. Malware is a malicious code that can take over the victim's computer hard drive, giving the person remote access to the computer. The malware gives the person's passwords and other information to the fraudster.

5. *Paper check phone call.* A person, falsely representing to be an IRS employee, claims to have sent a check to the taxpayer but says that it was returned. The false IRS employee asks for the taxpayer's bank account number. In many cases, the caller may have a foreign accent. In reality, the IRS does not ask for or have a need to know a taxpayer's bank account number. If a taxpayer chooses to have direct deposit, then the taxpayer must put the bank routing number and bank account number on the 1040 return. The IRS does not contact the taxpayer to verify the information. If the taxpayer does not get their tax refund deposited into their bank account, then they must go to an IRS office to solve the problem.

6. *Abuse charitable organizations and deductions.* The IRS has reported an increase in the use of tax exempt organizations to improperly shield income or assets from taxation. This can be done when a taxpayer moves assets or income to a tax exempt organization. The owner maintains control over the assets and income, thereby

obtaining a tax deduction without transferring a commensurate benefit to charity. Some taxpayers have been advised to transfer all their income and assets (home, vehicle, etc.) to a church, which is set up by an unscrupulous tax preparer. Universal Life Church is the most common charity organization used in this type of tax evasion scheme. They even will provide degrees in theology for a fee and without any theological training.

7. *Offshore transactions.* Individuals try to avoid U.S. taxes by illegally hiding income in offshore bank and brokerage accounts or using offshore credit cards, wire transfers, foreign trusts, employee leasing schemes, private annuities, or life insurance. Unscrupulous tax accountants can get taxpayers involved in these types of schemes. The IRS requires taxpayers to report all their income from all sources, including offshore investments. Failure to report offshore bank and brokerage accounts can result in heavy penalties and interest as well as possible criminal prosecution.

If a taxpayer receives a questionable e-mail or telephone call, then the e-mail should be forwarded to Phishing.irs.gov. If the taxpayer received a telephone call, then advise the IRS by e-mail at Phishing.irs.gov.

Suspected tax fraud can also be reported by using form 3949-A, Information Referral. The form can be downloaded from the IRS Web site at www.irs.gov. The form can be sent to the Internal Revenue Service, Fresno, CA 93888.

If a taxpayer has become a victim of a scam involving the IRS, then the taxpayer should call the local office of the Treasury Inspector General for Tax Administration or the Criminal Investigation Division.

17.93   Telemarketing

Telemarketing is a fast growing business. Many telemarketers are legitimate; however, there are many fraudulent ones. The scheme involves selling products or services that are not delivered. Telemarketing is referred to as "boiler room" operations. It involves hiring telephone solicitors who call customers using high-pressure sales tactics. The customer orders the product or service and makes payment in advance. The product or service is either not provided or an inferior product or service is provided. In most cases, these products or services cost more than what is available in local stores. There are many scheme variations. One scheme is the telemarketer tells the customer that he/she won a prize, but in order to receive it, they must send in money for shipping, handling, or taxes. The customer sends in the money but either receives an inferior product or does not receive any product. The unscrupulous telemarketer will make misrepresentations about their product or service. This is evident in such statements as "the best deal or investment ever made" or "it's too good to be true." When contacted by a telemarketer, the consumer should follow these guidelines:

If the telemarketer is "pushy" in using high-pressure sales tactics, then hang up the telephone. The consumer should treat the telemarketer as an obscene telephone caller.

Some states have passed laws requiring telemarketers to be licensed or registered. The consumer should obtain identification of the telemarketer, as well as information about the company that they represent.

1. If the deal sounds too good to be true, then you can be assured that it is not good. So, if the telemarketer makes claims about their product or service that in any way seems too good to be true, do not order it.
2. Some products or services are forbidden to be sold over the telephone in many states. It is unlawful to sell fraudulent securities using the telephone or mail. Some states have laws against certain professions of soliciting customers by mail or telephone, for example, accounting, legal, and medical.
3. The consumer should compare prices of products and services that the telemarketer is selling to the same products and services in the local area. In many cases, the products and services cost more than what the local merchants provide. Shipping and handling charges should be considered when ordering from telemarketers. These drive up the costs.
4. It is advisable to use a credit card for making a purchase. It provides the ability for the consumer to have the credit card company cancel the charge, provided that it is done so within 30 days from date of purchase. Also, U.S. postal regulations require that the company ship the goods within 30 days. However, the consumer should review their monthly credit card statements for any possible charges by the company at a later date or fraudulent use of their credit card number at another location.
5. The consumer should make inquiries with the Better Business Bureau or the state consumer affairs department about any complaints about the company.

17.94   Mail Order

Many consumers receive "junk" mail that solicits them to purchase goods through the mail. Consumers can see advertisements on television and in the newspapers. Most advertisements are done by legitimate businesses; however, there are unscrupulous mail order houses. Mail order houses operate like fraudulent telemarketers, except they lack the element of direct communication and therefore the ability for the consumer to make inquiries about the product and company before placing the order. The consumer should take the following steps:

1. The consumer should compare mail order prices of products and services with those in the local area. Shipping and handling charges should be considered because they can drive up the total costs of the product.
2. If the product or service sounds too good to be true, then do not order it.
3. The consumer should make inquiries with the Better Business Bureau or the state consumer affairs department about any complaints or company existence. Some states require an out-of-state company to be registered in that state before it can do business in that state.
4. Local merchants should be consulted about the special ordering of the products that are not generally available. In some cases, local merchants can obtain the product or service at lower costs than by direct mail.
5. If the product is not received within 30 days, then the consumer should call the company and find out the status. If the consumer gets no satisfactory response, then he/she should notify the U.S. Postal Inspection Office near them.

6. The consumer should keep in mind that some products are not allowed to be shipped through the mail. This is particularly true for dangerous or flammable products. Also, illegal products, such as illegal drugs and pornographic material, are not allowed to be mailed.

17.95   Identity Thefts

It is easier to prevent identity theft than it is to get it corrected. There are individuals and criminal groups who specialize in identity theft. It can cost a victim from hundreds to thousands of dollars to get corrected. Some preventive measures are:

1. Do not give out any information unless the party requesting it needs to know your personal data. Banks and credit card companies know your account number and your mother's maiden name, so if someone calls asking for it, do not give it.
2. When traveling, mail should be held at your post office or collected by a family member or close friend.
3. When calling someone, never pass on personal financial information. Someone nearby may be listening.
4. Check your financial information regularly and look for what should be there and what should not be there. You should reconcile your bank account(s) each month and review your credit card statement(s) each month. If you fail to get a bank or credit card statement, then you should call. You should not wait. Also, you should check for unauthorized charges or withdrawals.
5. You should obtain a credit report. The credit report should list all bank and financial accounts under your name and will provide indications of whether someone has wrongfully opened or used any accounts in your name.
6. Records containing your personal data should be kept or destroyed. Credit card receipts and bank statements or cancelled checks contain personal data.
7. Never throw away credit card statements, bank statements, and cancelled checks without shredding or burning them. Thieves go through trash cans and can steal your identity.
8. When you receive requests to open a credit card, then you should shred or burn it. Thieves can use these applications to get credit using your name.

17.96   Religious/Nonprofit Organizations

There are religious cults and nonprofit organizations that exist for the purpose of committing fraud. There are many criminals who will either call on the telephone or approach a victim on the street. They ask the person to contribute to their particular cause or organization. These causes or organizations either do not exist or are only fronts. Many criminals will claim that they are tax exempt. Nonprofit organizations, except for religious organizations, must apply to the Internal Revenue Service to get a tax exemption. The consumer can call or write to the Internal Revenue Service and find out if a particular nonprofit organization is tax exempt. If it is not tax exempt, then any contributions made are not tax deductible. The United Way is an organization that conducts campaigns to raise funds for various charitable organizations. The United Way can provide contributors a list of tax exempt organizations that need donors.

Religious organizations present a different problem. By federal statute, religious organizations (churches, synagogues, temples, etc.) are tax exempt. This is due to the Constitution, which separates church and state. There are various evangelists who prey on people's emotions and feelings so that they will open their pocketbooks. Some religious leaders try to control member's lives. They become cults. The danger signs of a corrupt religious organization are as follows:

1. The leaders claim to be the only true church.
2. The leaders never accept criticism and denounce any criticism as a negative attitude.
3. The leadership attempts to control a person's life. It starts to tell the members what to wear, give, where to work, play, and do or say.
4. The leader tells the member what is right and wrong. The leader makes contradictory statements, actions, and attitudes.
5. The religious organization is isolated mostly from the rest of the outside world. Its only contact is to improve its image to outsiders and recruit new members.
6. The religious organization wants to keep its financial affairs secret. The leadership lives a high lifestyle.

17.97   Telephone Fraud

Most people nowadays have telephones in their homes. In addition, many people are using cell phones. The phone bills can get high if a person makes a lot of long distance telephone calls. Crooks have found a way to make calls where the telephone bill is charged to someone else. The most prevalent group of scammers who are doing this are people in jail who want to make calls to someone else. The scammer will call a person from jail or some other location to a person usually just listed in the telephone directory. They ask the person to make a call for them by having them call *72 and the number to which they are calling from including the area code. This allows the person to make calls from their location to anyone across the country. When the telephone bill comes to the telephone subscriber, they are shocked by the number of calls and, of course, the amount of the bill. Another sign is the lack of incoming calls. Most people receive calls every day from someone, even if it is for solicitation. The bill could be up in the thousands of dollars. To avoid this scam, the telephone subscriber should refuse making any calls using the *72. If the subscriber does use *72, it can be cancelled by using *73 plus the telephone number. What makes the problem worse, the telephone company will not cancel the charges because the subscriber used *72. If an inmate in jail made the call, then the subscriber can report the incident to the correctional authorities. The correctional authorities can add criminal charges for making the telephone charges. However, the subscriber will have to sue the criminal for the money.

17.98   Timeshare Sales and Resales

Vacation timeshares provide consumers the right to use a vacation home for a limited and preplanned period. Timeshare scams affect both the front end, the time at original purchase, and the back end, the time the consumer tries to resell the timeshare. Victims of timeshare fraud are usually contacted by telephone or mail. The following should be considered when either buying or selling a timeshare:

- The salesperson may want you to sign a contract right away; the consumer should not do it. They should take a day or two and consider the details of the purchase. Some timeshares are leased, while others are to be purchased. In case of a purchase, the timeshare owner is usually billed for insurance and property taxes, which can be high. The consumer should also be considered if he/she wants to vacation each year at the same place. Also, timeshares are very hard to resell.
- The consumer should be skeptical of claims made by the salesperson. The salesperson may claim the market is hot. In reality, the market is not hot. Therefore, the consumer should be skeptical of too good to be true claims.
- Many resale companies require you to pay an advance fee before selling your timeshare. In typical real estate transactions, the fee is paid from the proceeds of the sale.
- The consumer should verify that the salesperson is a licensed real estate salesperson or broker. This can be done by calling the state board of realtors. Also, the consumer should check for any complaints or legal actions against the broker or the salesperson.
- The consumer may want to list the timeshare in the area with a real estate broker in the area.
- The consumer may want to exchange the timeshare unit with another in another area by contacting the company from whom he/she purchased the timeshare.

The consumer can file complaints with the state consumer protection agency or real estate board. Also, file a complaint with the Federal Trade Commission in Washington, DC.

17.99   Toy Ads on TV

Children usually want toys that are advertised on television. However, parents should be aware and advise their children about the television ads. The toys shown on television may not be what are expected when purchased.

- Parents should advise their children about how television can overplay the product.
- Parents should advise their children that some toys are more difficult to use than what appears on television.
- Toys are not always sold as they appear on television. Some parts may have to be bought separately. If the advertisement says "pieces sold separately" or "batteries not included," then it means these items will have to be purchased in addition to the main items.
- Parents should ensure the toys are age appropriate. The age level on the toy packaging can give the parent the appropriate age and skill level.
- The parent should find out about the toy before purchasing. The parent should ask the store or friends about their knowledge and/or experience. The parent should

try to find out how the toy actually performs, which pieces come with it, and how much assembly is required.

Any complaints about toys should be directed to the state and local consumer protection agency.

17.100 Travel Scams

Travel scams are a bait and switch scheme. Travel agents advertise tour packages as a too good to be true package. After the consumer purchases the tour package, then they are told the tour is blocked because of the State Department or Treasury Department. The consumer is refused a refund and he/she is out their money. However, the company may offer another tour package, but it will be for a lot more money.

Another version of this scheme is to allow the consumer to travel to the destination. On arrival, the consumer finds their accommodations are below standard. To upgrade, they are charged a large fee. In some cases, the consumer has no upgrade option. The consumer has only the option of remaining or going to another hotel in the area. Before purchasing a tour package, the consumer should:

- Check the hotel accommodations in advance of purchasing the tour package.
- Check with other travel agents on tour packages for the destination desired.
- Check the U.S. State Department for warnings of places the consumer wants to go.
- Check the local Better Business Bureau for any complaints about the travel agent and/or travel agency.

If you have become a victim, then you should file a complaint with the state attorney general's office and the Federal Trade Commission. You should provide:

- Copy of the tour contract
- Copy of your payment(s)
- Identify the travel agent and agency in detail, for example, address, phone, and name of agent

17.101 Viatical Scams

This is an investment in insurance policies for terminally ill patients. The investor purchases an insurance policy of a terminally ill person. Upon the death of the patient, the investor collects the insurance proceeds. This was introduced in the 1990s to help dying AIDS patients get cash to pay their bills. The ill policyholder sells his/her life insurance policy at a discount rate to investors. When the policyholder dies, the investor gets the full face value. However, the longer the patient lives, the longer the investor has to pay monthly premiums and the smaller the return on the policy. Investors become victims in viaticals when they are given phony death estimates and false promises of guaranteed payoffs. They often do not find out what happens to the sick policyholder. Promoters also charge large sales commissions. To prevent becoming a victim of viaticals scams, the investor should:

- Not invest in viaticals.
- Obtain the insurance policy of the ill patient. It should not be held by the promoter.
- Communicate with the policyholder to be sure that he/she is the true policyholder and is ill. It would be best to talk to the policyholder face-to-face.
- Obtain an update on the ill policyholder on a periodic basis, usually every 3 to 6 months.

If you become a victim of a viatical scam, then you should file a complaint with the state insurance commissioner and/or the state securities regulator. You should provide:

- Copy of payments on the insurance policy
- Copy of the insurance policy
- Copy of correspondence and promotional material by the promoter
- Provide information about the policyholder, for example, name, address, telephone, and illness diagnosis

17.102   Unordered Merchandise

Occasionally, a person may receive merchandise that was not ordered. This may be a ballpoint pen, a key chain, or something of little value. Legally speaking, the consumer can only receive two types of merchandise through the mail without their consent or agreement. They are:

- Free samples that are clearly and conspicuously marked as such
- Merchandise mailed by a charitable organization that is soliciting contributions

The rules are shown in 39 USC 3009. The rules are made to protect the consumer from unordered merchandise under unfair methods of competition and unfair trade practices.
If this happens, you can do one of the following:

- If you did not order the merchandise, then you have a legal right to keep the merchandise.
- You do not have an obligation to notify the seller; therefore, you may keep it if you wish. However, it is advisable to notify the company by certified mail with return receipt of your intention to keep the merchandise. You should keep a copy of the letter. If you receive a bill or a letter stating you owe the money for the unordered merchandise, then you can send a letter to the company that you never ordered the merchandise and therefore have a legal right to keep it for free.
- If the unordered merchandise is the result of a shipping error, then contact the seller and offer to return the merchandise at the company's expense. You should give a specific or reasonable time, about 30 days, in which to pick up the merchandise or arrange to have it returned at no expense to you. If the seller, after the specified period of time, does not respond, then you should advise the company of your right to keep or dispose of it as you wish.
- You may receive merchandise that was not ordered but is labeled as "free gifts." You may keep such shipments as free gifts. Charitable organizations usually send

address labels, decorative stamps, and other merchandise and are asking for donations. You may keep such shipments as free gifts.

- The consumer should be aware of participating in sweepstakes or ordering goods advertised as "free" or "trial" at an unusually low price. You should read the fine print to determine if you have any obligations to make future purchases or to purchase the merchandise after the trial period. If you do not wish to keep the merchandise during the trial period, then you should return the merchandise and call or write the company of your intention of not keeping the item.
- If you have not opened the package, you may mark it "Return to Sender" and the postal service will return it with no additional postage charged to you.
- If you open the package and do not like what you find, you may throw it away.

It is illegal for a company to send you unordered merchandise to follow the mailing with a bill or dunning communications. If you have difficulty in dealing with unordered merchandise problems, then you should attempt to resolve it with the company. However, if you cannot resolve it with the company, then you should contact your local U.S. Postal Inspector. You can also contact the Better Business Bureau in your area, the Direct Marketing Association, 6 East 43rd Street, New York, NY 10017, or the Federal Trade Commission.

17.103 Vacation Scam

Consumers sometimes get mail that claims they have won a free vacation at some exotic spot. The consumer is asked to call a company to claim the vacation. There is a catch. For the consumer to be eligible, he/she is required to pay a service charge or purchase membership in a travel club. The cost usually runs $200 to $500. Do not pay it. Also, the consumer should not provide their credit card number or even the expiration date. If the consumer joins the travel club, they will get a travel packet describing the vacation. There are usually many restrictions if the consumer takes the trip. There is usually an additional charge for booking the reservation. The travel dates will be restricted to certain times of the year. If the consumer complains, he/she may be offered an upgraded plan for more additional fees. In some cases, the operator will close down operations and move elsewhere to bilk other consumers.

If you have been victimized by a free vacation scam or fraudulent travel club, then you should contact the local postmaster or the local postal inspector's office and the state attorney general's office. You should provide:

- Copy of the mailing the consumer received
- Copy of cancelled checks or money orders paid to the company
- Copy of credit card statements if paid by credit card

17.104 Variable Annuities

A variable annuity is a contract that provides future payments to the holder after a number of years. The benefit is determined by the performance of the portfolio's securities and the amount invested over the years. Many variable annuities are placed in mutual funds as an insurance wrapper for tax deferred investment growth. Annuity products are legitimate investments. Annuities are generally not suitable for older investors because of the high surrender charges, significant up-front fees, illusory tax, and probate benefits. There are steep penalties for early withdrawals that make them unsuitable for short-term investors. For younger investors, annuities are a good tax deferred investment. For retired persons, these types of investments are inappropriate. Retired people who are drawing retirement from social security or some other retirement plan should not invest. They are only providing commissions to sellers and get a negative return on investments.

If you have invested in a variable annuity and are retired, then you should file a complaint with the state regulatory agency.

17.105   Varicose Vein Treatments

Many women and men consider getting treatment for varicose veins and spider veins. Advertisements for treating venous disease sometimes claim unique, painless, and safe treatments. The consumer should always consult his/her physician.

Some people get veins that become enlarged with pools of blood because of poor blood circulation. These veins become visible in the legs and thighs and can rupture or form open ulcers on the skin. Small spider veins appear on the skin's surface and become web-like formations. They are common in the thighs, ankles, feet, and face.

Normally, treatment is not necessary; however, doctors will recommend treatment in severe cases. Some doctors may make claims of "major breakthroughs," "absolutely painless," and "unique treatments." These claims should be documented and the consumer should ask for proof. Surgery and sclerotherapy are the most commonly used techniques in treating varicose and spider veins. Your doctor should recommend the best treatment based on your diagnosis and personal medical history. You should question your doctor about the various procedures available, safety, side effects for each type of treatment, and amount of pain and scarring you might experience. Also, you should ask about how long the results will last and if the veins will come back.

You should find out what it will cost. You should also contact your insurance company about the coverage under your insurance policy.

You should consult more than one doctor before deciding on any kind of treatment. You should find out about the doctor's experience. You should check with the local hospital about a physician referral service that can give you information about doctors.

If you have a problem with a doctor, then you should contact the state board of medical examiners.

17.106   Voter Registration Scams

Scammers may send e-mail or telephone calls asking for your social security number or financial information supposedly to register you to vote or to confirm your registration, when they really want to commit identity theft. Organizations conducting legitimate voter registration either contact you in person or give a voter registration form to you to fill out. They will never ask for financial information.

To register to vote, a person should contact the local election office about whether a social security number is required. It does not require any citizen to pay a fee to vote. The person usually has to fill out a form and either mail or deliver it to the local election office. Some states require you to come to the election office and bring a driver's license and either a property tax bill or a utility bill to confirm your residence.

If you have become a victim, then you should file a complaint with the local law enforcement agency. Also you should notify your bank if you wrote a check or call the credit card company if paid by credit card. Also, you should notify the credit bureaus of possible identity theft.

17.107   Water Treatment Devices

Many people are having concerns about their water. News reports of leaking landfills, corroding lead pipes, and deterioration of gasoline storage tanks have painted a gloomy picture of toxic wastes, pesticides, and other chemicals seeping into both well and municipal water supplies. For the most part, water from public sources is not a concern for consumers. However, there are unscrupulous salespeople who prey on concerned consumers by using scare tactics and fraudulent practices to sell their water treatment devices.

Fraudulent sellers advertise free home water testing. They are only interested in selling you their water treatment systems, whether you need it or not. The salesperson will add chemicals to your water that will change color or particles form if the water is contaminated. When the water changes color, the salesperson will say the water is polluted and can cause disease. In almost all cases, the water will fail the company's test.

Some salespeople will notify you of being selected to win a prize. To qualify, the consumer must buy a water treatment device, costing hundreds or even thousands of dollars. In many cases, the prize and water treatment device are of little value.

Some salespeople will claim some government agency either requires or recommends consumers to use water purification systems. These claims are false. If the consumer sees an EPA registration number on a water treatment product label, it means only the manufacturer has registered the product with the Environmental Protection Agency. It does not mean the EPA has approved the product.

The consumer should check with the superintendent of their water supply and compare it with state and federal standards. If the consumer uses well water, then they should consult their local health department. They offer free water testing.

The consumer can obtain information about drinking water regulations and general information from the EPA's Safe Drinking Water Hotline at 1-800-426-4791 or www.epa.gov/safewater/.

If the consumer has established water contaminants in their water, then they should determine what type of system the consumer needs to treat their water. There is a wide variety of water treatment devices and systems. Some devices are simple like low cost filter devices for faucets or expensive systems that can solve every problem. The consumer can ask local government officials what system is best for their needs.

17.108   Weight Loss Fraud

There are salespeople who lure people into buying diet pills without dieting or exercising. Medical science has not created a pill for weight loss. Such claims will only slim down your bank account. The consumer should always be skeptical. The consumer should consider.

- Advertisements that use words such as "breakthrough discovery," "secret," "exclusive," or "miraculous" are indicators of false advertising. They have no scientific meaning.
- The consumer should be aware of claims that sound too good to be true. There are no pills that will make pounds melt away.
- The consumer should be skeptical of glowing testimonials. They are impossible to verify and often are fancy sounding clinics.
- The consumer should check with their doctor, a licensed nutritionist, or registered dietitian about weight loss products. Many diet pills are strong laxatives or diuretics that can cause serious health problems.

The consumer should check with the local Better Business Bureau and consumer protection agency in both the state of residence and the state where the company is located. The consumer can file complaints with the Federal Trade Commission and the Food and Drug Administration.

17.109   Wi-Fi Scam

When a person is out in a public place, they try to find a place where they can get connected to the Internet. Many places, particularly airports, offer free Wi-Fi connections. Unfortunately, a hacker can steal the information a person sends over the Internet including usernames and passwords. They can also steal files and your identity; they infect your PC with spyware and malware, and turn it into a spam-spewing zombie. Windows Vista users are more susceptible to attacks than Windows XP. They use an ad hoc, computer-to-computer network. The hacker sets up his/her computer to trap someone using their computer. When the victim gets on the Internet, they are, in fact, using the hacker's computer. All traffic goes through the hacker's computer. The hacker can see everything you do online including usernames and passwords. The victim cannot see anything happening. Depending on how you are connected to the ad hoc network, the next time the person's computer is turned on, it may automatically broadcast the Free Wi-Fi network ID to the world and anyone nearby can connect to it in a peer-to-peer mode without the person's knowledge and can do damage if sharing files. If a company laptop is connected to one of those networks and gets infected, then it can damage the company's network. The best protection against these kinds of attacks is: Never connect to an ad hoc network. However, if the person is using Windows XP and needs to access the Internet, they can take the following steps.

1. Click the wireless icon in the System Tray.
2. Click "Change advanced settings."
3. Select the Wireless Network tab.
4. Click "Advanced."
5. On the screen that appears, select "Access point (infrastructure) networks only."
6. Click Close and click OK for the dialog boxes to disappear.

The only way to distinguish between ad hoc and normal wireless hot spots is to look at the network icon on the screen. An ad hoc network's icon is made up of several PCs; a normal network is made up of one PC.

A person cannot file a complaint on a free Wi-Fi scam. However, a person should immediately check and report the incident to their bank and credit card companies. The hacker may have your identity so they can commit identity theft.

17.110 Wireless Cable Investment

The Federal Communications Commission awards licenses for wireless cable, known as Multi-channel Multipoint Distribution Service through a lottery. If you are considering investing in wireless cable, you may be approached by an application preparation service or an investment company selling shares of wireless cable companies. You should consider the following before investing in this technology:

- The winner of the lottery is awarded a conditional license if it remedies any deficiency in the application. The license is forfeited if the wireless cable station is not constructed and operational within 1 year. Application preparation services charge thousands of dollars for their services. The investor should consider using a lawyer to assist the investor in completing the application process.
- You should consider the geographic area being considered. Is it suitable for this type of service? You should determine if the population can support a wireless cable television station. Also, there may be a lot of competition. In hill or mountainous areas, transmission may be too poor to generate enough subscribers to make the venture profitable.
- You should contact the state attorney general's office or the Federal Trade Commission about any complaints or legal actions. If the company is offering share of stock in the company, then they may be required to register with the Securities and Exchange Commission and the state Division of Securities. You should not rely on business organizations where membership is based on a payment of a fee.

17.111 Work-at-Home Schemes

Newspapers, television, and magazines are carrying advertising that claims huge earnings from working at home. Earnings can be hundreds of dollars a day or week and thousands of dollars in a year. These ads ask you to send money today at some address, usually a drop box or post office box. These work-at-home schemes have hidden costs. These costs can involve huge fees for supplies or require you to spend money on advertising. Work-at-home schemes have defrauded consumers out of millions of dollars.

The targets of work-at-home schemes are those who need extra money but who are not able to work outside their homes. Victims typically include mothers at home caring for young children, the unemployed, the elderly, handicapped persons, and people with low incomes. The most common work-at-home schemes are envelope stuffing, product assembly, or craft work. The consumer never gets any envelope stuffing work. Modern mailing techniques and equipment have virtually eliminated the need for home workers to perform legitimate envelope stuffing, addressing, and mailing services from their homes. In product assembly or craft work, the consumer is hit with extra costs for supplies, equipment, etc. The company will usually reject anything assembled or made because of substandard work.

A legitimate company will put all the terms in writing before you pay a fee. The contract will spell out what work must be performed, how you will be paid, when payments will begin, and the total costs for fees and supplies. Even then, the consumer should scrutinize the contact carefully.

If you become defrauded, then you can file a complaint with the state or local consumer protection agency and the state attorney general's office. You can also file a complaint with the U.S. Postal Inspection Service in your area. You also should call the newspaper or magazine where the ad appeared and let them know about the problems you experienced.

17.112 Worthless Bank Checks

In most states, the passing of worthless checks is a criminal act. Returned checks that are stamped NSF or Account Not Found indicate worthless checks. These types of checks are subject to criminal prosecution. Checks returned with "Refer to Maker" or "Uncollected Funds" require further investigation before criminal charges can be made.

Checks that are stamped "Stop Payment" might be subject to criminal prosecution. In most cases, stop payment is usually a means of a legitimate dispute. Stop payment checks are resolved in Small Claims Court.

Checks stamped with "Unauthorized Drawer's Signature" are worthless checks but are forgeries signed by someone other than the checking account holder. These checks should be given to the local sheriff's department or local police department.

If you are a victim of a worthless check, then you should contact the local state or district attorney. They will provide you with procedures to be taken before they can prosecute a person for writing a worthless check. If the state or district attorney is unable to pursue the case, then you can file a civil suit in small claims court. The clerk of the court can assist you in the process.

You do not have to accept a check for payment for goods and services. You can insist on payment by certified check or money order. However, if you decide to accept a check, then you should follow these guidelines:

1. Do not accept checks that are postdated or checks with no date listed on them. Postdated checks cannot be prosecuted for the crime of passing worthless checks.
2. Do not agree to hold a check, even for a few hours. Accepting a check and agreeing to hold it for any period of time gives you notice the check has insufficient funds available. If the check is dishonored by the bank, then you cannot prosecute the passer of the check. It will have to be resolved in small claims court.
3. Do not accept third party checks. The person who wrote the check is not the person giving it to you for payment. You may be accepting a forged or stolen check.
4. When accepting a check, you should ask for some type of picture identification. The identification should be something issued by a governmental agency, for example, driver's license, passport, or a card issued by a government agency. You should be

sure the document is not altered. You should examine the card to be sure it is a legitimate card.

5. The person should have printed identifying information on the check. If it does not appear on the check, then write it on the front or back of the check. Such information should include:
   a. Name.
   b. Address.
   c. Home telephone number.
   d. Date of birth.
   e. Race.
   f. Height.
   g. Place of employment.
   h. Employer's telephone number.
   i. Driver's license number and state.
   j. Make sure that the information on the check matches the data on the ID card.
6. Be sure there is a signature on the check. Compare the signature on the check to the signature on the ID card.
7. Review the check. Make sure the check is made out in the proper amount, both in the number amount and the written amount.
8. If there is no name printed on the check, then have the person print their name under the signature line.
9. You can call the financial institution that maintains the bank account to verify whether the check has sufficient funds. However, it may have sufficient funds at the time of the call, but when the check is presented for payment, the account may not have sufficient funds.

17.113   800 Prefix Telephone Service

Not all 800 telephone numbers are free. Some 800 numbers access information or entertainment that costs money. They will ask you to pay with a credit card or make billing arrangements. If you call an 800 number, then it might be transferred to a 900 or 976 number (pay per call) or to an international number that has prefixes of 011 or 809. This is illegal. Blocking 900 or 976 numbers will not prevent calls from 800 numbers or international numbers. The company should tell you its name and address, its rates, and personal identification number (PIN) for you to use in obtaining service. Your children should receive permission before using the telephone to make calls for obtaining services or products using an 800 number.

You should review your phone bills for 800 number charges. If there are 800 number charges, then you should follow the instructions on the billing statement for disputes.

17.114   900 Prefix Telephone Numbers (Pay-per-Call)

900 numbers are pay-per-call services because you pay for the call and for the services or products. Charges for 900 number calls are set by the 900 number companies and not by

the government or the telephone companies. The costs are much higher than with regular long distance rates.

When you call a 900 prefix number, you should hear:

- The 900 number company's name
- The cost of the call
- A description of the information, goods, or services to be provided
- A notice that you can hang up and not be charged for the call within 3 seconds of hearing a certain tone or signal
- A warning that kids under 18 need their parents' permission to stay on the line

You cannot be billed for listening to the beginning message. It is illegal to be transferred from a toll-free 800 number to a 900 number. Bills for 900 numbers should tell you who to contact if there is a problem and provide a local or toll free number that you can call to dispute charges. The local and long distance service provider cannot shut off service if you refuse to pay a disputed 900 number charge. You must pay the rest of the bill by the due date. You can ask the local telephone company to block any 900 number calls so children or other people cannot make these calls.

The following can help the consumer from becoming a victim of a 900 number fraud:

- Be suspicious when you receive a prize notification or other promotion that asks you to call a 900 number. There is always a charge for a 900 number call.
- Never dial a 900 number unless you are absolutely sure of how much you will be charged and are willing to pay it.
- Be wary if after dialing a 900 number you hear a message asking you to dial a second 900 number.
- If you are unfamiliar with the company making the promotion, check it out with the local Better Business Bureau or the state consumer protection agency.
- Trust your common sense. If it sounds too good to be true, it probably is.

If you have been defrauded by a 900 number scheme, then file a complaint with the state consumer protection agency. If U.S. mail has been used in any way, then report it to the local postal inspector's office.

17.115 Summary

The consumer should observe the following rules:

1. If the deal seems too good to be true, it probably is.
2. Investigate the company and/or product being offered. The local library is an excellent source. The Internet can also be used to investigate a company.
3. Never purchase any product or service from anyone who solicits you by telephone, Internet, mail, or in person.
4. Never give anyone control over any part of your financial affairs unless you really know the person or company.

5. Keep your checks, credit cards, and ATM cards in a safe place and separate from other things or valuables. Never give account numbers over the telephone, Internet, or to solicitors unless you contacted them.
6. Review all bank statements, credit card statements, and brokerage statements for accuracy.

Fraud Prevention for Business 18

18.1 Introduction

There are many precautions that businesses can take to prevent fraud. If businesses, like consumers, will take the appropriate steps and procedures to prevent fraud, then their losses can be nonexistent or minimal. In some cases, fraud can be prevented by just making appropriate inquiries. While in other cases, implementing proper internal controls can help prevent fraud. It should be stressed that all precautions that can be taken do not guarantee that businesses will not become victims; however, it will reduce their chances of becoming victims. There are many "con" artists, who can "take your shoes while you are standing in them," regardless of all the precautions taken.

18.2 Business

Businesses can be victims of fraud in three primary areas:

1. Customers
2. Employees
3. Vendors and suppliers

Businesses should be aware of fraud that is committed by these three groups. If fraud is uncovered by any of the three groups, then prosecution should be initiated. Failure to prosecute only encourages more fraud. Large corporations and many medium and small companies do not like to prosecute because they rationalize that it could hurt their image. This is not so. Many of the consumer frauds also apply to businesses, for example, insurance, legal and accounting, banking, construction, and repairs. Therefore, those preventative measures apply to businesses. Fraud issues that concern businesses are addressed here.

18.3 Customers

Shoplifting is the most common fraud committed by customers. It involves the customer walking out of the business establishment with the merchandise either open in his/her hands or concealed in bags or undergarments. Detecting shoplifting can be done by observing or detecting the customer in some manner. However, some customers commit fraud in other ways. The two principal methods, outside of shoplifting, are known as the refund method and the other is commonly called the "bust-out" artist.

18.4   Refund Method

The refund method of committing fraud is becoming more prevalent. This is used by crime organizations in recent years in "fencing" stolen property. The customer purchases merchandise on one day and returns it later, for various reasons, for a refund. The customer later brings in more merchandise using a receipt, either forged or the same old receipt, for another refund. The second or subsequent refund claim usually involves merchandise that is stolen or purchased from another store. Organized crime groups use it to fence stolen property. If done often enough, law enforcement agencies will believe that the business establishment is owned or controlled by organized crime. In the case of large chain stores, if internal controls are not implemented and followed, then this scheme can become enormous, resulting in losses. For the business to prevent such a scheme, the following precautions are recommended:

1. When making a refund, the cashier should take back the original receipt and match up with the refund slip. This will prevent the customer from reusing the purchase slip.
2. The business should establish a policy that is posted for both customers and cashiers to follow. This policy should not allow refunds after 30 days. No refunds should be allowed for some small consumer items, for example, paper products, shoes, pencils, pens, flashlight batteries, and cleaning agents.
3. For merchandise that has serial numbers or some specific identification that requires some detailed accounting, returned merchandise should be matched with sales records to find if it was the same item that was sold.
4. For refunds that are made by credit card credit slips, account numbers should be analyzed to identify customers with excessive refunds. Excessive refunds should be gauged to the number of refunds made to the same customer within one month. Names and credit card account numbers should be scrutinized. Some fraudulent customers will use more than one credit card.

Most refund fraud will usually involve merchandise with low dollar prices. The principal target of refund fraud is almost solely the retailers. Wholesalers and manufacturers are rarely victims.

18.5   Bust-Out Artists

Businesses that extend credit to customers become easy victims of credit fraud. They ship goods to a customer with the expectation of getting paid in the normal 30 days or sooner with a discount. However, payment is never received. Letters requesting payment are sent. Telephone calls are made to only find out that the telephone has been disconnected or is not operating. This usually happens within a month after shipment of merchandise. The credit manager finds the business premises empty. Inquiries about the business turn up nothing. The credit manager reports back that the business is nonexistent and the merchandise is gone. The company controller then has to make a write-off of the accounts receivable to bad debts. This causes the company to have a loss or a reduction of earnings on their financial statements. For some companies, this can be devastating. It could even cause the company to close shop. This kind of fraud is called "bust out." There are many bust-out artists around that make a living doing this kind of fraud. The surprising part of all of this is that the company does not pursue the bust-out artist. The La Cosa Nostra, called the Mafia, and other organized crime groups have been doing this for years. They have become experts in this field.

The extent of business credit fraud is not known. The primary reason for this is that businesses do not report such losses, nor do they pursue any criminal prosecution. It is estimated by the National Association of Credit Management that businesses lose tens of hundreds of thousands of dollars. They also have records of people who have operated credit frauds for many years. There are measures that can be taken to prevent this kind of fraud. They are:

1. The sales department should not control the credit department. The credit department should make the final decision based on their inquiries about the creditor. Remember, it is better to have unsold inventory than to have a bad debt write-off.
2. The company should obtain and study a credit report. The credit manager should call all previous creditors. However, the credit manager should be cautious of references in the same geographical area, as well as post office boxes and private mailboxes, because these indicate "singers" (i.e., phony references).
3. Businesses should call the Better Business Bureaus and/or local or state Consumer Affairs Departments about any complaints and how many. Complaints are danger signs.
4. Bust-out artists like to have rush orders. This is a ploy to get shipment before a full credit check is made. They usually want orders shipped immediately without any credit checks.
5. Credit managers should be wary of unsolicited orders. Bust-out artists try to obtain as many suppliers as possible.
6. Credit managers should be wary of references located around the country. There is a strong danger sign if the references turn out to be answering machines or answering services.
7. Increases in orders are a danger sign. The bust-out artist sometimes buys small and gradually increases his/her orders. He/she also pays promptly, or pays slower on each order. He/she tries to get your confidence before he/she makes his/her last and largest order.
8. Credit managers should be careful of business names that are almost identical to well known and highly credit worthy corporations. The address given may even be on the same street as that of the reputable concern.
9. The business comes under new management and the change of ownership is not publicly announced and the identity of the new owners is obscure. This is a danger sign.
10. The business should be aware of orders unrelated to the usual line (like grocery stores ordering jewelry as door prizes) during the business's busy season or the customer's off-season.
11. The customer orders increased quantities that are contradictory to the seasonal nature of the customer's business.
12. Financial statements of the customer are unaudited, unverified, and appear inconsistent or unusual. A cash flow should be done to see if the cash balances agree.

Also, check ratios to see if they are consistent. Vertical and horizontal analysis should be performed on the financial statements. If the company is new, they will not have multiperiod financial statements. Therefore, you should compare this with industry statistics and other data to see if they are consistent.

13. If racketeers or those with a criminal record are in positions of importance in a customer being serviced, then credit should not be extended.

14. Credit managers should be aware of an abnormal amount of credit inquiries. Bust-out artists attempt to order from as many companies as possible. The credit manager should be alert to other legitimate references that tell him/her of receiving many inquiries. Credit inquiry rates indicate a strong danger sign.

15. The credit manager should check the background of the principals. The business must know with whom they are dealing. Credit reports and other financial information should be obtained on the principals as to their backgrounds and businesses that they have operated in the past.

16. Front men are used by organized crime organizations. Organized crime uses front men because they have clean backgrounds. The credit manager must determine if the front men have the capital to start or control the business. Also, if the front men have the experience, education, and knowledge to successfully operate such a business.

17. Payments are made on time at first. As purchases are made, the payments become slower and sometimes these checks begin to bounce. When the checks begin to bounce, this is a danger sign. Credit should be terminated when customer checks start to bounce. This is especially true when orders are also increasing.

18.6   Employee Fraud

Employee theft and embezzlement are the most common forms of fraud in businesses. Most employees are not dishonest when they are first hired. They only become dishonest when the opportunity becomes available. Fraud only occurs when three elements come together. These elements are:

1. Items of value
2. A perpetrator
3. Given an opportunity

These elements will equal fraud. There are three basic areas where businesses can take steps to help prevent fraud by employees. They are:

1. Hiring
2. Work environment
3. Internal controls

18.7   Hiring

Hiring honest employees is the first step. Screening prospective employees can do this. Personnel managers should implement and maintain a thorough selection process. The prospective employee should be screened for both character traits and financial stability. Obtaining the following information can do this:

1. *Application.* The business should obtain a complete application and/or résumé from the prospective employee. The application and résumé should contain:
   a. *Full name.* The applicant's full name should be obtained along with any and all aliases and nicknames.
   b. *Identification data.* This should consist of date of birth, social security number, and driver's license number. If the applicant is a resident alien, then obtain the Immigration and Naturalization Service (INS) alien number and country of origin passport number and country.
   c. *History.* This should contain work history back to the age of 21. The work history should show the name of company, address, and manager's name of past employers. Any gaps of employment should be questioned and explanations obtained.
   d. *Character references.* The prospective employee should give a minimum of three character references. These character references should not be former employers or relatives.
   e. *Relatives.* A listing of close relatives should be obtained. This includes spouse, parents (both applicant and spouse), children (with dates of birth), and brothers and sisters (with ages or dates of birth).
2. *Character examination.* The business should have prospective employees take a personal (psychological) character examination. This is strongly urged for prospective employees applying for positions of trust.
3. *References.* The prospective employee character and employment references should be checked. For character references, personnel managers should make inquiries as to the applicant's moral values and religious affiliations. Past time activities should be identified. The character reference should be examined as to the extent of his/her association with the applicant. The applicant's former employers should be asked about his/her job performance and skills, reason for leaving the employment, and punctuality.
4. *Drug test.* The applicant should be examined for any signs of drug and alcohol abuse. Many employees commit fraud because of drug or alcohol abuse. They need the funds to support such a habit.
5. *Credit history.* The applicant's credit history should be obtained. This will show the applicant's financial history and current status. An applicant with a high debt service has a potential of committing fraud. Also, the question should be answered if the applicant can live off the income from what the employer expects to start him/her out.
6. *Public records.* Public records should be examined to determine whether the applicant has any criminal or civil actions. Traffic infractions should not be considered unless the applicant is applying for a driver's position. Also, real and personal property that is owned by the applicant should be identified in public records.

This information will help the employer to evaluate the applicant as to his/her fraud potential. It will supply information about the applicant in case he/she commits fraud. This information will help law enforcement to track the fraudulent employee. It will also help in civil tort cases. Subjecting the applicant to such scrutiny will discourage some dishonest individuals from applying and informs employees that fraud will not be tolerated.

18.8   Work Environment

After an employee is hired, an environment should be created that will discourage dishonesty. Treating employees fairly can do this. Employers also can provide amenities that do not cost very much. They can implement policies that will discourage employees from being dishonest. Internal controls and physical security procedures can be maintained to discourage theft. All of these environmental controls are discussed in the following list:

1. *Amenities.* The business should have amenities that will benefit the employee. These include such things as clean rest rooms, a decent break room, parking space, and clean workspace.
2. *Ethical standards.* The business has to promote and display good ethical and moral standards. These standards must be equally applied to employees, managers, and officers. These ethical and moral standards should be applied to employees, vendors and suppliers, and customers alike.
3. *Performance evaluation.* Job performance goals should be high, but not unrealistic. Employees should be encouraged to perform to the best of their abilities. If a business sets unrealistic goals, this will force employees and managers to lie or cheat. Outstanding employees and managers should be rewarded for their performance. Incentives such as bonuses, time off, and stock options, should be made available. These awards should be based on performance. Different employees will perform differently. The greater the performance should result in greater rewards.
4. *Benefits.* The employer should provide various benefits that should be available to officers, managers, and employees alike. Health insurance, disability insurance, retirement, and stock options (if public held company) should be made available. Small companies are not financially able to provide many of these benefits because of the expense; however, they can make them available to employees at their expense (payroll deductions). Even if the employee has to pay (through payroll deductions) for these benefits, it can be a boost to employee morale and performance. Most employees, especially in hard economic times, want security. If a business has to downsize for whatever reason, then it is management's responsibility to advise the employees. In some cases, particularly for small businesses, management should solicit the cooperation of employees to reduce the downsizing. They should be considered an asset to the business and not an expense.
5. *Internal controls.* Management should implement and maintain internal controls. Internal controls mean more than just establishing administrative procedures. They should include enforcing employees to take vacations, making periodic rotations, and providing training for different assignments. Remember the more responsibilities that an employee can take on, the more valuable the employee becomes to the business. However, a business should not rely too heavily on any one or two employees for a particular assignment. Internal controls should also encompass security procedures. Change or rotation of guards should be made periodically. Lunch boxes, handbags, etc., should be inspected before managers and employees

leave the business site. Limit access to various areas to only employees who work in the area. This is especially true for computers. Work areas should be locked after hours. Access to keys should be limited to appropriate personnel.

6. *Internal auditors.* For medium and large businesses, internal auditors should be employed to act as "watch dogs." They should ensure compliance with company policies and procedures. Internal auditors should be hired by and report to the board of directors. Management should not have any control over internal auditors. Many corporate fraud cases involve upper management who can control internal auditors by directing them away from the area where the fraud is being committed.

Employee theft usually involves the following schemes:

1. Cash register thefts
2. Payroll falsification
3. Issuing fraudulent refunds
4. Kickbacks
5. Embezzlement
6. Lapping schemes
7. Check kiting

See chapter 24 for more detail. However, prevention is the primary key to preventing fraud by employees. If items of value and the opportunity do not exist, then employee fraud will be minimal or nonexistent.

18.9   Employee Theft

Employee theft usually involves the following schemes:

- Cash register thefts
- Payroll falsification (called ghost employees)
- Payroll tax withholding
- Issuing fraudulent refunds
- Kickbacks
- Embezzlement
- Credit memos and lapping schemes
- False invoices for goods and services
- Skimming

18.10   Accounts Payable Fraud

Accounts payable fraud involves paying falsified bills. It can be done by either the employee having a bill be paid on their behalf or a vendor has submitted a bill for services or products not rendered or received. This can be prevented by:

- Having the prepared check attached to the invoices being paid.
- A tape showing the total amount of invoices being paid to a vendor.
- Invoices should be marked paid along with the date and check number listed.
- Shipping receipts should be attached to each invoice. This shows the merchandise has been received.
- The officer/partner or sole proprietor should not sign the check until he/she has verified the invoices and shipping receipts are in agreement with the check amount.
- The bookkeeper/clerk should never be able to sign checks for the company. Only the corporate officer, partner, or sole proprietor should sign checks.

If fraud is discovered in payment of false invoices, then the business should provide copies of the cancelled check(s) and the false invoice(s) to local law enforcement. The small business should always prosecute the criminal. Not doing so will send a message for other employees to do the same. The company should keep a copy of the canceled check(s) and false invoice(s). Also, the canceled checks and false invoices can be evidence in a civil suit. A civil law suit should not be instituted until the criminal case has been completed. Remember, the employee rarely ever pays back the stolen funds. However, if the employee has the ability to repay the loss funds, then a civil suit is advisable.

18.11   Accounts Receivable Fraud

Besides employee theft of cash from sales, they can also steal cash and checks from receipt of accounts receivable. The cash or checks are diverted to their personal account. They will, in turn, record either a credit memo to offset the account receivable or post another receipt to the account from which the funds were diverted. One may ask how can a check made payable to the company be diverted to a personal account. It is done by the employee opening a bank account in the company's name with only their signature shown. The bank account is usually at a different bank from the company bank. Lapping accounts receivable refers to the application of one customer receipt to another customer's account. To avoid lapping accounts receivable or diverting customer receipts, a corporate officer, partner, or sole proprietor should:

- Review an aging schedule of all accounts receivable each month. The principal should call customers who have an account more than 30 days old. If the customer said the bill was paid, then the principal should review deposit records to locate the receipt on the expected date(s) of receipt.
- The employee(s) who keep the books should not make any contact with customers.
- Credit memos should be approved by a corporate officer, partner, or sole proprietor. They should not be made by the employee.

If the small business has found fraud in their business dealings with diversion or lapping of accounts receivable, then they should:

- Get a copy of the canceled check, both front and back, from the customer. The small business can get a copy of the check from their bank but usually will only show the front of the check and not the back. The endorsement on the back of the check will identify where the funds went.

- Notify local law enforcement of the crime.
- Provide copy of canceled check(s) and invoice(s) to law enforcement.
- Prosecute the employee for theft. Not doing so will encourage other employees to commit theft.
- If the defendant has the ability to make restitution, then file a civil law suit for recovery of loss. It is not cost-effective if the defendant has no means of repaying the loss funds.

18.12 Cash Register Sales

Some employees will steal from the cash register. They come up short when closing out for the day. If an employee comes up short only occasionally, this does not mean the employee is stealing. Some companies have found new employees do not always give out proper change. One reason is that the public school system does not teach basic mathematics too well. However, if this shortage occurs regularly, then there is a high probability of fraud by the cashier. To help prevent theft by the cashier, the company should:

- Bond all employees who perform cashier duties or handle cash.
- Test the applicant before hiring as to their basic mathematical skills.
- Do not let multiple employees use the same cash register.
- Do not let employees cash personal checks without management approval.
- Do not let employees borrow funds from their assigned cash register.

If an employee is caught stealing from the cash register, it is advisable to just dismiss them if the amount is small. The cost of prosecution and getting restitution is prohibitive. Most restitution agreements are generally not complied with by the perpetrator. However, if the amount is large, then the company should provide all cash shortages slips to the local police or sheriff's office.

18.13 Embezzlement

Embezzlement is the taking of funds from a company and hiding it on the books. There are various ways of doing this. An employee can write a check to himself/herself or on their behalf and record it as an expense. This requires the employee to have access to the checking account and the accounting books and records. For small businesses, the management needs to:

- Review all bank statements and canceled checks each month.
- Never let an employee be a signatory on any bank account.
- Bank statements and canceled checks should be opened by a corporate officer, partner, or sole proprietor.

If an employee is caught embezzling funds, then the local police or sheriff's office should be notified. The company should always pursue prosecution. A civil case for restitution should not be started until the criminal case has been completed. The company should provide the following evidence to local law enforcement:

- Copy of the front and back of canceled checks. These checks should not only include those paid to the employee but all checks paid on their behalf, for example, telephone, credit card bills, or some other personal expense.

18.14   Kickbacks

Kickbacks come in two schemes. Both involve an employee(s) and a vendor or supplier. One scheme involves the sale of unreported inventory that is sold and shared by the vendor and employee. The other scheme involves the business paying for inventory at inflated prices and the employee receives a portion of the excess back. Internal controls can help prevent this, but the key indicators are:

- The same vendor is constantly used.
- The current vendor has prices higher than other vendors do in the same line.
- Inventory reveals more goods in stock that cannot be accounted for.
- Payments to vendors show more than one endorsement.
- Manager or purchasing agent has excessive debts.
- Purchasing agent or manager does not take any vacation time.
- Only photocopies of invoices are provided.

If a company believes an employee is receiving kickbacks, then they should obtain the following evidence for local law enforcement:

- Get a copy of vendor's catalogs that shows their prices. Many times the prices paid are higher than what is shown in the catalogs.
- Provide copies of shipping receipts.
- Provide copies of invoices that show the items sold.
- Provide copies of canceled checks that might show multiple endorsements.
- Provide copies of any false invoices.

18.15   Payroll Fraud

Some payroll clerks have been known to put a friend on the payroll. Ghost employees are people who do not work for the company but are receiving payroll checks. This has happened to companies with as few as 10 employees. It is usually done because the corporate officer, partner, or sole proprietor do not sign the checks or are in a hurry and do not pay attention. Companies with a high turnover rate of employees are the most vulnerable. If a company has a high turnover rate, then they should review their hiring practices and management style (see section 8.7). To prevent having ghost employees, the company should do the following:

- Do not allow the payroll clerk to sign checks.
- Management should review the checks before signing to ensure the people being paid are actual employees.
- Review state and federal employment tax returns for accuracy.
- Management should pass out the checks instead of the payroll clerk.

When payroll checks to ghost employee(s) are discovered, the company should call the local police or sheriff's office. The company should provide the following evidence to law enforcement:

- Copies or original checks made payable to ghost employees. Be sure both front and back of the checks are provided.
- Copy of the employee's employment application.

18.16 Payroll Tax Withholding

Payroll clerks can manipulate the payroll by showing a higher salary and a higher income tax withholding. The net pay remains the same. When the employee gets their W-2 wage statement, he/she will file their tax return and get a large tax refund. The W-2 wage statement will show the higher salary and the higher income tax withholding. Management should:

- Check the Federal 941 withholding report to the gross wages and taxes withheld for the quarter for their accuracy with the company records and books.
- Management should review and sign the Federal 941 and state employment returns.
- Management should ensure the tax deposits have been made. This can be done by reviewing the canceled checks made payable to the bank or the U.S. Treasury.
- Payroll checks should be made payable to the U.S. Treasury and not the Internal Revenue Service (IRS).
- If direct deposits are being made, then the bank statements should reflect charges to the U.S. Treasury.

This is more of an IRS matter. The payroll tax returns, both federal and state, should be corrected to show the correct salary and withholding. The company can apply the overages to future tax liabilities.

18.17 Skimming

Skimming is the method of diverting cash receipts to an employee before it can be deposited into the company's bank account and recorded in the accounting records. Skimming usually only involves cash, but sometimes it can involve checks. Unlike stealing from the cash register after the sale was rung up, the cash sale will not be made on the cash register. In some cases, the sales on one cash register would not be deposited nor recorded in the accounting records. This could lead to hundreds and thousands of dollars being lost. A good indicator of missing sales is when the gross profit margin percentages declines. Gross margin is computed by subtracting cost of sales from gross sales. Gross profit percentage is gross profit divided by total sales, then multiplied by 100. Some steps to prevent skimming are:

- Do not let a cashier have access to more than one cash register.
- Cash registers should be secured when not in normal operation.
- Only management should have keys to cash registers.
- Checks should be endorsed immediately upon receipt with an endorsement stamp. This will prevent a check from being deposited into some other account. If it does, then the bank is liable for the funds.

For businesses in the bar and pub business, it has been known for employees to bring in their own liquor and sell it to customers. These sales, of course, are not rung up on the cash register. In addition, it does not affect the gross profit percentages because the liquor was not purchased by the company. The only prevention here is for management to keep close observation on sales and inventory. It would be advisable for the bartenders to provide cash register receipts to customers. In fact, a sign should be posted whereby any sale without a receipt is free. This gives customers notice and many will ask for a receipt when paying for a drink. This will cause the gross profit percentages to increase.

If an employee is caught skimming, then the local police or sheriff's office should be called. Any civil settlements should be done after a criminal conviction. Evidence should be provided to local law enforcement.

- Provide a list of inventory that is missing.
- Provide the sales price of the missing inventory.
- Prepare a schedule showing the amount of sales not recorded on the cash register or the accounting records.

18.18   Internal Controls

Every business should have some internal controls. The extent of internal controls depends on the size of the business and the number of employees in the company. For small businesses with fewer than 25 employees, not including the corporate officer, partner, or sole proprietor, these internal controls are:

- Internal bookkeepers or accountants should never be a signatory on any bank account.
- Petty cash should be kept on an imprest basis. This means the total amount of cash and receipts should total to a set sum, for example, $100 or $500. The size of the petty cash should be large enough to cover any cash expenses that are normally made by the business in a week or month depending on the volume.
- The principal, corporate officer, partner, or sole proprietor should review all bank statements before the bookkeeper or accountant does a bank reconciliation.

- A bank reconciliation should be done immediately after the principal has reviewed the bank statements. After the bank statements have been reconciled, the principal should review the bank reconciliation and question any outstanding deposit that is more than a week old and any outstanding checks that are more than 30 days old.
- The principal should review all accounts receivable that are more than 30 days old.
- The principal should review all payments to vendors and suppliers. This requires the principal to review the invoices being paid along with shipping receipts and purchase orders. The small business owner should mark the invoices "PAID" after signing the checks.
- All merchandise should be ordered by purchase order.
- The small business owner should review the payroll as to gross wages, deductions, and net pay before signing the payroll checks.

18.19   Fraud by Vendors, Suppliers, and Other Providers

A third source of fraud on businesses is by vendors and suppliers. Small businesses have to be aware of fraud perpetrated by their suppliers, vendors, and other providers of goods and services. Like consumers, businesses use many of the same kind of goods and services. Some of these providers use various schemes to defraud businesses. In this scenario, the business is basically the consumer. The subsequent consumer section addresses the various areas where the consumer can be defrauded. This also applies to businesses as well; however, businesses face additional areas. These are addressed in the following.

18.20   Accountant Fraud

Most small businesses use outside accountants to prepare their tax returns, both federal and state. Accountants generally charge by the hour to prepare business tax returns, for example, Corporate Tax Return (1120 or 1120S), Partnership Return (1065), and Schedule C to the Individual Income Tax Return (1040) for self-employed individuals. However, there are some unscrupulous accountants who charge high fees and fill out fraudulent tax returns. You must remember that the taxpayer is responsible for the complete and accurate return, not the accountant or tax preparer.

For businesses that are incorporated, a corporate tax return is required to be filed every year. There are two types of corporate tax returns, the 1120 for fully taxable corporations and the 1120S for corporations whose earnings are taxed at the shareholder level. The K-1 schedules are used to show the prorate share of corporate earnings for each shareholder. If an accountant has prepared your corporate return, then the corporate officer/owner should review the corporate tax return for accuracy. This can be done for corporation and partnership, Form 1065, returns by doing the following steps.

- Verify sales are correct, whether on the accrual method of recognizing income or the cash basis of recognizing income. Scrupulous accountants often lower income figures so a loss is shown on the bottom line.

- Verify the cost of sales. Cost of sales is the cost of merchandise sold. All businesses have cost of sales if their income is derived from selling merchandise. There should be no cost of sales for services rendered. Scrupulous accountants will sometimes bury other expenses into cost of sales.
- Check the math. Some returns are rejected because of mathematical errors in addition and subtraction. On the income and expense side on page one of the corporate return, the additions and subtractions should agree with the bottom line. The balance sheet on page four should total to the bottom line for each column.
- The M-1 schedule should be checked for math accuracy and proper items. The M-1 schedule is used to reconcile the differences between book income and the tax return. The most common items where there is a difference are disallowed charitable contributions because of the 10% limitation and disallowed entertainment expenses because of the 50% limitation on deductibility.
- The M-2 schedule should be checked for math accuracy and proper items. Any personal expenses paid on behalf of a shareholder/officer should be reflected in this schedule. This is assuming the shareholder/officer has not loaned the corporation any funds. If the shareholder/officer has loaned the corporation funds, then personal expenses paid by the corporation should reduce the shareholder loan account.

For sole proprietorships, the self-employed individual should review their 1040 return and pay particular attention to Schedule C. Like corporate and partnership returns, the sole proprietor should check for:

- *Verify sales.* Most sole proprietorships are usually on a cash basis of accounting; therefore, total sales should agree with the total deposits into the bank account for the year.
- *Verify cost of sales.* Cost of sales is the cost of merchandise sold. All businesses have cost of sales if their income is derived from selling merchandise. There should be no cost of sales for services rendered.
- *Check the math.* The income and expenses on Schedule C should be computed accurately.
- *Check repairs and maintenance expenses.* Many accountants bury personal expenses in this account heading.
- *Check entertainment expenses.* These expenses are only allowed 50% of the total cost.

If a corporate officer/shareholder, partner, or sole proprietor finds any mistakes from analyzing one of the above tax returns, then they should have the accountant change the return or else find a more competent accountant or tax preparer. Remember, the accountant is not liable for the tax, only the taxpayers are responsible for the taxes. An IRS audit can cost the taxpayer more money if the tax returns are not properly prepared. Also, it could lead to criminal prosecution.

A business should never allow the accountant, whether internal or external, to sign checks. There have been many instances where payroll tax deposits go to the accountant and not the Internal Revenue Service. There are many instances where the accountant has embezzled funds by making checks to himself, other businesses associated with the accountant, and friends and relatives. Only the business owner, whether a corporate officer, partner, or sole proprietor, should sign checks.

18.21 Advertising Material

Many small businesses like to advertise their business by using place mats, calendars, pencils, pens, and other materials because of the lower costs compared to other advertising mediums. The company or person who produces the materials for the client business in most cases also does the distribution. Before a company contracts with an advertising company who produces and distributes advertising material, they should verify the following:

- The company should get references for previous jobs and call those companies about the advertiser's performance.
- The company should see samples of jobs previously produced.
- The company should not be pressured into anything immediately.
- The company should shop around and compare products, services, and prices.
- The company should inquire about any complaints or legal actions with the state or local consumer protection agency and the Better Business Bureau.
- The company should obtain a written contract. The contract should show the company's name, address, telephone numbers (office and fax), internet address (if any), price, payment schedule, description of the product to be produced, and dates of production and distribution.
- The company should never pay for the full amount up front. Some amount should be withheld until the final production and distribution.
- Payments should always be made by check.

If the company suspects fraud or has been defrauded, then this should be reported to the local police or sheriff's office or the state attorney general's office. It would also be advisable to report it to the Better Business Bureau and the state board of accountancy, and National Fraud Information Center (NFIC) at a hotline: 1-800-876-7060. The company should provide the following evidence to the local police or sheriff's office when they become a victim of fraud:

- Original or certified copy of canceled checks to the advertiser.
- Original or copy of the contract.
- A statement or affidavit providing information about the advertiser who obtained the contract. It should provide information about dates and times of meetings, identifiers of the person (age, physical characteristics, and vehicle driven), and company (address, phone numbers, etc.).

18.22 Arson

Arson is the deliberate burning of real and personal property for gain. It also can be done for revenge or to eliminate competition. A disgruntled employee will commit arson for revenge. A competitor will do it to eliminate competition. Many arson cases are done by organized crime for the purpose of eliminating competition. A failing business will commit arson to collect insurance proceeds. This is one of the most frequent motives for arson in small businesses.

In the case of a disgruntle employee, the business owner should:

- Observe and listen to the disgruntled employee for signs of animosity and bitterness.
- Talk to coworkers about the conversations with the disgruntled employee. Most disgruntled employees will tell coworkers what they might do.
- Have the police or security guard check the place periodically, particularly during hours when the business is closed (nighttime and weekends).
- Keep all financial records in a fire proof cabinet(s). Financial records include checkbooks, backup disks/tapes of accounting records, employee records (pay and employment applications), and insurance contracts.

The above records will help in prosecuting the arsonist if arson is perpetrated and help make an insurance claim. If arson is done to reduce competition, then the company should:

- Beware of any offers to buy the company. A record of any unsolicited offers should be noted in writing. The person who makes the offer should be fully identified and his/her relation to any company being represented.
- Threats against the company should be reported immediately to law enforcement.
- Law enforcement should be supplied with as much information as possible about the person making the threat. Law enforcement will usually know who the person making the threat is and his/her involvement in illegal activities. It is best to get them involved as soon as possible.
- Keep all financial records in a fireproof cabinet(s). Financial records should include checkbooks, backup accounting records, payroll records, employment applications, and all types of contracts.

When arson is committed by a shareholder, partner, or sole proprietor, law enforcement can easily obtain records from third parties and put a case together for prosecution. The fire department can determine whether a fire is caused by arson or by something else. Insurance companies will work with law enforcement to develop a case for prosecution. In many states, if a person is killed in a fire caused by arson, the perpetrator could face homicide charges.

18.23 Attorney

See section 17.11 (Attorney Fraud) in chapter 17.

18.24 Bankers

Bank employees can be thieves in various ways. First, they can embezzle funds from the bank account using various schemes. Second, they can overcharge for their services. One way to steal from customers is to provide encoded deposit slips for their own account instead of the customer's account. Many banks have tried to prevent this by not having deposit slips displayed in the lobby. However, some customers will not have any deposit slips and will ask to obtain them from their banker. The banker then gives them some with an encoded account number not belonging to the customer. The customer makes a deposit, but the funds go to the banker. When a customer makes a deposit using "counter" deposit slips, he/she should check the encoded number on the bottom to see if it matches their account number on their checks.

Bankers also overcharge for obtaining a bank loan. In the case of car and boat loans, they will inflate the expenses of obtaining an appraisal for the used car or boat. In recent years, this has been a common practice in granting home equity loans. Also, bankers charge high rate of interest or large "points" for customers obtaining home equity loans. Points are bank fees for processing loan applications, principally, real estate loans. Customers should be aware of points over 4%. Home mortgages should not be more than 3 points over the prime rate. The prime rate is what banks charge their preferred customers. This is published daily in most newspapers across the country.

With the advent of automatic teller machines (ATMs), unscrupulous bankers have been able to embezzle funds from customer accounts. The banker can get the personal identification number (PIN) if the bank's internal controls are deficient. Also, they can obtain duplicate cards, allegedly by the customer's request. The banker, with duplicate ATM cards and PIN numbers, can access the customer's account and withdraw funds. To prevent this, the customer should review and reconcile his/her bank statements every month; otherwise, these withdrawals by the banker will go undetected. Also, federal law requires the customer to report the fraud within 30 days from the date the bank statement was issued. Otherwise, the customer will be out the loss.

18.25   Bogus Invoices

Some companies may receive invoices for office supplies, janitorial supplies, renewal ads in the Yellow Pages, or some other product or service in which the invoice amounts range from around $100 to $500 and even more. The company did not order the supplies or services. There are Yellow Pages that are produced by an out of town company that does not really service your local area. They will send bogus invoices. Local telephone companies produce Yellow Pages that are distributed by the local telephone company. Some precautions against bogus invoices are:

- If mailing looks like an invoice but is only a solicitation, then do not pay the bill unless you want the service. Title 39 USC 3001 makes it illegal to mail solicitation in the form of an invoice, bill, or statement of account due unless it conspicuously bears notice on its face that it is merely a solicitation. The U.S. Postal Regulations require a solicitation to read, "THIS IS NOT A BILL. THIS IS A SOLICITATION. YOU ARE UNDER NO OBLIGATION TO PAY THE AMOUNT STATED ABOVE UNLESS YOU ACCEPT THIS OFFER."
- The company should be checked out and the offer carefully examined.
- The company should be very skeptical of any invoice that does not have a telephone number. Nowadays, invoices are showing an internet address or an e-mail

address. Fraudulent companies do not want people to call them with any questions or complaints.

- The company should compare the account number on the invoice with your regular vendor.
- The company should not be pressured into paying for goods or services they did not order. Fraudulent companies sometimes use threats of collection or legal action to get payment for goods and services not ordered.
- The company should always use purchase orders when ordering for goods and services. These purchase orders should be matched with invoices and shipment receipts before paying the invoices.

If your company gets bogus invoices, then they should contact local law enforcement, U.S. Postal Inspector's Office, or the state attorney general's office. A solicitation whose appearance does not conform to the requirements of 39 USC 3001 constitutes prima facie evidence of violation of the federal False Representation Statute and should be reported to the local postmaster or the local postal inspector's office. If you have become a victim, then you should provide evidence:

- Copy of the check
- Copy of the invoice(s)

18.26   Calling Card Charges

Many companies have employees use calling cards when out of the office or building. When officers and employees use calling cards, they can be stolen or compromised. When the company gets their telephone bills, they find long distances charges that employees did not make. Calling cards with PIN numbers are usually not required, but they can be required and should be required. The calling card does not have to be used. It only requires the calling card number and the PIN if required. PIN numbers can be compromised by someone nearby watching the employee use the PIN numbers or by using binoculars or zoom cameras while the employee is using the calling card. Some precautions to prevent calling card fraud are:

- Employees should shield the key pad with their body and hands when dialing.
- If asked by the operator for your number, then speak softly so no one can hear you.
- Do not make any calls using a calling card when a lot of people are close by.
- The accounting clerk should verify all charges before paying.
- Do not allow PIN numbers be printed on the calling card.
- Do not allow the calling card out in plain sight.
- Do not allow anyone access to a calling card who is not authorized to use it.
- The account number should be changed immediately if there are suspicious charges.

If you know someone is using the calling card without authorization, then this should be reported to the telephone company who issued the card. If the charges are large, then a complaint should be filed with the local police or sheriff's department. Also, the company should file a complaint with the state attorney general's office.

18.27   Charitable Solicitations

Like consumers, businesses can be scammed by people soliciting charitable contributions. Many solicitations are done for police and fire associations. However, there are many other people who solicit for various organizations that are either bogus or the organizations for which they solicit funds either get little or no funds. A business should:

- Not make an immediate decision if unfamiliar with the charity.
- Get the name of the charity, the address, and the telephone number.
- Ask how the donation will be used.
- Ask for details. If the solicitation is to sponsor a children's event, then ask how many children will be participating, where they are coming from, and what the children's activities are.
- Verify the children's program and the facilities involved.
- Not immediately donate until they have verified the charity and on how the money will be spent. Many con artists ask for donations for disaster victims, for example, hurricanes, floods, earthquakes, blizzards, and other disasters.
- Check with the state attorney general's office to determine how to verify status of a charity. Some states require charities and fundraisers to be licensed.
- Check the IRS Web site and look at Publication 78 to see if the charity is recognized by the IRS. Charitable contributions are not tax deductible unless they have been approved by the IRS.
- Never give cash. Also, the business should obtain a receipt. Some charities will accept payments by credit card.

If the business becomes suspicious of a charitable solicitation, then they should call local law enforcement or the state attorney general's office. If a small business owner has become a victim, then he/she should file a complaint with the local law enforcement agency, the state attorney's office, and the state consumer protection agency. The needed information for prosecution is:

- Cancelled checks
- Identity of person and charity, including name, address, and telephone number

18.28   Cramming

Cramming is a scam by a telephone company that charges for optional services such as voice mail, paging, or Internet access that were not agreed to by the business owner. Some telephone companies contract with other companies that sell telecommunication-related services. All that is needed for the criminal is your business name and telephone number. The business should:

- Call the telephone company when someone calls and asks about your service, wants to provide a new service, or notifies you of a service charge.
- Not provide any information or agree to anything. You should get the person's name and telephone number. After the call, you should call your telephone company to verify the caller and that the purpose of the call is legitimate.
- Look at "junk mail" very carefully before it is disposed of. Some solicitations have a "negative option" that will provide an optional service unless you call the vendor to refuse it.
- Not return calls to numbers on answering machines that you do not recognize.
- The accounting clerk should know what services you have when paying the telephone bill. The clerk should question terms such as "monthly service fee."
- The telephone bill should be carefully examined each month before being paid. Some charges may reappear even after being previously reversed.

If your business is a victim of cramming, then you should report it to the local police or sheriff's office. Also, the company should advise the state attorney's office and the Federal Trade Commission. The company should provide:

- Copy of telephone bill
- Copy of payments (canceled checks)
- Copy of junk mail
- Date and times called number with answering machine

18.29 Loan Fraud

Small businesses sometimes borrow money from banks, credit unions, and finance companies. The purpose is usually to make payroll or pay vendors when cash flow is tight. Before signing the loan contract, the business owner should verify the terms of the loan for interest rate, fees, and payment terms. Unscrupulous loan companies tend to charge a high rate of interest. Also, they can charge large fees if the payment is late, even by one day. In fact, they have been known to charge a late fee when the payment was made on the due date in the afternoon. The business owner should check the date and time on the receipt. For instance, banks and finance companies will defer payment to the next day when the payment is made after a certain time in the afternoon, usually 2:00 PM. The business owner should be aware of the time when making payment on the due date. Business owner(s) should be aware of the interest rate. Many banks and finance companies will start with a low interest rate, but over time, the interest rates increase to double digits, for example, 18% or 20%. High interest rates cut into profits. It is best not to borrow funds unless it is absolutely necessary.

Unfortunately, the law is on the side of banks and finance companies. Therefore, one should consult an attorney before taking any legal action, whether civil or criminal. In recent years, title loan companies have been charging as much as 300% on loans. This has caused some state legislatures to pass laws to restrict the interest on title loan companies.

18.30   Computer Fraud

Computer fraud makes deliberate misrepresentations of the truth. They can range from simple actions to very complex schemes. The most common types of computer fraud are:

- E-mails requesting money for products and services.
- Pyramid schemes or investment schemes via the computer with the intent to take and use someone's money.
- E-mails attempting to gather personal information to be used to access and use credit card accounts, bank accounts, and social security numbers for identity theft.
- Using computers to solicit minors into sexual alliances.
- Violating copyright laws by copying information with the intent to sell the information.
- Hacking into computer systems to gather information for illegal purposes.
- Hacking into computer systems to change information, for example, grades and work reports.
- Sending computer viruses or worms with the intent to destroy or ruin someone's computer.

Even though there are stiff penalties for committing computer fraud, the laws governing against it may be difficult to enforce. Some e-mail scams for investment opportunities and get rich schemes originate outside the United States. It may be difficult to instigate investigations on foreign soil. It is advisable to follow these rules:

- Do not give personal information to anyone or to any company you have never heard of before. This includes your full name, address, phone number, credit card data, bank account data, date of birth, or information about the people in your household or company.
- Do not pay attention to get rich schemes or loan scams.
- Do not open e-mails from strangers. Install antiviral software and spam-blocking programs on your computer and on your e-mail program.
- Do not download attachments from people you do not know.
- Teach children about safe communication on the Internet to protect them from Internet predators.
- Do not keep passwords on your computer and do not use common passwords like the names of your kids, birthdays, social security number, or any guessable words.
- Never give your password to anyone.
- Business computers for small businesses should never be hooked up to the Internet. If a small business keeps all their financial records on a computer, then it can be accessed by hackers who can steal information about the business by using spyware. Hackers also can install malware, which can destroy your accounting records.
- Limit access to the computer to employees who have a need to use the computer.
- The company should have written policies about the use of company computers. The policies should state what is allowed and what is not allowed, for example, no access to porn sites.

If you have become a victim of computer fraud, then the owner should file a complaint with the local law enforcement agency. It is also advisable to file a complaint with the Federal Trade Commission and the state consumer protection agency. You will need to hire a forensic computer specialist who can obtain the evidence off the computer in cases involving spyware, viruses, or malware. In case of e-mails, you should provide copies to law enforcement.

18.31   Coupon Fraud

Many retailers and manufacturers offer coupons. They are a good promotional device and are very effective in generating sales. If one has used coupons at the grocery store, then one knows how they work. The customer presents a coupon to the cashier. She scans the coupon, resulting in a discount. The discount can be anywhere from $.50 to $1.00. For the store to get the cash, it must mail the coupons to the manufacturer or a clearinghouse. On the back of the coupon, the manufacturer lists the mailing address and states it will reimburse the store less a small charge for processing. For many stores, the amount of the reimbursement can be quite large. One can be talking hundreds of thousands of dollars. Many small retail stores will accept coupons. They bundle them up and send them to a clearinghouse. The clearinghouse sends the coupons to the manufacturer who, in turn, reimburses the store. In some cases, the clearinghouse will send the reimbursement. The three common scams involving coupons are:

- Counterfeit coupons
- Coupon certificate books
- Work-at-home scams involving coupon clipping

There are some scam artists who will counterfeit coupons. These counterfeit coupons will have indicators that can be identified. These are:

- Pictures on the coupon are fuzzy.
- Coupon text is misspelled.
- Longer-than-normal expiration dates.
- Coupon does not scan at the register.
- Physical coupons printed only on one side.
- Multiple coupons for the same product with the identical bar code numbers or PINs.
- Internet coupons missing vendor security features.
- Some manufacturers do not issue Internet print-at-home coupons.

Legitimate sources of coupons are the manufacturer's Web site or from their authorized vendors, for example, Cool Savings and Coupons, Inc.

No one is allowed to sell coupons. It is prohibited under "Terms and Conditions." Small business owners should not purchase coupons or allow any employee to do so. However, there are nonprofit organizations that are allowed to sell coupon books.

There are scam artists who hire housewives to clip coupons from newspapers and magazines. They bundle up these coupons and send them to a clearinghouse. The clearinghouse or the manufacturer will send a check to the "phony store" for the coupon amount. One law enforcement agency investigated a store front that was cutting coupons and sending them to the clearinghouse. It had eight women clipping coupons from stale newspapers. The phony store had no merchandise, just empty store shelves. They were making over $100,000 per month. They were caught because the manufacturer found the phony store never purchased any of their products.

If the small business has become a victim of a coupon fraud, then they should call their local law enforcement agency and file a complaint with the Federal Trade Commission. They should provide:

- The name of the store submitting the coupons
- Copies of the coupons submitted for payment
- Copies of all payments made to the store

18.32 Promissory Note Fraud

Sometimes businesses will accept payment for goods and services by accepting a promissory note from a third party. Some promissory notes charge a high interest rate, for example, 18%. The small business should be wary of such notes. They usually are just empty promises or maybe just falsified promissory notes. Before accepting such third party promissory note(s), the business owner should:

- Contact the company making the promissory note to find out if it is binding and true.
- Check a credit bureau for the credit standing of the company making the promissory note.
- Check with the Better Business Bureau and the Chamber of Commerce for any complaints against the company who made the promissory note.

If you have become a victim, then file a complaint with the state attorney's office against the company who gave you the promissory note. You may also have to file a civil lawsuit against the company providing the promissory note.

18.33 Vendors and Suppliers

A third source of fraud on businesses is by vendors and suppliers. In this scenario, the business is basically the consumer. The previous consumer section addressed the various areas where the consumer can be defrauded. This also applies to businesses as well; however, businesses face additional areas.

18.34 Kickbacks

Kickbacks come in various schemes. In any case, it involves an employee(s) and a vendor or supplier. One scheme involves the sale of unreported inventory, which is sold and shared by the vendor and employee. The other scheme involves the business paying for inventory at inflated prices and the employee receives a portion of the excess back. Internal controls can help prevent this, but the key indicators are:

1. The same vendor is constantly used.
2. The current vendor has prices higher than other vendors do in the same line.
3. Inventory reveals more goods in stock that cannot be accounted for.
4. Payments to vendors show more than one endorsement.
5. Manager or purchasing agent has excessive debts.
6. Purchasing agent or manager does not take any vacation time.
7. Only photocopies of invoices are provided.

18.35   Worker's Compensation

Worker's compensation fraud is the most common fraud committed. What usually begins as a minor injury on the job develops into a golden opportunity for an early retirement, a paycheck without having to work, or an income supplemented from the insurance company. False information is presented to the worker's compensation carrier. The report describes the claimant as totally or partially disabled and either unable to work at all or only able to work part time. In many cases, these schemes are enhanced with the assistance of an unscrupulous doctor who, for an extra fee, provides a false diagnosis of the claimant's condition and fabricates medical records for phony treatments. Greedy claimants have collected worker's compensation benefits and still work at full- or part-time jobs elsewhere. Some claimants use another name or alias. Workman's compensation claims cause businesses to pay higher rates for workman's compensation insurance. Therefore, fraud is perpetrated on both the business and the insurance carrier. The indicators are:

1. The employee has a history of prior worker's compensation claims.
2. Injuries are soft tissue kinds.
3. The employee claims to be incapacitated but is seen engaging in activities that require full mobility.

18.36   Surety Bonds

Surety and performance bonds guarantee that certain events will or will not occur. A performance bond guarantees the completion of a construction project; whereas a surety bond protects the public against damages sustained on a construction project. Certain insurance agents specialize in this kind of market and earn an excellent income. Others use the bond market to generate a far greater income by issuing worthless bonds. In this scheme, the unscrupulous salesperson manufactures worthless paper, which is issued to the consumer, usually for high-risk coverage. This might include bridge construction, building demolition, fireworks displays, transportation or storage of explosives, or other potentially hazardous situations. The agent issues the bonds in hopes that no claims will be made. If a claim is made, the agent pays the claim with available funds from other clients, uses delay tactics, or skips out. The indicators of fraudulent agents are:

1. No bond or endorsements are received from the agent.
2. The bond is a photocopy or the bond papers bear no company watermark.
3. The agent requests payments by cash, money order, or cashier's check made payable to him/her or to a company other than the insurance carrier.
4. Checks are returned, having been cashed or deposited to the agent's personal account.
5. The insurance company allegedly issuing the coverage is not authorized to sell insurance in the state or is unknown to the state insurance department.

18.37   Banks

Criminals like to target banks for various fraud schemes because that is where the money is located. Also, insiders cause many bank frauds. Banks offer many types of services. Each of these services is an area that criminals can target for fraud. The Federal Deposit Insurance Corporation (FDIC) has identified the following danger signs:

1. Loan participations
   a. Excessive participation of loans among closely related banks, correspondent banks, and branches or departments of the lending bank.
   b. Absence of a formal participation agreement.
   c. Poor or incomplete loan documentation.
   d. Investing in out-of-territory participation.
   e. Reliance on third-party guaranties.
   f. Large pay down or payoff of previously classified loans.
   g. Some indication that there may be informal repurchase agreements on some participations.
   h. Lack of independent credit analysis.
   i. Volume of loan participations sold is high in relation to the size of the bank's own loan portfolio.
   j. Evidence of lapping of loan participations. For example, the sale of loan participation in an amount equal to or greater than, and at or about the same time as, participation that has matured or is about to mature.
   k. Disputes between participating banks over documentation, payments, or any other aspect of the loan participation agreements.
2. Secured lending, real estate, and other type of collateral
   a. Lack of independent appraisals.
   b. Out-of-territory loans.
   c. Evidence of land flips. A land flip is a process in which individuals or businesses buy and sell properties among themselves, each time inflating the sales price to give the appearance of rapidly increasing property values. The mortgage amounts increase with each purchase until, in many cases, the amounts of the mortgages greatly exceed the actual values of the mortgaged property.

   d. Loans with unusual terms and conditions.
   e. Poor or incomplete documentation.
   f. Loans that are unusual considering the size of the bank and the level of exper-
      tise of its lending officers.
   g. Heavy concentration of loans to a single project or to individuals related to the
      project.
   h. Concentrations of loans to local borrowers with the same or similar collateral
      that is located outside the bank's trade area.
   i. Asset swaps. Sale or other real estate or other distressed assets to a broker at an
      inflated price in return for favorable terms and conditions on a new loan to a
      borrower introduced to the bank by the broker. The new loan is usually secured
      by property of questionable value and the borrower is in a weak financial condi-
      tion. Borrower and collateral are often outside the bank's normal trade area.
   j. Failure to consider the risk of decline in collateral value.
3. Insider transactions
   a. Financing the sale of insider assets to third parties.
   b. From a review of personal financial statement, evidence that an insider is lend-
      ing his/her own funds to others.
   c. Improper fees to major shareholders.
   d. Frequent changes of auditors or legal counsel.
   e. Unusual or unjustified fluctuations in insider or officer's personal financial
      statements or statements of their interests.
   f. Frequent appearances of suspense items relating to accounts of insiders, offi-
      cers, and employees.
   g. An insider's borrowing money from someone who borrows from the bank.
   h. Purchase of bank assets by an insider.
   i. A review of the bank's fixed assets or other asset accounts reveals that the bank
      owns expensive artwork, expensive automobiles, yachts, airplanes, or other
      unusual items that are out of character for a bank of its size and location.
   j. A review of the bank's expense accounts reveals expenditures for attorney's fees,
      accountant's fees, broker's fees, and so forth that do not appear to correspond
      to services rendered to the bank or that appear unusually high for services
      rendered.
   k. Heavy lending to the bank's shareholders, particularly in conjunction with
      recent capital injections.
   l. A large portion of the insider's bank stock has been pledged to secure debts to
      other financial institutions.
   m. An insider has past due obligations at other financial institutions.
   n. An insider is receiving all or part of the proceeds of loans granted to others.
   o. An insider is receiving special consideration or "favors" from bank customers.
      For example, an insider may receive favorable lease terms or favorable purchase
      terms on an automobile obtained from a bank customer.
4. Credit card and electronic funds transfer
   a. Lack of separation of duties between the card-issuing function and the issuance
      of a PIN.
   b. Poor control of unissued cards and PINs.
   c. Poor control of returned mail.

    d. Customer complaints.

    e. Poor control of credit limit increases.

    f. Poor control of name and address changes.

    g. Frequent malfunction of payment authorization system.

    h. Unusual delays in receipt of cards and PINs by customers.

    i. Bank does not limit amount of cash that a customer can extract from an ATM in a given day.

    j. Evidence that customer credit card purchases have been intentionally structured by a merchant to keep individual amounts below the "floor limit" to avoid the need for transaction approval.

5. Wire transfers

    a. Indications of frequent overrides of established approval authority and other internal controls.

    b. Intentional circumvention of approval authority by splitting transactions.

    c. Wire transfers to and from bank secrecy haven countries.

    d. Frequent large wire transfers to persons who do not have an account relationship with the bank.

    e. In a linked financing situation, a borrower's request for immediate wire transfer of loan proceeds to one or more banks where the funds for brokered deposits originated.

    f. Large or frequent wire transfers against uncollected funds.

    g. Wire transfers involving cash where the amount exceeds $10,000.

    h. Inadequate control of password access.

    i. Customer complaints and frequent error conditions.

6. Offshore transactions

    a. Loans made on the strength of a borrower's financial statement when the statement reflects major investments and income from businesses incorporated in bank secrecy countries.

    b. Loans to offshore companies.

    c. Loans secured by obligations of offshore banks.

    d. Transactions involving an offshore "shell" bank whose name may be very similar to the name of a major legitimate institution.

    e. Frequent wire transfers of funds to and from bank secrecy countries.

    f. Offers of multimillion dollar deposits at below market rates from a confidential source to be sent from an offshore bank or somehow guaranteed by an offshore bank through a letter, telex, or other "official" communication.

    g. Presence of telex or facsimile equipment in a bank where the usual and customary business activity would not appear to justify the need for such equipment.

7. Third-party obligations

    a. Incomplete documentation.

    b. Loans secured by obligations of offshore banks.

    c. Lack of credit information on third-party obligor.

    d. Financial statements reflect concentrations of closely held companies or businesses that lack audited financial statements to support their value.

8. Corporate culture ethics

    a. Absence of a code of ethics.

    b. Absence of a clear policy on conflicts of interest.

    c. Lack of oversight by the bank's board of directors, particularly outside directors.

    d. Absence of planning, training, hiring, and organizational policies.

    e. Absence of clearly defined authorities and lack of definition of the responsibilities that go along with authorities.

    f. Lack of independence of management in acting on recommended corrections.

9. Miscellaneous

    a. Indications of frequent overrides of internal controls or intentional circumvention of bank policy.

    b. Unresolved exceptions of frequently recurring exceptions on exception reports.

    c. Out-of-balance conditions.

    d. Purpose of loan is not recorded.

    e. Proceeds of loan are used for a purpose other than purpose recorded.

    f. A review of checks paid against uncollected funds indicates that a customer is offsetting checks with deposits of the same or similar amount and maintains a relatively constant account balance, usually small in relation to the amount of activity and the size of the transactions.

18.38 Summary

The best things that businesses can do to prevent fraud are:

1. Establish and adhere to high moral and ethical standards by management.
2. Prosecute any employee who commits fraud. Failure to do so will only encourage other employees to do the same.
3. Establish and adhere to internal controls.
4. Install and use various detection devices for customer-oriented business. For areas where customers and most employees have no business or need, restrict access to only certain employees.

Money Laundering

19

19.1 Introduction

Money laundering was not considered a crime until the 1980s when Congress passed a series of laws. Organized crime groups have laundered gains from illegal activities for many years. However, it has not been until the 1980s when laws were passed to address the money laundering activities. Fraud examiners are called on to unravel various money laundering schemes. There are many accounting and auditing techniques that can be used to detect these schemes, and the fraud examiner should be well versed in their use.

19.2 Definition

Money laundering is defined as "washing" proceeds to disguise their true source. The source of these proceeds can be from either legal or illegal activities. The things that a money launderer wants to accomplish are to move money, reduce its volume, and change its character to allow for spending or investing, while sheltering it from detection and taxation. All of these actions are forms of money laundering. While this occurs quite often in drug trafficking and other organized crime operations, it is not limited to that area. It also occurs in bookmaking, loan sharking, skimming business receipts, and many others. With the passage of the Patriot Act in 2001, financing terrorism has been included in money laundering. The Patriot Act has also increased the civil and criminal penalties for money laundering.

19.3 History

Congress began a long series of steps to combat money laundering. The first step was the passage of the Bank Secrecy Act in 1970. Its purpose was to identify money launderers and tax evaders. In 1984, Congress passed the Deficit Reduction Act, commonly known as the Tax Reform Act of 1984. Congress added Internal Revenue Code Section 6050I to enable the Internal Revenue Service (IRS) to discover unreported income from legal or illegal sources by identifying taxpayers involved in large cash transactions. Section 6050I requires information returns to be filed by all trades or businesses for cash transactions over $10,000. Using Form 8300 does this. It further requires that these forms be filed within 15 days after the cash is received. It also requires the filing of Form 8300 when all payments aggregate to more than $10,000. Also, the reporting requirement is imposed to any receipt of cash in connection with a trade or business whether or not the receipt constitutes income in the trade or business. Cash is defined as coin and currency of the United States or any other country that is circulated in and are customarily used and accepted as money in the country in which it is issued. Cash does not include bank checks, traveler's checks, bank drafts, wire transfers, or other negotiable or monetary instruments.

In 1986, Congress passed the Anti-Drug Abuse Act. This act subjects persons to criminal liability for knowingly participating in any laundering of money. It added money laundering schemes to include wire transfers. It increased fines and penalties and promotes the international exchange of information.

In 1988, Congress passed the Omnibus Drug Bill II, commonly called the Anti-Drug Abuse Act of 1988. This bill forbids financial institutions from issuing or selling bank checks, traveler's checks, or cashier's checks in connection with cash of $3000 or more unless the person has an account. It also requires additional record keeping requirements. Additional penalties are imposed on financial institution officers, directors, and employees. The Treasury Department is required to negotiate with foreign countries.

In 2001, Congress passed the USA PATRIOT Act. This act has increased penalties, civil and criminal, for money laundering activities. It has also imposed requirements on various financial institutions. For U.S. banks, it requires their foreign correspondent banks and subsidiaries to maintain information about their customers. A U.S. bank cannot administer, manage, or establish a correspondent bank in a foreign country that does not have a physical presence in any country. The Patriot Act has allowed financial institutions to share information about their customers with other banks.

19.4   Government Reporting Forms

The laws passed by Congress require various forms to be filed with the Internal Revenue Service at the Detroit Computing Center in Detroit, Michigan. Financial Crimes Enforcement Network, called FinCen, is empowered to assess penalties for failure to file or to file fraudulent forms. Some forms are required to be filed with the Internal Revenue Service.

19.4.1   FinCen Form 104

FinCen Form 104 is the former Form 4789 Currency Transaction Report (CTR). This form is to be filled out by financial institutions that report currency transactions exceeding $10,000 to the Treasury Department, thus its name Currency Transaction Report. Financial institutions are broadly defined and have been expanded since. Some of these institutions that are defined as financial institutions are:

1. Banks and trust companies
2. Thrift institutions
3. Brokers and dealers in securities
4. Pawn brokers
5. Currency exchangers
6. Check cashing stores
7. Auto dealers
8. Real estate businesses
9. U.S. Postal Service money orders

10. Issuers, sellers, or redeemers of money orders, traveler checks, and cashier checks
11. Transmitters of funds
12. Telegraph companies
13. Casinos
14. Loan companies

These financial institutions must file these reports within the 15th calendar day from the date of the transaction. Also, the financial institution must retain copies or maintain a log of these transactions for five years. Currency is defined to include coins or paper of the United States or any other country, but not negotiable instruments.

19.4.2   FinCen Form 105

FinCen Form 105 is the former Form 4790 Report of International Transportation of Currency or Monetary Instruments (CMIR). Any person who transports cash or bearer instruments into or out of the United States requires this form. The title of this form is Report of International Transportation of Currency or Monetary Instruments (CMIR). The CMIR is to be filed at the time of entry or departure from the United States with U.S. Customs. Monetary instruments is defined, as amended, to include:

1. U.S. and foreign coin and currency
2. Bearer negotiable instruments (personal checks, business checks, bank checks, cashier's checks, promissory notes, and money orders)
3. Bearer stock and securities

Transportation is defined to include physical mailing and shipping as well as carrying.

19.4.3   Form 90-22.1

Form 90-22.1 is the Report of Foreign Bank Accounts (FBAR). This form requires a person to report any transaction that they have with a foreign financial institution. Accounts with domestic branches of foreign banks are exempt from this requirement. The report requires the aggregation of separate accounts regardless of whether they are located in one or more foreign countries. This form is required to be filed by June 30 of each calendar year with respect to foreign financial accounts exceeding $10,000 during the previous calendar year. This requirement is in addition to the block on Form 1040, Schedule B.

19.4.4   Form 8300

Form 8300 is the Report of Cash Payments over $10,000 Received in a Trade or Business. This form requires any business that receives more than $10,000 in cash in one or more related transactions. Transactions are related even if they are longer than 24 hours. Example: A jewelry dealer sells a diamond ring for $18,000. He receives $9000 and 2 weeks later gets the remaining $9000. At the time of receiving the second $9000, the jewelry dealer must file the 8300 within fifteen (15) days.

19.4.5 FinCen Form 103

FinCen Form 103 is the former Form 8362 Currency Transaction Report by Casinos. This form requires that casinos in the U.S. report cash received or disbursed of more than $10,000 in a gaming day. Multiple transactions must be treated as a single transaction. The report must be filed by the 15th day following the transaction.

19.4.6 FinCen Form 107

FinCen Form 107 is the former Form TD F 90-22.55 Registration of Money Services Business. Any money service business must register by filling out this form and sending it to the IRS Detroit Computing Center within 180 days after the business begin operations. Money service businesses must renew their registration every 2 years on or before December 31. Money service businesses include currency dealers or exchangers totaling more than $1000 for any one customer on any day; check cashers who cash checks totaling more than $1000 for any one customer on any day; issuers of traveler's checks and money orders of more than $1000 for any one customer; seller's of traveler's checks, money orders, or stored value who sell more than $1000 for any one customer on any day; redeemers of traveler's checks, money orders, or stored value of more than $1000 for any one customer.

19.4.7 Form 3520

Form 3520 is the Annual Return to Report Transactions with Foreign Trusts and Receipt of Certain Foreign Gifts. This form is due at the same time that the Individual Income Tax Return is due or filed. A joint 3520 can only be filed when a joint return is filed. This form goes to the Internal Revenue Service Center in Philadelphia, Pennsylvania 19255.

19.4.8 FinCen Form 9022-47

FinCen Form 9022-47 is the Suspicious Activity Report (SAR). All financial institutions are required to file a suspicious activity report when they suspect violations. This form helps the institution in providing the necessary information. The report is to be filed no later than 30 days after the date of initial detection of facts; however, an additional 30 days can be used to identify a suspect. The report is not required for robberies and burglaries that are reported to local authorities. This does not alleviate filing the CTR. There are special SAR forms for brokers, casinos, and money service businesses (FinCen Form 109).

19.5 Forms and Instructions

The preceding forms are provided in this chapter. The instructions for the forms are also provided. The instructions provide more detailed information about the forms and provide more information.

19.5.1   Penalties

There are penalties for not filing or filing false forms to the government. The penalties are divided into two categories: civil and criminal. Both civil and criminal penalties for each form are summarized.

1. *FinCen Form 104, formerly Form 4789.* The civil and criminal penalties for failure to file or filing false forms are:
   a. *Civil.* For any willful violation, a civil penalty of not more than $100,000 involved in the transaction or $25,000. The penalty can be assessed upon the person or institution for the amount of coins or currency involved in the transaction but shall be reduced by any forfeiture. A separate violation occurs for each day the violation continues and at each office, branch, or place of business.
   b. *Criminal.* For any willful violation of failure to file or filing false reports shall be fined upon conviction not more than $250,000 or be imprisoned not more than 10 years, or both. If the criminal acts are committed as part of a pattern of illegal activity involving transactions exceeding $100,000 in any 12-month period, then the penalty, upon conviction, may be a fine not more than $500,000 or imprisonment not more than 10 years, or both.
2. *FinCen Form 105, formerly Form 4790.* The civil and criminal penalties for failure to file or filing false forms are the same, both civil and criminal. A fine of not more than $500,000 and imprisonment of not more than 10 years can be imposed. Also, the currency or monetary instrument may be subject to seizure and forfeiture.
3. *Form 8300.* The penalties for willful failure to file or filing false reports are as follows:
   a. *Civil.* If the person or business fails to file or provide the required statement to those named in the Form 8300, then the minimum penalty is $25,000 or the amount of cash received.
   b. *Criminal.* The criminal penalties for willful failure to file, filing false or fraudulent forms, stopping or trying to stop filing, and setting up, helping to set up, or trying to set up a transaction in a way that would make it seem unnecessary to file, can be fined up to $250,000 ($500,000 for corporations) or sentenced up to 5 years, or both.
4. *Form 90-22.1. Report of Foreign Bank and Financial Accounts.* The civil and criminal penalties for failure of individuals or businesses for not filing or filing false reports are:
   a. *Civil.* For failure to file or filing false reports, the penalty is $25,000 or the amount of the transaction not to exceed $100,000.
   b. *Criminal.* Any person or business that violates this provision shall be fined not more than $250,000 or be imprisoned not more than 5 years, or both. In cases of a pattern of illegal activity involving transactions exceeding $100,000 in any 12-month period, the criminal penalties, upon conviction, may be a fine not more than $500,000 or imprisonment not more than 10 years, or both.
5. *FinCen Form 103, formerly Form 8362. Currency Transaction Report by Casinos.* The civil and criminal penalties for failure to file or filing false forms by casinos are:
   a. *Civil.* For any willful violation, a civil penalty of not more than $100,000 involved in the transaction or $25,000. The penalty can be assessed upon the

person or institution for the amount of coins or currency involved in the transaction but shall be reduced by any forfeiture. A separate violation occurs for each day the violation continues and at each office, branch, or place of business.

  b. *Criminal.* For any willful violation of failure to file or filing false reports shall be fined upon conviction not more than $250,000 or be imprisoned not more than 5 years, or both. If the criminal acts are committed as part of a pattern of illegal activity involving transactions exceeding $100,000 in any 12-month period, then the penalty, upon conviction, may be a fine not more than $500,000 or imprisonment not more than 10 years, or both.

6. *FinCen Form 107. Registration of Money Services Business.* Failure to register a money service business can result in penalties as follows:
  a. *Civil.* Any person who fails to register, keep records, or maintain agent lists shall be liable for a penalty of $5000 for each violation.
  b. *Criminal.* The criminal penalty is a fine and imprisonment up to 5 years.
7. *Form 3520. Annual Return to Report Transactions with Foreign Trusts and Receipt of Certain Foreign Gifts.* A penalty generally applies if Form 3520 is not timely filed or if the information is incomplete or incorrect. Generally, the penalty is one of the following:
  a. Thirty-five percent of the gross value of any property transferred to a foreign trust for failure by a U.S. transferor to report the transfer.
  b. Thirty-five percent of the gross value of the distributions received from a foreign trust for failure by a U.S. person to report receipt of the distribution.
  c. Five percent of the amount of certain foreign gifts for each month for which the failure to report continues (not to exceed 25%).

If a foreign trust has a U.S. owner and the trust fails to file the required annual reports on trust activities and income, the U.S. owner is subject to a penalty equal to 5% of the gross value of the portion of the trust's assets treated as owned by the U.S. person.

19.6 Schemes

Suppose a person receives income, whether legal or illegal, and wants to hide it from others. The person can hide it under his/her mattress or elsewhere, but that would leave the person vulnerable to theft and would not get the benefit of spending or investing the money. If the proceeds are in small denominations, then the person has the problem of exchanging the smaller bills for larger bills. Spending large bills could cause unwanted attention to the person. Also, a large amount of bills is cumbersome to carry or transport. A million dollars in $20 bills weighs 113 pounds and can fill nearly four file storage boxes. The person usually starts to convert the money to readily acceptable forms (e.g., money orders and traveler's checks). In many cases, the person will open more than one bank account and make frequent deposits into them. There is usually more than one bank involved. "Smurfing" is the term used for a person making deposits into various accounts and banks on the same or subsequent days. "Structuring" is the term used for a person making more than one deposit into the same or various bank accounts at the same bank or financial institution. If the person has no legitimate source of income, then the person will want to acquire a business so that money can be run through it. The business would pay a salary or show it loaning the person money. The person may even transfer money to foreign bank accounts with bank secrecy laws.

A financial institution can be involved in money laundering. A drug dealer drops off cash at the bank. The bank wires the funds to an offshore account, usually to a certificate of deposit. Then the bank makes a loan to the drug dealer and gives him back some of the cash or deposits it into a bank account. The certificate of deposit is the collateral for the loan. The Bank of Credit and Commerce International (BCCI) was convicted of this scheme in the United States.

Another scheme is to buy gold and diamonds. The dealer, of course, does not file any 8300 forms. Gold and diamonds are not as bulky as currency; thus, they can be transported easily.

Sophisticated money launderers will deposit cash in offshore bank accounts. The bank account is in a corporation name. The corporation, in turn, issues bearer bonds or stock. Bearer bonds or stock can be used the same way as cash. They can be redeemed for the face amount. The face value can be for large amounts, such as $100,000 or more. A drug dealer can pay for his/her drugs using bearer bonds. In the United States, bearer bonds and stock are not legal but are legal in some countries including some tax haven countries.

19.7   Hawala

A hawala is a money transfer without the movement of money. A person gives funds to another person (called a hawala) for transfer to another country. The hawala sends a fax or calls his/her contact in another country to provide funds to someone there. The person gives the funds to the other person in the other country. The hawala in this country charges a commission for making the transfer and keeps a record of the amount owed to the person in the other country. The person in the other country shows a receivable on their books. In time, the two hawala's books will be balanced by either settling up or by other transactions. This scheme requires a great amount of trust between the two hawalas.

19.8   Business

Money laundering in businesses involves three principal methods. They are:

1. *Balance sheet.* Balance sheet money laundering encompasses making cash deposits into a business bank account. The person writes checks using that money. The deposits are credited to shareholder loans or an equivalent account and the checks are charges against shareholder loans. The taxpayer avoids paying income taxes on the funds in this case.
2. *Overstating revenue.* The person makes deposits into the business bank accounts and charges it to legitimate income. The person uses the funds to pay himself/herself or relative's salaries or expenses.
3. *Overstating expenses.* In this case, the person pays wages for nonexistent employees or pays for supplies or services that it never receives. Another version is to pay

cash for items at a discount. The discount is not recorded on the invoice. The books show the full price paid for the item.

4. *Shifting of income.* Another method used by criminals is to shift income offshore. For terrorists, they want to shift income to the United States. This scheme involves selling goods to an offshore entity at below market value. The goods are sold in the offshore country at market value. In essence, the income is shifted to offshore. Terrorists sell goods to an offshore entity at market or above prices, and the income is transferred to the United States. In some cases, the organization in the states is a nonprofit entity, so no income is reported and no taxes are paid.

19.9   Trusts

Some criminals use trusts to hide funds or assets. It can be as simple as having an individual, such as an attorney, hold title to real or personal property in their name as "trustee." Trusts can be complex. The trustee holds income-producing property, real or personal, for the grantor. The trustee collects the income and pays the expenses for the trust property. The trustee will charge fees for this service, usually based on the time spent in administering the trust. The trustee will file tax returns for the trust and pay the taxes. The grantor of the trust can also be the beneficiary. In some cases, the trust does not pay taxes but passes the income down to grantors or beneficiaries. The trustee can be almost anyone. They can be a bank or trust company, insurance company, an attorney, accountant, relative, or close friend.

The fraud examiner must view trusts in terms of hiding assets by the criminals. The difficulty with trusts is connecting the trust and its assets to the grantor or beneficiary. Trust agreements are not recorded in public records for the most part. They are generally not filed with federal or state tax authorities, except during tax examinations. Therefore, other investigative techniques have to be used. Criminals like to and want to hide ownership of real or personal property; however, they do not want to relinquish control over the property. Fraud examiners and law enforcement must look to the control factor for uncovering hidden ownership. Observing the following can do this:

1. The criminal constantly uses the property, while it is titled to a trustee.
2. Title to the property is transferred to the trust, but the liability is still retained by the grantor.
3. The grantor has inadequate income history to have allowed for such cash accumulation or asset purchase.
4. The grantor and trustee sign documents jointly for the property and related liabilities.
5. The grantor transfers property to the trust during a bond hearing after just being arrested for criminal activities.
6. The grantor is present when the purchase is made.
7. The grantor has possession of personal property titled to the trust.
8. The grantor pays rent to the trust for use of trust property. Usually, the grantor pays rent either at below or higher than market values in the same area.
9. The grantor has to provide funds to the trust to keep it liquid or stable.

10. The grantor owned the property prior to the trust. The grantor made the transfer prior to his/her criminal activities so as to have future or current benefit of the property or his/her children to have an inheritance.

19.10 Nominees

A nominee is a person designated to act for another as an agent or trustee. Criminals use nominees to hide assets. In some cases, nominees are involved with the criminals in the illegal activities. Another version of nominees is called the alter ego. Alter ego refers to entities, corporate, and business entities that are intermixed so that their income and assets are not separable. The fraud examiner must look to the possibility of criminals using nominees and alter egos (when businesses are involved) for hiding assets. The indicators of nominees and alter egos are as follows:

1. A close or suspected relationship exists between the parties. These include:
   a. Blood or marriage relationship
   b. Length of association
   c. Common address
   d. Same corporate stockholders, directors, officers, employees, attorney, accountant, etc.
2. Inadequate consideration by nominee/alter ego is given for asset purchased from the criminal. Examples include:
   a. An asset transfer without a transfer of the matching liabilities.
   b. Inadequate deed stamps.
   c. Book value transfer of an appreciated property.
   d. Use of the term "gift" on vehicle title transfers (usually done to evade state sales tax).
   e. Payment of a long-term, low interest note without adequate security.
   f. Alleged consideration was for an "assumption of liabilities" by the purchaser. If so were the assumed liabilities less than the value of the transferred property and did the criminal continue to satisfy the liabilities?
3. The nominee/alter ego does not have the ability to pay for the asset. Examples:
   a. Inadequate income history reported by the nominee to have allowed such cash accumulation.
   b. Interest deductions on tax returns showing large debts of nominee/alter ego.
   c. Lack of dividend/interest income sources.
   d. Nominee is too young to have accumulated funds.
   e. Financial statements in obtaining credit cards or applying for bank loans, opening bank accounts, or making installment purchase show inability to acquire asset.
   f. Cosigning by the criminal may show that the nominee's credit record or the criminal's collateral was responsible for the loan.
   g. There is a lack of a "paper trail" through the bank/savings account.
   h. The nominee is on welfare or social security.
4. Prove the ability of the criminal to have paid for the asset. Examples:
   a. Likely source of income from illegal acts

     b. Criminal's lifestyle

     c. Liquidations by the criminal prior to the nominee's purchase of an asset

     d. Criminal was present when the seller received the proceeds

5. Prove the ability of the nominee to operate the asset. Examples:

     a. Inexperience or lack of education of nominee

     b. Complexity, special skill, or experience required by nominee and possessed by the criminal

     c. No business or occupational license by nominee

     d. Lack of physical strength or stamina by nominee

     e. Lack of zoning clearance with the nominee's alter ego location

6. Prove continued use and possession by the criminal. Examples:

     a. Asset at criminal's address

     b. Insurance shows criminal as operator or occupant

     c. Criminal physically drives, occupies, repairs, maintains, etc., the asset

     d. No change of asset use after the supposed transfer

     e. The keys (to car, house, safety deposit box, business, etc.) in criminal's or his/her attorney's possession

     f. Criminal uses but pays no rent to nominee or pays grossly excessive rent.

7. The criminal maintains control. Examples:

     a. Criminal's senior status in the family.

     b. Criminal's supervision, hiring, firing of employees and officers.

     c. Criminal has access and signatory authority over nominee's bank accounts.

     d. Criminal makes contracts or orders repairs for nominee's assets.

     e. Personal expenses or "perks" are by the nominee.

8. The nominee knew or should have known of skimming or other unclean funds. Examples:

     a. Spouse or other close relative can almost never claim ignorance, especially if they work in the business with the criminal.

     b. Related corporations have the same officers, accountants, employees, etc., and are in an awkward position to allege ignorance.

     c. Illegal use of corporation is a valid ground for piercing the corporate veil or dissolving the corporation.

9. The nominee fails to observe corporate formalities.

     a. Improper incorporation

     b. Undercapitalization

     c. Failure to file tax returns, federal and state

     d. Acting outside corporate charter

     e. Failure to obtain various tax numbers

     f. Failure to file tax returns

     g. Failure to maintain corporate books and minutes

     h. Failure to obtain stock subscription payments from stockholders

     i. Failure to appoint officers

     j. Failure of directors to meet

     k. Loss of charter or dissolution by proclamation

     l. Failure to register in state

     m. Commingling of assets

10. The criminal has continued financial liability in addition to the nominee financial liability. Examples:
    a. Mortgage or installment debt is still in criminal's name
    b. State or local property tax records in criminal's name
    c. Utility bills (phone, water, and electric) in criminal's name
    d. Rent paid by criminal
    e. Criminal co-signed note
11. The nominee committed perjury, propensity for concealment, or inherent untrustworthiness. Examples:
    a. Nominee makes misrepresentations either orally or on financial statements.
    b. Nominee has a criminal record or pending charges.
    c. Foreign corporation (offshore) loans or invests funds to the nominee or corporation.
12. The criminal has the propensity, history, or habit to use fraudulent devices. Examples:
    a. The criminal has an illegal occupation.
    b. Past history of successful or unsuccessful fraudulent transfers.
    c. Lies to law enforcement.
13. Times shows fraud. Examples:
    a. There is extreme haste in incorporating, in closing on real estate, or in weekend/holiday asset transfers.
    b. The transfer is prior to incorporation or while the corporation is inactive or dissolved.
    c. The transfer or sale occurs in the middle of busy or lucrative season or before contract completion and right to receive payment.
    d. Nominee acquires an asset just after the criminal obtains money from sale of a different asset.
14. There are purchase or transfer irregularities. Examples:
    a. Undocumented or unrecorded transfer.
    b. "Oral" agreement.
    c. The purchase contract is signed by the criminal, but title taken by nominee.
    d. The criminal sells or conveys to nominee without:
        1) Appraisal
        2) Competitive bid
        3) Advertising
        4) Showing or exhibiting property to nominee
        5) Nominee never learning about the conveyance
        6) Advising mortgage holder
        7) No cash to criminal, only a note
        8) A written rental agreement for future use by the criminal.
15. Use admissions of ownership by the criminal. Examples:
    a. Failure by criminal to report gain or loss on alleged sale of asset to nominee to tax authorities.
    b. Criminal lists nominee assets on financial statements given to creditors.
    c. Statements of ownership to customers, suppliers, or neighbors.
    d. Testimony in divorce proceedings as to ownership.

    e. Statements under oath of ownership on homestead exemption forms or required contractual disclosure statements in litigation against third parties, on license applications, etc.

    f. Statements to accountants, employees who are fired, or to spouses or relatives.

19.11   Offshore

More sophisticated money launderers like to smuggle currency offshore and deposit into a foreign bank account. These funds are later wired back to the United States as foreign investment in some form, for example, loans or capital investments. Tax authorities and accountants call most of these foreign countries as tax havens. Tax haven countries are those that have the following characteristics:

1. *No or low taxes.* Tax haven countries have either no or low taxes, which attract deposits and capital investments.

2. *No exchange controls.* Tax haven countries have no monetary exchange controls. A person can transfer funds in and out of a tax haven country without any interference from local authorities. Also, funds can be exchanged from one currency to another. Funds can be transferred quickly in and out of the country by electronic means. Additionally, currency can be converted to various commodities, for example, gold, silver, and platinum.

3. *Bank facilities.* Tax haven countries attract many foreign and domestic banks. They encourage banks to have modern facilities and provide the services offered in other industrialized countries. Tax haven countries have banking laws that control and encourage the industry.

4. *Bank secrecy.* Tax haven countries have bank secrecy laws or customs. They do this primarily to help people conceal the fact that they have accounts in that country. Tax authorities in other countries are not allowed any information about people's bank accounts in the tax haven country. However, some tax haven countries will provide banking information if the request clearly shows violations that are not related to taxes. Some tax haven countries do not want the image of being a haven for criminals (e.g., drug traffickers).

5. *Stability.* Tax haven countries have both good political and economic stability. People do not want to have bank accounts in countries that are politically or economically unstable. Why should someone deposit funds in a country that is being ravished by civil or guerrilla warfare?

6. *Communications.* Tax haven countries have good communication facilities. This is necessary for people to be able to transfer funds back and forth. Large amounts of money can be wired from one country to another very rapidly. If communication facilities were not available, then this would not be possible. Criminals have to have easy access to funds.

7. *Corruption.* Tax haven countries have to be free of corruption. People do not like to make payoffs to public officials for hiding or maintaining funds in that country. However, organized crime organizations like to make payoffs to public officials for them to ignore or not interfere with their operations.

Multinational corporations use tax haven countries to avoid various taxes as well as route funds to subsidiaries. This is legal. Avoiding taxes is legal; evading taxes is illegal. Some elements use tax havens to hide their gains or assets. Other people use tax havens for investment. The difference between hiding gains or assets and investment can be a very fine line. Some people will form a corporation offshore and deposit funds into a bank account for that corporation. A case where this is legal is when a professional forms an insurance company offshore. The professional writes checks to the foreign insurance corporation and expenses it on the business books. Policies are written for malpractice or liability insurance from the offshore insurance company. If a claim is made, the offshore corporation pays the claim. This is legal. However, it would be illegal if the funds are solely used to hide gains or assets and no claims are paid. Also, if the funds are small, the amount of coverage or claim would strongly indicate hiding assets, especially if no claims are made or the policy is not issued or disclosed. The ratio of premiums to the face amount of coverage should be compared to industry averages. If premiums are lower or coverage is higher than industry averages, then this indicates money laundering.

19.12   Offshore Entities

When a fraud examiner comes across an offshore entity, a determination has to be made as to whether this entity is legitimate. The following factors can help determine this:

1. *No payments or repayments.* The subject has no evidence of making payments or repayments. The offshore entity does not loan or provide products or services without some compensation or repayments. The absence of any payment or repayments clearly indicates a shell entity.
2. *Not U.S. registered.* Under most states, foreign entities cannot do business in that state unless they are registered with the appropriate agency. Failure to get registered bars their legal rights in that state. If an offshore entity makes a loan to a customer but is not registered in that state, then it does not have any recourse if the customer fails to make payments.
3. *Failure to file tax returns.* If the offshore entity does business in the United States, it is required to file income tax returns, even if no tax liability exists. Foreign entities are required to pay taxes on income earned in the United States.
4. *No place of business.* If the offshore entity has no business location in this country or in the country of origin, then this is a shell entity. Tax haven countries commonly have entities that are registered. Only the registered agent or representative is listed on the country's register. However, when the fraud examiner tries to find such entity, the entity is nothing more than a book or piece of paper in an attorney's office. It has no business location either in the United States or the country of origin.

If a financial transaction meets all or most of the above criteria, then this is a sham entity. It only serves to cover up the true source and ownership of the funds used. Many criminals and organized crime groups use this scheme to hide income and assets. In one case, a drug trafficker borrowed $800,000 from a Panamanian corporation to finance a house. The mortgage was duly filed in the county public records. The Panamanian corporation had no business location either in the United States or in Panama nor was it registered in the United States. Further investigation revealed that the corporation was a shell. In another case, an individual borrowed funds to finance a house. The mortgage was written so that the borrower would not have to make repayments on the mortgage until 30 years later when principal and interest was due. The individual was 60 years old. Also, the individual's son was the sole shareholder of the mortgage company and a known drug trafficker. The corporation was an offshore corporation located in the Cayman Islands, which is a tax haven country. The corporation had no business location in the Cayman Islands or the United States. These are examples of using offshore entities to cover up illegal gains or assets.

19.13   Record Keeping

Taxpayers are required to keep records as to both taxes and to banking. Title 26, Section 6001, requires taxpayers to keep permanent books of accounts or records, including inventories, as are sufficient to establish the amount of gross income, deductions, credits, or other matters required to be shown by such person on any return or information. The regulations empowered area directors to require any person, by notice served upon him, to keep such specific records as will enable the area director to know whether or not such person is liable for tax. Taxpayers are required to keep records for at least 3 years, and in some cases, even longer. Title 31 requires more specific record keeping and retention. Congress found that adequate records maintained by banks, businesses, individuals engaging in business of carrying on as a financial institution, defined in 31 USC 5312(a) and 12 USC 1953. Individuals engaging in transactions or maintaining a relationship with a foreign financial agency have a high degree of usefulness in criminal, tax, and regulatory investigations and proceedings. In 31 CFR 103, the secretary promulgated regulations requiring records to be maintained for 5 years and filed or stored in such a way as to be accessible within a reasonable period of time. A person having financial interests in foreign financial institutions is required to file the FBAR and retain records containing:

1. The name in which each such account is maintained
2. The number or other designation of such account
3. The name and address of the foreign bank or other person with whom such account is maintained
4. The type of such account
5. The maximum value of each such account

The 5-year retention period is extended by any period beginning with a date on which the taxpayer is indicted or information instituted on account of the filing of a false or fraudulent federal income tax return, and ending with the date on which final disposition is made of the criminal proceeding.

Financial institutions must retain either the original or a microfilm or other copy or reproduction of records containing the name, amount, the nature or purpose, and the date regarding extension of credit exceeding $10,000, which are not secured by real property. In addition, the financial institutions are required to keep records regarding advice, request, or instruction received or given concerning any transaction resulting in the transfer of currency or other monetary instruments, funds, checks, investment securities, or credit of more than $10,000 to or from any person with an account or place outside the United States.

Additionally, banks are required to keep customer's name, address, and identification number for all accounts opened after June 30, 1972 or certificates of deposit sold or redeemed after May 31, 1978. Also, banks are required to keep documents granting signature authority and any notations of specific identifying information such as driver's license or credit card number. They must keep account statements showing each transaction. Checks, drafts, or money orders issued or payable by the bank or other debit items unless $100 or less or certain checks drawn on accounts that can be expected to have drawn on them an average of at least 100 checks per year. Deposit slips or credit tickets reflecting a transaction in excess of $100 containing the amount of currency must be maintained.

Brokers, dealers in securities, casinos, and currency dealers or exchangers are required to keep records identifying name, address, social security number, and documents granting signature or tracing authority over each customer's account. A record of each remittance or transfer of funds, or of currency, checks, other monetary instruments, investment securities, or credit, of more than $10,000 to a person, account, or place, outside of the United States must be maintained. A record of each extension of credit in excess of $2500, the terms and conditions of such extension of credit or repayments must be retained.

Businesses and individuals who are involved in cashing checks are required to maintain the name, address, and social security number of each individual that this service is provided for. In addition, records must be maintained of each check draft, money order, and cashier's check in excess of $100. The front and back of the instrument or document must be maintained or a copy retained.

19.14 Terminology

There are terms used in money laundering activities that have their special meanings. These terms also define the particular scheme or purpose.

19.14.1 Structuring

Structuring is an activity that describes a person or persons who conduct or attempt to conduct one or more transactions in currency in any amount at one or more financial institutions on one or more days in any manner for the purpose of evading various cash reporting requirements.

19.14.2 Smurfing

Smurfing is an activity that describes a person who goes to various financial institutions and makes deposits or obtains cashier checks, money orders, travel checks, etc., on the same day or consecutive days.

19.14.3 Layering

Layering describes the scheme of making financial transactions to disguise the audit trail of the illegal proceeds. It involves converting cash into monetary instruments, for example, cashier checks, money orders, traveler checks, stocks, and bonds. Layering encompasses making multiple deposits and making wire transfers or purchasing expensive assets.

19.14.4   Integration

The money launderer needs to provide a legitimate looking explanation for his/her wealth. Integration is the process of routing money into the banking system so as to make it appear that it comes from normal business earnings. Using front companies, sham loans, and false export-import invoices commonly does this. Money launderers will purchase property at high cost with partial payment (down payment) made in cash. The purchase documents are prepared showing a lower price by excluding the down payment or "under the table" payments. Over valuation of exports are used to justify deposits as funds from foreign sources.

19.15   Know Your Customer

The Federal Reserve Board issued a booklet, "Know Your Customer—Internal Compliance and Check Lists to Identify Abuses," to help financial institutions guard against illegal activities that could cause heavy penalties and bad publicity. It advises financial institutions to be aware of unusual banking practices that are not consistent with the customer's business. Financial institutions must verify new customer's identities and true ownership of accounts. Internal controls must be maintained to insure compliance and detection. This booklet gives the following danger signs of money laundering activities:

1. Large number of cash deposits while balance remains low and constant.
2. Large volume of cashier's checks, money orders, or traveler's checks sold for cash.
3. Large number of cash deposits to more than one account with transfers to a single account.
4. Large cash deposits from a business that is not normally a cash business.
5. CTRs are incorrect or lack important information.
6. Transactions with offshore banks in tax haven countries.
7. Loans or investments to offshore companies.
8. Offshore banks or companies are "shell" companies, meaning no physical location.
9. Frequent wire transfers to tax haven countries, especially to the same person or corporation.
10. Prepayment of interest on accounts used as collateral on loans.
11. Merchants structure credit card purchases to avoid the need for approval.
12. Purpose of loan is not recorded on the loan proceeds or used for purposes other than intended.
13. Loan proceeds are sent offshore.
14. Loan proceeds are used to purchase certificates of deposits or certificates of deposits are used for loans.
15. Customer requests to be placed on the bank's exemption list.
16. Safe deposit box has heavy traffic.
17. Cash deposits are made at the same time when the safe deposit box is accessed.

19.16   Summary

The federal government, as well as some states, have many laws, regulations, and require the reporting of various kinds of financial transactions by various business and institutions. Some businesses are well aware of these laws, regulations, and reporting forms while others are not aware. Many financial institutions and businesses have been fined for non-compliance. The fraud examiner should also become familiar with the laws, regulations, and the forms. This is one area that fraud examiners are most often called on to unravel.

19.17   Exhibits

Form 103 Currency Transaction Report by Casinos	4 pages
Form 104 Currency Transaction Report	4 pages
Form 105 Report of International Transportation of Currency or Monetary Instruments	2 pages
Form 3520 Annual Return to Report Transaction with Foreign Trusts and Receipts of Certain Foreign Gifts (form and instruction 19 pages)	
Form 8300 Report of Cash Payments over $10,000	5 pages
Form TDF 90-22.1 Report of Foreign Bank and Financial Accounts	8 pages
Form 107 Registration of Money Services Business	5 pages
Form 109 Suspicious Activity Report by Money Services Business	6 pages
Form 9022-47 Suspicious Activity Report	5 pages

FINCEN Form **103**	**Currency Transaction Report by Casinos**	

FINCEN Form **103**
(Rev. August 2008)
Department of the Treasury
FINCEN

Currency Transaction Report by Casinos
► Previous editions will not be accepted after February, 2009.
► **Please type or print. Items marked with an asterisk* are considered critical. (See instructions.)**
(Complete all applicable parts--See instructions)

OMB No. 1506-0005

1 If this is an **amended report** check here: ☐ and attach a copy of the original CTRC to this form.

Part I   Person(s) Involved in Transaction(s)

Section A--Person(s) on Whose Behalf Transaction(s) Is Conducted (Customer)   2 ☐ Multiple persons

*3 Individual's last name or Organization's name	*4 First name	5 M.I.

6 Doing business as (DBA)

*7 Permanent address (number, street, and apt. or suite no.)   *8 SSN or EIN

*9 City	*10 State	*11 ZIP code	*12 Country code (if not U.S.)	*13 Date of birth / / M M D D Y Y Y Y

*14 Method used to verify identity: **a** ☐ Examined identification credential/document   **b** ☐ Known Customer - information on file   **c** ☐ Organization

*15 Describe identification credential: **a** ☐ Driver's license/State ID **b** ☐ Passport **c** ☐ Alien registration **z** ☐ Other
     Issued by: Number:

16 Customer's Account Number

Section B--Individual(s) Conducting Transaction(s) - If other than above (Agent)   17 ☐ Multiple agents

18 Individual's last name	19 First name	20 M.I.

21 Address (number, street, and apt. or suite no.)   22 SSN

23 City	24 State	25 ZIP code	26 Country code (if not U.S.)	27 Date of birth / / M M D D Y Y Y Y

28 Method used to verify identity: **a** ☐ Examined identification credential/document   **b** ☐ Known Customer - information on file

29 Describe identification credential: **a** ☐ Driver's license/State ID **b** ☐ Passport **c** ☐ Alien registration **z** ☐ Other
     Issued by: Number:

Part II   Amount and Type of Transaction(s). Complete all items that apply.   30 ☐ Multiple transactions

*31 CASH IN: (in U.S. dollar equivalent)		*32 CASH OUT: (in U.S. dollar equivalent)	
a Purchase(s) of casino chips, tokens, and other gaming instruments	$ _____ .00	**a** Redemption(s) of casino chips, tokens, TITO tickets, and other gaming instruments	$ _____ .00
b Deposit(s) (front money or safekeeping)	_____ .00	**b** Withdrawal(s) of deposit (front money or safekeeping)	_____ .00
c Payment(s) on credit (including markers)	_____ .00	**c** Advance(s) on credit (including markers)	_____ .00
d Currency wager(s) including money plays	_____ .00	**d** Payment(s) on wager(s) (Including race book and OTB or sports pool)	_____ .00
e Currency received from wire transfer(s) out	_____ .00	**e** Currency paid from wire transfer(s) in	_____ .00
f Purchase(s) of casino check(s)	_____ .00	**f** Negotiable instrument(s) cashed (including checks)	_____ .00
g Currency exchange(s)	_____ .00	**g** Currency exchange(s)	_____ .00
h Bills inserted into gaming devices	_____ .00	**h** Travel and complimentary expenses and gaming incentives	_____ .00
z Other (specify): _____	_____ .00	**i** Payment for tournament, contest or other promotions	_____ .00
		z Other (specify): _____	_____ .00
Enter total of CASH IN transaction(s) $ _____ 0 .00		Enter total of CASH OUT transaction(s) $ _____ 0.00	

*33 Date of transaction (see instructions) / / M M D D Y Y Y Y	34 Foreign currency used: _____ (Country)

Part III   Casino Reporting Transactions

*35 Casino's trade name	*36 Casino's legal name	*37 Employer Identification Number (EIN)

*38 Address where transaction occurred (See instructions)	*39 City

*40 State	*41 ZIP code	*42 Type of gaming **a** ☐ State licensed casino **b** ☐ Card club **c** ☐ Tribal authorized casino Institution (Check only one) **z** ☐ Other (specify) _____

Sign ► Here	43 Title of approving official	44 Signature of approving official	45 Date of signature / / M M D D Y Y Y Y
	46 Type or print preparer's name	47 Type or print name of person to contact	48 Contact telephone number ( )

For Paperwork Reduction Act Notice, see page 4.   Cat. No. 37041B   (Rev. 8-08)

FinCEN Form 103 (Rev. 8-08)   Page **2**

Multiple Persons or Multiple Agents
(Complete applicable parts below if box 2 or box 17 on page 1 is checked.)

Part I	**Person(s) Involved in Transaction(s)**

Section A--Person(s) on Whose Behalf Transaction(s) Is Conducted (Customer)

*3 Individual's last name or Organization's name	*4 First name	5 M.I.

6 Doing business as (DBA)

*7 Permanent address (number, street, and apt. or suite no.)	*8 SSN or EIN

*9 City	*10 State	*11 ZIP code	*12 Country (if not U.S.)	*13 Date of birth / / MM DD YYYY

*14 Method used to verify identity: **a** ☐ Examined identification credential/document   **b** ☐ Known Customer - information on file   **c** ☐ Organization

*15 Describe identification credential: **a** ☐ Driver's license/State ID **b** ☐ Passport **c** ☐ Alien registration **z** ☐ Other
Issued by: Number:

16 Customer's Account Number

Section B--Individual(s) Conducting Transaction(s) - If other than above (Agent)

18 Individual's last name	19 First name	20 M.I.

21 Address (number, street, and apt. or suite no.)	22 SSN

23 City	24 State	25 ZIP code	26 Country (if not U.S.)	27 Date of birth / / MM DD YYYY

28 Method used to verify identity: **a** ☐ Examined identification credential/document   **b** ☐ Known Customer - information on file

29 Describe identification credential: **a** ☐ Driver's license/State ID **b** ☐ Passport **c** ☐ Alien registration **z** ☐ Other
Issued by: Number:

General Instructions

Form 103. Use this revision of Form 103 for filing on reportable transactions.

Suspicious Transactions. If a transaction is greater than $10,000 in currency as well as suspicious, casinos must file a Form 103 and must report suspicious transactions and activities on FinCEN Form 102, Suspicious Activity Report by Casinos (SARC). Also, casinos are required to use the SARC form to report suspicious activities involving or aggregating at least $5,000 in funds. **Do not** use Form 103 to **(a)** report suspicious transactions involving $10,000 or less in currency or **(b)** indicate that a transaction of more than $10,000 is suspicious.

In situations involving suspicious transactions requiring immediate attention, such as when a reportable transaction is ongoing, the casino or card club shall immediately notify, by telephone, appropriate law enforcement and regulatory authorities in addition to filing a timely suspicious activity report.

Who must file. Any organization duly licensed or authorized to do business as a casino, gambling casino, or card club in the United States and having gross annual gaming revenues in excess of $1 million must file Form 103. This includes the principal headquarters and every domestic branch or place of business of the casino or card club. The requirement includes state-licensed casinos (both land-based and riverboat), tribal casinos, and state-licensed and tribal card clubs. Since card clubs are subject to the same reporting rules as casinos, the term "casino" as used in these instructions refers to both a casino and a card club.

What to file. A casino must file Form 103 for each transaction involving either currency received (Cash In) or currency disbursed (Cash Out) of more than $10,000 in a gaming day. A gaming day is the normal business day of the casino by which it keeps its books and records for business, accounting, and tax purposes. Multiple transactions must be treated as a single transaction if the casino has knowledge that: **(a)** they are made by or on behalf of the same person, and **(b)** they result in either Cash In or Cash Out by the casino totaling more than $10,000 during any one gaming day. Reportable transactions may occur at a casino cage, gaming table, and/or slot machine/video lottery terminal. The casino should report both Cash In and Cash Out transactions by or on behalf of the same customer on a single Form 103. **Do not** use Form 103 to report receipts of currency in excess of $10,000 by non-gaming businesses of a casino (e.g., a hotel); instead, use **Form 8300**, Report of Cash Payments Over $10,000 Received in a Trade or Business.

Exceptions. A casino does **not** have to report transactions with:
• domestic banks; or
• currency dealers or exchangers, or check cashers, as defined in 31 C.F.R. § 103.11(uu), and which are conducted pursuant to a contractual or other agreement covering the financial services in 31 C.F.R. §§103.22(b)(2)(i)(H), 103.22(b)(2)(ii)(G), and103.22(b)(2)(ii)(H).
Also, a casino does **not** have to report the following types of transactions:
• Cash ins when it is the same physical currency previously wagered in a money play on the same table game without leaving the table;
• Bills inserted into electronic gaming devices in multiple transactions (unless a casino has knowledge pursuant to 31 C.F.R. 103.11(c)(3));
• Cash outs won in a money play when it is the same physical currency wagered, (**Note:** However, when a customer increases a subsequent cash bet (*i.e.*, money play), at the same table game without departing, the increase in the amount of the currency bet would represent a new bet of currency and a transaction in currency.) or,
• Jackpots from slot machines or video lottery terminals.

Identification requirements. All individuals (except employees conducting transactions on behalf of armored car services) conducting a reportable transaction(s) for themselves or for another person must be identified by means of an official or otherwise reliable record.

Acceptable forms of identification include a driver's license, military or military dependent identification card, passport, alien registration card, state issued identification card, cedular card (foreign), or a combination of other unexpired documents that contain an individual's name and address and preferably a photograph and are normally acceptable by financial institutions as a means of identification when cashing checks for persons other than established customers.

For casino customers granted accounts for credit, deposit, or check cashing, or on whom a CTRC containing verified identity has been filed, acceptable identification information obtained previously and maintained in the casino's internal records may be used as long as the following conditions are met. The customer's identity is reverified periodically, any out-of-date identifying information is updated in the internal records, and the date of each reverification is noted on the internal record. For example, if documents verifying an individual's identity were examined and recorded on a signature card when a deposit or credit account was opened, the casino may rely on that information as long as it is reverified periodically.

When and where to file: This form can be e-filed through the Bank Secrecy Act E-filing System. Go to http://bsaefiling.fincen.treas.gov/index.jsp to register. This form is also available for download on the Web at www.fincen.gov, or may be ordered by calling the IRS Forms Distribution Center at (800) 829-3676.

File each Form 103 by the 15th calendar day after the day of the transaction with the:

> IRS Enterprise Computing Center-Detroit
> ATTN: CTRC
> P.O. Box 32621
> Detroit, MI 48232

A casino must retain a copy of each Form 103 filed for 5 years from the date of filing.

Penalties. Civil and/or criminal penalties may be assessed for failure to file a CTRC or supply information, or for filing a false or fraudulent CTRC. See 31 U.S.C. 5321, 5322, and 5324.

Definitions. For purposes of Form 103, the terms below have the following meanings:

Agent. Any individual who conducts a currency transaction on behalf of another individual or organization.

Currency. The coin and paper money of the United States or of any other country that is circulated and customarily used and accepted as money.

Customer. Any person involved in a currency transaction whether or not that person participates in the casino's gaming activities.

Person. An individual, corporation, partnership, trust or estate, joint stock company, association, syndicate, joint venture, or any other unincorporated organization or group.

Organization. Person other than an individual.

Transaction In Currency (Currency Transaction). The **physical** transfer of currency from one person to another.

Negotiable Instruments. All checks and drafts (including business, personal, bank, cashier's, and third-party), traveler's checks, money orders, and promissory notes, whether or not they are in bearer form.

Specific Instructions

Note: Items marked with an asterisk (3, 4, 7 – 12, 13, 14, 15, 31- 33 and items 35-42 in Part III) are considered critical and must be completed as required by line item instruction. Social Security Number, Item 8, must be completed unless: Country Code, Item 12, is recorded (as long as it is **not** the U.S.), Passport Number, Item 15 b, issued by, and number are recorded, or Nonresident Alien Registration Number, Item 15 c, issued by, and number, are recorded.

Item 1. Amends prior report.—Check Item 1 if this Form 103 amends a previously filed report. Staple a copy of the original report behind the amended one. Complete Part III in its entirety, but complete only those other entries that are being amended.

Part I. Person(s) Involved in Transaction(s)

Note: Section A **must** be completed in all cases. If an individual conducts a transaction on his/her own behalf, complete only section A. If a transaction is conducted by an individual **on behalf of** another person(s), complete Section A for each person on whose behalf the transaction is conducted; complete Section B for the individual conducting the transaction.

Section A. Person(s) on Whose Behalf Transaction(s) Is Conducted (Customer)

Item 2. Multiple persons.—Check Item 2 if this transaction is being conducted on behalf of more than one person. For example, if John and Jane Doe cash a check made out to them jointly at the casino, more than one individual has conducted the transaction. Enter information in Section A for one of the individuals; provide information for the other individual on page 2, Section A. Attach additional sheets as necessary.

Items *3, *4, and 5. Individual/Organization name.— If the person on whose behalf the transaction(s) is conducted is an individual, put his/her last name in Item 3, first name in Item 4 and middle initial in Item 5. If there is no middle initial, leave Item 5 BLANK. If the transaction is conducted on behalf of an organization, enter the name in Item 3, enter XX in item 4, and identify the individual conducting the transaction in Section B.

Item 6 Doing business as (DBA) name.—If an organization has a separate "doing business as" (DBA) name, first enter in Item 3 the organization's legal name (e.g., Smith Enterprises, Inc.) and then enter here in Item 6 the DBA name of the business (e.g., Smith Casino Tours). If no DBA name leave item 6 BLANK.

Items *7, *9, *10, *11, and *12. Address.—Enter the permanent street address, city, two-letter state abbreviation used by the U.S. Postal Service, and ZIP code of the person identified in Item 3. Also, enter in Item 7 the apartment or suite number and road or route number. Do not enter a P. O. box number unless the person has no street address. If the person is from a foreign country, enter any state/territory code (Canada/Mexico only) as well as the appropriate two-letter country code (For state/country code list go to www.fincen.gov/reg_bsaforms.html or call 1-800-949-2732 option 5). If country is U. S., leave Item 12 BLANK. Enter XX in any item that is unknown/not applicable.

Item *8. Social security number (SSN) or Employer identification number (EIN).—Enter the SSN (if an individual) or EIN (if other than an individual) of the person identified in Items 3 through 5. If that individual is a nonresident alien individual who does not have an SSN, enter "XX" in this space

Item *13. Date of birth.—Enter the customer's date of birth (DOB) if it is known to the casino through an existing internal record or reflected on an appropriate identification document or credential presented to the casino to verify the customer's identity (see **Identification Requirements** above). Internal casino records can include those for casino customers granted accounts for credit, deposit, or check cashing, or for whom a CTRC containing verified identity has been filed. If such records do not indicate the DOB, a casino should ask the customer for the DOB. If the DOB is not available from any of these sources, the casino should enter "XX" in the "mm" month position of the date field. Eight numerals must be inserted for each date. Enter the date in the format "mm/dd/yyyy", where "mm" is the month, "dd" is the day, and "yyyy" is the year. Zero (0) should precede any single-digit number. For example, if the individual's birth date is June 1, 1948, enter "06/01/1948" in Item 13.

Item *14. Method used to verify identity.—If an individual conducts the transaction(s) on his/her own behalf, his/her name and address **must** be verified by examination of an official credential/document or internal record containing identification information on a known customer (see **Identification Requirements** above). Check box **a** if you examined an official identification

credential/document. Check box **b** if you examined an acceptable internal casino record (i.e., credit, deposit, or check cashing account record, or a CTRC worksheet) containing previously verified identification information on a "known customer." Check box **c** if the transaction is conducted on behalf of an organization. If box **a** or **b** is checked, you **must** complete Item 15. If box **c** is checked, do not complete Item 15.

Item *15. Describe identification credential.— If item 14c above is checked, leave item 15 blank. If a driver's license, passport, or alien registration card was used to verify the individual's identity, check as appropriate box **a, b,** or **c.** If you check box **z,** you must specifically identify the type of document used (e.g., enter "military ID" for a military or military/dependent identification card). A statement such as "known customer" in box **z** is **not** sufficient for completion of Form 103. Enter in Item 15, issued by, the two-letter state postal code, two-letter country code, or the name of the issuer for that document, and enter in Item 15 the number shown on that official document in the space provided. If item 15 information is unknown, check box "z" other, and enter XX in the text field provided.

Item 16. Customer account number.—Enter the account number which corresponds to the transaction being reported and which the casino has assigned to the person whose name is entered in Item 3. If the person has more than one account number affected by the transaction, enter the account number that corresponds to the majority of currency being reported. If the transaction does not involve an account number, enter "XX" in the space.

Section B. Individual(s) Conducting Transaction(s) – If Other Than Above (Agent)

Complete Section B if an individual conducts a transaction on behalf of another person(s) listed in Section A. If an individual conducts a transaction on his/her own behalf, leave Section B BLANK.

Item 17. Multiple agents.—If, during a gaming day, more than one individual conducts transactions on behalf of an individual or organization listed in Section A, check this box and complete Section B. List one of the individuals on the front of the form and the other individual(s) on page 2, Section B. Attach additional sheets as necessary.

Items 18, 19, and 20. Name of individual.— Refer to and follow instructions for completing items 3, 4, and 5.

Items 21, 23, 24, 25, and 26. Address.— Refer to and follow instructions for completing items 7, 9, 10, 11, and 12.

Item 22. Social security number (SSN).— Refer to and follow instructions for completing item 8.

Item 27. Date of birth.—Enter the individual's date of birth. For proper format, see the instructions under **Item 13** above.

Item 28. Method used to verify identity.—Any individual listed in Items 18 through 20 must present an official document to verify his/her name and address. See the instructions under **Item 14** above for more information. After completing Item 28, you must also complete Item 29.

Item 29. Describe identification credential.— Describe the identification credential used to verify the individual's name and address. See the instructions under **Item 15** above for more information.

Part II. Amount and Type of Transaction(s)

Part II identifies the type of transaction(s) reported and the amount(s) involved. You must complete all items that apply.

Item 30. Multiple transactions.—Check this box if multiple currency transactions, **none** of which individually exceeds $10,000, comprise this report.

Items *31 and *32. Cash in and cash out.— Enter in the appropriate spaces provided in Items 31 and/or 32, the specific currency amount for each "type of transaction" for a reportable Cash In or Cash Out. If the casino engages in a Cash In or a Cash Out transaction that is not listed in Items 31a through 31h or Items 32a through 32i, specify the type of transaction and the amount of currency in Item 31z or 32z, respectively. Enter the total amount of the reportable Cash In transaction(s) in Item 31 in the space provided. Enter the total amount of the reportable Cash Out transaction(s) in Item 32 in the space provided.

If less than a full dollar amount is involved increase the figure to the next higher dollar. For example, if the currency total is $20,500.25, show it as $20,501.00.

If there is a currency exchange, list it separately with both the Cash In and Cash Out totals. If foreign currency is exchanged, use the U.S. dollar equivalent on the day of the transaction.

Payment(s) on credit, Item 31c, includes all forms of cash payments made by a customer on a credit account or line of credit, or in redemption of markers or counter checks. Currency received from wire transfer(s) out, Item 31e, applies to cash received from a customer when the casino sends a wire transfer on behalf of a customer.

Bills inserted into gaming devices (Item 31h), includes the amount of all paper currency inserted into a bill validator on a slot machine, video lottery terminal, or other electronic gaming device, used in conjunction with a customer's "slot club account" (magnetic strip card), aggregated by that account and which is posted to a casino's slot monitoring system.

Redemptions of chips, tokens, TITO tickets and other gaming instruments, Item 32a, includes all cash redemptions of slot machine or video lottery tickets to a customer. Payments on wagers, Item 32d, includes all cash paid on race book or sports pool betting tickets to a customer. Currency paid from wire transfer(s) in, Item 32e, applies to cash paid to a customer when the casino receives a wire transfer on behalf of a customer. Travel and complimentary expenses and gaming incentives, Item 32h, includes reimbursements of a customer's travel and entertainment expenses and cash complementaries ("comps").

Determining Whether Transactions Meet The Reporting Threshold

Only cash transactions that, alone or when aggregated, exceed $10,000 should be reported on Form 103. A casino must report multiple currency transactions when it has knowledge that such transactions have occurred. This includes knowledge gathered through examination of books, records, logs, information retained on magnetic disk, tape or other machine-readable media, or in any manual system, and similar documents and information that the casino maintains pursuant to any law or regulation or within the ordinary course of its business.

Cash In and Cash Out transactions for the same customer are to be aggregated separately and must not be offset against one another. If there are both Cash In and Cash Out transactions which **each** exceed $10,000, enter the amounts in Items 31 and 32 and report on a single Form 103.

Example 1. Person A purchases $11,000 in chips with currency (one Cash In entry); and later receives currency from a $6,000 redemption of chips and a $2,000 credit card advance (two Cash Out entries). Complete Form 103 as follows:
  Cash In of "$11,000" is entered in Item 31a (purchase of chips) and also in the Total Cash In entry at the bottom of Item 31. No entry is made for Cash Out. The two Cash Out transactions equal only $8,000, which does not meet the BSA reporting threshold.

Example 2. Person B deposits $5,000 in currency to his front money account and pays $10,000 in currency to pay off an outstanding credit balance (two Cash In entries); receives $7,000 in currency from a wire transfer (one Cash Out entry); and presents $2,000 in small denomination U.S. Currency to be exchanged for an equal amount in U.S. $100 bills. Complete Form 103 as follows:

  Cash In of "$5,000" is entered in Item 31b (deposit), "$10,000" is entered in Item 31c (payment on credit), "$2,000" is entered in Item 31g (currency exchange), and Cash In Total of "$17,000" is entered in Item 31 in the space provided for "total Cash-in." In determining whether the transactions are reportable, the currency exchange is aggregated with both the Cash In and the Cash Out amounts. The result is a reportable $17,000 Cash In transaction. No entry is made for Cash Out. The total Cash Out amount only equals $9,000, which does not meet the BSA reporting threshold.

Example 3. Person C deposits $7,000 in currency to his front money account and pays $9,000 in currency to pay off an outstanding credit balance (two Cash In entries); receives $2,500 in currency from a withdrawal from a safekeeping account, $2,500 in currency from a wire transfer and cashes a personal check of $7,500 (three Cash Out entries); and presents Canadian dollars which are exchanged for $1,500 in U.S. Dollar equivalent. Complete Form 103 as follows:

  Cash In of "$7,000" is entered in Item 31b (deposit), "$9,000" is entered in Item 31c (payment on credit), "$1,500" is entered in Item 31g (currency exchange), and a Cash In total of "$17,500" is entered in Item 31 in the space provided for "total Cash-in." Cash Out of "$2,500" is entered in Item 32b (withdrawal of deposit), "$2,500" is entered in Item 32e (wire transfer), "$7,500" is entered in Item 32f (negotiable instrument cashed), "$1,500" is entered in Item 32g (currency exchange) and a Cash Out Total of "$14,000" is entered in Item 32 in the space provided for "total Cash-out." In this example, both the Cash In and Cash Out totals exceed $10,000, and each must be reflected on Form 103.

Example 4. Person D purchases $10,000 in chips with currency and places a $10,000 cash bet (two Cash In entries); and later receives currency for an $18,000 redemption of chips and $20,000 from a payment on a cash bet (two Cash Out entries). Complete Form 103 as follows:

  Cash In of "$10,000" is entered in Items 31a and 31d and a Cash In total of "$20,000" is entered in Item 31 in the space provided for "total Cash-in." Cash Out of "$18,000" is entered in Item 32a (redemption of chips), "$20,000" is entered in Item 32d (payment on bets) and a Cash Out Total of "$38,000" is entered in Item 32 in the space provided for "total Cash-out." In this example, both the Cash In and Cash Out totals exceed $10,000, and each must be reflected on Form 103.

Item *33. Date of transaction.—Enter the gaming day on which the transaction occurred (see **What To File** above). For proper format, see the instructions for **Item 13** above.

Item 34. Foreign currency.—If foreign currency is involved, identify the country of issuance by entering the appropriate two-letter country code. If multiple foreign currencies are involved, identify the country for which the largest amount in U.S. Dollars is exchanged.

Part III. Casino Reporting Transaction(s)

Item *35. Casino's trade name.—Enter the name by which the casino does business and is commonly known. Do not enter a corporate, partnership, or other entity name, unless such name is the one by which the casino is commonly known.

Item *36. Casino's legal name.—Enter the legal name as shown on required tax filings. This name will be defined as the name indicated on a charter or other document creating the entity, and which is identified with the casino's established EIN.

Item *37. Employer identification number (EIN).— Enter the casino's EIN.

Items *38, *39, *40, and *41. Address.—Enter the street address, city, state, and ZIP code of the casino (or branch) where the transaction occurred. **Do not** use a P.O. box number.

Item *42. Type of gaming institution.—Check the appropriate box to indicate the type of gaming institution. Check box "a" for a land-based or riverboat casino that is duly licensed by a state, territory or insular possession of the United States; check box "c" to indicate a tribal casino (e.g., a Class III gaming operation or a Class II gaming operation using video lottery terminals). Check box "b" for a card club, gaming club, and card room or gaming room (including one operating on Indian lands). If you check box "z" for "other" specify the type of gaming institution (e.g., racino).

Items 43 and 44. Title and signature of approving official.—The official who is authorized to review and approve Form 103 must indicate his/her title and sign the form.

Item 45. Date the form is signed.—The approving official must enter the date the Form 103 is signed. For proper format, see the instructions for **Item 13** above.

Item 46. Preparer's name.—Type or print the full name of the individual preparing Form 103. The preparer and the approving official may be different individuals.

Items 47 and 48. Contact person/telephone number.—Type or print the name and commercial telephone number of a responsible individual to contact concerning any questions about this Form 103.

Paperwork Reduction Act Notice.—The requested information is useful in criminal, tax, and regulatory investigations and proceedings. Financial institutions are required to provide the information under 31 U.S.C. 5313 and 31 CFR Part 103, commonly referred to as the Bank Secrecy Act (BSA). The BSA is administered by the U.S. Department of the Treasury's Financial Crimes Enforcement Network (FinCEN). You are not required to provide the requested information unless a form displays a valid OMB control number. The time needed to complete this form will vary depending on individual circumstances. The estimated average time is 30 minutes. Send comments regarding this burden estimate, including suggestions for reducing the burden, to the Office of Management and Budget, Paperwork Reduction Project, Washington, DC 20503 and to the Financial Crimes Enforcement Network, Attn.: Paperwork Reduction Act, P.O. Box 39, Vienna VA 22183-0039.

FINCEN Form **104**
(Formerly Form 4789)
(Eff. December 2003)
Department of the Treasury
FinCEN

Currency Transaction Report

▶ Previous editions will not be accepted after August 31, 2004.

▶ Please type or print.

(Complete all parts that apply--See Instructions)

OMB No. 1506-0004

1   Check all box(es) that apply: **a** ☐ Amends prior report   **b** ☐ Multiple persons   **c** ☐ Multiple transactions

Part I   Person(s) Involved in Transaction(s)

Section A--Person(s) on Whose Behalf Transaction(s) Is Conducted

2 Individual's last name or entity's name	3 First name	4 Middle initial

5 Doing business as (DBA)	6 SSN or EIN

7 Address (number, street, and apt. or suite no.)	8 Date of birth __/__/__ MM DD YYYY

9 City	10 State	11 ZIP code	12 Country code (if not U.S.)	13 Occupation, profession, or business

14 If an individual, describe method used to verify identity: **a** ☐ Driver's license/State I.D.   **b** ☐ Passport   **c** ☐ Alien registration

d ☐ Other _____   **e** Issued by: _____   **f** Number: _____

Section B--Individual(s) Conducting Transaction(s) (if other than above).

If Section B is left blank or incomplete, check the box(es) below to indicate the reason(s)

a ☐ Armored Car Service   **b** ☐ Mail Deposit or Shipment   **c** ☐ Night Deposit or Automated Teller Machine   **d** ☐ Multiple Transactions   **e** ☐ Conducted On Own Behalf

15 Individual's last name	16 First name	17 Middle initial

18 Address (number, street, and apt. or suite no.)	19 SSN

20 City	21 State	22 ZIP code	23 Country code (If not U.S.)	24 Date of birth __/__/__ MM DD YYYY

25 If an individual, describe method used to verify identity: **a** ☐ Driver's license/State I.D.   **b** ☐ Passport   **c** ☐ Alien registration

d ☐ Other _____   **e** Issued by: _____   **f** Number: _____

Part II   Amount and Type of Transaction(s).   Check all boxes that apply.

26   Total cash in $ _____ 0.00   **27**   Total cash out $ _____ 0.00   **28** Date of transaction __/__/__ MM DD YYYY

26a   Foreign cash in _____ 0.00 *(see instructions, page 4)*   **27a**   Foreign cash out _____ 0.00 *(see instructions, page 4)*

29 ☐ Foreign Country _____   **30** ☐ Wire Transfer(s)   **31** ☐ Negotiable Instrument(s) Purchased

32 ☐ Negotiable Instrument(s) Cashed   **33** ☐ Currency Exchange(s)   **34** ☐ Deposit(s)/Withdrawal(s)

35 ☐ Account Number(s) Affected (if any):   **36** ☐ Other (specify):

Part III   Financial Institution Where Transaction(s) Takes Place

37 Name of financial institution	Enter Regulator or BSA Examiner code number ▶ (see instructions)

38 Address (number, street, and apt. or suite no.)	39 EIN or SSN

40 City	41 State	42 ZIP code	43 Routing (MICR) number

Sign Here ▶

44 Title of approving official	45 Signature of approving official	46 Date of signature __/__/__ MM DD YYYY
47 Type or print preparer's name	48 Type or print name of person to contact	49 Telephone number (___) ___ - ____

▶ For Paperwork Reduction Act Notice, see page 4.   Cat. No. 37683N   FinCEN Form **104** (Formerly Form 4789) **(Rev. 08-03)**

FinCEN Form 104 (formerly Form 4789) (Eff. 12-03) Page 2

Multiple Persons
Complete applicable parts below if box 1b on page 1 is checked

Part I Person(s) Involved in Transaction(s)

Section A--Person(s) on Whose Behalf Transaction(s) Is Conducted

2 Individual's last name or entity's name	3 First name	4 Middle initial

5 Doing business as (DBA)	6 SSN or EIN

7 Address (number, street, and apt. or suite no.)	8 Date of birth MM DD YYYY

9 City	10 State	11 ZIP code	12 Country code (if not U.S.)	13 Occupation, profession, or business

14 If an individual, describe method used to verify identity: a ☐ Driver's license/State I.D. b ☐ Passport c ☐ Alien registration

d ☐ Other _____ e Issued by: _____ f Number: _____

Section B--Individual(s) Conducting Transaction(s) (if other than above).

15 Individual's last name	16 First name	17 Middle initial

18 Address (number, street, and apt. or suite no.)	19 SSN

20 City	21 State	22 ZIP code	23 Country code (if not U.S.)	24 Date of birth MM DD YYYY

25 If an individual, describe method used to verify identity: a ☐ Driver's license/State I.D. b ☐ Passport c ☐ Alien registration

d ☐ Other _____ e Issued by: _____ f Number: _____

Part I Person(s) Involved in Transaction(s)

Section A--Person(s) on Whose Behalf Transaction(s) Is Conducted

2 Individual's last name or entity's name	3 First name	4 Middle initial

5 Doing business as (DBA)	6 SSN or EIN

7 Address (number, street, and apt. or suite no.)	8 Date of birth MM DD YYYY

9 City	10 State	11 ZIP code	12 Country code (if not U.S.)	13 Occupation, profession, or business

14 If an individual, describe method used to verify identity: a ☐ Driver's license/State I.D. b ☐ Passport c ☐ Alien registration

d ☐ Other _____ e Issued by: _____ f Number: _____

Section B--Individual(s) Conducting Transaction(s) (if other than above).

15 Individual's last name	16 First name	17 Middle initial

18 Address (number, street, and apt. or suite no.)	19 SSN

20 City	21 State	22 ZIP code	23 Country code (if not U.S.)	24 Date of birth MM DD YYYY

25 If an individual, describe method used to verify identity: a ☐ Driver's license/State I.D. b ☐ Passport c ☐ Alien registration

d ☐ Other _____ e Issued by: _____ f Number: _____

Suspicious Transactions

This Currency Transaction Report (CTR) should NOT be filed for suspicious transactions involving $10,000 or less in currency OR to note that a transaction of more than $10,000 is suspicious. Any suspicious or unusual activity should be reported by a financial institution in the manner prescribed by its appropriate federal regulator or BSA examiner. (See the instructions for Item 37). If a transaction is suspicious and in excess of $10,000 in currency, then both a CTR and the appropriate Suspicious Activity Report form must be filed.

In situations involving suspicious transactions requiring immediate attention, such as when a reportable transaction is ongoing, the fianacial institution shall immediately notify, by telephone, appropriate law enforcement and regulatory authorities in addition to filing a timely suspicious activity report.

General Instructions

Who Must File. Each financial institution (other than a casino, which instead must file FinCEN Form 103, and the U.S. Postal Service for which there are separate rules) must file FinCEN Form 104 (CTR) for each deposit, withdrawal, exchange of currency, or other payment or transfer, by, through, or to the financial institution which involves a transaction in currency of more than $10,000. Multiple transactions must be treated as a single transaction if the financial institution has knowledge that (1) they are by or on behalf of the same person, and (2) they result in either currency received (Cash In) or currency disbursed (Cash Out) by the financial institution totaling more than $10,000 during any one business day. For a bank, a business day is the day on which transactions are routinely posted to customers' accounts, as normally communicated to depository customers. For all other financial institutions, a business day is a calendar day.

Generally, financial institutions are defined as banks, other types of depository institutions, brokers or dealers in securities, money transmitters, currency exchangers, check cashers, and issuers and sellers of money orders and traveler's checks. Should you have questions, see the definitions in 31 CFR Part 103.

When and Where To File. This form should be e-filed through the Bank Secrecy Act E-filing System. Go to http: //bsaefiling.fincen.treas.gov/index.jsp to register. This form is also available for download on the Financial Crimes Enforcement Network's Web site at www.fincen.gov, or may be ordered by calling the IRS Forms Distribution Center at (800) 829-3676. File this CTR by the 15th calendar day after the day of the transaction with the:

> Enterprise Computing Center - Detroit
> ATTN: CTR
> P.O. Box 33604
> Detroit, MI 48232-5604

Keep a copy of each CTR for five years from the date filed.

A financial institution may apply to file the CTRs magnetically. To obtain an application to file magnetically, write to the:

> IRS Detroit Computing Center
> ATTN: CTR Magnetic Media Coordinator
> P.O. Box 33604
> Detroit, MI 48232-5604

Identification Requirements. All individuals (except an employees of armored car services) conducting a reportable transaction(s) for themselves or for another person, must be identified by means of an official document(s). Acceptable forms of identification include driver's license, military and military/dependent identification cards, passport, state issued identification card, cedular card (foreign), non-resident alien identification cards, or any other identification document or documents, which contain name and preferably address and a photograph and are normally acceptable by financial institutions as a means of identification when cashing checks for persons other than established customers.

Acceptable identification information obtained previously and maintained in the financial institution's records may be used. For example, if documents verifying an individual's identity were examined and recorded on a signature card when an account was opened, the financial institution may rely on that information. In completing the CTR, the financial institution must indicate on the form the method, type, and number of the identification. Statements such as "known customer" or "signature card on file" are not sufficient for form completion.

Penalties. Civil and criminal penalties are provided for failure to file a CTR or to supply information or for filing a false or fraudulent CTR. See 31 U.S.C. 5321, 5322 and 5324.

For purposes of this CTR, the terms below have the following meanings:

Currency. The coin and paper money of the United States or any other country, which is circulated and customarily used and accepted as money.

Person. An individual, corporation, partnership, trust or estate, joint stock company, association, syndicate, joint venture or other unincorporated organization or group.

Organization. Entity other than an individual.

Transaction in Currency. The **physical** transfer of currency from one person to another. This does not include a transfer of funds by means of bank check, bank draft, wire transfer or other written order that does not involve the physical transfer of currency.

Negotiable Instruments. All checks and drafts (including business, personal, bank, cashier's and third-party), money orders, and promissory notes. For purposes of this CTR, all traveler's checks shall also be considered negotiable instruments whether or not they are in bearer form.

Foreign exchange rate. If foreign currency is a part of a currency transaction that requires the completion of a CTR, use the exchange rate in effect for the business day of the transaction to compute the amount, in US dollars, to enter in item 26/27. The source of the exchange rate that is used will be determined by the reporting institution.

Specific Instructions
Because of the limited space on the front and back of the CTR, it may be necessary to submit additional information on attached sheets. Submit this additional information on plain paper attached to the CTR. Be sure to put the individual's or entity's name and identifying number (items 2, 3, 4, and 6 of the CTR) on any additional sheets so that if it becomes separated, it may be associated with the CTR.

Item 1a. Amends Prior Report. If this CTR is being filed because it amends a report filed previously, check Item 1a. Staple a copy of the original CTR to the amended one, complete Part III fully and only those other entries which are being amended.

Item 1b. Multiple Persons. If this transaction is being conducted by more than one person or on behalf of more than one person, check Item 1b. Enter information in Part I for one of the persons and provide information on any other persons on the back of the CTR.

Item 1c. Multiple Transactions. If the financial institution has knowledge that there are multiple transactions, check Item 1c.

PART I - Person(s) Involved in Transaction(s)

Section A **must** be completed. If an individual conducts a transaction on his own behalf, complete Section A and leave Section "B" BLANK. If an individual conducts a transaction on his own behalf and on behalf of another person(s), complete Section "A" for each person and leave Section "B" BLANK. If an individual conducts a transaction on behalf of another person(s), complete Section "B" for the individual conducting the transaction, and complete Section "A" for each person on whose behalf the transaction is conducted of whom the financial institution has knowledge.

Section A. Person(s) on Whose Behalf Transaction(s) Is Conducted. See instructions above.

Items 2, 3, and 4. Individual/Organization Name. If the person on whose behalf the transaction(s) is conducted is an individual, put his/her last name in Item 2, first name in Item 3, and middle initial in Item 4. If there is no middle initial, leave item 4 BLANK. If the transaction is conducted on behalf of an entity, enter the name in Item 2 and leave Items 3 and 4 BLANK.

Item 5. Doing Business As (DBA). If the financial institution has knowledge of a separate "doing business as" name, enter it in Item 5. For example, if Smith Enterprise is doing business as MJ's Pizza, enter "MJ's Pizza" in item 5.

Item 6. SSN or EIN. Enter the Social Security Number (SSN) or Individual Taxpayer Identification Number (ITIN) or Employer Identification Number (EIN) of the person or entity identified in Item 2. If none, write NONE.

Items 7, 9, 10, 11, and 12. Address. Enter the permanent address including ZIP Code of the person identified in Item 2. Use the U.S. Postal Service's two letter state abbreviation code. A P. O. Box should not be used by itself, and may only be used if there is no street address. If a P. O. Box is used, the name of the apartment or suite number, road or route number where the person resides must also be provided. If the address is outside the U.S., provide the street address, city, province or state, postal code (if known), and the two letter country code. For country code list go to www.fincen.gov/reg_bsaforms.html or telephone 800-949-2732 and select option number 5. If U.S., leave item 12 blank.

Item 8. Date of Birth. Enter the date of birth. Eight numerals must be inserted for each date. The first two will reflect the month, the second two the day, and the last four the year. A zero (0) should precede any single digit number. For example, if an individual's birth date is April 3 1948, Item 8 should read 04 03 1948.

Item 13. Occupation, profession, or business. If known, identify the occupation, profession or business that best describes the individual or entity in Part I (e.g., attorney, car dealer, carpenter, doctor, farmer, plumber, truck driver, etc.). Do not use nondescript terms such as businessman, merchant, store owner (unless store's name is provided), or self employed. If unemployed, or retired are used enter the regular or former occupation if known.

Item 14. If an Individual, Describe Method Used To Verify Identity. If an individual conducts the transaction(s) on his/her own behalf, his/her identity must be verified by examination of an acceptable document (see **General Instructions**). For example, check box **a** if a driver's license is used to verify an individual's identity, and enter the state that issued the license and the number in items **e** and **f**. If the transaction is conducted by an individual on behalf of another individual not present, or on behalf of an entity, check box "14d" "Other" and enter "NA" on the line provided.

Section B. Individual(s) Conducting Transaction(s) (if other than above). Financial institutions should enter as much information as is available. However, there may be instances in which Items 15-25 may be left BLANK or incomplete. If Items 15-25 are left BLANK or incomplete, check one or more of the boxes provided to indicate the reasons.

Example: If there are multiple transactions that, if only when aggregated, the financial institution has knowledge the transactions exceed the reporting threshold, and therefore, did not identify the transactor(s), check box **d** for Multiple Transactions.

Items 15, 16, and 17. Individual's Name. Complete these items if an individual conducts a transaction(s) on behalf of another person. For example, if John Doe, an employee of XY Grocery Store, makes a deposit to the store's account, XY Grocery Store should be identified in Section A and John Doe should be identified in section B.

Items 18, 20, 21, 22, and 23. Address. Enter the permanent street address including ZIP Code of the individual. (See the instructions for Items 7 and 9 through 12.) Enter country code if not U.S. (Reference item 12).

Item 19. SSN/ITIN. If the individual has a Social Security Number, or Individual Taxpayer Indentification Number, enter it in Item 19. If the individual does not have an SSN/ITIN, enter NONE.

Item 24. Date of Birth. Enter the individual's date of birth. (See the instructions for Item 8.)

Item 25. If an Individual, Describe Method Used To Verify Identity. Enter the method used to identify the individual's identity. (See **General Instructions** and the instructions for Item 14.)

PART II - Amount and Type of Transaction(s)
Complete Part II to identify the type of transaction(s) and the amount(s) involved.

Items 26 and 27. Total Cash In/Total Cash Out. In the spaces provided, enter the total amount of currency received (Total Cash In) or total currency disbursed (Total Cash Out) by the financial institution. If foreign currency is exchanged, use the U.S. dollar equivalent on the day of the transaction (See "Foreign exchange rates"), and complete item 26a or 27a, whichever is appropriate.

If less than a full dollar amount is involved, increase that figure to the next highest dollar. For example, if the currency totals $20,000.05, show the total as $20,001.00.

Items 26a and 27a. Foreign cash in/Foreign cash out. If foreign currency is exchanged, enter the amount of foreign currency (Do not convert to U.S. dollars) in items 26a and 27a. Report country of origin in item 29.

Item 28. Date of Transaction. Insert eight numerals for each date. (See instructions for Item 8.)

Item 29. Foreign Country. If items 26a and/or 27a are completed indicating that foreign currency is involved, check Item 29 and identify the country. If multiple foreign currencies are involved, check box 36 and identify the additional country(s) and/or currency(s) involved.

Determining Whether Transactions Meet the Reporting Threshold.

Only cash transactions that, if alone or when aggregated, exceed $10,000 should be reported on the CTR. Transactions shall not be offset against one another.

If there are both Cash In and Cash Out transactions that are reportable, the amounts should be considered separately and not aggregated. However, they may be reported on a single CTR.

If there is a currency exchange, it should be aggregated separately with each of the Cash In and Cash Out totals.

Example 1: A person deposits $11,000 in currency to his savings account and withdraws $3,000 in currency from his checking account. The CTR should be completed as follows:
Cash In $11,000 and no entry for Cash Out. This is because the $3,000 transaction does not meet the reporting threshold.

Example 2: A person deposits $11,000 in currency to his savings account and withdraws $12,000 in currency from his checking account. The CTR should be completed as follows:
Cash In $11,000, Cash Out $12,000. This is because there are two reportable transactions. However, one CTR may be filed to reflect both.

Example 3: A person deposits $6,000 in currency to his savings account and withdraws $4,000 in currency from his checking account. Further, he presents $5,000 in currency to be exchanged for the equivalent in Euro's. The CTR should be completed as follows:
Cash In $11,000 and no entry for Cash Out. This is because in determining whether the transactions are reportable, the currency exchange is aggregated with each of the Cash In and Cash Out amounts. The result is a reportable $11,000 Cash In transaction. The total Cash Out amount is $9,000, which does not meet the reporting threshold. Therefore, it is not entered on the CTR.

Example 4: A person deposits $6,000 in currency to his savings account and withdraws $7,000 in currency from his checking account. Further, he presents $5,000 in currency to be exchanged for the equivalent in Euro's. The CTR should be completed as follows:
Cash In $11,000, Cash Out $12,000. This is because in determining whether the transactions are reportable, the currency exchange is aggregated with each of the Cash In and Cash Out amounts. In this example, each of the Cash In and Cash Out totals exceed $10,000 and must be reflected on the CTR.

Items 30-33. Check the appropriate item(s) to identify the following type of transaction(s):
30. Wire Transfer(s)
31. Negotiable Instrument(s) Purchased
32. Negotiable Instrument(s) Cashed
33. Currency Exchange(s)

Item 34. Deposits/Withdrawals. Check this item to identify deposits to or withdrawals from accounts, e.g. demand deposit accounts, savings accounts, time deposits, mutual fund accounts, or any other account held at the financial institution. Enter the account number(s) in Item 35.

Item 35. Account Numbers Affected (if any). Enter the account numbers of any accounts affected by the transactions that are maintained at the financial institution conducting the transaction(s).

Example 1: If a person cashes a check drawn on an account held at the financial institution, the CTR should be completed as follows:
Indicate negotiable instrument(s) cashed and provide the account number of the check.

If the transaction does not affect an account, make no entry.

Example 2: A person cashes a check drawn on another financial institution. In this instance, negotiable instrument(s) cashed would be indicated, but no account at the financial institution has been affected. Therefore, Item 35 should be left BLANK.

Item 36. Other (specify). If a transaction is not identified in Items 30-34, check Item 36 and provide an additional description. For example, a person presents a check to purchase "foreign currency." If multiple (more than one) foreign currencies are involved in the transaction, enter the amount of the largest foreign currency transaction in item 26a or 27a and that currency's country-code of origin in item 29. Then check box 36 and enter the additional foreign currencies amount(s) and country-code(s) of origin in the space provided.

PART III - Financial Institution Where Transaction(s) Take Place

Item 37. Name of Financial Institution and Identity of Regulator or BSA Examiner. Enter the financial institution's full legal name and identify the regulator or BSA examiner, using the following codes:

Regulator or BSA Examiner	CODE
Comptroller of the Currency (OCC)	1
Federal Deposit Insurance Corporation (FDIC)	2
Federal Reserve System (FRS)	3
Office of Thrift Supervision (OTS)	4
National Credit Union Administration (NCUA)	5
Securities and Exchange Commission (SEC)	6
Internal Revenue Service (IRS)	7
U.S. Postal Service (USPS)	8
Commodity Futures Trading Commission (CFTC)	9
State Regulator	10

Items 38, 40, 41, and 42. Address. Enter the street address, city, state, and ZIP Code of the financial institution where the transaction occurred. If there are multiple transactions, provide information of the office or branch where any one of the transactions has occurred.

Item 39. EIN or SSN. Enter the financial institution's EIN. If the financial institution does not have an EIN, enter the SSN of the financial institution's principal owner.

Item 43. Routing (MICR) Number. If a depository institution, enter the routing (Magnetic Ink Character Recognition (MICR)) number.

SIGNATURE

Items 44 and 45. Title and signature of Approving Official. The official who reviews and approves the CTR must indicate his/her title and sign the CTR.

Item 46. Date of Signature. The approving official must enter the date the CTR is signed. (See the instructions for Item 8.)

Item 47. Preparer's Name. Type or print the full name of the individual preparing the CTR. The preparer and the approving official may not necessarily be the same individual.

Items 48 and 49. Contact Person/Telephone Number. Type or print the name and telephone number of an individual to contact concerning questions about the CTR.

Paperwork Reduction Act Notice. The requested information is useful in criminal, tax, and regulatory investigations and proceedings. Financial institutions are required to provide the information under 31 U.S.C. 5313 and 31 CFR Part 103, commonly referred to as the Bank Secrecy Act (BSA). The BSA is administered by the U.S. Department of the Treasury's Financial Crimes Enforcement Network (FinCEN). You are not required to provide the requested information unless a form displays a valid OMB control number. The time needed to complete this form will vary depending on individual circumstances. The estimated average time is 19 minutes. If you have comments concerning the accuracy of this time estimate or suggestions for making this form simpler, you may write to the **Financial Crimes Enforcement Network, P. O. Box 39, Vienna, VA 22183. Do not** send this form to this office. Instead, see **When and Where to File** in the instructions.

DEPARTMENT OF THE TREASURY
FINANCIAL CRIMES ENFORCEMENT NETWORK

**REPORT OF INTERNATIONAL
TRANSPORTATION OF CURRENCY
OR MONETARY INSTRUMENTS**

FinCEN Form **105**
(Formerly Customs Form 4790)
(Rev. July 2003)
Department of the Treasury
FinCEN

▶ Please type or print.

OMB NO. 1506-0014

▶ To be filed with the Bureau of Customs and Border Protection
▶ For Paperwork Reduction Act Notice and Privacy Act Notice, see back of form.

31 U.S.C. 5316; 31 CFR 103.23 and 103.27

PART I FOR A PERSON DEPARTING OR ENTERING THE UNITED STATES, OR A PERSON SHIPPING, MAILING, OR RECEIVING CURRENCY OR MONETARY INSTRUMENTS. (IF ACTING FOR ANYONE ELSE, ALSO COMPLETE PART II BELOW.)

1. NAME *(Last or family, first, and middle)*	2. IDENTIFICATION NO. *(See instructions)*	3. DATE OF BIRTH *(Mo./Day/Yr.)*

4. PERMANENT ADDRESS IN UNITED STATES OR ABROAD	5. YOUR COUNTRY OR COUNTRIES OF CITIZENSHIP

6. ADDRESS WHILE IN THE UNITED STATES	7. PASSPORT NO. & COUNTRY

8. U.S. VISA DATE *(Mo./Day/Yr.)*	9. PLACE UNITED STATES VISA WAS ISSUED	10. IMMIGRATION ALIEN NO.

11. IF CURRENCY OR MONETARY INSTRUMENT IS ACCOMPANIED BY A PERSON, COMPLETE 11a OR 11b

A. EXPORTED FROM THE UNITED STATES		B. IMPORTED INTO THE UNITED STATES	
Departed From: *(U.S. Port/City in U.S.)*	Arrived At: *(Foreign City/Country)*	Departed From: *(Foreign City/Country)*	Arrived At: *(City in U.S.)*

12. IF CURRENCY OR MONETARY INSTRUMENT WAS MAILED OR OTHERWISE SHIPPED, COMPLETE 12a THROUGH 12f

12a. DATE SHIPPED *(Mo./Day/Yr.)*	12b. DATE RECEIVED *(Mo./Day/Yr.)*	12c. METHOD OF SHIPMENT *(e.g. u.s. Mail, Public Carrier, etc.)*	12d. NAME OF CARRIER

12e. SHIPPED TO *(Name and Address)*

12f. RECEIVED FROM *(Name and Address)*

PART II INFORMATION ABOUT PERSON(S) OR BUSINESS ON WHOSE BEHALF IMPORTATION OR EXPORTATION WAS CONDUCTED

13. NAME *(Last or family, first, and middle or Business Name)*

14. PERMANENT ADDRESS IN UNITED STATES OR ABROAD

15. TYPE OF BUSINESS ACTIVITY, OCCUPATION, OR PROFESSION	15a. IS THE BUSINESS A BANK? ☐ Yes ☐ No

PART III CURRENCY AND MONETARY INSTRUMENT INFORMATION (SEE INSTRUCTIONS ON REVERSE)(To be completed by everyone)

16. TYPE AND AMOUNT OF CURRENCY/MONETARY INSTRUMENTS		17. IF OTHER THAN U.S. CURRENCY IS INVOLVED, PLEASE COMPLETE BLOCKS A AND B.
Currency and Coins	▶ $	A. Currency Name
Other Monetary Instruments *(Specify type, issuing entity and date, and serial or other identifying number.)*	▶ $	B. Country
(TOTAL)	▶ $	

PART IV SIGNATURE OF PERSON COMPLETING THIS REPORT

Under penalties of perjury, I declare that I have examined this report, and to the best of my knowledge and belief it is true, correct and complete.

18. NAME AND TITLE (Print)	19. SIGNATURE	20. DATE OF REPORT *(Mo./Day/Yr.)*

CUSTOMS AND BORDER PROTECTION USE ONLY		COUNT VERIFIED Yes ☐ No ☐	VOLUNTARY REPORT Yes ☐ No ☐
DATE	AIRLINE/FLIGHT/VESSEL	LICENSE PLATE STATE/COUNTRY / NUMBER	INSPECTOR *(Name and Badge Number)*

FinCEN FORM 105
(Formerly Customs Form 4790)

GENERAL INSTRUCTIONS

This report is required by 31 U.S.C. 5316 and Treasury Department regulations (31 CFR 103).

WHO MUST FILE:

(1) Each person who physically transports, mails, or ships or causes to be physically transported, mailed, or shipped currency or other monetary instruments in an aggregate amount exceeding $10,000 at one time from the United States to any place outside the United States or into the United States from any place outside the United States, and

(2) Each person who receives in the United States currency or other monetary instruments In an aggregate amount exceeding $10,000 at one time which have been transported, mailed, or shipped to the person from any place outside the United States.

A TRANSFER OF FUNDS THROUGH NORMAL BANKING PROCEDURES, WHICH DOES NOT INVOLVE THE PHYSICAL TRANSPORTATION OF CURRENCY OR MONETARY INSTRUMENTS, IS NOT REQUIRED TO BE REPORTED.

Exceptions: Reports are not required to be filed by:

(1) a Federal Reserve bank,

(2) a bank, a foreign bank, or a broker or dealer in securities in respect to currency or other monetary instruments mailed or shipped through the postal service or by common carrier,

(3) a commercial bank or trust company organized under the laws of any State or of the United States with respect to overland shipments of currency or monetary instruments shipped to or received from an established customer maintaining a deposit relationship with the bank, in amounts which the bank may reasonably conclude do not exceed amounts commensurate with the customary conduct of the business, industry, or profession of the customer concerned,

(4) a person who is not a citizen or resident of the United States in respect to currency or other monetary instruments mailed or shipped from abroad to a bank or broker or dealer in securities through the postal service or by common carrier,

(5) a common carrier of passengers in respect to currency or other monetary instruments in the possession of its passengers,

(6) a common carrier of goods in respect to shipments of currency or monetary instruments not declared to be such by the shipper,

(7) a travelers' check issuer or its agent in respect to the transportation of travelers' checks prior to their delivery to selling agents for eventual sale to the public,

(8) a person with a restrictively endorsed traveler's check that is in the collection and reconciliation process after the traveler's check has been negotiated, nor by

(9) a person engaged as a business in the transportation of currency, monetary instruments and other commercial papers with respect to the transportation of currency or other monetary instruments overland between established offices of banks or brokers or dealers in securities and foreign persons.

WHEN AND WHERE TO FILE:

A. Recipients—Each person who receives currency or other monetary instruments in the United States shall file FinCEN Form 105, within 15 days after receipt of the currency or monetary instruments, with the Customs officer in charge at any port of entry or departure or by mail with the Commissioner of Customs, Attention: Currency Transportation Reports, Washington DC 20229.

B. Shippers or Mailers—If the currency or other monetary instrument does not accompany the person entering or departing the United States, FinCEN Form 105 may be filed by mail on or before the date of entry, departure, mailing, or shipping with the Commissioner of Customs, Attention: Currency Transportation Reports, Washington DC 20229.

C. Travelers—Travelers carrying currency or other monetary instruments with them shall file FinCEN Form 105 at the time of entry into the United States or at the time of departure from the United States with the Customs officer in charge at any Customs port of entry or departure.

An additional report of a particular transportation, mailing, or shipping of currency or the monetary instruments is not required if a complete and truthful report has already been filed. However, no person otherwise required to file a report shall be excused from liability for failure to do so if, in fact, a complete and truthful report has not been filed. Forms may be obtained from any Bureau of Customs and Border Protection office.

PENALTIES: Civil and criminal penalties, including under certain circumstances a fine of not more than $500,000 and Imprisonment of not more than ten years, are provided for failure to file a report, filing a report containing a material omission or misstatement, or filing a false or fraudulent report. In addition, the currency or monetary instrument may be subject to seizure and forfeiture. See 31 U.S.C.5321 and 31 CFR 103.57; 31 U.S.C. 5322 and 31 CFR 103.59; 31 U.S.C. 5317 and 31 CFR 103.58, and U.S.C. 5332.

DEFINITIONS:

Bank—Each agent, agency, branch or office within the United States of any person doing business in one or more of the capacities listed: (1) a commercial bank or trust company organized under the laws of any State or of the United States; (2) a private bank; (3) a savings association, savings and loan association, and building and loan association organized under the laws of any State or of the United States; (4) an insured institution as defined in section 401 of the National Housing Act; (5) a savings bank, industrial bank or other thrift institution; (6) a credit union organized under the laws of any State or of the United States; (7)

any other organization chartered under the banking laws of any State and subject to the supervision of the bank supervisory authorities of a State other than a money service business; (8) a bank organized under foreign law; and (9) any national banking association or corporation acting under the provisions of section 25A of the Federal Reserve Act (12 U.S.C. Sections 611-632).

Foreign Bank—A bank organized under foreign law, or an agency, branch or office located outside the United States of a bank. The term does not include an agent, agency, branch or office within the United States of a bank organized under foreign law.

Broker or Dealer in Securities—A broker or dealer in securities, registered or required to be registered with the Securities and Exchange Commission under the Securities Exchange Act of 1934.

Currency —The coin and paper money of the United States or any other country that is (1) designated as legal tender and that (2) circulates and (3) is customarily accepted as a medium of exchange in the country of issuance.

Identification Number—Individuals must enter their social security number, if any. However, aliens who do not have a social security number should enter passport or alien registration number. All others should enter their employer identification number.

Monetary Instruments— (1) Coin or currency of the United States or of any other country, (2) traveler's checks in any form, (3) negotiable instruments (including checks, promissory notes, and money orders) in bearer form, endorsed without restriction, made out to a fictitious payee, or otherwise in such form that title thereto passes upon delivery, (4) incomplete instruments (including checks, promissory notes, and money orders) that are signed but on which the name of the payee has been omitted, and (5) securities or stock in bearer form or otherwise in such form that title thereto passes upon delivery. Monetary instruments do not include (i) checks or money orders made payable to the order of a named person which have not been endorsed or which bear restrictive endorsements, (ii) warehouse receipts, or (iii) bills of lading.

Person—An individual, a corporation, a partnership, a trust or estate, a joint stock company, an association, a syndicate, joint venture or other unincorporated organization or group, an Indian Tribe (as that term is defined in the Indian Gaming Regulatory Act), and all entities cognizable as legal personalities.

SPECIAL INSTRUCTIONS:

You should complete each line that applies to you. PART I. — Block 12A and 12B; enter the exact date you shipped or received currency or monetary instrument(s). PART II. -Block 13; provide the complete name of the shipper or recipient on whose behalf the exportation or importation was conducted. PART III. — Specify type of instrument, issuing entity, and date, serial or other identifying number, and payee (if any). Block 17, if currency or monetary instruments of more than one country is involved, attach a list showing each type, country of origin and amount.

PRIVACY ACT AND PAPERWORK REDUCTION ACT NOTICE:

Pursuant to the requirements of Public law 93-579 (Privacy Act of 1974), notice is hereby given that the authority to collect information on Form 4790 in accordance with 5 U.S.C. 552a(e)(3) is Public law 91-508; 31 U.S.C. 5316; 5 U.S.C. 301; Reorganization Plan No.1 of 1950; Treasury Department Order No. 165, revised, as amended; 31 CFR 103; and 44 U.S.C. 3501.

The principal purpose for collecting the information is to assure maintenance of reports or records where such reports or records have a high degree of usefulness in criminal, tax, or regulatory investigations or proceedings. The information collected may be provided to those officers and employees of the Bureau of Customs and Border Protection and any other constituent unit of the Department of the Treasury who have a need for the records in the performance of their duties. The records may be referred to any other department or agency of the Federal Government upon the request of the head of such department or agency. The information collected may also be provided to appropriate state, local, and foreign criminal law enforcement and regulatory personnel in the performance of their official duties.

Disclosure of this information is mandatory pursuant to 31 U.S.C. 5316 and 31 CFR Part 103. Failure to provide all or any part of the requested information may subject the currency or monetary instruments to seizure and forfeiture, as well as subject the individual to civil and criminal liabilities.

Disclosure of the social security number is mandatory. The authority to collect this number is 31 U.S.C. 5316(b) and 31 CFR 103.27(d). The social security number will be used as a means to identify the individual who files the record.

An agency may not conduct or sponsor, and a person is not required to respond to, a collection of information unless it displays a currently valid OMB control number. The collection of this information is mandatory pursuant to 31 U.S.C. 5316, of Title II of the Bank Secrecy Act, which is administered by Treasury's Financial Crimes Enforcement Network (FINCEN).

Statement required by 5 CFR 1320.8(b)(3)(iii): The estimated average burden associated with this collection of information is 11 minutes per respondent or record keeper depending on individual circumstances. Comments concerning the accuracy of this burden estimate and suggestions for reducing this burden should be directed to the Department of the Treasury, Financial Crimes Enforcement Network, P.O. Box 39 Vienna, Virginia 22183. DO NOT send completed forms to this office—See When and Where To File above.

FinCEN FORM 105

Form **3520**	**Annual Return To Report Transactions With Foreign Trusts and Receipt of Certain Foreign Gifts**	OMB No. 1545-0159
Department of the Treasury Internal Revenue Service	▶ See separate instructions.	2008

Note: *All information must be in English. Show all amounts in U.S. dollars. File a **separate** Form 3520 for **each** foreign trust.*

For calendar year 2008, or tax year beginning _____ , 2008, ending _____ , 20 _____

A Check appropriate boxes: ☐ Initial return ☐ Final return ☐ Amended return

B Check box that applies to person filing return: ☐ Individual ☐ Partnership ☐ Corporation ☐ Trust ☐ Executor

Check all applicable boxes:

☐ **(a)** You are a U.S. transferor who, directly or indirectly, transferred money or other property during the current tax year to a foreign trust, **(b)** You held an outstanding obligation of a related foreign trust (or a person related to the trust) issued during the current tax year, that you reported as a "qualified obligation" (defined in the instructions) during the current tax year, or **(c)** You are the executor of the estate of a U.S. decedent and (1) the decedent made a transfer to a foreign trust by reason of death, (2) the decedent was treated as the owner of any portion of a foreign trust immediately prior to death, or (3) the decedent's estate included any portion of the assets of a foreign trust. See the instructions for Part I.

☐ You are a U.S. owner of all or any portion of a foreign trust at any time during the tax year. See the instructions for Part II.

☐ **(a)** You are a U.S. person who, during the current tax year, received a distribution from a foreign trust, or **(b)** You are a U.S. person and you are also a grantor or beneficiary of a foreign trust that has made a loan of cash or marketable securities directly or indirectly to you during the current tax year that you reported as a "qualified obligation" (defined in the instructions) during the current tax year. See the instructions for Part III.

☐ You are a U.S. person who, during the current tax year, received certain gifts or bequests from a foreign person. See the instructions for Part IV.

Service Center where U.S. person's income tax return is filed ▶ _____

1a Name of person(s) filing return (see instructions)	**b** Identification number

c Number, street, and room or suite no. (if a P.O. box, see instructions)	**d** Spouse's identification number

e City or town	**f** State or province	**g** ZIP or postal code	**h** Country

2a Name of foreign trust (if applicable)	**b** Employer identification number (if any)

c Number, street, and room or suite no. (if a P.O. box, see instructions)

d City or town	**e** State or province	**f** ZIP or postal code	**g** Country

3 Did the foreign trust appoint a U.S. agent (defined in the instructions) who can provide the IRS with all relevant trust information? . . . . ☐ **Yes** ☐ **No**
If "Yes," complete lines 3a through 3g.

3a Name of U.S. agent	**b** Identification number (if any)

c Number, street, and room or suite no. (if a P.O. box, see instructions)

d City or town	**e** State or province	**f** ZIP or postal code	**g** Country

4a Name of U.S. decedent (see instr.)	**b** Address	**c** TIN of decedent
d Date of death		**e** EIN of estate

f Check applicable box:
☐ U.S. decedent made transfer to a foreign trust by reason of death.
☐ U.S. decedent treated as owner of foreign trust immediately prior to death.
☐ Assets of foreign trust were included in estate of U.S. decedent.

Under penalties of perjury, I declare that I have examined this return, including any accompanying reports, schedules, or statements, and to the best of my knowledge and belief, it is true, correct, and complete.

▶ _____ Signature	_____ Title	_____ Date
▶ _____ Preparer's signature	_____ Preparer's SSN or PTIN	_____ Date

For Privacy Act and Paperwork Reduction Act Notice, see instructions.   Cat. No. 19594V   Form **3520** (2008)

Form 3520 (2008)   Page **2**

Part I **Transfers by U.S. Persons to a Foreign Trust During the Current Tax Year** (see instructions)

5a Name of trust creator (if different from line 1a)	**b** Address	**c** Identification number (if any)

6a Country code of country where trust was created	**b** Country code of country whose law governs the trust	**c** Date trust was created

7a Will any person (other than the U.S. transferor or the foreign trust) be treated as the owner of the transferred assets after the transfer? ☐ **Yes** ☐ **No**

b	(i) Name of other foreign trust owners, if any	(ii) Address	(iii) Country of residence	(iv) Identification number, if any	(v) Relevant code section

8 Was the transfer a completed gift or bequest? If "Yes," see instructions . . . . ☐ Yes ☐ No
9a Now or in the future, can any part of the income or corpus of the trust benefit any U.S. beneficiary? . . . ☐ Yes ☐ No
b If "No," could the trust be revised or amended to benefit a U.S. beneficiary? . . . . ☐ Yes ☐ No
10 Will you continue to be treated as the owner of the transferred asset(s) after the transfer? . . . . ☐ Yes ☐ No

Schedule A—Obligations of a Related Trust (see instructions)

11a During the current tax year, did you transfer property (including cash) to a related foreign trust in exchange for an obligation of the trust or an obligation of a person related to the trust? See instructions . . . . ☐ Yes ☐ No
If "Yes," complete the rest of Schedule A, as applicable. If "No," go to Schedule B.

b Were any of the obligations you received (with respect to a transfer described in 11a above) qualified obligations? ☐ Yes ☐ No
If "Yes," complete the rest of Schedule A with respect to each qualified obligation.
If "No," go to Schedule B and, when completing columns (a) through (i) of line 13 with respect to each nonqualified obligation, enter "-0-" in column (h).

(i) Date of transfer giving rise to obligation	(ii) Maximum term	(iii) Yield to maturity	(iv) FMV of obligation

12 With respect to each qualified obligation you reported on line 11b: Do you agree to extend the period of assessment of any income or transfer tax attributable to the transfer, and any consequential income tax changes for each year that the obligation is outstanding, to a date 3 years after the maturity date of the obligation? . . . . . ☐ Yes ☐ No
Note: *Generally, you must answer "Yes," if you checked "Yes" to the question on line 11b.*

Schedule B—Gratuitous Transfers (see instructions)

13 During the current tax year, did you make any transfers (directly or indirectly) to the trust and receive less than FMV, or no consideration at all, for the property transferred? . . . . ☐ Yes ☐ No
If "Yes," complete columns (a) through (i) below and the rest of Schedule B, as applicable.
If "No," go to Schedule C.

(a) Date of transfer	(b) Description of property transferred	(c) FMV of property transferred	(d) U.S. adjusted basis of property transferred	(e) Gain recognized at time of transfer	(f) Excess, if any, of column (c) over the sum of columns (d) and (e)	(g) Description of property received, if any	(h) FMV of property received	(i) Excess of column (c) over column (h)
Totals ▶				$				$

14 You are required to attach a copy of each sale or loan document entered into in connection with a transfer reported on line 13. If these documents have been attached to a Form 3520 filed within the previous 3 years, attach only relevant updates.

Are you attaching a copy of:	Yes	No	Attached Previously	Year Attached
a Sale document?	☐	☐	☐	_____
b Loan document?	☐	☐	☐	_____
c Subsequent variances to original sale or loan documents?	☐	☐	☐	_____

Form **3520** (2008)

Form 3520 (2008)   Page **3**

Part I   **Schedule B—Gratuitous Transfers** *(Continued)*

Note: *Complete lines 15 through 18 only if you answered "No" to line 3.*

15

(a) Name of beneficiary	(b) Address of beneficiary	(c) U.S. beneficiary?		(d) Identification number, if any
		Yes	**No**	

16

(a) Name of trustee	(b) Address of trustee	(c) Identification number, if any

17

(a) Name of other persons with trust powers	(b) Address of other persons with trust powers	(c) Description of powers	(d) Identification number, if any

18   If you checked "No" on line 3 (or did not complete lines 3a through 3g), you are required to attach a copy of all trust documents as indicated below. If these documents have been attached to a Form 3520-A filed within the previous 3 years, attach only relevant updates.

Are you attaching a copy of:	**Yes**	**No**	**Attached Previously**	**Year Attached**
a Summary of all written and oral agreements and understandings relating to the trust? . .	☐	☐	☐	_____
b The trust instrument?	☐	☐	☐	_____
c Memoranda or letters of wishes?	☐	☐	☐	_____
d Subsequent variances to original trust documents?	☐	☐	☐	_____
e Trust financial statements.	☐	☐	☐	_____
f Other trust documents?	☐	☐	☐	

Schedule C—Qualified Obligations Outstanding in the Current Tax Year (see instructions)

19   Did you, at any time during the tax year, hold an outstanding obligation of a related foreign trust (or a person related to the trust) that you reported as a "qualified obligation" in the current tax year? . . . .   ☐ **Yes**   ☐ **No**
If "Yes," complete columns (a) through (e) below.

(a) Date of original obligation	(b) Tax year qualified obligation first reported	(c) Amount of principal payments made during the tax year	(d) Amount of interest payments made during the tax year	(e) Does the obligation still meet the criteria for a qualified obligation?	
				Yes	**No**

Form **3520** (2008)

Form 3520 (2008)   Page **4**

Part II   **U.S. Owner of a Foreign Trust** (see instructions)

20	(a) Name of other foreign trust owners, if any	(b) Address	(c) Country of residence	(d) Identification number, if any	(e) Relevant code section

21	(a) Country code of country where foreign trust was created	(b) Country code of country whose law governs the foreign trust	(c) Date foreign trust was created

22   Did the foreign trust file Form 3520-A for the current year? . . . . ☐ **Yes**   ☐ **No**

If "Yes," attach the Foreign Grantor Trust Owner Statement you received from the foreign trust.
If "No," to the best of your ability, complete and attach a substitute Form 3520-A for the foreign trust.
See instructions for information on penalties.

23   Enter the gross value of the portion of the foreign trust that you are treated as owning . . . . . . ▶ $

Part III   **Distributions to a U.S. Person From a Foreign Trust During the Current Tax Year** (see instructions)

24   Cash amounts or FMV of property received, directly or indirectly, during the current tax year, from the foreign trust (exclude loans included on line 25).

(a) Date of distribution	(b) Description of property received	(c) FMV of property received (determined on date of distribution)	(d) Description of property transferred, if any	(e) FMV of property transferred	(f) Excess of column (c) over column (e)

Totals. . . . . ▶ $

25   During the current tax year, did you (or a person related to you) receive a loan from a related foreign trust (including
an extension of credit upon the purchase of property from the trust)? . . . . ☐ **Yes**   ☐ **No**
If "Yes," complete columns (a) through (g) below for each such loan.
Note: The FMV of an obligation (column (f)) is -0- unless it is a "qualified obligation."

(a) FMV of loan proceeds	(b) Date of original loan transaction	(c) Maximum term of repayment of obligation	(d) Interest rate of obligation	(e) Is the obligation a "qualified obligation?"		(f) FMV of obligation	(g) Amount treated as distribution from the trust (subtract column (f) from column (a))
				Yes	No		

Total . . . . ▶ $

26   With respect to each obligation you reported as a "qualified obligation" on line 25: Do you agree to extend the
period of assessment of any income or transfer tax attributable to the transaction, and any consequential income
tax changes for each year that the obligation is outstanding, to a date 3 years after the maturity date of the
obligation? . . . . ☐ **Yes**   ☐ **No**
Note: Generally, you must answer "Yes" if you checked "Yes" in column (e) of line 25.

27   Total distributions received during the current tax year. Add line 24, column (f), and line 25, column (g). . . ▶ $

28   Did the trust, at any time during the tax year, hold an outstanding obligation of yours (or a person related to you)
that you reported as a "qualified obligation" in the current tax year? . . . . ☐ **Yes**   ☐ **No**
If "Yes," complete columns (a) through (e) below for each obligation.

(a) Date of original loan transaction	(b) Tax year qualified obligation first reported	(c) Amount of principal payments made during the tax year	(d) Amount of interest payments made during the tax year	(e) Does the loan still meet the criteria of a qualified obligation?	
				Yes	No

Form **3520** (2008)

Part III	**Distributions to a U.S. Person From a Foreign Trust During the Current Tax Year** *(Continued)*

29   Did you receive a Foreign Grantor Trust Beneficiary Statement from the foreign trust with respect to a distribution?   ☐ **Yes**   ☐ **No**
If "Yes," attach the statement and do not complete the remainder of Part III with respect to that distribution.
If "No," complete Schedule A with respect to that distribution. Also complete Schedule C if you enter an amount
greater than zero on line 37.

30   Did you receive a Foreign Nongrantor Trust Beneficiary Statement from the foreign trust with respect to a distribution?   ☐ **Yes**   ☐ **No**
If "Yes," attach the statement and complete either Schedule A or Schedule B below (see instructions). Also complete
Schedule C if you enter an amount greater than zero on line 37 or line 41.
If "No," complete Schedule A with respect to that distribution. Also complete Schedule C if you enter an amount
greater than zero on line 37.

Schedule A—Default Calculation of Trust Distributions (see instructions)

31	Enter amount from line 27	
32	Number of years the trust has been a foreign trust (see instructions) ▶ _____	
33	Enter total distributions received from the foreign trust during the 3 preceding tax years (or during the number of years the trust has been a foreign trust, if fewer than 3)	
34	Multiply line 33 by 1.25	
35	Average distribution. Divide line 34 by 3 (or the number of years the trust has been a foreign trust, if fewer than 3) and enter the result	
36	Amount treated as ordinary income earned in the current year. Enter the smaller of line 31 or line 35 . . .	
37	Amount treated as accumulation distribution. Subtract line 36 from line 31. If -0-, do not complete the rest of Part III	
38	Applicable number of years of trust. Divide line 32 by 2 and enter the result here ▶	

Schedule B—Actual Calculation of Trust Distributions (see instructions)

39	Enter amount from line 27	
40	Amount treated as ordinary income in the current tax year	
41	Amount treated as accumulation distribution. If -0-, do not complete Schedule C, Part III	
42	Amount treated as capital gains in the current tax year	
43	Amount treated as distribution from trust corpus	
44	Enter any other distributed amount received from the foreign trust not included on lines 40, 41, 42, and 43 (attach explanation)	
45	Amount of foreign trust's aggregate undistributed net income	
46	Amount of foreign trust's weighted undistributed net income	
47	Applicable number of years of trust. Divide line 46 by line 45 and enter the result here ▶	

Schedule C—Calculation of Interest Charge (see instructions)

48	Enter accumulation distribution from line 37 or 41, as applicable	
49	Enter tax on total accumulation distribution from line 28 of Form 4970	
50	Enter applicable number of years of foreign trust from line 38 or 47, as applicable (round to nearest half-year) ▶ _____	
51	Combined interest rate imposed on the total accumulation distribution (see instructions)	
52	Interest charge. Multiply the amount on line 49 by the combined interest rate on line 51	
53	Tax attributable to accumulation distributions. Add lines 49 and 52. Enter here and as "additional tax" on your income tax return	

Part IV   **U.S. Recipients of Gifts or Bequests Received During the Current Tax Year From Foreign Persons** (see instructions)

| 54 | During the current tax year, did you receive more than $100,000 that you treated as gifts or bequests from a nonresident alien or a foreign estate? See instructions for special rules regarding related donors and gifts or bequests from "covered expatriates" . . . . | ☐ Yes | ☐ No |

If "Yes," complete columns (a) through (c) with respect to each such gift or bequest in excess of $5,000. If more space is needed, attach schedule.

(a) Date of gift or bequest	(b) Description of property received	(c) FMV of property received
Total . . . . ▶		$

| 55 | During the current tax year, did you receive more than $13,561 that you treated as gifts from a foreign corporation or a foreign partnership? See instructions regarding related donors . . . . | ☐ Yes | ☐ No |

If "Yes," complete columns (a) through (g) with respect to each such gift. If more space is needed, attach schedule.

(a) Date of gift	(b) Name of donor	(c) Address of donor	(d) Identification number, if any

(e) Check the box that applies to the foreign donor		(f) Description of property received	(g) FMV of property received
Corporation	Partnership		

| 56 | Do you have any reason to believe that the foreign donor, in making any gift or bequest described in lines 54 and 55, was acting as a nominee or intermediary for any other person? If "Yes," see instructions . . . . . . | ☐ Yes | ☐ No |
| 57 | During the current tax year, did you receive a "covered gift or bequest" (as defined in section 2801(e)) of more than $12,000 from a "covered expatriate" (as defined in section 877A(g)(1)) (see instructions)? . . . . | ☐ Yes | ☐ No |

If "Yes," complete and file Form 708, U.S. Return of Tax for Gifts and Bequests Received From Expatriates.

Form **3520** (2008)

20**08**

Department of the Treasury
Internal Revenue Service

Instructions for Form 3520

Annual Return To Report Transactions With Foreign Trusts and Receipt of Certain Foreign Gifts

Section references are to the Internal Revenue Code unless otherwise noted.

What's New

Line 57 of the form is new. U.S. persons who receive a covered gift or bequest of more than $12,000 from a covered expatriate are subject to a new tax under section 2801. See the instructions for line 57 for details.

General Instructions

Purpose of Form

U.S. persons (and executors of estates of U.S. decedents) file Form 3520 to report:
• Certain transactions with foreign trusts and
• Receipt of certain large gifts or bequests from certain foreign persons.

A separate Form 3520 must be filed for transactions with **each** foreign trust.

Who Must File

File Form 3520 if:

1. You are the responsible party for reporting a reportable event that occurred during the current tax year, or you held an outstanding obligation of a related foreign trust (or a person related to the trust) that you treated as a qualified obligation during the current tax year. Responsible party, reportable event, and qualified obligation are defined on pages 3 and 4.

Complete the identifying information on page 1 of the form and the relevant portions of Part I. See the instructions for Part I.

2. You are a U.S. person who, during the current tax year, is treated as the owner of any part of the assets of a foreign trust under the grantor trust rules.

Complete the identifying information on page 1 of the form and Part II. See the instructions for Part II.

3. You are a U.S. person who received (directly or indirectly) a distribution from a foreign trust during the current tax year **or** a related foreign trust held an outstanding obligation issued by you (or a person related to you) that you treated as a qualified obligation (defined on page 3) during the current tax year.

Complete the identifying information on page 1 of the form and Part III. See the instructions for Part III.

4. You are a U.S. person who, during the current tax year, received either:

a. More than $100,000 from a nonresident alien individual or a foreign estate (including foreign persons related to that nonresident alien individual or foreign estate) that you treated as gifts or bequests; or

b. More than $13,561 from foreign corporations or foreign partnerships (including foreign persons related to

such foreign corporations or foreign partnerships) that you treated as gifts.

Complete the identifying information on page 1 of the form and Part IV. See the instructions for Part IV.

Note. You may also be required to file Form TD F 90-22.1, Report of Foreign Bank and Financial Accounts.

Exceptions To Filing

Form 3520 does not have to be filed to report the following transactions.
• Transfers to foreign trusts described in sections 402(b), 404(a)(4), or 404A.
• Most fair market value (FMV) transfers by a U.S. person to a foreign trust. However, some FMV transfers must nevertheless be reported on Form 3520 (e.g., transfers in exchange for obligations that are treated as qualified obligations, transfers of appreciated property to a foreign trust for which the U.S. transferor does not immediately recognize all of the gain on the property transferred, transfers involving a U.S. transferor that is related to the foreign trust). See Section III of Notice 97-34, 1997-25 I.R.B. 22.
• Transfers to foreign trusts that have a current determination letter from the IRS recognizing their status as exempt from income taxation under section 501(c)(3).
• Transfers to, ownership of, and distributions from a Canadian registered retirement savings plan (RRSP) or a Canadian registered retirement income fund (RRIF), where the U.S. citizen or resident alien holding an interest in such RRSP or RRIF is eligible to file Form 8891, U.S. Information Return for Beneficiaries of Certain Canadian Registered Retirement Plans, with respect to the RRSP or RRIF.
• Distributions from foreign trusts that are taxable as compensation for services rendered (within the meaning of section 672(f)(2)(B) and its regulations), so long as the recipient reports the distribution as compensation income on its applicable federal income tax return.
• Distributions from foreign trusts to domestic trusts that have a current determination letter from the IRS recognizing their status as exempt from income taxation under section 501(c)(3).
• Domestic trusts that become foreign trusts to the extent the trust is treated as owned by a foreign person, after application of section 672(f).

Joint Returns

Two transferors or grantors of the same foreign trust, or two U.S. beneficiaries of the same foreign trust, may file a joint Form 3520, but only if they file a joint income tax return.

Additional Reporting Information

For more information on foreign trust reporting, including abusive foreign trust schemes, go to the IRS website at *www.irs.gov.*

Cat. No. 23068I

When and Where To File

In general, Form 3520 is due on the date that your income tax return is due, including extensions. In the case of a Form 3520 filed with respect to a U.S. decedent, Form 3520 is due on the date that the estate tax return is due (or would be due if the estate were required to file a return), including extensions. Send Form 3520 to the Internal Revenue Service Center, P.O. Box 409101, Ogden, UT 84409.

Form 3520 must have all required attachments to be considered complete.

Note. If a complete Form 3520 is not filed by the due date, including extensions, the time for assessment of any tax imposed with respect to any event or period to which the information required to be reported in Parts I through III of such Form 3520 relates, will not expire before the date that is 3 years after the date on which the required information is reported. See section 6501(c)(8).

Who Must Sign

If the return is filed by:
• An individual or a fiduciary, it must be signed and dated by that individual or fiduciary.
• A partnership, it must be signed and dated by a general partner or limited liability company member.
• A corporation, it must be signed and dated by the president, vice president, treasurer, assistant treasurer, chief accounting officer, or any other corporate officer (such as a tax officer) who is authorized to sign.

The paid preparer must complete the required preparer information and:
• Sign the return in the space provided for the preparer's signature.
• Give a copy of the return to the filer.

Inconsistent Treatment of Items

The U.S. beneficiary and U.S. owner's tax return must be consistent with the Form 3520-A, Annual Information Return of Foreign Trust With a U.S. Owner, filed by the foreign trust unless you report the inconsistency to the IRS. If you are treating items on your tax return differently from the way the foreign trust treated them on its return, file Form 8082, Notice of Inconsistent Treatment or Administrative Adjustment Request (AAR). See Form 8082 for more details.

Penalties

A penalty generally applies if Form 3520 is not timely filed or if the information is incomplete or incorrect. Generally, the penalty is:
• 35% of the gross value of any property transferred to a foreign trust for failure by a U.S. transferor to report the transfer,
• 35% of the gross value of the distributions received from a foreign trust for failure by a U.S. person to report receipt of the distribution, or
• 5% of the amount of certain foreign gifts for each month for which the failure to report continues (not to exceed a total of 25%). See section 6039F(c).

If a foreign trust has a U.S. owner and the trust fails to file the required annual reports on trust activities and income, the U.S. owner is subject to a penalty equal to 5% of the gross value of the portion of the trust's assets treated as owned by the U.S. person (the gross reportable amount). See Form 3520-A.

Additional penalties may be imposed if noncompliance continues after the IRS mails a notice of failure to comply with required reporting. However, this penalty may not exceed the gross reportable amount. Also, penalties will only be imposed to the extent that the transaction is not reported. For example, if a U.S. person transfers property worth $1 million to a foreign trust but only reports $400,000 of that amount, penalties could only be imposed on the unreported $600,000.

For more information, see section 6677.

Reasonable cause. No penalties will be imposed if the taxpayer can demonstrate that the failure to comply was due to reasonable cause and not willful neglect.

Note. The fact that a foreign country would impose penalties for disclosing the required information is not reasonable cause. Similarly, reluctance on the part of a foreign fiduciary or provisions in the trust instrument that prevent the disclosure of required information is not reasonable cause.

Definitions

Distribution

A distribution is any gratuitous transfer of money or other property from a trust, whether or not the trust is treated as owned by another person under the grantor trust rules, and without regard to whether the recipient is designated as a beneficiary by the terms of the trust. A distribution includes the receipt of trust corpus and the receipt of a gift or bequest described in section 663(a).

A distribution also includes constructive transfers from a trust. For example, if charges you make on a credit card are paid by a foreign trust or guaranteed or secured by the assets of a foreign trust, the amount charged will be treated as a distribution to you by the foreign trust. Similarly, if you write checks on a foreign trust's bank account, the amount will be treated as a distribution.

Also, if you receive a payment from a foreign trust in exchange for property transferred to the trust or services rendered to the trust, and the FMV of the payment received exceeds the FMV of the property transferred or services rendered, the excess will be treated as a distribution to you.

Examples

1. If you sell stock with an FMV of $100 to a foreign trust and receive $150 in exchange, you have received a distribution of $50.

2. If you receive $100 from the trust for services performed by you for the trust, and the services have an FMV of $20, you have received a distribution of $80.

See the instructions for Part III, line 25, on page 7, for another example of a distribution from a foreign trust.

Foreign Trust and Domestic Trust

A foreign trust is any trust other than a domestic trust.

A domestic trust is any trust if:

1. A court within the United States is able to exercise primary supervision over the administration of the trust; and

2. One or more U.S. persons have the authority to control all substantial decisions of the trust.

Grantor

A grantor includes any person who creates a trust or directly or indirectly makes a gratuitous transfer of cash or other property to a trust. A grantor includes any person treated as the owner of any part of a foreign trust's assets under sections 671 through 679, excluding section 678.

Note. If a partnership or corporation makes a gratuitous transfer to a trust, the partners or shareholders are generally treated as the grantors of the trust, unless the partnership or corporation made the transfer for a business purpose of the partnership or corporation.

If a trust makes a gratuitous transfer to another trust, the grantor of the transferor trust is treated as the grantor of the transferee trust, except that if a person with a general power of appointment over the transferor trust exercises that power in favor of another trust, such person is treated as the grantor of the transferee trust, even if the grantor of the transferor trust is treated as the owner of the transferor trust.

Grantor Trust

A grantor trust is any trust to the extent that the assets of the trust are treated as owned by a person other than the trust. See the grantor trust rules in sections 671 through 679. A part of the trust may be treated as a grantor trust to the extent that only a portion of the trust assets are owned by a person other than the trust.

Gratuitous Transfer

A gratuitous transfer to a foreign trust is any transfer to the trust other than (a) a transfer for FMV or (b) a distribution to the trust with respect to an interest held by the trust (i) in an entity other than a trust (e.g., a corporation or a partnership) or (ii) in an investment trust described in Regulations section 301.7701-4(c), a liquidating trust described in Regulations section 301.7701-4(d), or an environmental remediation trust described in Regulations section 301.7701-4(e).

A transfer of property to a trust may be considered a gratuitous transfer without regard to whether the transfer is a gift for gift tax purposes (see Chapter 12 of Subtitle B of the Code).

For purposes of this determination, if a U.S. person contributes property to a trust in exchange for any type of interest in the trust, such interest in the trust will be disregarded in determining whether FMV has been received. In addition, a U.S. person will not be treated as making a transfer for FMV merely because the transferor is deemed to recognize gain on the transaction.

If you transfer property to a foreign trust in exchange for an obligation of the trust (or a person related to the trust), it will be a gratuitous transfer unless the obligation is a qualified obligation. Obligation and qualified obligation are defined below.

Gross Reportable Amount

Gross reportable amount is:
• The gross value of property involved in the creation of a foreign trust or the transfer of property to a foreign trust (including a transfer by reason of death);
• The gross value of any portion of a foreign trust treated as owned by a U.S. person under the grantor trust rules or any part of a foreign trust that is included in the gross estate of a U.S. citizen or resident;
• The gross value of assets deemed transferred at the time a domestic trust to which a U.S. citizen or resident previously transferred property becomes a foreign trust, provided such U.S. citizen or resident is alive at the time the trust becomes a foreign trust (see section 679(a)(5)); or
• The gross amount of distributions received from a foreign trust.

Gross Value

Gross value is the FMV of property as determined under section 2031 and its regulations as if the owner had died on the valuation date. Although formal appraisals are not generally required, you should keep contemporaneous records of how you arrived at your good faith estimate.

Guarantee

A guarantee:
• Includes any arrangement under which a person, directly or indirectly, assures, on a conditional or unconditional basis, the payment of another's obligation;
• Encompasses any form of credit support, and includes a commitment to make a capital contribution to the debtor or otherwise maintain its financial viability; or
• Includes an arrangement reflected in a "comfort letter," regardless of whether the arrangement gives rise to a legally enforceable obligation. If an arrangement is contingent upon the occurrence of an event, in determining whether the arrangement is a guarantee, you must assume that the event has occurred.

Nongrantor Trust

A nongrantor trust is any trust to the extent that the assets of the trust are not treated as owned by a person other than the trust. Thus, a nongrantor trust is treated as a taxable entity. A trust may be treated as a nongrantor trust with respect to only a portion of the trust assets. See *Grantor Trust* above.

Obligation

An obligation includes any bond, note, debenture, certificate, bill receivable, account receivable, note receivable, open account, or other evidence of indebtedness, and, to the extent not previously described, any annuity contract.

Owner

An owner of a foreign trust is the person that is treated as owning any of the assets of a foreign trust under the grantor trust rules.

Property

Property means any property, whether tangible or intangible, including cash.

Qualified Obligation

A qualified obligation, for purposes of this form, is any obligation only if:
1. The obligation is reduced to writing by an express written agreement;
2. The term of the obligation does not exceed 5 years (including options to renew and rollovers) and it is repaid within the 5-year term;
3. All payments on the obligation are denominated in U.S. dollars;
4. The yield to maturity of the obligation is not less than 100% of the applicable federal rate under section 1274(d) for the day on which the obligation is issued and not greater than 130% of the applicable federal rate;
5. The U.S. person agrees to extend the period for assessment of any income or transfer tax attributable to the transfer and any consequential income tax changes for each year that the obligation is outstanding, to a date not earlier than 3 years after the maturity date of the obligation, unless the maturity date of the obligation does not extend beyond the end of the U.S. person's tax year and is paid within such period (this is done on Part I, Schedule A, and Part III, as applicable); and
6. The U.S. person reports the status of the obligation, including principal and interest payments, on Part I, Schedule C, and Part III, as applicable, for each year that the obligation is outstanding.

Related Person

A related person generally includes any person who is related to you for purposes of section 267 and 707(b). This includes, but is not limited to:

- A member of your family—your brothers and sisters, half-brothers and half-sisters, spouse, ancestors (parents, grandparents, etc.), lineal descendants (children, grandchildren, etc.), and the spouses of any of these persons.
- A corporation in which you, directly or indirectly, own more than 50% in value of the outstanding stock.

See section 643(i)(2)(B) and the regulations under sections 267 and 707(b).

Person related to a foreign trust. A person is related to a foreign trust if such person, without regard to the transfer at issue, is a grantor of the trust, a beneficiary of the trust, or is related to any grantor or beneficiary of the trust. See the definition of related person on page 3.

Reportable Event

A reportable event includes:

1. The creation of a foreign trust by a U.S. person.
2. The transfer of any money or property, directly or indirectly, to a foreign trust by a U.S. person, including a transfer by reason of death. This includes transfers that are deemed to have occurred under sections 679(a)(4) and (5).
3. The death of a citizen or resident of the United States if:

- The decedent was treated as the owner of any portion of a foreign trust under the grantor trust rules or
- Any portion of a foreign trust was included in the gross estate of the decedent.

Responsible Party

Responsible party means:
- The grantor in the case of the creation of an inter vivos trust,
- The transferor, in the case of a reportable event (defined above) other than a transfer by reason of death, or
- The executor of the decedent's estate in any other case (whether or not the executor is a U.S. person).

U.S. Agent

A U.S. agent is a U.S. person (defined below) that has a binding contract with a foreign trust that allows the U.S. person to act as the trust's authorized U.S. agent in applying sections 7602, 7603, and 7604 with respect to:
- Any request by the IRS to examine records or produce testimony related to the proper U.S. tax treatment of amounts distributed, or required to be taken into account under the grantor trust rules, with respect to a foreign trust; or
- Any summons by the IRS for such records or testimony.

A U.S. grantor, a U.S. beneficiary, or a domestic corporation controlled by the grantor or beneficiary may act as a U.S. agent. However, you may not treat the foreign trust as having a U.S. agent unless you enter the name, address, and taxpayer identification number of the U.S. agent on lines 3a through 3g. See *Identification numbers* on page 5.

If the person identified as the U.S. agent does not produce records or testimony when requested or summoned by the IRS, the IRS may redetermine the tax consequences of your transactions with the trust and impose appropriate penalties under section 6677.

The agency relationship must be established by the time the U.S. person files Form 3520 for the relevant tax year and must continue as long as the statute of limitations remains open for the relevant tax year. If the agent resigns or liquidates, or its responsibility as an agent of the trust is terminated, see Section IV(B) of Notice 97-34.

U.S. Beneficiary

A U.S. beneficiary generally includes any U.S. person that could possibly benefit (directly or indirectly) from the trust (including an amended trust) at any time, whether or not the person is named in the trust instrument as a beneficiary and whether or not the person can receive a distribution from the trust in the current year. In addition, a U.S. beneficiary includes:
- A foreign corporation that is a controlled foreign corporation (as defined in section 957(a)),
- A foreign partnership if a U.S. person is a partner of the partnership, and
- A foreign estate or trust if the estate or trust has a U.S. beneficiary.

A foreign trust will be treated as having a U.S. beneficiary unless the terms of the trust instrument specifically prohibit any distribution of income or corpus to a U.S. person at any time, even after the death of the U.S. transferor, and the trust cannot be amended or revised to allow such a distribution.

U.S. Person

A U.S. person is:
- A citizen or resident alien of the United States (see Pub. 519, U.S. Tax Guide for Aliens, for guidance on determining resident alien status),
- A domestic partnership,
- A domestic corporation,
- Any estate (other than a foreign estate, within the meaning of section 7701(a)(31)(A)), and
- Any domestic trust (defined on page 2).

U.S. Transferor

A U.S. transferor is any U.S. person who:

1. Creates or settles a foreign trust.
2. Directly or indirectly transfers money or property to a foreign trust. This includes a U.S. citizen or resident who has made a deemed transfer under section 679(a)(4) or a U.S. resident who has made a deemed transfer under section 679(a)(5).
3. Makes a sale to a foreign trust if the sale was at other than arm's-length terms or was to a related foreign trust, or makes (or guarantees) a loan to a related foreign trust.
4. Is the executor of the estate of a U.S. person and:

a. The decedent made a testamentary transfer (a transfer by reason of death) to a foreign trust,

b. Immediately prior to death, the decedent was treated as the owner of any portion of a foreign trust under the grantor trust rules, or

c. Any portion of a foreign trust's assets were included in the estate of the decedent.

Generally, the person defined as the transferor is the responsible party (defined above) who must ensure that required information be provided or pay appropriate penalties.

Specific Instructions

Period Covered

File the 2008 return for calendar year 2008 and fiscal years that begin in 2008 and end in 2009. For a fiscal year, fill in the tax year space at the top of the form.

Item A—Initial Return, Final Return, Amended Return

Initial return. If this is the first return you are filing concerning the foreign trust identified, check the "Initial return" box.

Final return. If no further returns for transactions with the foreign trust are required, check the "Final return" box.

Example. If you annually filed Part II, Form 3520, because you were the owner of the trust for U.S. income tax purposes and the trust has terminated within the tax year, that year's return would be a final return with respect to that foreign trust.

Amended return. If this Form 3520 is filed to amend a Form 3520 that you previously filed, check the "Amended return" box.

Identifying Information

Service Center. Generally, enter the name of the Service Center where you file your income tax return. However, if you are an executor filing a Form 3520 with respect to a U.S. decedent, provide both the name of the Service Center where the decedent's final income tax return will be filed, and the name of the Service Center where the estate tax return will be filed. Please enter the information as follows. First enter the name of the Service Center where the decedent's final income tax return will be filed. Then enter the name of the Service Center where the estate tax return will be filed, followed by "(estate tax return)."

If your income tax return is filed electronically, enter "e-filed."

Identification numbers. Use social security numbers or individual taxpayer identification numbers to identify individuals. Use employer identification numbers to identify estates, trusts, partnerships, and corporations.

 Do not enter a preparer tax identification number (PTIN) in any entry space on Form 3520 other than the entry space for "Preparer's SSN or PTIN" at the bottom of page 1 of the form.

Address. Include the suite, room, or other unit number after the street address. If the post office does not deliver mail to the street address and the U.S. person has a P.O. box, show the box number instead.

Foreign address. Do **not** abbreviate the country name.

Line 1. This line identifies the person that is filing Form 3520. If you and your spouse are both making transfers to the same trust and you file joint returns, you may file only one Form 3520. Put the names and taxpayer identification numbers in the same order as they appear on your Form 1040.

Line 4. If you are the executor of the estate of a U.S. citizen or resident, you must provide information about the decedent on lines 4a through 4e. You must also check the applicable box on line 4f to indicate which of the following applies: the U.S. decedent made a transfer to a foreign trust by reason of death, the U.S. decedent was treated as the owner of a portion of a foreign trust immediately prior to death, or the estate of the U.S. decedent included assets of a foreign trust.

Part I—Transfers by U.S. Persons to a Foreign Trust During the Current Tax Year

Complete Part I for information on a reportable event (defined on page 4).

Note. Although the basic reporting requirements for Form 3520 are contained in section 6048 (and are clarified by Notice 97-34), the reporting requirements have been clarified by the regulations under sections 679 and 684. Accordingly, the regulations under sections 679 and 684 should be referred to for additional clarification for transfers that are required to be reported in Part I of Form 3520.

Line 5. If you are not the trust creator, enter the name of the person that created or originally settled the foreign trust.

Line 6. See the list of country codes on pages 11, 12, and 13. If the country is not included in the list, enter "OC" for "other country" and enter the country's name.

Lines 7, 8, and 10. If you are reporting multiple transfers to a single foreign trust and the answers to lines 7, 8, or 10 are different for various transfers, complete a separate line for each transfer on duplicate copies of the relevant pages of the form.

Line 7a. If "Yes," you must comply with the reporting requirements that would apply to a direct transfer to that other person. For example, if that other person is a foreign partnership, you must comply with the reporting requirements for transfers to foreign partnerships (see Form 8865, Return of U.S. Persons With Respect to Certain Foreign Partnerships).

Line 8. If the transfer was a completed gift (see Regulations section 25.2511-2) or bequest, you may have to file Form 706, United States Estate (and Generation-Skipping Transfer) Tax Return, or Form 709, United States Gift (and Generation-Skipping Transfer) Tax Return.

Line 9. See definition of U.S. beneficiary on page 4.

Line 10. If you are treated as the owner of any portion of the foreign trust under the grantor trust rules, answer "Yes" to this question and complete Part II.

Schedule A—Obligations of a Related Trust

Line 11a. The FMV of an obligation of the trust (or an obligation of another person related to the trust) that you receive in exchange for the transferred property equals zero, unless the obligation meets the requirements of a qualified obligation. See page 3 for the definitions of obligation and qualified obligation. See page 4 for the definition of person related to a foreign trust.

Lines 12 and 26. If you answered "Yes" to the question on line 11b (line 25, column (e)) with respect to any obligation, you generally must answer "Yes" to the question on line 12 (line 26). By so doing, you agree to extend the period of assessment of any income or transfer tax attributable to the transfer and any consequential income tax changes for each year that the obligation is outstanding. This form will be deemed to be agreed upon and executed by the IRS for purposes of Regulations section 301.6501(c)-1(d).

If you answer "No" to the question on line 12 (line 26), you generally may not treat an obligation as a qualified obligation on line 11b (line 25, column (e)). The one exception to this is if the maturity date of the obligation does not extend beyond the end of your tax year for which you are reporting and such obligation is paid within that tax year.

Schedule B—Gratuitous Transfers

Complete the applicable portions of Schedule B with respect to all reportable events (defined on page 4) that took place during the current tax year.

Line 13
• In your description, indicate whether the property is tangible or intangible.
• You may aggregate transfers of cash during the year on a single line of line 13.

- If there is not enough space on the form, please attach a statement.
- For transfers reported on attachments, you must enter "Attachment" on one of the lines in column (b), and enter the total amount of transfers reported on the attachment on line 13, columns (c), (d), (e), (f), (h), and (i).

Note. Penalties may be imposed for failure to report all required information. See *Penalties* on page 2.

Line 13, column (e). Only include gain that is immediately recognized at the time of the transfer.

Note. For any transfer by a U.S. person to a foreign nongrantor trust after August 4, 1997, the transfer is treated as a sale or exchange and the transferor must recognize as a gain the excess of the FMV of the transferred property over its adjusted basis. Although the gain is not recognized on Form 3520, it must be reported on the appropriate form or schedule of the transferor's income tax return. See section 684.

Line 13, column (f). Generally, if the reported transaction is a sale, you should report the gain on the appropriate form or schedule of your income tax return.

Line 15. Enter the name, address, whether the person is a U.S. beneficiary (defined on page 4), and taxpayer identification number, if any, of all reportable beneficiaries. Include specified beneficiaries, classes of discretionary beneficiaries, and names or classes of any beneficiaries that could be named as additional beneficiaries. If there is not enough space on the form, please attach a statement.

Line 17. Enter the name, address, and taxpayer identification number (if any) of any person, other than those listed on line 16, that has significant powers over the trust (e.g., "protectors," "enforcers," any person that must approve trustee decisions or otherwise direct trustees, any person with a power of appointment, any person with powers to remove or appoint trustees, etc.). Include a description of each person's powers. If there is not enough space, attach a statement.

Line 18. If you checked "No" on line 3 (or you did not complete lines 3a through 3g) attach:
- A summary of the terms of the trust that includes a summary of any oral agreements or understandings you have with the trustee, whether or not legally enforceable.
- A copy of all trust documents (and any revisions), including the trust instrument, any memoranda of wishes prepared by the trustees summarizing the settlor's wishes, any letter of wishes prepared by the settlor summarizing his or her wishes, and any similar documents.
- A copy of the trust's financial statements, including a balance sheet and an income statement similar to those shown on Form 3520-A. These financial statements must reasonably reflect the trust's accumulated income under U.S. income tax principles. For example, the statements must not treat capital gains as additions to trust corpus.

Schedule C—Qualified Obligations Outstanding in the Current Tax Year

Line 19. Provide information on the status of outstanding obligations of the foreign trust (or person related to the foreign trust) that you reported as a qualified obligation in the current tax year. This information is required in order to retain the obligation's status as a qualified obligation. If relevant, attach a statement describing any changes in the terms of the qualified obligation.

If the obligation fails to retain the status of a qualified obligation, you will be treated as having made a gratuitous transfer to the foreign trust, which must be reported on Schedule B, Part I. See Section III(C)(2) of Notice 97-34.

Part II—U.S. Owner of a Foreign Trust

Complete Part II if you are considered the owner of any assets of a foreign trust under the grantor trust rules during the tax year. You are required to enter a taxpayer identification number for such foreign trust on line 2b.

Line 20. Enter information regarding any person other than yourself who is considered the owner of any portion of the trust under the grantor trust rules. Also, enter in column (e) the specific Code section that causes that person to be considered an owner for U.S. income tax purposes. See the grantor trust rules under sections 671 through 679.

Line 21. See the list of country codes on pages 11, 12, and 13. If the country is not included in the list, enter "OC" for "other country" and the country's name.

Line 22. If "Yes," the copy of the Foreign Grantor Trust Owner Statement (page 3 of Form 3520-A) should show the amount of the foreign trust's income that is attributable to you for U.S. income tax purposes. See Section IV of Notice 97-34.

If "No," you may be liable for a penalty of 5% of the trust assets that you are treated as owning, plus additional penalties for continuing failure to file after notice by the IRS. See section 6677. Also see *Penalties* on page 2.

Line 23. Enter the FMV of the trust assets that you are treated as owning. Include all assets at FMV as of the end of the tax year. For this purpose, disregard all liabilities. The trust should send you this information in connection with its Form 3520-A. If you did not receive such information (line 9 of the Foreign Grantor Trust Owner Statement) from the trust, complete line 23 to the best of your ability. At a minimum, include the value of all assets that you have transferred to the trust. Also use Form 8082 to notify the IRS that you did not receive a Foreign Grantor Trust Owner Statement. However, filing Form 8082 does not relieve you of any penalties that may be imposed under section 6677. See *Penalties* on page 2.

Part III—Distributions to a U.S. Person From a Foreign Trust During the Current Tax Year

If you received an amount from a portion of a foreign trust of which you are treated as the owner and you have correctly reported any information required on Part II and the trust has filed a Form 3520-A with the IRS, do not separately disclose distributions again in Part III. If you received an amount from a foreign trust that would require a report under both Parts III and IV (gifts and bequests) of Form 3520, report the amount only in Part III.

Line 24. Report any cash or other property that you received (actually or constructively, directly or indirectly) during the current tax year, from a foreign trust, whether or not taxable, unless the amount is a loan to you from the trust that must be reported on line 25. For example, if you are a partner in a partnership that receives a distribution from a foreign trust, you must report your allocable share of such payment as an indirect distribution from the trust.

Line 24, column (c). The filer is permitted to enter the basis of the property in the hands of the beneficiary (as determined under section 643(e)(1)), if lower than the FMV of the property, but only if the taxpayer is not required to complete Schedule A (lines 31 through 38) due to lack of documentation. For these purposes, lack of documentation refers to a situation in which the filer checked "No" on line 29 or 30 because (a) the beneficiary did not receive a Foreign Grantor Trust Beneficiary Statement or a Foreign Nongrantor Trust Beneficiary Statement from the trust or (b) such statement did not contain all six of the items specified under the instructions for line 29 or line 30 below.

Line 25. If you, or a person related to you, received a loan from a related foreign trust, it will be treated as a distribution to you unless the obligation you issued in exchange is a qualified obligation.

For this purpose, a loan to you by an unrelated third party that is guaranteed by a foreign trust is generally treated as a loan from the trust.

Line 25, column (e). Answer "Yes" if your obligation given in exchange for the loan is a qualified obligation (defined on page 3).

Line 26. See *Lines 12 and 26* on page 5.

Line 27. Penalties may be imposed for failure to accurately report all distributions received during the current tax year. See *Penalties* on page 2.

Line 28. Provide information on the status of any outstanding obligation to the foreign trust that you reported as a qualified obligation in the current tax year. This information is required in order to retain the obligation's status as a qualified obligation. If relevant, attach a statement describing any changes to the terms of the qualified obligation. If the obligation fails to retain the status of a qualified obligation, you will be treated as having received a distribution from the foreign trust, which must be reported as such on line 25. See Section V(A) of Notice 97-34.

Lines 29 and 30. If any of the six items required for the Foreign Grantor Trust Beneficiary Statement (see *Line 29* below) or for the Foreign Nongrantor Trust Beneficiary Statement (see *Line 30* below) is missing, you must check "No" on line 29 or line 30, as applicable.

Also, if you answer "Yes" to line 29 or line 30, and the foreign trust or U.S. agent does not produce records or testimony when requested or summoned by the IRS, the IRS may redetermine the tax consequences of your transactions with the trust and impose appropriate penalties under section 6677.

Line 29. If "Yes," attach the Foreign Grantor Trust Beneficiary Statement (page 4 of Form 3520-A) from the foreign trust and do not complete the rest of Part III with respect to the distribution. If a U.S. beneficiary receives a complete Foreign Grantor Trust Beneficiary Statement with respect to a distribution during the tax year, the beneficiary should treat the distribution for income tax purposes as if it came directly from the owner. For example, if the distribution is a gift, the beneficiary should not include the distribution in gross income.

In addition to basic identifying information (i.e., name, address, TIN, etc.) about the foreign trust and its trustee, this statement must contain these items:

1. The first and last day of the tax year of the foreign trust to which this statement applies.

2. An explanation of the facts necessary to establish that the foreign trust should be treated for U.S. tax purposes as owned by another person. (The explanation should identify the Code section that treats the trust as owned by another person.)

3. A statement identifying whether the owner of the trust is an individual, corporation, or partnership.

4. A description of property (including cash) distributed or deemed distributed to the U.S. person during the tax year, and the FMV of the property distributed.

5. A statement that the trust will permit either the IRS or the U.S. beneficiary to inspect and copy the trust's permanent books of account, records, and such other documents that are necessary to establish that the trust

should be treated for U.S. tax purposes as owned by another person. This statement is not necessary if the trust has appointed a U.S. agent.

6. A statement as to whether the foreign trust has appointed a U.S. agent (defined on page 4). If the trust has a U.S. agent, include the name, address, and taxpayer identification number of the agent.

Line 30. If "Yes," attach the Foreign Nongrantor Trust Beneficiary Statement from the foreign trust. A Foreign Nongrantor Trust Beneficiary Statement must include the following items:

1. An explanation of the appropriate U.S. tax treatment of any distribution or deemed distribution for U.S. tax purposes, or sufficient information to enable the U.S. beneficiary to establish the appropriate treatment of any distribution or deemed distribution for U.S. tax purposes.

2. A statement identifying whether any grantor of the trust is a partnership or a foreign corporation. If so, attach an explanation of the relevant facts.

3. A statement that the trust will permit either the IRS or the U.S. beneficiary to inspect and copy the trust's permanent books of account, records, and such other documents that are necessary to establish the appropriate treatment of any distribution or deemed distribution for U.S. tax purposes. This statement is not necessary if the trust has appointed a U.S. agent.

4. The Foreign Nongrantor Trust Beneficiary Statement must also include items 1, 4, and 6, as listed for line 29 above as well as basic identifying information (e.g., name, address, TIN, etc.) about the foreign trust and its trustee.

Schedule A—Default Calculation of Trust Distributions

If you answered "Yes" to line 30, you may complete either Schedule A or Schedule B. Generally, however, if you complete Schedule A in the current year (or did so in the prior years), you must continue to complete Schedule A for all future years, even if you are able to answer "Yes" to line 30 in that future year. (The only exception to this consistency rule is that you may use Schedule B in the year that a trust terminates, but only if you are able to answer "Yes" to line 30 in the year of termination.)

Line 32. To the best of your knowledge, state the number of years the trust has been in existence as a foreign trust and attach an explanation of your basis for this statement. Consider any portion of a year to be a complete year. If this is the first year that the trust has been a foreign trust, do not complete the rest of Part III (you do not have an accumulation distribution).

Line 33. Enter the total amount of distributions that you received during the 3 preceding tax years (or the number of years the trust has been a foreign trust, if less than 3). For example, if a trust distributed $50 in year 1, $120 in year 2, and $150 in year 3, the amount reported on line 33 would be $320 ($50 + $120 + $150).

Line 35. Divide line 34 by 3 (or the number of years the trust has been a foreign trust if fewer than 3). Consider any portion of a year to be a complete year. For example, a foreign trust created on July 1, 2006, would be treated on a 2008 calendar year return as having 2 preceding years (2006 and 2007). In this case, you would calculate the amount on line 35 by dividing line 34 by 2. Do not disregard tax years in which no distributions were made. The IRS will consider your proof of these prior distributions as adequate records to demonstrate that any distribution up to the amount on line 31 is not an accumulation distribution in the current tax year.

Line 36. Enter this amount as ordinary income on your tax return. Report this amount on the appropriate schedule of your tax return (e.g., Schedule E (Form 1040), Part III).

Note. If there is an amount on line 37, you must also complete line 38 and *Schedule C — Calculation of Interest Charge*, to determine the amount of any interest charge you may owe.

Schedule B—Actual Calculation of Trust Distributions

You may only use Schedule B if:
- You answered "Yes" to line 30,
- You attach a copy of the Foreign Nongrantor Trust Beneficiary Statement to this return, and
- You have never before used Schedule A for this foreign trust or this foreign trust terminated during the tax year.

Line 40. Enter the amount received by you from the foreign trust that is treated as ordinary income of the trust in the current tax year. Ordinary income is all income that is not capital gains. Report this amount on the appropriate schedule of your tax return (e.g., Schedule E (Form 1040), Part III).

Line 42. Enter the amount received by you from the foreign trust that is treated as capital gain income of that trust in the current tax year. Report this amount on the appropriate schedule of your tax return (e.g., Schedule D (Form 1040)).

Line 45. Enter the foreign trust's aggregate undistributed net income (UNI). For example, assume that a trust was created in 2002 and has made no distributions prior to 2008. Assume the trust's ordinary income was $0 in 2007, $60 in 2006, $124 in 2005, $87 in 2004, $54 in 2003, and $25 in 2002. Thus, for 2008, the trust's UNI would be $350. If the trust earned $100 and distributed $200 during 2008 (so that $100 was distributed from accumulated earnings), the trust's 2009 aggregate UNI would be $250 ($350 + $100 - $200).

Line 46. Enter the foreign trust's weighted undistributed net income (weighted UNI). The trust's weighted UNI is its accumulated income that has not been distributed, weighted by the years that it has accumulated income. To calculate weighted UNI, multiply the undistributed income from each of the trust's years by the number of years since that year, and then add each year's result. Using the example from line 45, the trust's weighted UNI in 2008 would be $1,260, calculated as follows:

Year	No. of years since that year	UNI from each year	Weighted UNI
2007	1	$ 0	$ 0
2006	2	60	120
2005	3	124	372
2004	4	87	348
2003	5	54	270
2002	6	25	150
TOTAL		$350	$1,260

To calculate the trust's weighted UNI for the following year (2009), the trust could update this calculation, or the weighted UNI shown on line 46 of the 2008 Form 3520 could simply be updated using the following steps:

1. Begin with the 2008 weighted UNI.
2. Add UNI at the beginning of 2008.
3. Add trust earnings in 2008.
4. Subtract trust distributions in 2008.
5. Subtract weighted trust accumulation distributions in 2008. (Weighted trust accumulation distributions are the

trust accumulation distributions in 2008 multiplied by the applicable number of years from 2008.)

Using the examples above, the trust's 2009 weighted UNI would be $1,150, calculated as follows.

2008 weighted UNI	$1,260
UNI at beginning of 2008	+ 350
Trust earnings in 2008	+ 100
Trust distributions in 2008	- 200
Weighted trust accumulation distributions in 2008 ($100 X 3.6)	- 360
2009 weighted UNI	$1,150

Line 47. Calculate the trust's applicable number of years by dividing line 46 by line 45. Using the examples in the instructions for lines 45 and 46, the trust's applicable number of years would be 3.6 in 2008 (1,260/350) and 4.6 in 2009 (1,150/250).

Note. Include as many decimal places as there are digits in the UNI on line 45 (e.g., using the example in the instructions for line 45, include three decimal places).

Schedule C—Calculation of Interest Charge

Complete Schedule C if you entered an amount on line 37 or line 41.

Line 49. Include the amount from line 48 of this form on line 1, Form 4970. Then compute the tax on the total accumulation distribution using lines 1 through 28 of Form 4970. Enter on line 49 the tax from line 28 of Form 4970, Tax on Accumulation Distribution of Trusts.

Note. Use Form 4970 as a worksheet and attach it to Form 3520.

Line 51. Interest accumulates on the tax (line 49) for the period beginning on the date that is the applicable number of years (as rounded on line 50) prior to the applicable date and ending on the applicable date. For purposes of making this interest calculation, the applicable date is the date that is mid-year through the tax year for which reporting is made (e.g., in the case of a 2008 calendar year taxpayer, the applicable date would be June 30, 2008). Alternatively, if you received only a single distribution during the tax year that is treated as an accumulation distribution, you may use the date of that distribution as the applicable date.

For portions of the interest accumulation period that are prior to 1996 (and after 1976), interest accumulates at a simple rate of 6% annually, without compounding. For portions of the interest accumulation period that are after 1995, interest is compounded daily at the rate imposed on underpayments of tax under section 6621(a)(2). This compounded interest for periods after 1995 is imposed not only on the tax, but also on the total simple interest attributable to pre-1996 periods.

If you are a 2008 calendar year taxpayer and you use June 30, 2008, as the applicable date for calculating interest, use the table below to determine the combined interest rate and enter it on line 51. If you are not a 2008 calendar year taxpayer or you choose to use the actual date of the distribution as the applicable date, calculate the combined interest rate using the above principles and enter it on line 51.

-8-

Table of Combined Interest Rate Imposed on the Total Accumulation Distribution

Look up the applicable number of years of the foreign trust that you entered on line 50. Read across to find the combined interest rate to enter on line 51. Use this table only if you are a 2008 calendar year taxpayer and are using June 30, 2008, as the applicable date.

Applicable number of years of trust (from line 50)	Combined interest rate (enter on line 51)
1	0.0753
1.5	0.1189
2	0.1649
2.5	0.2060
3	0.2462
3.5	0.2807
4	0.3100
4.5	0.3396
5	0.3704
5.5	0.4048
6	0.4479
6.5	0.4916
7	0.5452
7.5	0.6117
8	0.6863
8.5	0.7591
9	0.8314
9.5	0.9009
10	0.9791
10.5	1.0642
11	1.1600
11.5	1.2586
12	1.3631
12.5	1.4652
13	1.5391
13.5	1.6131
14	1.6870
14.5	1.7610
15	1.8349
15.5	1.9089
16	1.9828
16.5	2.0568
17	2.1308
17.5	2.2047
18	2.2787
18.5	2.3526
19	2.4266
19.5	2.5005
20	2.5745
20.5	2.6484
21	2.7224
21.5	2.7963
22	2.8703
22.5	2.9443
23	3.0182
23.5	3.0922
24	3.1661
24.5	3.2401
25	3.3140
25.5	3.3880
26	3.4619
26.5	3.5359
27	3.6098
27.5	3.6838
28	3.7578
28.5	3.8317
29	3.9057
29.5	3.9796
30	4.0536
30.5	4.1275
31	4.2015
All Years Greater than 31	4.2754

(**Note.** Interest charges began in 1977.)

Line 53. Report this amount as additional tax (ADT) on the appropriate line of your income tax return (e.g., for Form 1040 filers, include this amount as part of the total for line 61 of your 2008 Form 1040 and enter "ADT" to the left of the line 61 entry space).

Part IV—U.S. Recipients of Gifts or Bequests Received During the Current Tax Year From Foreign Persons

Note. Penalties may be imposed for failure to report gifts that should be reported. See *Penalties* on page 2.

A gift to a U.S. person does not include any amount paid for qualified tuition or medical payments made on behalf of the U.S. person.

If a foreign trust makes a distribution to a U.S. beneficiary, the beneficiary must report the amount as a distribution in Part III, rather than as a gift in Part IV.

Contributions of property by foreign persons to domestic or foreign trusts that have U.S. beneficiaries are not reportable by those beneficiaries in Part IV unless they are treated as receiving the contribution in the year of the transfer (e.g., the beneficiary is an owner of that portion of the trust under section 678).

A domestic trust that is not treated as owned by another person is required to report the receipt of a contribution to the trust from a foreign person as a gift in Part IV.

A domestic trust that is treated as owned by a foreign person is not required to report the receipt of a contribution to the trust from a foreign person. However, a U.S. person should report the receipt of a distribution from such a trust as a gift from a foreign person in Part IV.

Line 54. To calculate the threshold amount ($100,000), you must aggregate gifts from different foreign nonresident aliens and foreign estates if you know (or have reason to know) that those persons are related to each other (see definition of related person on page 3) or one is acting as a nominee or intermediary for the other. For example, if you receive a gift of $75,000 from nonresident alien individual A and a gift of $40,000 from nonresident alien individual B, and you know that A and B are related, you must answer "Yes" and complete columns (a) through (c) for each gift.

If you answered "Yes" to the question on line 54 and none of the gifts or bequests received exceeds $5,000, do not complete columns (a) through (c) of line 54. Instead, enter in column (b) of the first line: "No gifts or bequests exceed $5,000."

Note. Include gifts or bequests from a "covered expatriate" (as defined in section 877A(g)(1)) when calculating the $100,000 threshold amount.

Line 55. Answer "Yes" if you received aggregate amounts in excess of $13,561 during the current tax year that you treated as gifts from foreign corporations or foreign partnerships (or any persons that you know (or have reason to know) are related to such foreign corporations or foreign partnerships).

For example, if you, a calendar-year taxpayer during 2008, received $6,000 from foreign corporation X that you treated as a gift, and $8,000 that you received from nonresident alien A that you treated as a gift, and you know that X is wholly owned by A, you must complete columns (a) through (g) for each gift.

Note. Gifts from foreign corporations or foreign partnerships are subject to recharacterization by the IRS under section 672(f)(4).

Line 56. If you answered "Yes" to the question on line 56 and the ultimate donor on whose behalf the reporting donor is acting is a foreign corporation or foreign partnership, attach an explanation including the ultimate foreign donor's name, address, identification number (if any), and status as a corporation or partnership.

If the ultimate donor is a foreign trust, treat the amount received as a distribution from a foreign trust and complete Part III.

Line 57. Answer "Yes" if, during the current tax year, you received a "covered gift or bequest" (as defined in section 2801(e)) of more than $12,000 from a "covered expatriate" (as defined in section 877A(g)(1)).

Important. Answer "Yes" only in the case of "covered gifts and bequests" received on or after June 17, 2008 from transferors (or from the estates of transferors) whose expatriation date is on or after June 17, 2008.

Note. If you answer "Yes" to the question on line 57, complete and file Form 708. Presently, the IRS is developing this form. When available, this form will be posted at *www.irs.gov*. If Form 708 is not available at the time you file your income tax return, attach a separate statement to your income tax return which shows your computation of the section 2801 tax.

Privacy Act and Paperwork Reduction Act Notice. We ask for the information on this form to carry out the Internal Revenue laws of the United States. You are required to give us the information. We need it to ensure that you are complying with these laws and to allow us to figure and collect the right amount of tax.

Our authority to ask for information is sections 6001, 6011, and 6012(a) and their regulations, which require you to file a return or statement with us for any tax for which you are liable. Your response is mandatory under these sections. Section 6109 requires filers and return preparers to provide their identification numbers. This is so we know who you are, and can process your return and other papers. You must fill in all parts of the tax form that apply to you.

You are not required to provide the information requested on a form that is subject to the Paperwork Reduction Act unless the form displays a valid OMB control number. Books or records relating to a form or its instructions must be retained as long as their contents may become material in the administration of any Internal Revenue law. Generally, tax returns and return information are confidential, as required by section 6103. However, section 6103 allows or requires the Internal Revenue Service to disclose or give the information shown on your tax return to others as described in the Code. For example, we may disclose your tax information to the Department of Justice to enforce the tax laws, both civil and criminal, and to cities, states, the District of Columbia, and U.S. commonwealths or possessions to carry out their tax laws. We may also disclose this information to other countries under a tax treaty, to federal and state agencies to enforce federal nontax criminal laws, or to federal law enforcement and intelligence agencies to combat terrorism. Failure to provide this information, or providing false information, may subject you to fines or penalties.

Please keep this notice with your records. It may help you if we ask you for other information. If you have any questions about the rules for filing and giving information, please call or visit any Internal Revenue Service office.

The time needed to complete and file this form and related schedules will vary depending on individual circumstances. The estimated burden for individual taxpayers filing this form is approved under OMB control number 1545-0074 and is included in the estimates shown in the instructions for their individual income tax return. The estimated burden for all other taxpayers who file this form is shown below.

Recordkeeping	42 hr., 48 min.
Learning about the law or the form	4 hr., 50 min.
Preparing the form	6 hr., 40 min.
Sending the form to the IRS	16 min.

If you have comments concerning the accuracy of these time estimates or suggestions for making this form simpler, we would be happy to hear from you. You can write to the Internal Revenue Service, Tax Products Coordinating Committee, SE:W:CAR:MP:T:T:SP, 1111 Constitution Ave. NW, IR-6526, Washington, DC 20224. Do not send the tax form to this office. Instead, see *When and Where To File* on page 2.

Country Codes

Enter on lines 6a and 6b and line 21, columns (a) and (b), the codes from the list below.

Country	Country Code
Afghanistan	AF
Akrotiri	AX
Albania	AL
Algeria	AG
American Samoa	AQ
Andorra	AN
Angola	AO
Anguilla	AV
Antarctica	AY
Antigua and Barbuda	AC
Argentina	AR
Armenia	AM
Aruba	AA
Ashmore and Cartier Islands	AT
Australia	AS
Austria	AU
Azerbaijan	AJ
Bahamas	BF
Bahrain	BA
Baker Island	FQ
Bangladesh	BG
Barbados	BB
Belarus	BO
Belgium	BE
Belize	BH
Benin	BN
Bermuda	BD
Bhutan	BT
Bolivia	BL
Bosnia-Herzegovina	BK
Botswana	BC
Bouvet Island	BV
Brazil	BR
British Indian Ocean Territory	IO
Brunei	BX
Bulgaria	BU
Burkina Faso	UV
Burma	BM
Burundi	BY

Country	Country Code
Cambodia	CB
Cameroon	CM
Canada	CA
Cape Verde	CV
Cayman Islands	CJ
Central African Republic	CT
Chad	CD
Chile	CI
China, People's Republic of (including Inner Mongolia, Tibet and Manchuria)	CH
Christmas Island	KT
Clipperton Island	IP
Cocos (Keeling) Islands	CK
Colombia	CO
Comoros	CN
Congo (Brazzaville)	CF
Congo, Democratic Republic of (Kinshasa)	CG
Cook Islands	CW
Coral Sea Islands	CR
Costa Rica	CS
Cote d'Ivoire (Ivory Coast)	IV
Croatia	HR
Cuba	CU
Cyprus	CY
Czech Republic	EZ
Denmark	DA
Dhekelia	DX
Djibouti	DJ
Dominica	DO
Dominican Republic	DR
East Timor	TT
Ecuador	EC
Egypt	EG
El Salvador	ES
Equatorial Guinea	EK
Eritrea	ER
Estonia	EN
Ethiopia	ET
Falkland Islands (Islas Malvinas)	FK

Country	Country Code
Faroe Islands	FO
Fiji	FJ
Finland	FI
France	FR
French Polynesia	FP
French Southern & Antarctic Lands	FS
Gabon	GB
Gambia	GA
Georgia	GG
Germany	GM
Ghana	GH
Gibraltar	GI
Greece	GR
Greenland	GL
Grenada	GJ
Guadeloupe	GP
Guam	GQ
Guatemala	GT
Guernsey	GK
Guinea	GV
Guinea-Bissau	PU
Guyana	GY
Haiti	HA
Heard Island and McDonald Islands	HM
Holy See	VT
Honduras	HO
Hong Kong	HK
Howland Island	HQ
Hungary	HU
Iceland	IC
India	IN
Indonesia	ID
Iran	IR
Iraq	IZ
Ireland	EI
Isle of Man	IM
Israel	IS
Italy	IT
Jamaica	JM
Jan Mayen	JN
Japan	JA
Jarvis Island	DQ
Jersey	JE

Country	Country Code
Johnston Atoll	JQ
Jordan	JO
Kazakhstan	KZ
Kenya	KE
Kingman Reef	KQ
Kiribati	KR
Korea, North	KN
Korea, South	KS
Kosovo, Republic of	KV
Kuwait	KU
Kyrgyzstan	KG
Laos	LA
Latvia	LG
Lebanon	LE
Lesotho	LT
Liberia	LI
Libya	LY
Liechtenstein	LS
Lithuania	LH
Luxembourg	LU
Macau	MC
Macedonia	MK
Madagascar	MA
Malawi	MI
Malaysia	MY
Maldives	MV
Mali	ML
Malta	MT
Marshall Islands	RM
Martinique	MB
Mauritania	MR
Mauritus	MP
Mayotte	MF
Mexico	MX
Micronesia, Federated States of	FM
Midway Islands	MQ
Moldova	MD
Monaco	MN
Mongolia	MG
Montenegro	MJ
Montserrat	MH
Morocco	MO
Mozambique	MZ

Country	Country Code
Namibia	WA
Nauru	NR
Navassa Island	BQ
Nepal	NP
Netherlands	NL
Netherlands Antilles	NT
New Caledonia	NC
New Zealand	NZ
Nicaragua	NU
Niger	NG
Nigeria	NI
Niue	NE
Norfolk Island	NF
Northern Mariana Island	CQ
Norway	NO
Oman	MU
Pakistan	PK
Palau	PS
Palmyra Atoll	LQ
Panama	PM
Papua New Guinea	PP
Paracel Island	PF
Paraguay	PA
Peru	PE
Philippines	RP
Pitcairn Islands	PC
Poland	PL
Portugal	PO
Puerto Rico	RQ
Qatar	QA
Reunion	RE
Romania	RO
Russia	RS
Rwanda	RW
Samoa	WS
San Marino	SM
Sao Tome and Principe	TP
Saudi Arabia	SA
Senegal	SG
Serbia	RB
Seychelles	SE
Sierra Leone	SL
Singapore	SN

Country	Country Code
Slovakia	LO
Slovenia	SI
Solomon Islands	BP
Somalia	SO
South Africa	SF
South Georgia and South Sandwich Islands	SX
Spain	SP
Spratly Islands	PG
Sri Lanka	CE
St. Bartholemy	TB
St. Helena	SH
St. Kitts and Nevis	SC
St. Lucia	ST
St. Martin	RN
St. Pierre and Miquelon	SB
St. Vincent and The Grenadines	VC
Sudan	SU
Suriname	NS
Svalbard	SV
Swaziland	WZ
Sweden	SW
Switzerland	SZ
Syria	SY
Tajikistan	TI
Tanzania	TZ
Thailand	TH
Timor-Leste	TT
Togo	TO
Tokelau	TL
Tonga	TN
Trinidad and Tobago	TD
Tunisia	TS
Turkey	TU
Turkmenistan	TX
Turks and Caicos Islands	TK
Tuvalu	TV
Uganda	UG
Ukraine	UP
United Arab Emirates	AE
United Kingdom	UK

-12-

Country	Country Code
United States	US
Uruguay	UY
Uzbekistan	UZ
Vanuatu	NH
Venezuela	VE

Country	Country Code
Vietnam	VM
Virgin Islands	VI
Virgin Islands, U.S.	VQ
Wake Island	WQ
Wallis and Futuna	WF

Country	Country Code
Western Sahara	WI
Yemen	YM
Zambia	ZA
Zimbabwe	ZI
Other Countries	OC

IRS Form **8300** (Rev. March 2008) OMB No. 1545-0892 Department of the Treasury Internal Revenue Service	**Report of Cash Payments Over $10,000 Received in a Trade or Business** ▶ See instructions for definition of cash. ▶ Use this form for transactions occurring after March 31, 2008. Do not use prior versions after this date. For Privacy Act and Paperwork Reduction Act Notice, see page 5.	FinCEN Form **8300** (Rev. March 2008) OMB No. 1506-0018 Department of the Treasury Financial Crimes Enforcement Network

1 Check appropriate box(es) if: **a** ☐ Amends prior report; **b** ☐ Suspicious transaction.

Part I   Identity of Individual From Whom the Cash Was Received

2 If more than one individual is involved, check here and see instructions . . . . ▶ ☐

3 Last name	**4** First name	**5** M.I.	**6** Taxpayer identification number

7 Address (number, street, and apt. or suite no.)	**8** Date of birth . . ▶ M M D D Y Y Y Y (see instructions)

9 City	**10** State	**11** ZIP code	**12** Country (if not U.S.)	**13** Occupation, profession, or business

14 Identifying document (ID) **a** Describe ID ▶ .... **b** Issued by ▶ .... **c** Number ▶

Part II   Person on Whose Behalf This Transaction Was Conducted

15 If this transaction was conducted on behalf of more than one person, check here and see instructions . . . . ▶ ☐

16 Individual's last name or Organization's name	**17** First name	**18** M.I.	**19** Taxpayer identification number

20 Doing business as (DBA) name (see instructions)	Employer identification number

21 Address (number, street, and apt. or suite no.)	**22** Occupation, profession, or business

23 City	**24** State	**25** ZIP code	**26** Country (if not U.S.)

27 Alien identification (ID) **a** Describe ID ▶ .... **b** Issued by ▶ .... **c** Number ▶

Part III   Description of Transaction and Method of Payment

28 Date cash received M M D D Y Y Y Y	**29** Total cash received $ .00	**30** If cash was received in more than one payment, check here . . . . ▶ ☐	**31** Total price if different from item 29 $ .00

32 Amount of cash received (in U.S. dollar equivalent) (must equal item 29) (see instructions):

- **a** U.S. currency $ .... .00 (Amount in $100 bills or higher $ .... .00)
- **b** Foreign currency $ .... .00 (Country ▶ ....)
- **c** Cashier's check(s) $ .... .00 Issuer's name(s) and serial number(s) of the monetary instrument(s) ▶
- **d** Money order(s) $ .... .00 ....
- **e** Bank draft(s) $ .... .00 ....
- **f** Traveler's check(s) $ .... .00

33 Type of transaction

- **a** ☐ Personal property purchased
- **b** ☐ Real property purchased
- **c** ☐ Personal services provided
- **d** ☐ Business services provided
- **e** ☐ Intangible property purchased
- **f** ☐ Debt obligations paid
- **g** ☐ Exchange of cash
- **h** ☐ Escrow or trust funds
- **i** ☐ Bail received by court clerks
- **j** ☐ Other (specify in item 34) ▶

34 Specific description of property or service shown in 33. Give serial or registration number, address, docket number, etc. ▶ ....

Part IV   Business That Received Cash

35 Name of business that received cash	**36** Employer identification number

37 Address (number, street, and apt. or suite no.)	Social security number

38 City	**39** State	**40** ZIP code	**41** Nature of your business

42 Under penalties of perjury, I declare that to the best of my knowledge the information I have furnished above is true, correct, and complete.

Signature ▶ .... Authorized official   Title ▶ ....

43 Date of signature M M D D Y Y Y Y	**44** Type or print name of contact person	**45** Contact telephone number ( )

IRS Form **8300** (Rev. 3-2008)   Cat. No. 62133S   FinCEN Form **8300** (Rev. 3-2008)

IRS Form 8300 (Rev. 3-2008)   Page **2**   **FinCEN Form 8300** (Rev. 3-2008)

Multiple Parties
(Complete applicable parts below if box 2 or 15 on page 1 is checked)

Part I   Continued—Complete if box 2 on page 1 is checked

3 Last name	4 First name	5 M.I.	6 Taxpayer identification number

7 Address (number, street, and apt. or suite no.)	8 Date of birth . . ▶ (see instructions)	M M D D Y Y Y Y

9 City	10 State	11 ZIP code	12 Country (if not U.S.)	13 Occupation, profession, or business

14 Identifying document (ID)	a **Describe ID** ▶	b **Issued by** ▶ ....
	c **Number** ▶	

3 Last name	4 First name	5 M.I.	6 Taxpayer identification number

7 Address (number, street, and apt. or suite no.)	8 Date of birth . . ▶ (see instructions)	M M D D Y Y Y Y

9 City	10 State	11 ZIP code	12 Country (if not U.S.)	13 Occupation, profession, or business

14 Identifying document (ID)	a **Describe ID** ▶	b **Issued by** ▶ ....
	c **Number** ▶	

Part II   Continued—Complete if box 15 on page 1 is checked

16 Individual's last name or Organization's name	17 First name	18 M.I.	19 Taxpayer identification number

20 Doing business as (DBA) name (see instructions)	Employer identification number

21 Address (number, street, and apt. or suite no.)	22 Occupation, profession, or business

23 City	24 State	25 ZIP code	26 Country (if not U.S.)

27 Alien identification (ID)	a **Describe ID** ▶	b **Issued by** ▶ ....
	c **Number** ▶	

16 Individual's last name or Organization's name	17 First name	18 M.I.	19 Taxpayer identification number

20 Doing business as (DBA) name (see instructions)	Employer identification number

21 Address (number, street, and apt. or suite no.)	22 Occupation, profession, or business

23 City	24 State	25 ZIP code	26 Country (if not U.S.)

27 Alien identification (ID)	a **Describe ID** ▶	b **Issued by** ▶ ....
	c **Number** ▶	

Comments – Please use the lines provided below to comment on or clarify any information you entered on any line in Parts I, II, III, and IV

_____
_____
_____
_____

IRS Form **8300** (Rev. 3-2008)   FinCEN Form **8300** (Rev. 3-2008)

Section references are to the Internal Revenue Code unless otherwise noted.

Important Reminders

• Section 6050I (26 United States Code (U.S.C.) 6050I) and 31 U.S.C. 5331 require that certain information be reported to the IRS and the Financial Crimes Enforcement Network (FinCEN). This information must be reported on IRS/FinCEN Form 8300.

• Item 33 box i is to be checked only by clerks of the court; box d is to be checked by bail bondsmen. See the instructions on page 5.

• The meaning of the word "currency" for purposes of 31 U.S.C. 5331 is the same as for the word "cash" (See *Cash* on page 4).

General Instructions

Who must file. Each person engaged in a trade or business who, in the course of that trade or business, receives more than $10,000 in one transaction or in two or more related transactions, must file Form 8300. Any transactions conducted between a payer (or its agent) and the recipient in a 24-hour period are related transactions. Transactions are considered related even if they occur over a period of more than 24 hours if the recipient knows, or has reason to know, that each transaction is one of a series of connected transactions.

Keep a copy of each Form 8300 for 5 years from the date you file it.

Clerks of federal or state courts must file Form 8300 if more than $10,000 in cash is received as bail for an individual(s) charged with certain criminal offenses. For these purposes, a clerk includes the clerk's office or any other office, department, division, branch, or unit of the court that is authorized to receive bail. If a person receives bail on behalf of a clerk, the clerk is treated as receiving the bail. See the instructions for Item 33 on page 5.

If multiple payments are made in cash to satisfy bail and the initial payment does not exceed $10,000, the initial payment and subsequent payments must be aggregated and the information return must be filed by the 15th day after receipt of the payment that causes the aggregate amount to exceed $10,000 in cash. In such cases, the reporting requirement can be satisfied either by sending a single written statement with an aggregate amount listed or by furnishing a copy of each Form 8300 relating to that payer. Payments made to satisfy separate bail requirements are not required to be aggregated. See Treasury Regulations section 1.6050I-2.

Casinos must file Form 8300 for nongaming activities (restaurants, shops, etc.).

Voluntary use of Form 8300. Form 8300 may be filed voluntarily for any suspicious transaction (see *Definitions* on page 4) for use by FinCEN and the IRS, even if the total amount does not exceed $10,000.

Exceptions. Cash is not required to be reported if it is received:

• By a financial institution required to file Form 104, Currency Transaction Report.

• By a casino required to file (or exempt from filing) Form 103, Currency Transaction Report by Casinos, if the cash is received as part of its gaming business.

• By an agent who receives the cash from a principal, if the agent uses all of the cash within 15 days in a second transaction that is reportable on Form 8300 or on Form 104, and discloses all the information necessary to complete Part II of Form 8300 or Form 104 to the recipient of the cash in the second transaction.

• In a transaction occurring entirely outside the United States. See Publication 1544, Reporting Cash Payments of Over $10,000 (Received in a Trade or Business), regarding transactions occurring in Puerto Rico and territories and possessions of the United States.

• In a transaction that is not in the course of a person's trade or business.

When to file. File Form 8300 by the 15th day after the date the cash was received. If that date falls on a Saturday, Sunday, or legal holiday, file the form on the next business day.

Where to file. File the form with the Internal Revenue Service, Detroit Computing Center, P.O. Box 32621, Detroit, MI 48232.

Statement to be provided. You must give a written or electronic statement to each person named on a required Form 8300 on or before January 31 of the year following the calendar year in which the cash is received. The statement must show the name, telephone number, and address of the information contact for the business, the aggregate amount of reportable cash received, and that the information was furnished to the IRS. Keep a copy of the statement for your records.

Multiple payments. If you receive more than one cash payment for a single transaction or for related transactions, you must report the multiple payments any time you receive a total amount that exceeds $10,000 within any 12-month period. Submit the report within 15 days of the date you receive the payment that

causes the total amount to exceed $10,000. If more than one report is required within 15 days, you may file a combined report. File the combined report no later than the date the earliest report, if filed separately, would have to be filed.

Taxpayer identification number (TIN). You must furnish the correct TIN of the person or persons from whom you receive the cash and, if applicable, the person or persons on whose behalf the transaction is being conducted. You may be subject to penalties for an incorrect or missing TIN.

The TIN for an individual (including a sole proprietorship) is the individual's social security number (SSN). For certain resident aliens who are not eligible to get an SSN and nonresident aliens who are required to file tax returns, it is an IRS Individual Taxpayer Identification Number (ITIN). For other persons, including corporations, partnerships, and estates, it is the employer identification number (EIN).

If you have requested but are not able to get a TIN for one or more of the parties to a transaction within 15 days following the transaction, file the report and attach a statement explaining why the TIN is not included.

Exception: *You are not required to provide the TIN of a person who is a nonresident alien individual or a foreign organization if that person or foreign organization:*

• *Does not have income effectively connected with the conduct of a U.S. trade or business;*

• *Does not have an office or place of business, or a fiscal or paying agent in the United States;*

• *Does not furnish a withholding certificate described in §1.1441-1(e)(2) or (3) or §1.1441-5(c)(2)(iv) or (3)(iii) to the extent required under §1.1441-1(e)(4)(vii); or*

• *Does not have to furnish a TIN on any return, statement, or other document as required by the income tax regulations under section 897 or 1445.*

Penalties. You may be subject to penalties if you fail to file a correct and complete Form 8300 on time and you cannot show that the failure was due to reasonable cause. You may also be subject to penalties if you fail to furnish timely a correct and complete statement to each person named in a required report. A minimum penalty of $25,000 may be imposed if the failure is due to an intentional or willful disregard of the cash reporting requirements.

Penalties may also be imposed for causing, or attempting to cause, a trade or business to fail to file a required report; for causing, or attempting to cause, a trade or business to file a required report containing a material omission or misstatement of fact; or for structuring, or attempting to structure, transactions to avoid the reporting requirements. These violations may also be subject to criminal prosecution which, upon conviction, may result in imprisonment of up to 5 years or fines of up to $250,000 for individuals and $500,000 for corporations or both.

Definitions

Cash. The term "cash" means the following:

• U.S. and foreign coin and currency received in any transaction.

• A cashier's check, money order, bank draft, or traveler's check having a face amount of $10,000 or less that is received in a designated reporting transaction (defined below), or that is received in any transaction in which the recipient knows that the instrument is being used in an attempt to avoid the reporting of the transaction under either section 6050I or 31 U.S.C. 5331.

Note. Cash does not include a check drawn on the payer's own account, such as a personal check, regardless of the amount.

Designated reporting transaction. A retail sale (or the receipt of funds by a broker or other intermediary in connection with a retail sale) of a consumer durable, a collectible, or a travel or entertainment activity.

Retail sale. Any sale (whether or not the sale is for resale or for any other purpose) made in the course of a trade or business if that trade or business principally consists of making sales to ultimate consumers.

Consumer durable. An item of tangible personal property of a type that, under ordinary usage, can reasonably be expected to remain useful for at least 1 year, and that has a sales price of more than $10,000.

Collectible. Any work of art, rug, antique, metal, gem, stamp, coin, etc.

Travel or entertainment activity. An item of travel or entertainment that pertains to a single trip or event if the combined sales price of the item and all other items relating to the same trip or event that are sold in the same transaction (or related transactions) exceeds $10,000.

Exceptions. A cashier's check, money order, bank draft, or traveler's check is not considered received in a designated reporting transaction if it constitutes the proceeds of a bank loan or if it is received as a payment on certain promissory notes, installment sales contracts, or down payment plans. See Publication 1544 for more information.

Person. An individual, corporation, partnership, trust, estate, association, or company.

Recipient. The person receiving the cash. Each branch or other unit of a person's trade or business is considered a separate recipient unless the branch receiving the cash (or a central office linking the branches), knows or has reason to know the identity of payers making cash payments to other branches.

Transaction. Includes the purchase of property or services, the payment of debt, the exchange of a negotiable instrument for cash, and the receipt of cash to be held in escrow or trust. A single transaction may not be broken into multiple transactions to avoid reporting.

Suspicious transaction. A suspicious transaction is a transaction in which it appears that a person is attempting to cause Form 8300 not to be filed, or to file a false or incomplete form.

Specific Instructions

You must complete all parts. However, you may skip Part II if the individual named in Part I is conducting the transaction on his or her behalf only. For voluntary reporting of suspicious transactions, see Item 1 below.

Item 1. If you are amending a prior report, check box 1a. Complete the appropriate items with the correct or amended information only. Complete all of Part IV. Staple a copy of the original report to the amended report.

To voluntarily report a suspicious transaction (see *Suspicious transaction* above), check box 1b. You may also telephone your local IRS Criminal Investigation Division or call 1-866-556-3974.

Part I

Item 2. If two or more individuals conducted the transaction you are reporting, check the box and complete Part I for any one of the individuals. Provide the same information for the other individual(s) on the back of the form. If more than three individuals are involved, provide the same information on additional sheets of paper and attach them to this form.

Item 6. Enter the taxpayer identification number (TIN) of the individual named. See *Taxpayer identification number (TIN)* on page 3 for more information.

Item 8. Enter eight numerals for the date of birth of the individual named. For example, if the individual's birth date is July 6, 1960, enter 07 06 1960.

Item 13. Fully describe the nature of the occupation, profession, or business (for example, "plumber," "attorney," or "automobile dealer"). Do not use general or nondescriptive terms such as "businessman" or "self-employed."

Item 14. You must verify the name and address of the named individual(s). Verification must be made by examination of a document normally accepted as a means of identification when cashing checks (for example, a driver's license, passport, alien registration card, or other official document). In item 14a, enter the type of document examined. In item 14b, identify the issuer of the document. In item 14c, enter the document's number. For example, if the individual has a Utah driver's license, enter "driver's license" in item 14a, "Utah" in item 14b, and the number appearing on the license in item 14c.

Note. You must complete all three items (a, b, and c) in this line to make sure that Form 8300 will be processed correctly.

Part II

Item 15. If the transaction is being conducted on behalf of more than one person (including husband and wife or parent and child), check the box and complete Part II for any one of the persons. Provide the same information for the other person(s) on the back of the form. If more than three persons are involved, provide the same information on additional sheets of paper and attach them to this form.

Items 16 through 19. If the person on whose behalf the transaction is being conducted is an individual, complete items 16, 17, and 18. Enter his or her TIN in item 19. If the individual is a sole proprietor and has an employer identification number (EIN), you must enter both the SSN and EIN in item 19. If the person is an organization, put its name as shown on required tax filings in item 16 and its EIN in item 19.

Item 20. If a sole proprietor or organization named in items 16 through 18 is doing business under a name other than that entered in item 16 (for example, a "trade" or "doing business as (DBA)" name), enter it here.

Item 27. If the person is not required to furnish a TIN, complete this item. See *Taxpayer Identification Number (TIN)* on page 3. Enter a description of the type of official document issued to that person in item 27a (for example, a "passport"), the country that issued the document in item 27b, and the document's number in item 27c.

Note. You must complete all three items (a, b, and c) in this line to make sure that Form 8300 will be processed correctly.

Part III

Item 28. Enter the date you received the cash. If you received the cash in more than one payment, enter the date you received the payment that caused the combined amount to exceed $10,000. See *Multiple payments* on page 3 for more information.

Item 30. Check this box if the amount shown in item 29 was received in more than one payment (for example, as installment payments or payments on related transactions).

Item 31. Enter the total price of the property, services, amount of cash exchanged, etc. (for example, the total cost of a vehicle purchased, cost of catering service, exchange of currency) if different from the amount shown in item 29.

Item 32. Enter the dollar amount of each form of cash received. Show foreign currency amounts in U.S. dollar equivalent at a fair market rate of exchange available to the public. The sum of the amounts must equal item 29. For cashier's check, money order, bank draft, or traveler's check, provide the name of the issuer and the serial number of each instrument. Names of all issuers and all serial numbers involved must be provided. If necessary, provide this information on additional sheets of paper and attach them to this form.

Item 33. Check the appropriate box(es) that describe the transaction. If the transaction is not specified in boxes a–i, check box j and briefly describe the transaction (for example, "car lease," "boat lease," "house lease," or "aircraft rental"). If the transaction relates to the receipt of bail by a court clerk, check box i, "Bail received by court clerks." This box is only for use by court clerks. If the transaction relates to cash received by a bail bondsman, check box d, "Business services provided."

Part IV

Item 36. If you are a sole proprietorship, you must enter your SSN. If your business also has an EIN, you must provide the EIN as well. All other business entities must enter an EIN.

Item 41. Fully describe the nature of your business, for example, "attorney" or "jewelry dealer." Do not use general or nondescriptive terms such as "business" or "store."

Item 42. This form must be signed by an individual who has been authorized to do so for the business that received the cash.

Comments

Use this section to comment on or clarify anything you may have entered on any line in Parts I, II, III, and IV. For example, if you checked box b (Suspicious transaction) in line 1 above Part I, you may want to explain why you think that the cash transaction you are reporting on Form 8300 may be suspicious.

Privacy Act and Paperwork Reduction Act Notice. Except as otherwise noted, the information solicited on this form is required by the Internal Revenue Service (IRS) and the Financial Crimes Enforcement Network (FinCEN) in order to carry out the laws and regulations of the United States Department of the Treasury. Trades or businesses, except for clerks of criminal courts, are required to provide the information to the IRS and FinCEN under both section 6050I and 31 U.S.C. 5331. Clerks of criminal courts are required to provide the information to the IRS under section 6050I. Section 6109 and 31 U.S.C. 5331 require that you provide your social security number in order to adequately identify you and process your return and other papers. The principal purpose for collecting the information on this form is to maintain reports or records which have a high degree of usefulness in criminal, tax, or regulatory investigations or proceedings, or in the conduct of intelligence or counterintelligence activities, by directing the federal Government's attention to unusual or questionable transactions.

You are not required to provide information as to whether the reported transaction is deemed suspicious. Failure to provide all other requested information, or providing fraudulent information, may result in criminal prosecution and other penalties under Title 26 and Title 31 of the United States Code.

Generally, tax returns and return information are confidential, as stated in section 6103. However, section 6103 allows or requires the IRS to disclose or give the information requested on this form to others as described in the Code. For example, we may disclose your tax information to the Department of Justice, to enforce the tax laws, both civil and criminal, and to cities, states, the District of Columbia, to carry out their tax laws. We may disclose this information to other persons as necessary to obtain information which we cannot get in any other way. We may disclose this information to federal, state, and local child support agencies; and to other federal agencies for the purposes of determining entitlement for benefits or the eligibility for and the repayment of loans. We may also provide the records to appropriate state, local, and foreign criminal law enforcement and regulatory personnel in the performance of their official duties. We may also disclose this information to other countries under a tax treaty, or to federal and state agencies to enforce federal nontax criminal laws and to combat terrorism. In addition, FinCEN may provide the information to those officials if they are conducting intelligence or counter-intelligence activities to protect against international terrorism.

You are not required to provide the information requested on a form that is subject to the Paperwork Reduction Act unless the form displays a valid OMB control number. Books or records relating to a form or its instructions must be retained as long as their contents may become material in the administration of any law under Title 26 or Title 31.

The time needed to complete this form will vary depending on individual circumstances. The estimated average time is 21 minutes. If you have comments concerning the accuracy of this time estimate or suggestions for making this form simpler, you can write to the Internal Revenue Service, Tax Products Coordinating Committee, SE:W:CAR:MP:T:T:SP, 1111 Constitution Ave. NW, IR-6526, Washington, DC 20224. Do not send Form 8300 to this address. Instead, see *Where to File* on page 3.

TD F 90-22.1

(Rev. October 2008)
Department of the Treasury

Do not use previous editions of this form after December 31, 2008

REPORT OF FOREIGN BANK AND FINANCIAL ACCOUNTS

Do NOT file with your Federal Tax Return

OMB No. 1545-2038

1 This Report is for Calendar Year Ended 12/31

_ _ _ _

Amended ☐

Part I   **Filer Information**

2   Type of Filer

a ☐ Individual   b ☐ Partnership   c ☐ Corporation   d ☐ Consolidated   e ☐ Fiduciary or Other—Enter type _____

3 U.S. Taxpayer Identification Number	4 Foreign identification (Complete only if item 3 is not applicable.)	5 Individual's Date of Birth MM/DD/YYYY
If filer has no U.S. Identification Number complete Item 4.	a Type: ☐ Passport ☐ Other _____ b Number _____ c Country of Issue _____	

6 Last Name or Organization Name	7 First Name	8 Middle Initial

9   Address (Number, Street, and Apt. or Suite No.)

10 City	11 State	12 Zip/Postal Code	13 Country

14   Does the filer have a financial interest in 25 or more financial accounts?

☐ Yes   If "Yes" enter total number of accounts _____

(If "Yes" is checked, do not complete Part II or Part III, but retain records of this information)

☐ No

Part II   **Information on Financial Account(s) Owned Separately**

15 Maximum value of account during calendar year reported	16 Type of account a ☐ Bank b ☐ Securities c ☐ Other—Enter type below

17   Name of Financial Institution in which account is held

18 Account number or other designation	19 Mailing Address (Number, Street, Suite Number) of financial institution in which account is held

20 City	21 State, if known	22 Zip/Postal Code, if known	23 Country

---

Signature

44 Filer Signature	45 Filer Title, if not reporting a personal account	46 Date (MM/DD/YYYY)

File this form with: U.S. Department of the Treasury, P.O. Box 32621, Detroit, MI 48232-0621

This form should be used to report a financial interest in, signature authority, or other authority over one or more financial accounts in foreign countries, as required by the Department of the Treasury Regulations (31 CFR 103). No report is required if the aggregate value of the accounts did not exceed $10,000. **See Instructions For Definitions.**

PRIVACY ACT AND PAPERWORK REDUCTION ACT NOTICE

Pursuant to the requirements of Public Law 93-579 (Privacy Act of 1974), notice is hereby given that the authority to collect information on TD F 90-22.1 in accordance with 5 USC 552a (e) is Public Law 91-508; 31 USC 5314; 5 USC 301; 31 CFR 103.

The principal purpose for collecting the information is to assure maintenance of reports where such reports or records have a high degree of usefulness in criminal, tax, or regulatory investigations or proceedings. The information collected may be provided to those officers and employees of any constituent unit of the Department of the Treasury who have a need for the records in the performance of their duties. The records may be referred to any other department or agency of the United States upon the request of the head of such department or agency for use in a criminal, tax, or regulatory investigation or proceeding. The information collected may also be provided to appropriate state, local, and foreign law enforcement and regulatory personnel in the performance of their official duties. Disclosure of this information is mandatory. Civil and criminal penalties, including in certain circumstances a fine of not more than $500,000 and imprisonment of not more than five years, are provided for failure to file a report, supply information, and for filing a false or fraudulent report. Disclosure of the Social Security number is mandatory. The authority to collect is 31 CFR 103. The Social Security number will be used as a means to identify the individual who files the report.

The estimated average burden associated with this collection of information is 20 minutes per respondent or record keeper, depending on individual circumstances. Comments regarding the accuracy of this burden estimate, and suggestions for reducing the burden should be directed to the Internal Revenue Service, Bank Secrecy Act Policy, 5000 Ellin Road C-3-242, Lanham MD 20706.

Cat. No. 12996D   Form **TD F 90-22.1** (Rev. 10-2008)

Part II Continued—Information on Financial Account(s) Owned Separately		Form TD F 90-22.1
Complete a Separate Block for Each Account Owned Separately		Page Number
This side can be copied as many times as necessary in order to provide information on all accounts.		___ of ___

1 Filing for calendar year

3–4 Check appropriate Identification Number

☐ Taxpayer Identification Number
☐ Foreign Identification Number
Enter identification number here:

6 Last Name or Organization Name

---

15 Maximum value of account during calendar year reported   **16** Type of account **a** ☐ Bank **b** ☐ Securities **c** ☐ Other—Enter type below

17 Name of Financial Institution in which account is held

18 Account number or other designation | **19** Mailing Address (Number, Street, Suite Number) of financial institution in which account is held

20 City | **21** State, if known | **22** Zip/Postal Code, if known | **23** Country

---

15 Maximum value of account during calendar year reported   **16** Type of account **a** ☐ Bank **b** ☐ Securities **c** ☐ Other—Enter type below

17 Name of Financial Institution in which account is held

18 Account number or other designation | **19** Mailing Address (Number, Street, Suite Number) of financial institution in which account is held

20 City | **21** State, if known | **22** Zip/Postal Code, if known | **23** Country

---

15 Maximum value of account during calendar year reported   **16** Type of account **a** ☐ Bank **b** ☐ Securities **c** ☐ Other—Enter type below

17 Name of Financial Institution in which account is held

18 Account number or other designation | **19** Mailing Address (Number, Street, Suite Number) of financial institution in which account is held

20 City | **21** State, if known | **22** Zip/Postal Code, if known | **23** Country

---

15 Maximum value of account during calendar year reported   **16** Type of account **a** ☐ Bank **b** ☐ Securities **c** ☐ Other—Enter type below

17 Name of Financial Institution in which account is held

18 Account number or other designation | **19** Mailing Address (Number, Street, Suite Number) of financial institution in which account is held

20 City | **21** State, if known | **22** Zip/Postal Code, if known | **23** Country

---

15 Maximum value of account during calendar year reported   **16** Type of account **a** ☐ Bank **b** ☐ Securities **c** ☐ Other—Enter type below

17 Name of Financial Institution in which account is held

18 Account number or other designation | **19** Mailing Address (Number, Street, Suite Number) of financial institution in which account is held

20 City | **21** State, if known | **22** Zip/Postal Code, if known | **23** Country

---

15 Maximum value of account during calendar year reported   **16** Type of account **a** ☐ Bank **b** ☐ Securities **c** ☐ Other—Enter type below

17 Name of Financial Institution in which account is held

18 Account number or other designation | **19** Mailing Address (Number, Street, Suite Number) of financial institution in which account is held

20 City | **21** State, if known | **22** Zip/Postal Code, if known | **23** Country

---

15 Maximum value of account during calendar year reported   **16** Type of account **a** ☐ Bank **b** ☐ Securities **c** ☐ Other—Enter type below

17 Name of Financial Institution in which account is held

18 Account number or other designation | **19** Mailing Address (Number, Street, Suite Number) of financial institution in which account is held

20 City | **21** State, if known | **22** Zip/Postal Code, if known | **23** Country

Form **TD F 90-22.1** (Rev. 10-2008)

Part III   **Information on Financial Account(s) Owned Jointly**   Form TD F 90-22.1

Complete a Separate Block for Each Account Owned Jointly   Page Number

This side can be copied as many times as necessary in order to provide information on all accounts.   ____ of ____

1 Filing for calendar year	3–4 Check appropriate Identification Number	6 Last Name or Organization Name
____ ____ ____ ____	☐ Taxpayer Identification Number ☐ Foreign Identification Number Enter identification number here:	

15 Maximum value of account during calendar year reported	16 Type of account **a** ☐ Bank **b** ☐ Securities **c** ☐ Other—Enter type below

17 Name of Financial Institution in which account is held

18 Account number or other designation	19 Mailing Address (Number, Street, Suite Number) of financial institution in which account is held	
20 City	**21** State, if known	**22** Zip/Postal Code, if known	**23** Country

24 Number of joint owners for this account	25 Taxpayer Identification Number of principal joint owner, if known. See instructions

26 Last Name or Organization Name of principal joint owner	27 First Name of principal joint owner, if known	28 Middle initial, if known

29 Address (Number, Street, Suite or Apartment) of principal joint owner, if known

30 City, if known	31 State, if known	32 Zip/Postal Code, if known	33 Country, if known

15 Maximum value of account during calendar year reported	16 Type of account **a** ☐ Bank **b** ☐ Securities **c** ☐ Other—Enter type below

17 Name of Financial Institution in which account is held

18 Account number or other designation	19 Mailing Address (Number, Street, Suite Number) of financial institution in which account is held
20 City	**21** State, if known	**22** Zip/Postal Code, if known	**23** Country

24 Number of joint owners for this account	25 Taxpayer Identification Number of principal joint owner, if known. See instructions

26 Last Name or Organization Name of principal joint owner	27 First Name of principal joint owner, if known	28 Middle initial, if known

29 Address (Number, Street, Suite or Apartment) of principal joint owner, if known

30 City, if known	31 State, if known	32 Zip/Postal Code, if known	33 Country, if known

15 Maximum value of account during calendar year reported	16 Type of account **a** ☐ Bank **b** ☐ Securities **c** ☐ Other—Enter type below

17 Name of Financial Institution in which account is held

18 Account number or other designation	19 Mailing Address (Number, Street, Suite Number) of financial institution in which account is held
20 City	**21** State, if known	**22** Zip/Postal Code, if known	**23** Country

24 Number of joint owners for this account	25 Taxpayer Identification Number of principal joint owner, if known. See instructions

26 Last Name or Organization Name of principal joint owner	27 First Name of principal joint owner, if known	28 Middle initial, if known

29 Address (Number, Street, Suite or Apartment) of principal joint owner, if known

30 City, if known	31 State, if known	32 Zip/Postal Code, if known	33 Country, if known

Form **TD F 90-22.1** (Rev. 10-2008)

Part IV	Information on Financial Account(s) Where Filer has Signature or Other Authority but No Financial Interest in the Account(s)	Form TD F 90-22.1

Complete a Separate Block for Each Account

This side can be copied as many times as necessary in order to provide information on all accounts.

Page Number

_____ of _____

1 Filing for calendar year ___ ___ ___ ___	3–4 Check appropriate Identification Number ☐ Taxpayer Identification Number ☐ Foreign Identification Number Enter identification number here:	6 Last Name or Organization Name

15 Maximum value of account during calendar year reported	16 Type of account a ☐ Bank b ☐ Securities c ☐ Other—Enter type below

17 Name of Financial Institution in which account is held

18 Account number or other designation	19 Mailing Address (Number, Street, Suite Number) of financial institution in which account is held

20 City	21 State, if known	22 Zip/Postal Code, if known	23 Country

34 Last Name or Organization Name of Account Owner	35 Taxpayer Identification Number of Account Owner

36 First Name	37 Middle initial	38 Address (Number, Street, and Apt. or Suite No.)

39 City	40 State	41 Zip/Postal Code	42 Country

43 Filer's Title with this Owner

15 Maximum value of account during calendar year reported	16 Type of account a ☐ Bank b ☐ Securities c ☐ Other—Enter type below

17 Name of Financial Institution in which account is held

18 Account number or other designation	19 Mailing Address (Number, Street, Suite Number) of financial institution in which account is held

20 City	21 State, if known	22 Zip/Postal Code, if known	23 Country

34 Last Name or Organization Name of Account Owner	35 Taxpayer Identification Number of Account Owner

36 First Name	37 Middle initial	38 Address (Number, Street, and Apt. or Suite No.)

39 City	40 State	41 Zip/Postal Code	42 Country

43 Filer's Title with this Owner

15 Maximum value of account during calendar year reported	16 Type of account a ☐ Bank b ☐ Securities c ☐ Other—Enter type below

17 Name of Financial Institution in which account is held

18 Account number or other designation	19 Mailing Address (Number, Street, Suite Number) of financial institution in which account is held

20 City	21 State, if known	22 Zip/Postal Code, if known	23 Country

34 Last Name or Organization Name of Account Owner	35 Taxpayer Identification Number of Account Owner

36 First Name	37 Middle initial	38 Address (Number, Street, and Apt. or Suite No.)

39 City	40 State	41 Zip/Postal Code	42 Country

43 Filer's Title with this Owner

Form **TD F 90-22.1** (Rev. 10-2008)

Part V	Information on Financial Account(s) Where Corporate Filer Is Filing a Consolidated Report	Form TD F 90-22.1

Complete a Separate Block for Each Account

This side can be copied as many times as necessary in order to provide information on all accounts.

Page Number

____ of ____

1 Filing for calendar year ___ ___ ___ ___	3-4 Check appropriate Identification Number ☐ Taxpayer Identification Number ☐ Foreign Identification Number Enter identification number here:	6 Last Name or Organization Name

15 Maximum value of account during calendar year reported	16 Type of account **a** ☐ Bank **b** ☐ Securities **c** ☐ Other—Enter type below

17 Name of Financial Institution in which account is held

18 Account number or other designation	19 Mailing Address (Number, Street, Suite Number) of financial institution in which account is held

20 City	21 State, if known	22 Zip/Postal Code, if known	23 Country

34 Corporate Name of Account Owner	35 Taxpayer Identification Number of Account Owner

38 Address (Number, Street, and Apt. or Suite No.)

39 City	40 State	41 Zip/Postal Code	42 Country

15 Maximum value of account during calendar year reported	16 Type of account **a** ☐ Bank **b** ☐ Securities **c** ☐ Other—Enter type below

17 Name of Financial Institution in which account is held

18 Account number or other designation	19 Mailing Address (Number, Street, Suite Number) of financial institution in which account is held

20 City	21 State, if known	22 Zip/Postal Code, if known	23 Country

34 Corporate Name of Account Owner	35 Taxpayer Identification Number of Account Owner

38 Address (Number, Street, and Apt. or Suite No.)

39 City	40 State	41 Zip/Postal Code	42 Country

15 Maximum value of account during calendar year reported	16 Type of account **a** ☐ Bank **b** ☐ Securities **c** ☐ Other—Enter type below

17 Name of Financial Institution in which account is held

18 Account number or other designation	19 Mailing Address (Number, Street, Suite Number) of financial institution in which account is held

20 City	21 State, if known	22 Zip/Postal Code, if known	23 Country

34 Corporate Name of Account Owner	35 Taxpayer Identification Number of Account Owner

38 Address (Number, Street, and Apt. or Suite No.)

39 City	40 State	41 Zip/Postal Code	42 Country

Form **TD F 90-22.1** (Rev. 10-2008)

General Instructions

Who Must File this Report. Each United States person who has a financial interest in or signature or other authority over any foreign financial accounts, including bank, securities, or other types of financial accounts, in a foreign country, if the aggregate value of these financial accounts exceeds $10,000 at any time during the calendar year, must report that relationship each calendar year by filing this report with the Department of the Treasury on or before June 30, of the succeeding year.

Exceptions

An officer or employee of a bank which is currently examined by Federal bank supervisory agencies for soundness and safety need not report that he has signature or other authority over a foreign bank, securities or other financial account maintained by the bank, if the officer or employee has NO personal financial interest in the account.

An officer or employee of a domestic corporation whose equity securities are listed upon any United States national securities exchange or which has assets exceeding $10 million and has 500 or more shareholders of record need not file such a report concerning signature or other authority over a foreign financial account of the corporation, if he has NO personal financial interest in the account and he has been advised in writing by the chief financial officer or similar responsible officer of the corporation that the corporation has filed a current report, which includes that account. An officer or employee of a domestic subsidiary of such a domestic corporation need not file this report concerning signature or other authority over the foreign financial account if the domestic parent meets the above requirements, he has no personal financial interest in the account, and he has been advised in writing by the responsible officer of the parent that the subsidiary has filed a current report which includes that account. If a United States subsidiary is named in a consolidated FBAR of the parent, the subsidiary will be deemed to have filed a report for purposes of this exception. An officer or employee of a foreign subsidiary more than 50% owned by such a domestic corporation need not file this report concerning signature or other authority over the foreign financial account if the employee or officer has no personal financial interest in the account, and he has been advised in writing by the responsible officer of the parent that the parent has filed a current report which includes that account.

General Definitions

United States Person. The term "United States person" means a citizen or resident of the United States, or a person in and doing business in the United States. See 31 C.F.R. 103.11(z) for a complete definition of "person." The United States includes the states, territories and possessions of the United States. See the definition of United States at 31 C.F.R. 103.11(nn) for a complete definition of United States. A foreign subsidiary of a United States person is not required to file this report, although its United States parent corporation may be required to do so. A branch of a foreign entity that is doing business in the United States is required to file this report even if not separately incorporated under U.S. law.

Financial Account. This term includes any bank, securities, securities derivatives or other financial instruments accounts. Such accounts generally also encompass any accounts in which the assets are held in a commingled fund, and the account owner holds an equity interest in the fund (including mutual funds). The term also means any savings, demand,

checking, deposit, time deposit, or any other account (including debit card and prepaid credit card accounts) maintained with a financial institution or other person engaged in the business of a financial institution. Individual bonds, notes, or stock certificates held by the filer are not a financial account nor is an unsecured loan to a foreign trade or business that is not a financial institution.

Account in a Foreign Country. A "foreign country" includes all geographical areas located outside the United States. See "United States Person" above 31 C.F.R. 103.11(nn) for a definition of United States. The geographical location of the account, not the nationality of the financial entity institution in which the account is found determines whether it is in an account in a foreign country. Report any financial account (except a military banking facility) that is located in a foreign country, even if it is held at an affiliate of a United States bank or other financial institution. Do not report any account maintained with a branch, agency, or other office of a foreign bank of other institution that is located in the United States.

Military Banking Facility. Do not consider as an account in a foreign country, an account in an institution known as a "United States military banking facility" (or "United States military finance facility") operated by a United States financial institution designated by the United States Government to serve U.S. Government installations abroad, even if the United States military banking facility is located in a foreign Country, is not an account in a foreign country.

Financial Interest. A financial interest in a bank, securities, or other financial account in a foreign country means an interest described in one of the following three paragraphs:

1. A United States person has a financial interest in each account for which such person is the owner of record or has legal title, whether the account is maintained for his or her own benefit or for the benefit of others including non–United States persons.

2. A United States person has a financial interest in each bank, securities, or other financial account in a foreign country for which the owner of record or holder of legal title is: (a) a person acting as an agent, nominee, attorney, or in some other capacity on behalf of the U.S. person; (b) a corporation in which the United States person owns directly or indirectly more than 50 percent of the total value of shares of stock or more than 50 percent of the voting power for all shares of stock; (c) a partnership in which the United States person owns an interest in more than 50 percent of the profits (distributive share of income, taking into account any special allocation agreement) or more than 50 percent of the capital of the partnership; or (d) a trust in which the United States person either has a present beneficial interest, either directly or indirectly, in more than 50 percent of the assets or from which such person receives more than 50 percent of the current income.

3. A United States person has a financial interest in each bank, securities, or other financial account in a foreign country for which the owner of record or holder of legal title is a trust, or a person acting on behalf of a trust, that was established by such United States person and for which a trust protector has been appointed. A trust protector is a person who is responsible for monitoring the activities of a trustee, with the authority to influence the decisions of the trustee or to replace, or recommend the replacement of, the trustee.

Correspondent or "nostro" accounts (international interbank transfer accounts) maintained by banks that are used solely for the purpose of bank-to-bank settlement need not be reported on this form, but are subject to other Bank Secrecy Act filing requirements. This exception is intended to encompass those accounts utilized for bank-to-bank settlement purposes only.

Signature or Other Authority Over an Account. A person has signature authority over an account if such person can control the disposition of money or other property in it by delivery of a document containing his or her signature (or his or her signature and that of one or more other persons) to the bank or other person with whom the account is maintained. Other authority exists in a person who can exercise comparable power over an account by communication with the bank or other person with whom the account is maintained, either directly or through an agent, nominee, attorney, or in some other capacity on behalf of the U.S. person, either orally or by some other means.

Filing Information—Do NOT file with your Federal Income Tax Return

When and where to file. This report must be filed on or before June 30 of the year following the calendar year reported. The report is required annually. File by mailing this report to the Department of the Treasury, Post Office Box 32621, Detroit, MI 48232-0621, or by hand-carrying it to any local office of the Internal Revenue Service for forwarding to the Department of the Treasury, Detroit, MI. Tax attaches are located in the U.S. embassies in some countries. A filer can receive instructions for verifying that a report has been filed by calling the Detroit Computing Center Hotline at 1-800-800-2877.

Extensions of time to file federal tax returns do not extend the time for filing this report. **There is no extension of time available for filing this report.** If a delinquent FBAR is filed, also attach a statement explaining the reason for the late filing. See "When and where to file" (above) for filing instructions.

An amendment of a previously filed FBAR is accomplished by checking the "Amended" box in the upper right hand corner of the first page of the form, making the needed additions or corrections, and then stapling it to a copy of the original form. Please also attach a statement explaining the changes. See "When and where to file" (above) for filing instructions.

Record Keeping Requirements. If this Report is required, certain records must be retained. Such records must contain the name in which each such account is maintained, the number or other designation of such account, the name and address of the foreign bank or other person with whom such account is maintained, the type of such account, and the maximum value of each account during the reporting period. Retaining filed copies of this report will help to meet these requirements. The records must be retained for a period of five years and must kept at all times available for inspection as provided by law.

Explanations for Specific Items

Part I

Item 1. The Report of Foreign Bank and Financial Accounts (FBAR) is an annual report. Enter the calendar year being reported.

Amendment of a previously filed FBAR is accomplished by checking the "Amended" box in the upper right hand corner of the first page of the form, making the needed additons and corrections, and then stapling it to a copy of the original report. See "When and where to file" (above) for filing instructions.

Item 2. Check the appropriate box describing the filer. A corporation which owns directly or indirectly more than a 50 percent interest in one or more other entities required to file this Report will be permitted to file a consolidated report on TD F 90-22.1, on behalf of itself and such other entities.

Check box "d" in Item 2 and complete Part V. Consolidated reports should be signed by an authorized official of the parent corporation. Trusts and other entities, including tax-exempt organizations, should check box "e" and describe the filer on the line following box "e."

Item 3. A filer should provide the filer's taxpayer identification number. Generally this is the filer's U.S. social security number (SSN) or employer identification number (EIN). Numbers should be entered with no spaces, dashes, or other punctuation throughout this report. If the filer does not possess such U.S. identification, the filer should complete Item 4.

Item 4. Complete Item 4 only if the filer has no U.S. taxpayer identification number. Item 4 requires the filer to provide the information about an official foreign government document evidencing the filer's nationality or residence. The filer should write in the document number followed by the country of issuance. The filer may check off the type of document. If "other" is checked, the filer should write in the type of document. For example, an individual who is not a U.S. citizen would provide a passport number, the name of the country of issuance, and check off "passport."

Item 5. Enter the date of birth of the filer using the month, day, and year convention.

Items 6, 7 and 8. Enter the name of the filer. An organization should enter its name in the Last Name space.

Items 9, 10, 11, 12 and 13. Enter the address of the filer. An individual filer residing in the United States should enter the street address of filer's United States residence, not a post office box. An individual filer residing outside the United States should enter the filer's United States mailing address. If the filer has no U.S. mailing address the filer may provide a foreign address. An organization should enter its United States mailing address.

Item 14. If the filer has a financial interest in 25 or more foreign financial accounts, the filer should check the yes box, sign and date the report (Items 44, 45 and 46) and leave blank Part II (Continuation of Separate Accounts) or Part III (Joint Accounts) of the report. If the group of entities covered by a consolidated report has a financial interest in 25 or more foreign financial accounts, the reporting parent corporation need only complete Part V (for consolidated reporting) Items 34 through 42, for the identity information of the account owners, but need not complete the account information. Detailed information about each account, including all information called for on this report, must be recorded and retained for five years from June 30 of the year following the calendar year reported. Any person who reports 25 or more foreign financial accounts must provide all the information omitted from Part II, III or V as appropriate.

Part II

Item 15. Provide the maximum value of the account during the calendar year being reported. The maximum value of an account is the largest amount of currency or non-monetary assets that appear on any quarterly or more frequent account statement issued for the applicable year. If periodic account statements are not issued, the maximum account asset value is the largest amount of currency and non-monetary assets in the account at any time during the year. Convert foreign currency by using the official exchange rate at the end of the year. In valuing currency of a country that uses multiple exchange rates, use the rate which would apply if the currency in the account were converted into United States dollars at the close of the calendar year. The value of stock, other securities, or other non-monetary assets in an account reported on TD F 90-22.1 is the fair market value at the end of the calendar year or, if withdrawn from the account, at the time of the withdrawal. For purposes of Item 15, if the filer had a financial interest in more than one account, each account is to be valued separately in accordance with the foregoing two paragraphs. If the filer had a financial interest in one or more but fewer than 25 accounts, and is unable to determine whether the maximum value of these accounts exceeded $10,000 at any time during the year, complete Part II, III, or V for each of these accounts and enter "value unknown" in Item 15 for these accounts.

Item 16. Indicate the type of account. If "Other" is selected describe the account.

Item 17. Provide the name of the financial institution with which the account is held.

Item 18. Provide the account number which the financial institution uses to designate the account.

Item 19—23. Provide the complete mailing address of the financial institution where the account is located. If the foreign state or postal code is not known leave them blank.

Part III

Item 24. Enter the number of joint owners for the account. If the exact number is not known, provide an estimate. In determining the number of joint owners, the filer is not counted.

Items 25—33. Enter this identity information about the joint owner. If there is more than one joint owner, enter the identity information about the principal joint owner. The filer may leave blank items for which no information is available. A spouse having a joint financial interest in an account with the filing spouse should be included as a joint account owner in Part III of this report. The filer should write (spouse) on Line 26 after the last name of the joint spousal owner. If the only reportable accounts of the filer's spouse are those reported as joint accounts, the filer's spouse need not file a separate report. If the accounts are owned jointly by both spouses, the filer's spouse should also sign the report. See the instructions for Item 44. If the filer's spouse has a financial interest in other accounts that are not jointly owned with the filer or has signature or other authority over other accounts, the filer's spouse should file a separate report for all accounts including those owned jointly with the other spouse.

Part IV—No Financial Interest in Account

Items 34-42. You must provide the name, address, and identifying number of the owner of a foreign financial account over which you had signature or other authority but no

financial interest in the account. If there is more than one owner of the account over which you have authority, providethe information in Items 34-43 for the primary owner for which you have authority. If you complete the account information for more than one account of the same owner, you need identify the owner only once. Write "Same Owner" in Item 34 for the succeeding accounts of the same owner.

Item 43. Enter filer's title for the position which gives him authority over the account.

Part V—Consolidated Report for Corporate Parent & Subsidiary Corporations

A corporation which owns directly or indirectly more than a 50 percent interest in one or more other entities required to file this report will be permitted to file a consolidated report on TD F 90-22.1, on behalf of itself and such other entities. Check box "d" in Item 2 in Part I and complete Part V.

Items 34—42. You must provide the corporate name, identifying number and address of the owner of the foreign financial account as shown on the books of the financial institution.

If you complete the account information for more than one account of the same owner you need identify the owner only once. Write "Same Owner" in Item 34 for the succeeding accounts of the same owner.

Signatures

This report must be signed by the person named in Part I. If the report is being filed on behalf of a partnership, corporation, fiduciary or other legal entity, it must be signed by an authorized individual. Consolidated reports should be signed by an authorized official of the parent corporation. Enter the title of the individual signing for a legal entity, such as a corporation, which is shown as the filer. A spouse included as a joint owner, who elects not to file a separate report in accordance with the instructions in Part III, must also sign this report. See the instructions for Part III.

Enter the title of the individual signing for a legal entity, such as a corporation, which is shown as the filer. Leave "Filer's Title" blank if the filer is only reporting as an individual. An individual filing because of a financial interest in his individual accounts is filing as an individual. An individual filing because of signature or other authority over a foreign financial account is filing as an individual. If the filer only has signature authority over the account, he should enter his title in Part IV Item 43, Filer's Title with this Owner, to show his relationship to the account. Enter the actual date signed.

FinCEN Form 107	Registration of Money Services Business	
August, 2008 Previous editions will not be accepted after December 31, 2008.	Please type or print. Always complete entire report. See instructions for items marked with an asterisk (*).	 OMB No.1506-0013

Complete and send to: Enterprise Computing Center-Detroit, Attn: Money Services Business Registration, P. O. Box 33116, Detroit, MI 48232-0116

Part I   Filing Information

1 Indicate the type of filing by checking a, b, or d below (Check only one). If filing a <u>correction</u>, check "c" **and** either a, b, or d.

  a ☐ Initial registration   b ☐ Renewal   c ☐ Correcting a prior filing   d ☐ Re-registration

2 If you checked item 1 d please indicate the reason(s). Check all that apply.

  a ☐ Re-registered under state law   b ☐ More than 10 percent transfer of equity interest   c ☐ More than 50 percent increase in agents

Part II   Registrant Information

*3 Legal name of the money services business

4 Doing business as

*5 Address	*6 City	*7 State	8 ZIP Code

*9 EIN (entity), SSN/ITIN (individual)	10 Telephone number (include area code)	11 E-mail address (If available)

Part III   Owner or Controlling Person

12 Individual's last name, or organization's name	13 First name	14 Middle initial

15 Address

16 City	17 State	18 ZIP Code/Postal Code	19 Country (if other than US)

20 Telephone number - (include area code)	21 Date of birth ___ / ___ / ___ MM DD YYYY	22 SSN/ITIN (individual), EIN (entity)

23 Skip this item if you completed item 22.

    If the owner or controlling person is an individual enter their form of identification, the ID number, and the issuing state or country.

  a ☐ Driver's license/state ID   b ☐ Passport   c ☐ Alien registration   z ☐ Other _____

  e ID number |__|__|__|__|__|__|__|__|__|__|__|__|__|__|__| f Issuing state or country _____

Part IV   Money Services and Product Information

24 States and/or territories where the registrant, its agents or branches are located. Check box a, b, or c as appropriate (<u>Check only one</u>) and
   do not check individual state/territory boxes. If box a, b, or c **does not apply**, check as many state/territory boxes as necessary.

a ☐ All States & Territories   b ☐ All States   c ☐ All Territories

☐ Alabama (AL)	☐ Georgia (GA)	☐ Maryland (MD)	☐ New York (NY)	☐ South Dakota (SD)
☐ Alaska (AK)	☐ Guam (GU)	☐ Massachusetts (MA)	☐ North Carolina (NC)	☐ Tennessee (TN)
☐ American Somoa (AS)	☐ Hawaii (HI)	☐ Michigan (MI)	☐ North Dakota (ND)	☐ Texas (TX)
☐ Arizona (AZ)	☐ Idaho (ID)	☐ Minnesota (MN)	☐ N. Mariana Isls. (MP)	☐ Utah (UT)
☐ Arkansas (AR)	☐ Illinois (IL)	☐ Mississippi (MS)	☐ Ohio (OH)	☐ Vermont (VT)
☐ California (CA)	☐ Indiana (IN)	☐ Missouri (MO)	☐ Oklahoma (OK)	☐ Virgin Islands (VI)
☐ Colorado (CO)	☐ Iowa (IA)	☐ Montana (MT)	☐ Oregon (OR)	☐ Virginia (VA)
☐ Connecticut (CT)	☐ Kansas (KS)	☐ Nebraska (NE)	☐ Palau (PW)	☐ Washington (WA)
☐ Delaware (DE)	☐ Kentucky (KY)	☐ Nevada (NV)	☐ Pennsylvania (PA)	☐ West Virginia (WV
☐ District of Columbia (DC)	☐ Louisiana (LA)	☐ New Hampshire (NH)	☐ Puerto Rico (PR)	☐ Wisconsin (WI)
☐ FS of Micronesia (FM)	☐ Maine (ME)	☐ New Jersey (NJ)	☐ Rhode Island (RI)	☐ Wyoming (WY)
☐ Florida (FL)	☐ Marshall Islands (MH)	☐ New Mexico (NM)	☐ South Carolina (SC)	

Part IV   (continued)   2

25 Enter the number of branches of the registrant. **Reminder: do not separately register each branch.**
See instructions for an explanation of the term "branch".

26 Money services business activities of the registrant. Check as many as apply. See instructions for an explanation of the terms " issuer",
"seller", "redeemer", "check casher", and "money transmitter".

a ☐   Issuer of traveler's checks   d ☐   Issuer of money orders   g ☐   Currency dealer or exchanger

b ☐   Seller of traveler's checks   e ☐   Seller of money orders   h ☐   Check casher

c ☐   Redeemer of traveler's checks   f ☐   Redeemer of money orders   i ☐   Money transmitter

27 Is any part of the registrant's money services business an informal value transfer system?
See the explanation of "money transmitter" in the instructions.   a ☐ Yes   b ☐ No

28 Is any part of the registrant's money services business conducted as a mobile operation?
a ☐ Yes   b ☐ No

29 Enter the number of agents authorized to conduct each money services business activity. Do not include branches, or persons who are
solely employees. See instructions for an explanation of the term "agent".

a   Traveler's check sales   e   Currency exchange
or dealer

b   Traveler's check redemption   f   Check cashing

c   Money order sales   g   Money transmission

d   Money order redemption

Part V   **Primary Transaction Account for MSB Activities**

30 If the registrant has more than one transaction account for money services business activities check here. ☐
See instructions for an explanation of the term "transaction account".
The registrant's primary transaction account is the one that has the greatest annual dollar amount of money services business activity.
In items 31 through 36 enter information about the registrant's primary transaction account for money services business activities.

31 Name of financial institution where the primary transaction account is held

32 Address   33 City

34 State | 35 ZIP Code | 36 Primary transaction account number

Part VI   **Location of Supporting Documentation**

If the supporting documentation is kept at the U.S. location reported in Part II check here ☐ and continue to Part VII.

37 Address

38 City   39 State | 40 ZIP Code

Part VII   **Authorized Signature**

I am authorized to file this form on behalf of the money services business listed in Part II. I declare that the information provided is true, correct and
complete. I understand that the money services business listed in Part II is subject to the Bank Secrecy Act and its implementing regulations. See 31
CFR Part 103. The money services business listed in Part II maintains a current list of all agents, an estimate of its business volume in the coming
year, and all other information required to comply with 31 U.S.C. 5330 and the regulations thereunder. **The signature of the owner, controlling
person or authorized corporate officer is mandatory.**

41 Signature   42 Print name

43 Title   44 Date of signature

_____ / _____ / _____
MM   DD   YYYY

Rev. 8/08

FinCEN Form 107a   Registration of Money Services Business Instructions ▮1

General Information

Who Must Register

Generally each money services business must register with the Department of the Treasury. This form must be used by a money services business (also referred to as an MSB) to register. However, not all MSBs are required to register. For example, if you are an MSB solely because you are an agent of another MSB, you are not required to register. The discussion below will help you determine whether or not you are an MSB that is required to register. For more information visit **www.msb.gov**.

The term money services business includes:
1. Currency dealers or exchangers who exchange more than $1,000 for any one customer on any day.

2. Check cashers who cash checks totaling more than $1,000 for any one customer on any day.

3. Issuers of traveler's checks, money orders or stored value who issue more than $1,000 in traveler's checks, money orders or stored value for any one customer on any day.

4. Sellers of traveler's checks, money orders or stored value who sell more than $1,000 in traveler's checks, money orders or stored value for any one customer on any day.

5. Redeemers of traveler's checks, money orders or stored value who redeem more than $1,000 in traveler's checks, money orders or stored value for any one customer on any day.

6. Money transmitters.

7. U.S. Postal Service.

The following are not required to register:
1. A business that is an MSB solely because it serves as an agent of another MSB. For example, a supermarket corporation that sells money orders for an issuer of money orders is not required to register. This is true even if the supermarket corporation serves as an agent for two or more MSBs. However, an MSB that serves as an agent of another MSB and engages in MSB activities on its own behalf must register. For example, a supermarket corporation must register if, in addition to acting as an agent of the money order issuer, it provides check cashing or currency exchange services on its own behalf in an amount greater than $1,000 for any one person on any day.

2. The United States Postal Service, any agency of the United States, of any state, or of any political subdivision of any state.

3. At this time, persons are not required to register to the extent that they issue, sell or redeem stored value. If, however, a money services business provides money services in addition to stored value, the provision of stored value services does not relieve it of the responsibility to register, if required, as a provider of those other services.

For the regulatory definition of "money services business" see 31 CFR 103.11(n) and (uu).

The following terms are used in the form and instructions to describe a money services business:

1. An "agent" is a separate business entity from the issuer that the issuer authorizes, through written agreement or otherwise, to sell its instruments or, in the case of funds transmission, to sell its send and receive transfer services. A person who is solely an employee of the MSB is not an agent of that MSB.

2. A "branch" is an owned location of either an issuer or agent at which financial services are sold. An MSB should not separately register each of its branches. A mobile operation owned by an MSB is a branch of that MSB. The MSB's headquarters is not a branch. If the MSB has only one location, that location is not a branch.

3. A "check casher" is a person engaged in the business of providing cash to persons in return for a check.

4. A "currency dealer or exchanger" is a person who engages in the physical exchange of currency for retail customers.

5. "Informal value transfer system". See explanation of the term money transmitter.

6. An "issuer" is the business that is ultimately responsible for payment of money orders or travelers checks as the drawer of such instruments, or a money transmitter that has the obligation to guarantee payment of a money transfer.

7. A "money transmitter" is a person that engages as a business in the transfer of funds through a financial institution.
Generally, acceptance and transmission of funds as an integral part of the execution and settlement of a transaction other than the funds transmission itself (for example, in connection with the bona fide sale of securities) will not cause a person to be a money transmitter.
An "informal value transfer system" is a kind of money transmitter. An informal value transfer system includes any person who engages as a business in an informal money transfer system or any network of people who engage as a business in facilitating the transfer of money domestically or internationally outside of the conventional financial institutions system.
8. A "person" is an individual, a corporation, a partnership, a trust or estate, a joint stock company, an association, a syndicate, joint venture, or other unincorporated organization or group, an Indian Tribe (as that term is defined in the Indian Gaming Regulatory Act), and all entities cognizable as legal personalities.

9. A "redeemer" is a business that accepts instruments in exchange for currency or other instruments for which it is not the issuer. You are not a redeemer if you take the instruments in exchange for goods or general services, provided that the amount of cash returned is not more than $1,000 for any one customer on any day.

10. A "seller" is a business that issuers authorize, through written agreement or otherwise, to sell their instruments or their send and receive transfer services.

11. A "transaction account" is a deposit or account on which the depositor or account holder is permitted to make withdrawals by negotiable or transferable instrument, payment orders of withdrawal, telephone transfers, or other similar items for the purpose of making payments or transfers to third persons or others. Such terms include demand deposits, negotiable order of withdrawal accounts, savings deposit subject to automatic transfers, and share draft accounts. See 12 USC 461(b)(1)(c).

When to Register

Initial registration: File the form within 180 days after the date the business is established.

Renewal: Each MSB must renew its registration every two years, on or before December 31. See 31 CFR 103.41(b)(2). For example, if an MSB registered on October 15, 2003, it must file a renewal by December 31, 2004, and then every 24 months thereafter (on or before December 31, 2006, then December 31, 2008, etc.). **Renewals must be submitted on a new Form 107. Photo copies of previously submitted forms or facsimiles will not be accepted for renewal purposes**

Correction: Use the form to correct a prior report. Complete Part I in its entirety and only those other entries that are being added or changed. Staple a copy of the prior report (or the acknowledgment from ECC-D if received) to the corrected report.

Re-registration: Refile a new registration form when one of the following events occurs:
1. a change in ownership requiring re-registration under state registration law;
2. more than 10 percent of voting power or equity interest is transferred (except certain publicly-traded companies) or;
3. the number of agents increases by more than 50 percent.

Where to Register

Send your completed form to:

Enterprise Computing Center - Detroit
Attn: Money Services Business Registration
P.O. Box 33116
Detroit, MI 48232-0116

FinCEN Form 107   Registration of Money Services Business Instructions   **2**

The Enterprise Computing Center-Detroit (ECC-D) will send an acknowledgment of receipt to the registrant listed in Part II within approximately 60 days after the form is processed (See note below). ECC-D can respond to general questions over the phone at telephone (800) 800-2877.

General Instructions

NOTE: All items on FinCEN Form 107 should be completed fully and accurately. Items marked with an asterisk (*) must be completed for the registration to be accepted, processed, and recorded. Acknowledgment letters will not be provided if these items are not complete.

1. This form is available on the Financial Crimes Enforcement Network's web site for MSBs at www.msb.gov, or FinCEN's web site at www.fincen.gov, or by calling the IRS Forms Distribution Center at (800) 829-2437.

2. Unless there is a specific instruction to the contrary, leave blank any items that do not apply or for which information is not available.

3. Complete the form by providing as much information as possible.

4. Do not include supporting documents with this form.

5. Type or complete the form using block written letters.

6. Enter all dates in MM / DD / YYYY format where MM=month, DD=day, and YYYY=year. Precede any single number with a zero, i.e., 01,02, etc.

7. List all U.S. telephone numbers with area code first and then the seven-digit phone number, using the format (XXX) XXX-XXXX.

8. Always enter an individual's name as last name, first name, and middle initial (if known). If a legal entity is listed, enter its name in the last name field.

9. Enter identifying numbers starting from left to right. Do not include spaces, dashes, or other punctuation. Identifying numbers include social security number (SSN), employer identification number (EIN), individual taxpayer identification number (ITIN), alien registration number, driver's license/state identification, foreign national identification, and passport number.

10. Enter all Post Office ZIP Codes from left to right with at least the first five numbers, or with all nine (ZIP + 4) if known.

11. Addresses: Enter the US permanent street address, city, two-letter state or territory abbreviation used by the U.S. Postal Service and ZIP Code (ZIP+4 if known) of the individual or

entity. A post office box number should not be used for an individual, unless no other address is available. For an individual, also enter any apartment number, suite number, or road or route number. If a P.O. Box is used for an entity, enter the street name, suite number, and road or route number. If the address of the individual or entity in PART III is in a foreign country, enter the city, province or state, postal code and the name of the country. Complete any part of the address that is known, even if the entire address is not known. If the address is in the United States leave country code blank.

Specific Instructions

Part I   Filing Information

See "When to Register" in the General Information part of these instructions.

Item 1-- Check either box a, b, or d (only one) for the type of filing. If this report corrects an earlier filing. check box **"c" and** either box a, b, or d.

Item 2-- If you checked box 1d, please indicate the reason by checking boxes a, b, or c (check all that apply).

Part II   Registrant Information

Enter the US State or Territory operating location.

Item *3--Legal name of the money services business. Enter the full legal name of the registrant money services business as it is shown on the charter or other document creating the entity. For example, enter Good Hope Enterprises, Inc. when the money services business is Good Hope Enterprises, Inc. If a sole proprietorship, enter the business name of the proprietorship.

Item 4-- Doing business as. If applicable, enter separate doing business as name of the registrant. For example, if Good Hope Enterprises, Inc., is doing business as "Joe's Check Cashing" enter in item 4, Joe's Check Cashing.

Items *5, *6, *7 and 8-- Address. Enter the permanent United States address of the registrant's US operations that is being registered.

Item *9--EIN (entity), SSN/ITIN (individual). If the registrant is an entity enter its employer identification number (EIN). If the registrant is an individual and a U. S. Citizen or an alien with a social security number, enter his/her SSN. If the registrant is an individual who is an alien and has an individual taxpayer identification number, enter his/her ITIN.

Item 10-- Telephone number. Enter the telephone number of the MSB listed in item 3.

Item 11-- E-mail address (Optional). If the MSB has an e-mail address please enter it here. An e-mail address may be used to contact the MSB should questions arise regarding their registration.

Part III   Owner or Controlling Person

General: Any person who owns or controls a money services business is responsible for registering the MSB. Only one registration form is required for any business in any registration period. If more than one person owns or controls the business, they may enter into an agreement designating one of them to register the MSB. The designated owner or controlling person must complete Part III and provide the requested information. In addition, that person must sign and date the form as indicated in Part VII. Failure by the designated person to register the business does not relieve any other person who owns or controls the business of the liability for failure to register the business.

An "Owner or Controlling Person" includes the following:

Registrant Business	Owner or Controlling Person
Sole Proprietorship	the individual who owns the business
Partnership	a general partner
Trust	a trustee
Corporation	the largest single shareholder

If two or more persons own equal numbers of shares of a corporation, those persons may enter into an agreement as explained above that one of those persons may register the business. If the owner or controlling person is a corporation, a duly authorized officer of the owner-corporation may execute the form on behalf of the owner-corporation.

Item 12--Individual's last name, or organization's name. If the registrant is a publicly held corporation, it is sufficient to write "public corporation" in item 12. Where registrant is a public corporation, a duly authorized officer of the registrant must execute the form in Part VII.

Items 13 to 22--Enter the applicable information for the owner or controlling person. Their home address and phone number should not be used, unless a business address and phone number are unavailable.

Item 23--Identification information. If you completed item 22, you may omit this item. If you did not complete item 22, enter separately the form of identification, the ID number, and the issuing state or country. Do not provide "other" identification unless no driver's license/state ID, passport or alien registration number is available. "Other" identification includes any unexpired official identification that is issued by a governmental authority. If you check item 23z, give a brief description of the "other" identification.

Part IV   Money Services and Product Information

Item 24--States and/or territories where the registrant, its agents or branches are located. Check box "a" for All States and Territories, "b"

FinCEN Form 107   Registration of Money Services Business Instructions   **3**

for All States, or "c" for All Territories (Check only one) as appropriate, and **do not** check any individual state or territory boxes. If box a, b, or c **does not apply,** check as many state or territory boxes as necessary. If a service is offered on tribal lands, mark the box for the state, territory or district in which the tribal lands are located.

Item 25--Enter the number of branches of the registrant. Enter the number of branches of the money services business at which one or more MSB activities are offered. If there are no branches, enter zero. See the General Information for an explanation of the term "branch".

Item 26--MSB activities of the registrant. Items 25a through 25i are MSB activities. Check the box of each MSB activity conducted by the registrant at its branches. See the General Information for an explanation of the terms "issuer", "seller", "redeemer", "check casher", and "money transmitter".

Item 27--Informal value transfer system. If any part of the registrant's money services business is an informal value transfer system, check yes. An informal value transfer system is a kind of money transmitter. See the General Information explanation of the term "money transmitter".

Item 28--Mobile operation. If any part of the registrant's money services business is conducted as a mobile operation, check yes. A mobile operation is one based in a vehicle. For example, a check cashing service offered from a truck is a mobile operation. For purposes of Item 25, each mobile operation should be counted as a separate branch.

Item 29--Number of agents. Enter the number of agents that the registrant has authorized to sell or distribute its MSB services. Do not count branches or any person who is solely an employee of the MSB. A bank is not an agent for this purpose. See the General Information for an explanation of the term "agent".

Part V Primary Transaction Account for MSB Activities

Item 30--Check the box if the registrant has more than one primary transaction account for money services business activities. Example: If the registrant is both an issuer of money orders and an issuer of traveler's checks and the registrant has separate clearing accounts for money orders and traveler's checks, the box should be checked.

Item 31--Name of the financial institution where the primary transaction account is held. Enter the name of the bank or other financial institution where the registrant has its primary transaction account. If you indicated that the registrant has more than one primary transaction account in Item 30, enter information about the account with the greatest money service activity transaction volume as measured by value in dollars. See the General

Information for an explanation of the term "transaction account".

Items 32 to 35--Enter the permanent address for the financial institution.

Item 36--Primary transaction account number. Enter the primary transaction account number.

Part VI   Location of Supporting Documentation

General: The registrant must retain for five (5) years certain information at a location within the United States. That information includes:
1. A copy of the registration form.
2. Annual estimate of the volume of the registrant's business in the coming year.
3. The following information regarding ownership or control of the business: the name and address of any shareholder holding more than 5% of the registrant's stock, any general partner, any trustee, and/or any director or officer of the business.
4. An agent list.
If the registrant has agents it must prepare and maintain a list of its agents. That agent list must be updated annually and retained by the business at the location in the United States reported on this registration form in Part II or Part VI. The agent list **should not** be filed with this registration form.
The agent list must include:
   a. Each agent's name,
   b. Each agent's address,
   c. Each agent's telephone number,
   d. The type of service(s) provided by each agent on behalf of the registrant,
   e. A listing of the months in the immediately preceding 12 months in which the gross transaction amount of each agent with respect to financial products/ services issued by the registrant exceeds $100,000,
   f. The name and address of any depository institution at which each agent maintains a transaction account for the money services business activities conducted by the agent on behalf of the registrant,
   g. The year in which each agent first became an agent of the registrant, and
   h. The number of branches or subagents of each agent.

Items 37 to 40--If the supporting documentation is retained at a location other than the address listed in Part II, enter the location information in items 37 through 40.

Part VII Authorized Signature

Items 41 to 44--The owner or controlling person listed in Part III must sign and date the form as indicated in Part VII. If the owner or controlling person is a corporation, a duly authorized officer of the corporation must execute the form on behalf of the corporation. Enter the date this document was signed.

Penalties for failure to comply: Any person who fails to comply with the requirements to register, keep records, and/or maintain agent lists pursuant

to 31 CFR 103.41 may be liable for civil penalties of up to $5,000 for each violation. Failure to comply also may subject a person to criminal penalties, which may include imprisonment for up to five (5) years and criminal fines. See 18 USC 1960. Note: This registration does not satisfy any state or local licensing or registration requirements.

Paperwork Reduction Act Notice.
The purposes of this form are to provide an effective and consistent means for money services businesses to register with the Financial Crimes Enforcement Network, and to assure maintenance of reports or records where such reports or records have a high degree of usefulness in criminal, tax, or regulatory investigations or proceedings. This report is required by law, pursuant to authority contained in Public Law 103-305; 31 USC 5330; 5 USC 301; 31 CFR 103. The information collected may be provided to those officers and employees of any constituent unit of the Department of the Treasury who have a need for the records in the performance of their duties. The records may be referred to any other department or agency of the United States, to any State, or Tribal Government. Public reporting and recordkeeping burden for this information collection is estimated to average 30 minutes per response, and includes time to gather and maintain data for the required report, review the instructions, and complete the information collection. Send comments regarding this burden estimate, including suggestions for reducing the burden, to the Office of Management and Budget Paperwork Reduction Project, Washington, DC 20503 and to the Paperwork Reduction Act; Department of the Treasury, Financial Crimes Enforcement Network, P.O. Box 39, Vienna, VA 22183-0039. The agency may not conduct or sponsor, and an organization (or a person) is not required to respond to, a collection of information unless it displays a currently valid OMB control number.

Privary Act Notice.
Pursuant to the requirements of Public Law 93-579 (Privacy Act of 1974), notice is hereby given that, in accordance with 5 U.S.C. 552a(e), the authority to collect information on **FinCEN Form 107** is Public Law 103-305; 31 USC 5330; 5 USC 301; 31 CFR 103. The Department of the Treasury may use and share the information with any other department or agency of the United States, to any State, or Tribal Government, or part thereof, upon the request of the head of such department or agency, or authorized State or Tribal Government official for use in a criminal, tax, or regulatory investigation or proceeding, and to foreign governments in accordance with an agreement, or a treaty. Disclosure of this information is mandatory. Civil and criminal penalties, including in certain circumstances a fine of not more than $5,000 per day and imprisonment of not more than five years, are provided for failure to file the form, supply information requested by the form, and for filing a false or fraudulent form. Disclosure of the social security number or taxpayer identification number is mandatory. The authority to collect is 31 CFR 103. The social security number/taxpayer identification number will be used as a means to identify the individual or entity who files the report.

FinCEN Form **109** March 31, 2007 Previous editions will not be accepted after September 30, 2007 (Formerly Form TD F 90-22.56)	**Suspicious Activity Report by Money Services Business** ► Please type or print. Always complete entire report. Items marked with an asterisk * are considered critical. (See instructions.)	 OMB No. 1506-0015

1 ☐ Check this box only if amending or correcting a prior report (see item 1 instructions)   1a ☐ Check this box if this is a recurring report

Part I   Subject Information   2 ☐ Multiple subjects (see item instructions)

3 Subject type (check only one box)   a ☐ Purchaser/sender   b ☐ Payee/receiver   c ☐ Both a & b   z ☐ Other

*4 Individual's last name or entity's full name

*5 First name

6 Middle initial

*7 Address

*8 City

*9 State

*10 ZIP Code

*11 Country Code (If not US)

*12 Government issued identification (if available)

a ☐ Driver's license/state I.D.   b ☐ Passport   c ☐ Alien registration   z ☐ Other _____

e Number | | | | | | | | | | | | | | | | | | | | | f Issuing state/country _____

*13 SSN/ITIN (individual) or EIN (entity)

*14 Date of birth   ___/___/___   MM DD YYYY

15 Telephone number   (___)___-____

Part II   Suspicious Activity Information

*16 Date or date range of suspicious activity

From ___/___/___   To ___/___/___
MM DD YYYY   MM DD YYYY

*17 Total amount involved in suspicious activity   a ☐ Amount unknown

$ _____ .00

*18 Category of suspicious activity (check all that apply)

a ☐ Money laundering   b ☐ Structuring   c ☐ Terrorist financing   z ☐ Other (specify) _____

*19 Financial services involved in the suspicious activity and character of the suspicious activity, including unusual use (check all that apply).

    a ☐ Money order   b ☐ Traveler's check   c ☐ Money transfer

    z ☐ Other _____   e ☐ Currency exchange

Check all of the following that apply

(1) ☐ Alters transaction to avoid completing funds transfer record
    or money order or traveler's check record ($3,000 or more)

(2) ☐ Alters transaction to avoid filing CTR form (more than $10,000)

(3) ☐ Comes in frequently and purchases less than $3,000

(4) ☐ Changes spelling or arrangement of name

(5) ☐ Individual(s) using multiple or false identification documents

(6) ☐ Two or more individuals using the similar/same identification

(7) ☐ Two or more individuals working together

(8) ☐ Same individual(s) using multiple locations over a short time period

(9) ☐ Offers a bribe in the form of a tip/gratuity

(10) ☐ Exchanges small bills for large bills or vice versa

If mailing, send each completed SAR report to:
Enterprise Computing Center - Detroit
Attn: SAR-MSB
P.O. Box 33117
Detroit, MI 48232-0980

A free secure e-filing system is available to file this report.
Go to http://bsaefiling.fincen.treas.gov for more
information and to register.

Catalog No. 49340J

(Rev. 3/07)

| Part II | Suspicious Activity Information, Continued | 2 |

*20 Purchases and redemptions (check box "P" for purchase or box "R" for redemption).

Instrument	P	R	Issuers	Total Instruments	Total Amount (US Dollars)
Money Orders:	☐	☐	_____	____	$_____ .00
	☐	☐	_____	____	$_____ .00
	☐	☐	_____	____	$_____ .00
Traveler's Checks:	☐	☐	_____	____	$_____ .00
	☐	☐	_____	____	$_____ .00
	☐	☐	_____	____	$_____ .00
Money Transfers:	☐	☐	_____	____	$_____ .00
	☐	☐	_____	____	$_____ .00
	☐	☐	_____	____	$_____ .00

*21 Currency Exchanges: Tendered Currency/Instrument   Country   Received currency   Country   Amount (US Dollars)

☐ If bulk small currency   _____   ____   _____   ____ $_____ .00

☐ If bulk small currency   _____   ____   _____   ____ $_____ .00

| Part III | Transaction Location | 22 ☐ Multiple transaction locations |

23 Type of business location (check only one)   a ☐ Selling location   b ☐ Paying location   c ☐ Both

| *24 Legal name of business | 25 Doing business as |

| *26 Permanent address (number, street, and suite no.) | *27 City | *28 State | *29 ZIP Code |

| *30 EIN (entity) or SSN/ITIN (individual) | *31 Business telephone number | 32 Country Code (If not US) | 33 Internal control/file number (If available) |
| (___) ___ — ____ |

| Part IV | Reporting Business | 34 ☐ The Reporting Business is the same as the Transaction Location (go to Part V) |

| *35 Legal name of business | 36 Doing business as |

| *37 Permanent address (number, street, and suite no.) | *38 City | *39 State | *40 ZIP Code |

| *41 EIN (entity) or SSN/ITIN (individual) | *42 Business phone number (include area code) | 43 Country Code (If not US) | 44 Internal control/file number (If available) |
| (___) ___ — ____ |

| Part V | Contact for Assistance |

| *45 Designated contact office | *46 Designated phone number (Include area code) | 47 Date filed (See instructions) |
| | (___) ___ — ____ | ___ / ___ / _____ MM DD YYYY |

48 Agency (If not filed by a Money Services Business)

| **Part VI** | **Suspicious Activity Information - Narrative*** | 3 |

Explanation/description of suspicious activity(ies). This section of the report is **critical**. The care with which it is completed may determine whether or not the described activity and its possible criminal nature are clearly understood by investigators. Provide a clear, complete and chronological description of the activity, including what is unusual, irregular or suspicious about the transaction(s). Use the checklist below, as a guide, as you prepare your description. The description should cover the material indicated in Parts I, II and III, but the money services business (MSB) should describe any other information that it believes is necessary to better enable investigators to understand the suspicious activity being reported.

a. **Describe** conduct that raised suspicion.

b. **Explain** whether the transaction(s) was completed or only attempted.

c. **Describe** supporting documentation and retain such documentation for your file for five years.

d. **Indicate** a time period, if it was a factor in the suspicious transaction(s). For example, specify the time and whether it occurred during AM or PM. If the activity covers more than one day, identify the time of day when such activity occurred most frequently.

e. **Retain** any admission or explanation of the transaction(s) provided by the subject(s) or other persons. Indicate when and to whom it was given.

f. **Retain** any evidence of cover-up or evidence of an attempt to deceive federal or state examiners, or others.

g. **Indicate** where the possible violation of law(s) took place (e.g., main office, branch, agent location, etc.).

h. **Indicate** whether the suspicious activity is an isolated incident or relates to another transaction.

i. **Indicate** for a foreign national any available information on subject's passport(s), visa(s), and/or identification card(s). Include date, country, city of issue, issuing authority, and nationality.

j. **Indicate** whether any information has been excluded from this report; if so, state reasons.

k. **Indicate** whether any U.S. or foreign instrument(s) were involved. If so, provide the amount, name of currency, and country of origin.

l. **Indicate** whether any transfer of money to or from a foreign country,

or any exchanges of a foreign currency were involved. If so, identify the currency, country, and sources and destinations of money.

m. **Indicate** any additional account number(s), and any foreign bank(s) account numbers which may be involved in transfer of money.

n. **Identify** any employee or other individual or entity (e.g., agent) suspected of improper involvement in the transaction(s).

o. **For issuers, indicate** if the endorser of money order(s) and/or traveler's check(s) is different than payee. If so, provide the individual or entity name; bank's name, city, state and country; ABA routing number; endorser's bank account number; foreign non-bank name (if any); correspondent bank name and account number (if any); etc.

p. **For selling or paying locations, indicate** if there is a video recording medium or surveillance photograph of the customer.

q. **For selling or paying locations,** if you do not have a record of a government issued identification document, **describe** the type, issuer and number of any alternate identification that is available (e.g., for a credit card specify the name of the customer and credit card number.)

r. **For selling or paying locations,** describe the subject(s) if you do not have the identifying information in Part I or if multiple individuals use the same identification. Use descriptors such as male, female, age, etc.

s. **If amending** a prior report, complete the form in its entirety and note the changes here in Part VI.

t. If a law enforcement agency has been contacted, list the name of the agency and the name of any person contacted, their title, their telephone number, and when they were contacted.

Supporting documentation should not be filed with this report. Maintain the information for your files.

Enter the explanation/description narrative in the space below. If necessary, continue the narrative on a duplicate of this page or a blank page.

Tips on SAR form preparation and filing are available in the SAR Activity Reviews at **www.fincen.gov/pub_reports.html.**

Legal disclaimers will not be included in this narrative. Also, do not include charts or tables.

FinCEN Form 109a   Suspicious Activity Report by Money Services Business -- Instructions   1

Safe Harbor

Federal law (31 U.S.C. 5318(g)(3)) provides complete protection from civil liability for all reports of suspicious transactions made to appropriate authorities, including supporting documentation, regardless of whether such reports are filed pursuant to this report's instructions or are filed on a voluntary basis. Specifically, the law provides that a financial institution, and its directors, officers, employees and agents, that make a disclosure of any possible violation of law or regulation, including in connection with the preparation of suspicious activity reports, "shall not be liable to any person under any law or regulation of the United States, any constitution, law, or regulation of any State or political subdivision of any State, or under any contract or other legally enforceable agreement (including any arbitration agreement), for such disclosure or for any failure to provide notice of such disclosure to the person who is the subject of such disclosure or any other person identified in the disclosure".

Notification Prohibited

Federal law (31 U.S.C. 5318(g)(2)) provides that a financial institution, and its directors, officers, employees, and agents, who report suspicious transactions to the government voluntarily or as required by 31 CFR 103.20, may not notify any person involved in the transaction that the transaction has been reported.

Notification Required

In situations involving suspicious transactions requiring immediate attention, such as ongoing money laundering schemes, a money transmitter; a currency dealer or exchanger; or an issuer, seller, or redeemer of money orders and/or traveler's checks shall immediately notify, by telephone, an appropriate law enforcement authority. In addition, a timely SAR-MSB form shall be filed, including recording any such notification in Part VI on the form.

A. When To File A Report:

1. Money transmitters; currency dealers and exchangers; and issuers, sellers and redeemers of money orders and/or traveler's checks that are subject to the requirements of the Bank Secrecy Act and its implementing regulations (31 CFR Part 103) are required to file a suspicious activity report (SAR-MSB) with respect to:

a. Any transaction conducted or attempted by, at, or through a money services business involving or aggregating funds or other assets of at least $2,000 (except as described in section "b" below) when the money services business knows, suspects, or has reason to suspect that:

i. The transaction involves funds derived from illegal activity or is intended or conducted in order to hide or disguise funds or assets derived from illegal activity (including, without limitation, the nature, source, location, ownership or control of such funds or assets) as part of a plan to violate

or evade any Federal law or regulation or to avoid any transaction reporting requirement under Federal law or regulation;

ii. The transaction is designed, whether through structuring or other means, to evade any regulations promulgated under the Bank Secrecy Act; or

iii. The transaction has no business or apparent lawful purpose and the money services business knows of no reasonable explanation for the transaction after examining the available facts, including the background and possible purpose of the transaction.

iv. The transaction involves the use of the money services business to facilitate criminal activity.

b. To the extent that the identification of transactions required to be reported is derived from a review of clearance records or other similar records of money orders or traveler's checks that have been sold or processed, an issuer of money orders or traveler's checks shall only be required to report a transaction or a pattern of transactions that involves or aggregates funds or other assets of at least $5,000.

2. File a SAR-MSB no later than 30 calendar days after the date of initial detection of facts that constitute a basis for filing the report.

3. The Bank Secrecy Act requires that each financial institution (including a money services business) file currency transaction reports (CTRs) in accordance with the Department of the Treasury implementing regulations (31 CFR Part 103). These regulations require a financial institution to file a CTR (FinCEN Form 104) whenever a currency transaction exceeds $10,000. If a currency transaction exceeds $10,000 and is suspicious, a money transmitter, or issuer, seller or redeemer of money orders and/or traveler's checks or currency dealer or exchanger must file two forms, a CTR to report the currency transaction and a SAR-MSB to report the suspicious aspects of the transaction. If the suspicious activity involves a currency transaction that is $10,000 or less, the institution is only required to file a SAR-MSB. Appropriate records must be maintained in each case. See 31 CFR Part 103

B. Abbreviations and Definitions

1. EIN -- Employer Identification Number
2. IRS -- Internal Revenue Service
3. ITIN -- Individual Taxpayer Identification Number
4. SSN -- Social Security Number
5. Instruments -- includes Money order(s) and/or Traveler's Check(s)

6. Redeemer --A business that accepts instruments in exchange for currency or other instruments for which it is not the issuer is a redeemer. The MSB definition in 31 CFR 103.11(u)(4) extends to "redeemers" of money orders and traveler's checks only insofar as the

instruments involved are redeemed for monetary value — that is, for currency or monetary or other negotiable or other instruments. The taking of the instruments in exchange for goods or general services is not redemption under BSA regulations.

C. General Instructions

1. **This form should be e-filed through the Bank Secrecy Act E-filing System. Go to http://bsaefiling.fincen.treas.gov to register.** This form is also available for download on the Financial Crimes Enforcement Network's Web site at www.fincen.gov, or may be ordered by calling the IRS Forms Distribution Center at (800) 829-3676.

2. If not filed electronically, send each completed suspicious activity report to:

Enterprise Computing Center-Detroit
ATTN: SAR-MSB
P.O. Box 33117
Detroit, MI 48232-5980

3. While all items should be completed fully and accurately, items marked with an asterisk (*) must be completed according to the provisions of paragraph 4 below.

4. If the information for a data item marked with a asterisk (*) is not known or not applicable, enter special response "XX" (**Exception: Items 11, 20, 21, and 34 - see instructions in Section D**) NOTE: Check boxes are not data items. To indicate "Total amount" as unknown, check the box provided. Non-asterisk fields should be left blank if the information is unknown or not applicable.

5. Complete each suspicious activity report by providing as much information as possible on initial and amended or corrected reports.

6. Do not include supporting documents when filing the suspicious activity report . Retain a copy of the suspicious activity report and all supporting documentation or business record equivalent in your files for five (5) years from the date of the report. All supporting documentation (such as copies of instruments; receipts; sale, transaction or clearing records; photographs, surveillance audio and/or video recording medium) must be made available to appropriate authorities upon request.

7. Type or complete the report using block written letters.

8. If more than one subject is being reported, use as many copies of the Part I Subject Information page as necessary to record the additional subjects. Attach the additional page(s) behind page 1. If more than one transaction location is being reported, use as many copies of the Part III Transaction Location Information page as necessary to record the additional locations. Attach the additional page(s) behind page 2. If more space is needed for the Part VI Narrative, add as many blank continuation pages as necessary to complete the narrative. Attach the additional pages behind page 3.

If more space is needed to complete any other item, identify that item in Part VI by "item number" and provide the additional information.

9. Enter all **dates** in MM/DD/YYYY format where MM = month, DD = day, and YYYY = year. Precede any single number with a zero, i.e., 01, 02, etc.

10. Enter all **telephone numbers** with (area code) first and then the seven numbers, using the format (XXX) XXX-XXXX. List fax and international telephone numbers in Part VI.

11. Always enter an **individual's name** by entering the last name, first name, and middle initial (if known). If a legal entity is listed, enter its legal name in the last name item. If the legal entity has a trade name that is different, list the trade name in Part VI.

12. Enter all **identifying numbers** (alien registration, driver's license/state ID, EIN, ITIN, Foreign National ID, passport, SSN, vehicle license number, etc.) starting from left to right. Do not include spaces or other punctuation.

13. Enter all **ZIP Codes** with at least the first five numbers (ZIP+4, if known).

14. Enter all **monetary amounts** in U.S. Dollars. Use whole dollar amounts rounded up when necessary. Use this format: $000,000,000. If foreign currency is involved, record the currency amount in U.S. Dollars, name, and country of origin in the Part VI narrative.

15. Addresses, general. Enter the permanent street address, city, two letter state/territory abbreviation used by the U.S. Postal Service, and ZIP code (ZIP+4, if known) of the individual or entity. A post office box number should not be used for an individual, unless no other address is available. For an individual also enter any apartment number or suite number and road or route number. If a P.O. Box is used for an entity, enter the street name, suite number, and road or route number. If the address is in a foreign country, enter the city, province or state if Canada or Mexico, and the name of the country. Complete any part of the address that is known, even if the entire address is not known. If the street address, city, ZIP Code or country is unknown, enter "XX" in the item.

Lists of two-digit country and state codes are available on the FinCEN web site at www.fincen.gov/reg_bsaforms.html, or by calling 1-800-949-2732 and selecting option 5 to request a list by mail.

D. Item Preparation Instructions

Item 1. Check the box if this report amends (adds missing data) or corrects errors in the prior report. (See Part VI, item "s").

Item 1a-- Check this box if this is a recurring report filed on continuing activity.

Part I   Subject Information

Note: Enter information about the person(s) or entity involved that caused this report to be filed, not the victim of the activity.

Item 2 -- Multiple Subjects. If there are multiple subjects involved, check box "2" and complete a separate Part I for each subject. If **ANY** subject information is available, record that information in Part 1, and insert the appropriate special response in any critical item for which data is missing.

Item 3   Subject type. Check box "a" if the subject purchased a money order(s) or traveler's check(s) or sent a money transfer(s). Check box "b" if the subject cashed a money order(s) or traveler's check(s) or received payment of a money transfer(s). Check box "c" if both "a" and "b" apply. If the transaction is a currency exchange check box "c." Check box "z" Other and describe in Part VI if the subject is an individual other than a customer. Examples are MSB employees and agents.

Items 4, 5, and 6 *Name of subject. See General Instruction 11. Enter the name of the subject individual in Items 4 through 6. If the MSB knows that the individual has an "also known as" (AKA) or "doing business as" (DBA) name, enter that name in Part VI. If the subject is an entity, enter the legal name in Item 4 and the trade or DBA name in item 5. If the legal name is not known, enter the DBA name in Item 4. If there is more than one subject, use as many Part I Subject Information continuation pages as necessary to provide the information about each subject. Attach the additional copies behind page 1. When there is more than one purchaser and/or payee (e.g., two or more transactions), indicate in Part VI whether each subject is a purchaser or payee and identify the instrument or money transfer information associated with each subject. If part of an individual's name is unknown, enter "XX" in the appropriate name item. If the subject is an entity, enter "XX" in Item 5 (if the trade or legal name is not known) and in Item 6.

Items 7 - 11 *Permanent address. See General Instructions 13 and 15. Enter "XX" if the street address, city, and ZIP Code items are unknown or not applicable. Enter "XX" if the state or country is not known. If country is US, always leave country code blank.

Item 12 *Government issued identification (if available). See General Instruction 12. Check the box showing the type of document used to verify subject identity. If you check box "z" **Other**, be sure to specify the type of document used. In box "e" list the number of the identifying document. In box "f" list the issuing state or country. If more space is required, enter the additional information in Part VI. If the subject is an entity or an individual's identification was not available, check box "z" and enter "XX" in "Other."

Item 13 *SSN/ITIN (individual) or EIN (entity). See General Instruction 12 and

definitions. If the subject named in Items 4 through 6 is a U.S. Citizen or an alien with a SSN, enter his or her SSN in Item 13. If that person is an alien who has an ITIN, enter that number. For an entity, enter the EIN. If the SSN, ITIN, or EIN was unknown or not applicable, enter "XX" in this item.

Item 14 *Date of birth. See General Instruction 9. If the subject is an individual, enter the date of birth. If the month and/or day is not available or unknown, fill in with zeros (e.g., "01/00/1969" indicates an unknown date in January, 1969). If entire date is unknown, or if an entity, enter XX in the MM part of the date field.

Item 15 Telephone number. See General Instruction 10. Enter the U.S. home or business number for individual or entity. List foreign telephone numbers and any additional U.S. numbers (e.g., hotel, etc.) in Part VI.

Part II Suspicious Activity Information

Item 16 *Date or date range of suspicious activity. See General Instruction 9. Enter the date of the reported suspicious activity in the "From" field. If more than one day is involved, indicate the duration of the activity by entering the first date in the "From" field and the last date in the "To" field.

Item 17 *Total dollar amount. See General Instruction 14. **If unknown, check box 17a.** If the suspicious activity only involved purchases, or redemptions, or currency exchanges, enter the total U.S. Dollar value involved in the reported activity. For instance, if multiple money orders from more than one issuer were redeemed, enter the total of all money orders redeemed. If multiple activities are involved, such as a redemption of money orders combined with purchase of a money transfer, enter the largest activity amount in Item 17. For instance, if the transaction involved redeeming $5,000 in money orders and purchase of a $3,500 money transfer , the Item 17 amount would be $5,000.

Item 18 *Category of suspicious activity. Check the box(es) which best identifies the suspicious activity. Check box "b Structuring" when it appears that a person (acting alone, in conjunction with, or on behalf of other persons) conducts or attempts to conduct activity designed to evade any record keeping or reporting requirement of the Bank Secrecy Act. If box "z" is checked, specify the type of suspicious activity which occurred. Describe the character of such activity in Part VI. Box "z" should only be used if no other type of suspicious activity box adequately categorizes the transaction.

Item 19 *Financial services involved. Check any of boxes "a" through "e" that apply to identify the services involved in the suspicious activity. If box "z" is checked, briefly explain the service on the following line. If "unusual use" is involved, check the appropriate service box(s) and box "z" and note "unusual use" and explain in Part VI. Check all of boxes "1" through "10" that apply to describe the character of the suspicious activity.

3

Item 20 *Purchases and redemptions (See definition 6 on page 1 of the instructions). Enter information about purchases or redemptions of money orders, traveler's checks, or money transfers. Check the appropriate box in column "P" or "R" to identify the entry as a purchase or redemption. If reporting a money transfer(s) check "P" if subject is sending money and "R" if subject is receiving money. Enter the name of the issuers, the total number of instruments purchased or the total redeemed, and the total amount of the instruments. You can enter up to three issuers in each instrument category. If more than three issuers are involved, enter the information on the additional issuers in Part VI. The use of "XX" for unknown only applies if reporting on a particular transaction, i.e, "XX" should not be entered on non-reporting blank lines.

Item 21 *Currency Exchanges.   Record up to two currency exchanges made by the subject(s). Check the box "If bulk small currency" if a large number of small bills was used to pay for the currency exchange. Enter the name of the currency or type of monetary instrument used to pay for the exchange, and the two-letter code for the country that issued the currency. An example of this would be "Pesos" for the name of the currency and "MX" representing Mexico as issuer of the currency. Enter the name of the currency received in exchange and the two-digit code for the country that issued the currency. Enter the value of the exchange in U.S. Dollars. If there were more than two currency exchanges, enter the information about the additional exchanges in Part VI. The use of "XX" for unknown only applies if reporting a currency exchange, i.e., "XX" should not be entered on non-reporting blank lines.

Part III Transaction Location Information

Item 22 Multiple selling and/or paying business locations. Check the box if the reported activity occurred at multiple selling and/or paying business locations. Fill out as many Part III Transaction Location Information sections as necessary to record all locations. Attach the additional sections behind page 2 of the SAR-MSB.

Item 23 Type of business location(s). Check box "a" if this is the selling location where the customer purchases a money order(s) or traveler's check(s), or initiated a money transfer(s), or exchanged currency. Check box "b" if this is the paying location where the customer cashed a money order(s) or traveler's check(s) or received payment of a money transfer(s). Check box "c" if multiple transactions are reported and the business was both a selling and paying location for one or more transactions.

Item 24 *Legal name of business. Enter the legal name of the business where the transactions took place.

Item 25 Doing business as. Enter the trade name by which the business is commonly known.

Items 26-29, 32 *Transaction location address. Enter the transaction location address by following General Instructions 13 and 15.

Item 30   *EIN (entity) or SSN/ITIN (individual). See General Instruction 12 and definitions. If the business identified in Item 24 has an EIN, enter that number in Item 30. If not, enter individual owner's SSN or ITIN.

Item 31 *Business telephone number. See General Instruction 10. Enter the telephone number of the business listed in Item 24.

Item 32 Country code. Enter the 2-letter country code if not US.

Item 33 Internal control/file number (If available). Enter any internal file or report number assigned by the reporting institution to track this report. This information will act as an identification aid if contact is required.

Part IV Reporting Business Information

Item 34 Check this box and go to Part V if the reporting business is the same as the Part III Transaction Location. If the reporting business is different, complete Part IV. **If item 34 is checked, leave items 35 through 44 blank and do not enter "XX" in these items.**

Item 35 *Legal name of business. Enter the legal name of the reporting business.

Item 36 Doing business as. Enter the trade name by which the reporting business is commonly known (if other than the legal name).

Items 37-40, 43   *Reporting business address. Enter the reporting business address by following General Instructions 13 and 15.

Item 41   *EIN (entity) or SSN/ITIN (individual). See General Instruction 12 and definitions. If the business identified in Item 35 has an EIN, enter that number in Item 41. If not, enter individual owner's SSN or ITIN.

Item 42 *Business phone number. Enter the telephone number of the reporting business. If the reporting business telephone number is a foreign telephone number, leave Item 42 blank and enter the number in the Part VI Narrative. See General Instruction 10.

Item 43 Country code. Enter the 2-letter country code if not US.

Item 44 Internal control/file number (If available). Enter any internal file or report number assigned by the reporting institution to track this report. This information will act as an identification aid if contact is required.

Part V Contact for Assistance

Item *45-- Designated contact office. Enter the name of the office that the financial institution has designated to receive request for assistance with this report.

This office must have an individual knowledgeable of this report available during regular business hours.

Item *46--Phone number. See General Instruction B10. Enter the work telephone number of the contact office.

Item *47--Date filed. See General Instruction B9. Enter the date this report was filed. For electronic filing, it is the date that the report was e-filed using BSA Direct. For all other filers, it is the date the financial institution completed the final review and mailed/submitted the report to ECC-D.

Item 48--Agency. If this report is filed by an agency other than an MSB, such as a federal or state examiner, enter the name of the reporting agency in Item 48.

Part VI Suspicious Activity Information -- Narrative*

Enter a narrative describing all aspects of the suspicious activity not covered by form data items. See page 3 of the form for instructions on completing the narrative. If the initial Part VI narrative page is not sufficient, continue on plain bond paper and attach the additional pages after the initial narrative page. **Do not include charts or tables. Legal disclaimers will not be included in this narrative.**

Paperwork Reduction Act Notice

The purpose of this form is to provide an effective means for a money services business (MSB) to notify appropriate law enforcement agencies of suspicious transactions and activities that occur by, through, or at an MSB. This report is authorized by law, pursuant to authority contained in 31 U.S.C. 5318(g). Information collected on this report is confidential (31 U.S.C. 5318(g)). Federal regulatory agencies, State law enforcement agencies, the U.S. Departments of Justice and Treasury, and other authorized authorities may use and share this information. Public reporting and record keeping burden for this form is estimated to average 60 minutes per response, and includes time to gather and maintain information for the required report, review the instructions, and complete the information collection. Send comments regarding this burden estimate, including suggestions for reducing the burden, to the Office of Management and the Budget,   Paperwork   Reduction   Project, Washington, DC 20503 and to the Financial Crimes Enforcement Network, Attn.: Paperwork Reduction Act. P.O. Box 39, Vienna VA 22183-0039. The agency may not conduct or sponsor, and an organization (or a person) is not required to respond to, a collection of information unless it displays a currently valid OMB control number.

Suspicious Activity Report		1

Suspicious Activity Report

July 2003

Previous editions will not be accepted after December 31, 2003

FRB:	FR 2230	OMB No. 7100-0212
FDIC:	6710/06	OMB No. 3064-0077
OCC:	8010-9,8010-1	OMB No. 1557-0180
OTS:	1601	OMB No. 1550-0003
NCUA:	2362	OMB No. 3133-0094
TREASURY:	TD F 90-22.47	OMB No. 1506-0001

ALWAYS COMPLETE ENTIRE REPORT
(see instructions)

1 Check box below only if correcting a prior report.
   ☐ Corrects Prior Report (see instruction #3 under "How to Make a Report")

Part I   Reporting Financial Institution Information

2 Name of Financial Institution

3 EIN

4 Address of Financial Institution

5 Primary Federal Regulator

   a ☐ Federal Reserve   d ☐ OCC
   b ☐ FDIC   e ☐ OTS
   c ☐ NCUA

6 City   7 State   8 Zip Code

9 Address of Branch Office(s) where activity occurred   ☐ Multiple Branches (include information in narrative, Part V)

10 City   11 State   12 Zip Code   13 If institution closed, date closed
                                                    ___/___/___
                                                    MM   DD   YYYY

14 Account number(s) affected, if any   Closed?   Closed?
    a _____ ☐ Yes ☐ No   c _____ ☐ Yes ☐ No
    b _____ ☐ Yes ☐ No   d _____ ☐ Yes ☐ No

Part II   Suspect Information   ☐ Suspect Information Unavailable

15 Last Name or Name of Entity   16 First Name   17 Middle

18 Address   19 SSN, EIN or TIN

20 City   21 State   22 Zip Code   23 Country (Enter 2 digit code)

24 Phone Number - Residence (include area code)   25 Phone Number - Work (include area code)
    (   )   (   )

26 Occupation/Type of Business   27 Date of Birth   28 Admission/Confession?
                                       ___/___/___   a ☐ Yes   b ☐ No
                                       MM   DD   YYYY

29 Forms of Identification for Suspect:
    a ☐ Driver's License/State ID   b ☐ Passport   c ☐ Alien Registration   d ☐ Other _____
       Number _____   Issuing Authority _____

30 Relationship to Financial Institution:
    a ☐ Accountant   d ☐ Attorney   g ☐ Customer   j ☐ Officer
    b ☐ Agent   e ☐ Borrower   h ☐ Director   k ☐ Shareholder
    c ☐ Appraiser   f ☐ Broker   i ☐ Employee   l ☐ Other _____

31 Is the relationship an insider relationship?   a ☐ Yes   b ☐ No   32 Date of Suspension, Termination, Resignation
    If Yes specify: c ☐ Still employed at financial institution e ☐ Terminated   ___/___/___
                     d ☐ Suspended   f ☐ Resigned   MM   DD   YYYY

IRS Cat. No. 22285L

Part III	Suspicious Activity Information		2

33 Date or date range of suspicious activity

From: ___/___/_____   To: ___/___/_____
    MM DD   YYYY   MM DD   YYYY

34 Total dollar amount involved in known or suspicious activity

$ | | | | | | | | | | | .00

35 Summary characterization of suspicious activity:

a ☐ Bank Secrecy Act/Structuring/ Money Laundering
b ☐ Bribery/Gratuity
c ☐ Check Fraud
d ☐ Check Kiting
e ☐ Commercial Loan Fraud

f ☐ Computer Intrusion
g ☐ Consumer Loan Fraud
h ☐ Counterfeit Check
i ☐ Counterfeit Credit/Debit Card
j ☐ Counterfeit Instrument (other)
k ☐ Credit Card Fraud

l ☐ Debit Card Fraud
m ☐ Defalcation/Embezzlement
n ☐ False Statement
o ☐ Misuse of Position or Self Dealing
p ☐ Mortgage Loan Fraud
q ☐ Mysterious Disappearance
r ☐ Wire Transfer Fraud
t ☐ Terrorist Financing
u ☐ Identity Theft

s ☐ Other _____
                    (type of activity)

36 Amount of loss prior to recovery

$ | | | | | | | | | .00

37 Dollar amount of recovery (if applicable)

$ | | | | | | | | | .00

38 Has the suspicious activity had a material impact on, or otherwise affected, the financial soundness of the institution?

a ☐ Yes   b ☐ No

39 Has the institution's bonding company been notified?

a ☐ Yes   b ☐ No

40 Has any law enforcement agency already been advised by telephone, written communication, or otherwise?

a ☐ DEA
b ☐ FBI
c ☐ IRS

d ☐ Postal Inspection
e ☐ Secret Service
f ☐ U.S. Customs

g ☐ Other Federal
h ☐ State
i ☐ Local

j ☐ Agency Name (for g, h or i) _____

41 Name of person(s) contacted at Law Enforcement Agency

42 Phone Number (include area code)

(   )

43 Name of person(s) contacted at Law Enforcement Agency

44 Phone Number (include area code)

(   )

Part IV	Contact for Assistance

45 Last Name

46 First Name

47 Middle

48 Title/Occupation

49 Phone Number (include area code)

(   )

50 Date Prepared

___/___/_____
MM DD YYYY

51 Agency (if not filed by financial institution)

| Part V | Suspicious Activity Information Explanation/Description | 3 |

Explanation/description of known or suspected violation of law or suspicious activity.

This section of the report is **critical**. The care with which it is written may make the difference in whether or not the described conduct and its possible criminal nature are clearly understood. Provide below a chronological and **complete** account of the possible violation of law, including what is unusual, irregular or suspicious about the transaction, using the following checklist as you prepare your account. **If necessary, continue the narrative on a duplicate of this page.**

a   **Describe** supporting documentation and retain for 5 years.
b   **Explain** who benefited, financially or otherwise, from the transaction, how much, and how.
c   **Retain** any confession, admission, or explanation of the transaction provided by the suspect and indicate to whom and when it was given.
d   **Retain** any confession, admission, or explanation of the transaction provided by any other person and indicate to whom and when it was given.
e   **Retain** any evidence of cover-up or evidence of an attempt to deceive federal or state examiners or others.

f   **Indicate** where the possible violation took place (e.g., main office, branch, other).
g   **Indicate** whether the possible violation is an isolated incident or relates to other transactions.
h   **Indicate** whether there is any related litigation; if so, specify.
i   **Recommend** any further investigation that might assist law enforcement authorities.
j   **Indicate** whether any information has been excluded from this report; if so, why?
k   If you are correcting a previously filed report, describe the changes that are being made.

For Bank Secrecy Act/Structuring/Money Laundering reports, include the following additional information:
l   **Indicate** whether currency and/or monetary instruments were involved. If so, provide the amount and/or description of the instrument (for example, bank draft, letter of credit, domestic or international money order, stocks, bonds, traveler's checks, wire transfers sent or received, cash, etc.).
m   **Indicate** any account number that may be involved or affected.

Tips on SAR Form preparation and filing are available in the SAR Activity Review at www.fincen.gov/pub_reports.html

Paperwork Reduction Act Notice: The purpose of this form is to provide an effective and consistent means for financial institutions to notify appropriate law enforcement agencies of known or suspected criminal conduct or suspicious activities that take place at or were perpetrated against financial institutions. This report is required by law, pursuant to authority contained in the following statutes. Board of Governors of the Federal Reserve System: 12 U.S.C. 324, 334, 611a, 1844(b) and (c), 3105(c) (2) and 3106(a). Federal Deposit Insurance Corporation: 12 U.S.C. 93a, 1818, 1881-84, 3401-22. Office of the Comptroller of the Currency: 12 U.S.C. 93a, 1818, 1881-84, 3401-22. Office of Thrift Supervision: 12 U.S.C. 1463 and 1464. National Credit Union Administration: 12 U.S.C. 1766(a), 1786(q). Financial Crimes Enforcement Network: 31 U.S.C. 5318(g). Information collected on this report is confidential (5 U.S.C. 552(b)(7) and 552a(k)(2), and 31 U.S.C. 5318(g)). The Federal financial institutions' regulatory agencies and the U.S. Departments of Justice and Treasury may use and share the information. Public reporting and recordkeeping burden for this information collection is estimated to average 30 minutes per response, and includes time to gather and maintain data in the required report, review the instructions, and complete the information collection. Send comments regarding this burden estimate, including suggestions for reducing the burden, to the Office of Management and Budget, Paperwork Reduction Project, Washington, DC 20503 and, depending on your primary Federal regulatory agency, to Secretary, Board of Governors of the Federal Reserve System, Washington, DC 20551; or Assistant Executive Secretary, Federal Deposit Insurance Corporation, Washington, DC 20429; or Legislative and Regulatory Analysis Division, Office of the Comptroller of the Currency, Washington, DC 20219; or Office of Thrift Supervision, Enforcement Office, Washington, DC 20552; or National Credit Union Administration, 1775 Duke Street, Alexandria, VA 22314; or Office of the Director, Financial Crimes Enforcement Network, Department of the Treasury, P.O. Box 39, Vienna, VA 22183. The agencies may not conduct or sponsor, and an organization (or a person) is not required to respond to, a collection of information unless it displays a currently valid OMB control number.

Suspicious Activity Report
Instructions

Safe Harbor Federal law (31 U.S.C. 5318(g)(3)) provides complete protection from civil liability for all reports of suspicious transactions made to appropriate authorities, including supporting documentation, regardless of whether such reports are filed pursuant to this report's instructions or are filed on a voluntary basis. Specifically, the law provides that a financial institution, and its directors, officers, employees and agents, that make a disclosure of any possible violation of law or regulation, including in connection with the preparation of suspicious activity reports, "shall not be liable to any person under any law or regulation of the United States, any constitution, law, or regulation of any State or political subdivision of any State, or under any contract or other legally enforceable agreement (including any arbitration agreement), for such disclosure or for any failure to provide notice of such disclosure to the person who is the subject of such disclosure or any other person identified in the disclosure".

Notification Prohibited Federal law (31 U.S.C. 5318(g)(2)) requires that a financial institution, and its directors, officers, employees and agents who, voluntarily or by means of a suspicious activity report, report suspected or known criminal violations or suspicious activities may not notify any person involved in the transaction that the transaction has been reported.

In situations involving violations requiring immediate attention, such as when a reportable violation is ongoing, the financial institution shall immediately notify, by telephone, appropriate law enforcement and financial institution supervisory authorities in addition to filing a timely suspicious activity report.

WHEN TO MAKE A REPORT:

1. All financial institutions operating in the United States, including insured banks, savings associations, savings association service corporations, credit unions, bank holding companies, nonbank subsidiaries of bank holding companies, Edge and Agreement corporations, and U.S. branches and agencies of foreign banks, are required to make this report following the discovery of:

   a. **Insider abuse involving any amount.** Whenever the financial institution detects any known or suspected Federal criminal violation, or pattern of criminal violations, committed or attempted against the financial institution or involving a transaction or transactions conducted through the financial institution, where the financial institution believes that it was either an actual or potential victim of a criminal violation, or series of criminal violations, or that the financial institution was used to facilitate a criminal transaction, and the financial institution has a substantial basis for identifying one of its directors, officers, employees, agents or other institution-affiliated parties as having committed or aided in the commission of a criminal act regardless of the amount involved in the violation.

   b. **Violations aggregating $5,000 or more where a suspect can be identified.** Whenever the financial institution detects any known or suspected Federal criminal violation, or pattern of criminal violations, committed or attempted against the financial institution or involving a transaction or transactions conducted through the financial institution and involving or aggregating $5,000 or more in funds or other assets, where the financial institution believes that it was either an actual or potential victim of a criminal violation, or series of criminal violations, or that the financial institution was used to facilitate a criminal transaction, and the financial institution has a substantial basis for identifying a possible suspect or group of suspects. If it is determined prior to filing this report that the identified suspect or group of suspects has used an "alias," then information regarding the true identity of the suspect or group of suspects, as well as alias identifiers, such as drivers' licenses or social security numbers, addresses and telephone numbers, must be reported.

   c. **Violations aggregating $25,000 or more regardless of a potential suspect.** Whenever the financial institution detects any known or suspected Federal criminal violation, or pattern of criminal violations, committed or attempted against the financial institution or involving a transaction or transactions conducted through the financial institution and involving or aggregating $25,000 or more in funds or other assets, where the financial institution believes that it was either an actual or potential victim of a criminal violation, or series of criminal violations, or that the financial institution was used to facilitate a criminal transaction, even though there is no substantial basis for identifying a possible suspect or group of suspects.

   d. **Transactions aggregating $5,000 or more that involve potential money laundering or violations of the Bank Secrecy Act.** Any transaction (which for purposes of this subsection means a deposit, withdrawal, transfer between accounts, exchange of currency, loan, extension of credit, purchase or sale of any stock, bond, certificate of deposit, or other monetary instrument or investment security, or any other payment, transfer, or delivery by, through, or to a financial institution, by whatever means effected) conducted or attempted by, at or through the financial institution and involving or aggregating $5,000 or more in funds or other assets, if the financial institution knows, suspects, or has reason to suspect that:

i. The transaction involves funds derived from illegal activities or is intended or conducted in order to hide or disguise funds or assets derived from illegal activities (including, without limitation, the ownership, nature, source, location, or control of such funds or assets) as part of a plan to violate or evade any law or regulation or to avoid any transaction reporting requirement under Federal law;

ii. The transaction is designed to evade any regulations promulgated under the Bank Secrecy Act; or

iii. The transaction has no business or apparent lawful purpose or is not the sort in which the particular customer would normally be expected to engage, and the financial institution knows of no reasonable explanation for the transaction after examining the available facts, including the background and possible purpose of the transaction.

The Bank Secrecy Act requires all financial institutions to file currency transaction reports (CTRs) in accordance with the Department of the Treasury's implementing regulations (31 CFR Part 103). These regulations require a financial institution to file a CTR whenever a currency transaction exceeds $10,000. If a currency transaction exceeds $10,000 and is suspicious, the institution must file both a CTR (reporting the currency transaction) and a suspicious activity report (reporting the suspicious or criminal aspects of the transaction). If a currency transaction equals or is below $10,000 and is suspicious, the institution should only file a suspicious activity report.

2. **Computer Intrusion.** For purposes of this report, "computer intrusion" is defined as gaining access to a computer system of a financial institution to:

a. Remove, steal, procure, or otherwise affect funds of the institution or the institution's customers;
b. Remove, steal, procure or otherwise affect critical information of the institution including customer account information; or
c. Damage, disable or otherwise affect critical systems of the institution.

For purposes of this reporting requirement, computer intrusion does not mean attempted intrusions of websites or other non-critical information systems of the institution that provide no access to institution or customer financial or other critical information.

3. A financial institution is required to file a suspicious activity report no later than 30 calendar days after the date of initial detection of facts that may constitute a basis for filing a suspicious activity report. If no suspect was identified on the date of detection of the incident requiring the filing, a financial institution may delay filing a suspicious activity report for an additional 30 calendar days to identify a suspect. In no case shall reporting be delayed more than 60 calendar days after the date of initial detection of a reportable transaction.

4. This suspicious activity report does not need to be filed for those robberies and burglaries that are reported to local authorities, or (except for savings associations and service corporations) for lost, missing, counterfeit, or stolen securities that are reported pursuant to the requirements of 17 CFR 240.17f-1.

HOW TO MAKE A REPORT:

1. Send each completed suspicious activity report to:

Detroit Computing Center, P.O. Box 33980, Detroit, MI 48232-0980

2. For items that do not apply or for which information is not available, leave blank.
3. If you are correcting a previously filed report, check the box at the top of the report (line 1). Complete the report in its entirety and include the corrected information in the applicable boxes. Then describe the changes that are being made in Part V (Description of Suspicious Activity), line k.
4. **Do not include any supporting documentation with the suspicious activity report.** Identify and retain a copy of the suspicious activity report and all original supporting documentation or business record equivalent for five (5) years from the date of the suspicious activity report. All supporting documentation must be made available to appropriate authorities upon request.
5. If more space is needed to report additional suspects, attach copies of page 1 to provide the additional information. If more space is needed to report additional branch addresses, include this information in the narrative, Part V.
6. Financial institutions are encouraged to provide copies of suspicious activity reports to state and local authorities, where appropriate.

Interviewing 20

20.1 Introduction

Interviewing is an important part of a quality investigation and examination. It is important to have an initial dialogue with a person who has sufficient knowledge about the areas of interest. This person must be in a position to provide timely information that can be relied on. The determination of whether or not a person is knowledgeable will depend on the examiner's judgment. It is as important as any technical ability to examine documents, prepare work papers, or conduct audits.

20.2 Purpose

The purpose of interviewing is to obtain and develop information. Interviewing provides leads in developing a case. The examiner can meet, talk, and evaluate witnesses or victims. The examiner should record the interview in some form that will later help witnesses to remember their statements at trials or hearings. Interviews also establish evidence. Cases are presented to a jury through the testimony of witnesses. Therefore, it is the examiner's duty to interview every witness connected with the case.

20.3 Types of Witnesses

There are three types of witnesses: the cooperative or friendly witness, the neutral witness, and the hostile or adverse witness.

20.3.1 Cooperative Witness

The cooperative witness is more than willing to give information. This is particularly true if they are also the victims. A cooperative witness not only gives facts but also mixes the facts with opinions. Sometimes, they want something in exchange. Cooperative witnesses should be evaluated very closely. They might not be suitable witnesses on the witness stand because of biases and lack of objectivity.

20.3.2 Neutral Witness

Neutral witnesses have no or little interest in the case. Even though they make the best witnesses, they do not always provide all the necessary evidence. This is particularly true in cases of custodians of records. Most have never seen the subject and sometimes have difficulty in locating all their records.

20.3.3 Hostile Witness

The hostile witness is harder for the examiner to interview. A witness who lies or becomes uncooperative or evasive may be indicating "dishonest intent" or has close association with the subject under investigation. The interview should be conducted professionally and with a high degree of formality. The interview should start with identification of the witness and later the identification of the subject. A hostile witness can be softened up by not accusing them even though the evidence is clear and convincing. The examiner should let the witness have an "out" or offer an excuse for their behavior. Rewards for cooperation or punishment for being uncooperative should be pointed out. Under no circumstances should the examiner make any promises or guarantees. The examiner should never reveal his/her knowledge or lack of to the witness. The more the witness talks, the better because more information or evidence can be obtained.

20.4 Planning the Interview

Proper planning of the interview is important. The examiner must have a general idea as to what the witness knows, what he/she can provide, and their relationship to the subject. Prior to any interview, the examiner should review all the information and data relating to the case. Such information can be divided into three general categories.

1. Information that can be documented and need not be discussed
2. Information that may be documented but needs to be discussed
3. Information that must be developed by testimony

The examiner should prepare a file that contains only data or information arranged in the order it is to be discussed or covered in the interview. The examiner should determine the purpose or goal for questioning. An outline should be prepared, more or less in detail. The outline should contain only information that is relevant and material including hearsay. Important topics should be set off or underscored and related topics listed in their proper sequence. The examiner should keep specific questions to a minimum because they tend to reduce the flexibility of the examiner. The examiner should cover as much information as possible. The time and place can be scheduled for cooperative witnesses. The best place to interview them is at their place of business or where they keep documents. In the case of hostile witnesses, it is best to approach them unannounced. This prevents the witness from contacting the subject or an attorney, or from disappearing. The interview outline should cover at least the following:

1. Name, address, employment, and contact telephone numbers
2. Witness connection to the subject
3. Meetings and telephone conversations with subject
4. Documents furnished by the subject to the witness
5. Other potential witnesses
6. Financial dealings, including any losses
7. Information about the history and background of the subject
8. Any other material or relevant information or evidence

20.5   Conducting the Interview

During the interview, you must keep an open mind that is receptive to all information regardless of the nature and be prepared to develop it. If you are not flexible, you may waste a great deal of time and ask unnecessary questions, resulting in a voluminous statement of little or no value. Although you may find it easier to adhere to a fixed pattern of interviewing or to rely on a series of questions or topics, rigid adherence to any notes or outline will seriously impair flexibility. The outline and data should serve only as aids and not as substitutes for original and spontaneous questioning. A carefully planned outline will provide enough leeway to allow the examiner to better cope with any situations that may occur and permit him/her to develop leads that may arise.

Establishing good communications with the witness in the initial interview is essential because it provides an opportunity to obtain information, which may not be readily available at a later date. A skilled examiner leads the interview so that he or she obtains as much information as possible. The examiner encourages the witness to discuss himself/herself, family, hobbies, financial history, and relations with others including the subject of the investigation. After the initial contact, some witnesses may procrastinate or become less communicative. Therefore, plan for and conduct your initial interview so that you obtain as much information as possible. Let the witness talk; you be a good listener. The obvious fact about interviewing is that it involves communication between two or more people. It is a specialized, professional type of conversation, requiring all the facilities and tools of good speech and communication.

Techniques should be developed that lead witnesses into answering desired questions. The examiner should gain a clear understanding of the witness or subject's lifestyle and financial dealings. Statements made by the witness or subject may be used later as a test of their truthfulness and accuracy. Always be alert for any indications of fraud on the part of the witness or subject. Witnesses or subjects may have had unusual good or bad luck. Let them discuss their failures or successes. These are leads that are obtained in the interview and should alert you to follow up with questions to document these failures or successes. Nonresponse to specific questions should be enough to note the answer or the lack of it. Follow through on every pertinent lead and incomplete answer. Continue asking questions until all information that can reasonably be expected has been secured.

The following suggestions will help the examiner follow through and obtain answers that are complete and accurate:

1. Use short questions confined to one topic that can be clearly and easily understood.
2. Ask questions that require narrative answers; avoid "yes" and "no" answers whenever possible.
3. Question the witness about how he/she learned what is stated to be fact. The subject should also be required to give the factual basis for any conclusions stated.
4. Whenever possible, avoid questions that suggest part of an answer, "leading questions."
5. Be alert to prevent the witness from aimlessly wandering. Where possible, require a direct response.
6. Prevent the witness from leading you far afield. Do not allow the witness to confuse the issue and leave basic questions unanswered.

7. Concentrate more on the answers than on the next questions.
8. To avoid an unrelated and incomplete chronology, clearly understand each answer and ensure that any lack of clarity is eliminated before continuing.
9. When all-important points have been resolved, terminate the interview; if possible, leave the door open for further meetings.

The witness or subject should completely answer the following basic questions:

1. *Who.* Complete identification should be made of all persons referred to. This includes the following: description, address, alias, "trading as," "also known as," citizenship, reputation, and associates.
2. *What.* Complete details as to what happened. Questions should relate to events, methods, and systems. A complete answer should be developed. Trace the event from its inception to its ultimate termination.
3. *Where.* Complete details regarding financial records and affairs, including their location, witnesses, clients, customers, and the like.

20.6 Recording of Interview

The principal purpose of interviews is to obtain all the facts helpful in resolving the case. Thus, it is necessary to prepare a permanent record of every interview to be preserved for future use. The methods used to record and document the interview are as follows:

20.6.1 Affidavit

An affidavit is a written or printed declaration or statement made voluntarily and confirmed by the oath or affirmation of the party, making it before an officer having authority to administer such oath. The procedures for taking an affidavit are:

1. *When to take an affidavit.* An affidavit should be taken when an affiant presents information, written or oral, relating to his/her knowledge about the matter under investigation that has a material effect.
2. *How to take an affidavit.* Ideally, two examiners or investigators should be present, although it is permissible for one representative to be present. One representative will swear in the affiant after the affidavit is filled out by asking the following:
   "Do you swear or affirm that the foregoing facts are true to the best of your knowledge?" The affiant must have his/her right hand raised at the time of reply to this statement.
3. An affidavit should contain, at a minimum, the following:
   a. *Name.* This could contain current full legal name or any current or prior aliases.
   b. *Address.* This should be the most current address.
   c. *Occupation.* This is the present occupation of the person giving the affidavit. If the information relates to a prior occupation, that should be given.

d. *Identified document.* If the person giving the affidavit is presenting a document, it should be described as precisely as possible.

e. *When prepared.* If a document is presented, when it was prepared should be noted.

f. *Who prepared it.* The preparer must be noted.

g. *Source prepared from.* If the information contained in the document was taken from another source, state what the source was.

20.6.2   Memorandum of Interview

Memorandum of interview is an informal method of recording an interview. It is basically putting down on paper what the examiner learned from the interview. The memorandum of interview should be done as soon as possible after the interview because the examiner's knowledge is fresh in his/her mind. The examiner should have taken notes to help in writing his/her memorandum. The memorandum of interview should contain at least the following:

1. Date and time of interview
2. Place or location of interview
3. The people present at the interview
4. Date the memorandum was prepared
5. A summary of the conversation that took place
6. It should provide as much information as possible about the interview and what the subject or witness said

The examiner should sign the memorandum of interview.

20.6.3   Question-and-Answer Statement

The question and answer statement is a formal method of interviewing a witness or subject. It sometimes requires that the court reporter present will generally administer an oath and record the proceedings verbatim. If a court reporter is not used, then a tape recording is used and is later transcribed. The witness is always administered an oath. The witness may be later required to read and swear or affirm to the transcribed proceedings. Even though this is a preferred method to use because it precludes a witness or subject from changing his/her testimony, it may not be admissible in court because cross-examination has not taken place. If the subject provides such a statement, then his/her legal rights should be explained to him before taking such a statement. If a tape recorder is used in lieu of a reporter or as a backup to the reporter, consent must be obtained on the record from the witness or subject. The question and answer statement is similar to a deposition, except in a deposition, cross-examination is done by the opposing counsel or party.

An experienced reporter will be able to transcribe notes made under adverse conditions. However, if recording conditions are improved, then the reporter will be able to transcribe notes much more rapidly and with less chance of error.

The following techniques will help the reporter to do a better job.

20.6.3.1 Brief Your Reporter before the Interview

The examiner should provide the names of the people that are expected to be present. The reporter must identify each speaker. It will be helpful if the reporter knows the witness's line of business and has a general idea of the line of questioning to be pursued. The reporter should read any correspondence or memorandums that you have that would be helpful, particularly where unusual names may be involved.

20.6.3.2 Control the Interview

Remind those present to speak one at a time. The reporter cannot record two voices simultaneously. This is essential even if you are using a tape recorder. The machine will not encounter any difficulty in recording several voices at once, but when you play it back, you will not be able to understand a word of it.

20.6.3.3 Open the Interview in a Formal Manner

Open the interview by saying, "This is the testimony of (name of witness) taken in (complete address) at (time) on (date) in the matter of (suspected crime). Those present are: (List all persons present at the interview)." This information is necessary for preparing your transcript, and by opening in this manner, you can be sure that these facts are accurately recorded. This formal opening also affords a built-in "warm up" for both examiner and reporter. It also alerts all participants that anything they say after this time will be recorded.

20.6.3.4 Avoid Overlapping

Overlapping is the practice of breaking in with another question before the witness has finished speaking. The transcript will have a better appearance if all parties have spoken in complete sentences. Also, it is necessary to listen carefully to the replies of your witness rather than thinking ahead to the next question.

20.6.3.5 Guard against Multiple Questions

The interviewer should keep questions short, concise, and to the point. The interviewer can do a lot to head off the witness who tends to ramble on without giving a specific answer. Questions that require more than one answer or that are leading should not be asked.

20.6.3.6 Assist Your Reporter with a Witness Difficult to Record

The interviewer may have a witness with an extraordinary rapid rate of speech or with a heavy accent or other speech peculiarity that makes it very difficult for the reporter to follow. A break of only one or two seconds in the flow of difficult language makes a world of difference to the reporter. Some helpful things that an interviewer can do in such situations are:

1. Speak more slowly than usual when asking your questions.
2. If you have a document that you wish to show the witness, reach for it in a leisurely manner.
3. Glance at the reporter to see if he/she is ready before you ask your next question.

20.6.3.7 Remember There Are No Shortcuts to Writing Figures

Speak slowly when giving a number with several digits. There are no shortcuts to writing figures, and they have no context. A rapidly spoken 13-digit number followed immediately by a flow of words will force the reporter to try to carry possibly 5 digits and 7 or 8 words in her head simultaneously. The possibility of error will be greatly reduced if you speak more slowly when numbers are involved.

20.6.3.8 *Identify Documents*

If you have occasion to refer to documents, identify them specifically, such as "cash disbursement book, advertising expense column." If you say "this book" and "that column," a reviewer examining the transcript will not be sure which documents or columns you have made reference to.

20.6.3.9 *Be Aware of the Required Transcription Time*

When the reporter prepares a transcript of an interview, he/she must set up in question and answer form, numbering each question and answer and identifying all speakers. This adds to typing time. The required transcription time for the reporter's examination is 1 hour for 5 minutes dictation at 160 words per minute. This would mean 6 hours are needed to transcribe a 30-minute interview. If the examiner knows the transcription time required, he/she will not expect to record a 6-hour interview on Monday and find a finished transcript on his/her desk by Wednesday morning. When you need a completed transcript by a certain date, take this factor into consideration when setting the date of the interview.

20.6.4 Statement

A statement is a written record by the witness or subject as to his/her knowledge of an offense that possibly took place. The interviewer should be sure that the statement is dated, and in some instances signed. A statement does not have to be sworn to. The witness should write down everything that he has seen or heard before, during, and after the event. This helps the witness later to recall the events in detail, even things that were not put in the statement.

20.7 Interviews

The fraud examiner should be very aware of the importance of interviews, particularly, of witnesses. Interviews are just as important as the document evidence. Remember, especially in criminal cases, there must be both physical evidence and a witness. With no witness, the documentary evidence may not be admissible. Witnesses do not only furnish evidence in the case, but they also furnish leads to other evidence and witnesses. The fraud examiner should follow up on these leads. When making interviews of witnesses or the subject, the fraud examiner should always take a professional attitude. The fraud examiner is only interested in getting the facts. Witnesses not only give facts but also opinions. The fraud examiner has to take great care to differentiate facts from opinions. Keep in mind that you can "get more flies with honey than you get with vinegar."

20.8 Interview Techniques

Over many decades, criminologists have developed various interview techniques. One technique is called "kinesic" interviewing that encompasses the answers to questions as well as observing his/her body movements (language), for example, movements of head, hands, and arms. Certain movements by the subject can indicate deception when they answer particular questions. This method has the disadvantage of the interviewer being present with the subject. The presence of an authority figure tends to make the subject less talkative. Another method of interviewing is to have the subject or witness take a polygraph test.

Similar to kinesic interviewing, the polygraph relies on body responses to answers. The polygraph machine measures various bodily changes that occur when a person lies. During the test, tubes are placed on the chest and abdomen to collect respiratory data. Metal connectors are placed on the finger to record sweat gland activity and blood pressure. The polygraph records significant changes in the subject's baseline physiological data. A lie will cause identifiable changes in one or more of the physical changes in one or more of the physical responses measured by the polygraph. The polygraph examiner will begin with asking yes or no questions. The questions gradually become more intense and relevant to the particular act under investigation. Its disadvantage is that it makes the subject feel the interviewer is intrusive and becomes less informative. Also, if the subject is nervous or jittery during the whole session or the questions have no physiological response, the polygraph test has no meaning. Subjects of polygraphs try to deceive it. One method is by taking sedatives before the test in hope of altering results. Sedatives lower blood pressure and enhance relaxation that the polygraph measures. A subject may apply deodorant to his/her fingertip to help prevent perspiration. A subject may step on a tack inside his/her shoe to cause anxiety. Another tact is that the subject might bite down on his/her tongue or cheek in hopes that the pain will increase anxiety levels.

20.8.1   Kinesic Interviewing

This technique observes the body movements. The body movements can indicate deception or lying. Some body language signs can indicate deception or lying. They are:

1. Crossing legs
2. Hand over mouth
3. Shifting in chair
4. Arms crossed
5. Shaking head
6. Biting lips
7. Leaning forward
8. Steepled hands
9. Avoiding eye contact

20.8.2   Statement Analysis

Another technique is to obtain an open-ended statement from the subject or witness. The statement is analyzed to determine deception or to gather more information about an event. A disadvantage to this technique is that the subject or witness may refuse to provide a written statement. However, it does have several advantages over other techniques. First, the interviewer does not need to be present. In fact, it is better for the interviewer not to be present because a person will not feel as threatened. Second, a questionnaire can be given to many people at one time. This saves time and effort. The next chapter will discuss the theory and procedures in the use of statement analysis.

20.9 Summary

Subjects and witnesses author are very important. It basically comprises about half the case in terms of importance. Criminal cases require witnesses to introduce evidence, physical or documented. The most serious obstacle to obtaining information is the interviewer. The interviewer either does not ask the proper questions or influences the person to lie. In many cases, the interviewer does not listen to what a person says.

Investigative Interview Analysis

21

21.1 Introduction

Investigative interview analysis is conducted on the subject's statement to determine deception. This statement can be oral or written. Best practice is to transcribe oral statements so that they can be analyzed in the future. The resulting transcript is nothing more than a transcript of an interview.

The purpose of the interview or interrogation is to obtain information about an event or a series of events. Investigative interview analysis is not the process of interviewing. It has nothing to do with making people talk; instead, it looks at how to use what people have said. Analysis is the breaking down of the whole into its parts to determine their nature. The analyst looks for what is there and notices what is not there. Investigative interview analysis is the process of studying the nature of the statement and determining its essential elements.

One of the principle functions of law enforcement and compliance personnel is to interview people to get facts about a crime or event. Usually, the first people to be interviewed are witnesses and/or victims. For law enforcement, it is important to gather the facts of a case as soon as possible. The investigator must obtain information not only about the crime or event but also about suspects, witnesses, and victims. The investigator must get answers as to who, what, where, when, why, and how. Sometimes, the investigator may interview a subject at the scene of a crime without knowing that he/she would become a suspect. This suspect will provide information that tends to direct attention away from him/her or to make it seem that he/she is only a witness. The investigator may obtain a statement from a person and still not get any useful information.

The purpose of investigative interview analysis is to identify a person who is deceptive. Investigative interview analysis is cost-effective and more accurate than a polygraph examination. Scientific interview analysis is effective about 95% of the time. However, it is not effective for attorneys. Attorneys lack commitment to their statements because of their training. It does not matter if the subject is careful, deliberate, or selective. The point is whether the subject is truthful and accurate. It is cost-effective in one aspect. Statements can be taken from various witnesses of an event at the same time. These statements can be gathered and analyzed at a later date. Also, the subject can write down his/her own narrative at home or in his/her office. If the subject becomes a suspect, this option can help eliminate his/her claiming coercion or intimidation because his/her account will have been written in a comfortable environment, for example, his/her home. There is another cost aspect. Investigative interview analysis does not require expensive equipment or a high degree of training. One can use a computer, but it is not required. The investigator can type a question at the top of the page and let the subject type out his/her response. Only paper and pencil/pen are required.

Criminals rarely come forward voluntarily. Witnesses are usually reluctant to become involved. These are barriers for the investigator to overcome. The investigator usually has no problem with neutral witnesses, and victims will usually cooperate fully. The victim's drawback is lack of objectivity and biases. Victims can also become very emotional.

Witnesses who have observed an event or crime will be reluctant to testify in court or provide a statement. Our society has become more apathetic in recent years. In the past, strangers would come to the aide of the victim, but now they are reluctant to do so. There are many reasons for this. One reason is people do not want to be involved in the judicial proceedings. Witnesses have to take time from work to attend court proceedings. Another reason is the fear of retribution from the criminals. In many cases, an investigator can overcome this reluctance by having the person write down his/her statement. It is harder for a person to talk to another person, but it is very easy to express oneself in writing. People disclose more of themselves on the computer in "chat rooms" and e-mails than they do face to face.

Many investigators prefer to bring the person into the office for an interview. It is best to start the interview process by having the person write down his/her statement. Afterward, the investigator analyzes the statement and follows up with subsequent interview questions.

Some investigators prefer to bring the person into an interview room and commence the interview with an open-ended question. During this interview, the person and the investigator are being taped or videotaped. The audiotape is later transcribed and analyzed. For videotapes, the audio portion is transcribed and analyzed while the video portion is studied by the investigator for body language. Body language can help confirm deception or truthfulness to the audio transcript.

21.2 Purpose

The primary purpose of an interview is to get as much information as possible. The interview should tell a story. That story is analyzed to determine deception. The speed of thinking is faster than the speed of speech. The speed of speech is faster than the speed of writing. Because of this, there is a tendency to take shortcuts in speaking and writing. It is expected that a subject will take a shortcut when introducing someone. Society rules of etiquette apply to statements as well as to everyday life. People will use titles, for example, my wife/my husband, when talking to strangers. A social introduction is a necessary part of every statement. One person will introduce another person into the picture. An improper social introduction indicates something has prevented the subject from introducing the other person. If the subject does not mention "my wife" or "my husband," then he/she is not his/her spouse.

Investigative interview analysis deals with information, written or verbal, and not with the person. The purpose of interview analysis is to obtain information and detect deception. This information is called a statement, which consists of two parts: structure and content.

Structure is more important than content. The structure reveals more about the person. The first interview is the most important. It should give a picture of the event. It will not be a complete picture, but it will be the basis for further inquiry. The investigator asks an open-ended question. The subject answers with a story or long narrative. The question should be much shorter than the response.

If a person likes to talk, then the interviewer should let him/her talk. The subject who talks without being asked will provide more information than can be gained from asking a question. The interviewer should not interrupt when the person is talking, that is, the interviewer should only listen.

21.3 Interview Stages

There are three stages of interviews. The first stage is the first time interview. This is referred to as the original version because subsequent interviews are based on this one. The second stage involves subsequent interviews, where various points from the initial interview are cleared up. The questions and answers should be about equal in length. The last stage, called interrogation, is used to obtain a confession from a suspect. The interrogation is based on prior interviews as well as other evidence. These three stages are discussed further in the following.

The first stage is most important. During the initial interview, the subject gives the interviewer only what the subject thinks is important for the interviewer to know. The following suggestions will help the interviewer obtain the best picture of the event:

1. Ask only open-ended questions. Allow the subject to "tell the story."
2. Do not use prepared lists of questions. A conversation involves spontaneity and flexibility. Investigators who use prepared lists of questions, invariably, do not get good responses.
3. Do not ask questions for which you already know the answer. This is a waste of time and effort.
4. Listen to the subject's answer and try not to predict it. People are more afraid of asking questions than answering questions.
5. Do not explain a question to a subject.
6. Do not ask leading questions, which tend to give the suspect answers that you are looking for. It also has a tendency to teach the person to lie.

    Examples of open-ended questions are: "Tell me what you saw and heard on Friday," or "What did you do from the time you arrived at the office until the time you left the office yesterday?"
7. Do not ask questions that require a "yes" or "no" answer because they do not give details. Attorneys like to ask this type of question to people on the witness stand. One reason is to ignore the details behind the question. Another reason is to either deny or confirm something without giving any explanation.

The time gap between the interview and the event reported in the statement can influence the statement. Statements have never been given at the time of the event. They are given after the event, and that time can range from a few minutes to years later. One's memory about an event diminishes over time unless it was a very traumatic event.

The main point of the interview is to determine whether the subject is truthful and accurate. People are more open when they are on the computer than they are face to face with someone. This is true of children and especially teenagers. This is why pedophiles use chat rooms on the Internet. They play on the child's emotions. To take advantage of this openness, an investigator can allow the subject to write the answer to the questionnaire on a computer and e-mail it back. It is important that, after obtaining the initial interview statement, the investigator create an impression of appreciation. This will encourage witnesses to contact the investigator if they recall additional information. Establishing good rapport with a subject reduces anxiety. The investigator should ask the subject to "think of anything else that might be important."

The second stage of the interview involves subsequent interviews. The object is to clear up points and to obtain information omitted from the initial interview, that is, to get a complete picture. This is called the subsequent inquiry. Questions should be short and only deal with one issue. Specific questions are designed to detect deception. There should be equal time between the question and the answer. At subsequent inquiries, the investigator should go over the initial interview and ask questions to obtain details. This will not affect a truthful person, but it will cause distress for a guilty person.

By discussing facts, the stress of interviewing is removed. Witnesses must feel confident. They must have time to think, speak, reflect, and speak again. The interviewer should not use any word or term that the person did not use before.

During the initial interview, recording every word is necessary. During subsequent interviews, it is only recommended, unless there is a high probability that the subject is lying. If that's the case, an interview transcript is necessary.

A person cannot give the investigator all the information about an event or crime. He/she edits the information and gives only what is important to him/her. Both truthful and deceptive people edit their story. If an investigator asks a person why he/she did not tell about something, then the person would probably answer, "I didn't think it was important." The investigator should get a complete story, but he/she can only do this by conducting subsequent interviews.

The presence of a question within the initial statement might indicate a person took out sensitive information. People usually will ask a question in order to avoid telling sensitive information which the subject is trying not to tell. In subsequent interviews, the investigator should ask questions, but they should be careful not to provide too much information and not to ask too many questions. Provide too much information and the subject may use it to lie. When the subject receives too much information, he/she tends to feed it back to the investigator. For the same reason, the investigator should not ask too many questions, which could give information to the subject. While the investigator would like to know the information, it will be false information.

During these interviews, the investigator must consider a person's feelings and emotions. Not doing so will prevent him/her from obtaining information. This is particularly true with victims. The investigator should also be aware of communication barriers such as fear, anger, and grief.

21.4 The Interviewer

The interviewer should not argue with the subject. It is a waste of time and does not accomplish anything. In fact, arguing causes the subject to provide less information, making him/her more reluctant to talk to the investigator. The interviewer should avoid personal conflicts, even though the subject might try to push the interviewer into one. The subject may feel stronger than the interviewer. The subject will not blame the interviewer if the interviewer is just doing his/her job.

The object of an interview is to find out if a person is truthful or deceptive. The investigator cannot be fully objective because he/she has some information. The investigator usually reads all available information in a file before interviewing a subject. His/her knowledge can influence his/her opinion as to whether or not a person is deceptive. Investigators by nature look on each subject as potentially deceptive because of his/her adversary role. When the investigator analyzes a statement, he/she should disregard anything known outside the statement. The investigator should only consider what is said in the statement. The reader should not add to the statement and should not disregard anything in the statement. The statement should be taken literally. It is best for the investigator to analyze a statement a few days after taking it without referring to other data. This will help him/her focus on the statement and not the subject.

A person likes to talk more to a stranger than to a family member or friend. There are cases where a criminal has talked to another person about his/her crime(s). The other person then reports it to the authorities, who then arrest the criminal. The other person then testifies what the criminal told him/her about the crime. This often results in a conviction.

21.5 Deception

Deception depends on the speaker. A deceptive person knows he/she is lying. A truthful person can give a false opinion, but he/she cannot give false facts. A lie is defined by the speaker. There are no synonyms, or two different words that mean the same thing, in a statement. A guilty person likes to profess their innocence. They try to give information to convince the investigator of his/her innocence, but they cannot rely on facts. People "lie by omission and not by commission." In other words, the person lies by not telling something.

The following sections discuss the various parts of a statement. These include the use of nouns, pronouns, certain verbs, connections, unimportant or out-of-sequence information, conversation, and times. The last section discusses how to analyze a statement using statistics.

21.5.1 Nouns and Pronouns

Nouns are words that identify persons, places, and things. Pronouns replace nouns so that the speaker does not have to continually repeat the name. Nouns and pronouns are objective. A truthful person will identify a person, place, or thing, which is followed up by using pronouns to relate to the noun. Every pronoun has an antecedent, the noun. A subject who does not introduce a person, place, or thing is deceptive. Therefore, the introduction is very important.

An investigator obtains information from a person about an event or crime that took place in the past. To do this, the investigator questions the subject on his/her past history. For the investigator to establish a connection between the subject and the event, the subject's statement must

1. Connect himself/herself by using the pronoun I
2. Connect statement to past tense

These two connections use the first person singular, past tense, which establishes commitment on the part of the subject. This is called the commitment test. The investigator expects the subject to establish commitment. However, if the statement passes this test, it does not mean that the subject is truthful. A subject can provide a statement without using the first person singular past tense. The subject can use the past tense and not use "I." There are six ways to give a statement without using "I."

1. We
2. You, second person
3. He/she, third person
4. It was done, passive language
5. Omitting pronouns altogether
6. Use first or last name

An investigator should not force the person during an initial interview to use "I" or past tense because the investigator must not influence the statement. However, after the first statement, the investigator should not let the person get away from using "I" and/or past tense. In fact, forcing the subject to use past tense and/or the "I" will cause the person to be truthful.

It is important for the investigator to be certain of who the subject is referring. If the subject does not want the investigator to understand to whom he/she is referring, then the misunderstanding was intentional on the part of the subject. Pronouns give responsibility and possession to a person. Pronouns are one of the parts in a statement that are not subject to personal language or interpretation. Pronouns are objective, that is, they the same for everyone. When the subject says "I," it means he/she was alone. When the subject says "we," it means someone was with him/her. The use or misuse of pronouns produces almost 80–90% of admissions and confessions within a statement.

First Person Pronouns:
    I, me, we, us, my, myself, ourselves
Second Person Pronouns:
    You, your
Third Person Pronouns:
    He, she, her, they, them, his, her, our, their, him, herself, himself, ourselves, it, their, us

The first time a person is mentioned, it is the same as a social introduction. The proper way to introduce a person is to identify him/her by name or title, for example, John, Sue, wife, husband, son. First names are usually used when the subject has been previously introduced. Titles are usually used in talking to strangers. In a statement, if pronouns come before the person is identified, then it is considered rude and impolite and might indicate a bad relationship. If "we" appears before the social introduction, then it is equivalent linguistically to identifying the motive for a crime or event.

Example:

"I got up and went to the kitchen. My wife, Suzy, was in the kitchen making breakfast."

This is the best kind of introduction. The subject identifies the person as his wife and gives her name. If the subject repeats the social introduction, then it is an indication of something wrong in the relationship. If the subject uses a short introduction then a long introduction, it is a signal that indicates tension and possibly a bad relationship.

Example:

"My wife was in the kitchen. My wife, Suzy, was preparing breakfast."

The subject is expected to go from a long, social introduction to a short introduction. When the subject goes from a short introduction to a long one, something took place to downgrade the person. If the subject mentions a person without his/her title, this indicates tension between the subject and the person. The lack of pronouns is a strong indication of an attempt on the part of the subject to conceal identity. Missing pronouns indicate distance, whether physical or emotional. If the subject does not commit himself, then the statement is unreliable.

A change in pronouns indicates the subject is playing around with pronouns.

If "I" is present, it does not necessarily mean the subject is truthful.
If "we" is missing, it does not necessarily mean the subject is truthful.
If "I" is used a lot in part of a statement, then the statement is unreliable for the parts where the "I" is not used.
The use of small "i" is a strong indication of deception.
The lack of "I" in a statement or in a block in the statement indicates tension and might show deception.
Overuse of "I" is not good. The sentences are cut, meaning that the subject is very much on alert. This is associated with tension and eventually deception.

"We" means one is a willing partner. Investigators do not expect the "we" in a violent crime or incident. A missing "we" can indicate tension or friction in the relationship between two parties. "We" is important, especially when dealing with partnerships and corporations. Partnerships can be defined as two or more persons working together for a particular purpose. A statement without "we" requires further analysis because no one functions alone in a partnership. The investigator should note the frequency of "we" in a statement because it gives an indication of whether the subject was relaxed or not. The lack of "we" indicates distance and a great deal of tension in the relationship. The presence of "our" or "we" without an introduction indicates a bad relationship.

"We" is important in:

- White collar crimes
- Personal relationships
- Assault cases
- Kidnappings

Possessive pronouns show ownership or relationship. The lack of possessive pronouns strongly indicates possible deception in the statement. Usually, when people are deceptive, they change the possessive pronoun to "the" instead of "my" or "our." When the change of a possessive pronoun occurs, this is the point where the statement becomes deceptive unless the statement reflects the reason for the change.

Example:

"My dog and I went fishing."

In the above example, the word "my" means a close relationship with the dog. It also means I am a dog lover because I have a dog and I take him fishing with me.

Example:

"I came home and washed the dog."

In this example, the "my" is missing. It was replaced with the word "the." This indicates a bad relationship. However, when reading the sentence carefully, the reader can see "I" does not like washing the dog. If the sentence does not reflect the reason for changing the "I" to "the," this indicates deception.

Example:

"I went to the store with the wife."

In this example, the word "the" is used instead of the word "my." Also, the word "with" is used. The word "with" always indicates distance in the relationship. When the words "with" and "the" are used together, it indicates a bad relationship. For example, it could indicate that the couple is about to get a divorce or is getting a divorce.

Change from "my" to "the" is important in:

- Dispute about possession
- Child/spousal abuse cases

Passive language refers to sentences where an activity is described, but the sentence does not reveal who did the activity. This involves a form of the verb "to be," which resembles a past participle that ends in "ed."

Example:

"The books and records were lost."

In this case, the subject does not know who lost the books and records. This is an indication of deception.

The lack of names throughout a statement indicates distance in the relationship. People who are mentioned in a statement are very important. The investigator should check how the subject labels these people or things to see if the subject changes his/her language. If it does not change, then the investigator should determine whether the subject justifies the language change by the content in the sentence. If the change is justified, then the subject is truthful.

Repetition of pronouns in the same place indicates a heightened level of distress. The scale of anxiety can be measured. If the repetition occurs twice, then it is mild distress. If it occurs three or four times, then it is moderate. If it occurs five to seven times, then it is extreme distress. Extreme distress is found in murder cases, which involve deep, emotional problems.

The investigator should review the pronouns to see how the subject utilizes them throughout the narrative. Pronouns can provide insight into the status of relationships. They also define the subject places or events, circumstances, and actions. The investigator should also review nouns throughout the narrative, paying particular attention to the introduction. If a noun is used in reference to an individual change, then there must be an antecedent that causes the change. If there is no antecedent for the change, then the statement is deceptive.

Second-person referencing allows the subject to divert attention from herself/himself. The subject feels no personal responsibility for whatever happened. Therefore, it is imperative for the investigator to pay attention to pronouns. Change of pronouns in the same sentence indicates deception. The investigator should develop the statement in detail in such a way that the subject would not be able to fill in the gaps with detail.

21.5.2   Prepositions

Prepositions connect a noun or pronoun to another element in a sentence. Prepositions can give the investigator a sense of location or position of a person, as well as the relationship between individuals and things.

Prepositions are: at, by, in, from, off, on above, around, before, behind, over, through, until, with.

21.5.3   Verbs and Adverbs

Verbs are words that describe an action, existence, or occurrence. Adverbs are words used to modify a verb, adjective, or another adverb. They express time, place, and degree. Verbs show a time frame, or tense, within the statement. There are three basic tenses:

1. Past
2. Present
3. Future

There are three kinds of verbs.

1. **Action verbs without an object**. Example: He ran. The plane flew.
2. **Action verbs with an object**. Example: She cooked supper.
3. **Linking verbs**. Example: I am hungry.

The most common linking verbs are:

- Forms of "to be" (am, is, was, were, has been, etc.)
- Become
- Remain
- Turn

- Seem
- Appear
- Pertaining to the five senses (see, touch, hear, smell, feel)

In a statement, it is very important for the investigator to notice when verb tense changes. This is an indication of deception. If the verb tense changes, then there must be some antecedent that caused the change. If there is no antecedent, then the statement where the verb tense changed is deceptive.

The interviewer should pay particular attention to six types of verbs:

1. Anything about leaving a place.
2. Verbs that indicate missing time or information.
3. Anything about communication with someone by the subject.
4. Verbs that lack commitment.
5. Verbs that do not describe what happened.
6. Verbs of what did not happen.

1. *Verbs about leaving a place.* Verbs that refer to leaving a place are very significant. The more times "left" or its equivalent is used, the more sensitive the statement becomes. In most cases, the word "left" or its equivalent is used because the subject was pressured for time, for example, being in a rush or late. However, in about a third of cases, the word "left" or its equivalent is used because of strong sensitivity, thus deception. Many deceptive statements start and end with "left." "Left" or its equivalent also indicates missing information or time. To find this information, the investigator should ask more questions during subsequent interviews.

2. *Verbs that indicate missing time or information.* The investigator should look for the following verbs: started, began, commenced, continued, proceeded, resumed, completed, finished, returned, coming, going, attempted, ended, needed, was finishing/completing/about to, etc.

The above verbs indicate missing information or missing time. If the person explains in the statement why he/she said "began, etc.," then it is fine. If the person does not explain it, then the interviewer should ask questions about it in a subsequent interview. Remember that the first interview must be unadulterated. If these expressions are used right before the main issue, then the missing time or information has something to do with the main issue. "Began" and "started" indicate a break in activity during which there is no account. In other words, the investigator does not know what the subject did during this time. "Continued" and "proceeded" are also a break in activity during which there is no account. In subsequent interviews, the investigator should ask questions to determine what happened. "Getting" or "coming" should be noticed for change in language. The common reason for change in language in "returning" is that people use one term when alone and another term when someone is present. "Returning" is very important in murder cases. Repeating the term "returning" indicates some significant information was intentionally left out of the statement. Mentioning "getting dressed" in an initial statement indicates significant information was intentionally taken out of the statement. "Getting undressed" in an initial statement indicates the subject has problems with his/her sex life.

3. *Verbs about communication.* Verbs that refer to communication are also very significant. These verbs include said, talk, speak, chat, discuss, and conversed.

When the subject uses "talking" in the first statement, it is an important conversation. If the subject says it is an important conversation, then it is fine. However, if the subject denies the conversation is not important, then it is not important. However, in having the conversation was important. In subsequent interviews, the investigator should ask about the content of the conversation. The nouns should be checked closely in regard to the conversation. If the "we" is present in the conversation, then the conversation had a good atmosphere. If the "we" is not present in the conversation, then the conversation resulted in disagreement or even an argument. A discussion indicates a strong difference of opinions and sometimes it is on the verge of an argument. A conversation between two people is normally two sided. If the subject says, "told me" and immediately after says, "told me," then the subject's answer or response is missing. In a subsequent interview, the interviewer should ask the subject about his/her answer. If the subject said, "He/she went on to say...," then the subject intentionally took out his/her part of the conversation. The investigator in a subsequent interview should have the subject write down his/her part of the conversation.

Example:

> She/he: (type in the exact quotation.)
> You:
> She/he: (type in the exact quotation.)

If the subject never mentions what is said, then nothing was said. The word "said" indicates a one-sided communication. The word "told" indicates a two-sided communication. The word "discussion" indicates disagreement and conflict. If the change in language from "told" to "said" is unjustified by the sequence of events, then deception is present at the point of change. "Said" has a softer tone, while "told" is a command or order.

4. *Verbs that lack commitment.* When the subject uses terms, for example, think, believe, don't remember, and don't know, the subject is not committed to his/her statement. The subject is expressing his/her own thoughts and not describing the event. The subject may also use present tense to describe a past occurrence. This shows lack of commitment by the subject. One should pay attention to changes in tenses. It will probably be deceptive at the point where the verb tense changes to present tense. The word "would" is a form of future tense. This shows lack of commitment and should be noted. If these expressions are used right before the main issue, then the missing information has something to do with the main issue.

There are other terms that show a lack of commitment. These include: little, believe, guess, sort of, kind of, probably, usually, almost, would appear, seldom, possibility, think, not sure, guess, suppose, figure, presume, assume, like, almost, mainly, and maybe.

These terms are used to modify or qualify. Qualifying terms show lack of commitment. The word "but" can also be used as a modifier or qualifier, but it is usually used as a conjunction or adverb.

- Did the subject use present tense during the event? This shows lack of commitment.
- Did the subject use third person to talk about himself? This shows lack of commitment in the statement.

- Did the subject use passive language in the statement? This also shows lack of commitment in the statement.
- Does the subject talk about the future? If not, then the investigator should not expect the subject to establish commitment.

The conjunction "but" is an example of a qualifier. It modifies or rebuts the previous statement. The term "when" indicates missing elements that the subject has leaped over or left something out of the narrative.

Linguistic signals that indicate deception are present when the subject is not sure of the information furnished to the investigator. Some examples of not being sure are: Maybe, might, could have, perhaps, you might say, I would say, about, approximately, more or less, would have been, can't say for sure, and it's hard to say.

Information can be unreliable because of deception or uncertainty on the part of the subject. Crimes or events that happened a long time ago will show uncertainty.

5. *Verbs that do not describe what happened.* Verbs that do not describe what happened are: suggested, declined, convinced, started, began, continued, proceeded, and needed.

When a person does not describe what happened, he/she is outside of the parameters of the question. This is considered out of sequence of events. Thus, it becomes sensitive and is important information. When the subject says "suggested," it indicates the subject may have wanted to do something, but did not do it.

6. *Verbs of what did not happen.* The story should tell us what happened, not what did not happen. As in the example with "suggested," the same applies to the words "decline" and "convinced." Both terms indicate what could have happened but did not happen. Another way of describing what did not happen is to use a negative, for example, "wasn't," "didn't."

The object is to get the subject to say "I did it." People do not like to confess. "Never" is not as strong as "didn't." When a person says, "I never did it," it is a weak assertion. Sometimes it means just the opposite: he/she did do it. President Clinton went on television and said, "I never had sex with that woman." What the President is actually saying is, "I had sex." Notice the word "with" in the sentence. It indicates the relationship was not close. If the subject says "I am telling the truth," then this is a strong indication of truthfulness, which is not found in deceptive people. However, if the person says, "I am telling you the truth," then the person is deceptive. He/she is addressing the interviewer.

A deceptive person will relate events vaguely to actions or blocks of time summed up in phrases, for example, messed around, talked for awhile. Avoidance by the subject begins with verbs or description of activities that the subject was a participant but he/she gives no reference to his/her involvement.

21.6 Changes in Language

Changes in language are very important. When a change in language occurs, it indicates deception. The change in language can take place by:

1. Changes in pronouns
2. Changes in verbs

21.6.1 Connections

A connection is a phrase that connects two different events in the statement. Connections identify parts that have been left out, such as time, and are used to determine cause and effect. Conjunctions connect or link the narrative. A missing link is any link without which the story cannot continue.

Example:

"I woke up at seven o'clock. I went to the bathroom then I took a shower. After leaving the bathroom, I went to the kitchen."

In the above example, the unnecessary connection is "After leaving the bathroom." In a subsequent interview, the investigator should take the subject back a sentence or two before the unnecessary connection and ask, "You are now at . . . (specific time and place). Go on."

The common connectors are: After, after this/that, later on, sometime after, shortly thereafter, afterward, after this/that, the next thing I remember/knew, finally, eventually, from there, and after X I did Y.

If the unnecessary connection appears after food (breakfast, lunch, dinner, supper) or church, then it should be disregarded. The word "then" is not considered an unnecessary connection.

There are two basic ways a person can lie: strategic and tactical.

In the strategic (or strategy) type, the subject is aware of his/her lying but is not aware of the choice of words used. The subject's personality affects strategy. The subject is usually truthful at first, but he/she is not telling everything. Out-of-sequence information or unnecessary connection is an indicator of strategy. The subject may have taken some information out of the statement, but the effects of the missing information remain. The only way the subject can give an incomplete truthful statement is by leaping over the crime or event. At this point, it becomes necessary for the investigator to identify this gap and ask questions to account for the missing time. The investigator should check the specific location in the statement to determine if it corresponds to the area that is the focus of the investigation. Another strategy is for the subject to make accusations against the investigator.

Example:

"You are against me because I am (race, sex, nationality, etc.)."

Example:

"I am against you."

In the tactical (or tactics) type, the subject uses a word or sentence that has no relevant connection to the statement. Tactics help the subject get through an interview. He/she will use them to answer specific questions, and he/she tends to use many of them. Because of their professional positions, tactics do not apply to lawyers or investigators. Some examples of tactical phrases are:

1. "I don't think so."
2. "I guess not."
3. "I'm telling you."
4. "I don't remember."
5. "It's impossible."
6. "It cannot be."
7. "It's illogical."
8. "I don't remember."

Another tactic is when the subject provides an answer that ends in a question. This is a sign of resistance, indicating that the question preceding the answer is sensitive for the subject.

Example:

"I went to the bathroom then I took a shower. What would you like to know now?"

Sometimes the subject wants to either "fight" or give "flight." These are tactics used by subjects. In "fights," the subject is trying to confront the interviewer. In "flights," the subject is trying to evade the interviewer questions.
Examples of fight against authority:

"I don't like your questions."
"I am not going to answer."
"You don't have any authority/power to say that."

Examples of "flight" from authority:

1. Flattery
2. Another department/store, etc.
3. One common tactic is the person uses own name instead of "I"

21.7   Objective Times

Times mentioned in a statement, for example, 8 o'clock, are important. They are referred to as objective times, and they are not subject to the subject's personal language. Objective times mentioned in the statement should match times identified by other sources. If they do not, then the subject is deceptive. Further, if the subject did not mention any objective times, then the investigator should follow up in a subsequent interview. For example:

1. When did you get up?
2. When did you have breakfast?
3. When did you have lunch?
4. When did you have dinner/supper?
5. When did you go to bed?

In statements that encompass the whole day, the subject should mention the times when he/she had breakfast, lunch, and dinner. Lunch is expected to take place around one-third of the way into the statement. Dinner is expected to take place about two-thirds of the way into the statement. Any deviation is significant. In statements that only cover a part of the day, for example, only the morning or afternoon, the investigator should check for the times when the subject had breakfast and lunch or lunch and dinner. The time is objective only if the subject mentioned it and does not include going to a scheduled or promised time.

Example:

"I went to an eight o'clock appointment." This is not an objective time.

Example:

"I got to my appointment at eight o'clock." This is an objective time.

An objective time gives the investigator a solid reference point. The only way the subject can give an incomplete truthful statement is by skipping the time of the crime. The investigator should search for that missing time. It is interesting to note that many criminals put the time of the crime inside the story. If there is any objective time mentioned in the statement, the investigator should ask himself/herself if this time corresponds to the time of the crime. If it does, then there is a serious suspicion that the person might have committed the crime. If the subject does not mention any time, it does not usually mean he/she is deceptive. It only means time was not important to him/her. The investigator should not instruct the subject to put time inside the statement at the initial interview. Such instruction would influence the statement and would not allow the investigator to ascribe the importance to the points where the subject mentioned time.

If we can find missing information, we would be able to solve most cases. One way to find what the subject did not want the investigator to know is by identifying missing time. If the statement indicates a jump in time, then the time that the subject leaped over is called "missing time." The easiest way to find that time is to check the objective times mentioned in the statement. In an initial statement, the subject does not have to mention time. Time becomes important because the subject mentioned it.

Example:

"I got home at 5:00 P.M. At 5:30 P.M., I . . . ." In this case, we have 30 minutes missing.

Subjective time is the amount of time it takes the subject to write the statement. In a truthful statement, the subjective time will correspond to the objective time. If something took longer in objective time, then the statement will have more lines written than in something that took less time. If there is any deviation from the normal pace in the statement, then the statement is unbalanced. Any deviation of more than 30% should raise a red flag. Small deviations are not relevant. Any change in a regular pattern to describe his/her day indicates a problem. Subjective time is an excellent tool for identifying sensitive areas. It also is good for pointing out what the person did not want the interviewer to know.

The investigator should search for objective times by asking:

1. Are there objective times mentioned in the statement?
2. Is there only one time mentioned in the statement?
3. Did the subject correct an objective time?
4. Are there differences between the subject's commitments to time? For example, the subject said, "... at ..." while in another place the subject said, "... about..."
5. Is there any time that is mentioned more than once?

Missing time is determined by the number of lines in the statement. In most cases, the subject will describe an event by three or four lines. If the subject writes more than four lines, then the statement is sensitive at this point. If the statement has less than three lines about an event, then the statement is sensitive to the subject at this point. Normally, a subject will write three to four lines per hour. Any deviation is meaningful.

In the original statement, if the subject did not mention people at time of food during the day, the investigator should ask the subject to mention other people and time in a subsequent interview. If the subject did not mention any time in the initial statement, the investigator should ask the subject about the time he had breakfast, lunch, and dinner in a subsequent interview. The investigator should pay attention to "at" and "about."

21.8 Unimportant and Out-of-Sequence Information

A truthful story will have unnecessary links. Unnecessary links are any links that can be taken out of the statement by the investigator and the story will flow smoothly. There are six types of unnecessary information.

1. Why something happened
2. Emotions
3. What did not happen
4. Information that does not make sense
5. Ambivalent sentence(s)
6. Unimportant information

21.8.1 Why Something Happened

If a person provides explanatory terms for the cause of an event, then he/she is outside the parameters of the question. Explanatory terms are used to give reason or cause of an event. It does not describe the event. Very often, statements describing why something happened are usually preceded by conjunctions. A common deceptive maneuver is providing a small amount of relevant information and intermingling explaining information. When a subject uses explanatory terms, it shows lack of commitment and undermines his/her story. A person who provides a lot of explanations of why something happened is usually deceptive.

Conjunctions are used to describe why something happened. They include: Because, since, so, due to, on account of, and as.

21.8.2 Emotions

In cases where some type of violence or threats are made, the subject will express emotions. Emotions are any strong feelings. They include love, hate, fear, and anger. Emotions are usually expressed right after the main event. If the subject expresses emotion during the main event, then the subject is deceptive. People do not have time to deal with emotions during the main event. They are too busy concentrating on what to do or say during the main event.

21.8.3 What Did Not Happen

When the subject explains what did not happen, he/she is out of bounds. This is considered "out-of-sequence" of events. A suspect will deny or negate what did not happen or what he did not know, do, or observe. The most common indicators of what did not happen are sentences written in the negative, for example, "wasn't" and "didn't."

Examples:

"I didn't even know." Or "I don't remember," or "I didn't see/her . . . ."

21.8.4 Information That Does Not Make Sense

The subject may provide information which does not make sense. The interviewer should regard this information as very important. It does not make sense to the reader/listener, but it does make sense to the subject. In a follow-up interview, the subject should explain the information that does not make sense.

21.8.5 Ambivalent Sentences

Ambivalent sentences or part of a sentence are those addressed to the reader/listener.

Examples of ambivalent sentences or part of a sentence are: excuse me, should I continue, or any question present in the statement.

21.8.6 Unimportant Information

Unimportant information is any information that seems inconsequential to the reader/listener. This information is actually usually important information. Unimportant information could be: "brushed my teeth," "said good-bye/good morning/good night," "turned on/off the lights," "got dressed," etc. Inconsequential statements are those that are out of place or chronological order in the statement. They do not fit into the story; yet, the speaker included them. Unnecessary phrases that suggest editing may have more sinister meaning when provided by the suspect. A suspect who reduces an important event to three sentences but provides two pages of preliminary trivia raises serious questions. Extraneous information often reveals effects to justify or mislead. Editing phrases provides clues to missing information. Present tense verbs imply fabrication. Unbalanced statements lack credibility. Mentioning a mundane activity is usually found in many cases to be a strong signal for concealing significant information later in the statement by the subject.

Out-of-sequence information is a specific case of an "unnecessary link." This means every "out-of-sequence" information is an unnecessary link. However, an unnecessary link is not always out of sequence. The two types of unnecessary links are:

1. By the sequence of events.
2. By the change of language

An unnecessary link is any link that can be taken out of the statement by the reader/listener and still the story flows smoothly. Out-of-sequence information is a specific case of an "unnecessary link." This means out-of-sequence information is an unnecessary link. However, an unnecessary link is not always out-of-sequence. The two types of unnecessary link are by change in pronouns or by change in vocabulary. If the changes in language are justified by the sequence of events, then the subject is truthful. However, if the change of language is not justified by the sequence of events, then the subject is deceptive. Amplifying questions should be employed in instances where out-of-sequence statements occur in the narrative.

21.9   Narrative Balance

A statement should have three parts. The first part is the introduction and events leading up to the main issue. This is called the prologue (P). This is important because it includes the date, time, place, and people involved. It is also important for the investigator because it provides information about location to be checked, witnesses to be interviewed, and where to search for physical evidence. The second part is the main event or the critical event (CE). This describes what happened to him/her or what they saw. It should identify what people did and how they did it. This is when the crime took place, for example, theft, murder, rape, arson, fraud, etc. The last part deals with actions after the critical event, which is known as the aftermath (A). It describes what the subject did following the main event. The first and last parts are the trivial issues, while the second (middle part) part is the critical event.

A truthful person will balance his/her statement about equally between the three parts of the statement. A deceptive person will devote more time to the first part of the statement than they do to the critical issue or the last part of the statement. If the main part has not been discussed in the first one-third of the statement, then deception is present. If the subject provides a title to the statement, then this is not the main issue. There are two competing issues in a statement: the statement itself and the subject.

The interviewer should test statements by the total number of words on page(s) and determine the number of words for each of the three different parts of the statement (i.e., prologue, the critical event, and aftermath). After the number of words has been determined by part, then the interviewer should compute the percentages for each of the three parts. This is detection of deception by the subjective time by the subject. There are four possible structures in the statement. The structures are:

1. (P) (CE) (A) = S   A truthful statement   (1/3+/–) (1/3+/–) (1/3+/–)
2. (P) (CE) = S   A deceptive statement   MI is less than 40%
3. (CE) (A) = S   A deceptive statement   MI is less than 40%
4. (CE) = S   A deceptive statement   MI is greater than 85%

The first statement structure indicates a truthful statement. The statement balanced between each of the three parts. Each part could vary by 10 or 15%. The first part could be 40%, the middle part 30%, and the last part 30%. In any case, all three parts must be present in the statement.

The second statement structure indicates a deceptive statement. The statement is missing the last part of the statement.

The third statement structure indicates a deceptive statement. The statement does not give any introduction or give the time, place, or identity of the people in the event. An introduction must be in the statement about time, place, and people involved.

The fourth statement structure indicates a deceptive statement. It does not provide an introduction or give any information as to who, what, where, or when. Also, it does not provide any information as to what the subject did after the main event.

If the investigator is using a computer, then he/she can determine the balance of the three parts by the total word counts for each part by the total word count in the story.

21.10 Analysis

This section shows how quantitative analysis can be used. Quantitative analysis uses a grid showing the number of occurrences for each word that is identified as deceptive. This may be a single word, a phrase, or a sentence. Whether it is a single word, phrase, or sentence, each word is counted and recorded on the analysis form. The word count for each component is added up and placed at the bottom of the form. The total deceptive words are compared to the total words in the statement. A percentage is computed. A scale is provided to show the degree of deception. The degree of deception is based on a percentage. On the basis of case studies, statistics show:

- 0–20% shows no deception or very mild. The subject is basically truthful.
- 21–50% shows mild deception. The subject is not fully truthful.
- 51–80% shows a high degree of deception. The subject is definitely hiding important information.
- 81–100% shows extreme deception. The subject is totally fabricating his/her statement.

In the case of the last component in the statement analysis form, the statement balance should not use all the words in each section of the statement. The parts of the statement are:

- Introduction and events leading to the main event or crime
- The main event or crime
- Events after the main event

The investigator should instead identify the number of words for the introduction and events leading to the main event or crime; the number of words for the main event or crime; and the events following the main event or crime. This is because many words in the statement are not deceptive. The statement analysis form only wants the deceptive word count. The investigator should use a single number of 0, 1, or 2. If the statement has all three parts of a narrative, then the investigator should place 0 (zero). If the statement has only two parts of a narrative, then the investigator should place one (1). If the statement contains only one part of a statement, then he/she should place two (2). Example:

0—All three parts of the statement are present.
1—Only two parts of the statement are present.
2—Only one part of the statement is present.

Statement Analysis Form

Narrative Components	Word #
Changes in nouns, e.g., car to vehicle	
Changes in pronouns, e.g., my to the	
Lack of pronouns, e.g., I or We	
Words leaving a place, e.g., left, went, departed.	
Words or phrases of why something happened. Usually follows words: since, so, because, or but	
Changes in verb tense, e.g., from past tense to present or future tense	
Unnecessary connections, e.g., Later on, sometime later, shortly thereafter, afterward, after X I did Y, the next thing I remember, and the next thing I knew	
Missing times, e.g., 9:00 A.M. or ten o'clock	
Unimportant information, e.g., brushed my teeth, turned off the lights	
Out-of-sequence information, e.g., emotions during the main event or crime, it does not make sense	
Ambivalent sentences, e.g., addresses the listener, excuse me, should I continue, or ask the interviewer a question	
Lack of commitment terms, e.g., think, believe, don't remember, don't know, little, guess, sort of, kind of, usually, probably, almost, would appear, seldom, possibility, not sure	
Does not describe what happened, e.g., suggested, declined, convinced	
Passive language use, e.g., The books were on the table	
Words regarding conversation, e.g., said, told, spoke, discussed, talking, chatting, conversation, etc.	
Statement balance, i.e., introduction and events leading to main event or crime; the main event or crime; actions after the main event	
Total Deceptive Words:	

Using the formula below, one can determine the percentage of the statement that shows deception:

$$\frac{\text{Total deceptive words}}{\text{Total words in statement}} \times 100 = \text{Percent of deceptive statement}$$

Statements showing the following percentages indicate the degree of deception:

0–20%	Truthful or very low deception
21–50%	Mild deception
51–80%	High level of deception
81–100%	Extreme deception (subject is totally deceptive)

21.11 Summary

Investigative interview analysis means analyzing a statement by breaking it down into its individual components. The structure is more important than context. How a person uses nouns, pronouns, certain types of verbs, and conjunctions can indicate deception. How the suspect uses time and statement balance can also indicate deception. Using statistical analysis, the investigator can determine the degree of deception. A truthful statement can be considered anything below 20% in using deceptive language. A mild statement is anything from 21% to 50%. A deceptive statement is anything over 50%. An 80% or higher is considered a fully deceptive statement, indicating that the person is not truthful in any part of his/her statement.

Banking and Finance 22

22.1 Introduction

Fraud examiners find that their best and probably most useful evidence is bank records. Banks maintain various kinds of records, some of which the customer does not have available to them. Many customers like using one or more banks on a regular basis. They want to establish a working relationship, which, in turn, gives a sense of security. Money launderers particularly want good relationships with bankers, so that they might look "the other way" when money launderers do business. Bank records are perhaps the single most important financial source. Bank records can provide leads to sources of funds, expenditures, and personal affairs, and they may be used as evidence to prove criminal and civil violations.

22.2 Bank Services

Many banks offer all or many of the following services:

1. *Checking accounts.* These are sometimes called "demand accounts" because the customer can make deposits and withdrawals at will. This is probably the most common service at banks. Many banks offer checking accounts, which have service charges of a flat fee or low fees, for individuals. In some areas, checking accounts are provided free to certain types of customers, for example, elderly and minors. Corporate or business checking accounts have service charges based on account activity and/or minimum daily balances.
2. *Savings accounts.* Banks offer various types of savings accounts, often referred to as "time deposits." Banks usually offer three types of savings accounts.
   a. *Passbook.* This is a savings account where the customer has ready access to their funds, but the bank pays interest on the average balances. However, the customer cannot write checks but must physically withdraw the funds at the bank. Banks require a minimum balance, usually between $200 and $1000.
   b. *Money market.* This is a savings account where the customer has ready access to their funds. The customer can write checks against the account with some limitations. The bank pays interest on these accounts at market rates.
   c. *Certificates of deposits.* The customer buys a certificate of deposit, basically a savings account, where the customer cannot withdraw the funds over a period of time that ranges from 3 months to 2 or 3 years. Interest is paid periodically and usually deposited into their checking account. Early withdrawals can result in penalties. Many banks will renew the certificates of deposit if the customer does not tell the bank not to do so.

d. *Individual retirement accounts.* Financial institutions, banks, and savings and loans offer customers a savings plan in which the individual cannot withdraw without penalties until they reach age 59½ years old or older. These accounts usually offer a higher return because the customer cannot withdraw it until retirement. In effect, these are tax-deductible savings accounts for the customer. The bank has to file the appropriate forms with the Internal Revenue Service, showing that the customer has an individual retirement account.

3. *Loans.* Banks make their money from making loans to customers. Many customers not only have checking and savings accounts but also borrow funds from the bank for purchasing items. Banks will lend money provided that the customer has collateral, for example, automobiles, boats, and real estate. Banks make loans to businesses using inventory or equipment of the business for collateral. Banks do not make loans to customers unless they have a good credit standing in the community.

4. *Safe deposit box.* Banks offer customers safe deposit boxes for rent. These safe deposit boxes are locked boxes in a highly secured vault. The boxes come in various sizes. Customers can use these vaults to store important papers, documents, and other valuables with safety and security.

5. *Credit cards.* Banks offer customers access to bank credit cards, Master Card or Visa. Banks like their customers using credit cards because they charge a very high interest rate on the use of them. Customers can use these cards to purchase goods and services, as well as getting cash advances.

6. *Trust services.* Many banks offer trust services. These services vary widely, depending on what the customer wants done on their behalf. The bank, as trustee, could manage anything from simple trusts, for example, collecting investment income, to complex trusts involving managing huge amounts of assets, investments, and income for the grantor. The grantor will probably have the bank, as trustee, provide funds to beneficiaries as set forth in the trust agreement.

7. *Exchange instruments.* Banks offer customers various vehicles of transferring funds. They are:

    a. *Cashier's checks.* Cashier's checks are bank checks. The customer purchases these checks for a small fee. Cashier's checks are usually issued for large amounts, $500 and up.

    b. *Money orders.* Money orders are similar to cashier's checks, but they are issued for small amounts, usually $500 or less.

    c. *Certified checks.* Certified checks are customer's checks on which "certified" is written or stamped across the front of the check. This certification is a guarantee that the bank will pay the check. Certified checks are liabilities of the bank and, when paid, are kept by the bank. However, the customer can obtain the checks by surrendering debit memorandums which the bank has charged the customer's account.

    d. *Wire transfers.* Banks can transfer funds from an internal account to another bank account at another bank by electronic means. The customer's account is charged for the amount of the transfer plus a fee. The customer can have this done in minutes. These electronic transfers can be done in minutes. These electronic transfers can be done to any bank in the United States or any foreign country that has the ability to accept wire transfers.

22.3 Checking Account Operation

A customer goes to his/her neighborhood bank and opens a checking account. The customer will go through the following procedures in opening and operating a checking account.

1. *Opening.* The customer will be asked to provide the following:
    a. *Signature card.* The signature card wants full name, address, city, state, zip code, telephone number, social security number, and signatures of each person who is going to sign on the account. It is called a signature card because each person who can sign checks must sign the card.
    b. *Initial deposit.* The customer is required to make a minimum deposit. This is usually between $200 and $500.
    c. *Corporations.* If a corporation is opening a checking account, then it must submit a Corporate Resolution, which shows the corporate officers who can sign on the account. In many instances, the corporation may require that two corporate officers jointly sign checks.
2. *Checks.* The customer writes checks to various people for various purposes. The check requires the customer to complete the following items:
    a. *Date.* The customer must put the date that the check is written. However, some customers may postdate or backdate a check.
    b. *Payee.* The customer writes the name of the payee who is to receive the funds. Sometimes, customers write checks to cash in order to obtain cash.
    c. *Amount.* The customer puts the dollar amount of the check. This is written in figures.
    d. *Written amount.* The customer writes out in long hand the amount of the check. This amount should agree to the dollar amount written above. If the amounts between the figure and the written amount are different, banks usually will pay the written amount.
    e. *Signature.* The customer must sign the check. The signature must correspond to the signature that the customer signed on the signature card when the account was initially opened.
3. *Deposits.* The customer must deposit funds, currency and checks, into the checking account to cover withdrawals. The customer must complete the following:
    a. *Deposit slip.* The customer must complete a deposit slip. The deposit slip requires the customer to complete the following:
       Date. The customer must record the date the deposit is made.
       Cash. The customer must record the amount of currency or coins being deposited.
       Items. The customer must list every check or draft that is being deposited. This column shows from whom the check was received. Some people list the bank routing number of the customer's check while others list the name of the sender. Corporations sometimes list the customer's internal account number.
       Amount. The customer fills in the amount of the customer's check that was received and being deposited.

Total deposit. The customer must total up all cash and checks and place the total at the bottom of the deposit slip. Some banks even want a total count of checks being deposited.

4. *Statement.* The bank sends the customer a statement each month showing each deposit and check, and summarizes deposits and checks. It also gives the beginning and ending balances according to the bank. The customer is now obligated to reconcile his/her statement to their check register. For corporations, the bank statement must be reconciled to the cash receipts and disbursement journals and general ledger for that bank account. Most banks include the deposit slips and each canceled check received by the bank with the bank statement. Many banks show not only the date and amount of checks but also the check number. In a few cases, the bank shows the payee on the check and whether the deposit is checks or cash.

22.4   Savings Account Operation

Savings accounts operate mostly identical to checking accounts. Money market accounts function the same as checking accounts, except that they receive interest on account balances. The interest can be computed on either the average balance (most are) or the monthly ending balance. Passbook and certificates of deposit accounts are issued periodic statements, which show principal and interest earned for the period and year to date. In the case of certificates of deposit, when the term has expired, the customer must notify the bank as to whether the certificate of deposit is to be renewed, transferred, or refunded to the customer. If the customer fails to notify the bank of his/her intentions, then the bank will automatically renew the certificate of deposit, which could be at either a higher or lower rate than the original rate.

22.5   Loans

Banks offer a variety of loans. They offer installment loans, home equity loans, business loans, signature loans, and mortgages. Banks earn their income from the interest on loans. A performing loan is one that the customer pays on time. A nonperforming loan is one that the customer is constantly late in making repayments or does not pay at all. Banks usually commence foreclosure proceedings when the nonperforming loan reaches 90 days past due.

1. *Installment loans.* Installment loans are the most common loans provided by banks. They are also the most profitable. The interests on installment loans are computed on the "add-on" interest method. Interest is rebated on the rule of 78's. The add-on interest method is basically taking the interest rate and multiplying it by the number of years the loan is to run. The rule of 78's is basically adding total months the loan is to run. It is rebated by the factor of adding the months remaining over the total months of the loan. This is multiplied to the total interest charged on the loans. For example:

Term:	12 months
Interest charged:	$1000
Payoff period:	6 months has elapsed

The payoff would be computed as follows:

$$(1 + 2 + 3 + 4 + 5 + 6) = 21/78 \times \$1000 = \$269.23$$

Note: 78 is the sum of the numbers 1 through 12, thus the rule of 78.

2. *Mortgages.* Banks can provide prospective homeowners with mortgages to pur-chase a home. Banks usually requires a better credit rating and better income than other financial institutions. Banks can provide mortgages that range from 15 to 30 years. Interest rates range from prime to several points above prime. Also, they offer both fixed rates and variable rate mortgages. Simple interest is charged on the monthly balances. Banks also charge the customer "points" for providing the loan. These points are for the costs the bank incurs in preparing and providing the mort-gage. Many banks require the mortgagee to deposit funds into an escrow account for the payment of taxes and insurance. The bank uses these escrow accounts to pay property taxes and homeowners insurance directly.

3. *Home equity loans.* Home equity loans are loans based on the homeowner's equity in the house. It is defined by banks as the difference between the mortgage on the property and the fair market value. Banks will loan funds up to the amount of fair market value less 10% and the mortgage. Home equity loans usually have an inter-est rate of two or more points above the prime rate. Most home equity loans have variable interest rates. Some banks offer revolving loans in which the loan balances can go up and down as the homeowner borrows and repays the loan.

4. *Business loans.* Banks make loans to businesses. Inventory, accounts receivable, or equipment usually secures these loans. The loans are usually for a short term, which range from one month to a few years. Many business loans are rolled over. Interest rates range from prime and up depending on the business credit rating.

5. *Signature loans.* Banks will provide loans to individuals with no collateral. However, these loans are rare and are only provided to customers with a high credit rating. Interest rates range from prime and up to the maximum rate allowed by law.

22.6   Safe Deposit Box

Banks offers customers the renting of a box in a secured vault. Banks do not have access to this box except by court order or nonpayment of rental charges. Customers use these boxes to store important papers and documents. They are also used to store jewelry, cash, and negotiable instruments. These boxes come in various sizes. Banks maintain a log of every person who accesses their safe deposit box. This log generally shows the name of the person, their signature, and date and time they entered. Heavy access to a safe deposit box can indicate a cash hoard, especially when deposits are made on the same date.

22.7   Credit Cards

Credit cards are becoming more widespread in their use. Some businesses will only accept credit cards, while others will accept only cash or credit cards but no checks of any kind. Many businesses have electronic terminals which can verify that the credit card is good.

If it is bad, the business is supposed to confiscate the card. Most banks have a credit card division which issues and maintains customer's accounts. When a customer uses his/her credit card, the business establishment deposits the slips into the bank or sends them to the card issuer for payment.

1. *Credit card companies.* There are currently five major credit card companies. Each company has a number, which is the card number prefix, indicating the kind of credit card. They are:

   a. Carte Blanche   3
   b. American Express   3
   c. Visa   4
   d. MasterCard   5
   e. Discovery   6

   Carte Blanche, American Express, and Discovery require the merchant to send their charge slips directly to them. The merchant is sent a draft less the fees. Visa and MasterCard require the merchant to deposit the charge slips into their bank account. The bank charges the merchant's bank account for the fees. Banks become members of Visa and/or MasterCard companies who operate the system. The bank mails out statements to customers and collects the customer's payments. In turn, the credit card companies forward earnings (interest) to the banks. For banks, credit cards are very profitable because of the high interest charged. Even with fraud committed by either customers or merchants, banks earn more than they receive on other types of loans. The bank credit card companies publish a book, which shows the bank's identification numbers (BIN). This book is not made available to the general public.

2. *Card numbers.* Visa and MasterCard use a 16-digit number grouped in fours. The first eight digits (on the left) indicate the type of credit card, the bank identification number, and routing number. The last eight digits represent the customer's account number.

22.8   Trust Services

Many banks offer trust services. These services vary depending on what the customer wants. Banks have the ability to service many kinds of trusts, ranging from simple to complex. Fees are based on the amount of services required to be performed. Trustees are required to file state and federal income tax returns. Some trusts are taxed on their earnings, while others pass the income down to the grantor. The grantor is deemed to be the owner of the trust's assets. The most common trusts are:

1. *Decedent's Trust.* The trustee takes control over the decedent's assets, liabilities, income, and expenses. The trustee distributes the net income and assets to the beneficiaries after the estate is probated and taxes, expenses, and liabilities have been paid. A simple version of this is called the Insurance Trust. The grantor assigns his/her life insurance policies to the trustee. The trustee distributes the insurance proceeds after death of the grantor to the beneficiaries based on the grantor's wishes.

2. *Intervivos Trust.* The grantor transfers all or part of his/her assets to the trustee. The grantor is still living. The trustee administers the trust assets in accordance with

the grantor's wishes. The grantor can make the trust an Irrevocable Trust in which the grantor loses control of his/her assets. A Revocable Trust is one in which the grantor can terminate the trustee at any time and gain control of his/her assets.

Many criminal elements use trusts to hide their assets in order to keep it out of the reach of the government and law enforcement agencies.

22.9   Exchange Instruments

Banks offer the following exchange services for customers. Exchange instruments are basically the withdrawals of funds from their bank accounts for various bank instruments.

1. Cashier's checks
2. Money orders
3. Certified checks
4. Wire transfers

22.10   Magnetic Ink Character Recognition (MICR)

MICR was developed by the American Bankers Association (ABA) as a machine language and as a standard in check design to which all banks must conform. Numeric information is printed in magnetic ink on the bottom of bank checks and other documents. This coding is electronically scanned by computers, which convert the magnetic ink notations into electronic impulses intelligible to a computer. MICR information is printed in groupings called fields. On bank checks, the first field on the left is the Federal Reserve check routing code and the next is the ABA transit number. These numbers also appear in the upper right corner of the check. The middle group of numbers shows the drawer's assigned account number at the bank. The MICR information in these two fields is imprinted on the blank checks furnished to the customer. The right field contains a control number used for processing and the amount of the check. The dollar amount of the check should be compared with the encoded amount to be sure the subject did not alter the returned check. Many banks are adding an additional field for the check number. Some place this field after the account number, while others place it before the account number.

22.11   Bank Reconciliation

The bank sends a statement along with the canceled checks, deposit slips, and credit and debit memorandum each month. It is up to the customer to reconcile his/her bank account with his/her check register. Many banks provide the customer a bank reconciliation schedule on the back of the statements. A typical example of bank reconciliation is as follows:

Balance per Banks Statement	\$_____
Add: Deposits in Transit	_____
Less: Outstanding Checks	_____
Balance per Reconciliation	\$_____

The customer will usually have to make adjustments to their check register to show current bank charges, interest earned, and any deposits or checks that cleared the bank but were not recorded. Otherwise, the customer will not be able to reconcile to the above example.

22.12   Government Securities

Banks also sell and redeem government securities. They sell U.S. bonds, bills, and notes. Bills are of very short duration, usually 60–360 days. Notes are short term, usually 3–10 years. Bonds are long term, usually 20 or more years.

22.13   Currency Transactions Reports

Banks are required to file Currency Transaction Reports with the U.S. Treasury Department whenever a customer makes a cash withdrawal or deposit, purchases cashier's checks, or makes payments on loans of $10,000 or more. These reports are discussed in more detail in another chapter.

22.14   Correspondence

Banks maintain a file of all letters to and from customers. Most bank customer correspondence relates to granting and servicing loans. However, banks maintain files of customer complaints. The bank's internal auditors review these letters to determine adherence to bank policies and internal controls.

22.15   Letters of Credit

Banks issue an official form of correspondence called "letters of credit." A letter of credit is an official bank correspondence, which asks other banks to extend credit to the holder of the letter. These letters are generally issued to bank customers who have an established banking relationship. The customer must have an approved credit line or funds on account that can cover the letter of credit amount.

22.16   Foreign Currency Exchange

Many banks offer customers the ability to exchange foreign currency into U.S. dollars or vice versa. Banks charge a small fee for this service, and they must keep records of any foreign currency exchanges. Currency Transactions Reports will have to be filed if it involves $10,000 or more in terms of U.S. dollars.

22.17   Bank Records

Of all the sources of financial information, banks rank at the top of the list. They can provide a wealth of financial data. These data can help the fraud examiner determine the customer's lifestyle, financial patterns, and show the degree of sophistication. Examiners and investigators, when requesting and obtaining copies of bank records, should use the following checklist.

1. Records of checking accounts
   a. Monthly statements
   b. Deposit tickets
   c. Canceled checks
   d. Signature cards
   e. Debit and/or credit memorandums
   f. Deposit items
2. Records of savings accounts, certificates of deposit, or any other income producing positive balance instruments
   a. Ledger cards and/or monthly account statements
   b. Deposit slips
   c. Deposited items
   d. Transfer slips
   e. Withdrawals slips
   f. Canceled checks used for withdrawals
   g. Signature cards
   h. Items of withdrawals
   i. Debit and/or credit memorandums
   j. Interest statements (Form 1099, etc.)
3. Records of loan accounts
   a. Ledger cards
   b. Repayment schedule
   c. Canceled loan checks
   d. Signature cards
   e. Application, including supporting documents and escrows statements
   f. Financial statements
   g. Credit bureau reports
4. Records of credit card accounts
   a. Monthly statements
   b. Sales drafts
   c. Payment schedules
   d. Interest schedules
   e. Applications
   f. Financial statements
   g. Credit bureau reports
5. Safe deposit box records
   a. Application
   b. Entry record
   c. Signature card

6. Agreements, statements, account ledger sheets, and checks disbursed from or for any trust account established by or for the benefit of the person(s) specified.
7. Wire transfer records
8. Cashier checks or registers
9. Letters of credit
10. Cash transit letters
11. Money order records
12. Currency Transaction Reports, including records and source documents indicating transfer of funds prepared in compliance with currency and Foreign Transaction Reporting Act (31 USC 1051)
13. Individual retirement accounts
    a. Signature card
    b. Ledger card and/or account statements
    c. Canceled checks
    d. Deposit slips
14. Correspondence

22.18 Security Brokers

The second most important source of financial information comes from security dealers. Securities fall into two basic markets: trading of stocks and bonds and commodities. Both markets operate under similar structures. The Securities and Exchange Commission regulates the security industry. The broker is an agent who handles the public's orders to buy and sell securities, usually for a commission. A broker may be a corporation, partnership, or individual and is often a member of an exchange. A registered representative (also known as a securities salesperson or account executive) personally places customer's orders and maintains their accounts. While commonly referred to as a broker, a registered representative is usually an employee of a brokerage firm rather than a member.

22.19 Security Markets

The security markets are classified into two categories: organized securities exchanges and over-the-counter market.

1. *Organized securities exchanges.* Securities exchanges or stock exchanges neither buy nor sell securities themselves. An exchange functions as a central marketplace and provides facilities for executing orders. Member brokers representing buyers and sellers carry out the transactions. The two major exchanges are the New York Stock Exchange (NYSE) and the American Stock Exchange (AMEX); both are located in New York City. While there are various regional exchanges, the NYSE and AMEX together handle more than 90% of the trading done through organized exchanges. If a security is to be traded on an exchange, the issue must be approved for listing by that exchange. Securities traded on the NYSE and AMEX may also be listed and traded on the regional exchanges, but no security is listed on both the NYSE and AMEX.

2. *Over-the-counter market.* The over-the-counter securities market handles most of the security transactions that take place in the United States. The over-the-counter market does not handle the purchase or sale of securities that actually occur on securities exchanges, but it handles everything else in the way of securities transactions. Thus, securities not listed on a securities exchange are "unlisted," that is, traded over the counter. The over-the-counter market is not located in any one central place. It consists of thousands of security houses located in hundreds of different cities and towns all over the United States. These security houses are called brokers or dealers and are engaged in buying and selling securities, usually for their own account and risk.

22.19.1   Ownership of Securities

There are two principal ways securities are held, in the name of the account holder and in street name. In the first instance, the customer's name is reflected on the security and the account. When securities are held in street name, they are registered in the name of the broker. This occurs when securities have been bought on margin or when a cash customer wishes the security to be held by the broker, rather than in his/her own name.

22.19.2   Over-the-Counter Trading

There are many more types of securities that are traded in the over-the-counter market than what are traded on the national or regional exchanges. These include:

1. Bank stocks
2. Insurance company stocks
3. U.S. Government securities
4. Municipal bonds
5. Open-end investment company shares (mutual funds)
6. Most corporate bonds
7. Stocks of a large number of industrial and utility corporations, including nearly all-new issues
8. Securities of many foreign corporations

22.19.3   Stock Classes

When a corporation is formed, capital stock representing the ownership of the corporation is authorized in the corporate charter. There are two principal classes of stock: common and preferred. If only one class of stock is authorized, it is common stock. The number of shares authorized can be changed by formal approval of the stockholders. Shares issued and subsequently reacquired by the corporation through purchase or donation are referred to as Treasury Stock. The number of shares outstanding will always equal the number of shares issued less the number of shares of treasury stock, unless stock has been repurchased and canceled. Each stockholder is part owner of the corporation, because each share of stock represents a fractional interest in the corporation. The stockholder is entitled to a stock certificate showing ownership of a specific number of shares of stock in the corporation. If a stockholder desires to buy more stock, it is not necessary to obtain the permission of the corporation. The stockholder acquires it by purchase in the open market or privately. Conversely, if a stockholder desires to sell shares, he/she cannot demand the corporation to buy the stock. Instead, a stockholder is free to seek a buyer for the stock either in the market or by private sale. After the sale terms have been agreed on, the mechanics of transfer are simple. The seller signs his/her name on the back of the stock certificate and delivers it to the buyer or the buyer's broker. A record of all outstanding certificates is kept by the corporation or by its duly appointed transfer agents, often a bank. The transfer agent has a record of the names and addresses of the stockholders and the number of shares owned by each. After determining that the old certificate is in proper form for transfer, the transfer agent issues a new certificate to a new owner. Most companies have a registrar. The duty of the registrar is to double-check the actions of the transfer agent to prevent improper issue of stock or fraudulent transfer.

22.19.4 Stock Rights

A common stockholder may usually subscribe (at a stated discount price) to new issues of common stock in proportion to his/her holdings. This privilege, known as a stock right, is usually offered to stockholders for a limited time. During this period, the stockholders may exercise the right to purchase additional shares under the terms of the offer or may choose to sell the rights. If the stockholder allows the time limit to run out without acting, the rights become worthless.

22.19.5 Stock Warrants

A stock warrant is a certificate that gives the holder the privilege to purchase common stock at a stated price within a specified time limit or perpetually. Warrants are often issued with bonds or preferred stock as an added inducement to investors. The stockholder may exercise the right to purchase additional shares or choose to sell the warrants.

22.19.6 Stock Splits

When the price of the common stock of a corporation reaches a high market value, the corporation may choose to bring the price down to a more favorable trading range. To do this, the corporation splits its shares; that is, it increases the number of shares outstanding without issuing additional stock. If, for example, a stockholder owned 100 shares that had a market value of $200 per share, a 4 to 1 stock split would increase the stockholder's shares to 400 and decrease the market value to $50 per share. Although the stockholder now owns a greater number of shares, the value of the stock and proportionate interest remains unchanged.

22.19.7 Dividends

A corporation may pay a dividend in cash, in stock, or in property. When cash dividends are paid, the company, or its dividend-disbursing agent (usually a bank), sends checks to all the stockholders whose names appear on the books of the company on a so-called record date. A dividend is a prorated distribution among stockholders. Cash dividends are paid in terms of so much per share. Some companies, in order to conserve cash, pay dividend in their own stock. A stock dividend has an effect similar to that of a stock split in that the stockholder's proportionate share of the ownership remains unchanged. A stock dividend is usually stated as a percentage of the outstanding shares (up to a maximum of 25%, above which it is called a stock split). When a corporation pays a property dividend, it is usually in the form of stock in another corporation that has been acquired for investment or some other purpose.

22.20 Bonds

When a corporation or government unit wishes to borrow money for some period, usually for more than 5 years, it will sell a bond issue. Each bond, generally of $1000 denominations, is a certificate of debt of the issuer and serves as evidence of a loan to the corporation or governmental unit. The bondholder is a creditor of the issuer. A bond pays a stated rate of interest and matures on a stated date when the fixed sum of money must be repaid to the bondholder. Railroad, public utility, and industrial bonds are called corporate bonds. The obligations of states, counties, cities, towns, school districts, and authorities are known as municipal bonds. U.S. Treasury certificates, notes, and bonds are classified as government securities. Bonds are issued in two principal forms: coupon bonds and registered bonds.

1. *Coupon bonds.* Coupon bonds have interest coupons attached to each bond by the corporation that issues it. Because the corporation keeps no record of the owner of the bonds, they are called bearer bonds. On the due dates for the interest, the owner clips the coupons and presents them to the authorized bank for payment. The principal, when due, is payable to the holder or bearer of the bonds.
2. *Registered bonds.* Registered bonds have the name of the owner written on the front of the bond. The company, or its authorized agent (usually a bank), has a record of the name and address of the owner. When interest is due, it is paid to the bondholder by check.

22.20.1 Types of Transactions

There are two types of transactions: long and short.

1. *Long transactions.* In a long transaction an account holder purchases a security with the expectation that the market price of that security will appreciate or advance. Long simply means ownership of a security.
2. *Short transactions.* In a short transaction an account holder sells a security that he/she does not own with the expectation that the market price of that security will decline. Short signifies a liability position in a security.

22.20.2 Records

The broker can furnish all documents relating to securities account activity. The principal documents available from a broker are:

1. *Customer account cards.* This is a broker's record of the customer's account.
2. *Application for account.* This form contains basic information about the customer. Its primary purpose is to identify the customer and be able to contact the customer when needed.
3. *Signature cards and margin account agreements.* The customer must fill out a signature card, much like that of a signature card with a bank or other financial institution. In addition, the customer must sign a margin agreement if the customer opens a margin account.
4. *Securities receipts.* The broker keeps copies of security receipts for securities received from the customer.
5. *Cash receipts.* The broker keeps copies of receipts for funds received from the customer.
6. *Confirmation slips.* The broker keeps copies of confirmation receipts. Confirmation slips are used to confirm the customer's buys and sells of securities.
7. *Securities delivered receipts.* The broker keeps copies of receipts of securities that are delivered to the customer.
8. *Canceled checks.* The broker keeps canceled checks of payments made to the customer.
9. *Monthly account statements.* The broker issues monthly statements. These statements show all transactions for the month. Unlike bank statements, brokerage statements show the customer's holdings and their market values at the end of the month. This serves as a barometer for the customer as to how his/her holdings are faring in the market place.
10. *IRS reporting forms.* The broker is required to keep copies of all forms that report earnings and sales of securities to the Internal Revenue Service.

22.20.3   Types of Accounts

There are two types of accounts that a customer can have with a broker. They are:

1. *Cash.* This type of account requires the customer to pay securities in full at time of purchase.
2. *Margin.* This type of account allows securities to be purchased on credit. Margin is the percentage of the purchase price of a security that the customer must pay. The Federal Reserve Board establishes the margin requirement. To open a margin account, there must be a minimum deposit by the customer. Stock purchased on margin must be registered in street name while in the account. If the customer's margin falls below the minimum, then the broker can liquidate the account without permission of the customer if the customer fails to bring the margin up to proper requirements.

22.20.4   Security Account Statements

The customer's security account statement (issued monthly) contains all transactions from the last statement date. These statements are the basic documents used to reconstruct a customer's security position. The following guidelines are applicable when analyzing security account statements:

1. *Buying.* The buy column will show the following entries.
   a. *Bought or Received.* This shows whether the customer either bought the security or received the security that was previously purchased.
   b. *Description.* This is the name of the security.
   c. *Price or Symbol.* This gives the purchase price per share.
   d. *Debit.* This is the amount of the purchase price paid by the customer including the broker's commission.
2. *Selling.* The sold column will show the following entries.
   a. *Sold or Delivered.* This column shows whether the customer sold a security or delivered a security to the broker.
   b. *Description.* This identifies the security that is sold or delivered to the broker.
   c. *Price or Symbol.* This shows the unit sales price per share.
   d. *Credit.* This shows the proceeds from the sales credited to the customer's account.

When a customer purchases stock, he/she has the option of taking "delivery" of the certificates from the broker or leaving them in the broker's custody. The customer usually indicates this when he/she opens up a brokerage account.

If a customer takes delivery of the certificates, the number of shares would be noted in the Sold or Delivered column and the Date column would show the date of delivery. In addition, there would be no entry in the Price or Symbol column.

If there are no entries indicating delivery of securities, the broker is, in fact, holding them and the customer is in what is commonly referred to as a "long" position. The broker will list at the bottom of the customer's statement a summary of customer's long position; that is, a listing of the number of shares of each stock being held for the customer and their market values.

22.20.5 Transfer Agent

The transfer agent keeps a record of the name and address of each stockholder and the number of shares owned and checks that certificates presented for transfer are properly canceled and that new certificates are issued in the name of the transferee. In many small firms, the transfer agent is usually an attorney, a bank, or the corporation itself. In most large firms, the transfer agent is a bank. The transfer agent maintains the following information:

1. Stockholder identification
2. Stockholder position
3. Stock certificate numbers
4. Number of shares represented by certificates
5. Date certificates were issued or surrendered
6. Evidence of returned certificates
7. Names of transferees and transferors

The principal documents available from the transfer agent are:

1. Stockholder ledger card
2. Stock certificates

The names and addresses of transfer agents may be found in Moody's or Standard and Poor's for publicly held companies or may be obtained from the main offices of the corporations.

22.20.6   Dividend Disbursing Agent

Most large corporations distribute their dividends through agents known as dividend disbursing agents. The dividend disbursing agent is generally a bank and can furnish the following information:

1. Stockholder identification
2. Stockholder position
3. Amount of dividends
4. Form of dividend
5. Dates paid
6. Evidence of payments

The principal documents available from the dividend disbursing agent are:

1. Cancelled checks
2. Form 1099, which reports dividends paid to the customer to the Internal Revenue Service

It is common practice for separate financial institutions to serve as transfer agent and dividend disbursing agent. However, a single financial institution can serve both functions. Names and addresses of institutions providing these services can be found for publicly held companies in security publications such as:

a. Financial Stock Guide Service
b. Moody's Investors Service, Inc.
c. Standard and Poor's Corporation

22.21   Summary

Bank and other financial records are the most important documents for a fraud examiner. The importance cannot be overemphasized. These records should be the starting point for the fraud examiner. Bank and other financial records will either make or break the case. Without this evidence, the fraud examiner has no case.

22.22   Sample Check

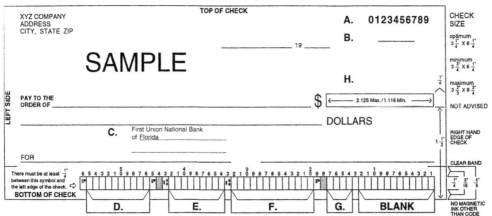

SAMPLE CHECK FOR: FIRST UNION NATIONAL BANK OF FLORIDA

A. Serial Number: Must be in the upper right corner and match the serial number in the MICR line. (See "D" for further explanation.)

B. Fractional Routing Transit Number: Must be in the upper right corner and must match the routing transit number in the MICR line with the exception of the state prefix number, FL = 63

C. Bank Name, State, City, etc.: The First Union Logo is optional. Name of bank (First Union National Bank of "State"), city, state, and zip where the account will be assigned/opened is a required field.

D. Serial Number: (46-55) This is a required field if the customer desires services offered by FUNB which require a serial number. The serial number can be 4 to 10 digits for commercial accounts, and must be zero filled to accommodate a minimum of 4 positions (example: 0123, 123456, etc.). A & D must match.

E. Routing Transit Number: (34-42) Designates the Federal Reserve district, city and branch. Preceding zeros are not needed in the fractional number in the upper right corner. Each city, state or region that First Union serves has a unique institution identifier with the city name printed in field "C". IMPORTANT: position 35-42 is the Routing Transit #. Position 34 is the check digit.

F. Account Number: (20-32) This is a unique 13 digit number assigned to the customer.

G. Optional Serial Number: (14-17) Used for personal accounts (checks only). A 4 digit zero filled field, that must match the serial number in the upper right corner. If field "D" is used, then this field must be blank.

H. Courtesy Amount Box should be in the general location shown above in the diagram.

Additional Information
Positions 1-12 blank
Positions of required symbols:

19 -	On-Us Symbol
33 -	Transit No. Symbol
43 -	Transit No. Symbol
45 -	On-Us Symbol
50-56 -	On-Us Symbol Depending on serial field length and must be right justified

See Bank Management Publication #147 by American Bankers Association for detailed printing specifications.

533761 (50/pad)

See Reverse Side for Important Information

Reports and Case Files

23

23.1 Introduction

The fraud examiner has two important administrative duties to perform. The first is to obtain and maintain proper files. These files must be maintained so that evidence, statements, interviews, and financial information is readily and easily accessible. Second, the fraud examiner must prepare reports that are factual, clear, and relevant. This chapter is directed to help the fraud examiner set up and maintain his/her case files and prepare proper reports.

23.2 Purpose

There are various reasons why reports and files are important. The primary reasons are:

1. They give the attorney all the evidence that was obtained, so it can be evaluated as to its admissibility and success in court, whether civil or criminal.
2. It helps evaluate the fraud examiner's work product as to thoroughness, reliability, objectivity, and relevancy.
3. It forces the fraud examiner to review his/her evidence and witness interviews or statements. If material or relevant facts have been omitted or not obtained, then the fraud examiner can go seek them out. Remember, fraud examiners will most often have to interview witnesses more than once to obtain all the facts.
4. The report should give the attorney or reviewer all the material and relevant facts. It omits immaterial information whether or not it was obtained.
5. It helps the fraud examiner to ensure that all the evidence and witness statements have been obtained and are available. In quoting witnesses in the report, the fraud examiner should guard against misquoting or taking facts out of context.
6. The fraud examiner's report is a work product of the fraud examiner. It tells the reviewer what the fraud examiner has done and what the fraud examiner feels to be material and relevant. The report must be true and correct. The reviewer or attorney may uncover additional evidence and witnesses that may alter or render the fraud examiner's report invalid.

23.3 Report Characteristics

The fraud examiner's report should consist of the following characteristics:

1. *Accuracy.* The report should contain all material and relevant evidence and witness statements. Any computational schedules should be correct. Any misquotes or mathematical errors can render the report useless. Times, dates, figures, and supporting information should be reaffirmed with witnesses or subject.
2. *Clarity.* The report should use clear and simple language. The report should not use slang or technical terminology. Those reading the report usually are not familiar with slang or technical language. If slang or technical language must be used, then explain its meaning before continuing use. Witnesses may use such language in statements and interviews. The fraud examiner's report should definitely explain their meaning so the reader can understand.
3. *Prejudice.* The report should only give the facts. The report should not give the fraud examiner's biases or partialities. All facts should be shown regardless of which side it favors. The U.S. Supreme Court in *Brady v. Maryland*, 373 U.S. 83 (1963) better known as "Brady" held that the government's failure to disclose evidence favorable to a defendant who specifically requested it violated the defendant's due process rights because the evidence was material to guilt or punishment. In addition, a defendant is also entitled to disclosure of information that might be used to impeach the government or plaintiff's witnesses. These include, but are not limited to, payments to witnesses, immunity, any promises, witness biases, and rewards offered or collected.
4. *Relevance.* The fraud examiner should ensure that all relevant information is in the report. If in doubt as to the relevance of information, then include it in the report. Any information that has either a direct or indirect bearing on the case should be reflected in the report. Immaterial or irrelevant information only confuses the reader and can lead to questions of the examiner's capabilities and methodologies.
5. *Promptness.* The fraud examiner should take notes during interviews of witnesses or possible subjects. These notes should be reduced to memorandums of interview or statements as soon as possible. The longer the examiner waits, the less the examiner will remember. The interim or final report should be prepared as soon as possible following the investigation. Delaying will result in the report missing material or relevant information. It is recommended that the fraud examiner does not work on more than three cases at any one time, unless there are extenuating circumstances.
6. *Opinions or conclusions.* The fraud examiner should never express an opinion of any kind on the guilt or innocence of the subject. The fraud examiner should never express any opinions or conclusions about a witness testimony or statements. Witnesses or subjects statements will clearly show conflicting statements. Confidential informants should never be identified in either statements or the body of the report. The report should only identify confidential informants by codes or numbers. Some law enforcement agencies require "conclusions" in their reports. Actually, the conclusions are in reality recommendations. Law enforcement agencies want recommendations as to all possible courses of action that are available. Conclusions or opinions as to the guilt or innocence of the subject are not what they want.

23.4 Discovery

The courts have held that investigator's notes can be used as evidence in court and must be made available to the defense. Therefore, the fraud examiner should never destroy or dispose of his/her interview notes, whether a witness or subject. The fraud examiner does not have the right to privilege communications. However, there are two exceptions to the general rule. They are:

1. The fraud examiner is conducting the investigation under the retainer of an attorney. In this case, the fraud examiner is working for the attorney and comes under the rules of the attorney-client privilege communications.
2. The fraud examiner is retained or hired by a law enforcement agency. This is considered privileged communications by the courts, especially in grand jury cases. Grand jury information cannot be disclosed unless authorized by the court.

23.5 Report Format

There is no formal or set format for the fraud examiner's report. However, the fraud examiner should identify and cover the following items.

1. *Date.* The date of the report should be when the report is finally finished.
2. *Retainer.* The report should be addressed to the person and entity that has retained the fraud examiner. If the fraud examiner is an employee of an entity, then the report should be addressed to the employer.
3. *Subject.* The report should identify the subject of the investigation, including the subject's full name, address, date of birth, and in some instances the social security number.
4. *Case description.* The first paragraph should identify what type of case, such as embezzlement, kickbacks, or theft. It should never state that the subject committed an offense, but it should allege that the subject committed an offense.
5. *Investigator.* The report should identify all the investigators involved in the investigation and their respective roles.
6. *Type.* The report should identify the type of case under examination and investigation. There are basically three choices: criminal, civil, and administrative. A criminal investigation involves the potential conviction and imprisonment of the offender. A civil examination encompasses potential monetary damages. An administrative case involves the possibility of disciplinary action on the job such as dismissal or demotion.
7. *History.* The report should give a brief history about the subject. It should include the following items:
   a. *Identifiers.* The full name of the subject and immediate family members should be identified. This should include the dates of births, social security numbers, place of births, driver's license numbers, alien numbers if foreigners, etc.

b. *Health.* The subject's health condition and his immediate family should be disclosed. This can have an effect on whether a criminal prosecution will be pursued or not pursued.

c. *Employment or business history.* The employment history of the subject should be fully identified. This should describe the skills and knowledge acquired from past and present employment. The employment history of the spouse may also be included if it has a bearing on the case. If the subject has operated businesses in the past or present, then they should also be identified.

d. *Education.* The educational history of the subject should also be disclosed. If the subject has a college degree, then this should be disclosed. More sophisticated crimes are committed by well-educated people.

e. *Residence.* The subject's residence should be disclosed. This should include not only the primary residence but also any and all secondary residences, for example, vacation homes and the residences of relatives and friends frequented by the subject.

f. *Associates.* Friends, close business associates, and other relatives should be identified in the report and their specific relationships.

g. *Travel.* The subject's travel experiences should be disclosed in the report. This should include not only the past few years but should go back two or more decades.

8. *Evidence.* The report should summarize the evidence that has been obtained to show that a crime has been committed and who committed the crime. It should identify both physical evidence as well as oral (testimony) evidence. In a large case, this should be a brief summary since many witness statements and physical evidence will be obtained which can explain it. The evidence should be categorized and indexed in a logical order. The index should contain a brief description and identify the witness and physical evidence. This can encompass large volumes of documents and witness statements or depositions. In small cases, the evidence, both oral and physical, can be summarized and referenced as attachments.

9. *Intent.* The report should identify the evidence, both oral and physical, that shows the state of mind of the subject. Most cases require the prosecution or plaintiff to show intent to commit fraud on the part of the subject. Intent is a state of mind. The state of mind to defraud someone is based on the actions and statements of the subject. These conditions and statements should be identified and referenced to the physical evidence, statements, or depositions.

10. *Defenses.* The report should identify any defenses made by either the defendant or any other witness on behalf of the defendant. In addition, any evidence that contradicts the defenses should also be identified and referenced. This will help the prosecutor or plaintiff attorney to be prepared for these defenses.

11. *Referrals.* The report should identify any referrals made to law enforcement agencies, state attorneys, or outside counsel. A copy of the referral report should be attached. If the fraud examiner is working for law enforcement, then this section is not required because the report will be processed according to local procedures.

12. *Financial data.* The report should disclose the total investigative costs. This should include fees charged, investigative expenses, administrative expenses, and other direct costs that are charged the client. An itemized statement should be attached to the report. In addition, the investigative costs and the amount of the client's

loss should be identified. A schedule should be attached to the report showing the details of the loss or illegal gains.

13. *Recommendation.* The report should express all recommendations and actions that are available. The fraud examiner should not express any opinion as to the guilt or innocence of the subject.

23.6 Sources/Informants

The identity of a confidential informant should never be disclosed in the report. They should only be identified by a code (number or letter). Files on each confidential source or informant should be maintained. The files should contain:

1. *Identifiers.* There should be a profile or personal data sheet, which contains information about the source or confidential informant. Such information should include, but is not limited to, full name, aliases, address, date and place of birth, driver's license number, social security number, INS alien number if applicable, names and addresses of relatives, friends, and associates.

2. *Evaluation.* The fraud examiner should make notes of the confidential source or informant as to their reliability. This evaluation of reliability should be objective. These notes should reflect the information provided by the informant. The information provided by the informant should be corroborated or verified. This fact should be noted in the file. One method is to write a "memorandum of interview" of the informant. When the information that the confidential informant has been verified or corroborated then another memorandum to file should be prepared showing what information was corroborated and what was not corroborated. A comparison of this data will show in an objective manner how reliable the confidential informant is. The more information the informant gives that is corroborated, the more reliable the informant becomes. The converse also holds true.

3. *Financial data.* Any financial dealings with the confidential informant should be documented. The fraud examiner or investigator should obtain a receipt from the informant for any funds paid to or on behalf of the informant. Failure to get receipts can put the examiner or investigator in an awkward position in court. Also, the Internal Revenue Service requires receipts for any deduction taken on a tax return. Failure to have a receipt will cause the disallowance of a deduction, which will result in a higher tax liability.

Confidential informants and source files should be kept in a highly secured place. The investigator or examiner should never pledge total secrecy. This can cause problems at a later date. The examiner or investigator can be jailed for failure to disclose a confidential informant when ordered by a court to disclose. Remember the fraud examiner or investigator must kept his word for any promises that are made. Otherwise, the fraud examiner will lose his/her credibility on the "streets." Therefore, the fraud examiner can prevent this situation by only making a limited commitment.

23.7 Report Writing Mistakes

There are other mistakes in report writing besides the normal misspelling and grammar errors. Reports should always be reviewed for any misspelling and grammar errors. Other mistakes include:

1. *Opinions.* The fraud examiner should never express an opinion about the guilt or innocence of the subject. This opens up the door for the defense attorney to show bias on the part of the fraud examiner.
2. *Data.* Information presented in the report should be accurate. Even mistakes in small details can leave doubts about the accuracy of the report as a whole. A wrong date of birth of a subject can lead the case being thrown out because it is not the date of birth of the subject, but someone else. This is especially true if it is constantly used.
3. *Quotes.* The examiner should not misquote a witness or subject. Misquotes can lead to doubts about the examiners reliability. The fraud examiner should always have the witness or subject repeat statements that are important. In reports, the fraud examiner should cross-check any quotes made by a witness or subject.

23.8 Case Disposition

When a case has been completed, its final disposition should be noted on the report. It is recommended that a disposition report be prepared and attached to the final report. The disposition report should provide:

1. *Fines.* The amount of fines imposed by the court should be shown.
2. *Prison sentence.* The prison sentence imposed by the court should be disclosed.
3. *Probation.* The probation term imposed by the court should be shown.
4. *Forfeitures and seizures.* All assets that were seized and forfeited to law enforcement agencies should be delineated. Each asset should be identified that was seized by law enforcement, along with its costs or market values. Also, if these assets were sold by law enforcement, then the sale proceeds should be noted. This may be impossible to find out in some cases, for example, autos, boats, and furniture, when all seized assets are pooled and auctioned off.
5. *Dropped.* If the case was dropped, then this should be noted. An explanation should be given as to why the case was dropped. There are many reasons why a case is dropped. It could be the lack of funds to pursue prosecution or a lawsuit, the lack of collectibility, insufficient evidence, deceased subject, negative public image, and various others.
6. *Judgments.* In civil cases, the amount of judgments awarded by the court should be noted. Copy of the judgment should be included in the case file.
7. *Restitution.* If the court ordered any restitution, the case file should note this fact. Also, a copy of the restitution order should be attached to the report.

23.9   Disclosure

A log should be maintained on all people who have or have had access to the case files. This log should identify the person, date, reason for access to files, and who authorized the access. Also, the fraud examiner should issue a memorandum, which identifies only those people that should have regular access to the case files. These people are generally the case examiner(s), clerical staff, and client attorney. Staff members should be instructed on disclosure of case files and information. Cases should never be discussed outside the office. Case files should never be taken outside the office. Only copies of files should be taken for witness interviews. These instructions should also be included in the memorandum. Improper disclosure can result in the case being dropped, or the examiner and client being sued. In cases involving undercover work or similar actions, this can put the examiner at risk of not being able to perform the job as planned. In criminal cases, it can put the examiner's life at risk.

23.10   Witness List

The fraud examiner or investigator should keep a witness list. This witness list should identify the name of the witness, but also it should include title or capacity, address, both home and business telephone numbers, and identify, in summary, the physical evidence that the witness can provide. Remember witnesses should keep files. The witness files should contain statements, depositions, and physical evidence. Some tangible evidence because of size or other characteristics may have to be kept in a separate property room. The witness file should have a note that describes in detail where the evidence is located and its description.

Using the scenario problem, the following witness list is presented in Figure 23.1 as an example. Besides identifying the witness, it also identifies the specific exhibits that the witness will introduce into court. Each witness and exhibit is assigned a number. "W" before the number identifies the number as a witness and not an exhibit. Exhibit numbers must be associated with the witness number and name.

Figure 23.1 shows a condensed witness list; however, this list should include the names, address, home and business telephone numbers, and business or agency name. This witness list mostly covers the evidence introduced in the Financial Data Section of the scenario problem. If witnesses can be obtained in offshore countries, then they and the evidence should be listed. Offshore public records can be obtained by consular officers of the U.S. Department of State. The consular officer has the authority to introduce these documents into court (see the Rules of Evidence in a preceding chapter). The bank records from Barclays Bank of London, England, were not introduced into evidence because a witness from that bank institution must be used to authenticate these records. The case detective who executed the search warrant could be used to introduce these records into court; however, he could not testify as to the authenticity.

The examiner should keep the witness list on a computer database. This can help the examiner counsel or prosecutor plan and schedule witnesses for trial. Costs can be reasonably estimated for paying witness expenses (e.g., witness fees, parking, travel, and lodging) if required.

Witness and Exhibit List

WITNESS NUMBER	WITNESS	EXHIBIT NUMBER	EXHIBIT DESCRIPTION
W-1	Case Detective	1	Property receipt for money seized
		2	Property receipt and laboratory report cocaine
		3	Barclays Bank statements
		4	Gold bullion property receipt
		5	Copy of search warrant with court signatures
W-2	Public Records Administrator	1	100 Alpha Street deed
		2	100 Bravo Street deed
W-3	Records Custodian Life Insurance Co.	1	Insurance policy
		2	Payment receipts
W-4	Furniture Company Records Custodian	1	Purchase invoice
W-5	Cabinet Company Records Custodian	1	Purchase invoice
W-6	Art Dealer Records Custodian	1	Purchase invoice
W-7	Fixture Company Records Custodian	1	Purchase invoice
W-8	Pool and Tennis Contractor	1	Builders contract
		2	Payment schedule
W-9	Appliance Dealer Records Custodian	1	Purchase invoice
W-10	Electronic Store Records Custodian	1	Purchase invoice
W-11	Security System Dealer Records Custodian	1	Purchase contract
		2	Payment schedule
W-12	IRS Representative	1	1040 return 19X0
		2	1040 return 19X1
		3	1040 return 19X3

Figure 23.1 Witness and exhibit list.

		4	1120 return 19X1
		5	1120 return 19X2
		6	1120 return 19X3
		7	1120S return 19X1
		8	1120S return 19X2
		9	1120S return 19X3
		10	1065 return 19X1
		11	1065 return 19X2
		12	1065 return 19X3
W-13	I. M. Balance, CPA	1	Financial statements for 19X2 store
		2	Financial statements for 19X3 store
		3	Lounge Doe, Inc. work papers for 19X1
		4	Lounge Doe, Inc. work papers for 19X2
		5	Lounge Doe, Inc work papers for 19X3
		6	Doe's Kwik Stop, Inc. work papers for 19X1
		7	Doe's Kwik Stop, Inc. work papers for 19X2
		8	Doe's Kwik Stop, Inc. work papers for 19X3
		9	Real Property, Ltd. work papers for 19X1
		10	Real Property, Ltd. work papers for 19X2
		11	Real Property, Ltd. work papers for 19X3
		12	Work papers 1040 for 19X1
		13	Work papers 1040 for 19X2
		14	Work papers 1040 for 19X3
W-14	Bookkeeper for Suzy's Sexy Clothes	1	Books and records 19X2
		2	Books and records 19X3
W-15	First National Bank Records Custodian	1	Bank account records for 19X1
		2	Bank account records for 19X2
		3	Bank account records for 19X3

Figure 23.1 Continued

		4	IRA account records for John Doe
		5	IRA account records for Suzy Que
		6	Trust account for sister
		7	Trust account for brother one
		8	Trust account for brother two
		9	Trust account for parents
		10	Mercedes Benz loan documents and payment schedule
		11	Toyota loan documents and payment schedule
W-16	Credit Card Co. Records Custodian	1	Credit card records 19X1
		2	Credit card records 19X2
		3	Credit card records 19X3
W-17	Utility Company Records Custodian	1	Billing and payment schedule 19X1
		2	Billing and payment schedule 19X2
		3	Billing and payment schedule 19X3
W-18	Telephone Company Records Custodian	1	Billing and payment schedule 19X1
		2	Billing and payment schedule 19X2
		3	Billing and payment schedule 19X3
W-19	Insurance Company Records Custodian	1	Policy and payment schedule 19X1
		2	Policy and payment schedule 19X2
		3	Policy and payment schedule 19X3
		4	Policy and payment schedule for apartment building
W-20	Church Donation Records Custodian	1	Receipt schedule for 19X2
		2	Receipt schedule for 19X3
W-21	Auto Dealership Records Custodian	1	Mercedes Benz purchase documents
		2	Toyota purchase documents

Figure 23.1 Continued

| W-22 | Apartment Building | 1 | Lease agreements and |
| | Tenants | 2 | payment schedules |

Note: Each apartment building tenant is a witness along with the documentary evidence. For simplicity here, only one tenant and related evidence is shown.

W-23	Florida Mortgage Co.	1	Mortgage documents
	Records Custodian	2	Payment schedule
W-24	Maintenance Co.	1	Maintenance records
	Records Custodian	2	Payment schedules
W-25	Administrator State Unemployment Compensation Office	1	Earnings records
W-26	Brokerage Firm	1	Account application
	Records Custodian	2	Monthly statements
		3	Buy and sell confirmation slips
W-27	Fraud Examiner Summary Witness	1	Net worth schedule
W-28	Jewelry Store Store owner	1	Gold bullion invoice
W-29	U.S. State Department Consular Officer	1	Bahamian public records
W-30	County Tax Collector Records Custodian	1	Property tax bills

Figure 23.1 Continued

23.11   Case Files

Case files are very important. They contain all of the evidence and witness statements or depositions. The two principal methods of keeping case files are:

1. *Originals.* Original or primary evidence and statements should be kept by witness. A witness statement or deposition along with any physical evidence should be kept together. For trial purposes, it makes it easier for the witness to review his previous statements or depositions and examine the evidence that they provided earlier. It often takes years from the time the witness is interviewed and evidence is obtained to the time the trial takes place. Both physical evidence and statements should be kept in files that are secured. Original evidence should be kept in clear plastic envelopes and properly labeled. Under no circumstances should original evidence be marked on.

2. *Working Copies.* Copies of original evidence and statements should be made for use as working copies. These copies can be marked on. If doing an indirect method

(e.g., net worth or expenditure methods), these working copies should be filed according to the method being used. In the case of the net worth method, the working copies should be kept by assets, liabilities, expenses, and known or non-taxable income. In the case of specific items, the files should be kept in chronological order. This can help the examiner to determine what items are missing or identify areas where more investigation work is required or additional evidence needs to be obtained.

23.12 Sample Report

This section will provide a condensed version of a fraud examiner's report. Its primary purpose is to provide a guideline for the fraud examiner in preparing their investigative report. The basic elements of the fraud examiner's report are:

1. Fraud examiner's memorandum
2. Table of contents
3. Witness list
4. Schedule of losses or net worth/expenditure schedules with references to witnesses and evidence
5. Interview memorandums/depositions
6. Copies or photos of evidence

Copies or photos of evidence will not be provided in this example. Figure 23.2 shows an example of a fraud examiner's report.

The next part of the fraud examiner's report is the Table of Contents. Figure 23.3 shows an example.

The fraud examiner should list each witness and index him or her to the statements and/or depositions in the table of contents. Also, copies of documents should be listed and indexed. For simplicity, it is not done here.

The next section of the report is the witness list. The witness list has been presented in an earlier section. It will not be presented here.

After the witness list, see the section showing the financial loss or the indirect method being used. The net worth schedule shows the account description, the witness number, evidence number, and a brief description of the evidence. Figure 23.4 shows a net worth schedule witness list; the figures have been omitted because they are shown in an earlier chapter (see chapter 8 for the RICO net worth schedule, pages 2 and 3).

The next section of the fraud examiner's report should list the interviews and/or depositions of witnesses. In this case, most of the witnesses are record custodians. This section is important in that it gives the witnesses statements. These statements can be in the form of casual statements, formal statements, and depositions. Some witnesses may have more than one statement. Figure 23.5 shows an example of the index of interview and/or depositions.

Figure 23.6 shows an example of a record custodian memorandum of interview.

Mr. Paul Jones is the record custodian for the XYZ Auto Dealership. Mr. Jones has never met the subject. He only processes the paperwork that the salesmen provide when customers purchase new or used cars.

Investigation Report

May 10, 19X4

U.S. State Attorney
Any County, USA

In re: John Doe
SSN: 000-00-0000
DOB: 1/24/XX
100 Alpha St
Any City, State XXXXX
Case #: XXXXXXX
Criminal-Drug Trafficking and
Money Laundering, RICO
FINAL REPORT

HISTORY

John Doe is a 24-year-old man. He dropped out of the 10th grade. He has two brothers, a sister, and parents who are still living in the area. He has not married but is currently living with a girlfriend, Suzy Que. John Doe has only had menial jobs during his career. Past employees have stated that John Doe has a talent of being a boat mechanic. John Doe is considered the "black sheep" of the family. His parents are highly educated. His father was a doctor in Cuba but now is working as a laboratory technician. His mother is a registered nurse. His brothers and sister are continuing their education. He has been seen on many occasions with Ramon Calderone, a known drug trafficker by local and federal law enforcement. John Doe, being young, is in excellent health. He has been seen jogging, swimming, and doing heavy lifting. Doe has not worked for any employer since 19X1. He quit his last job but gave no reason to the employer as to why. The employer offered to give him a $1.00 per hour raise if he would stay. Doe refused. Doe lived with his parents up until the time that he purchased the house on 100 Alpha Street. John Doe uses pay telephones quite often. He visits his family regularly. After meeting Suzy Que, Doe has spent less time visiting his family and more time courting Suzy. Doe does extensive travel around town and offshore. Suzy, his girlfriend, occasionally goes with Doe on his trips. It is documented that he has been to Europe, South and Central America, and various Caribbean Islands. This case was instituted because of testimony of former drug pushers in court who identify John Doe as the supplier. The former drug pushers have all been convicted and are incarcerated.

TYPE OF CASE

This is a net worth case. The purpose of the Net Worth is to determine Doe's alleged illegal gains from his drug trafficking and money laundering activities. In addition, it will serve as a basis for both civil and criminal forfeitures.

EVIDENCE

Since this is a net worth case, most of the witnesses are record custodians who have records of transactions conducted with the subject. Some of the record custodians have personal knowledge and possible friendship with the subject. The key witness will be the summary witness, who will have to summarize the financial evidence introduced into court. To place the subject in the drug trafficking and money laundering activities, witnesses will have to testify that they purchased drugs from or on behalf of the subject. Unfortunately, all the drug witnesses have been incarcerated for drug trafficking, which lends them to lack of credibility. Ramon Calderone is an indicted drug trafficker who has fled the United States. It is well documented that the subject had a close association with Calderone.

INTENT

The use of the net worth method of proving illegal gains shows that the subject did not fully hide his illegal gains. The subject maintained offshore bank accounts to hide his illegal gains. The subject did not operate his legitimate businesses on a day-to-day basis like normal businessmen. He traveled to offshore countries where he did not have any legitimate business dealings. He made cash deposits exceeding $10,000 and the bank did not file the appropriate CTRs because of inside contacts. He made various investment purchases in cash in order not to leave a paper trail. Mortgages were obtained from offshore companies with no record of repayments. The offshore mortgage company is not registered in the United States nor does it do any other business activities. The girlfriend is known to be a drug

Figure 23.2 Investigation report.

user by her coworkers and friends. Wiretapped conversations show that the subject is involved in drug trafficking by discussing drug deals. There were many telephone calls made to offshore tax havens, many of which were to banks.

DEFENSES

The most common defenses in this type of case will be the cash hoard. In this case, the fact that the subject is young and was unable to accumulate enough cash to make the investments and expenditures that he made negate the cash hoard story. His income prior to the prosecution period was very small. His relatives were financially unable to provide the funds for the subject to make the investments and expenditures. Of course, the defense will try to discredit the witnesses who had drug dealings with the subject. The net worth method of proving income will overcome these defenses.

FINANCIAL DATA

See the attached net worth schedule as to the illegal or unidentified gains by the subject. The fees and costs of this investigation are as follows:

Fees	$50,000
Investigation	10,000
Administrative	5,000
Total	$65,000

RECOMMENDATIONS

It is recommended that the subject be prosecuted for drug trafficking and money laundering under Federal Statutes, Title 18 USC 1956, 1963, and Title 21 USC 855 by the U.S. Attorney. If the U.S. Attorney declines to prosecute, then the State Attorney should prosecute under State Statute XXXX.

Fraud Examiner

Copy to:
File
Case Detective

Figure 23.2 Continued

Mr. Jones provided information about the regular course of business in keeping records. These procedures are as follows:

1. The salesman completes the sales contract and has the customer sign the contract. The salesman also obtains a down payment or full payment.
2. The credit department gets approval from a local financial institution for financed purchases after the salesman gets a signed contract and down payment. Once approved, the customer and the financial institution get a copy of the contract.

Table of Contents

1. Witness list
2. Net worth schedule
3. Witness interviews and depositions
4. Copies or photos of evidence

Figure 23.3 Table of contents sample.

John Doe's Net Worth Schedule

ACCOUNT	NUMBER	WITNESS NUMBER	EXHIBIT DESCRIPTION
1. Cash on hand	W-1	1	Property receipt
2. Cocaine, 2 kilos	W-1	2	Property receipt and lab report
3. First National Bank (FNB)	W-15	1-3	Bank account records
4. FNB savings	W-15	1-3	Bank account records
5. Business cash in bank	W-14	1-2	Books and records
	W-15	13-14	Bank account records 19X2-X3
6. Accounts receivable	W-13	1-2	Financial statements and
	W-14	1-2	work papers
7. Inventory	W-13	1-2	Financial statements and
	W-14	1-2	work papers
8. Business assets	W-13	1-2	Financial statements and
	W-14	1-2	work papers
9. Security system	W-11	1-2	Contract and payment schedule
10. Electronic equipment	W-10	1	Purchase invoice
11. Appliances	W-9	1	Purchase invoice
12. Fixtures	W-7	1	Purchase invoice
13. Furniture	W-4	1	Purchase invoice
14. Cabinets	W-5	1	Purchase invoice
15. Paintings	W-6	1	Purchase invoice
16. Pool and tennis court	W-8	1-2	Contract and payment schedule
17. 100 Alpha Street	W-2	1	Deed and mortgage
18. 100 Bravo Street	W-2	2	Deed and mortgage
19. Gold bullion	W-1	1	Case detective and property receipts
	W-28	1	Purchase invoice
20. Lounge Doe, Inc.	W-12	4-5-6	1120 tax returns
	W-13	3-4-5	Work papers
21. Doe's Kwik Stop, Inc.	W-12	7-8-9	1120S tax return
	W-13	6-7-8	Work papers
22. Real Property, Ltd.	W-12	10-12	1065 tax returns
	W-13	9-11	Work papers
23. Mercedes Benz	W-21	1	Purchase documents
24. Toyota	W-21	2	Purchase documents
25. IRA—John Doe	W-15	4	Bank records
26. IRA—Suzy Que	W-15	5	Bank records
27. Bahamas residence	W-29	1	Public records
28. Mercedes loan	W-15	10	Loan documents
29. Toyota loan	W-15	11	Loan documents
30. Credit card	W-16	1-2-3	Credit card records
31. Accounts payable	W-13	1-2	Financial statements and work papers
	W-14	1-2	Books and records
32. Florida Mortgage Co	W-23	1-2	Mortgage documents and payment schedule
33. Business Bank Loan	W-15	12	Loan documents

Figure 23.4 Net worth schedule witness list.

34. Purchases	W-13	1-2	Financial statements and work papers
	W-14	1-2	Books and records
35. Inventory change	W-13	1-2	Financial statements and work papers
	W-14	1-2	Books and records
36. Cost of sales	W-13	1-2	Financial statements and work papers
	W-14	1-2	Books and records
37. Advertising	W-13	1-2	Financial statements and work papers
	W-14	1-2	Books and records
38. Interest loan	W-13	1-2	Financial statements and work papers
	W-14	1-2	Books and records
39. Insurance	W-13	1-2	Financial statements and work papers
	W-14	1-2	Books and records
40. Professional fees	W-13	1-2	Financial statements and work papers
	W-14	1-2	Books and records
41. Office expenses	W-13	1-2	Financial statements and work papers
	W-14	1-2	Books and records
42. Rent expenses	W-13	1-2	Financial statements and work papers
	W-14	1-2	Books and records
43. Repairs	W-13	1-2	Financial statements and work papers
	W-14	1-2	Books and records
44. Supplies	W-13	1-2	Financial statements and work papers
	W-14	1-2	Books and records
45. Taxes and license	W-13	1-2	Financial statements and work papers
	W-14	1-2	Books and records
46. Utilities	W-13	1-2	Financial statements and work papers
	W-14	1-2	Books and records
47. Wages	W-13	1-2	Financial statements and work papers
	W-14	1-2	Books and records
48. Miscellaneous	W-13	1-2	Financial statements and work papers
	W-14	1-2	Books and records
49. Florida Mortgage Co.	W-23	1-2	Mortgage documents and payment schedule
50. Utilities	W-17	1-3	Billing and payment schedules

Figure 23.4 Continued

51. Telephone	W-18	1-3	Billing, payments, and toll schedules
52. Insurance	W-19	1-3	Policy and payment schedule
53. Life Insurance	W-3	1-2	Policy and payment schedule
54. Interest loans for automobiles	W-15	10-11	Bank loan documents and payment schedule
55. Income tax W/H	W-12	1-3	1040 tax return
56. Property taxes	W-13	12-13	Property tax bills
	W-30	1	Assessment and payments
57. Credit card	W-16	1-2-3	Credit card statements
58. Church donations	W-20	1-2	Payment receipts
59. Trust funds	W-15	6-9	Bank records and trust agreements
60. Loss XYZ stock	W-26	1-3	Brokerage records
61. Wages/salaries	W-12	1-3	W-2 records
	W-13	12-14	Work papers
	W-12	1	1099 records
62. Dividends	W-12	1	1099 records
	W-13	3, 12	Work papers
63. Rental income	W-12	1,2,3	1040 tax returns
	W-12	9-11	1065 tax returns
64. Gain ABC stock	W-26	1-3	Brokerage records
65. IRA interest	W-15	4	Bank records
66. IRA interest	W-15	5	Bank records
67. Tax refunds	W-12	1-3	IRS payment records
68. Sale XYZ stock	W-26	1-3	Brokerage records
69. Business income	W-13	1-2	Financial statements and work papers
	W-14	1-2	Books and records

Figure 23.4 Continued

The dealership keeps a copy of the contract. It is sent to the accounting department for processing.

3. The accounting department gets a copy of the contract for processing. The sale is recognized through the books after it has been approved by the financial institution. Mr. Jones is the controller of the dealership and the official record custodian. After the contract and sale is recognized, the contract is filed by customer name and stored.

Mr. Jones provided the following records of purchase.

1. The Purchase and Installment Sale Contract. This document shows the purchase, down payment, principal financed, rate of interest, payments, and term.
2. A copy of the sales journal is showing the receipt of the down payment.

INDEX OF INTERVIEWS/DEPOSITIONS

1. Case Detective	Police reports
2. Administrator, Public Records	Interview memorandum
3. Records Custodian, Life Insurance Co.	Interview memorandum
4. Records Custodian, Furniture Company	Interview memorandum
5. Records Custodian, Cabinet Company	Interview memorandum
6. Records Custodian, Art Dealer	Interview memorandum
7. Records Custodian, Fixture Company	Interview memorandum
8. Records Custodian, Pool and Tennis Contractor	Interview memorandum
9. Records Custodian, Appliance Dealer	Interview memorandum
10. Records Custodian, Electronics Store	Interview memorandum
11. Records Custodian, Security System Dealer	Interview memorandum
12. IRS Representative	Interview memorandum
13. I.M. Balance, CPA	Sworn statement and interview memorandum
14. Bookkeeper, Suzy's Clothing Store	Interview memorandum
15. Records Custodian, First National Bank	Interview memorandum
16. Records Custodian, Credit Card Company	Interview memorandum
17. Records Custodian, Utility Company	Interview memorandum
18. Records Custodian, Telephone Company	Interview memorandum
19. Records Custodian, Insurance Company	Interview memorandum
20. Records Custodian, Christian Church	Interview memorandum
21. Records Custodian, Auto Dealership	Interview memorandum
22. Tenants, Apartment Building	Interview memorandum
23. Records Custodian, Florida Mortgage Co.	Interview memorandum
24. Records Custodian, Maintenance Company	Interview memorandum
25. Administrator, State Unemployment Compensation Office	Interview memorandum
26. Records Custodian, Brokerage Firm	Interview memorandum
27. Fraud Examiner	Examiner's report
28. Records Custodian, Jewelry Store	Interview memorandum
29. Consular Officer, U.S. State Department	Interview memorandum
30. Records Custodian, County Tax Collector	Interview memorandum

Figure 23.5 Index of interviews/depositions.

MEMORANDUM OF INTERVIEW

Date: February 1, 19X4

Present: Records Custodian
            Case Detective/Agent
            Fraud Examiner

Place: XYZ Auto Dealership
            300 Main Street
            Any City, State XXXXX

Figure 23.6 Memorandum of interview sample.

3. A copy of the sales journal showing the payment by the financial institution.
4. A copy of the delivery receipt, which shows that the customer picked up the automobile four days after the contract was signed.
5. A copy of the maintenance contract and a record of service done on the vehicle while under warranty.

Figure 23.7 shows an example of a witness-sworn statement.

STATEMENT

I, IM Balance, CPA, provide the following statement about my client John Doe.

1. I obtained John Doe as a client by a referral. I don't recall who referred John Doe to me.

2. I prepared John Doe's individual tax returns, 1040s, for the years 19X1 and 19X3. I obtained the data to prepare John Doe's individual tax return for 19X2 but did not prepare it because I was missing some data. I don't recall what data that I was missing.

3. I prepared the 1120 federal corporate income tax returns for 19X1, 19X2, and 19X3 for Lounge Doe, Inc. These returns were prepared based on the bank statements, canceled checks, accounts payable, inventory, and asset listings which were provided by the client. These items were processed by generating a general journal, general ledger, trial balance, and financial statements. The financial statements were used to prepare the corporate tax return.

4. I prepared the 1120S federal corporate income tax returns for 19X1, 19X2, and 19X3 for Doe's Kwik Stop, Inc. These returns were also prepared based on the bank statements, canceled checks, accounts payable, inventory, and asset listings that were provided by the client. These items were processed by generating a general journal, general ledger, trial balance, and financial statements. The financial statements were used to prepare the corporate tax return.

5. I prepared the 1065 federal partnership income tax returns for 19X1, 19X2, and 19X3 for Real Property, Ltd. These returns were also prepared based on the bank statements, canceled checks, closing statement, and mortgage information. Generating a general ledger, trial balance, and financial statements also processed these items. The financial statements were used to prepare the partnership return. I never met the other partner, Ramon Calderone. All my dealings were with John Doe. Doe was given a copy of the return for his partner to complete his individual tax return.

6. I was retained by John Doe to do a certified audit on Suzy's Women Clothes Store. This is a sole proprietorship. John Doe is the sole owner. His girlfriend and Betsy Low took care of the books and managed the store. They had about 8–10 employees at any one time. Suzy Que and Betsy Low received a salary to operate the business. They maintained a general journal and general ledger. In addition, they maintained accounts receivable, accounts payable, and purchase journals. I used these journals to prepare a trial balance and produce financial statements. I also made test of the records in accordance with General Accepted Accounting Principals and General Accepted Audit Standards as promulgated by the AICPA. In addition, I prepared a Schedule C for John Doe for reporting on his individual income tax return. John Doe retained me to do the certified audit and oversee operations because he would be busy in his other business ventures.

7. I advised John Doe to obtain an Individual Retirement Account. In addition, I have counseled John Doe on taxes, management of businesses, and various investments. I advised John Doe to acquire Doe's Kwik Stop, Inc. store. This advice was based on the fact that John Doe wanted to supply boater's fast food items and supplies. Doe obtained a boat that he said was going to be used for this purpose. I never observed the boat.

8. John Doe was a friendly and personable individual. He is young and has many innovative ideas that I thought were good. He followed my advice on his business decisions. We worked well together.

I have read the foregoing statement. I fully understand that this statement is true, accurate, and complete to the best of my knowledge. I made this statement freely and voluntarily, without any threats or rewards, or promises of rewards having been made to me in return for it.

/s/ I. M. Balance

Witness signature   Date

Witness signature

Figure 23.7 Statement sample.

23.13 Summary

Maintaining proper files and producing reports are very important. It helps the fraud examiner and his client in evaluating the case. The fraud examiner's report is the final product that is produced. It reflects the capabilities of the examiner. Sloppy reports indicate that the examiner is sloppy. Maintaining proper files also helps the examiner. The examiner may find that he is missing evidence. If so, then the examiner has to obtain it. It also helps the examiner in trial. First, it tells him what evidence must be introduced into court before his summaries can be used. Second, it tells him exactly what he is going to testify about and gives the basis of his opinion as an expert witness.

Audit Programs 24

24.1 Introduction

Audit programs are procedures to be followed by accountants and auditors in the course of their examination of a business entity. The examiner must collect various kinds of evidence relating to the propriety of the recording of economic events and transactions. Audit programs are guidelines for the examiner in obtaining and collecting financial evidence. The auditor must collect and analyze evidence to support his/her attest function as to the business entity's financial condition. The fraud examiner must collect and analyze evidence to uncover possible fraud by employees, management personnel, or outsiders. While the auditor is primarily interested in obtaining evidence to support the attest function, the fraud examiner must obtain evidence that will convince a jury of peers that certain individual(s) have committed an economic crime. The evidence required to convince a jury and to be admissible in court is much greater than it is to support the attest function. This chapter gives the general guidelines that a fraud examiner must follow at a minimum. The fraud examiner's judgment should always overrule any audit program.

24.2 General Guidelines

The fraud examiner, like other accountants and auditors, must have a general outline of the engagement that should be followed. They are:

1. *Industry data.* The fraud examiner must know how the industry operates. He/she should obtain as much data, both financial and nonfinancial, as possible.
2. *Financial analysis.* The fraud examiner should make various comparisons and analysis to identify possible fraud areas.
3. *Internal controls.* The fraud examiner must review the internal controls in order to identify problem areas.
4. *Evidence gathering.* This is the stage where the fraud examiner searches and obtains evidence of possible fraud activity.
5. *Evaluation.* The fraud examiner must analyze evidence to confirm whether fraud was actually committed.
6. *Report.* The fraud examiner must report his/her findings to the appropriate parties.

24.3 Industry Data

Companies that are in the same business operate and report financial and nonfinancial data in a similar manner. This is particularly true with the Internal Revenue Service (IRS), because their regulations set forth tax principles that various industries must follow. The IRS annually publishes industry data and statistics. There are also other governmental and publishing companies that provide industry data. (See chapter on Sources of Information.) Comparing a business entity with others can identify problem areas, for example, inventory, receivables, payables, and sales.

24.4 Financial Analysis

Financial statements should be analyzed to determine trends, relationships, and comparison with nonfinancial data in order to identify significant irregularities and unexplained fluctuations. This can help in identifying possible areas where fraud can occur. There are three types of techniques that are commonly used. They are:

1. Ratio analysis
2. Vertical analysis
3. Horizontal analysis

24.4.1 Ratio Analysis

Ratios are useful in determining if financial statements are reasonable. Ratios can identify material fluctuations. These fluctuations must be researched for a reasonable explanation. Significant fluctuations from period to period can be a result of changing economic conditions, management strategy and policy, errors in record keeping, or fraud. The cause must be determined. Fraud could be one cause, but it is not proof that it occurred. Company ratios should be compared to industry statistics and data.

1. $\text{Current ratio} = \dfrac{\text{Current assets}}{\text{Current liabilities}}$

2. $\text{Quick ratio} = \dfrac{\text{Cash} + \text{Securities} + \text{Receivables}}{\text{Current liabilities}}$

3. $\text{Cash ratio} = \dfrac{\text{Cash} + \text{Securities}}{\text{Current liabilities}}$

4. $\text{Accounts receivable turnover} = \dfrac{\text{Sales}}{\text{Average receivables}}$

5. $\text{Days to collect receivables} = \dfrac{365}{\text{Account receivable turnover}}$

6. $\text{Inventory turnover} = \dfrac{\text{Cost of goods sold}}{\text{Average inventory}}$

7. $\text{Days to sell inventory} = \dfrac{365}{\text{Inventory turnover}}$

8. $\begin{array}{c}\text{Days to convert}\\\text{inventory to cash}\end{array} = \begin{array}{c}\text{Days to sell}\\\text{inventory}\end{array} + \begin{array}{c}\text{Days to collect}\\\text{cash receivables}\end{array}$

9. Debt to equity ratio $= \dfrac{\text{Total liabilities}}{\text{Total equity}}$

10. Times interest earned $= \dfrac{\text{Net income}}{\text{Interest expense}}$

11. Profit margin ratio $= \dfrac{\text{Net income}}{\text{Net sales}}$

12. Asset turnover $= \dfrac{\text{Net sales}}{\text{Average total assets}}$

13. Return on equity $= \dfrac{\text{Net income}}{\text{Average equity}}$

14. Earnings per share $= \dfrac{\text{Net income}}{\text{Number of shares of stock}}$

15. Gross profit % $= \dfrac{(\text{Cost of sales}) \times 100}{\text{Sales}}$

24.4.2 Vertical Analysis

This method is used in comparing items on the balance sheet and income statement by reflecting all components in terms of percentages. For the balance sheet, total assets are assigned 100%. For the income statement, net sales are assigned 100%. All other items on both the balance sheet and income statement are shown as a percentage of those two figures, respectively.

24.4.3 Horizontal Analysis

This method is used in comparing percentage changes in the balance sheet and income statement from one period to the next. Horizontal analysis compares both the dollar amount and change percentage from year to year. Any unusual fluctuation must be investigated to determine if it is due to fraud or some other cause. It is by no means proof that fraud exists. It is only an indication that fraud may exist.

24.5 Nonfinancial Data

Financial statements should reflect what actually happened. If inventory and fixed assets are shown on the financial statements, then these assets should be observable. There is a direct relationship between financial statements and the physical goods and movement of assets. Comparing financial statement data with nonfinancial data is a good method of detecting fraud. The fraud examiner should make further inquiries when things appear out of order or sequence. Some things that should be reviewed are as follows:

1. If sales increase, then accounts receivable should likewise increase.
2. If sales increase, then inventory should increase.
3. If profits increase, then cash should increase.

4. If sales increase, then the cost of outbound freight should increase.
5. If purchases increase, then the cost of inbound freight should increase.
6. If manufacturing volume is increasing, then per unit costs should be decreasing.
7. If manufacturing volume is increasing, then scrap sales and purchase discounts should also increase.
8. If inventory increases, then storage space must be available to contain it.
9. When sales increase, there are usually other expense accounts that increase in the same proportion.
10. Over-aged receivables could indicate not only slow payment by the customer but also possible fraud. The receivable could have been received but not recorded.

24.6   Cash Flow Statement

The cash flow statement can identify potential fraud. The cash flow statement identifies how a company uses and applies its funds and explains the net increase or decrease in cash during the period. It is particularly useful to identify problem areas. There is a close relationship between the balance sheet and income statement. The cash flow statement ties the balance sheet and income statement together with detail. There are many cases where fraudulent balance sheets and income statements were prepared. When a cash flow statement was prepared, it was discovered that there were discrepancies. These discrepancies help confirm that the financial statements are incorrect and can identify fraudulent areas.

The cash flow statement can be very complicated. Its primary purpose is to explain the increase in cash accounts from one period to another. Figure 24.1 outlines the general steps in preparing a cash flow statement.

The result should equal the net increase/decrease in cash accounts.

Cash Flow from Operations
    Net income
    Adjustments to net income
    Depreciation expense
    Amortization expense
    Increase/decrease receivables
    Increase/decrease inventory
    Increase/decrease payables

    Net cash inflow from operations

Other Sources of Funds
    Sales of fixed assets
    Borrowing from banks, etc.
    Capital investment

Application of Funds
    Purchase of fixed assets
    Debt reduction
    Dividends

    Net increase/decrease in cash

Figure 24.1 Cash flow statement.

24.7 Cash Flow Theory

The theory behind the cash flow statement is to start with the net income from operations. The first step is to convert the net income from the income statement into the net cash flow from operations. Eliminating the noncash items on the income statement does this. The second step is to add other sources of cash flow. This is additional cash that comes from sources other than normal operations. The third step is to identify cash expenditures that do not affect current income statement operations. After the net income from operations is adjusted for noncash items, the total other cash sources are added and the other cash expenditures are subtracted from the net cash from operations. This gives the net increase in the cash accounts. This should equal the net increase/decrease in the total cash accounts. If it does not, then the financial statements will have to be further analyzed to determine the area where the potential fraud has occurred.

24.8 Net Income Adjustments

There are five types of items that will be used to adjust the net income from operations. They are as follows:

1. Depreciation
2. Amortization
3. Receivables
4. Payables
5. Inventory

The theory for these adjustments is explained further.

24.8.1 Depreciation

This is a noncash expense. It is solely a journal entry by accountants to expense in a systematic method the writing off the cost of fixed assets on the balance sheet. Therefore, the depreciation expense shown as an expense must be added back to the net income from operations.

24.8.2 Amortization

This expense does not involve the use of cash. It is an entry used to systematically write off the cost of some tangible or intangible asset, for example, leasehold improvements, organization costs, goodwill, and various prepaid expenses.

24.8.3 Receivables

Many business enterprises keep their books on the accrual method of accounting. The accrual method requires that sales be recognized when they occur and not when the funds are collected. This method results in the business enterprise having an asset called accounts receivable. The IRS and the American Institute of Certified Public Accountants require many business enterprises to be on the accrual method of accounting. The sales accounts have to be adjusted for noncash sales. Finding the difference in accounts receivable between the beginning and ending of the period can do this. If the receivables increase, then the net income will have to be decreased by that difference. If the receivables decrease, then the net income will have to be increased by that difference.

24.8.4 Payables

Payables, like account receivables, recognize expenses when they are incurred and not when they are paid. Again, this is the accrual method of accounting. The expenses on the income statement will have to be adjusted for noncash items. This is done by getting the difference between the beginning and ending balances in the accounts payable for the period. If the payables increase for the period, then the net income will have to be increased. Conversely, if the payables decrease for the period, then the net income will have to be decreased.

24.8.5 Inventory

Inventories are goods that a business enterprise has on hand that are not sold. When inventory is sold, it is expensed to the cost of goods sold on the income statement. Inventory can be purchased in a prior period and sold in the current period. This causes an outlay of cash in the prior period but not the current period. The current period has to be adjusted for inventory and cost of goods sold that does not require any cash outlay. This can be done by finding the difference in inventory at the beginning and end of the period. If the inventory increases over the period, then net income should be increased by the difference. Conversely, if the inventory decreases over the period, then the net income should be decreased by the difference.

24.9   Internal Controls

Internal control describes an entity's organization and system of procedures that provide reasonable assurance that errors or irregularities will be prevented or detected on a timely basis. The objectives of internal controls are:

1. Transactions are executed in accordance with management's authorization.
2. Transactions are properly recorded. This entails that the transaction has substance (existence), is properly valued, classified, and recorded in the proper period.
3. Assets must be safeguarded. This entails restricting access to assets and segregation of duties.
4. Actual assets are required to be periodically compared to accounting records.

24.9.1 Basic Concepts

There are ten basic concepts on internal controls. The first four concepts relate to accounting controls. The last six concepts relate to essential characteristics of internal controls. These concepts are as follows:

24.9.1.1 Management Responsibility

Management must establish, maintain, supervise, and modify, as required, a system of internal controls for the company. They should have proper attitude. Setting a good example for others to follow can do this. Management can issue a code of conduct, provide training, and enforce policy. If employees see management being dishonest, then they will commit fraudulent acts.

24.9.1.2 Reasonable Assurance

The costs of controls should not exceed their expected benefit. Yet, there must be controls in place that can detect fraud or other irregularities. Organizational structure that clearly defines lines of responsibility and authority can deter internal fraud. An audit committee that reports to the board of directors is an important control element. The audit committee should control both financial and operational audit functions as well as be responsible for security. They should never be controlled by or report to management.

24.9.1.3 Methods of Data Processing

Most business enterprises today are using computers. This is primarily due to the low cost of both hardware and software. Computers also save time and costs in processing financial information. Computer systems, however, provide internal control problems. Transaction trails may exist for a short period of time or only in computer-readable form. Program errors are less frequent. Computer controls may become more important than segregation of functions. It also becomes more difficult to detect unauthorized access to the computer system. There is less documentation of initiation and execution of transactions. Manual control procedures using computer output is dependent on the effectiveness of computer controls.

24.9.1.4 Limitations

Auditors should not rely entirely on internal control, even if it seems outstanding, because the best system may break down owing to misunderstandings, mistakes in judgment, carelessness, collusion, and being overridden by management.

24.9.1.5 Segregation of Functions

The segregation of functions is an essential element of internal control. The basic premise is that no employee performs more than one function. The functions of recordkeeping, custodianship, authorization, and operations should always be kept separate.

24.9.1.6 Personnel

Personnel policies are an important ingredient for internal control systems. A business enterprise should obtain reliable employees. This can be done by screening prospective employees. References should be verified for both competence and trustworthiness. Employees in responsible positions should be bonded. Management should supervise employees in a professional manner. They should not be overbearing, critical, intimidate, instill fear, or treat employees unfairly. Any of these behaviors will encourage employee fraud. If management encourages team effort, ideas, gives recognition for good performances, then employee fraud is greatly reduced. Employees should be required to take vacations.

24.9.1.7 *Access to Assets*

Physical control over assets should be the responsibility of a custodian. This custodian should never have access to financial records. However, the custodian should maintain records of assets as to physical description, location, and condition.

24.9.1.8 *Comparison of Accountability with Assets*

A control procedure of periodically comparing financial records with physical observation is an important internal control element. This should be done by an independent reviewing party. The reviewing party should not have responsibility for either record keeping or custodianship. Any discrepancies should be investigated.

24.9.1.9 *Execution of Transactions*

Every transaction should be authorized. The business enterprise should set up policies and guidelines that should be followed. The larger transaction should have various levels of authorization.

24.9.1.10 *Recording of Transactions*

There should be standardized procedures for recording transactions. These controls must insure that fraudulent or unauthorized transactions are not recorded. Insure that authorized transactions are properly included, valued, and classified at the proper time. Any exceptions should be investigated immediately. Transactions should involve more than one employee. Proper records should be maintained. An audit trail must be maintained at all times. Audit evidence must be available for inspection and review. Source documents (e.g., invoices, purchase orders, and checks) should be prenumbered and accounted for periodically.

24.9.2 Internal Control Checklist

The following checklist gives an outline of internal controls, which most businesses should have depending on the size of the company. For small businesses, many of the internal controls listed below are not applicable. Some of the internal controls should be used in the actual audit process.

A. General Controls
   1. Chart of accounts (both past and current)
   2. Accounting procedures manual
   3. Organizational chart showing definite responsibilities
   4. Review of journal entries
      a. No ledger references
      b. No journal entries for ledger entries
   5. Standard journal entries
   6. Use of prenumbered forms
   7. Supporting documents for journal entries
   8. Limited access to authorized personnel
   9. Rotation of accounting personnel
   10. Required vacations
   11. System of reviews
   12. Separation of record keeping from operations

13. Record retention policy and procedures
14. Bonding of employees
15. Conflict of interest policies
    a. Written policy
    b. Promulgation procedures

B. Cash on Hand
   1. Impress system
   2. Reasonable amount
   3. Completeness of vouchers
   4. Custodian responsibility
   5. Reimbursement checks to order of custodian
   6. Surprise audits
   7. No employee check cashing
   8. Physical security
   9. Custodian has no access to receipts
   10. Custodian has no access to accounting records

C. Cash Receipts
   1. Listing of mail receipts
   2. Special handling of postdated checks
   3. Daily deposits
   4. Cash custodians bonded
   5. Cash custodians apart from negotiable instruments
   6. Bank accounts properly authorized
   7. Proper handling of returned nonsufficient funds (NSF) items
   8. Duplicate deposit slip compared with cash book
   9. Duplicate deposit slip compared with customer subledgers
   10. Banks instructed not to cash checks to company
   11. Control of cash from other sources
   12. Separation of cashier personnel from accounting duties
   13. Separation of cashier personnel from credit duties
   14. Use of cash registers
   15. Retention and safekeeping of register tapes
   16. Numbered cash receipts tickets
   17. Outside salesmen cash controls
   18. Daily reconciliation of cash collections

D. Cash Disbursements
   1. Numbered checks
   2. Support for check signature
   3. Limited authorization to sign checks
   4. No signing of blank checks
   5. All checks accounted for
   6. Detailed listing of checks
   7. Mutilation of voided checks
   8. Proper authorization of personnel signing checks
   9. Control over signature machines
   10. Check listing compared to cash book
   11. Control over bank transfers

12. Checks not payable to cash
13. Physical security over unused checks
14. Cancellation of supporting documents
15. Control over long outstanding checks
16. Reconciliation of bank account(s)
17. Independence of person reconciling bank statements
18. Bank statement direct to person reconciling bank statements
19. No access to cash records or receipts by check signers

E. Investments
1. Proper authorization of transactions
2. Under control of custodian
3. Custodian bonded
4. Custodian separate from cash receipts
5. Custodian separate from investment records
6. Safety deposit box
7. Record of all safe deposit visits
8. Access limited to safe deposit box
9. Presence of two required for access
10. Periodic reconciliation of detail with control
11. Record of all aspects of all securities
12. Brokerage advises and statements
13. Periodic internal audit
14. Securities in name of company
15. Segregation of collateral
16. Physical control of collateral
17. Periodic appraisal of collateral
18. Periodic appraisal of investments

F. Accounts Receivable and Sales
1. Sales orders prenumbered
2. Credit approval
3. Credit and sales department independent
4. Control of back orders
5. Sales order and sales invoice comparison
6. Shipping invoices prenumbered
7. Names and addresses on shipping orders
8. Review of sales invoices
9. Control over returned merchandise
10. Credit memorandums prenumbered
11. Matching of credit memorandum receiving reports
12. Control over credit memorandums
13. Control over scrap sales
14. Control over sales to employees
15. Control over cash on delivery (COD) sales
16. Sales reconciled with cash receipts and accounts receivables
17. Sales reconciled with inventory change
18. Accounts receivable statements to customers
19. Periodic preparation of aging schedule

20. Control over payments of written off receivables
21. Control over accounts receivable write-off's, proper authorization
22. Control over accounts receivable written off, review for possible collection
23. Independence of sales, accounts receivable, receipts, billing, and shipping

G. Notes Receivable
1. Proper authorization of notes
2. Detailed records of notes
3. Periodic detail to control comparison
4. Periodic confirmation with makers
5. Control over notes discounted
6. Control over delinquent notes
7. Physical safety of notes
8. Periodic count of notes
9. Control over collateral
10. Control over revenue from notes
11. Custodian of notes independent from cash and record keeping

H. Inventory and Cost of Sales
1. Periodic inventory
2. Written inventory instructions
3. Counts by noncustodians
4. Controls over count tags
5. Control over inventory adjustments
6. Use of perpetual records
7. Periodic comparison of general ledger and perpetual records
8. Investigation of discrepancies
9. Control over consignment inventory
10. Control over inventory stored at warehouse
11. Control over returnable containers with customers
12. Receiving reports prepared
13. Receiving reports in numerical order
14. Independence of custodian from record keeping
15. Adequacy of insurance
16. Physical safeguard against theft
17. Physical safeguard against fire
18. Adequacy of cost system
19. Cost system tied into general ledger
20. Periodic review of overhead rates
21. Use of standard costs
22. Use of inventory requisitions
23. Periodic summaries of inventory usage
24. Control over intercompany inventory transfers
25. Purchase orders prenumbered
26. Proper authorization for purchases
27. Review of open purchase orders
28. Purchasing agents bonded
29. Three or more bids or quotes

I. Prepaid Expenses and Deferred Charges
1. Proper authorization to incur
2. Authorization and support of amortization
3. Detailed records
4. Periodic review of amortization policies
5. Control over insurance policies
6. Periodic review of insurance needs
7. Control over premium refunds
8. Beneficiaries of company policies
9. Physical control of policies

J. Intangibles
1. Authorization to incur
2. Detailed records
3. Authorization to amortize
4. Periodic review of amortization

K. Fixed Assets
1. Detailed property records
2. Periodic comparison with control accounts
3. Proper authorization of acquisition
4. Written policies for acquisition
5. Control over expenditures for self-construction
6. Use of work orders
7. Individual asset identification plates
8. Written authorization for sale
9. Written authorization for retirement
10. Physical safeguard from theft
11. Control over fully depreciated assets
12. Written capitalization and expense policies
13. Responsibilities charged for asset and depreciation records
14. Written depreciation records
15. Detailed depreciation records
16. Depreciation adjustments for sales and retirements
17. Control over intercompany transfers
18. Adequacy of insurance
19. Control over returnable containers

L. Accounts Payable
1. Designation of responsibility
2. Independence of accounts payable personnel from purchasing, cashier, and receiving functions
3. Periodic comparison of detail and control
4. Control over purchase returns
5. Clerical accuracy of vendor's invoice
6. Matching of purchase orders, receiving reports, and vendor invoices
7. Reconciliation of vendor statements with accounts payable detail
8. Control over debit memos
9. Control over advance payments
10. Review of unmatched receiving reports

    11. Mutilation of supporting documents at payment

    12. Review of debit balances

    13. Investigation of discounts not taken

M. Accrued Liabilities and Other Expenses

    1. Proper authorization for expenditures and concurrence

    2. Control over partial deliveries

    3. Postage meter

    4. Purchasing department

    5. Verification of invoices

    6. Impress cash account

    7. Detailed records

    8. Independence from general ledger and cashier functions

    9. Periodic comparison with budget

N. Payroll

    1. Authorization to employ

    2. Personnel data files

    3. Tax records

    4. Time clock

    5. Review of payroll calculations

    6. Impress payroll account

    7. Responsibility for payroll records

    8. Compliance with labor statutes

    9. Distribution of payroll checks

    10. Control over unclaimed wages

    11. Profit-sharing authorization

    12. Responsibility for profit-sharing computations

    13. Responsible employees bonded

    14. Employee benefit plans comparison with tax records

O. Long-Term Liabilities

    1. Authorization to incur

    2. Executed in company name

    3. Detailed records of long-term debt

    4. Reports of independent transfer agent

    5. Reports of independent registrar

    6. Otherwise adequate records of creditors

    7. Control over unissued instruments

    8. Signers independent of each other

    9. Adequacy of records of collateral

    10. Periodic review of debt agreement compliance

    11. Record keeping of detachable warrants

    12. Record keeping of conversion features

P. Shareholder's Equity

    1. Use of registrar

    2. Use of transfer agent

    3. Adequacy of detailed records

    4. Comparison of transfer agent's report with records

    5. Physical control over blank certificates

6. Physical control over treasury certificates
7. Authorization for transactions
8. Tax stamp compliance for canceled certificates
9. Independent dividend agent
10. Impress dividend account
11. Periodic reconciliation of dividend account
12. Adequacy of stockholder's ledger
13. Review of stock restrictions and provision
14. Valuation procedures for stock issuance
15. Other paid-in capital entries
16. Other retained earnings entries

24.10   Forensic Auditing

Auditing for fraud is known as forensic auditing. The accounting profession has not developed forensic auditing to the degree that it should entail. Public accountants, that is, certified public accountants, audit for financial statement presentation. Internal auditors examine for compliance with company policies and procedures. The Government Accounting Office audits for compliance with government programs. The IRS audits primarily for compliance with federal tax laws. However, the IRS has specialized auditors who do forensic auditing. Their numbers are few and their emphasis is tax evasion and recently has been expanded into money laundering.

24.10.1   Forensic Audit Phases

There are four phases of forensic auditing. They are:

1. Recognition and planning phase
2. Evidence collection phase
3. Evidence evaluation phase
4. Communication of results phase

24.10.1.1   *Recognition and Planning Stage*
The first phase of forensic auditing is the recognition and planning stage. There must be some reason to believe that fraud exists before a fraud examiner conducts an audit. The problem must be defined. All possible explanations should be explored. Also, the examination should be planned for staffing, methods, location, and needs.

24.10.1.2   *Evidence Collection*
The second phase of forensic auditing is evidence collection. The purpose is to determine whether initial evidence of fraud is misleading and if more procedures are needed to resolve the fraud.

24.10.1.3   *Evidence Evaluation*
The evidence evaluation phase determines what type of legal action should be taken, if any. Some cases will only warrant civil action, which is obtaining restitution. In other cases,

criminal action may be warranted. In civil cases, the degree of evidence must be "clear and convincing." In criminal cases, the evidence must prove "beyond a reasonable doubt." When using an indirect method, for example, net worth, expenditure, or bank deposit methods, evidence must prove "with reasonable certainty." This phase requires the cooperation of management, legal counsel, internal audit, and corporate security. If the evidence is strong enough to stand up in court, then strategy should be planned and followed.

24.10.1.4 *Communication of the Results*
The final phase of the forensic audit is communication of the results. An audit report should be prepared and presented to management. This report should encompass a good description of the fraud and who perpetrated it by presenting both documentary and testimony evidence.

24.11 Evidence-Gathering Techniques

There are various evidence-gathering techniques that can be used. In most cases, a combination of various techniques is required to support a case. The elements of fraud are the theft act, concealment, and conversion. The evidence-gathering techniques are designed to uncover these fraud elements.

24.11.1 Interviewing

Interviewing is an important evidence-gathering technique. It helps obtain information, which establishes elements of a crime, provides additional leads, gets cooperation of witnesses and victims, and obtains the economic motives of a perpetrator.

24.11.2 Vulnerability and Internal Control Charts

Vulnerability and internal control charts help examiners determine the best probabilities where fraud is likely to occur.

24.11.3 Document Examination

This technique uncovers concealment efforts of perpetrators by manipulating source documents.

24.11.4 Employee Searches

This technique involves examining an employee's desk, lockers, lunch boxes, etc. It is important not to violate a person's constitutional rights of illegal searches. Searches are legal if conducted in a proper manner and with adequate notice. If obtained illegally, evidence can be inadmissible in court.

24.11.5 Invigilation

Invigilation is a technique that involves close supervision of suspects during an examination period. It can be effective in identifying who and where the fraud is occurring. It is particularly useful in catching fraud that is committed by independent suppliers, night watchmen, warehouse supervisors, purchasing agents, and cashiers. Its drawbacks are high cost and the potential for causing low employee morale.

24.11.6   Observation

Observation is watching, looking, spying, or snooping to gather evidence. Such observations are recorded on various kinds of mediums. Observation can show how the fraud is being committed.

24.11.7   Undercover

Undercover operations require an agent or informant. This technique should be used for major criminal acts (e.g., organized crime activities). It is important that it remains secret. It is also very dangerous for the undercover agent.

24.11.8   Specific Item

Specific item evidence is locating and identifying specific documents that show fraud has occurred. This can be with one or more documents, for example, an altered contract or many canceled checks.

24.12   Fraud Indicators

There are clues that indicate that fraud exists. These symptoms do not guarantee that fraud exists but can be warning signs that fraud can or has occurred. There are environmental and personal symptoms called "red flags."

24.12.1   Environmental Symptoms

The most common environmental symptoms that encourage fraud are:

1. *Loose internal controls.* If internal controls are not enforced, then the opportunity of fraud occurring is great. Fraud occurs more often when internal controls are ignored.
2. *Poor management philosophy.* If top management is dishonest, then dishonesty will flow down to employees. When autocratic management sets budgets that are impossible to attain, lower managers will have to cheat, fail, or quit. If management does not prosecute fraud offenders, even if small, it only sends a signal that the company does not deal harshly with criminals.
3. *Poor financial position.* If a company has poor cash flow, then fraud is more likely to occur. Employees are more likely to take advantage of a company when they feel insecure about their jobs or the company's existence.
4. *Low employee morale.* When employee morale is low, they lack loyalty and feel like they are being wronged. Low employee morale can be either the result of

personal problems or work related. Perceived inequities at the work place can lead to decreased employee loyalty. Some identified reasons for employee fraud to "correct" injustice are:

a. Being passed over for a raise
b. Being passed over for a promotion
c. Being subjected to disciplinary action
d. Feeling that pay is inadequate
e. Favoritism to other employees
f. Resentment toward superiors
g. Frustration with job
h. Boredom

5. *Ethics confusion.* If a company does not have an ethics code, then this could lead to employee confusion. What is the line between a gift and a kickback? What is a company secret? A corporate code of conduct and policy statements should be promulgated. These policies should address what types of gifts are acceptable, access to certain operating units, and security policies.

6. *Background checks.* The lack of a background check or the failure to exercise due care when hiring new employees can be costly. Proper screening has many benefits.

a. More honest employees
b. Acts as a deterrent to employee dishonesty
c. Protects innocent employees from false accusations
d. Eliminates problem employees such as substance abusers, serial thieves, etc.
e. Eliminates poor security risks
f. Permits honest employees to work in harmony
   Some common problems that employers encounter are:

a. Previous arrests
b. Unstable work record
c. Fired from previous job
d. Employee theft
e. Mental instability
f. Drug/substance abuse
g. Personal/domestic problems
h. Health defects
i. Bad tempers

7. *Lack of employee support programs.* Job stress or personal problems can lead to fraud. An organization can help employees deal with job or personal problems. First, the company can establish employee assistance programs that confidentially counsels employees about their problems. Second, the organization can have an open door policy within the organization. Managers can encourage good employee relationships. If managers are alert, they can identify danger signs and be available to assist.

8. *General conditions.* Other symptoms that promote fraud are near-term mergers or acquisitions, regulatory problems, rapid turnover of employees, too much trust in key employees, and lack of physical security.

24.12.2   Personal Symptoms

There are three specific symptoms of possible employee fraud. They are:

1. *Personal financial factor.* Employees are likely to commit fraud when they have serious financial problems. They are more likely to commit fraud as a solution to their problems. The symptoms exhibited are employees taking expensive vacations, purchasing expensive vehicles, boats, cottages, cabins, personal items, and bragging about their money.
2. *Personal habits.* Employee habits can induce fraud. Drug abuse, gambling, speculative investments, and maintaining a second household because of divorce can be strong indications of potential fraud.
3. *Personal feelings.* Employee feelings are another symptom for committing fraud. Employees with high expectations, perception of being mistreated by management, frustration with the job, and poor family or community relationships are likely candidates.

24.13   Kiting

Check kiting is a form of embezzlement. It is a form of fraud that embezzles a bank out of funds. It involves two or more bank accounts at two or more different banks. The objective is to cover-up a check or withdrawal that is not recorded on the books by writing checks from each bank account to another bank account. When the interbank checks clear, one bank loses out by the check(s) that were cashed or withdrawn. A bank transfer schedule is effective in detecting this scheme. A four or plus column bank reconciliation would clearly uncover this scheme.

24.14   Lapping

Lapping is an embezzlement scheme in which cash collections from customers are stolen. To keep the embezzlement from being discovered, the embezzler corrects the customer's accounts within a few days by posting other customer cash receipts to the account for which the proceeds have been embezzled. Lapping occurs most frequently when one individual has both record-keeping responsibility and custody of cash. Lapping will increase the average age of receivables and decrease turnover. The examiner should watch for posting of cash after an unusually long time. Also, the examiner should compare deposit slips from banks with names, dates, and amounts on remittance advises. The examiner should investigate customer complaints.

24.15   Ghost Employees

Funds are channeled to fictitious or former employees through phony salary payments known as ghost employees. This should be examined closely when union members are employed. Organized crime figures use ghost employees to channel funds. A common practice is to employ people who do not work or even show up on the job. In such cases, the examiner should compare payroll files with personnel files, employment applications, tax statements, insurance and union deductions, and payroll checks. Also, the examiner should compare travel and expense vouchers to employment records and tax records.

24.16 Illegal Activities

Organized crime groups, as well as individuals, operate illegal activities. These illegal activities encompass the following activities.

24.16.1 Arson

Arson can have one of several motives. One is a nonfinancial motive, and the another is for economic gain. An example of a nonfinancial motive would be a disgruntled employee. Most financial motives in arson are related to insurance claims or the elimination of competition. In case of insurance claims, the financial condition of the enterprise should be examined thoroughly to determine profitability. A losing enterprise will try to bail out by committing arson and file insurance claims. In the case of elimination of competition, the competitor will commit arson to cause financial hardship to the victim so they may not be able to recover or to disrupt the victim's operations.

24.16.2 Counterfeiting

Counterfeiting involves not only counterfeiting money but also food stamps, coupons, bonds, stock, credit cards, and anything else of value that can be duplicated. A key element of examining counterfeiters is obtaining the records from suppliers and vendors.

24.16.3 Frauds

"Con" men or women commit various kinds of fraud. Individuals, corporations, and partnerships commit it. There are many kinds of fraud. Fraud involves any means that human ingenuity can devise to take advantage over another by false suggestion or suppression of the truth. It encompasses any surprises, tricks, cunning, or any means to cheat, steal, or take anything of value from an individual or business. The victim(s) of such crimes has the documents and can testify in such cases.

24.16.4 Gambling

Organized crime groups, as well as some individuals, get involved in gambling activities. The most common are sports bookmaking, bingo, racetracks, casinos, and bolito (lottery). Most states have strong laws against gambling activities. In some states, gambling is legal but is highly regulated. Some states even have their own gambling (e.g., lotteries). In a previous chapter, gambling is addressed in more detail.

24.16.5   Illegal Alcohol

The production, sale, and distribution of alcohol is illegal in most states as well as at a federal level. The primary reason for the illegal sale of alcohol is the lack of collection of sales and/or excise taxes. Another reason is the alcohol may be contaminated in ways that could cause death if someone drinks it. This was a popular method of getting extra funds by various individuals. However, since the introduction of drugs and marijuana into our society, alcohol has become less of a concern to local or federal law enforcement. The key element is obtaining financial data on ingredients from suppliers and vendors.

24.16.6   Loan Sharking

Loan sharking is the illegal activity of loaning money to people at exorbitant rates of interest. Interest rates are normally charged between 2 and 5% per week or day. The loan shark requires a business front from which to conceal his/her illegal activities. This can be any kind of business. In some cases, the business was acquired on a defaulted loan or the loan shark has taken over from a legitimate owner as a front. Some of the signs of loan sharking are:

1. The collateral for the loan is not commensurate with the amount loaned.
2. The lender requires no references or financial statements.
3. The effective rate of interest is beyond legal limits.
4. The lender has no connection with any legal lending institution.
5. The borrower has a history of extensive gambling.
6. The borrower is living beyond his/her means.
7. There are excessive losses in the stock or bond market by the borrower.
8. Finder's fees are paid for securing financing.
9. There are high rates of thefts in the business.
10. Endorsements on checks indicate payments to people with no legitimate business connection to the business.
11. Money received is in the form of cash rather than by check.
12. The paperwork and/or loan documents are skimpy or nonexistent.

24.16.7   Narcotics

Narcotics involve the sale of any type of illegal drugs. This encompasses drugs such as heroin, cocaine, marijuana, and various synthetic or pharmaceutical drugs, whether legal or illegal. The fraud examiner must focus on the lifestyle of the drug trafficker.

24.16.8   Prostitution

This crime involves the sale of sexual intercourse. Pimps are individuals who control prostitutes as their "Johns" and the amount that they can earn. Pimps usually get a big cut of the profits or gross receipts, leaving the woman or man with little income. The prostitutes usually have to be totally dependent on the pimp. One fraud examiner determined income by counting the towels being used. Generally, the fraud examiner must focus on the lifestyle.

24.16.9 Protection Rackets

Protection rackets usually involve organized crime groups. Protection rackets encompass the charging of businesses for protection. This is like insurance, except that no protection is guaranteed. There are no benefits paid out like insurance. This is more prevalent in oriental communities today than anywhere else. The fraud examiner will have to rely on the victim(s), who, because of retaliation, may not cooperate.

24.16.10 Smuggling

Smuggling is an activity that involves the secret transportation of illegal goods either into or out of the country or both. Profits are made by the subsequent selling of those goods. The smuggler has no cost of sales or purchases. If invoices are provided, they will be false documents. If the supplier supplies invoices, then he/she is part of the conspiracy and must also be examined as well.

24.16.11 Stolen Property

Organized crime groups, as well as individuals, steal or buy and sell stolen property. This is called "fencing." Investigators look for the following signs of fencing:

1. The costs of purchases are unusually low.
2. Payments are made in cash.
3. There are no invoices, bills of laden, or shipping receipts.
4. The supplier cannot be identified.
5. The business owners, sellers of the merchandise, have no knowledge about the products they are selling.
6. The business has not been in existence very long.

24.17 Legal Activities

People involved in illegal activities must somehow "launder" their profits through legitimate businesses. Businesses that are most susceptible to "laundering" profits are:

1. *Auto agencies.* This is used as a front for stolen vehicles.
2. *Factoring.* Criminals in laundering corporate skimming and showing up as sales use this or payments of accounts receivable from various businesses.
3. *Food products.* Criminals use food stores as a way to launder money from illegal activities, as well as skimming sales receipts.
4. *Garment manufacturing.* Organized crime groups use this industry to sell off-brands for well-known brands of clothing. This industry is also susceptible to labor racketeering, kickbacks, ghost employees, and extortion.
5. *Jukeboxes and video machines.* This is used by criminals to obtain income without reporting the income to federal and state tax authorities. Also, it is an excellent vehicle for money laundering.

6. *Liquor distribution.* This involves stealing and selling liquor at discounts to liquor stores and bars. The profits, of course, are not reported to federal and state tax authorities.
7. *Night clubs.* Because this is a cash business, it lends itself to skimming. Organized crime groups use this to operate prostitution rings and extort funds from the dancers.
8. *Trade associations.* This involves labor racketeering. It exploits funds from labor unions, especially pension funds.
9. *Trucking.* Organized crime groups use trucking to extort higher fees for transportation of goods.
10. *Vending machines.* Like jukeboxes and video machines, vending machines are used to obtain income without reporting it to the tax authorities. However, profits can be more readily determined by use of the gross profit method as discussed in a previous chapter.
11. *Waste collections.* Organized crime groups use this industry to obtain funds without paying for dumping fees and violating environmental laws. Their customers are reluctant to cooperate because they are violating environmental laws.
12. *Construction.* Organized crime groups use this industry to extort funds from contractors. They do this in controlling labor and using ghost employees on the contractor payroll.
13. *Hotels and motels.* This industry lends itself to skimming as well as money laundering.
14. *Real estate.* This industry is used primarily for laundering money from illegal activities as an investment for criminals. However, it is also used for selling property above market values.
15. *Securities.* Criminals use this industry as a front for counterfeit securities, as well as money laundering.
16. *Mortgages.* Criminals use this as a means of laundering money. They usually charge higher rates in order to later repossess the valuable real estate at bargain prices.
17. *Entertainment.* Organized crime uses the entertainment industry to skim profits and steal funds from entertainers by basing their percentage on lower amount of gross receipts. Also, they use this to "bust out," which leaves owners holding the bag.
18. *Credit cards.* Criminals use credit cards to obtain merchandise, which is later fenced. The credit cards are usually stolen from customers or their numbers are used to make purchases. Some criminal groups steal the cards from the mail before the customer is able to receive them.
19. *Insurance.* Criminals sell insurance policies for companies that do not exist. Some criminals set up their own insurance companies with the intent of not paying claims.
20. *Labor.* Organized criminal groups exploit various labor groups. They do this by embezzling labor union funds. The major target by criminal groups is labor union pension funds because they consist of large amounts that need to be invested so funds are available for future benefits of its members.
21. *Banking.* Criminals like to defraud banks either by obtaining bad loans or check kiting. Drug traffickers like to use banks for laundering their illegal profits.

24.18   Intelligence

Before a fraud examiner commences any examination, he/she should obtain as much information about the possible type of fraud that is being committed. This intelligence will help the fraud examiner determine where he/she should focus his/her examination. If the fraud examiner has intelligence that a particular type of fraud is being committed, then he/she can focus his/her efforts where that type of fraud is being committed. This intelligence can save time and money for the client because the time of investigation and examination will be cut to a minimum. Companies with internal and/or external auditors should use them to develop as much evidence about the fraud scheme as possible before a fraud examiner is retained. The fraud examiner is interested in uncovering fraud and not issuing an opinion as to a company's financial condition.

24.19   Summary

The audit program is only a guide for the fraud examiner. It helps focus the examiner to where the fraud is being committed. However, the examiner must first rely on intelligence before he/she can start gathering evidence. If no intelligence is available, then the examiner must search for "red flags." Various types of analysis, financial and nonfinancial, can help identify those red flags. The biggest problem for fraud examiners is determining the effectiveness of internal controls. On paper, internal controls of a business look good, but when they are observed, they are often deficient or nonexistent.

Seizures and Forfeitures   25

25.1   Introduction

Forfeitures and seizures by government entities have been in existence since the American Revolution. England and the American Colonies have used forfeitures to enforce customs and revenue laws, and they are still used today in England, Canada, Australia, New Zealand, and the United States. During the twenty-first century, forfeiture and seizure laws have been expanded to encompass crimes, including drug trafficking and other "white-collar" crimes. Forfeitures are used in both civil and criminal cases, and today, they are used to deprive criminals of their illegal gains.

25.2   Federal Laws

The U.S. Government has many forfeiture laws on the books. The following is a partial list of forfeiture laws commonly used by federal prosecutors:

1. Title 18—Criminal Code
   Section 492—Counterfeiting
   Section 545—Smuggling
   Section 981—Civil Forfeiture ("white-collar" transactions)
   Section 982—Criminal Forfeiture ("white-collar" transactions)
   Section 1467—Obscene Materials
   Section 1956—Money Laundering
   Section 1957—Money Laundering
   Section 1963—Racketeering – Criminal
   Section 1964—Racketeering – Civil
   Section 2339C—Financing Terrorism
2. Title 19—Customs
   Section 1595(a)—Conveyances and Items Used to Facilitate Illegally Introduced Items
3. Title 21—Drugs and Controlled Substances
   Section 848—Continuing Criminal Enterprises
   Section 853—Drug Felonies – Criminal
   Section 881—Controlled Substances – Civil
4. Title 26—Taxation
   Section 7301—Property Subject to Tax
   Section 7302—Property Used in Violation of Internal Revenue Laws
   Section 7303—Other Property Subject to Forfeiture

5. Title 31—Money and Currency
   Section 5111—Coin Melting
   Section 5317—Unreported Monetary Instruments
   Section 5321—Civil Penalties
   Section 5322—Criminal Penalties
6. Title 49—Transportation
   Section 782—Contraband Seizures
   Section 1474—Civil Aircraft

25.3 Property

All kinds of property are subject to seizure and forfeiture, including all real and personal property, as well as tangible and intangible property. Many states also have forfeiture laws that are usually patterned after the federal statutes with some modifications. However, both federal and state forfeiture laws subject forfeitable property in the following categories:

25.3.1 Illegal Goods

Illegal goods consist of drugs, cigarettes, liquor, and other personal and intangible property that has been specifically outlawed by federal or state statutes. These assets can be seized and forfeited at the point of discovery. Contraband property is usually destroyed after criminal trials of defendants.

25.3.2 Direct Ties

Legal property, whether personal, real, or intangible, can be seized and forfeited if it can be shown that it was obtained from the proceeds from illegal activities. An example of this is when a drug trafficker purchases a vehicle (legal property) with the profits from the sale of drugs (illegal income). Also, the property used in the manufacture, distribution, and sale of contraband is subject to seizure and forfeiture. If an aircraft is discovered with illegal contraband, then the aircraft is subject to immediate seizure and forfeiture. The connection, or Nexus, between the illegal activity and the assets is the key element in direct seizures and forfeitures.

25.3.3 Indirect Ties

Illegal profits are sometimes mingled with legal sources, which make them impossible to distinguish. This is particularly true with organized crime organizations, which launder their illegal gains in legitimate sources. Congress has passed laws during the twenty-first century to overcome this obstacle. Al Capone was the first subject convicted using the Internal Revenue Code. In his case, the Internal Revenue Service used the net worth method of determining unreported taxable income. This method has been expanded, particularly under the Racketeer Influenced and Corrupt Organizations (RICO) Act and the Continuing Criminal Enterprise (CCE), to use the net worth and expenditure methods in determining illegal gains. After illegal gains have been determined, the forfeiture is based on the amount of the gain.

25.4   Civil Forfeiture

Civil forfeitures are legal actions against property. These are called "in rem" actions because they are made against property, not individuals or corporations. The burden of proof is not as great as in criminal actions. In other words, the rules of evidence are more relaxed. Civil actions only require the government to show "clear and convincing" evidence. Hearsay evidence can be introduced, and opinions can be expressed. However, unauthorized searches and wiretaps are not admissible. Civil forfeiture actions present a dilemma to subjects of criminal actions. If the civil actions take place before criminal proceedings, then the property owner can be compelled to produce evidence, which can later be used in criminal proceedings. Also, civil forfeiture actions can be instituted, while criminal actions may never be made. In addition, the property owner must establish control in addition to just having a legal title. The government is not required to show a direct relationship between the property seized and a specific drug transaction.

25.5   Criminal Forfeiture

Criminal forfeitures are made against a subject who has been convicted of a crime. Criminal forfeitures are called "in personam" because they are directed against a person. The rules of evidence are strictly adhered to in these cases. Reasonable doubt or "with reasonable certainty," when the net worth and expenditure methods are used, must be established in criminal cases. All evidence introduced in criminal proceedings can be used in any civil proceedings.

25.5.1   Direct Ties

Forfeitures and seizures can be made based on direct evidence that illegal gains were directly invested in identified assets. Assets that are used in the transportation, storage, purchase, and sale can be seized and forfeited. Any assets that are used in promotion of any illegal contraband can be seized and forfeited.

25.5.2   Indirect Ties

In criminal proceedings, assets can be forfeited whether or not used or acquired from illegal gains. The RICO and Continuing Criminal Enterprise statutes provide for forfeitures based on twice the illegal gains. This provides forfeiture of legally obtained assets as well as assets acquired from illegal activities. The RICO net worth and expenditure methods are used to determine the illegal gains.

25.6   Innocent Owner

The federal forfeiture laws make provisions for seizure and forfeiture of property of innocent owners. The burden of proof rests on the innocent owner to prove that he/she

1. Had no knowledge of the illegal use of the property
2. Was not a party to the illegal activity
3. Would have prevented the use of the property in the illegal activity if known

25.7 Federal Guidelines

In 1987, the U.S. Department of Justice issued guidelines on Seized and Forfeited Property. These guidelines were formulated because of the Comprehensive Crime Control Act of 1984 and the Anti-Drug Abuse Act of 1986, which addresses the disposition of forfeited property. These guidelines were promulgated to:

1. Promote cooperative law enforcement efforts in drug trafficking and other investigations
2. Ensure equitable transfer of forfeited property to the appropriate state or local law enforcement

25.8 Use and Transfer of Forfeited Property

The U.S. Attorney General has the authority to retain any civilly or criminally forfeited property or to transfer the property to other federal, state, or local law enforcement agencies. In order for the Attorney General to transfer forfeited property to any federal, state, or local law enforcement agency, the law enforcement agency must have directly participated in the acts that led to the seizure or forfeiture. The Attorney General or his/her designee on an equitable basis will determine the transfer of forfeited property. The basis will generally be on the relative contribution of the participating agencies to the investigation leading to its seizure and forfeiture. Property that is transferred to federal, state, or local agencies is to be used to increase resources for that agency. It is not to be used for salaries and regular operating expenses. If the federal forfeiture action is concluded successfully and the property is not placed into official use or transferred to a federal, state, or local agency, it will be sold and the net proceeds of sale will be placed in the Assets Forfeiture Fund. Forfeited cash will also be placed in the Asset Forfeiture Fund. If real or tangible property is transferred to federal, state, or local agencies, the recipient must pay the liens and mortgages on the forfeited property as well as any expenses in transferring the property.

25.9 Assets Forfeiture Fund

The Attorney General has made the U.S. Marshal Service responsible for administering the Assets Forfeiture Fund. There are two categories of reimbursements from the fund:

1. *Asset-specific reimbursements.* Asset-specific expenses are reimbursements for the management expenses. These take priority over program-related expenses. Asset-specific expenses are:
   a. Expenses incurred for safeguarding, maintenance, or disposal of seized or forfeited property whether by federal, state, or local agencies

    b. Payments on orders of mitigation or remission

    c. Payments of valid liens and mortgages pursuant to court order

    d. Equitable transfer payments to state or local law enforcement agencies

    e. Payments for contract service relating to the processing of and accounting for seizures and forfeitures

    f. Payments for storage, protection, and destruction of controlled substances

    g. Case-specific expenses relating to travel and subsistence, cost of depositions, messenger services, expert witnesses, and other direct costs

2. *Program-related expenses.* The following are program-related expenses:

    a. Expenses for the purchase or lease of computer equipment and related services, at least 90% of which will be dedicated to seizure- or forfeiture-related record keeping

    b. Payments to authorized investigative agents for the purchase of controlled substances

    c. Expenses incurred to equip any conveyance

    d. Payment of awards in recognition of information or assistance given to an investigator

    e. Expenses for training that relates to the execution of seizure or forfeiture responsibilities

    f. Expenses incurred for printing training material

25.10 Liens and Mortgages

Liens and mortgages can only be paid pursuant to an order of remission or mitigation or an order of the court. Otherwise, such amounts shall be paid from the proceeds of sale. The payment of liens and mortgages can be paid if they are beneficial to the government. Two circumstances exist for this:

1. Payment prior to the sale will improve the government's ability to convey title.
2. The property is to be placed into official use by the government.

Payments to unsecured creditors of seized and forfeited property are generally not allowed. However, in the case of a business, claims incurred within 30 days before the seizure can be paid. In addition, payments can be made for reasonable salaries and benefits of employees not believed to have been involved in the unlawful activities giving rise to the forfeiture and not having any ownership interest in the firm. Third party contractors of goods and services can be paid in order to carry on the business activity of the firm in a regular manner. Utilities also can be paid.

25.11 Internal Revenue Service Rewards

The Internal Revenue Service has provisions under Title 26 of the U.S. Code to reward both informants and state and local law enforcement for providing information on violation of Federal Tax Laws. Employees of the Treasury Department and individuals who are employed by other federal, state, or local law enforcement are not eligible to receive any awards. Informants can have their identity anonymous. Rewards are divided into two categories.

25.11.1 Informants

Under Section 7623, Internal Revenue Code and related regulations, an informant can receive up to 10% of the amount of taxes, penalties, and fines that are recovered. However, this 10% ceiling does not bind the IRS to fix the amount with regard to any percentage or formula. Although the law indicates that an informant may be rewarded for supplying information to the IRS, it does not bind the IRS to reward all informants. The informant must file Form 211 with either the District Director of the district that he/she resides in or the Commissioner of the Internal Revenue Service in Washington, DC.

25.11.2 State and Local Law Enforcement

Under Section 7624, Internal Revenue Code and related regulations, state and local law enforcement can get reimbursed by the Internal Revenue Service for costs incurred (e.g., salaries, overtime pay, per diem, and similar reasonable expenses), but should not exceed 10% of the sum recovered. This is a cost reimbursement program and not a reward program. Therefore the state and local law enforcement must meet certain criteria:

1. The federal taxes imposed must be related to illegal drug trafficking or related money-laundering activities.
2. No other reimbursement has been made under federal or state forfeiture programs or state revenue laws.
3. The Internal Revenue Service must not have the individual already under investigation.
4. The taxes, penalties, and fines must aggregate more than $50,000 in order to be eligible for reimbursement. This is called the de minimis rule.
5. Reimbursement of expenses cannot exceed 10% of the total taxes, penalties, and fines collected.

25.12 Summary

Fraud examiners get involved in forfeitures; therefore, they should understand the legal reasons for the forfeitures and seizures. In many criminal cases, the fraud examiner's work product either directly or indirectly involves forfeitures. When an examiner determines the income from illegal activities, it is this figure that can be used to determine the forfeiture, whether a civil or criminal case. One of the primary purposes of forfeitures is to take away the profits gained from illegal activities.

Judicial System 26

26.1 Introduction

An important element that the fraud examiner should know is how the judicial system is organized and how it operates. When a fraud examiner uncovers fraud, the examiner must know how to get a case prosecuted. To do this, the fraud examiner must know to whom the crime must be reported, what procedures must be followed, and what the policies are. The fraud examiner should be aware of how the case progresses through the legal system to its ultimate conclusion. This chapter gives the fraud examiner an overview of the judicial system in the United States.

26.2 History

The law as we know it is the outgrowth of the legal systems of England and Rome. The English jurist Blackstone defined law as "a rule of civil conduct prescribed by the supreme power of the state, commanding what is right and prohibiting what is wrong." The Roman orator Cicero stated, "The State without law would be like the human body without a mind." Legal systems, which are based on Roman codes and customs, are commonly referred to as civil law jurisdictions, while those derived from Britain are known as common law jurisdictions. The civil law is followed in Europe, South and Central America; the common law is followed in the United States, Canada, and Australia, with the exceptions of Louisiana and Quebec, whose legal codes are based on civil law. In addition to the civil and common law, canon law has made an imprint on our jurisprudence system by the Roman Catholic and Anglican Churches. The law merchant, a body of rules governing medieval business affairs of the mercantile class, has also influenced modern jurisprudence.

During the early part of the fifth century B.C., the lower classes in Rome, unequally treated in the application of customs prevailing at the time, became increasingly discontented. As a result of their protests, in 449 B.C. the so-called Twelve Tables were promulgated, codifying the customs and making them applicable to all Romans. These tables remained in effect for 400 years.

By the opening of the Christian era, Rome had become a vast superstate, ruled by an emperor. During the ensuing centuries, economic and social conditions changed drastically, causing many imperial decrees and administrative orders to be added to the body of law. By the sixth century A.D., it was almost impossible to determine the law governing any particular controversy. The Byzantine Emperor Justinian began the task of clarifying and organizing this mass of Roman law. The Code of Justinian was published in 528–534 A.D. together with the Digest (excerpts from the writings of Roman jurists), the Institutes (a short manual for law students and jurists), and the Novels (a new constitution). The Code of Justinian established a legal and legislative reform that lasted until the fall of the eastern Roman Empire in the fourteenth century.

Interest in the civil law system was revived in medieval Italy during the Christian Renaissance period. While the Church originally was hostile to Roman law, probably because Justinian's code emphasized the secular against the clerical authority as the supreme power of the state, it soon encouraged the study of civil law and reemphasized the significance and benefits of a formal system of jurisprudence. The legal profession was then created and training in Latin and Roman law was required of all law students, who were later employed as administrators by members of royalty.

The English common law, upon which most all of our American law is founded, came into existence after the Norman Conquest in 1066 A.D. Before that there was no "law of England," and feudal law, with its system of manorial courts, was just in the process of creation. The ruling Anglo-Saxons governed various parts of England according to local custom, thereby eliminating any possibility of a uniform system of law. The clergy were separately governed by canon law, administered in the ecclesiastical courts (Courts Christian). Before the Norman Conquest, it was not unusual for the bishop to preside in the secular courts. After the conquest, William I introduced many administrative reforms, strengthened the feudal courts, and made real effort to separate the ecclesiastical from the secular jurisdictions.

The common law actually began under Henry I, after 1100 A.D. It developed into a system of separate royal courts, such as the Courts of the Exchequer, each court developing its own substantive and procedural law. The law was referred to then as the King's Justice and was administered by justices appointed by the ruling monarch. In nearly all cases, these justices were members of the ruling class. In most cases, these justices were members of the clergy who exerted royal jurisdiction by a system of writs. These writs were authorizations or directions to the sheriff to summon a litigant to appear before the court for the purpose of answering a claim of a royal officer, a member of the nobility, or a wealthy patron. General considerations of fairness and equity, according to prevailing views of society, were supposed to be the foundation of legal decisions by the justices. Roman legal scholars had boasted of their enlightened maxim: *Salus populi suprema lex* (the people's welfare is the supreme law). In England at this time, the Norman trial by battle or ordeal was a frequent means of determining legal rights in both civil and criminal actions.

Writs in the King's courts were not readily available to persons of ordinary means. They were extremely costly and limited to certain types of cases. This gave rise to the establishment of chancery courts and the development of a body of law known as equity law. The rapidly growing number of writs eventually made it possible to collect them and to put them into law books, which later became known as registers. The registers were the first formal collation of legal precedents. By 1297 A.D. and the appearance of the Magna Carta, the law of the King's court had acquired the special name of common law. Publications of the King's courts, written by legal scholars, gave a yearly record of all cases argued before the courts. These yearbooks contained the common law and laid the foundation for this system's reliance on precedent. Reliance on precedent is the most significant difference between the common law and the civil law.

The English colonists in America, despite the fact that they sought to free themselves of the British yoke, brought with them the prevailing English legal system. The common law of England found its way into many local ordinances and state constitutions. Most states have enacted many statutory reforms to replace the outmoded and narrow common law concepts to furnish a better basis for the simpler administration of the law and justice in our courts according to the needs of our growing and ever-changing society. The Anglo-American systems of jurisprudence, while relying on precedent as a guide, are notable for their ability to accept new ideas and principles by which equitable and speedy justice can be attained.

26.3 Local Law Enforcement

In the United States, law enforcement authorities have been decentralized down to the local communities. Local communities consist of municipalities that are cities or towns having their own incorporated government. These incorporated municipalities are organized into departments, which have a police department. The police department is under the control of local mayors and city commissioners. The city commission passes ordinances, which the police department is required to enforce. Also, the police departments are empowered to enforce federal and state laws. They operate with almost complete autonomy within its jurisdiction. The police have a great amount of discretion as to the laws that they will enforce and on whom they will impose the laws and ordinances. However, they do not and cannot enforce laws, including federal and state, outside their respective jurisdictions. On occasion, local police work with state or federal law enforcement agencies on "task forces." While on these task forces, they are granted temporary authority outside their jurisdiction.

States are divided into various counties, which have their own county governments. These county governments have a law enforcement department, usually called the sheriff's office or department. The sheriff's department, like the police department, is subject to local control; it is under the control of the county commissioners and mayors. It enforces county ordinances and state and federal laws and has autonomy within its jurisdiction. In addition, it can enforce the city ordinances that are located within its county. The sheriff's department has discretion regarding what laws and ordinances it will enforce and to whom it will enforce them. Sheriff departments have jurisdiction within the municipalities within their county. However, they will usually not interfere with the police in their jurisdiction.

26.4 Officers and Deputies

Police officers and deputy sheriffs normally come from middle class families with close family ties. Most people become police officers because they are attracted to a civil service job. Most recruits have only high school diplomas. In recent years, many local law enforcement agencies are requiring applicants to have associate and bachelor degrees before being hired. Some police departments recruit from the military because of the maturity, discipline, and training of such applicants. Since police carry weapons, wear uniforms, and are instructed into a military type of organization, police departments are sometimes viewed as paramilitary organizations. Many large police and sheriff departments have special weapons and tactics (SWAT) teams. These SWAT teams were formed to combat the more violent members of society. Members of SWAT teams are usually former military people because these tactics come from military operations.

The local police have greater contact with members of the community. As a result, they see and come into closer contact with criminals than anyone else. They see criminal acts or the aftermath firsthand. Horrible accidents and violent crime scenes cause police to become dispassionate. They view the court system as too lenient against the hardened criminal. Some police feel the bureaucracy within their department restricts them from doing their jobs. Even though corruption within a department may involve only a small number or percentage, it causes polarization of the community, those supportive versus those critical. Some police officers constantly see criminals with high living standards, far above their own. This, in turn, causes some police officers to cross over to the criminal's side and become corrupt. Those police officers that see corruption in the local political structure may become corrupt along with it. If they try to fight it, then they lose any promotion opportunities or are transferred to menial assignments.

26.5   State Law Enforcement

All states have their respective law enforcement agencies that are responsible for enforcing state laws. The state, unlike counties and municipalities, has more than one law enforcement agency. The states structure their agencies into specialty areas. The state police enforce traffic laws on the highways and other crimes that cross county lines. Other departments within the state have agencies that have law enforcement powers. Revenue departments have agents that go after tax evaders. The Insurance Department has agents that investigate and prosecute fraudulent claims and insurance companies. Departments of Business and Professional Regulations investigate and prosecute crimes relating to various businesses and professions. Business crimes might include improper liquor, cigarette, land, banking, and restaurant operations. Professional crimes would include investigating and prosecuting crimes relating to professional groups, for example, medical, law, engineering, accounting, nursing, and pharmacy.

States generally require higher standards and education for their agents. This is mostly because the crimes they have to investigate require greater skills. A normal high school graduate would not have the skills to investigate such crimes as medical malpractice, securities and banking fraud, racketeering, criminal enterprises, and insurance.

26.6   Federal Law Enforcement

Because Americans do not want a national police force similar to some countries, the federal government has established law enforcement agencies within each department. Each law enforcement agency is only responsible for enforcing the laws and regulations for that department. Americans have been reluctant to have a national police force because it would pose a threat of quasi-military power. Even the military in the United States comes under civilian control.

The U.S. Department of Justice is the primary department for prosecuting criminals. Within the Justice Department, there are many law enforcement agencies. The principal law enforcement agencies are as follows:

1. The Federal Bureau of Investigation is responsible for investigating most federal crimes. It also investigates criminals who cross state lines to avoid prosecution.
2. The U.S. Marshal Service is responsible for courtroom security and going after criminals who flee from prosecution. It produces prisoners for trials and is responsible for service of process.

3. The Border Patrol is responsible for patrolling U.S. borders and investigating alien smuggling and apprehending illegal aliens.
4. The Drug Enforcement Agency is responsible for investigating and apprehending drug traffickers and other drug violations.

The U.S. Treasury Department has many law enforcement agencies. These include the following:

1. The Secret Service protects the president and other federal and foreign officials. It investigates counterfeiting of currency and other government obligations and credit card fraud.
2. The U.S. Customs Service enforces customs laws, duties, and products entering or leaving the United States. It is responsible for drug interdiction into or out of the United States.
3. The Internal Revenue Service enforces the federal tax law. In the 1980s, it was made responsible for enforcing money-laundering statutes.
4. The Bureau of Alcohol, Tobacco, and Firearms is responsible for investigations involving firearms, explosives, interstate arson, and liquor violations.

The U.S. Postal Service has a law enforcement agency called Postal Inspection. Postal inspectors investigate mail fraud and mailing of obscene and dangerous materials. There are other federal law enforcement agencies in the other departments. The Defense Department has its investigative services. The Environmental Protection Agency enforces federal pollution laws. The list goes on.

Like the states enforcement agencies, the federal law enforcement agencies usually require higher standards and education. The crimes that federal agents investigate are sophisticated and require a high degree of knowledge and expertise in their respective areas. Each department not only trains its agents in law enforcement but also in the laws in the respective fields.

26.7 Foreign Law Enforcement

Most countries maintain a national police agency. Some countries have a national police agency that also doubles as a military force. In Britain, police are under local control, but the home office sets nationwide standards.

Several large criminal organizations operate on an international scale. This makes it hard for law enforcement to investigate and prosecute such people. Criminals will flee from one country and seek refuge in another to avoid prosecution. Police in one country have difficulty in obtaining information and cooperation from another country. In 1923, the International Criminal Police Organization (INTERPOL) was formed for the purpose of promoting mutual assistance among international law enforcement authorities. This assistance includes coordinating and aiding international arrests and extraditions and providing a way to expedite the exchange of criminal justice information. At the present time, there are 125 members of INTERPOL. INTERPOL is not an international police agency but a conduit for cooperative exchange of criminal information to help detect and combat international crime. Each participating country sets up a national central bureau that serves as the country's point of contact with the international law enforcement community. Each country operates its national central bureau within the parameters of its own national laws and policies. In the United States, the INTERPOL function rests by law with the Attorney General. The U.S. National Central Bureau (USNCB) is under the control of the departments of justice and treasury.

Agents, analysts, communicators, translators, and clerical support personnel staff the USNCB. Most employees are with the department of justice. However, other federal and state law enforcement personnel are detailed on a regular basis. With the increase of international crime, the USNCB has arranged with the states a point of contact for a full range of international services. The liaison office in that state forwards requests for investigative assistance from abroad, which requires action by the police of a particular state, to the USNCB. INTERPOL provides the following services:

1. Criminal history checks
2. License plate/driver's license check
3. Full investigation leading to arrest and extradition
4. Location of suspects, fugitives, and witnesses
5. International wanted circulars
6. Traces of weapons, motor vehicles abroad
7. Other types of criminal investigations

26.8   Misdemeanor versus Felony

In the United States, crimes are divided into two categories: misdemeanors and felonies. Misdemeanors are generally considered trivial crimes. They impose incarceration at local detention facilities and/or fines and penalties of relatively small amounts. Parking and traffic violations are considered misdemeanors. Improper use of property or authority can be classified as a misdemeanor. Misdemeanor crimes are usually heard before a county or municipal judge or magistrate. There are no juries. The judge or magistrate serves as both judge and jury. The people that are found guilty of misdemeanor crimes do not go to state detention facilities. In most cases, they only pay fines. Some states divide misdemeanors into grades according to the degree of seriousness, such as gross misdemeanors and petit or simple misdemeanors.

A felony is a crime that is or may be punishable by death or imprisonment in a state prison. The possible sentence, not the actual one imposed by the court, determines the grade of the violation of law and whether the crime is a felony or misdemeanor. Before a person can be punished, the person's acts must be plainly and unmistakably prohibited or compelled by a statute. Any and every reasonable doubt must be resolved in favor of the accused, inasmuch as personal liberty and perhaps life are at stake. This principle of strict construction does not require that a criminal statute be given a narrow meaning. The language of the law is to be given its natural, reasonable, and accepted meaning in an effort to determine the legislative intent. The law distinguishes crimes as *mala in se* (bad in themselves) and *mala prohibita* (bad because prohibited). Acts such as murder, arson, rape, and robbery, which obviously are so evil in themselves and inherently violate the mores of society, are classified as *mala in se*. Other acts, which are deemed wrong only because a specific law declares them to be wrong, are classified as *mala prohibita*.

26.9 Hearings

Hearings are informal trials before a county or municipal judge or magistrate. There are no juries. The local judge or magistrate acts as both judge and jury. These hearings handle misdemeanors, bond or bail arrangements, criminal arraignments, and small civil disputes. The federal courts use hearings for bail or bond arrangements, sentencing, and some civil disputes.

26.10 Grand Jury

A grand jury is so called because it normally has more members than the ordinary trial jury. A grand jury consists of 16–23 people. However, some states have statutes that mandate fewer people. Grand juries may be impaneled under either federal or state law and classified as a "regular" or "special" grand jury, depending on the reason they are convened. A regular grand jury is so designated because it is routinely impaneled to perform the function of a grand jury and is the forum for presentation of cases developed through the normal investigative processes of law enforcement agencies. The court, often at the request of a state or U.S. attorney to investigate specific complaints or allegations of crime, convenes special grand juries. Special grand juries may be convened to investigate potential crimes involving casinos, union pension plans, and corruption in public agencies or offices.

26.10.1 History

It is generally agreed that the grand jury originated in England as an investigatory tool for the crown, its development usually being traced from the Assize of Clarendon, which was proclaimed by Henry II in 1166. However, its defined purpose in exercising its accusatorial and investigative function emerged as one of protecting the accused against unfounded charges rather than of furthering arbitrary prosecutions at the will of the sovereign. By the time the grand jury was brought to this country by the early colonists, it was firmly established in the common law as an important institution for the protection of citizens' rights and privileges. This historical protective function of the grand jury was incorporated into the Fifth Amendment to the Constitution as a guarantee that "no person shall be held to answer for a capital, or other infamous crime, unless on a presentment or indictment of a Grand Jury." Scholars of U.S. constitutional law generally regard the modern grand jury as being part of the judicial rather than the executive or legislative branch of government.

26.10.2 Rule 6, Federal Rules of Criminal Procedure

The adoption of the Federal Rules of Criminal Procedure in the 1940s established the first concise definition of federal grand jury procedural requirements. Rule 6 defines the role and procedures for federal grand juries. The following is a synopsis of Rule 6.

1. *Generally.* The court shall order one or more grand juries to be summoned at such time as the public interest requires. The grand jury shall consist of not less than 16 nor more than 23 members.
2. *Objections.* The attorney for the government or a defendant who has been held to answer in the district court may challenge the array of jurors on the ground that the grand jury was not selected, drawn, or summoned in accordance with law. They may challenge an individual juror on the ground that the juror is not legally qualified. Challenges shall be made before the administration of the oath to the jurors and shall be tried by the court.
3. *Foreperson.* The court shall appoint one of the jurors to be foreperson and another to be deputy foreperson. The foreperson shall have power to administer oaths and affirmations and shall sign all indictments. The foreperson is responsible for keeping a record of concurring findings of every indictment. During the absence of the foreperson, the deputy foreperson shall act as foreperson.
4. *Who may be present.* Attorneys for the government, the witness under examination, interpreters when needed, and for the purpose of taking the evidence, a stenographer may be present while the grand jury is in session, but no person other than the jurors may be present while the grand jury is deliberating or voting.
5. *Disclosure.* A grand juror, an interpreter, a stenographer, an attorney for the government, or any person to whom disclosure is made shall not disclose matters occurring before the grand jury. A violation of Rule 6 may be punished as a contempt of court.
6. *Return of indictment.* An indictment may be found only upon the concurrence of 12 or more jurors. The indictment shall be returned by the grand jury to a federal magistrate in open court. If a complaint or information is pending against the defendant and 12 jurors do not concur in finding an indictment, the foreperson shall so report to a federal magistrate in writing forthwith.

26.10.3 Secrecy

The requirement that secrecy of grand jury proceedings be maintained is one which developed gradually in English common law to protect the independence of the grand jury. 5 reasons are traditionally given in modern common law for this requirement of secrecy:

1. To encourage the free expression of witnesses by affording them the maximum freedom of disclosure without fear of reprisal
2. To prevent perjury by witnesses who might otherwise come forward to falsely controvert or reinforce other grand jury evidence, which they might learn about
3. To permit confidentially of the grand jury's interest in order to prevent prospective defendants from fleeing
4. To prevent disclosing knowledge of investigations that results in no grand jury action
5. To assure the grand jury freedom from outside interference

26.10.4 Pretrial Procedures

After the information (complaint) or indictment has been rendered, the defendant will appear before a judge or magistrate for arraignment. The defendant's lawyer may force the prosecution by use of a writ of habeas corpus the substantive reasons for depriving the accused of liberty. Bail is also set during the arraignment. The defendant can file motions. These motions fall into two classes:

1. Motions to correct defects in the complaint
2. Motions for judgment upon the complaint in favor of the defendant

All motions addressed to the complaint must be made promptly. The rules of procedure governing this type of relief generally provide for specific time limitations within which such motion practice is available to the defendant.

In most states, provisions for the examination before trial of a party and of a witness were expanded and liberalized. The practice of taking the testimony of parties and witnesses is a common one. The main objective of examination before trial in all jurisdictions is to allow a party to obtain material and necessary evidence for the prosecution or defense of an action. Going on "fishing expeditions" is not permitted. Depositions must contain both direct examination and cross-examination of a witness before they can be admissible in court. The court can suppress (forbid the use of) depositions for a variety of reasons, including fraud, unfair and overreaching conduct, improper or irregular procedure in taking or returning a deposition, and evasiveness or refusal of witnesses to answer questions put to them on cross-examination.

26.11   Trial

After arraignment, pretrial motions have been ruled on, and discovery (providing the defense all the evidence that will be used in trial) has been made, the case is ready to go to trial. The purpose of the trial will be to determine the issues of fact. The court determines questions of law. The trial is conducted by stringent rules regarding both evidence and procedures. There are seven stages of a trial:

26.11.1   Jury Selection

Jury members have to be selected. Usually, there are 12 jurors who have to be selected along with one or more alternate jurors, so that if a juror becomes ill or otherwise unable to complete the trial, an alternate may be substituted for such disabled juror without any disruption of the proceedings. This selection process is called voir dire examination. Both prosecution and defense examine prospective jurors about their qualifications to serve. The objective is to determine which jurors will reach an objective verdict without any biases or prejudices. A challenge to the poll is an objection to an individual prospective juror. Such objection may be for cause or peremptory. A challenge for cause may ordinarily be either for principal cause or to the favor. Principal cause involves the legal presumption that a juror would not try the case fairly; for example, if there is a close relationship between the prospective juror and a party to the action. A challenge to the favor is merely an assertion of a suspicion rather than a legal presumption that the juror will be prejudiced in the trial of the case. The court may dismiss a juror at any time before evidence is given in the action. In a peremptory challenge, no reason need be given. Peremptory challenges vary according to the crime charged. If the crime charged is punishable by death, 30 or more peremptory challenges may be allowed. If the crime is punishable with imprisonment for life or for a term of 10 years or more, 20 challenges are normally available. In all other criminal cases, law permits about 5 peremptory challenges.

26.11.2 Opening Arguments

Opening addresses to the jury by both plaintiff and defendant are the next order of procedure. The purpose of counsel's opening remarks to the jury is merely to advise the jury of the general nature of the issues, which the jury ultimately will have to determine. Usually, counsel tells the jury what the counsel expects (or hopes) to prove during the trial.

26.11.3 Evidence by the Prosecution

The prosecution has to present its evidentiary facts. Although it is true that evidentiary facts, for the most part, are adduced by the testimony of witnesses, there are, in fact, four methods of proving a case:

1. Presenting oral statements of sworn witnesses
2. Requesting the court to take judicial notice of matters of law
3. Offering in evidence documents that require no witnesses for their introduction
4. Offering in evidence documents identified by the oral testimony of a sworn witness

It is apparent that witnesses are often necessary, not only to testify to material evidentiary facts within their own knowledge but also to identify documents which would otherwise be inadmissible in evidence. If proper identification is made and a foundation is laid for the introduction of such documents in evidence, the facts contained in them may then be used by counsel to prove the allegations of the pleadings. No unsworn testimony is admissible in courts. Defense counsel has the right and obligation to cross-examine the prosecution's witnesses.

26.11.4 Evidence by the Defense

After the prosecution has presented its case, the defense presents its case. Counsel's questions must be competent, relevant, and material, and should conform to the well-established rules of evidence. Except to the limited extent permitted by specific statute, parties may not impeach their own witnesses. By that is meant that parties may not call witnesses to prove that their prior witness's general reputation is bad, that the witness is unworthy of belief, or that the witness made contradictory statements out of court. A witness must generally be asked questions that the witness can answer with evidentiary facts within the witness's own knowledge, unless the witness is called as an expert witness, in which event the witness may give opinion evidence. Leading questions are not permissible on direct examination unless the witness called by counsel is a hostile witness or an adverse witness. If opposing counsel deems a question put to a witness to be improper in form or content, counsel may object and have the court rule on such objection. Regardless of the nature of the objection, it should always be made as soon as the question is put to the witness and before it is answered. Sometimes, the witness's answer comes so fast that counsel is unable to make the objection first. In this event, if the objection is a proper one, it will be deemed timely, and the court will order the answer stricken from the record. In reality, nothing is stricken from the record.

26.11.5 Closing Arguments

Both sides are allowed to make closing arguments after presenting their case. Closing arguments are basically a summation of their case. They make their points in their case as previously presented to the jury. The prosecution presents its closing argument first. The defense then presents its closing argument, which is followed by the prosecution's rebuttal.

26.11.6 Jury Deliberations

After the closing arguments, the court will give the jury instructions regarding the law and its application to the issues involved. The law must be applied as charged, as presented to the jury by the trial court, regardless of whether the jury agrees or disagrees with it. Simply stated, the jury is the trier of the facts, while the court determines and instructs as to the applicable principles of law. It is well established in this country that the jury alone is responsible for determining questions of fact. The jury is bound only by its recollections and interpretations of the evidence adduced at the trial and not by the court's statement of fact in its charge. In fact, if the court calls material facts not in evidence to the attention of the jury, the charge will be deemed improper and a reversal will undoubtedly result.

26.11.7 Verdict

After the court has charged the jury, the jury will be secluded for its deliberations. The jury will take the case and decide it on the evidence, without sympathy or prejudice, with the sole desire of eliciting the truth and establishing such truth by a fair verdict. The jury may vote either by open or secret ballot on the innocence or guilt of the defendant. The foreperson will usually count the votes. In capital cases, each member of the jury must find the defendant guilty. Any one dissension will result in a "hung" jury, in effect no verdict. After a verdict has been reached, the foreperson will either read the verdict in open court or will have the verdict delivered to the court for open reading.

If the defendant is found not guilty of the offense(s), then he or she is able to walk out of the courtroom as a free person. If the defendant is found guilty of all or part of the charges, then the defendant will be taken to the detention facilities for further disposition. The court will order a sentencing hearing. The prosecution and defense will have to prepare for this hearing.

26.11.8 Plea Bargaining

Some criminals, especially those who know that they are guilty, want to plea bargain. Plea bargaining is a way of getting more lenient treatment. They know that if they go to trial and are found guilty, then they could get a harsher sentence. In areas where the courts are overloaded with cases, plea bargaining is welcomed. It reduces the time and expense of trial and saves the taxpayer money. Plea bargaining could involve the reduction of charges from a felony to a misdemeanor. Also, it could mean that the defendant would serve less time in a local "stockade" instead of serving longer in a state prison. There are many arguments for and against plea bargaining. Plea bargaining can offer swift justice. Alternatively, it does not get hardened criminals off the streets and also does not rehabilitate criminals.

26.11.9   Sentencing

Before 1984, judges had a lot of leeway in determining sentences for convicted criminals. Sentences ranged from 2 years and up depending on the crime. However, in 1984, the Crime Control Act was passed. This act provided sentencing guidelines, which the U.S. court system must follow. It mandates the possible sentences for a particular crime. The U.S. Supreme Court, on January 18, 1989, upheld the new sentencing guidelines in *Mistretta v. United States*. These new sentencing guidelines came about because

1. A person, presumably, will not go "straight."
2. The system was unfair because of different sentences for the same type of crime.
3. The public was disillusioned with the rehabilitation process.

Before sentencing, the judge will order a presentencing investigation. The purpose of this investigation is to determine the appropriate sentence. Both the prosecution and defense will present their opinions and facts. The convicted criminal's background will be examined. Prior convictions for the same or similar acts will influence the judge to hand out a harsher sentence. However, the judge can be influenced to issue a lighter sentence because of family life, community involvement, and the seriousness of the offense.

At the sentencing hearing, the judge will hear arguments from both the prosecution and the defense. The defendant, also, will have the opportunity to express his/her case. In nolo contendere (no contest) cases, the judge will further ask the defendant if he or she knows the consequences of the decision not to contest the charges. Judges are not bound to give a lesser sentence if the defendant pleads out. After hearing all arguments, the judge pronounces the sentence.

26.11.10   Punishment

There are various forms of punishment that a judge can mete out:

1. *Jail.* The criminal will be sent to a local detention facility for a term of up to 1 year.
2. *Prison.* The criminal will be sent to a state or federal prison system for a term of 1 year or more. Most criminals would rather go to a federal prison than a state prison because conditions in state prisons are generally harsher and more inhumane than federal prisons. Criminals sentenced 10 years or less in the federal system will go to prisons that are called "Club Fed" because they do not have the harsher rules and regulations that the state prisons have imposed.
3. *Probation.* The criminal will not go to prison or jail but will be required to live by a set of rules, which are enforced by a probation officer. The criminal will only be allowed to do certain activities and will be forbidden to do others. The probation officer is expected to help the criminal and also to keep the criminal out of further lawbreaking activities. Another version of probation is house arrest. Criminals

are not allowed to leave their home without permission. They wear an electronic device, which will alert authorities of their whereabouts or if they leave a designated area. Removing the electronic device will alert authorities that they have violated the "probation" and result in a return to jail or prison.

4. *Community service.* In misdemeanor or minor felony cases, the judge may order the criminal to perform community services. These services include, but are not limited to, cleaning up parks, roads, and helping the elderly or children. This is done without any compensation. A specific number of hours or days is specified. This form of punishment is becoming more popular because it helps cities and municipalities in economic hard times by reducing the cost of detaining people in jails or prisons and by reducing the cost of hiring personnel to perform these functions. Another version of this form of punishment is the "halfway" house. These houses are mostly directed at rehabilitation of drug and alcohol offenders.

26.12 Summary

Forensic accountants must be familiar with the judicial system and how it works because they will be involved in the system in one way or another. It is not unusual for forensic accountants to be involved from the start to the finish. This means that they will be involved:

1. From the initial investigation
2. To present evidence to a grand jury
3. To testify in trial
4. To present expert testimony in civil proceedings following the criminal case

Forensic accountants are involved in all phases of the judicial system.

Criminology

27

27.1 Introduction

Criminologists study crime and justice within the social order. Sociologists study society and its social order. Some scholars think of criminology as a field of sociology, whereas others view it as a field of psychology. Criminology in recent years has become a separate field of study, and it has incorporated some of the theories from both sociology and psychology. Sociologists have been instrumental in helping law enforcement understand organized crime and youth gangs. Psychologists have helped law enforcement understand criminal behavior. The FBI has developed a method called "profiling." This method uses crime scene evidence to determine the psychological makeup of a criminal. It is also used by other law enforcement agencies to identify drug traffickers, serial killers, and rapists. This chapter provides an overview of the field of criminology and the basic theories.

27.2 History

The field of criminology did not emerge until the eighteenth century when an Italian, Cesare Beccaria (1764), wrote an essay "On Crime and Punishment." An English contemporary, Jeremy Bentham, wrote "Principals of Morals and Legislation" (1789). These two individuals are considered the founders of criminology. A century later, several other schools of criminology developed. One of the schools was labeled the Positivist School. This school was promoted by Cesare Lombroso and his followers, Enrico Ferri and Raffaele Garofalo. The other school was the Conflict School. This school was originated by the writings of Karl Marx in Das Kapital (1867–1895).

During the nineteenth century, other professional groups developed theories for criminal behavior. An Austrian physician, Dr. Franz Josef Gall, formulated the theory of phrenology. Charles Caldwell promoted this theory in the United States, and it was widely accepted. This theory was rebutted in 1913 by Charles Goring in his research. However, Ernest A. Hooton partially confirmed some of Caldwell's theories in 1939. In the field of psychology, Sigmund Freud had a big impact on criminology, even though it was not his intention. Criminologists still rely on many of his theories and methodologies.

Sociologists have become involved in criminology in various ways. They are classified into four groups or schools. These schools were developed during the late nineteenth and early twentieth centuries. These theories are:

- Control
- Strain
- Cultural deviance
- Symbolic interaction or differential association

The control theories were promoted by Travis Hirschi in his 1969 book, *Cause of Delinquency*. Control theories originated from Emile Durkheim in the late nineteenth century and were expanded on by Thorsten Sellin (1959).

The strain theories are also based on works of Emile Durkheim, but they were adapted by Robert Merton (1938) for application in the United States. Other sociologists have expanded on Merton's strain theories by developing additional theories, for example, deprivation theories and institutional anomie theories. Anomie, according to Durkheim, means a condition of an individual or society characterized by a breakdown of norms and values.

The cultural deviance theories were developed by Edwin H. Sutherland (1939) in his book, *Principles of Criminology*. He was influenced by colleagues at the Sociology Department of the University of Chicago. His theories are closely related to the symbolic interaction theories by George Mead and others.

The symbolic interaction theories and the differential association theories were developed by George Mead in *Mind, Self and Society* (1934). This symbolic interaction theory is usually referred to as labeling theory or just social interaction theory.

Another school in criminology is Radical Criminology. The founder of this school was Ralf Dahrendorf, a sociologist. Radical Criminology was directly applied to criminology by George Vold in his writing *Theoretical Criminology* (1958). Radical Criminology is closely associated with Marxist theories. Also, Radical Criminology is similar to conflict theories. Richard Quinney developed criminology theories that were closely related to Marxist ideas in his writing *The Social Reality of Crime* (1970). William Chambliss and Robert Seidman were proponents of Radical Criminology.

27.3   Schools of Criminology

There are many theories advocated in the field of criminology. These theories are classified as schools. The field of criminology has been influenced by other professions. The medical profession has made propositions that physical characteristics make criminals. This is especially true in the case of phrenology. Psychologists and psychiatrists believe mental disorders and processes produce criminals. Sociologists advocate that social influences cause people to become criminals. Some of the criminology theories are closely intertwined. This is especially true in the case of Marxist theories and the conflict and radical theories. It is hard for one to distinguish the differences. Criminologists are usually more concerned with justice and human rights, whereas sociologists are concerned with social order and harmony. In reality, human rights and justice are so intertwined with social order and harmony that they cannot always be clearly distinguishable.

27.3.1   Classical School

The Classical School, founded by Cesare Beccaria and Jeremy Bentham, was based on society that is composed of individuals. Society must impose laws to regulate the conduct of individuals within the society. Individuals form a society in order to obtain life, liberty, and happiness. This requires individuals to give up some liberties and be responsible to society for their actions and deeds. Their main concepts were:

1. Conduct is chosen by individuals within a society.
2. Punishment is a deterrent for unwanted conduct.
3. Punishment should fit the crime.

Bentham proposed his theory of "Felicity calculus," which was his mathematical model of determining the amount of punishment to be imposed in order to deter an individual from committing a crime. This model was based on his estimation of pain. The Classical School has had an influence on the founding fathers of the United States when they incorporated the cruel and unusual punishment into the Eighth Amendment of the Constitution.

27.3.2 Positivist School

The Positivist School was interested in criminal behavior at the individual level. Also, the Positivist School embraced scientific methodologies more than philosophizing as the Classical School had done. The major proponents of the Positivist School were Cesare Lombroso and his followers, Enrico Ferri and Raffaele Garofalo. Lombroso studied Italian criminals. On the basis of his studies, he formulated that degeneracy, called atavism, causes criminality. He also classified criminals into three categories:

1. Pseudocriminals—involuntary crimes such as self-defense
2. Criminaloids—predisposed to crimes because of environmental causes
3. Habitual criminals—criminals who chose to be because of environmental or biological factors

Lombroso and his colleagues were proponents of criminal anthropology. In other words, heredity was the cause of criminal behavior in some instances. In the United States, biological causes to crime were more acceptable than in Europe.

27.3.3 Conflict School

This school followed the theories of Karl Marx, a nineteenth century sociologist. Crime is considered a class struggle between the lower and upper classes for political and economic power. Crime is defined as acts of the lower class, which are prohibited by the ruling upper class. This conflict is over the control of scarce resources. Marx engenders a parasitic class of people whose interest is living off other classes, both upper and lower. This parasitic class consists of thieves, burglars, prostitutes, and gamblers.

27.4 Biological Theories

The Positivist School was the first to theorize biological causes for criminal behavior. Ernest A. Hooton, an anthropologist, conducted a 12-year research on more than 17,000 subjects. Nearly 14,000 subjects were incarcerated in jails and prisons, and the remainder were citizens. He concluded criminals have physiological differences that set them apart from the general population. He believed tattooing was done more by criminals than others. An Englishman, Charles Goring, previously made a similar study in England. He did an 8-year study on 3000 convicts. He concluded criminals have low intelligence and this is an indication of hereditary inferiority. Charles Caldwell, a phrenologist, conducted a study of 29 women convicted of infanticide. He found that most of them were poorly developed as to their sense of caring for children.

27.5 Psychological Theories

This school believes the minds of criminals are the cause of their behavior. The psychological theorists explain behavior as mental anomalies. The best-known psychologist was Sigmund Freud. He conceived mental conflict was due to three incompatible elements of personality. He identified these personality elements, which must be in balance, as:

1. *Id.* The unconscious, which is composed of forces called instincts and drives
2. *Ego.* The personality, which is conscious, that deals with reality
3. *Superego.* The conscience, which internalizes a person's values and norms

From the Freudian perspective, crime is caused by the dysfunction of the ego and superego. Criminologists rely on Freudian theories to explain the motives for criminal behavior. Freud's theories were not addressed to explain criminal behavior nor did he expect them to be used in this field.

27.6 Sociological Theories

Sociologists have developed many theories to explain normal and abnormal behavior. They have also presented theories on the causation of crime. Their basic theme is based on external factors, which involve political, economical, and ecological elements. Some of the sociological theories are intertwined. These theories can be grouped into four classifications:

1. Control
2. Strain
3. Cultural deviance
4. Symbolic interaction or differential association

27.7 Control Theory

There are many theories that can be classified as control theories. Some of these are containment and anomie theories. Durkheim was the earliest proponent of the social control theory. He believed order and conformity to rules were important for social solidarity. Criminals are individuals who will not adapt to the social norms of society. Robert Merton, as well as Travis Hirschi, formulated elements that would strengthen social bonds. They are:

1. *Attachment.* This refers to the individual's feelings about others.
2. *Commitment.* This refers to the individual's personal stake in society

3. *Involvement.* This refers to the amount of time and resources the individual provides to society.
4. *Belief.* This refers to the individual's beliefs in adhering to society's rules.

27.8 Strain Theory

The strain theory is very similar to the control theory. Both of these theories come from the Chicago School of Sociology. Merton views society in two parts: cultural and social structures. Cultural structure refers to society's goals, while social structure refers to society's means of achieving the goals. Merton proposes different ways people respond to strain:

1. *Innovation.* Deviant behavior is a response to blocking individual's goals by society.
2. *Ritualism.* This refers to individuals adhering to society's rules but at a lower degree.
3. *Retreatism.* This refers to individuals who drop out of society since they are unable to achieve the goals that society wishes for them.
4. *Rebellion.* This refers to individuals who do not accept cultural and social structure and seek to replace them.
5. *Conformity.* Most people accept society's goals and the means to achieving them.

27.9 Cultural Deviance Theory

Cultural deviance theory is closely related to the strain theory. Thorsten Sellin argued that crime is caused by the conflict between cultures. The society makes laws for the majority, the middle, or dominant class. These laws can conflict with the values and norms of minority or ethnic groups who have their own set of values. In a heterogeneous society, laws represent the majority or dominant cultures.

27.10 Differential Association Theory

Differential association theory is closely associated with cultural deviance theories. The chief proponent of differential association theory is Edwin Sutherland. He suggested nine propositions:

1. Criminal behavior is learned.
2. Criminal behavior is learned through a process of communication.
3. Criminal behavior occurs in close groups.
4. Learning criminal behavior includes how to commit crimes and provides the motives and drives to do them.
5. Motives and drives come from legal definitions.
6. It is more favorable to commit crimes solely.

7. Criminal behavior varies by the frequency, duration, priority, and intensity of association.
8. Criminal behavior is learned by association with other criminals.
9. Criminal behavior does not explain general needs and values.

27.11   Symbolic Interaction Theory

Symbolic interaction theory is based on the belief that people communicate through symbols. A symbol is anything that has meaning in an individual's life. The interpretation of symbols is dependent on each individual. Different individuals will have different interpretations based on one's experiences. Symbolic interaction is a forerunner to labeling theory.

27.12   Labeling Theory

Labeling theory expands on the symbolic interaction theories. It proposes that people are given various symbolic labels by interaction with people around them. These labels connote behavior and attitudes. Labeling has both a positive and negative effect. When a person is labeled as conscientious, intelligent, thrifty, trustworthy, then this implies a positive view of the person. Alternatively, if the person is labeled as lazy, dumb, or troublesome, then this implies a negative view of the person. These labels do not have to be truthful. Labeling does not only apply to individuals but also to various minority and ethnic groups. Labeling theorists believe police, courts, and other agencies promote criminal behavior by use of labeling. Label theorists point out that crime is a matter of definition. What may be illegal at one particular time or place may not be illegal at another time or place. Gambling and alcohol consumption is illegal in some areas, yet legal in others in the United States today.

27.13   Critical Criminology

Radical criminology is heavily influenced by critical criminology. The major proponents of critical criminology are Ralf Dahrendorf and George Vold. Dahrendorf is a sociologist who advocated that society is divided into two classes: the domineering class and the dominated class. He applied critical theories to societal issues. George Vold applied critical theories to criminology. Vold explained that crime and deviance were caused by conditions of inequality. This was made explicit by inner city riots and political protests. Conflict theory is limited to situations where criminal acts of one group collide with another group.

27.14   Radical Criminology

The chief spokesman for radical criminology is Richard Quinney. Other supporters are William Chambliss and Robert Seidman. Radical criminology is very much Marxist oriented, applying the social theories of Karl Marx to criminology. Quinney made six propositions concerning definition of crime. These definitions can be condensed to the premise that those in power make laws to benefit and maintain their power while restraining those who are not in power. Laws are always changing to reflect changes in the political climate of society. Chambliss and Seidman also advocate that the state, even though an instrument of the ruling class, must be concerned with maintaining good relations between classes. It must balance the capitalistic society and personal interest of individuals. They point out that law enforcement is selective. Just because a law is on the books does not mean that it is enforced.

27.15   Scientific Methodology

Scientific methodology encompasses procedures used to search for the truth. These procedures try to eliminate human intuition and hunches and make the research more objective and verifiable. Research methodology tries to guard against the following:

1. *Errors in observation.* Some people fail to recognize important features of a crime scene. People have observed witnesses in court who cannot remember details of an event. Some witnesses make up observations that have contradictions when analyzed.
2. *Selective observation.* People only see things that they are interested in seeing. Witnesses in trials can only give facts from their observations.
3. *Errors in interpretation.* Everyone has some biases and prejudices. These biases and prejudices cause misinterpretations.
4. *Dependence on authority.* People rely heavily on others in authority. Juries hear expert witnesses. Expert witnesses can only express opinions based on data supplied to them. Expert witnesses have their biases and prejudices. News media reports can be slanted or biased. The headlines of one media vehicle may not be reported by another or placed in lower priority.
5. *Inappropriate use of evidence.* Evidence may be appropriate in one situation but may be inappropriate in another situation. Police sometimes report more than one offender, but only arrest one offender.

There are two recognized research methods in academia: qualitative and quantitative. Criminology uses both research methods. Qualitative research is gathering data which is not normally reduce to numbers and can only be applied to specific population groups, usually relative small. Quantitative research gathers data which can be reduced to numbers and is usually applied to whole populations.

27.16   Organized Crime

Many criminologists study the various aspects of organized crime. They are interested in its motives, organization, criminal activities, and individual and group profiles. In chapter 12, different organized crime organizations have been identified along with their basic organization and criminal activities. Law enforcement is always gathering intelligence on criminal organizations and their activities. Many large city police departments as well as some states and federal agencies have units whose sole responsibility is to investigate various organized crime groups.

27.16.1 Organized Criminal Code

Organized criminal groups cannot function without some kind of code for its members to follow. This code is well defined in some organizations, while it is not well defined in others. The code can vary from one criminal organization to another. Criminologist Donald Cressey made an analysis of organized crime, and he suggested the following:

1. *Loyalty.* Don't be an informer.
2. *Be rational.* Conduct business in a quiet, safe, and profitable manner.
3. *Be a man of honor.* Respect women and elders.
4. *Be a stand-up guy.* Show courage and heart. Keep your mouth shut.
5. *Have class.* Be independent.

27.16.2 Rules of Behavior

Donald Cressey found three basic rules of behavior in studying the Lupollo crime family. They are:

1. Primary loyalty is vested in family, not in individual lineages.
2. Each family member must act like a man and not bring disgrace on the family.
3. Family business is secret; do not discuss it outside the group.

27.16.3 Survival Mechanisms

Organized crime contains mechanisms that ensure the survival of the organization. The La Cosa Nostra (LCN) has a long history in both the United States and Italy. The Triads and Yakuzas have a very long history. Even with losses from both external and internal forces, they have been able to survive and prosper. They have learned to become more sophisticated in their methods of operations and use of more professional people, for example, accountants, lawyers, and engineers. These survival mechanisms are classified into three imperative roles. They are:

1. *The enforcer.* A position in the organization that provides for enforcement of its rules and the directives of those in authority. The methods can range from murder to verbal warnings.
2. *The buffer.* A position primarily centered on internal communication and the flow of decisions in the hierarchy. This person keeps lines of communication between leaders and followers open, forewarning of internal dissentions and problems at the street level. The buffer may settle disagreements and conflicts.
3. *The corruptor.* A position in the organization whose job is to bribe, buy, intimidate, negotiate, persuade, and maneuver into a relationship with police, public officials, and anyone who will help the family.

27.17 Predatory Crimes

Crimes that members of society fear most are predatory crimes. These are defined as "illegal acts where someone intentionally takes or damages the person or property of another, from *Theories of Crime* by Daniel Curran and Claire Renzetti." Criminologist Lawrence Cohen says predatory criminal events involve the following elements:

1. Motivated offenders
2. Suitable targets
3. The absence of capable guardians

If any one of these elements is lacking, the predatory criminal event will not occur.

27.17.1 Legal Definition

According to law, specific criteria must be met for an act to be considered a crime and the predator a criminal. These criteria are:

1. There must be conduct (not mere thoughts).
2. The conduct must constitute social harm.
3. Law must prohibit the conduct.
4. The conduct must be performed voluntarily.
5. The conduct must be performed intentionally.
6. The conduct must be punishable by law.

Natural crime consists of acts that are repulsive to most people in society. This is *mala in se*, which means "evil in itself." *Mala prohibita in se* consists of acts that are illegal by legislation or custom. *Mala prohibita in se* means "evil because it is forbidden."

Procedural and substantive criminal law draws two basic issues in law:

1. How the authorities handle matters of law and deal with law violators—the question of procedures
2. Content of specific rules making up the body of criminal law—the question of substance

27.17.2 Primitive Law

Primitive law is a system of rules and obligations in preliterate and semiliterate societies that modern legal systems are based on. Primitive law contains three important features.

1. Acts that injured or wronged others were considered private wrongs.
2. The injured party or family typically took personal action against the wrongdoer.
3. This self-help justice usually amounted to retaliation in kind.

The Code of Hammurapi is the earliest law and covered a wide range of crimes. The four important observations are:

1. Most laws are a product of prevailing social, political, and economic conditions.
2. Some laws articulate long-established customs and traditions and can be thought of as formal restatements of existing mores.

3. Some laws reflect efforts to regulate and coordinate increasingly complex social relations and activities.
4. Some laws display prevailing ethical and moral standards and show close ties to religious ideas and sentiments.

27.18   Criminology and the Fraud Examiner

Fraud examiners should be aware of sociology and criminology. Sociology and criminology help fraud examiners understand the criminal and the motives involved. Sometimes, the examiner is questioned about personality profiles that would help distinguish those who would commit a particular crime from those who would not. There is no clear-cut answer to this question. Most employees do not take a job with the intent of committing a crime. Employees who commit a crime do so because of internal and external influences. The fraud examiner should be alert to all possible influences that would cause an employee to commit fraud. Some of these influences are:

1. Management committing fraudulent acts, for example, padded expense accounts, embezzlement, skimming, using ghost employees.
2. Failure to obtain a desired position or promotion.
3. Low morale by the employee and/or his/her coworkers, for example, as a result of bad policies or layoffs due to bad economic times.
4. The employee has problems at home, for example, divorce, drug or alcohol abuse, gambling debts, large medical bills.
5. Employees tempted to commit fraud if internal controls are weak and the opportunity is present.

People have daily and regular routines. Career criminals also have regular patterns. The fraud examiner should become aware of those patterns. A "bust-out" artist will open a business and "bust out" months later leaving creditors holding worthless receivables. "Boiler room" operators will operate in one location for weeks or a few months and then shut down operations. They do this to evade law enforcement. The boiler room operators move to a new location and start up operations again. Boiler room operators and bust out artists establish a regular pattern of crime. They usually remain in the same product or service because they are familiar with it. After the pattern is determined, the examiner can develop his/her case to a greater degree. In addition, law enforcement can take the appropriate steps to shut down these operations with minimum effort and a greater degree of prosecution success.

Criminals have various motives for committing the crimes that they do. One major motive is greed. Other motives are to obtain power, status, etc. The fraud examiner should be aware of the motives and patterns that criminals have mapped out.

27.19   Summary

Criminology is the study of crime and causation. Criminology has been influenced by other disciplines, for example, psychology, anthropology, biology, and sociology. Sociology has had the greatest impact. The theories for crime and causation vary widely. These theories are classified as schools. The major schools are:

1. *Classical School.* This school proposes punishment should fit the crime.
2. *Positivist School.* This school was the first to use scientific methodology. It theorized that physiology caused criminal behavior.
3. *Radical and Critical Criminology Schools.* These schools advocate that societal conditions caused criminal behavior. They are closely related to the Marxist ideas.
4. *Psychological School.* This school believes mental processes cause criminal behavior.
5. *Sociology Schools.* These schools present many theories for the causation of crime based on various social forces.

Criminologists study various criminal groups. The most common subjects are organized crime organizations. Criminologists want to learn how they operate and survive after being combated by external and internal forces. Fraud examiners and investigators need to be familiar with criminology. Criminology can help examiners and investigators understand criminals' motives for their criminal activities.

Physical Security

28

28.1 Introduction

Physical security is that aspect of security concerned with physical measures designed to safeguard personnel, to prevent unauthorized access to equipment, facilities, material, and documents, and to safeguard them against loss, damage, and theft. Loss prevention is particularly concerned with preventing loss of supplies, tools, equipment, and other materials in use, storage, and transit. Concern is not only focused on the threat of criminal activity and acts of wrongdoing by forces external to the organizational unit, but it is also specifically directed toward internal causes—theft and pilferage by those who have authorized access, inattention to physical security practices and procedures, and disregard for property controls and accountability. Physical security and loss prevention measures include instructions, procedures, plans, policies, agreements, systems, and resources committed and designed to safeguard personnel, protect property, and prevent losses. Physical security helps remove the opportunity from people who want to commit fraud. An ounce of prevention is worth a pound of cure, as the cliché goes.

28.2 Responsibilities

Security is the direct, immediate, legal, and moral responsibility of all people in a business organization. However, there are officers or other personnel who have a direct responsibility for physical security and loss prevention. These personnel have different titles, for example, Security Officer or Loss Prevention Officer. Whatever their title may be, it is their duty to:

1. Manage the organization security and loss prevention program.
2. Determine the adequacy of the organization's loss prevention program and identify areas where improvements are required.
3. Develop, prepare, and maintain loss prevention and security plans.
4. Establish personnel identification and access control system(s).
5. Provide technical assistance on security matters.
6. Participate in planning, directing, coordinating, and implementing procedures for crisis management situations, which pose a threat to the organization.
7. Establish and maintain liaison and working relationships with local law enforcement and fire protection authorities.
8. Maintain good relations with other managers in the organization with specialized skills or technology in security and loss prevention.

28.3   Plans

Loss prevention and security plans should cover the following points:

1. Identify real property and structures to be protected.
2. Identify security areas.
3. Identify by location and priority the assets to be protected.
4. Assess the threat to such areas.
5. Determine legal jurisdiction.
6. Determine and identify the necessary resources: funds, staff, and equipment.
7. Establish barriers and points of ingress and egress.
8. Prescribe the personnel identification and access control system(s).
9. Identify and procure equipment that will detect and/or prevent wrongful removal, damage, destruction, or compromise of protected property.
10. Determine the number of personnel needed and prescribe their duties.
11. Establish and maintain records relating to violations and breaches of security.
12. Identify procedures for timely internal reporting of losses.
13. Identify procedures for ensuring that all losses, inventory adjustments, and surveys of property are reported to management.
14. Advise of legal and administrative procedures and remedies applicable to those found responsible and liable for losses.

28.4   Evaluation

In evaluating the need for and the type of protection required for an organization, the following factors should be considered:

1. Overall importance to the organization
2. Importance to the business operations
3. Ease of access to vital equipment and materials
4. Tailoring of security measures to the organization operations and other local considerations
5. Geographic location
6. Legal jurisdiction of real property
7. Aid and assistance agreements with local authorities
8. Local political climate
9. Adequacy of storage facilities for valuable or sensitive material
10. Accessibility of the activity to disruptive, criminal, subversive, or terrorist elements
11. Possible losses on the organization and their impact on operations
12. Possibility or probability of expansion, curtailment, or other changes in operations
13. Overall cost of security
14. Availability of personnel and material
15. Coordination of security personnel

16. Calculated risk (when there are limited resources available for protection, possible loss or damage to some supplies or to a portion of the operations is risked in order to ensure a greater degree of security to the remaining assets, supplies, and operations)

28.5   Cost of Security

Security expenditures should generally be based on the cost of the item(s) to be protected and the damage their loss could cause to the organization and to others. The cost of security is frequently greater than the dollar value of the property and material.

28.6   Crisis Situations

In evaluating the need for security protection, the possibility of injury to security personnel must be considered. This is especially relevant when addressing measures taken during crisis situations (e.g., bomb threats, fires, robberies, or natural disasters) to limit damage and provide emergency services for containment of the incident to restore the activity to normal operation. Security plans should include preventive measures to reduce the opportunities for introduction of bombs; procedures for evaluating and handling threatening messages; procedures for obtaining assistance and support by local law enforcement; procedures in the event a bomb or suspected bomb is found on premises; and procedures to be followed in the event of an explosion.

28.7   Security Considerations

Security measures to be considered when developing security plans are as follows:

1. Personnel screening and indoctrination
2. Protection for vulnerable points/assets within the organization
3. Security force organization and training
4. Personnel identification and control systems
5. Installation of security hardware, for example, intrusion detection systems, barriers, and access control systems
6. Key and lock control
7. Coordination with other security agencies

28.8   Sabotage

Sabotage acts can cause destruction equal to acts of war but without fear of retaliation against the hostile war-making capability if successfully carried out. The tools and methods of the saboteur are limited only by skill and ingenuity. Readily available materials can be used to construct simple but deadly devices. The effectiveness of the saboteur is limited only by inability to gain access to targeted installations. The basic sabotage techniques are as follows:

1. *Mechanical.* This includes introduction of foreign objects into machinery, severing of wires or cables, removal of components, and the mishandling/abuse of equipment.
2. *Arson.* This includes firebombing, electrical shorting, and the use of incendiary agents.
3. *Explosive.* This includes use of commercial and homemade compounds, contact trip wire detonators, and timed devices.
4. *Psychological.* This includes such things as instigation of labor strikes, personnel disputes, distrust of supervisors, hostilities between coworkers. Organized crime organizations, particularly the La Cosa Nostra (LCN) and the Yakuzas, use these tactics to take over businesses.

28.9   Motives

Saboteurs can be classified into two categories:

1. *Internal.* Internal saboteurs are employees who are often motivated by feelings of revenge, emotional disorder, disgruntlement, or use of drugs or alcohol. Offenders perform these acts to "get even" with superiors, to halt business operations, to achieve momentary fame as the "alert discoverer" of a fire or other threat.
2. *External.* Saboteurs outside the business organization commit sabotage because they do not like the organization's policies or political affiliations. They consider the organization "exploitative" of people in the community.

28.10   Terrorism

Terrorism is the use of tactics, principally by small groups, designed to create panic and chaos through the use of deadly force, publicity, uncertainty, and coercive acts of violence directed against specific or general targets in the general population. Generally, the goal of terrorist acts is to disrupt or destroy the bond of trust and credibility between government and the population. Acts of terrorism directed at businesses have the potential to destroy facilities, injure or kill employees, impair or delay business operations, and cause incalculable damage through adverse publicity and public perceptions of the incident.

28.11   Terrorist Methods

Terrorists use the following methods:

1. *Bombs.* Bomb(s) used may be of any degree of sophistication and may be placed to destroy equipment, cause fires, create casualties, etc. Depending on the bomb size and placement, the impact may range from a minor to a major crisis.

2. *Ambush.* Rapid ambush attacks may be employed by individuals or small groups to assassinate individuals, eliminate a group of people, or destroy or steal assets in remote locations or in transit.
3. *Armed attack.* An armed assault usually involves one or more diversionary actions carried out by small groups against key personnel or critical assets with the objective of causing disruption of operations and creating adverse publicity. Hostage taking is not a usual tactic in this type of terrorist action unless the attackers are prevented from escaping.
4. *Hostage situations.* A terrorist group may undertake the seizure of a specific hostage for ransom or political bargaining purposes. An armed attack scenario may be used to seize a critical asset (factory, research facility, etc.) when personnel are present in order to use both the asset and the personnel as leverage to bargain for publicity and political advantage. Care must be taken to provide for this possibility in companies that develop or produce high-technology products.
5. *Sabotage.* Terrorist groups may engage in the use of various sabotage methods already previously discussed.

28.12 Surveys

The security manager should conduct a security survey at least once a year. These surveys should be designed to show management what security measures are in effect, to determine what areas need improvement, and to provide a basis for determining priorities for funding and work accomplishment.

28.13 Threat Assessments

On the basis of available information that can be obtained legally, the business organization should determine the short-, medium-, and long-term threats. Such information must be analyzed to determine what additional security measures are necessary where security requirements are inadequate. A close liaison with local law enforcement agencies is imperative.

28.14 Loss Prevention

A vigorous loss prevention program is essential. Losses of property may disrupt operations and cost millions of dollars. Losses must be minimized by application of a comprehensive loss prevention program consisting of loss analysis, proper use of available investigative resources, continuing employee loss prevention education, the application of firm corrective measures, administrative personnel action, and other loss prevention measures when necessary. As a minimum, loss prevention measures should consist of the following:

1. *Loss analysis.* To help identify trends and patterns of losses and gains, all incidents involving reportable property which is missing, lost, stolen, or recovered, reporting and investigation must be included in an ongoing program of analysis.

A continuing loss analysis process should consider the types of material lost; geographic location; times and dates; proximity of personnel; proximity of doorways, passageways, loading docks/ramps, gates, parking facilities; and other activities adjacent to loss locations. Resulting analyses of loss trends and patterns will be used to balance the allocation of resources available for crime prevention.

2. *Investigative resources.* To prevent or reduce losses of property, it is essential to assign investigative personnel to loss prevention functions. A preliminary investigative capability should exist during all working production shifts (especially night shifts). Local loss analysis program data should be used to program security resources to combat losses.

3. *Loss prevention equipment.* Exterior doors in warehouses, storage buildings, office buildings, and other structures that contain high-value, sensitive, or pilferable property, supplies, or office equipment will be afforded with security protection commensurate with the value and sensitivity of the structure's contents. At a minimum, hinges will either be nonremovable or be provided with inside hinge protection, which prevents locked doors from opening even if hinges are removed, and lock/hasp security systems.

4. *Employee education.* Each employee must be indoctrinated in local procedures for preventing property losses as well as responsibility for the care and protection of property under the employee's control. This indoctrination should be included in the employee's initial security education briefing upon employment and annually thereafter.

5. *Discipline.* Administrative actions should be taken against employees or others who are responsible for losses. Depending on the circumstances, civil and/or criminal actions should be taken. Civil actions should be taken to recover losses from the responsible person. If an organization just terminates an employee for theft or embezzlement, it is sending a message to other employees that they can get away with the crime. In addition, the bad employee will go elsewhere and will probably commit the offense again.

6. *Financial responsibility.* Procedures for the issue and control of company property will ensure that strict accountability is established for persons responsible for the property that is reported missing, lost, or stolen. Recoupment action must be undertaken against an individual in which negligence or intention results in a missing, lost, or stolen property. This recoupment action is independent of, may be taken parallel with, or be exclusive of any formal criminal procedures arising from the same event.

7. *Claims.* A business organization should have adequate insurance coverage to compensate for any losses due to theft, fire, or other natural disasters. Claims should be filed as soon as possible because the insurance company will probably want to investigate the circumstances of the loss and bring civil actions against the person responsible.

8. *Criminal actions.* Examination of the facts may indicate criminality sufficient to warrant a referral to appropriate legal authorities. This action strengthens the deterrent aspects of loss prevention policies and procedures. The security manager should ensure that the security portion of criminal cases is properly prepared and in sufficient detail to render them acceptable for prosecution in federal, state, or local courts. The security manager should monitor the progress of criminal issues and maintain liaison with the legal authorities.

28.15   Loss Reporting

Effective reporting of losses is basic to the determination of the scope of the loss prevention program that must be developed by the company. When reviewing property losses that are not critical to business operations and do not harm anyone, it is important to know whether or not the expenditure of funds on physical security will pay back in loss reductions. If real losses are extremely low, and involve only low-value and nonsensitive materials, it may be more cost-effective to absorb such losses. Nevertheless, actual losses must be reported so that an accurate decision can be made by management. Steps must be taken to ensure that reportable loss and accountable individuals are identified. This can be done by matching property inventories, inventory adjustments, etc., with loss reports submitted. Historically, many audits and inspection reports have shown that not all required reports are submitted and actual losses have greatly exceeded reported losses. In each case of loss, theft, or destruction of property, efforts should be made to determine if the event involved negligence or criminality. The individuals responsible should be determined whenever possible. If an investigation is initiated, the ongoing status of the investigation will be provided during pending or supplementary reports. Incidents involving the same type or class of material are often indicative of a lack of adequate loss prevention and inventory control procedures. Causative factors should be identified and prompt corrective action initiated. Care must be taken to explain the detailed circumstances of a loss. The narrative comments should identify security problems and deficiencies related to the incident. Every report should provide details of any real or perceived security deficiency and any action taken or planned to correct such deficiency.

28.16   Area Protection

It is important to perform an analysis to determine the degree of security required. Criticality and vulnerability of security interest must be evaluated in relationship to ranking potential losses and giving the level of security to ensure the best possible protection for the loss level at efficient costs. Protective area controls are the first steps in providing actual protection against security hazards. These controls are obtained through the use of protective barriers and other security measures. All areas within a business operation must be assigned security area designations. Different areas and tasks involve different degrees of security depending on their purpose, nature of the work performed, and the information and/or materials concerned. Areas should be designated as either restricted or nonrestricted. Restricted areas should be areas where public access is denied to both unauthorized employees and customers. Such areas can be as follows:

1. Offices where financial data are compiled or sensitive information is processed
2. Communication facilities, for example, telephone wires, cables, and switching boxes
3. Warehouses where inventory is kept
4. Power stations, transformers, master valve, and switch spaces
5. Open storage areas and yards
6. Intrusion detection systems–monitoring spaces
7. Central storage spaces for keys and locks

8. Cash storage spaces
9. Negotiable instrument storage spaces

28.17   Security Measures

Restricted areas should include measures that exclude or require the following:

1. *A clearly defined area or perimeter.* The perimeter may be a fence, exterior walls, building, or a space within a building.
2. *A personnel identification and control system.* This may include access list, entry/departure logs, and identification badges. For small companies, the issuance of keys to only authorized personnel may be adequate. Larger companies may require more sophisticated systems.
3. *Controlled ingress/egress.* Ingress and egress controlled by guards or personnel within the restricted area.
4. *Restricted access.* Admission allowed only to those people whose duties require access and who have been granted authorization.

   Signs should be posted that tell people the area is restricted or say "authorized personnel only."

28.18   Key and Lock Controls

Businesses should establish a strict key and lock control program, which is managed and supervised by the security manager. It should include controls over all keys, locks, padlocks, and locking devices used to protect or secure restricted areas, perimeters, facilities, critical assets, and sensitive materials and supplies. The program should not include keys, locks, and padlocks for convenience, privacy, or personnel use. Examples are employee lockers, employee restrooms, and employee desks. Store managers, department heads, branch managers, etc., should be responsible for all keys controlled in their respective spaces and areas. Security locks, padlocks, and/or lock cores should be rotated from one location to another or changed at least once a year to guard against the use of illegally duplicated keys and to afford the opportunity for regular maintenance or security violations due to malfunction because of dirt, corrosion, and wear. Keys for security locks and padlocks should be issued only to those with a need approved by management and/or the security manager. Convenience or status is not a sufficient criterion for issue of a security key. A central key room should be established. Also each key custodian and subcustodian must institute a system showing keys on hand, keys issued, to whom, date/time the keys were issued and returned, and the signatures of persons drawing or returning security keys. Continuous accountability of keys is required at all times. When the door, gate, or other equipment, which the padlock is intended to secure, is open or operable, the padlock should be locked into the staple, fence fabric, or other nearby securing point to preclude the switching of the padlock to facilitate surreptitious entry by a thief or others. Inactive or infrequently used gates and doors should be locked and have seals affixed.

28.19   Parking

As a general rule, to prevent property losses, employees should not be permitted to park immediately adjacent to work spaces. Privately owned vehicles, except those driven by handicapped employees, should not be parked within 100 feet of doorways leading into or from buildings primarily used for the manufacturing, repair, rework, storage, handling, packaging, or shipping of inventory, materials, and supplies. Businesses that have many employees, more than a guard can recognize, usually 50 or more, should have employee-parking permits issued to personnel to restrict parking. A system should be in place to collect parking permits when employees leave employment.

28.20   Protective Lighting

Protective lighting provides a means of continuing, during hours of darkness, a degree of security approaching that which is maintained during daylight hours. It has considerable value as a deterrent to thieves and vandals and makes the job for them more difficult. Requirements for protective lighting will depend on the situation. The mix between energy conservation and effective security must be carefully studied in each situation. The overall goal is to provide a proper environment to perform duties, prevent illegal entry, detect intruders, and inspect unusual or suspicious activities. The following basic principles apply to help ensure protective lighting effectiveness:

1. Provide adequate illumination to discourage or detect illegal attempts to enter restricted areas and to reveal the presence of unauthorized persons within such areas.
2. Avoid glare, which handicaps security personnel or is objectionable to traffic or occupants of adjacent properties.
3. Locate light sources so that illumination is directed toward likely intruder avenues of approach.
4. Illuminate areas shadowed by structures within or adjacent to restricted areas.
5. Design the system to provide overlapping light distribution; design equipment to resist the effects of environmental conditions; locate all components of the system to provide maximum protection against intentional damage.
6. Avoid drawing unwanted attention to restricted areas

28.21   Intrusion Detection Systems

An intrusion detection system (IDS) should be an essential element of any in-depth security program. IDS consists of sensors capable of detecting one or more types of phenomena, signal media, annunciators, and energy sources for signaling the entry or attempted entry into the area protected by the system. IDS is designed to detect, not prevent, actual or attempted penetrations. Therefore, IDS is useless unless it is supported by a prompt security force response when the system is activated.

28.21.1 IDS Purpose

IDS is used to accomplish one or more of the following:

1. Permit more economical and efficient use of security personnel through the employment of mobile responding guard forces or local law enforcement.
2. Provide additional controls at critical areas.
3. Substitute for other physical security measures, which cannot be used because of safety regulations, operational requirements, building layout, cost, or similar reasons.
4. Provide insurance against human failure or error.
5. Enhance security force capability to detect and defeat intruders.
6. Provide the earliest practical warning to security forces of any attempted penetration of protected areas.

28.21.2 IDS Determination Factors

The following factors must be considered in determining the feasibility and necessity of installing IDS equipment.

1. The type of business operation or facility
2. Criticality of the operation or facility
3. Threat to the operation or facility
4. Location of the operation or facility and the location of the areas within each facility
5. Accessibility to intruders
6. Availability of other forms of protection
7. Initial and recurring cost of the system
8. Personnel and money savings over expected life of the system
9. Construction of the building or facility
10. Hours of operation of the facility
11. Availability of a security force and expected response time to an alarm condition

28.21.3 Types of Systems

There are basically four types of IDS systems.

1. *Local alarm.* The protective circuits and alarm devices actuate a visual and/or audible signal in the immediate vicinity of the protected area, usually on the exterior and/or interior of the building. The alarm transmission/communication lines do not leave the building. Response is by local security forces that may be in the area when the alarm is sounded. Otherwise, the security force will only know of the alarm if reported by a passerby or during routine checks. The disadvantage of this type of system is that intruders know exactly when the alarm is activated and, in most cases, can easily elude capture. This type of system should be used only when guards or workers are always in close proximity to the audible or visual alarm and are able to respond to it.

2. *Central station.* The operation of alarm devices and electrical circuits are automatically signaled to, recorded in, maintained, and supervised from a central station, owned or managed either in-house or by a commercial firm, which has trained guards and operators in attendance at all times. These personnel monitor the signals of the system and provide the response force to any unauthorized entry into the protected area. Connection of alarm equipment to the central station is usually over telephone lines.

3. *Police connection.* The alarm devices and electrical circuits are connected via telephone lines to a monitoring unit located in nearby police stations. An agreement with the local police department must be arranged prior to establishment of this type of system.

4. *Proprietary IDS station.* This system is similar to a central station operation, except that the IDS monitoring/recording equipment for all IDS systems at the installation is located within a constantly manned security force communications center maintained and/or owned by a commercial company. The security force operates and responds to all IDS activations. Connection of the alarm equipment to the monitoring room can be over telephone lines or by separate cable installed by the equipment company. This system is the preferred IDS monitoring system for medium to large organizations.

28.21.4   Sensor Systems

Sensor systems are divided into two areas based on environmental use:

1. *Exterior sensors.* Exterior intrusion detection devices should be selected for the best performance under such prevailing local environmental conditions as soil, topography, weather, and any other factors that could adversely affect device performance or increase its false alarm rate. The detecting devices are designed for outside installation and are usually used in conjunction with barriers such as fences. Commonly used sensors include those that detect light beam interruption, motion, pressure, vibration, magnetic field distortions, and seismic disturbances or combinations of these.

2. *Interior sensors.* Interior intrusion detection devices should be selected and installed to provide the best reliable information to security personnel in the shortest possible time. The devices are primarily designed to operate within an environmentally protected area to overcome security weaknesses in buildings, rooms, etc. Commonly used devices include those that detect motion, light beam interruption, sound, pressure, vibration, capacitance change, heat, magnetic field change, penetration, and the breaking of an electrical circuit.

3. *Data/Signal Transmission system.* This system integrates the sensors and the control/monitoring capabilities into a complete functioning IDS. The transmission medium is used to send control signals and data between all sensors, control points, and annunciator display panels. It may be wire landlines, radio frequency, link, or a combination of both. This vital system is probably the weakest and most vulnerable of the entire IDS system and requires protection.

28.21.5 Control and Display System

This system provides equipment for central operational control and monitoring of the IDS. Through this equipment, the security personnel are instantly alerted to the status of any protected area. This system should be located in a separate area closed off from public view. Zone numbers shall be used to designate alarmed spaces or items, for example, buildings, room numbers, and inventory items.

28.21.6 Power System

Normal power to operate an IDS system is usually derived from the local electrical power. The importance of an IDS continuous function cannot be overstated. Therefore, each IDS system should have an emergency backup source of power in the event of a power failure to ensure the continuous operation of the system. The backup power source usually consists of batteries, which should be of a rechargeable type. Power supplies should be arranged so that batteries are maintained fully charged at all times when power is available. The system should automatically transfer from AC to battery power whenever the former fails, and return to AC power upon restoration of that power.

28.21.7 Maintenance

Proper maintenance of an IDS system is imperative. Systems that are not properly maintained may either fail to detect intrusion or yield a high number of bogus alarms, commonly referred to as false/nuisance alarms. Systems that generate frequent false or nuisance alarms lose their credibility and demoralize security personnel to the point where alarm activations are ignored. The contracting company should develop procedures to ensure that only appropriately cleared personnel install, inspect, or maintain the IDS system.

28.22 Security Audits

Each business organization should have a program to assess the degree of security within the organization. Security assessments should be done at least once a year to ensure compliance by management and employees. The assessment should cover compliance with security measures, loss prevention programs, and crisis management. Fire drills should be conducted periodically. Disaster plans should be reviewed. Management and employees should be trained or at least informed each year. Loss prevention and disaster plans should be evaluated each year.

28.23 Security Checklist

The purpose of the checklist show in Figure 28.1 is to provide business organization guidelines for evaluating existing security measures. It is not intended to be all-inclusive. It is more appropriate for larger organizations, but many questions are relevant to smaller businesses.

1. Is there a security manager?
2. Does the organization have a security plan?
3. Does the security plan contain instructions for:
   a. Fire?
   b. Natural disasters?
   c. Disturbances?
   d. Sabotage?
   e. Bomb threats?
   f. Theft?
   g. Robberies?
4. Does the security plan include procedures for:
   a. Evaluating and handling threatening messages?
   b. Evacuation of personnel and customers?
   c. Suspected bomb found on premises?
   d. Reporting robberies?
   e. Reporting internal theft?
5. Does the organization have a counterespionage program?
6. Are security plans reviewed annually?
7. Has security manager established liaison with local law and fire authorities?
8. Are the basic security measures for exclusion areas in effect?
9. Are security measures in effect to protect:
   a. Electric power supplies and transmission?
   b. Communication centers/equipment?
   c. Computer and financial data and files?
10. Is there a key and lock custodian?
11. Does the key and lock control program include
    a. A key control register?
    b. An inventory of keys?
12. Is the present security force strength and composition commensurate with the degree of security protection required?
13. Does the security manager inspect and brief personnel on a daily basis?
14. Does the organization have a crisis plan in effect?
15. Are security personnel available and trained in procedures to help police and fire authorities?
16. Is a pass or badge identification system used to identify all personnel in the confines of restricted areas?
17. Does the identification system provide the desired degree of security?
18. Does the identification system provide procedures for:
    a. Protection for the badges and passes?
    b. Designation for areas requiring special control measures?
    c. Control of the pass or badges issued?
    d. Mechanics of identification upon entering and leaving each restricted area, as applied to both employees and visitors?
    e. Details of where, when, and how badges shall be worn?
    f. Procedures to be followed in case of loss or damage to identification media?
    g. Procedures for recovery and invalidation?
19. If a badge system is used for any security area, does the system provide for:
    a. Comparison of badge, pass, and personnel?
    b. Physical exchange of pass/badge at time of entrance/exits?
    c. Accounting for each badge or pass?
    d. Location and verification of personnel remaining within the security area at the end of normal working hours?
    e. Security of badges and passes not in use?
20. Do guards at control points compare badges to bearers, both upon entry and exit?
21. Is supervision of the personnel identification and control system adequate at all levels?
22. Are badges and serial numbers recorded and controlled by rigid accountability procedures?
23. Are lost badges replaced with badges bearing different serial numbers?
24. Have procedures been established that provide for issuance of temporary badges for individuals who have forgotten their permanent badges?
25. Are temporary badges used?
26. Are lists of lost badges posted at guard control points?

Figure 28.1 Business checklist.

27. Are badges of such design and appearance as to enable guards and other personnel to recognize quickly and positively the authorizations and limitations applicable to the bearers?
28. Are procedures in existence to ensure the return of identification badges upon termination of employment or assignment?
29. Are special badges issued to contractor employees working within security areas?
30. Are all phases of the personnel identification and control system under supervision and control of the security manager?
31. Have effective visitor escort procedures been established?
32. What controls are employed to control visitor movements while in restricted areas?
33. Are visitors required to display identification media conspicuously on outer garments at all times while within restricted areas?
34. When visitors depart restricted areas, are they required to turn in identification badges and is the departure time in each case recorded in the visitor register?
35. Are visitors who indicate an intention to return at a later time permitted to retain identification badges?
36. Are permanent records of visits maintained? If so, by whom?
37. What measures are employed, other than the issuance of identification badges, to control the movement of contractor personnel working within restricted areas?
38. Have written procedures been issued and authorized for the registration of privately owned vehicles aboard business premises?
39. What type of pass is used and where is it affixed/located within/on the vehicle?
40. Are temporary passes issued to visitor vehicles?
41. Are automobiles allowed to be parked within restricted areas?
42. Are parking areas within restricted areas located away from restricted areas?
43. Does a fence or other type of physical barrier define the parking perimeter and all restricted areas?
44. Are openings such as culverts, tunnels, manholes for sewers and utility access, and sidewalk elevators, which permit access to the restricted area, properly secured?
45. Are gates and/or other entrances, which are not actively used, locked and equipped with seals and frequently inspected by other personnel?
46. Are locks rotated annually?
47. Are all normally used pedestrian and vehicular gates and other entrances effectively and adequately lighted to assure:
    a.   Proper identification of individuals and examination of credentials?
    b.   Interior of vehicles can be observed?
    c.   That glare from luminaries does not interfere with the guard's vision?
48. Are appropriate signs setting forth the provisions of entry conspicuously posted at all entrances?
49. Are "No Trespassing" signs posted on or adjacent to barriers at such intervals that at least one sign is visible at any approach to a barrier during daylight hours?
50. Are lumber, boxes, or other extraneous material not allowed to be stacked against or adjacent to the barriers or doors?
51. Do guards patrol perimeter areas?
52. Are any perimeters protected by intrusion detection systems?
53. Does any relocated function, newly designated security area, physical expansion, or other factor indicate necessity for installation of additional barriers or additional lighting?
54. Does the perimeter of the installation and security area provided adequate lighting?
55. Does a protective lighting meet adequate intensity requirement?
56. Are the cones of illumination from lamps directed downward and away from guard personnel?
57. Is perimeter lighting utilized so that guards remain in comparative darkness?
58. Are lights checked for proper operation prior to darkness?
59. Are repairs to lights and replacement of inoperative lamps effected immediately?
60. Is additional lighting provided for active doorways and points of possible intrusion?
61. Does the operation have a dependable source of power for its lighting system?
62. Does the operation have a dependable auxiliary source of power?
63. Is the power supply for the protective lighting system protected? How?
64. Is there a provision for standby or emergency protective lighting?
65. Is the standby or emergency equipment tested frequently?
66. Can the emergency equipment be rapidly switched into operation when needed?
67. Is wiring tested and inspected periodically to ensure proper operation?
68. Is parallel circuitry used in the wiring?
69. Are multiple circuits used?

Figure 28.1 Continued

70. Is closed loop used in multiple circuits?
71. Is wiring for protective lighting properly run?
    a. Is it in tamper-resistant conduit?
    b. Is it installed underground?
    c. If aboveground, is it high enough to preclude the possibility of tampering?
72. Are switches and controls properly located, controlled, and protected?
73. Is the protective lighting system designed and are locations available so that repair can be made rapidly in an emergency?
74. Are materials and equipment in shipping and storage areas properly arranged to provide adequate lighting?
75. Does the organization employ any intrusion detection systems (IDS)?
76. Does the IDS, where required or used, meet the following minimum requirements?
    a. Are balanced magnetic switches installed on all perimeter doors?
    b. Are sensors attached to windows and doors?
    c. Are sensors attached to structural sections which do not provide penetration resistance roughly equivalent to that required for the basic structure?
    d. Are IDS signals monitored at one central point, and is the guard force response initiated from that point?
    e. Are all sensor equipment, doors, drawers, and removable panels secured with key locks or screws and equipped with tamperproof switches?
    f. Have power supplies been protected against overload by fuses or circuit breakers?
    g. Have power supplies been protected against voltage transients?
    h. Have safety hazards been identified and controlled to preclude personnel exposure?
    i. Do IDS components meet electromagnetic interference/electromagnetic compatibility requirements?
    j. Do IDS components meet the spurious radiation requirements set by the Federal Communications Commission?
77. Do properly trained security alert teams back up the system?
78. Is the alarm system for active areas or structures placed in access mode during normal working hours?
79. Is the system tested prior to activation?
80. Is the system inspected regularly?
81. Is the system weatherproof?
82. Is an alternate or independent source of power available for use on the system in the event of power failure?
83. Is the emergency power source designed to cut in and operate automatically when normal power goes down?
84. Do trained and properly cleared personnel properly maintain the IDS system?
85. Are frequent tests conducted to determine the adequacy and promptness of response to alarm signals?
86. Are records kept of all alarm signals received to include time, date, location, action taken, and cause for alarm?
87. How frequent are nuisance alarms and what action is taken to reduce the number?
88. Does the organization have a current security education program?
89. Are all newly assigned personnel provided security indoctrination?
90. Is security education training conducted for all personnel at least annually?
91. Have security personnel been trained in procedures necessary for the implementation of emergency and disaster plans for their organization?
92. Are security personnel qualified in assigned weapons if required?
93. Have armed security personnel received instruction in the use of deadly force?
94. Does the security force have its own communication system with direct lines between security and restricted areas?
95. Does the security communication system provide the security personnel with the means of rapidly apprising their superiors of problem situations?
96. Does the organization use a security dog program?
97. Have direct communications with local municipal fire and police headquarters been established?

Figure 28.1 Continued

28.24   Self-Protection

Many assaults take place at either the workplace or home. Assaults in parking lots of shopping centers, office buildings, plants, etc., are becoming more prevalent. Some tips for self-protection are listed below:

1. Walk with someone. Arrange to meet other employees when entering and/or leaving the business premises. If security guards are available, you should have them escort you. This should be done when it is dark or at odd hours.
2. Stay in well-lighted areas. Stay near curbs, lighted entrances, light poles, etc. Avoid alleys, unlighted entrances, deserted stairwells, dark rooms, etc. Also, avoid walking near blind spots such as columns or between cars.
3. Stay near other people or crowds. Avoid shortcuts through parks, vacant lots, or deserted places.
4. Hold a purse close under your arm with latch in, not dangling. Long straps should be around the shoulder or neck. Never set a purse or wallet on store counters, in supermarket baskets, or on car or bus seats.
5. When shopping, do not put money or credit and debit cards on counter. Put it in the hand of the store clerk. Do not flash large amounts of money.
6. Pay attention to your surroundings. Keep alert. Pay attention to anything that is unusual, for example, people and vehicles.
7. If a driver stops to ask you questions, avoid getting near the car. Never reach in or get in a stranger's vehicle.
8. If you feel that you are being followed, then be prepared to take some action, for example, run. If someone is following you on foot, cross the street, change direction, or vary your pace. Proceed to a lighted store or home and call the police or relative or friend to pick you up. The police will usually escort you home. If someone is following you in a car, turn around and walk in the other direction. Record the license number and call the police.
9. When you go to your vehicle, have your key ready and check the front and back seats before entering.
10. If you have a dog, particularly of medium or large size, and you go to a park or other recreational area, or the neighborhood store, you should take the dog with you. The presence of a medium or large dog deters criminals even if the dog has a gentle personality.
11. If attacked, scream as loud as you can. It may scare the attacker away. Otherwise, kick in the groin or on the foot and foreleg. Doing this will give you a chance to escape.

28.25   Summary

Physical security measures help remove the opportunity for employees and customers to remove inventory, assets, and supplies from a business organization premises. Therefore, it cannot be overlooked. For small businesses, the costs of security measures can be onerous because businesses have to balance their needs and benefits to the costs. Various electronic and other devices are making rapid advances in technology. These new and improved systems are becoming cheaper. Many businesses, regardless of size, are using security systems. One system attaches labels that will set off an alarm if the item is not scanned at the checkout counter. In another system, clothing stores attach dye devices that will explode the dye over the clothing when a customer removes the merchandise from the store without it being scanned at the checkout counter. Each business organization will have to evaluate the various security measures to meet its particular requirements.

Search Warrants

29

29.1 Introduction

Law enforcement officers may be required to execute search warrants to obtain evidence. Subjects of an investigation will usually keep some culpatory evidence in their possession, either at their residence or business premises. A search warrant authorizes limited intrusion into an area where there is reasonable expectation of privacy to search and seize certain specified evidence of a crime based on probable cause. A judge or magistrate is usually willing to issue a search warrant when information is provided by a reliable source. Fraud examiners can be used as a reliable source when they uncover evidence that other financial records are available at some identified location. Generally, evidence obtained by a defective search warrant is no longer suppressed if the law enforcement officers relied on those defective warrants and have acted in good faith. However, search warrants may cause many motions to be filed, which can tie up a case. Also, they can trigger Fourth Amendment considerations such as staleness, overbreadth, and other issues.

29.2 Fourth Amendment

The Fourth Amendment to the U.S. Constitution, adopted in 1791, states,

> The right of the people to be secure in their persons, houses, papers, and effects, against unreasonable searches and seizures, shall not be violated, and no Warrants shall issue, but upon probable cause, supported by Oath or affirmation, and particularly describing the place to be searched, and the persons or things to be seized.

29.3 Criminal Procedure

Rule 41 of the Federal Rules of Criminal Procedure contains the procedures for obtaining a warrant:

> Rule 41(a) provides for the issuance of a warrant by a federal magistrate or a judge of a state court of record within the district where the property or person sought is located, upon request by a federal law enforcement officer or an attorney for the government.
>
> Rule 41(b) provides for issuance of a warrant to seize (1) property that constitutes evidence of the commission of a crime; or (2) contraband, the fruits of a crime, or things otherwise criminally possessed; or (3) property designed or intended to be used as an instrumentality of a crime; or (4) people, when there is probable cause for their arrest.

Rule 41(c) provides for issuance of a warrant based on a sworn affidavit, which establishes the grounds for issuance of the warrant. If the federal magistrate is satisfied that the grounds for the application exist or that there is probable cause to believe that they exist and approves the warrant, then the officer has 10 days to execute the warrant. The search should be performed between 6:00 A.M. and 10:00 P.M., or the officer should be able to show cause why this cannot be done.

Rule 41(d) requires the officer taking the property to provide a copy of the warrant and a receipt for the property taken. The return shall be made promptly and accompanied by a written inventory of the property taken to the magistrate.

Rule 41(e) provides that an aggrieved person of an unlawful search and seizure may move the district court for the return of said property.

Rule 41(f) provides that a motion to suppress evidence may be made in the court of the district of trial as provided by Rule 12.

29.4   Purpose

A search warrant authorizes a limited intrusion into an area protected by the Fourth Amendment. A neutral and detached magistrate may, upon a finding of probable cause, issue a search warrant. The search warrant must specify with particularity the area or premise to be searched and the persons or things to be seized. This requirement of particularity prevents any kinds of exploratory searches. The premises to be searched must be sufficiently described to enable the executing officers to ascertain and identify it with reasonable certainty. Also, the persons or things to be seized must be specifically identified without leaving any doubt. The test is whether the officer can identify the item to be seized.

29.5   Privacy Expectation

The Supreme Court has adopted a two-pronged test in determining that privacy interests are protected. First, the individual must show a subjective expectation of privacy. Second, the privacy expectation must be generally recognized as reasonable. The courts have found reasonable expectation of privacy as to a person's home, a public employee's desk or file cabinets in the office, a person's luggage, and on his/her person. However, the courts have found no reasonable expectation of privacy in a warrantless installation of a pen register on a telephone or goods displayed in a store.

29.6   Probable Cause

The Fourth Amendment requires a finding of probable cause before the issuance of a valid search warrant. This protects an individual's expectation of privacy. Probable cause has been defined as facts and circumstances that will cause a prudent person to believe that an offense has been committed and that seizable property can be found at the place or on the person to be searched. Law enforcement has probable cause to conduct a search if a reasonably prudent officer, based on the facts and circumstances known by the officer, would be justified in concluding that the items sought are connected with criminal activities and that they will be found in the area to be searched.

While proof beyond a reasonable doubt is not required, some factual showing is required and not suppositions or speculations. The following have been found to be insufficient in establishing probable cause:

- Mere conclusory statement or an officer's mere notification of bare conclusions from other(s) (*Illinois v. Gates*, 462 U.S. 213)
- An officer's mere suspicion of criminal activity (*Brinegar v. United States*, 338 U.S. 175)
- Mere association with known or suspected criminals (*Ybarra v. Illinois*, 444 U.S. 85)
- An individual's mere presence at a given location (*United States v. Butts*, 704 F.2d 70)

The conclusions by an affiant may be included in a search warrant affidavit and considered in determining whether there is probable cause. Factual conclusions are a normal, necessary, and perfectly acceptable part of an affidavit. However, such conclusions must be drawn from facts contained within the affidavit and cannot be premised on the conclusory statements of others.

29.7   Magistrate

Facts justifying probable cause to search must be subjected to the scrutiny of a neutral and detached magistrate. As the Supreme Court stated in *Steagald v. United States*, 451 U.S. 204:

> The placement of this checkpoint between the government and the citizen implicitly acknowledges that an officer engaged in the often competitive enterprise of ferreting out crime may lack sufficient objectivity to weigh correctly the strength of the evidence against the individual's interests in protecting his own liberty.

An officer, in seeking a search warrant, must present sufficient facts in the affidavit to enable a magistrate to make an independent determination as to the existence of probable cause. Probable cause may be based on hearsay information and need not reflect direct personal observations. The magistrate must be informed of the surrounding circumstances. The Supreme Court has strongly expressed preference for using search warrants because it imposes an orderly procedure and reduces the risks inherent in police actions.

29.8   Staleness

The amount of delay that will make information stale will depend on the facts of the case. Staleness cannot be resolved by reference to the number of days between the facts relied upon and the time the warrant is issued. If the items still have a reasonable chance of being present, then the warrant can be issued even after a lengthy time. The staleness test is not designed to create an arbitrary time limitation. The test is whether or not the affidavit sufficiently establishes a fair probability that contraband or evidence of a crime would be found on the premises. The facts and circumstances of the case, including the nature of the unlawful activity, the length of time, and the nature of the property to be seized, must be considered.

29.9　Probable Cause Based on Informants

Probable cause may be based on hearsay evidence whether in whole or in part [FRE Rule 41(c)(1)]. Prior to 1983, the court had a two-pronged test to determine an informant's reliability. First, the facts that the informant provided must show the informant is credible and reliable. Second, some of the information can be verified. In *Illinois v. Gates* (462 U.S. 213), the Supreme Court abandoned the two-pronged test and reinstated the totality-of-the-circumstance test for probable cause determinations. Elements of knowledge, reliability, and veracity were relevant considerations in the totality of circumstances. A deficiency in one element could be compensated for by a strong showing in another or by some other indication of reliability. The court reiterated the standard of review. A magistrate should review the evidence on the whole for substantial basis. It rejected any after-the-fact review by a magistrate for a probable cause determination. One way to establish credibility and reliability is by having two informants independently corroborate each other's statements. By telling consistent, yet independent, stories, the informants provided "cross-corroboration." This enhances the reliability on the application for a warrant.

29.10　Particularity

The Fourth Amendment requires that a search warrant "particularly" describe (1) the place to be searched and (2) the persons or things to be seized. The aim is to protect the privacy of citizens against general rummaging through their possessions. General exploratory searches are forbidden. The Supreme Court has interpreted this requirement to mean that the description of the place to be searched be such that the officer can easily ascertain and identify the place intended. Also, the Fourth Amendment requires particularity as to items to be seized. The purpose is to prevent general seizure of property. Only items listed in a warrant can be seized. In *Andresen v. Maryland* (427 U.S. 463) the court expounded searches and seizures of personal or business records. It stated:

> There are grave dangers inherent in executing a warrant authorizing a search and seizure of a person's papers that are not necessarily present in executing a warrant to search for physical objects whose relevance is more easily ascertainable. In searches for papers, it is certain that some innocuous documents will be examined, at least cursorily, in order to determine whether they are, in fact, among those papers authorized to be seized. In this kind of search, responsible officials, including judicial officials, must take care to assure that they are conducted in a manner that minimizes unwarranted intrusions on privacy.

The Ninth Circuit has suggested that an affidavit should always be incorporated into the warrant. The affidavit can be used to provide further guidance to seizing agents and save an otherwise deficient search warrant. Generally, it is not a search warrant if it contains standards that guide officers in avoiding seizure of items not relevant to the case. The

Ninth Circuit overturned a warrant because it was not specific enough. The warrant should have described particular items found in the possession of loan sharks and bookmakers, such as "pay and collection sheets, lists of loan customers, loan accounts and telephone numbers, line sheets, bet slips, tally sheets, and bottom sheets." A search warrant is valid if it fully describes the alleged criminal activities in connection with which the items were sought. In *United States v. Stubbs* (873 F.2d 210) the court decided the particularity issue by focusing on:

1. Whether probable cause existed to seize all items of a particular type described in the warrant.
2. Whether the warrant set out objective standards by which officers could differentiate items subject to seizure from those that are not.
3. Whether the government was able to describe the items more particularly in light of the information available to it at the time the warrant was issued.

The Ninth Circuit suppressed evidence in the Stubbs case because the warrant that authorized the seizure of all financial records was too general. The warrant should have been more specific because there were two former employees cooperating in the investigation who knew where various documents were stored.

29.11   Places to Be Searched

The Fourth Amendment requires that the warrant particularly describe the place to be searched. The Fourth Amendment does not require legal descriptions. It points to a definitely ascertainable place so as to exclude all others. The test for determining the sufficiency of a description is:

1. Whether the place is described sufficiently enough to enable an officer to locate and identify the premises with reasonable effort.
2. Whether there is reasonable probability that another premise might be mistakenly searched.

There have been situations when law enforcement has searched the wrong place, even though the warrant was stated correctly. The search of an entire apartment building where probable cause was limited to only one apartment was not permitted. The courts have ruled that the name of an apartment complex or business enterprise will prevail over a street address. Also, the name of the occupant with a description of the premises will prevail over the stated apartment number or floor.

29.12   Items to Be Seized

A search warrant must describe the items to be seized. The warrant must be worded in such a way to describe only those items directly related to the crime under investigation. It must be drafted so as to prevent indiscriminate seizing of both relevant and irrelevant evidence. The general rule is to describe with as much specificity as possible.

29.13 Generic Description

When the precise identity of items cannot be ascertained, then the use of generic class of items will suffice. Some courts have indicated that a general description of property will be acceptable provided the circumstances and nature of the activity under investigation are identified. The use of a generic term or general description is only acceptable when a more specific description of the items to be seized is not available. Failure to use specificity when information is available will invalidate a general description in a warrant. When there is probable cause to believe that the premises to be searched contain a class of generic items, a portion of which may be contraband, then a search warrant may direct inspection of the entire class. There must be articulated standards for the officers to follow in distinguishing between legal and illegal property. These standards may be contained in the search warrant or the accompanying affidavit. To determine if a search warrant containing a generic description satisfies the specificity requirement, the warrant must:

1. Establish that there is a reason to believe that a large collection of similar items, for example, evidence of a crime, is present on the premises to be searched.
2. Explain that the methods to be used by officers are to differentiate the evidence of a crime from items that are not.

29.14 Permeated-with-Fraud Concept

When a business operates in a way that every transaction is potential evidence of fraud, the "permeated-with-fraud" concept allows seizure of all business records. If the whole business is a fraud, a warrant may properly permit the seizure of everything the officer finds. To establish that a business was permeated with fraud, there must be a pattern of criminal conduct that shows the existence of a plan, scheme, or artifice. When investigating the business practices, the investigation should not focus just on a small segment of operations but should be based on a major portion of the business operations. The permeated-with-fraud concept does not allow for wholesale seizure of all books and records of a business. The search warrant or affidavit must accurately describe those books and records that relate to the pervasive scheme to defraud.

29.15 Plain-View Doctrine

Law enforcement officers sometimes find other articles that they desire to seize because of their apparent connection to some criminal activity. The plain-view doctrine provides that a law enforcement officer may seize evidence when the law enforcement officer is lawfully on the premises by virtue of:

- Searches pursuant to warrants issued for other purposes
- Searches pursuant to exceptions to the warrant requirement

or in the performance of general police duties inadvertently comes upon the item and:

- It is immediately apparent that the item is incriminating.
- It is incriminating evidence.

The plain-view doctrine does not allow the seizure of material when the incriminating or evidentiary character of the material becomes known only after close inspection. Also, it does not allow law enforcement officers to examine items to expand from observation into a general exploratory search. Probable cause is required to invoke the plain-view doctrine as it applies to seizures.

29.16   Inadvertent Discovery

Inadvertence is a common element of most plain-view seizures. It is not a necessary element. However, if police fail to particularize evidence in advance with the expectation that the evidence exists, then the warrant lacks probable cause for seizure of such evidence. The second circuit concluded that where proof indicated that the police conducted a thorough investigation of a crime and the means to prove it and the search is conducted in a manner reasonable in duration and intensity, the property seized may be found to be inadvertently discovered in plain view.

29.17   Immediately Apparent Requirement

The incriminating nature of the evidence must be immediately apparent. The immediately apparent requirement ensures that the police will not use this method as a way to justify exploratory searches. Also, the police must be aware of some facts and circumstances that can justify suspicion that items are fruits, instruments, or evidence of crime. The first circuit said that the plain-view doctrine allowed evidence discovered in plain view to be lawfully seized even though the police were not originally authorized to search for it when:

- The officer's presence at the point of discovery is lawful.
- Discovery of seized items is inadvertent.
- The evidentiary value of the item is immediately apparent to the searchers.

29.18   Affidavit Inaccuracies

A warrant may become invalidated if the supporting affidavit is inaccurate. The Supreme Court in *Frank v. Delaware* (438 U.S. 154) identified some circumstances that could mandate an evidentiary hearing. If a defendant challenges the truthfulness of statements contained in the affidavit, then the defendant is entitled to a "Frank" hearing. The defendant must show in a "Frank" hearing:

> The false statement was knowingly and intentionally made, or with a reckless regard for the truth; and the allegedly false statement is necessary to the magistrate's finding of probable cause.

The court must void the warrant if the defendant proves the allegations by a preponderance of the evidence and there is no support of probable cause.

29.19   Exclusionary Rule

The exclusionary rule prohibits introduction into evidence of any material seized during an illegal search. This rule also prohibits any derivative evidence that is the product of the primary evidence or is acquired as an indirect result of an illegal search. In *United States v. Leon* (468 U.S. 897) the Supreme Court modified the exclusionary rule for search warrants that were obtained in "good faith." The court did not want to penalize police who thought that they were acting properly in obtaining a warrant, even though the warrant failed for some technicality at a later date. The court provided the good faith factors:

- The warrants were facially valid.
- The warrants were properly approved by a neutral and detached judicial officer.
- The police relied on the magistrate's probable cause determination.
- The officer's reliance was objectively reasonable.

The evidence will not be suppressed if the exclusionary rule is not applied. The exclusionary rule is a judicial remedy which is designed to deter police misconduct. The appropriateness of excluding evidence must be evaluated by weighing the costs and benefits of suppression. Suppression is not appropriate if the police acted in good faith that the warrant was valid and authorized their conduct. The court defined good faith as the lack of disregard or conscious indifference to Rule 41.

29.20   Inevitable Discovery Exception

The Supreme Court in *Nix v. Williams* (467 U.S. 431) adopted the "inevitable discovery doctrine" as an exception to the exclusionary rule. Evidence discovered as a result of violations of Sixth Amendment rights can be admitted at trial if the prosecution can establish, by a preponderance of the evidence, that such evidence ultimately and inevitably would have been discovered by lawful means.

29.21   Independent Source Rule

The independent source rule is another exception to the exclusionary rule. It provides that evidence will not be suppressed if the government obtains the evidence from an independent and legal source.

29.22   Intermingling of Documents

Only specific and listed items in a search warrant may be seized. There are occasions where documents are so intermingled that they cannot be feasibly sorted on site. The wholesale seizure for later detailed examination of records not described in a warrant is prohibited. All items in a set of files may be inspected during a search, provided that sufficient guidelines for identifying the documents sought are provided in the search warrant and are followed by the officers conducting the search. Where documents are so intermingled that they cannot be sorted on site, the court has suggested that police should seal and hold the documents pending approval by a magistrate of a further search. If there is a need to transport the documents, then police should apply for specific authorization for large-scale removal of material to a site more suitable for searching.

29.23   Effect of Unauthorized Seizure on Valid Search

When a search is conducted and items are seized that are not specifically described in the warrant, the remedy by the court is to exclude the items that are improperly taken. The court fulfills three purposes in the following ways:

1. It erects a deterrent to illegal searches.
2. It prohibits the government from benefiting from its own wrongdoing by not using the illegally seized evidence to convict.
3. By removing the illegally seized items, it precludes itself from serving as an accomplice in the violation of the constitution.

It is permissible for federal agents to take along local law enforcement officers when executing search warrants. However, the local law enforcement officers must abide by the specifics and limitations of the search warrant.

29.24   Conforming Warrants to Technology

The search and seizure of data contained in computers and other electronic media raise various issues that must be considered. Information in computers is not evident like paper records but must be generated by particular commands. Also, the data contained in computers may not be in readable form and may be intermingled with information that is not relevant. When it comes to computers, the question of what can be searched and seized arises. Also, the Electronic Communications Privacy Act (ECPA) imposes various kinds of restrictions and obligations on law enforcement agencies. Some of the issues that relate to computer search warrants are as follows:

- Establishing probable cause
- Execution or access
- Segregation issues
- ECPA issues
- Privacy Protection Act issues
- Subpoenas for computer records

Probable cause does not authorize police to search any computer found on the premises. Police must describe their beliefs that the computer was used for the creation and/or storage of financial records. The officer must determine the computer's role in the offense. Key questions are:

- Is there probable cause to seize hardware?
- Is there probable cause to seize software?
- Is there probable cause to seize data?

In developing probable cause, the investigator should evaluate the record system in operation and determine if there are any network and backup systems. Additional considerations are:

- Functions of the computer
- Records processed and stored on the system
- Programs used
- Sophistication of system by users
- Type of storage facilities
- Media used

The seizing agent should describe the information and items to be seized as explicitly as possible in the affidavit. The seizing agent should ask for express authority to remove any hardware in order to conduct an off-site search. The agent should mention any manuals or instructions for the computer system. A "no-knock warrant" should be requested if destruction is a concern. Probable cause to seize a computer does not necessarily mean the entire computer system (e.g., all peripheral devices). The search warrant for computers needs to describe the computer system and the information contained therein in detail. For a computer not under the control of the suspect, subpoenas should be used for computerized information.

29.25 Electronic Communications Privacy Act

Title 18 U.S.C. 2702 prohibits anyone to access stored communications and transactional records unless that person or government follows established procedures. Law enforcement must have a valid search and seizure warrant in order to obtain electronic data files. The search warrant must comply with the Federal Rules of Criminal Procedure or the state equivalent. Prior notice to the subscriber or customer is required if a governmental unit uses an administrative subpoena or summons. The court must approve and issue a non-disclosure order to prevent subscriber or customer notification. Attorney's fees and other litigation costs are recoverable by aggrieved parties if they win their case.

29.26 Privacy Protection Act

The Privacy Protection Act (42 U.S.C. 2000aa et seq.) was enacted to protect the press and certain other persons not suspected of committing a crime with protections not provided by the Fourth Amendment. The Privacy Protection Act protects two classes of materials:

work product materials and documentary materials. Work product materials are defined to mean materials that:

- Are prepared or created by any person for communication to the public
- Are possessed for purposes of communication to the public
- Contain mental impressions, conclusions, opinions, or theories of the person who prepared or created such material

Documentary materials are defined to mean materials upon which information is recorded and includes written or printed materials, films, video, and any mechanically, magnetically, or electronically recorded cards, tapes, or disks. Both documentary materials and work product materials do not include contraband, fruits of a crime, or materials intended for criminal use. There are two exceptions:

1. A search is permitted if the person possessing the materials has committed the criminal offense to which the materials relate.
2. A search is permitted when it appears that the use of a subpoena or other less intrusive means of obtaining the materials would cause serious bodily injury to a human being.

Under this act, the aggrieved person may seek actual damages, but not less than $1000 liquidated damages. Attorney's fees and other litigation costs are also recoverable.

29.27   Summary

Search warrants are a very valuable tool for law enforcement. To obtain a search warrant, the officer/agent must present all the facts so that an independent magistrate can draw the same conclusions that the officer/agent has drawn. The search warrant and the probable cause affidavit must describe in detail the specific evidence the officer/agent is seeking. Without the specificity, a search warrant cannot be obtained or, even worse, the evidence obtained from a bad search may not be admissible in court under the exclusionary rule. Law enforcement should consider the use of a subpoena or summons before considering a search warrant. The requirements of a search warrant states that the officer/agent gather more facts in order to obtain a search warrant. Particular attention should be considered when dealing with financial records and computer files. Commingling of legal and illegal documents presents a litigation hazard for law enforcement.

Computer Crimes

30

30.1 Introduction

Computers are increasingly used in our daily lives. We use them at work and at home. We use computers to shop and bank. The banking industry is relying more and more on computers and for their customers to do banking online. It cuts down on payroll expenses. A person can make withdrawals, deposits, and transfers at Automatic Teller Machines (ATMs). The use of credit cards involves using computers. Most businesses use computers for conducting sales and making inventory purchases. Service businesses and governmental agencies are also relying on the Internet to conduct business. It is a new way of shopping. Some companies are solely on the Internet with Web sites. People use the Internet to shop and communicate with family and friends by using electronic mail, called e-mail.

Most computer crimes are just new ways to commit old crimes. Criminals who used the telephone or mail to commit crimes now use computers and the Internet. Computers have also made it possible to commit new types of crime.

30.2 Types of Computer Crimes

Computer crimes can be classified into six types.

30.2.1 Fraud

Fraud involves deception where a person makes a misrepresentation. It typically involves:

a. The creation of nonexistent companies to receive payments, obtain credit, etc. It is a version of corporate identity theft. A criminal can set up a bank account in the name of the company for which he/she works or has worked. He/she is in a position to deposit corporate funds to bank accounts that he/she controls and not the company. Former employees use the company for obtaining credit.
b. The criminal bills for nonexistent goods and services. If the company receiving the bills has poor internal controls, the bills are paid.
c. The criminal manipulates data to create a false picture of an individual or a corporation's financial assets. This is usually referred to as "cooking the books" as it relates to corporations. Its purpose is to present a good financial picture for the company. The purpose is to make the company look good for shareholders and/or creditors. This was one reason for the collapse for the Enron and ImClone debacles. This falsification can result in getting credit or paying dividends and/or bonuses to officers. For individuals, it is usually done to commit bank fraud by completing false applications for a loan or shopping for goods and services without paying for them.

d. Another form of misrepresentation involves using computer-generated records, for example, false documents, identification cards, and false accounting statements. This is done primarily in identity theft. It is very easy to use computers to generate false documents. It is often used by criminals to duplicate false credit cards or debit cards from stolen information. A criminal group in South Florida put a card reader in a shopping mall that would read credit and debit cards. It looked like an ATM machine. When a customer put his/her card into the machine, it would appear the machine would not work. In reality, it read the information on the card and the criminals made a duplicate and would go to an ATM machine and withdraw funds.

30.2.2 Embezzlement

Embezzlement involves employee diversion of company funds for personal use. This is an old type of crime, but a new method of committing it.

30.2.3 Misappropriation of Computer Time

Misappropriation of computer time involves unauthorized use of a company's computer facilities for private amusement or gain.

30.2.4 Theft of Programs

Theft of programs involves the unauthorized user to steal costly programs from the developer by internal theft or through telecommunications.

30.2.5 Theft of Information

Theft of information involves the following:

1. Information such as mailing or customer lists are duplicated and sold surreptitiously to the competition or other persons who value them.
2. This involves the illegal acquisition of valuable confidential information of a company. This is often referred to a corporate espionage. It includes:
   - Marketing plans
   - Secret processes
   - Product design
   - Copyrighted material
   - Electronically distributed internal communications
   - Technical data

30.2.6 Sabotage

Sabotage involves the damage of company property. It is referred to as corporate sabotage. It entails:

- Vandalism against the employer. This involves the destruction of computer equipment, for example, computer CPUs, printers, and other peripherals.

- The company's computer systems are disrupted by viruses or worms.
- Protests. The company's computer systems are invaded by protest groups. They place pop-up notices (a form of advertising) or send e-mails.

30.3 Computer Crime Warning Signs

There are warning signs that can alert one to possible problems with their computer system. When these warning signs appear, one should begin an investigation to uncover the problem.

1. *Suspicious circumstances.* When a person gets on his/her computer, there may be some things happening that are not normal. For example:
   a. You get pop-up advertisements when you are not connected to the Internet or you get a pop-up advertisement that addresses you by name.
   b. The home page has mysteriously changed.
   c. A search term is entered into the Internet Explorer's address bar and you get an unfamiliar site that handles the search.
   d. Your system runs noticeably slower than it did before.
2. *Forms not sequential.* Numbered control forms such as purchase orders, invoices, and checks are not recorded or filed in sequential order.
3. *Customer complaints.* There are a large number of customer complaints about billing errors. This usually means false or overbilling or overlapping of accounts receivable.
4. *Poor security.* Internal controls over receipts and disbursements are lacking. Also, poor controls over access to computers. Passwords are readily available to anyone.

30.4 Computer Crime Techniques

The following are some of the common techniques of computer crimes.

30.4.1 Salami Technique

The Salami technique involves the theft of small amounts of assets from a large number of sources without noticeably reducing the whole. Salami slicing uses computers to make electronic transfers of funds from hundreds or even thousands of separate accounts. The amounts stolen are small and most account holders do not notice the theft. However, small amounts add up and the thief can end up with a large amount of funds. This is usually found in programs where there are mathematical computations (e.g., mortgage payments, loan payments, and annuities).

30.4.2 "Logic Bomb"

A computer program executed at a specific time period or when a specific event occurs detonates these bombs. They are deliberately damaging, but they do not replicate. They are designed to lay dormant within a computer for a period of time. They are designed to explode at some predetermined date or event. Logic bombs are favorites among disgruntled ex-employees because they can set it off at any time after their departure.

30.4.3 Electronic Eavesdropping

Electronic eavesdropping involves the interception of electronic messages. This can be easily done if the computer system is using wireless means of communicating.

30.4.4 "Trapdoor"

Programmers insert debugging aids that provide breaks in the instructions for insertion of additional code and intermediate output capabilities. Programmers insert instructions that allow them to circumvent these controls.

30.4.5 Personation

The criminal uses a legitimate user's facilities to gain input into the computer system. This is usually an unauthorized person who uses the access codes of an authorized person to gain access to the computer system.

30.4.6 Masquerading

The criminal taps into communication lines of a computer network system. By doing so, he can intercept messages and change them or redirect messages or funds.

30.4.7 Data Diddling

This involves changing data before or during entry into the system, such as forging or counterfeiting documents used for data entry or exchanging valid disks with modified replacements.

30.4.8 Scavenging

Obtaining information left around a computer system, in computer room trashcans, and the like.

30.4.9 Wiretapping

Wiretapping involves tapping into a computer's communication links to read the information being transmitted between systems and networks.

30.4.10 Trojan Horse

Instructions are covertly placed in a program that causes the computer to perform unauthorized functions but usually allows the intended performance. This is most common in computer-based frauds and sabotage.

30.4.11 Computer Viruses

These are malicious codes that cause damage to system information or deny access to the information through self-replication. Viruses or "self-replicating programs" are written for the purpose of infecting a computer system. They are usually transmitted through a diskette, Internet, or electronic mail. Some viruses are known to erase all data from the hard drive, rendering the computer useless. They can even melt down the motherboard.

30.4.12 Rabbits

These are instructions that order a computer to perform useless tasks endlessly, multiplying ever more work orders until they finally overwhelm the computer and it shuts down.

30.4.13 Worms

Worms take up residence in a computer and use up space until the machine slows down or crashes.

30.4.14 Cyber Pirates

Cyber pirates involve creating "con" (confidence) schemes using the computer. They can involve various schemes, for example, investment schemes, work-at-home schemes, and insurance scams. In one instance, a cyber pirate lied to an insurance company to collect policy money. The cyber pirate created a phantom ship using the computers of the maritime agency. The cyber pirate took out an insurance policy and later wrecked the ship.

30.5 Computer Embezzler Profile

The FBI has profiled various types of criminals. When it comes to computer crimes, they found the following motivations and personal characteristics:

1. *Motivation.* Cyber criminals have three types of motivation factors.
   - *Financial commitments.* Like other white-collar criminals, they commit the crime for financial gain because of personal financial crises. This could be due to either a lavish lifestyle or some crises that caused a financial hardship.
   - *Rationalization.* A common characteristic for the criminal is to rationalize their action. They make claims to justify their action. Examples are: "I should have got the promotion." "The company owes it to me for the work I've done." "I deserve the money."
   - *Challenge.* Some people do it for the challenge of seeing whether they can get caught. Computer hackers like the challenge of breaking into computer systems.
2. Personal characteristics
   - The common gender is white male.
   - People who commit computer fraud usually do not have any criminal record. It is usually their first offense.

- The person is usually married with one or more children living at home. However, there are many cases where it is only a one parent family.
- The person lives a middle class lifestyle.
- The person's income is usually in the top 40% of the population. They generally earn between $50,000 and $120,000.
- The person usually works by himself/herself. He/she is not closely supervised and is a trusted employee.
- The most common age group for computer fraud is males in their mid-thirties.
- The average loss is about 120% of his salary.
- The computer criminal usually has a bachelor's degree. In some cases, they have postgraduate degrees. In a few cases, young men, 14 to 22 years of age, may hack into computer systems for the challenge of it.

30.6 Countermeasures

There are basic measures that a company should take to secure their computer systems. This becomes more important as more businesses rely on computer systems. There are four basic countermeasures.

1. *Audit trail.* The computer system should be able to identify and record:
   - *Terminal used to gain access.* It should identify what terminal the unauthorized access occurred at and by whom.
   - *When it was accessed.* The computer system should show when the unauthorized access occurred.
   - *Identification of the operator.* It should be able to identify the person who made the unauthorized access.
   - *Files accessed by the operator.* It should be able to determine what files were accessed by the unauthorized person.
   - *How they were used.* When files were accessed by an unauthorized person, those files should be reviewed to see what was done to them. This may mean to review those files in detail.
2. *Shared responsibility.* There should be more than one person who has access to the computer system or module. All personnel should be instructed on security control procedures. When a business has more than one computer and staff members, the company should institute computer controls. An employee handling billing should not be able to access payroll, accounts receivable, or accounts payable modules. Any overrides by management should be reviewed by senior management and/or the internal audit staff. Most commercial computer accounting programs have access controls built into them.
3. *Outside testing.* External and/or internal auditors should examine the integrity and security of the system. This should be done once a year at a minimum. If there has been a breach of security, then this should be done more often as necessary. If the computer is linked to the Internet, then any unauthorized access should be fully investigated.
4. *Hiring practices.* Companies should investigate the background and employment history of persons working in their computer operations. Credit reports should be

obtained for prospective new hires. Criminal record checks should also be done. References should be checked. It is unlawful for a reference to disclose the reason for dismissal. However, one can get around it if they ask, "Would you rehire this person?" If the answer is no, then this should send a red flag up for not hiring the person.

30.7 Computer Crime Investigation

In many fraud cases today, the criminal will use a computer to either plan, keep records, or communicate with other conspirators. In other cases, the computer will be the centerpiece of the investigation since it can be used as the tool of the crime or the object of the crime. Investigators are having to become more familiar with computer crimes since the computer is used as an instrument in committing fraud, either directly or indirectly.

30.7.1 Preparation

Law enforcement are now seizing computers, both hardware and software, in conducting search warrants, because more and more criminals are using computers. Therefore, the investigator must have the following skills:

a. Have a basic understanding of computer operations and terminology.
b. Develop the technical skills to direct an investigation that may draw on the expertise of private consultants.
c. Be aware of the various schemes used to penetrate computer systems.
d. Be able to identify the source documents that can be important evidence in proving your case.

30.7.2 Documentary Evidence

Documentary evidence is the most important element in computer crime investigation. One should get as much evidence as possible. Forensic science analysis can be used to analyze magnetic tapes, disks, cassettes, input documents, and other relevant material for:

a. Fingerprints
b. Hairs
c. Indented writing
d. Erasure and alterations
e. Handwriting analysis
f. Typewriter or printer identification
g. Trace any evidence that may be relevant

To identify a questioned document with its author, consider the following:

a. Origin of document
b. Contents
c. Circumstances of preparation
d. Nature of deletions, additions, or other alterations

e. Age of document
f. Paper source
g. Handwriting
h. Typewriting

30.7.3 Computer Systems Investigation

It is important to get as much information about a computer system before conducting a search. The following information should be obtained:

- System configuration. Is it a stand-alone, LAN connection, WAN connection, or some other type of connection?
- Type of hardware (CPU), memory, and storage capacity (hard drive(s), other media).
- Type of versions of application software, brand names.
- External or internal modem, brand, type, and speed.
- Security system (access controls, encryption). Is the computer password protected?
- Can it be accessed without the suspect's knowledge?
- Are there booby traps that destroy information if unauthorized access is attempted?
- There are antiseizure devices on the market. These devices can erase the hard drive.
- A VCR recorder on the hard drive will erase it. The removal of the CPU case will activate inverter, which will trash the hard drive.
- Where exactly is the system physically located? The investigator should be careful of the surroundings. It is best to remove the system to a forensic laboratory, but circumstances may require that the computer system be examined on the premises.
- Printers and other peripherals should be seized. Printers and peripherals may have memory that can contain important evidence. Other items to consider are multiplexers, routers, bridges, printer servers, and repeaters.

30.7.4 Crime Scene Tool Kit

It is important to have a portable tool kit when searching microcomputers consisting of operating system software, application software, hardware, a set of computer maintenance tools, for example, Phillips head screwdrivers and pliers. Current microcomputer software includes MS Windows, MS-DOS, and the latest OS software for IBM and Apple computers. Utility software should provide disk editing, data recovery, diagnostics, and virus scanning. Also, tools that may allow one to crack common application specific password systems should be in the tool kit. Other hardware to consider is cables, disk drives, tape drives, power supplies, dialed number recorders, surge protectors, and a wrist strap for grounding.

30.7.5 General Conduct of Searches

When conducting a search of computers, the following guidelines are provided:

1. Immediately get people away from the computer. This will prevent any suspect from destroying computer files or the computer itself.
2. Photograph and videotape the area, screen, front and back of each system, and peripherals.

3. If you decide to unplug the system, do so at the wall or outside power source. (Using the switch may invite an unwanted action, such as reformat the hard drive or initiate a virus.)
4. If an older system, park the hard drive.
5. Leave a system disk in the drive and tape it to prevent booting from the hard drive. Most computers will not boot if a disk is in the drive.
6. Label all hardware, documentation, disks, and so forth.
7. Take all documents along with the system.
8. Look for documentation containing passwords.
9. Before removing the equipment, check for magnetic fields at doors and sign on (use a compass).
10. Use surge protectors.
11. Use your own software to examine the system.
12. Create bit-stream backup copies from the original storage media to allow restoring to the exact condition.
13. Create forensic search images of seized storage media for review. Never use the evidence itself.
14. Secure the original media sources as critical evidence.
15. Review, search, and inspect the forensic search image system for relevant evidence.
16. Document all steps taken.
17. The defendant may help, but do not let him/her near the machine and ensure that the defendant's rights are not violated.
18. Ensure that a chain of custody is maintained and completely documented for all access and use of evidentiary materials.
19. Prepare detailed reports of findings that present information and support conclusions using a minimum of technical jargon.

30.7.6 Cautions

It should be kept in mind that computer evidence can be destroyed with the touch of a keyboard. Computer evidence must be reliable and complete. Search procedures must allow for replication of results by anyone. Defense attorneys will question every aspect of computer evidence. Investigators must follow search procedures, identification processes, and preservation of electronic evidence. Investigators should copy all data from the hard drives and work from the copies. The original hard drives should be safely secured.

30.7.7 Prevention Measures

The National Fraud Information Center offers the following suggestions in preventing fraud on the Internet:

- Never reveal checking account numbers, credit card numbers, or other personal financial data at any Web site or online service location unless you are sure you know where this information will be directed.
- After you have subscribed to an online service provider, you may be asked for credit card information or passwords. Do not provide it because the service provider has ready access to your credit card information and passwords.

- Never give your social security number to anyone on the Internet unless you are applying for credit or contacting the Social Security Administration.
- Beware of dangerous downloads from the Internet. In downloading programs to see pictures, hear music, play games, etc., you could be downloading a virus that wipes out your computer files or connects your modem to a foreign telephone number, resulting in expensive phone charges.
- Pay the safest way. Credit cards are the safest way to pay for online purchases because you can dispute the charges if you never get the goods or services or the offer was misrepresented. Federal law limits your liability to $50 if someone makes unauthorized charges to your account and most credit card issuers will remove them completely if you report the problem promptly.
- Do not believe promises of easy money. If someone claims that you can earn money with little or no work, get a loan or credit card even if you have bad credit, or make money on an investment with little or no risk, it is probably a scam.
- Understand the offer. A legitimate seller will give you all the details about the products or services, the total price, the delivery time, the refund and cancellation policies, and the terms of any warranty.
- Be cautious about unsolicited e-mails. They are often fraudulent. If you are familiar with the company or charity that sent you the e-mail and you do not want to receive further messages, send a reply asking to be removed from the e-mail list.

30.8   Child Exploitation

One concern by law enforcement is the exploitation of children using the Internet. Some individuals seduce children through attention, affection, kindness, and even gifts. These individuals devote considerable amount of time, money, and energy in the process. They engage in sexually explicit conversations with children. Some offenders collect and trade pornographic pictures, while others seek face-to-face contact for direct victimization. Computer sex offenders can be any age or sex.

30.8.1   Signs for At-Risk Children

The FBI provided the following online signs that a child might be at risk.

1. Your child spends large amounts of time online, especially at night.
2. You find pornography on your child's computer.
3. Your child receives phone calls from men you do not know.
4. Your child is making long distance calls to numbers you do not recognize.
5. Your child receives mail, gifts, or packages from someone you do not know.
6. Your child turns the computer monitor off or quickly changes the screen on the monitor when you come into the room.
7. Your child becomes withdrawn from the family. This could indicate that your child is a victim of sexual exploitation.
8. Your child has an online account belonging to someone else.

30.8.2 Steps for Parents of At-Risk Children

If you suspect that your child is communicating with a sexual predator, then you should take the following steps:

1. Consider talking openly with your child about your suspicions. You should tell them about the dangers.
2. Review what is on your child's computer. Pornography or any kind of sexual communication is a strong warning sign.
3. Use a caller ID service to determine who is calling your child.
4. Install devices that show telephone numbers that have been dialed from your home phone.
5. Monitor your child's access to all types of live electronic communications. Computer sex offenders usually meet potential victims via chat rooms and follow up with e-mails.

30.8.3 More Prevention Measures from Predators

The FBI provides the follow prevention measures to minimize the chances of your child becoming a victim:

1. Communicate with your child about the potential online danger.
2. Spend time with your children online. Let them show you about their favorite online destinations.
3. Keep the computer in a common room in the house, not in your child's bedroom.
4. Utilize parental controls provided by your service provider and/or blocking software. Chat rooms should be heavily monitored. However, parents should not totally rely on utility mechanisms.
5. Always maintain access to your child's online account and randomly check his/her e-mail.
6. Teach your child responsible use of the resources online. There is more to the online experience than chat rooms.
7. Find out what computer safeguards are utilized by your child's school, public library, and at the homes of your child's friends. These are places where your child could encounter an online predator.
8. Instruct your children to:
   a. Never arrange a face-to-face meeting with someone they met online.
   b. Never upload pictures of themselves onto the Internet or online service to people they do not personally know.
   c. Never give out identifying information such as their name, home address, school name, or telephone number.
   d. Never download pictures from an unknown source, as there is a good chance there could be sexually explicit images.
   e. Never respond to messages or bulletin board postings that are suggestive, obscene, belligerent, or harassing.
   f. Never believe everything to be true online.

30.9   Summary

Computers and the Internet have become very widespread to the point that it is impossible for businesses, government, and individuals to be without. Criminals are also relying on computers and the Internet to commit their crimes. It is the responsibility of businesses and individuals to be aware of the types of computer crimes and how to prevent becoming a victim. Businesses should be aware of the prevention measures to protect their computer systems. When businesses and individuals become victims, they should know the procedures to be taken so a successful prosecution can take place. Law enforcement needs to know the proper procedures for executing a search warrant and protecting the integrity and reliability of computer evidence. The rules of evidence should be strictly followed. Computer evidence can be destroyed just by a stroke on the keyboard or by placing near a magnetic or electronic pulse. Businesses and law enforcement should use outside computer consultants if they do not have any in-house experts. In many cases, computers are just a new way of committing old crimes, for example, mail fraud, telemarketing fraud, and confidence scams. However, the computers have provided new types of crimes, for example, viruses, worms, and Salami techniques.

Document Examination 31

31.1 Introduction

The fraud examiner will occasionally come across documents that are false and are used to commit the fraud. Many embezzlement cases involved false signature(s) on checks and bank drafts. Many types of fraud cases involve false documents, for example, contracts, wills, invoices, identification cards. The fraud examiner should be skeptical of any documents obtained in their investigation. In many cases, the fraud examiner can easily determine if a document has been falsified or altered in some manner. However, the fraud examiner may suspect a document is false but does not have the expertise in determining whether a document is false or not. In suspicious cases, the fraud examiner should refer the evidence to a qualified forensic document examiner. They have the expertise, equipment, and know the methodologies of determining whether a document is a fake. Also, the use of computers in falsifying signatures and documents has become more sophisticated. Therefore, the fraud examiner has to rely more heavily on forensic document examiners. Even when a fraud examiner can see a signature or document is obviously a fake, they usually have to have a forensic document examiner examine the signature or document for it to be admissible in court. The purpose of this chapter is to help the fraud examiner to identify possible false signatures and documents.

31.2 Handwriting

Handwriting is a characteristic that is not common to everyone. Everyone writes differently from others. In addition, no one writes the same every time. Over time, people's handwriting will change. Some will change a lot while others will only slightly change. A person's signature will usually change more than their other writing styles. The way a person writes is determined by their education when learning to write. Also, where a person learns to write is affected. People who live in England will write differently from a person, let us say, from France or Italy. In fact, no teacher has ever succeeded in making all his/her pupils write precisely the same way. Teachers can recognize a child's writing at a very early age. Therefore, everyone has a unique method of writing that is clearly distinguishable from any other person. This is due to how a person's muscles in their arm, hand, and fingers are controlled by the brain.

31.2.1 Types of Writing

In Western European languages, roman script is used. In Eastern Europe and Russia, Greek script is used. Writing can be classified into three forms: capital writing, cursive writing, and disconnected script. Disconnected script is cursive writing but is not connected.

Capital writing is often called block writing. It is written in capital style. Writers will subconsciously use the easiest method.

31.2.2   Construction Methods

The individual letter determines how a capital letter is written. It can take only one stroke or it can take as many as four strokes to write a capital letter. The letter O, C, and S will take only one stroke. The letters can be long and narrow or short and fat. The letter E can take one stroke by writing 3 backward or as many as four strokes, which is one vertical stroke and three horizontal strokes. The letter I can be written in one stroke or two strokes by going up or down again. The letter U can be written in one stroke or in two strokes by a down with a vertical line. Most capital letters are written with a left downward stroke. The remaining part of the letter can be written by retracing the line or by lifting the pen and making the rest as a separate entity.

31.2.3   Pen Movement

Pen movements can be determined in two ways. The first is to observe how a person moves the pen when writing. The second is to determine the method of construction from a written document. The movement of the pen is determined by how continuous a line is drawn. A continuous line is not broken. Also, the line may retrace back to form the remaining part of the letter. A broken line shows the pen has left the paper. The vertical line for letters A, R, and N is likely to be a retrace if it continues to form the next part of the letter. It is unusual for it to begin at the bottom. The use of a 20–40× magnifier can determine if a break occurs between two touching lines or has changed direction without being lifted from the paper. Retracing will deposit more ink on the line while the remaining part of the letter has a lighter line.

31.2.4   Ink Lines

Ink lines can determine the flow of lines. When a ballpoint pen begins to write, it will start with a thin line. As the ballpoint pen progresses, more ink is deposited onto the paper. Also, when the ballpoint pen changes direction, it may deposit excess ink. Excess ink will show up when the ballpoint pen crosses over a previously drawn line. Striations are thin lines found within a line made by a pen. They are caused by damage or dirt on the ball housing that prevents an even flow of ink. The line is made in the direction where striation is traveling.

31.2.5   Letter Proportion

The proportion of letters may indicate the writing of one person from another. Some people have greater variations than other people. It is incumbent on the fraud examiner to obtain as much written material as possible in order to determine how vast the variations are by one person. The fraud examiner must establish a pattern by the writer to determine how some letters are wider at the top than the bottom, or vice versa, the angle of the curvature between letters, how the stroke of the letter began (e.g., top, level, or bottom). Proportion of letters within a word is another factor. The writer may make some letters smaller than other letters. Sometimes lowercase script is introduced into the document. The curves may be smooth or shaky. The spacing between letters can show variations between one person and another. Margins can be straight or uneven. This can be a sign of different writers. Numbers are regarded the same way as letters.

31.2.6   Cursive Writing

Cursive is Latin, which means "to run." Cursive writing provides rapid execution and speed. It also provides many styles of writing. The style is determined by many factors, for example, fashion and education. A person can have more than one style of writing, for example, writing carefully or writing fast. Cursive writing varies greatly between people. There may be some similar writing, but all writing employs a wide range of proportions within and between letters. How a writer connects letters is important. The ratio between the length of the loops and tails may be similar between different letters, but they can show a wide variation between writers. The connections between letters can be short or long. Letters may not be connected to the next letter. Some writers may not join certain letters in the alphabet. How the letters are made and their consistency is also important. Some writers will use a combination of block capital letters with cursive writing. This is called disconnected script. Usually, the first letter is a block capital letter, and it is followed by cursive writing.

31.2.7   Signatures

Signatures are a form of cursive writing. Signatures can be divided into two forms: normal cursive writing and with a distinctive mark. The latter is often barely readable or completely illegible. Signatures are subject to wide variation. No one can produce a signature exactly alike. Signatures can vary because of difficulty in writing. People with arthritis can have signatures that can vary significantly from their earlier signatures.

31.2.8   Layout

How writing is arranged on the page can vary from one writer to another. The fraud examiner should take notice of the size of gaps between words and lines, the use of punctuation marks, the employment of margins on all sides, the separation of paragraphs, and where they begin. These can give clues to a particular writer. Envelopes and checks can provide diversity between writers. How the address is written on the envelope is a clue. The writer may position it high, middle, or low on the envelope. How is the spacing on the envelope? It could be long or short. Parts on the checks can be written in various combinations. The fraud examiner should look at how the money amount in both figures and writing are made, the position of payee's name, and other features because they can vary widely.

31.2.9   One Person Variations

A writer will have variations within their writing. No writer is consistent with each letter of the alphabet. However, they all should fall within a range that is relatively small and excludes many other variants. Some letters will show similarity, while others will be consistently different. When there are many significant differences, it is evidence of another writer. A writer may use different forms of letters within a document. Some people may use unusual features in writing letters. They are called "personal characteristics." Some writers may use a style consistently from when they were taught. This is called "style characteristics." In practice, a person's writing can be distinguished from another by size, slope, line quality, smoothness of curvature, and separation between block capital and cursive writing from another person.

31.2.10   Non-Roman Scripts

Any language based on phonetics can use script to determine variations between writers as they do in Roman script. The Greek alphabet is used in many Eastern European countries. In Arabic writing, some letters can be distinguished from each other and indicate whether a document is prepared by the same or different writers.

31.2.11   Handwriting Variation

Writing conditions in the day-to-day course of business are often not ideal. They can be influenced by physical causes. The quality of the pen or the writing surface can affect writing. The position and the health of the writer can affect writing.

31.2.12   Writing Instruments

There is a wide range of writing instruments. Today, there are fountain pens, ballpoint pens, and felt tip pens. Despite the variety of writing instruments, there is little difference found in the writing of one person using different types of pens or pencils. Wide felt tip pens can cause difficulty in moving at right angles or upward movements. The coarseness of the paper can affect the writing line. However, their affects are not noticeable. When a pen is defective, it can cause an uneven flow of ink on the paper. It will also cause the writer to lift up the pen more often, causing the appearance of a different method of construction. Glossy paper absorbs less ink and gives an unlinked impression. Lack of pen control can give odd pen movements, resulting in poorly shaped loops and/or strokes. Lack of pen control can be from awkward standing positions.

The health of the writer can affect the writing. Some signatures are disputed on wills because of severe illness. The elderly and people with debilitating diseases show effects depending on the degree of infirmity and the disease. Parkinson's disease produces a tremor. Arthritis affects the ability to hold the pen or to move the hand and fingers easily. A tremor found in writing will usually be found throughout the writing. Lack of control will be even within the writing. Drugs and alcohol can modify writing as muscular control deteriorates. In general, writing becomes larger and less well formed and coordinated. The method of construction and relative proportions remain the same. The writing of addicts and alcoholics will be affected by high concentrations of the drugs. Impairment of vision can affect writing. Writings will affect the lines running together or misplace the writing line. A common feature of a blind person is obvious errors are uncorrected.

31.2.13   Deliberate Handwriting Variations

In normal writing, detail is relegated to the subconscious and attention is not paid to every movement of the pen. Deliberate alteration of writing occurs on many occasions. Deliberate writing can be classified as the (1) disguise of writing by the person making the writing and (2) simulated writing of another person.

31.2.13.1 Disguised Writing

Disguised writings are used in threatening letters, obscene missive, and explosive devices. They are usually sent through the mail. Notes demanding money are given to bank tellers. In most cases, attempts are made to make the writing less characteristic of their writer. Samples of writing given for comparison purposes are also frequently disguised. An obvious feature of writing by any person is its overall appearance. How large and how it slants are features immediately noticed by close examination. The method of writing each letter and the general proportions used will remain mostly unchanged. The ratio between the height of loops and the middle zone of the writing tends to remain much the same. The wrong hand can be used to write a disguised passage, the left hand for the right and vice versa. This will result in a poorly controlled, untidy, and irregular effect. However, the same general features of movement and proportion remain the same. Some letters may be constructed with a different direction of stroke. A skillful writer can introduce evidence of a lack of ability, for example, imitating the poor quality of a near-illiterate person. Sometimes block letters are used, but this is more of a change in writing methods. The ability to disguise varies with the individual. There are some people who are good at disguising.

Sometimes a suspect is asked for samples of writing. This should be done after having the suspect complete a written statement. Signatures are often found in fraud cases. Sometimes criminals will sign a document and later disclaim it. The criminal will tell the investigator the differences. The investigator will find both obvious differences and closely matched letters.

31.2.13.2 Simulated Writings

There are two methods of copying the writing of another person. The first is to draw the writing like an artist. The other is to trace over the writing. In either case, both methods are forgeries. Some people will introduce elaborate rubric, which gives the forger a problem. Two conditions are required in order to get a well formed and flowing signature. First, there must be accuracy in shape and proportion within the signature. Second, there must be smoothness of line. Satisfying both conditions is nearly impossible. Accuracy is achieved by writing carefully and slowly. This causes the writing to be smooth and curves and loops become difficult. When writing is done naturally, the pressure to the paper is not consistent. Some lines are made quickly, which results in the pen barely touching the surface. When lines are done quickly or changes direction, more weight is applied to the pen on the paper. When the pen is raised to write the next word, the pressure is reduced and the line tails off. It is the variations in pressure that are difficult to reproduce. In a slow moving pen, the pressure remains the same and the line remains even and does not tail off. The copier may have to produce a signature in front of someone. This will produce inaccuracy but good quality. The copier will not be able to avoid inaccuracies, particularly when dealing with relative heights of letters, spacing between capitals, and shapes of loops.

31.2.13.3 Tracing Signature

Tracing a signature is more common than imitating. It requires the model signature to be placed in the right position on the document. Some copiers place the original over the document and trace heavily along the line of writing. This gives an impression on the paper below. The impressions on the document are filled in with ink. Another method is to trace the signature onto the document by using a light source or a window so the signature is seen below the document. In both cases, the signs of a slowly made production will appear on the document, for example, even lines and no tail offs. Copied writing will exhibit features that are not present in the original document but are identified in normal habits of the copier.

31.2.13.4 *Simulation*

Unlike fingerprints, typewriting, shoe prints, tool marks, and striations on bullets, handwriting is much harder to be linked to its source. No one writes exactly the same. The document examiner must look for similarities in method of construction, proportions, and general shapes of letters, indentations, and flow of inks. If these are found to be copied rather than by natural flow, the resemblances are due to stimulation and not by common authorship.

There could be other reasons where a document is not simulated but was produced by the same person. A person could write with their opposite hand. This will usually produce badly formed and poorly controlled writing. An ambidextrous writer can write with both hands, resulting in a change of methods. Whether the document is drawn or copied, traced, or done slowly by freehand, it will produce evidence of poor line quality, pen lifts, retouching, inaccuracy, and use of guide lines.

31.3 Typewriting and Typescripts

Typewriters have been around for well over 100 years. During this time, they have developed into various models with various designs. Some typewriters have become obsolete. No one sees anyone using a manual typewriter anymore. Electric and electronic typewriters have basically replaced the old manual typewriters. Unlike the manual typewriter, the electric and electronic typewriter can exchange type script. IBM produced an electric typewriter that could replace the ball script with various script types. Other companies produced typewriters with a "daisy wheel," which could change the script type. With the advent of computers, electronic typewriters are becoming obsolete. Computers now can produce many types of script by just changing the "font" and size on the menu.

31.3.1 Typeface

Manual typewriters only had one type of script. The size and style was determined by the manufacturer. The script was mounted on a type bar. The most common spacing was 10 or 12 letters to an inch. Pica machines produced 10 letters to an inch. Elite machines produced 12 letters to an inch. Electric typewriters produced either pica or elite script. With the advent of electronic typewriters, they could use either pica or elite script but also could have right-hand justification, meaning that the script was even on the right as well as on the left. This causes a variation in the letter spacing.

31.3.2 Typewriter Identification

When considering typewriters, the typewriter, the type bar, and the type face are considered as a whole. Manufacturers maintain quality control for the production of their machines. The tolerances for typewriters are very low after they are produced. However, after use over time, the typewriter will show wear or damage. The wear and damage will vary greatly for the same model and type of machine. This is important for the investigator. The investigator needs to tie the document to the machine that produced the document. This can lead to the person producing the false document. This can be done by comparing the typescript on the document to the type face on the machine. If there are differences in typescript, then this would not be the machine that produced the document. If the typescript on the document matches the typescript on the typewriter, then you may have tied the document to the typewriter. This is not enough. The investigator must look for imperfections that show up on the document and typescript of the machine.

First, there can be damage to individual letters. In manual typewriters, the letters can be damaged by two keys hitting one another. This can cause a chip in one or both letters on the metal. For ball type machines, the letters can wear down or there may be a defect in the ball that appears on the paper. Daisy wheels are also prone to damage. The plastic material deteriorates rapidly once the surface coating has been broken.

Second, typewriters can have a misalignment of certain characters. In manual typewriters, the letters on the type bar may not have consistency when made or repaired. This results in differences in positioning of printed characters to each other. If the type bar is twisted or bent, then the letters will be misplaced. The characters can be upward, downward, to the left or right, or at an angle. Twisting will produce an uneven image. In ball machines, the ball can be out of alignment because of the rotating mechanism. This will result in the letters being out of alignment, either horizontal or vertical. The defect will continue to happen even if the ball is replaced. On daisy wheel machines, misalignment can occur. The spokes on the wheel may become distorted. The letter distortion will only appear on the spoke which is out of alignment.

Third, the characters on the machine may be dirty. This will cause the circles in letters to become a solid. This is a temporary condition. It can be corrected by cleaning the machine.

Fourth, the mechanism holding the paper may be loose. This will result in lines of typescript to become unevenly separated. The platen can be out of alignment, which will cause characters to print heavily at the top or bottom. This can happen to all types of typewriters, for example, manual, ball, or daisy wheel.

Fifth, the ribbon on the typewriter can be out of alignment. This will cause a cutting off of either the top or bottom of the characters. If a duel ribbon is used, black and red, the misalignment will show some of both colors.

Sixth, some typewriters can type in both pica and elite. Therefore, the spacing between letters can be different. In pica, there will be 10 letters to an inch, which can be measured with a ruler. In elite, there will be 12 letters to an inch. The fraud examiner should determine which size type was used. Some typewriters justify the type to make the right margins even as well as the left. This can be determined by typing a sample. Creases and folds can affect the dimensions of a document. Humidity can make subtle differences in the spacing of characters.

31.3.3 Comparison

The fraud examiner should compare the two documents for similarities. The comparison should be made with a document suspected to be from a particular typewriter to a sample taken from a particular typewriter. The fraud examiner should note each letter, figure, comma, question mark, pound or dollar sign, and other characteristics. The whole picture of similarities and differences are noted. A conclusion can only be reached after comparison of all the elements including misalignment and spacing.

31.4   Dot Matrix Machines

With the advent of computers, a system of dots is used to create characters. Vertical mount of pins are mounted on a head that move horizontally across the page. The pins are pressed against a ribbon that forms an image on the paper. In some machines, the dots can be easily seen while others would require a microscope. The dot matrix is used by ink-jet printers, which deliver a drop of ink on each point of the matrix to form a character on the paper. The quality of printing is determined by the number of points in the head. The greater the number of points on the head will give better printing quality. The head can be removed when it is damaged. A blocked port will produce an unlinked line across the typed characters. The fraud examiner will have to have a document examiner to examine the document by microscope to determine the type of machine used.

31.5   Laser Printers

Laser printers use the principles of photocopy machines. A photosensitive drum is charged electrostatically. Toner is attracted to the drum and is transferred to the paper and fused. The characters and style are controlled by the computer. This method prohibits identification of any individual machine. Sometimes small marks can be found on the drum that are transferred to the paper. This can help to identify the machine used to produce the document.

31.6   Erasure

Typewritten documents are subject to alterations. One method is using "white out" to cover the mistake. After the "white out" is used, the typist can type over the mistake. Document examiners can use trichlorotrifluoroethane over the white out to see what was covered up. The white out becomes translucent. This process will not affect the document. Document examiners can use infrared or visible light luminescence to see what has been obliterated. This method is very useful in ballpoint writing. Ink can be removed by scraping the surface until all the visible ink has been removed. Another method of erasure is by using a bleaching solution, which converts the dye into a colorless compound. In all the processes, traces of ink will remain. The document examiner can use fluoresce or luminescence to detect what was erased or obliterated.

Typewriting can be erased by scraping the surface with a sharp blade or a hard rubber eraser. To identify what was erased, the document examiner can use indentations, oblique light, or traces of ink remaining.

Typewriting using carbon ribbons adhere to the surface of the paper. They can be removed by typing the same letter(s) over what was typed with an adhesive tape, called "correcting tape." This lifts the carbon from the paper but leaves a deeper impression on the paper. The corrected characters are then typed over. The indentations remain from the first typewritten letters.

31.7 Added Typescript

A person might claim certain typed script was not on the paper when they saw it. This would indicate some script was added later. This can be determined by showing the added script was not in both vertical and horizontal alignment. This is not easily done. However, a fold or crease on the paper can make misalignment in subsequent typing.

31.8 Typist Identification

Typists have different styles of writing. Like handwriting, there is an individual pattern to typing. The spacing in lines, the size of the margins, the depth of indentation at the beginning of paragraphs, the number of spaces after periods or commas, and the use of capitals are consistent to one typist. A nontypist will not have a proper lay of a letter and often has misspelling. Frequent use of certain words, unconventional punctuation, and similar features of style can indicate a particular writer. The questioned document will have to be compared to previous writing before any conclusions can be made.

31.9 Paper

Paper is made from pulped fibers, which originate from wood, linen, cotton rag, esparto, hemp, or straw. Wood is the most common fiber used in paper. The wood is broken down into fiber using mechanical or chemical means. The fiber is mixed with a variety of chemicals and water. Gelatin, resins, or similar mixtures are then added to bind the fibers. Later, dyes and whiteners are added to determine the color. The mixture is spread over a frame that drains the water and other chemicals. The frame may contain a device to reduce fiber content in an area with a recognizable shape. This produces a watermark that is more transparent than the rest of the paper. The fiber mat is pressed and heated until it is dried. Some paper is specially coated to produce a surface for a specific use. The mat is rolled into a large roll. Later, the paper is cut into specific dimensions. The methods of manufacture give rise to differences in the produced product. These different papers can provide the fraud examiner and/or document examiner the time and place it was manufactured. Most manufacturers can distinguish their features in their paper. There are also differences in paper between different manufacturers. This will help the fraud examiner to determine who the manufacturer is and whether a document is genuine or counterfeit.

American money is sometimes counterfeited by criminals. Counterfeit money cannot be produced exactly the same as genuine money because of kind of paper used, ink used, and the engravings. Criminals so far have never fully counterfeited American money because they fail to use all of its characteristics.

31.9.1 Watermarks

Watermarks are produced in the manufacture of paper by thinning out the fibers into a shape. One can see a watermark on paper when they hold it up to the light. The watermark can be used to identify the manufacturer. A watermark is a means of security. They are hard to copy on multitone high-quality paper. Some manufacturers regularly change the "dandy rolls," which produce watermarks, in order to know when the paper was made.

31.9.2 Paper Dating

The production methods of paper have changed over the centuries. Counterfeited antique documents can be authenticated by the paper. Paper used years or centuries ago will not have the chemicals used in present-day paper. The texture of the paper will also be different. Many manufacturers change methods or chemicals in their paper. This allows a document examiner to determine if the paper was produced at a known period of time.

31.10 Envelopes

Envelopes come in various sizes and shapes. The size and shape of the envelope, the shape of the flaps, and the type of glue vary between manufacturers and sometimes by batches. Some manufacturers imprint bar codes on the envelopes, which can provide the date of manufacture.

31.11 Pencils

Pencils use graphite mixed with other fillers. The fillers determine the hardness of the lead. Softer lead gives a higher percentage of graphite. Colored pencils or crayons are made of wax and colored pigment. Different waxes provide different hardness. The particles of lead or waxes are embedded onto the paper surface. The lead or wax does not penetrate into the fibers; thus, they can be removed by pressure of a rubber eraser. Fraud examiners will have to use document examiners since the techniques used require the use of electron microscopy. Even if the quantity is small, the lead or waxes can be distinguished between different products and manufacturers.

31.12 Liquid Inks

Inks have been around for many centuries and were based on carbon particles mixed in an aqueous dilute solution of glue. Later, iron, tannin, salts and glue mixture was developed. In the nineteenth century, indigo dye was used to modify the ink. This gave a blue color and became known as blue-black. Dyes later replaced the iron-tannin. It was also a time when fountain pens replaced the quill and iron nib pens. The ballpoint pen differs by using a quick drying paste. It has mostly replaced the fountain pen; however, fountain pens are still used and sold by stores. A new development is fiber-tipped and gel pens. These pens use a compressed fiber stylus, which transfers ink from a reservoir by capillary action through the gaps between the fibers. The inks used are dyes mixed with water or alcohol for quick drying.

A recent development is the gel pen. It is similar to the ballpoint pen but uses ink colored with pigments. It is sometimes important to show what kind of pen was used in producing a document. Therefore, it is necessary to show whether two inks on a document are the same. A document examiner will have to be used in order to determine the kind of pen and ink used on a document and requires the use of sophisticated equipment. The fraud examiner may notice ink lines are narrow on part of the document and wider on other parts of the document. Also, the fraud examiner may notice different shades of ink.

31.13 Ink Dating

The aging of ink cannot be put to a precise time on the act of the writing. However, if an ink can be shown to have been made only before or after a certain date, then any writing made not corresponding to the date when the ink was produced would make the document a counterfeit.

31.14 Printed and Photocopied Documents

The fraud examiner may find a printed or copied document that is suspected of being counterfeit. This can be important in cases involving bank notes, currency, checks, and other high-grade security printing. The document examiner needs to know how the document was produced and what other document was used to make the production. This requires a comparison of printing quality and inks or toners used. There are various methods of printing or photocopying documents.

31.15 Letterpress

The letterpress method requires the image to be raised above the background, inked, and then pressed onto the paper. This is a common method in printing counterfeit documents. The more elementary forms of letterpress printing are the rubber stamps, post office cancellation stamps, and toy printing. Letterpress depends on raised type, which transfers ink to the paper. This requires a lot of pressure. By touching the paper surface, the fraud examiner will feel the paper surface is not smooth.

31.16 Lithography

Modern lithographic methods use plates made by photographic processes and the image is offset rather than by direct printing. The plates are prepared by projecting an image onto a sensitized plate that reacts to light. After the plate is developed, it is treated with water repellent for the areas to be printed. The plate is inked, and the image is transferred to a blanket and later to the paper. Offset printing is widely used in commercial printing in both color and black and white. The process used will cause the image to lose some of the detail of the original. The document examiner can determine this by using microscopic examination.

31.17   Gravure

The gravure uses an image carrier where the design to be printed is below the surrounding surface. The plate is inked, and the ink on the surface is scraped away with a blade. The ink remaining will be in the depressions. The plate is pressed onto the paper, and the ink is transferred in the shape of the image. Gravure printing is used in high-quality products, especially for full color pictures. This printing method is used to produce bank notes, checks, and other high-grade security printing. A thickness of ink on the paper will give an indication of the method of printing. The cellular method of producing areas of tone leaves signs of separation at the edges.

31.18   Raised Printing

Embossed printing is raised from the surface of the paper. It is produced by two plates, one with the image to be printed in relief and the other with the image depressed into the surface.

31.19   Screen Printing

Screen printing squeezes ink through a mesh made of nylon, silk, or other material. The nonprinting areas are covered with a stencil. This method is used in short runs. It transfers a thick amount of ink onto the surface.

31.20   Photocopying

Photocopiers are like photography. They reproduce an already existing document. A number of different methods are used, but most employ static electricity. It is based on the principle where substances that have been charged with static electricity will be discharged into those areas where light falls.

31.21   Xerography

Xerography projects an image onto a previously charged drum or belt that has been specially coated and charged. It will discharge when illuminated. The charged toner power then forms the image on the drum that is transferred to paper.

31.22   Laser Printing

In copiers, the image on the drum is formed by a projection of the document being copied. It is made by many thousands of impulses of laser light. The laser beam scans each row and letter. Each row and letter receives an impulse or not depending on the signals given to the laser. When toner is applied, it is attracted to and adheres to those areas that retain the charge. Laser printing, as well as photocopying and xerographic copying, will produce jagged edges, especially on diagonals. Toner or ink varies between the different matrix of inks. Laser printing depends on the fusing by heat, pressure, or both, of small toner particles.

31.23 Photocopies

Photocopies are now widely used in producing documents. Plain paper copiers use resinous particles fusing or compressed onto the paper. Most copiers use dry toners that build up on the surface of the paper. Toners can be distinguished by microscope. The fraud examiner will need a document examiner to analyze the toner and paper. The photocopier uses mechanical means for handling paper. The paper apparatus can leave marks on the copies that can give an indication of the model used. They can range from indentations caused by the gripper or marks made by toners in certain parts of the copy. Photocopiers do not produce copies of the exact size of the originals. Many copy machines are capable of reduction and magnification. Other marks can appear on the copy because of dirt or damage. The most significant are those formed by dust or damage. Testing of paper and tone can establish the source of the copy machine. Copy machines will show staple holes, folds, tears, stains, and adventitious inclusions. Copies from copy machines only show a copy of an original or another copy. Because of this, a photocopy should never be accepted as an authentic record of a transaction or document. Many false documents are made by using copy machines. A signature can never be exactly the same, so if one on a document precisely matches one on a photocopy, then the latter is a forgery.

31.24 Facsimile Machines

Many fax machines can be used as photocopiers. However, their quality is not as good as conventional copy machines. The origins of a fax whether by sending or receiving can be important. Normally, a fax received will indicate the transmitting terminal with a line of data at either the top or bottom of the fax. Like photocopy machines, the fraud examiner or document examiner can use the same methods of identifying fax machines. Dirt can be reproduced on fax copies. The document examiner can access the memory of the fax machine to determine when and where fax copies were either sent or received.

31.25 Stamped Impressions

Rubber or metal stamps are used to make inked impressions onto paper. Hand stamps will leave inked impressions of variable quality because of the angle at which the paper is stamped. The amount of ink on the stamp and the pressure exerted can all differ with each action. It is also possible to identify copied impressions as to its source. Document examiners can use gas chromatography to confirm the type of wax used on the surface. Date stamps are usually made with rubber and produced in large quantities. It may be hard to distinguish one rubber stamp from another made by the same manufacturer. However, there may be faults from manufacturing, cuts, damage, or wear from constant use, or the day, month, accumulation of dirt in crevices between and in characters, variability in inking, and year may not be fully aligned; all will produce a lack of uniformity. Hand stamps are inked by a porous pad containing ink or incorporated into the stamp. Comparison of ink provides a means of finding a link between the document and the stamp.

31.26   Dry Transfer Methods

Lettering and other designs are manufactured where these can be transferred to paper. These come in many styles, designs, and shapes. They can be peeled off a sheet and placed on the document by compression. They usually have an adhesive on the back of the letters or designs. Criminals use these to fabricate letter headings, serial numbers, money amounts, demand notes, or anonymous communications. If the sheet from which the lettering came from is found, then it can be compared to the one on the document. A match of the two is very important. Documents with transfer lettering should be handled with care. They can easily be removed and liquids such as those in detecting fingerprints can cause them to dislodge.

31.27   Indented Impressions

When a person writes on a pad of paper, especially using a ballpoint pen, it will leave an impression on the paper underneath. The discovery of indented impressions can be very significant. If the original document is obtained, then it can be compared to the impression on the writing pad. If it matches, then the fraud examiner knows the source of the original document. Document examiners should be used to determine this because of the sophisticated equipment needed to verify the match.

31.28   Damaged Documents

Generally, minor damage to documents does not have much significance. The effect of a fold or crease can cause the pen to place more ink on the paper. It can be important to show that one's writing was made after another by the ink on the fold or crease. This same principle applies to typewriting, pencil lines, and rubber stamps. Staples are commonly used to keep a bundle of documents together. However, it may be important to know if two or more documents have been stapled and how many times. If a bundle of documents has been stapled, separated, and restapled, then it is unlikely the holes will match. Examination of staple marks can show whether photocopies originated from a particular bundle because the staple holes on the original will show up on the copies. Paperclips also leave marks but are less visible. They leave impressions on the paper. Burnt documents are totally lost. A document examiner may be able to determine the chemical composition of the paper and ink, but sophisticated equipment must be used in both charred and burnt documents.

31.29 Summary

A fraud examiner must be aware of falsified documents. Some forgeries can be determined by the fraud examiner, but other forgeries must be examined by a document/handwriting examiner, who can determine the authenticity by using various sophisticated and expensive equipment. New technologies are being developed to help document/handwriting examiners. Many times, the fraud examiner can see handwriting that does not match. If the handwriting looks the same on various documents, then the fraud examiner knows they are forgeries. The fraud examiner should always question photocopies of documents. A business can use photocopies of invoices to increase sales and accounts receivable on the books. This will increase business profits. The same goes for increasing accounts payable and various expenses. This can decrease business profits. In fraud cases, the investigator should seize typewriters, computer equipment, pens and pencils, and other documents that can be used in committing fraud. The more evidence available, the better.

Fraud Examiner

32

32.1 Introduction

Accountants and law enforcement personnel ponder about the future of fraud examiners. These two professions have many common threads: a fraud examiner must be part accountant and part detective. The accountant has a good working knowledge of books and records, the ability to analyze books and records, come up with various schedules and statements, and act as a forensic accountant in court. The detective has the ability to interview witnesses and discover evidence and has knowledge of criminal law, especially the rules of evidence. When these elements of both the accountant and the detective are combined, the fraud examiner role is formed.

32.2 Law Enforcement

Law enforcement in recent years has come to realize that economic crimes can only be solved with the assistance of financial information. In order to solve economic crimes, the investigator must have a good working knowledge of financial transactions. Society today has become very sophisticated and complex in doing business. The Internal Revenue Service (IRS) has met the needs by forming specialized groups to attack the sophisticated crimes. The Federal Bureau of Investigations (FBI) has formed specialized squads as well. Many large police departments have formed fraud squads to combat various types of sophisticated, complex fraud schemes. The biggest problem with law enforcement is the lack of adequate personnel and resources to combat white-collar crime. This is particularly true with shrinking budgets and the demand for more resources to combat violent crimes.

32.3 Accounting Profession

The accounting profession has not fully recognized fraud. One principal reason is the belief that fraud is the responsibility of management and law enforcement. Many certified public accounting firms have been successfully sued for failure to uncover fraud. The firms' main argument is that they are not there to detect fraud but to render an opinion on the "fair presentation" of financial statements. However, they do not realize that fraud can have a big impact on financial statements. It is well established that fraud has caused many businesses to go out of business because of fraud committed by employees and management.

32.4 Business

The business community for the most part has taken a laissez-faire attitude. When it finds an employee taking kickbacks or embezzling funds, it usually lets the employee go with the hope of some restitution. It fails to prosecute. When this happens, a signal is sent to other employees that they can steal and get off lightly. In the meantime, the bad employee goes to another employer and will commit the same offense. Businesses are reluctant to prosecute because of possible bad publicity. Actually, the reverse takes place. If a business prosecutes a bad employee or customer, then it sends a positive message.

32.5   Fraud Examiner

The future for the fraud examiner looks very good. The U.S. News and World Report reported in its November 11, 1991, issue that forensic accounting would be one of the top 20 professions in the 1990s. It continues to be one of the top professions. In 1988, the Association of Certified Fraud Examiners (ACFE) was established by the Institute for Financial Crime Prevention. This is the beginning of establishing credentials for fraud examiners. Following ACFE, the American College of Forensic Examiners (ACFEI) established the Certified Forensic Accountant. In 2001, the Association of Certified Anti-Money Laundering Specialists (ACAMS) was formed. It established the Certified Anti-Money Laundering Specialists (CAMS). Forensic accounting has been around for more than a century but has not been recognized as a special field of endeavor like other fields in accounting, for example, tax planning and management services.

32.6   Association of Certified Fraud Examiners

This association has established minimum qualifications and programs for people who want to choose this field as a career.

1. *Qualifications.* The association requires candidates to have:
   a. A baccalaureate degree from a recognized institution
   b. Two years of professional experience in fraud-related matters
   c. Successful completion of the Uniform Certified Fraud Examiners (CFE) examination
2. *Examination.* The Uniform CFE examination tests the candidate's knowledge in fraud detection and deterrence. The CFE examination is divided into four parts:
   a. *Investigation.* This part addresses principles of interview and interrogation techniques, sources of information, report writing, case files and evidence, and covert investigations.
   b. *Law.* This part addresses criminal law, rules of evidence, rights of the accused, privacy laws, and testifying as an expert witness.
   c. *Financial transactions.* This part covers accounting and auditing theory, evaluating internal controls, financial statement analysis, statistical sampling, audit evidence, and computer fraud.
   d. *Criminology.* This part covers crime theories, sociology and psychology of offenders, the criminal justice system, crime statistics, sentencing guidelines, plea bargains, and restitution.

32.6.1 Ethics

The association of CFEs has promulgated a Code of Professional Ethics. Even though this code of ethics applies to CFEs, it also equally applies to anyone who works in this field of endeavor. This Code of Professional Ethics is presented as follows:

1. A CFE shall, at all times, demonstrate a commitment to professionalism and diligence in the performance of his/her duties.
2. A CFE shall not engage in any illegal or unethical conduct, or any activity that would constitute a conflict of interest.
3. A CFE shall, at all times, exhibit the highest level of integrity in the performance of all professional assignments and will accept only assignments for which there is reasonable expectation that the assignment will be completed with professional competence.
4. A CFE will comply with lawful orders of the courts and will testify to matters truthfully and without bias or prejudice.
5. A CFE, in conducting examinations, will obtain evidence or other documentation to establish a reasonable basis for any opinion rendered. No opinion shall be expressed regarding the guilt or innocence of any person or party.
6. A CFE shall not reveal any confidential information obtained during a professional engagement without proper authorization.
7. A CFE shall reveal all material matters discovered during the course of an examination, which, if omitted, could cause a distortion of the facts.
8. A CFE shall continually strive to increase the competence and effectiveness of professional services performed under his/her direction.

32.6.2 Professionalism

The fraud examiner should possess a quality of professionalism. The characteristics of professionalism are as follows:

1. It is a specialized field of endeavor which can only be acquired by higher, formal education.
2. It has strict qualification standards.
3. It is recognized and accepted by society.
4. It has standards of conduct that govern members of the profession and their relationships with colleagues and the public.
5. It has a national organization or regulatory agency present to promote and regulate the professional group.

The CFE is not regulated by state or federal agencies. Like most other professional organizations, the CFE must maintain and increase professional competence by continuing professional education. This has become more imperative because of the advances in technology and the increase in sophistication of economic crimes.

32.6.3 Diligence

Fraud examiners should be diligent in performing their duties. These duties include, but are not limited to, planning assignments, supervising assistants, avoiding conflicts of interest, obtaining sufficient evidence to form opinions, maintaining confidentiality, and avoiding any distortions.

32.6.4 Illegal Conduct

The fraud examiner is forbidden to participate in any illegal activities. While this seems very clear, there are times when this is not so clear-cut. The fraud examiner has to be careful of libel or slander. Improper disclosure of the investigation can result in injury of a subject. The fraud examiner cannot detain any person without proper authority. Fraud examiners cannot make plea agreements. Only the court can accept plea agreements. Promises should never be made unless the fraud examiner has the authority to keep them.

32.6.5 Unethical Conduct

The fraud examiner is prohibited from unethical conduct. This is harder to define. The best definition would be any conduct that would discredit the fraud examiner and the profession. Some examples of this would be padding expenses; not fully disclosing all the facts; having financial interest in or with the client; using intoxicants while on duty; lending or borrowing funds from clients; misuse of title; working a case where the subject is a friend, relative, neighbor, and the like. The key to unethical conduct is how the public perceives the fraud examiner and his /her business and personal dealings. The Internal Revenue Manual states that agents cannot use their office for personal gain. This rule also applies to fraud examiners.

32.6.6 Integrity

The fraud examiner should have high integrity. Integrity consists of being honest, truthful, trustworthy, loyal, helpful, friendly, and courteous. In other words, the fraud examiner should have high morals.

32.6.7 Professional Competence

This relates to performance of duty. Fraud examiners should conscientiously perform their duties. They should keep abreast of current developments. Relations with associates, clients, and others should be conducted in a manner that will not cause dissension, discord, or disrupt business operations. The fraud examiner should become familiar with client's operations, respond to unusual events or conditions, and review evidence and assistants' work.

32.6.8 Testimony

The fraud examiner will have to testify in court on many cases. In some cases, the fraud examiner is the expert/summary witness. This is particularly true in cases involving indirect methods of proving illegal gains. The fraud examiner should only summarize evidence that is introduced into court. Opinions are admissible and sometimes required. However, no opinion as to the guilt or innocence of the subject is to be expressed. The fraud examiner should always respond to questions in examination or cross-examination, no more and no less. Answers should never express any bias or prejudice but always be truthful.

32.6.9 Orders of the Court

The fraud examiner should always obey the orders of the court. Whenever a subpoena or summons is issued by any judicial body of competent authority, it should be obeyed.

32.6.10 Obtaining Evidence

The fraud examiner should obtain sufficient and competent evidence to render an opinion. However, no opinion should be expressed on the guilt or innocence of any person. Evidence should be obtained by all means possible. This can include inspection, observation, and interviews. The evidence should be material and relevant.

32.6.11 Confidential Information

For all practical purposes, any information that fraud examiners obtain in the course of their assignment is confidential. Disclosure without proper authorization and to the improper people can jeopardize a case. In the case of a grand jury, disclosure is not allowed under any circumstances except by the court. Privileged information cannot be disclosed to anyone, not even the court. In some cases, the fraud examiner may be retained by an attorney who is representing a client and the examiner's services are for the attorney who has privileged communication status. All information that the fraud examiner obtains and analyzes belongs to the attorney. Even though the fraud examiner may retain various files and work papers and has been discharged by the client, confidentiality still remains. However, this confidentiality does not apply when an employee provides information about fraudulent acts, whether of another employee or of him or herself, because the client is the employer. Another complex situation occurs when the client is committing the fraud. The client holds the highest rank in management. The fraud examiner should withdraw from the engagement and issue a disengagement letter, which should state the facts. Fraud examiners are not required to blow the whistle, but circumstances may exist where the fraud examiner is legally required to take steps. An attorney should be consulted. The fraud examiner should never let the client promulgate false or misleading reports based on the examiner's work. Certain federal statutes require the fraud examiner to report criminal offenses to the appropriate federal agency.

32.6.12 Complete Reporting

The fraud examiner should always report all the facts whether they help or hurt the case. Evidence and facts are material if they can influence the report user to come to a different conclusion. An omission of facts or evidence is as much as a distortion as stretching the truth. The fraud examiner should gather all the evidence, oral and physical. The fraud examiner should never jump to conclusions.

32.6.13   Professional Improvement

The fraud examiner should always strive for improvements and greater knowledge. Most professionals, including fraud examiners, are required to have continuing education to learn new methods and techniques. Various organizations (e.g., AICPA, Institute of Internal Auditors [IIA], Institute of Management Accountants [IMA], and ACFE), offer various seminars and programs to enhance the examiner's knowledge. In addition, the fraud examiner should keep abreast of local and national news media. They report of new schemes or variations of old schemes that are taking place in one's area. Fraud examiners should be aware of current conditions around them. When new schemes or variations of old schemes are discovered, the fraud examiner should think and plan ways to prevent and detect them.

32.7   American College of Forensic Examiners

The American College of Forensic Examiners has two programs for certification. They are the Certified Forensic Accountant and the Certified Medical Investigator. Only the Certified Forensic Accountant is addressed here. It uses the designation of CrFA[(sm)].

32.7.1   Requirements

The Certified Forensic Accountant program requires the applicant to be a member of their State Board of Accountancy. In other words, it requires the prospective candidate to be a certified public accountant (CPA). The examination has two parts: Examination 1 and Examination 2. The examination also must be in compliance with local ordinances, state laws, and federal regulations. The candidate must hold a bachelor's degree in business or have 10 years of accounting-related experience. If a candidate is a CPA, then he/she does not have to take Examination 1. A fee of $450 is required for both exams and $225 is required for only examination 2. Also, the candidate must be a member of the American College of Forensic Examiners and provide three references.

32.7.2   Examination for Certified Forensic Accountant

One section of the examination covers judicial procedures and evidence applicable to forensic accounting. It also covers dispute resolution, professional responsibility, and ethics. It pays attention to the Federal Rules of Evidence. Another section discusses the role of forensic accountant in litigation engagements and testifying. A third section covers fraud investigations, fraudulent financial reporting, and the legal elements of fraud and fraud investigation. A fourth section addresses services of forensic accountants, damages analysis, and failure in audit, tax, and consulting services. The last section covers valuation of closely held businesses, professional practices, and interests in real estate businesses.

32.8   Association of Certified Anti-Money Laundering Specialists

The Association of Certified Anti-Money Laundering Specialists (ACAMS) was formed in 2001. The examination process started in 2003. It has a worldwide membership and attracts law enforcement personnel, people from various types of financial institutions, and law, accounting, and consulting companies. The September 11, 2001, terrorist attack was what spurred this organization into existence, along with the Financial Action Task Force with their 40 recommendations to 29 countries on money laundering in 1990.

32.8.1 Requirements

The candidate must pass an examination. To be eligible, candidates must have a minimum of 20 qualifying points based on education, certifications, and experience. The qualifying points are based on a Credit Award System. Documentation must be provided to support the education, certifications, and experience. This organization can schedule an in-house examination for members of an organization.

32.8.2 Examination for CAMS

The CAMS examination has four sections. They are:

a. *Money Laundering Risks and Methods.* This section discusses the various methods of money laundering and suspicious activity.
b. *International Standards of Money Laundering Compliance.* This section addresses the various international, regional, and national legal requirements and laws dealing with money laundering.
c. *Money Laundering Compliance Program.* This section discusses various anti-money laundering policies, procedures, and controls. The candidate should know what reports are made and to whom they are made.
d. *Conducting or Supporting the Investigation Process.* This section discusses procedures for working with law enforcement and gathering evidence. It addresses issues such as cooperation between countries in confiscation, mutual assistance, and extradition.

32.9 Summary

The fraud examiner has a bright future when it comes to employment opportunities. These opportunities exist in private industry, public accounting, and government. There are three certifications. Fraud examiners must be aware of their responsibilities, obligations, and duties. The fraud examiner must keep abreast of current events and new technologies. Fraud examiners in the public or private sectors must be aware of the code of ethics. Adherence ensures integrity and professionalism within the profession. Governmental fraud examiners must abide by their departmental rules of ethics and conduct. All federal agencies have their rules of ethics and conduct, which usually go far beyond those of the three associations. For instance, many federal agencies either restrict or prohibit outside employment.

Appendix A
Federal Reserve Districts

1. Boston
2. New York
3. Philadelphia
4. Cleveland
5. Richmond
6. Atlanta
7. Chicago
8. St. Louis
9. Minneapolis
10. Kansas City
11. Dallas
12. San Francisco

The Numerical System of the American Bankers Association

Index to Prefix Numbers of Cities and States

Numbers 1 to 49 inclusive are prefixes for cities
Numbers 50 to 99 inclusive are prefixes for states
Prefix numbers 50 to 58 are eastern states
Prefix numbers 59 is Hawaii
Prefix numbers 60 to 69 are southeastern states
Prefix numbers 70 to 79 are central states
Prefix numbers 80 to 88 are southwestern states
Prefix number 89 is Alaska

Prefix Numbers of Cities in Numerical Order

1. New York, NY	8. Pittsburg, PA	15. Washington, DC
2. Chicago, IL	9. Detroit, MI	16. Los Angeles, CA
3. Philadelphia, PA	10. Buffalo, NY	17. Minneapolis, MN
4. St. Louis, MO	11. San Francisco, CA	18. Kansas City, MO
5. Boston, MA	12. Milwaukee, WI	19. Seattle, WA
6. Cleveland, OH	13. Cincinnati, OH	20. Indianapolis, IN
7. Baltimore, MD	14. New Orleans, LA	21. Louisville, KY

22. St. Paul, MN
23. Denver, CO
24. Portland, OR
25. Columbus, OH
26. Memphis, TN
27. Omaha, NE
28. Spokane, WA
29. Albany, NY
30. San Antonio, TX
31. Salt Lake City, UT

32. Dallas, TX
33. Des Moines, IA
34. Tacoma, WA
35. Houston, TX
36. St. Joseph, MO
37. Fort Worth, TX
38. Savannah, GA
39. Oklahoma City, OK
40. Wichita, KS

41. Sioux City, IA
42. Pueblo, CO
43. Lincoln, NE
44. Topeka, KS
45. Dubuque, IA
46. Galveston, TX
47. Cedar Rapids, IA
48. Waco, TX
49. Muskogee, OK

Prefix Numbers of States in Numerical Order

50. New York
51. Connecticut
52. Maine
53. Massachusetts
54. New Hampshire
55. New Jersey
56. Ohio
57. Rhode Island
58. Vermont
59. Hawaii
60. Pennsylvania
61. Alabama
62. Delaware
63. Florida
64. Georgia
65. Maryland
66. North Carolina

67. South Carolina
68. Virginia
69. West Virginia
70. Illinois
71. Indiana
72. Iowa
73. Kentucky
74. Michigan
75. Minnesota
76. Nebraska
77. North Dakota
78. South Dakota
79. Wisconsin
80. Missouri
81. Arkansas
82. Colorado
83. Kansas

84. Louisiana
85. Mississippi
86. Oklahoma
87. Tennessee
88. Texas
89. Alaska
90. California
91. Arizona
92. Idaho
93. Montana
94. Nevada
95. New Mexico
96. Oregon
97. Utah
98. Washington
99. Wyoming
100. Territories

Appendix B
Money Laundering Acronyms

Government

AFMLS	Asset Forfeiture and Money Laundering Section Department of Justice
ATF	Bureau of Alcohol, Tobacco, and Firearms, Department of the Treasury
BJA	Bureau of Justice Assistance, Department of Justice
CFTC	Commodity Futures Trading Commission
DEA	Drug Enforcement Administration, Department of Justice
EOUSA	Executive Office of United States Attorneys, Department of Justice
FBI	Federal Bureau of Investigation, Department of Justice
FDIC	Federal Deposit Insurance Corporation
Fed	Federal Reserve Board
FinCEN	Financial Crimes Enforcement Network, Department of the Treasury
HIDTA	High Intensity Drug Trafficking Area
HIFCA	High Intensity Money Laundering and Related Financial Crime Area
INL	Bureau for International Narcotics and Law Enforcement Affairs, Department of State
IRS-CI	Internal Revenue Service—Criminal Investigations
MLCC	Money Laundering Coordination Center, U.S. Customs Service, Department of the Treasury
NCUA	National Credit Union Administration
OCC	Office of the Comptroller of the Currency, Department of the Treasury
OCDEFT	Organized Crime Drug Enforcement Task Force
OFAC	Office of Foreign Assets Control, Department of the Treasury
OJP	Office of Justice Programs, Department of Justice
ONDCP	Office of National Drug Control Policy
OTS	Office of Thrift Supervision, Department of the Treasury
SEC	Securities and Exchange Commission
SOD	Special Operations Division, Department of Justice
USPIS	United States Postal Inspection Service

U.S. Statutes, Laws, and Reports

BSA	Bank Secrecy Act
IEEPA	International Emergency Economic Powers Act
INCSR	International Narcotics Control Strategy Report

MLCA	Money Laundering Control Act of 1986
MLSA	Money Laundering Suppression Act of 1994
APEC	Asia Pacific Economic Cooperation
APG	Asia Pacific Group on Money Laundering
CHFI	Committee on Hemispheric Financial Issues
FAFT	Financial Action Task Force on Money Laundering
FIU	financial intelligence unit
FSF	Financial Stability Forum
GCC	Gulf Cooperation Council
ILEA	International Law Enforcement Academy
IFI	international financial institution
IMF	International Monetary Fund
NCCTs	non-cooperative countries or territories
OAS	Organization of American States
OECD	Organization for Economic Cooperation and Development
OFC	offshore financial center
OGBS	Offshore Group of Banking Supervisors

General Terminology

BMPE	Black Market Peso Exchange
GTO	Geographic Targeting Order
MOU	memorandum of understanding
MSB	money services businesses

BSA Forms

CMIR	Report of International Transportation of Currency or Monetary Instruments
CTR	Currency Transaction Report
FBAR	Foreign Bank Account Report
SAR	Suspicious Activity Report
SARC	Suspicious Activity Report for Casinos
SAR-S	Suspicious Activity Report for Securities Brokers and Dealers

Appendix C
Internet Sources of Information

Data Source	Free	Internet Address
Federal Government		
Copyright Office	Yes	www.loc.gov
Center for Disease Control	Yes	www.cdc.gov
Government Printing Office	Yes	www.gpo.gov
Government Accounting Office	Yes	www.gao.gov
Federal Election Commission	Yes	www.fec.gov
Federal Deposit Insurance Corp	Yes	www.fdic.gov
Federal Aviation Administration	Yes	www.faa.gov
Securities Exchange Commission	Yes	www.sec.gov
Census Bureau	Yes	www.census.gov
Federal Bureau of Investigation	Yes	www.fbi.gov
Federal Trade Commission	Yes	www.ftc.gov
FedWorld Information Network	Yes	www.fedworld.gov
Small Business Administration	Yes	www.sbaonline.gov
Library of Congress	Yes	www.loc.gov
U.S. Department of Justice	Yes	www.usdoj.gov
U.S. House of Representatives	Yes	www.house.gov
U.S. Senate	Yes	www.senate.gov
Federal Law Enforcement Training Center	Yes	www.ustreas.gov
U.S. Air Force	Yes	www.af.mil
U.S. Army	Yes	www.army.mil
U.S. Navy	Yes	www.navy.mil
U.S. Coast Guard	Yes	www.uscg.gov
Consumer Information Center	Yes	pueblo.gsa.gov
Central Intelligence Agency	Yes	www.odci.gov
Alcohol, Tobacco Firearms	Yes	atf.ustreas.gov
Bureau of Labor Statistics	Yes	stats.bls.gov
Bureau of Transportation	Yes	www.bts.gov
U.S. Courts	Yes	www.uscourts.gov
Bureau of Prisons	Yes	www.bop.gov
Department of Agriculture	Yes	www.usda.gov
Department of Commerce	Yes	www.doc.gov
Department of Education	Yes	www.ed.gov
Department of Energy	Yes	www.doe.gov
Department of Health and Human Services	Yes	www.hhs.gov
Department of Housing Urban Development	Yes	www.hud.gov

(continued)

Data Source	Free	Internet Address
Department of Labor	Yes	www.dol.gov
Department of State	Yes	www.dos.gov
Department of Transportation	Yes	www.dot.gov
Department of Veterans Affairs	Yes	www.va.gov
Equal Employment Opportunity Commission	Yes	www.eeoc.gov
Environmental Protection Agency	Yes	www.epa.gov
Federal Communications Commission	Yes	www.fcc.gov
U.S. Marine Corps	Yes	www.usmc.mil
National Oceanographic and Atmospheric Administration	Yes	www.noaa.gov
National Security Agency	Yes	www.nsa.gov
U.S. Postal Service	Yes	www.usps.gov
Social Security Administration	Yes	www.ssa.gov
Census Bureau	Yes	www.census.gov/epcd/www/naics.html
Office of Personnel Management	Yes	www.opm.gov
Department of Commerce	Yes	www.commerce.gov
State Governments		
Alabama	Yes	www.eng.auburn.edu/alabama/map.html
Alaska	Yes	www.state.ak.us
Arizona	Yes	www.state.az.us
Arkansas	Yes	www.state.ar.us
California	Yes	www.state.ca.us
Colorado	Yes	www.state.co.us
Connecticut	Yes	www.state.ct.us
Delaware	Yes	www.state.de.us
District of Columbia	Yes	www.dchomepage.net
Florida	Yes	www.state.fl.us
Georgia	Yes	www.state.ga.us
Hawaii	Yes	www.state.hi.us
Idaho	Yes	www.state.id.us
Illinois	Yes	www.state.il.us
Indiana	Yes	www.state.in.us
Iowa	Yes	www.state.ia.us
Kansas	Yes	www.state.ks.us
Kentucky	Yes	www.state.ky.us
Louisiana	Yes	www.state.la.us
Maine	Yes	www.state.me.us
Maryland	Yes	www.state.md.us
Massachusetts	Yes	www.state.ma.us
Michigan	Yes	www.state.mi.us
Minnesota	Yes	www.state.mn.us
Mississippi	Yes	www.state.ms.us
Missouri	Yes	www.state.mo.us
Montana	Yes	www.state.mt.us
Nebraska	Yes	www.nol.org/state/

(continued)

Data Source	Free	Internet Address
Nevada	Yes	www.state.nv.us
New Hampshire	Yes	www.state.nh.us
New Jersey	Yes	www.state.nj.us
New Mexico	Yes	www.state.nm.us
New York	Yes	www.state.ny.us
North Carolina	Yes	www.state.nc.us
North Dakota	Yes	www.state.nd.us
Ohio	Yes	www.state.oh.us
Oklahoma	Yes	www.state.ok.us
Oregon	Yes	www.state.or.us
Pennsylvania	Yes	www.state.pa.us
Rhode Island	Yes	www.state.ri.us
South Carolina	Yes	www.state.sc.us
South Dakota	Yes	www.state.sd.us
Tennessee	Yes	www.state.tn.us
Texas	Yes	www.state.tx.us
Utah	Yes	www.state.ut.us
Vermont	Yes	www.state.vt.us
Virginia	Yes	www.state.va.us
Washington	Yes	www.state.wa.gov/wahome.html
West Virginia	Yes	www.state.wv.us
Wisconsin	Yes	www.state.wi.us
Wyoming	Yes	www.state.wy.us
Puerto Rico	Yes	www.pr-edu.com
International		
Embassies in Washington, DC	Yes	www.embassy.org
Australian Legal Information	Yes	austlii.law.uts.edu.au
Canadian Criminal Justice System	Yes	www.criminaldefence.com
Central Adjudication Services UK	Yes	www.open.gov.uk/cas/cashome.htm
Centre for Defence and International Security	Yes	www.cdiss.org
Court Service UK	Yes	www.open.gov.uk/courts/court/
Crime Stopper on line Australia	Yes	www.crimestoppers.net.au
Foreign Government Resources	Yes	www.lib.umich.edu/libhome/Documents.center/foreign.html
HM Prison Service	Yes	www.open.gov.uk/prison/
International Association of Crime Analysts	Yes	www.iaca.net
National Criminal Intelligence Service UK	Yes	www.open.gov.uk/ncis/ncishome.htm
Office of International Criminal Justice	Yes	www.acsp.uic.edu
UK Police and Forensic Web	Yes	www.innotts.co.uk
UN Crime and Justice Info Network	Yes	www.ifs.univie.ac.at
Asia Far East Institute for the Prevention of Crime	Yes	www.unafei.or.jp
European Union Home Page	Yes	europa.eu.int/index.htm
International Money Laundering Information Network	Yes	www.imolin.org
UN Interregional Crime and Justice	Yes	www.unicri.it

(continued)

Data Source	Free	Internet Address
Forensic Science Society	Yes	www.demon.co.uk/forensic
UN Centre for International Crime	Yes	www.ifs.univie.ac.at
UN International Drug Control Policy	Yes	www.undcp.org
Atlas—Canadian	Yes	www.nais.ccm.emr.ca
Institute for International Economics	Yes	www.iie.com
International Monetary Fund	Yes	www.imf.org
Organization for Economic Development	Yes	www.oecd.org
World Bank	Yes	www.worldbank.org
World Trade Organization		
European Union Home Page	Yes	www.europa.eu
United Nations	Yes	www.un.org
UNESCO	Yes	www.unesco.org
UNAFRI	Yes	www.mukla.gn.apc.org
UNAFEI	Yes	www.niftyserve.or.jp
Australian Institute of Criminology	Yes	www.aic.gov.au
Helsinki Institute for Crime Prevention	Yes	www.joutsen.pp.fi
NATO	Yes	nato.int
International Money Laundering Info Network	Yes	www.imolin.org
Financial Action Task Force	Yes	www.fatf-gafi.org
International Crime Police Organization	Yes	www.interpol.int
Directories		
Switchboard	Yes	www.switchboard.com
Social Security Death Index	Yes	www.infobases.com/ssdi/query01.htm
Info Space	Yes	www.infospace.com
US and Canadian Links to Data	Yes	www.searchsystems.net
People Finder's Search Engine	Yes	www.databaseamerica.com/engine/gpfind.htm
Biz Finder Database	Yes	www.databaseamerica.com
SSN Validation Database	Yes	www.informus.com/ssnlkup.html
Military Locator	Yes	www.militarycity.com
World Yellow Pages	Yes	www.wyp.net/Search.html
The Big Book	Yes	www.bigbook.com
Four 11 People Finder (Internet)	Yes	www.Four11.com
Internet Address Finder	Yes	www.iaf.net
Net People Finder	Yes	www.whowhere.com
ESP Email Search Program	Yes	www.esp.co.uk
Newsgroup Locator Tools	Yes	www.cen.uiuc.edu
Newsgroup Locator Tools	Yes	tile.net/news/
Newsgroup Locator Tools	Yes	sunsite.unc.edu/usenet-I/home.html
Net Mailing List Locator Tool	Yes	www.liszt.com
Net Mailing List Locator Tool	Yes	www.nova.edu/Inter-Links/cgi-bin/lists
Net Usenet Filter	Yes	www.reference.com
Searchable Phonebooks	Yes	www.networkx.com
Searchable Phonebooks	Yes	www.animax.com
Searchable Phonebooks	Yes	www.tollfree.att.net
Searchable Phonebooks	Yes	www.bellcore.com

(continued)

Data Source	Free	Internet Address
Searchable Phonebooks	Yes	www.telephonebook.com
Searchable Phonebooks	Yes	www.payphones.com
Searchable Phonebooks	Yes	www.infospaceinc.com
Searchable Phonebooks	Yes	www.pagenet.net
Searchable Phonebooks	Yes	www.searchameria.com
Searchable Phonebooks	Yes	www.switchboard.com
Searchable Phonebooks	Yes	www.ypo.com
Searchable Phonebooks	Yes	www.c2.org
Teleport Internet Services	Yes	www.teleport.com/news/
World Email Directory	Yes	www.worldemail.com
Internet Sleuth	Yes	www.intbc.com/sleth/
Doctor Search Database	Yes	ama-assn.org
MediaFinder	Yes	www.mediafinder.com
ATT 800 Toll Free Directory	Yes	www.tollfree.att.net
Attorney Information Lookups	Yes	www.wld.com
Movie/Actor Information Lookup	Yes	www.internetdatabase.com/movie.htm
Pharmaceutical Information	Yes	www.pharminfo.com
Claim Providers of America	Yes	www.claims.com
Business Yellow Pages	Yes	www.ypo.com
Physician Database	Yes	www.medaccess.com/physician/phys01.htm
Envirosearch	Yes	www.envirosearch.com
Health Care Locator	Yes	www.medaccess.com/locator/hclocate.htm
ComFind	Yes	www.comfind.com
Medical and Mental Health	Yes	www.realtime.net/~mmjw/
World's Most Wanted People	Yes	www.mostwanted.com
MapQuest	Yes	www.mapquest.com
Index of Newspapers	Yes	www.teleport.com
American Medical Forensics	Yes	www.emeraldcity.com/crimefiles.htm
Directory of Database Services	Yes	www.facsnet.org/report_tools/CAR/cardirec.htm
Reunion Network	Yes	www.reunion.com
Sex Offender Registry Indiana	Yes	www.state.in.us/cji/index.html
American Medical Forensics	Yes	www.amfs.com
Yellow Pages Directory	Yes	www.bigyellow.com
800 Number Telephone Directory	Yes	www.dir800.att.net
Telephone Directory	Yes	www.switchboard.com
Dun & Bradstreet	Y/N	www.dnb.com
Who Where? Search for People	Yes	www.whowhere.com
Any Who People Finder	Yes	www.anywho.com
Will Yancey, PhD, CPA	Yes	www.willyancey.com
Search Engines		
Ask	Yes	www.ask.com
Yahoo	Yes	www.yahoo.com
Webcrawler	Yes	www.webcrawler.com
Lycos	Yes	www.lycos.com

(continued)

Data Source	Free	Internet Address
Alta Vista	Yes	www.altavista.com
Starting Point	Yes	www.stpt.com
Open Text	Yes	www.opentext.com
Metacrawler	Yes	www.metacrawler.com
U.S. Government Website Searches	Yes	www.firstgov.gov
Dogpile Search Engine	Yes	www.dogpile.com
Ask	Yes	www.ask.com
Copernic	Yes	www.copernic.com
Epilot	Yes	www.epilot.com
Google	Yes	www.google.com
Hot Bot	Yes	www.hotbot.com
Itools	Yes	www.itools.com
Infoseek	Yes	www.infoseek.com
Law Crawler	Yes	www.lawcrawler.com
Mamma	Yes	www.mamma.com
Northern Light	No	www.northernlight.com
Teoma	Yes	www.teoma.com
Tenkwizard	Yes	www.tenkwizard.com
Industry Data		
NAICS Codes and Descriptions	Yes	www.census.gov/epcd/www/naics.html
Medical Group Management Association	Y/N	www.mgma.com
Chemical Week	Yes	www.chemweek.com
Legal Information		
Cornell Law/Supreme Court	Yes	www.law.cornell.edu
Legal Information	Yes	www.law.cornell.edu
Tax Code	Yes	www.law.cornell.edu
Tax News	Yes	www.cch.com
Libraries and Publications		
Journal of Finance	Yes	www.afaof.org/jofihome.shtml
Book Stacks	Yes	www.books.com
Smithsonian Encyclopedia	Yes	www.si.edu
Reference Desk—General	Yes	www.refdesk.com
Concise Columbia Encyclopedia	Yes	www.encyclopedia.com
Business Statistics	Yes	www.bizstats.com
National Economics		
Fed—Boston	Yes	www.bos.frb.org
Fed—Chicago	Yes	www.bog.frbchi.org
Fed—Cleveland	Yes	www.clev.frb.org
Fed—Dallas	Yes	www.dallasfed.org
Fed—Kansas City	Yes	www.kc.frb.org
Fed—Minneapolis	Yes	www.mpls.frb.fed.us
Fed—New York	Yes	www.ny.frb.org
Fed—Philadelphia	Yes	www.phil.frb.org
Fed—Richmond	Yes	www.rich.frb.org

(continued)

Data Source	Free	Internet Address
Fed—San Francisco	Yes	www.frbsf.org
Fed—St. Louis	Yes	www.stls.frb.org
SIC Codes and Descriptions	Yes	www.ecrc.uofs.edu/sic.html
Telephone Directory	Yes	www.switchboard.com

Useful Resource Providers

American Society of Appraisers	Yes	www.apo.com
Independent Business Alliance	Yes	www.ibaonline.com
Institute of Business Appraisers	Yes	www.instbusapp.org
Mercer Capital	Yes	www.bizval.com
Shannon Pratt's Business Valuation	Yes	www.transport.com/~shannonp
Wealth Planning for Closely Held Corp	Yes	www.wealthinfo.net
International Business Brokers Association	Yes	www.ibba.org
D & B Reports	No	www.dbisna.com/dbis/dnbhome.htm
Dunn & Bradstreet	Yes	www.dnb.com
State Court Locator	Yes	www.law.vill.edu
Standard & Poor	No	mcgraw-hill.com
Business Information	Yes	www.business.com
Annual Report Gallery	Yes	www.ReportGallery.com
Annual Report Service	Yes	www.Annualreportservice.com
Annual Report Library	Yes	www.zpub.com/sf/arl
Global company annual report	Yes	www.carol.co.uk
Corpwatch	Yes	www.corpwatch.org
Direct Hit	Yes	www.directhit.com

Accounting Research

FASB	Yes	www.fasb.org
GASB	Yes	www.financenet.gov/gasb.htm
Accounting Net	Yes	www.accountingnet.com

Public Stock Information

Investment Resources	Yes	www.infomanage.com/investment
NASDAQ	Yes	www.nasdaq.com
Securities Exchange Commission	Yes	www.sec.gov
News Service Including Stock Prices	Yes	www.infobeat.com
Enhanced SEC EDGAR Reports	Yes	www.freedgar.com

Miscellaneous

Microsoft Online	Yes	www.microsolft.com
Personal Investments	Yes	www.INVESTools.com
Newsmaker Profiles—ABC	Yes	www.abcnews.com/reference
United Parcel Service	Yes	www.ups.com
Police Resource List	Yes	police.sas.ab.ca
The Legal Pad	Yes	www.legal-pad.com
Global Security Complex	Yes	www.guns-training.com
Insurance Fraud Research Register	Yes	www.ifb.org
PI Magazine	Yes	www.pimall.com
Investigative News Magazine	Yes	www.offshorebusiness.com

(continued)

Data Source	Free	Internet Address
Tax Prophet News (Scams)	Y/N	www.taxprophet.com
Scam News	Yes	www.quatloos.com
Currency Converter	Yes	www.oanda.com/comverter/classic
Associations and Nonprofit Organizations		
Police Officer's Internet Directory	Yes	www.officer.com
International Association of Chiefs of Police	Yes	www.theiacp.org
Crime Prevention	Yes	www.prevention.gc.ca
Internet Crime Archives	Yes	www.mayhem.net/Crime/archives.html
CopNet	Yes	www.copnet.org
National Association of Legal Investigators	Yes	www.nalionline.org
VERA Institute of Justice	Yes	www.vera.org
Association Investment Management and Research	Yes	www.cfainstitute.org
Investigative Reporters and Editors	Yes	www.ire.org
National Institute Computer Assisted Report	Yes	www.nicar.org
American Bar Association	Yes	www.abanet.org
Investigators Open Network	Yes	www.pihome.com
Association of British Investigators	Yes	www.uklegal.com
Justice Information Center	Yes	www.ncjrs.org
National Fraud Information Center	Yes	www.fraud.org
National Law Enforcement Technology Center	Yes	www.nletc.org
High Tech Crime Investigation Association	Yes	www.htcia.org
Rand	Yes	www.rand.org
C-SPAN	Yes	gopher://c-span.org
American Gaming Organization	Yes	www.americangaming.org
Cop Seek	Yes	www.copseek.com
International Association Personal Protection Specialists	Yes	www.iapps.org
American Institute of CPAs	Yes	www.aicpa.org
Association of Government Accountants	Yes	www.agacgfm.org
Institute of Internal Auditors	Yes	www.theiia.org
Institute of Management Accountants	Yes	www.imanet.org
North American Society of Tax Advisors	Yes	www.taxadvisors.com
Association of Communications Enterprises	Yes	www.ascent.org
Computer Security Institute	Yes	www.gocsi.com
Association of Certified Fraud Examiners	Yes	www.acfe.org
American Society for Industrial Security	Yes	www.asis.com
Institute of Internal Auditors	Yes	www.iia.org
Coalition Against Insurance Fraud	Yes	www.insurancefraud.org
News Sources		
ABC News Online	Yes	www.abcnews.com
Business Week	Yes	www.businessweek.com
CBS	Yes	www.cbs.com
CNN	Yes	www.cnn.com
Financial Times	Y/N	www.ft.com

(continued)

Data Source	Free	Internet Address
Forbes Magazine	Y/N	www.forbes.com
Fortune Magazine	Yes	www.fortune.com
Miami Herald	Yes	www.miami.com
Los Angeles Times	Yes	www.latimes.com
MSNBC	Yes	www.msnbc.com
New York Times	Yes	www.nytimes.com
Reuters News Service	Yes	www.reuters.com
Time Magazine	Yes	www.time.com
U.S. News & World Reports	Yes	www.usnews.com
USA Today	Yes	www.usatoday.com
Wall Street Journal	Yes	www.wsj.com
Washington Post	Yes	www.washingtonpost.com
World Net Daily	Yes	www.worldnetdaily.com
DEBKA	Yes	www.debka.com

Commercial Database Services

International Air Transport Association	No	www.iata.org
Carfax	No	www.carfax.com
Auto Check	No	www.autocheck.com
Data-Star/Dialog	No	www.dialog.com
Minital Services Company	No	www.minitel.fr
AMS	No	www.ams.com
Global Scan (USA) Inc.	No	www.iig-associates.com
Lexis/Nexis	No	www.lexisnexis.com
NCI	No	www.nciinc.com
Pacer	No	pacer.psc.uscourts.gov
Superior Online	No	www.superiorinfo.com
ASIS Net	No	www.infoinc.com
Merlin Information Services	No	www.merlindata.com
US Datalink	No	www.usdatalink.com
Choice Point	No	www.choicepoint.com

Appendix D
Internet Country Codes

AD	Andorra	CK	Cook Islands
AE	United Arab Emirates	CL	Chile
AF	Afghanistan	CM	Cameroon
AG	Antigua and Barbuda	CN	China
AI	Anguilla	CO	Colombia
AL	Albania	CR	Costa Rica
AM	Armenia	CS	Czechoslovakia (former)
AN	Netherlands Antilles	CU	Cuba
AO	Angola	CV	Cape Verde
AQ	Antarctica	CX	Christmas Island
AR	Argentina	CY	Cyprus
AS	American Samoa	CZ	Czech Republic
AT	Austria	DE	Germany
AU	Australia	DJ	Djibouti
AW	Aruba	DK	Denmark
AZ	Azerbaijan	DM	Dominica
BA	Bosnia and Herzegovina	DO	Dominican Republic
BB	Barbados	DZ	Algeria
BD	Bangladesh	EC	Ecuador
BE	Belgium	EE	Estonia
BF	Burkina Faso	EG	Egypt
BG	Bulgaria	EH	Western Sahara
BH	Bahrain	ER	Eritrea
BI	Burundi	ES	Spain
BJ	Benin	ET	Ethiopia
BM	Bermuda	FI	Finland
BN	Brunei Darussalam	FJ	Fiji
BO	Bolivia	FK	Falkland Islands (Malvinas)
BR	Brazil	FM	Micronesia
BS	Bahamas	FO	Faroe Islands
BT	Bhutan	FR	France
BV	Bouvet Island	FX	France, Metropolitan
BW	Botswana	GA	Gabon
BY	Belarus	GB	Great Britain (UK)
BZ	Belize	GD	Grenada
CA	Canada	GE	Georgia
CC	Cocos (Keeling) Islands	GF	French Guiana
CF	Central African Republic	GH	Ghana
CG	Congo	GI	Gibraltar

CH	Switzerland	GL	Greenland
CI	Cote D'Ivoire (Ivory Coast)	GM	Gambia
GN	Guinea	MA	Morocco
GP	Guadeloupe Equatorial Guinea	MC	Monaco
GR	Greece	MD	Moldova
GS	S. Georgia and S. Sandwich Islands	MG	Madagascar
GT	Guatemala	MH	Marshall Islands
GU	Guam	MK	Macedonia
GW	Guinea-Bissau	ML	Mali
GY	Guyana	MM	Myanmar
HK	Hong Kong	MN	Mongolia
HM	Heard Island and McDonald Islands	MO	Macau
HN	Honduras	MP	North Mariana Islands
HR	Croatia (Hrvatska)	MQ	Martinique
HT	Haiti	MR	Mauritania
HU	Hungary	MS	Montserrat
ID	Indonesia	MT	Malta
IE	Ireland	MU	Mauritius
IL	Israel	MV	Maldives
IN	India	MW	Malawi
IO	British Indian Ocean Territory	MX	Mexico
IQ	Iraq	MY	Malaysia
IR	Iran	MZ	Mozambique
IS	Iceland	NA	Nambia
IT	Italy	NC	New Caledonia
JM	Jamaica	NE	Niger
JO	Jordan	NF	Norfolk Island
JP	Japan	NG	Nigeria
KE	Kenya	NI	Nicaragua
KG	Kyrgyzstan	NL	Netherlands
KH	Cambodia	NO	Norway
KI	Kiribati	NP	Nepal
KM	Comoros	NR	Nauru
KN	Saint Kitts and Nevis	NT	Neutral Zone
KP	Korea (North)	NU	Niue
KR	Korea (South)	NZ	New Zealand
KW	Kuwait	OM	Oman
KY	Cayman Islands	PA	Panama
KZ	Kazakhstan	PE	Peru
LA	Laos	PF	French Polynesia
LB	Lebanon	PG	Papua New Guinea
LC	Saint Lucia	PH	Philippines
LI	Liechtenstein	PK	Pakistan
LK	Sri Lanka	PL	Poland
LU	Luxembourg	PM	St. Pierre and Miquelon
LV	Latvia	PN	Pitcairn
LY	Libya	PR	Puerto Rico
PT	Portugal	TJ	Tajikistan

PW	Palau	TK	Tokelau
PY	Paraguay	TM	Turkmenistan
QA	Qatar	TN	Tunisia
RE	Reunion	TO	Tonga
RO	Romania	TP	East Timor
RU	Russian Federation	TR	Turkey
RW	Rwanda	TT	Trinidad and Tobago
SA	Saudi Arabia	TV	Tuvalu
SB	Solomon Islands	TW	Taiwan
SC	Seychelles	TZ	Tanzania
SD	Sudan	UA	Ukraine
SE	Sweden	UG	Uganda
SG	Singapore	UK	United Kingdom
SH	St. Helena	UM	U.S. Minor Outlying Islands
SI	Slovenia	US	United States
SJ	Svalbard and Jan Mayen Islands	UY	Uruguay
SK	Slovak Republic	UZ	Uzbekistan
SL	Sierra Leone	VA	Vatican City State
SM	San Marino	VC	Saint Vincent and the Grenadines
SN	Senegal	VE	Venezuela
SO	Somalia	VG	Virgin Islands (British)
ST	São Tomé and Príncipe	VI	Virgin Islands (U.S.)
SU	USSR (former)	VN	Viet Nam
SV	El Salvador	VU	Vanuatu
SY	Syria	WF	Wallis and Futuna Islands
SZ	Swaziland	WS	Samoa
TC	Turks and Caicos Islands	YE	Yemen
TD	Chad	YT	Mayotte
TF	French Southern Territories	YU	Yugoslavia
TG	Togo	ZA	South Africa
LR	Liberia	ZM	Zambia
LS	Lesotho	ZR	Zaire
LT	Lithuania	ZW	Zimbabwe

Appendix E
Glossary of Common
Internet Terms

ADN: Advanced Digital Network. Usually refers to a 56-kbps leased line.

ADSL: Asymmetric Digital Subscriber Line. A method for moving data over regular phone lines. An ADSL circuit is much faster than a regular phone connection, and the wires coming into the subscriber's premises are the same (copper) wires used to regular phone service. An ADSL circuit must be configured to connect two specific locations, similar to a leased line.

Applet: A small Java program that can be embedded in an HTML page. Applets differ from full-fledged Java applications in that they are not allowed to access certain resources on the local computer, such as files and serial devices (modems, printers, etc.) and are prohibited from communicating with most other computers across a network. The current rule is that an applet can only make an Internet connection to the computer from which the applet was sent.

Archie: A tool (software) for finding files stored on anonymous FTP sites. You need to know the exact file name or a substring of it.

ASCII: American Standard Code for Information Interchange. This is the de facto worldwide standard for the code numbers used by computers to represent all the upper- and lowercase Latin letters, numbers, punctuation, etc. There are 128 standard ASCII codes, each of which can be represented by a seven-digit binary number: 0000000 through 1111111.

Bandwidth: How much stuff you can send through a connection; usually measured in bits-per-second. A full page of English text is about 16,000 bits. A fast modem can move about 15,000 bits in 1 second. Full-motion full-screen video would require roughly 10,000,000 bits-per-second, depending on compression.

Baud: In common usage, the baud rate of a modem is how many bits it can send or receive per second. Technically, baud is the number of times per second that the carrier signal shifts value; for example, a 1200 bit-per-second modem actually runs at 300 baud, but it moves 4 bits per baud (4 × 300 = 1200 bits per second).

BBS: Bulletin Board System. A computerized meeting and announcement system that allows people to carry on discussions, upload and download files, and make announcements without the people being connected to the computer at the same time. There are many thousands or millions of BBSs around the world; most are very small, running on a single IBM clone PC with one or two phone lines. Some are very large and the line between a BBS and a system such as CompuServe gets crossed at some point, but it is not clearly drawn.

Binhex: Binary hexadecimal. A method for converting non-text files (non-ASCII into ASCII). This is needed because Internet e-mail can only handle ASCII.

Bit: Binary digit. A single digit number in base 2; in other words, either a 1 or a 0. The smallest unit of computerized data.

Browser: A client program (software) used to look at various types of Internet resources.

BMP: A graphic bitmap image. The colors of dots or pixels make up the picture. BMP files use the .bmp extension in their filename.

Buried Web Site: A Web site that does not have a registered domain name. These are typically small sites consisting of Web pages on a host ISP.

Byte: A set of bits that represent a single character. Usually, there are 8 bits in a byte, sometimes more, depending on how the measurement is being made.

Client: A software program used to contact and obtain data from a server software program on another computer, often across a great distance. Each Client program is designed to work with one or more specific types of server programs, and each server requires a specific type of Client. A Web browser is a specific kind of Client.

Cookie: The most common meaning of "cookie" on the Internet refers to a piece of information sent by a Web server to a Web browser that the browser software is expected to save and to send back to the server whenever the browser makes additional requests from the server.

Depending on the type of cookie used, and the browser's settings, the browser may accept or not accept the cookie, and may save the cookie either for a short time or a long time. Cookies might contain information such as login or registration information, online "shopping cart" information, user preferences, etc. When a server receives a request from a browser that includes a cookie, the server is able to use the information stored in the cookie. For example, the server might customize what is sent back to the user, or keep a log of a particular user's requests.

Cookies are usually set to expire after a predetermined length of time and are usually saved in memory until the browser software is closed down, at which time they may be saved to disk if their expired time has not been reached. Cookies do not read your drive and send your life story to the CIA, but they can be used to gather more information about a user than would be possible without them.

Cyberspace: Term originated by author William Gibson in his novel *Neuromancer.* The word cyberspace is currently used to describe the whole range of information resources available through computer networks.

Domain Name: Domains divide World Wide Web sites into categories on the nature of their owner, and they form part of the site's address, or uniform locator (URL). Common top-level domains are:

.com for commercial enterprises
.org for nonprofit organizations
.net for networks
.edu for educational institutions
.gov for government organizations
.mil for military services
.int for organizations established by international treaty

Additional three-letter and four-letter top level domains have been proposed, and some are likely to be implemented in the near future. Each country linked to the Web has a two-letter top level domain, representing the country name (e.g., .ca for Canada).

E-mail: Electronic mail. Messages, usually text, sent from one person to another via computer. E-mails can also be sent automatically to a large number of addresses (mailing list).

Ethernet: A very common method of networking computers in a LAN. Ethernet will handle about 10,000,000 bits-per-second and can be used with almost any type of computer.

FAQ: Frequently asked questions. A FAQ file is a collection of common questions and answers for a particular subject matter.

FDDI: Fiber Distributed Data Interface. A standard for transmitting data on optical fiber cables at a rate of around 100,000,000 bit-per-second (10 times as fast as Ethernet, about twice as fast as T-3).

Firewall: Firewall refers to the concept of a security interface or gateway between a closed network and the outside Internet that blocks or manages communications in and out of the network. Passwords, authentication techniques, software, and hardware may provide the security.

FTP: File Transfer Protocol. The Internet protocol (IP) that permits you to transfer files between your system and another system. There are various FTP programs available to assist with file transfers and you can also transfer files directly using your browser from an FTP Web site.

GIF: Graphical interchange format. A bitmap graphical format that is widely used in WWW pages. It is particularly good for text art, cartoon art, poster art, and line drawings. GIF files use a .gif extension in their filename.

Gigabyte: 1000 or 1024 megabytes, depending on who is measuring.

HTML: HyperText Markup Language. The coding system used to create Web pages. A page written in HTML is a text file that includes tags in angle brackets that control the fonts and type sizes, insertion of graphics, layout of tables and frames, paragraphing, calls to short runnable programs, and hypertext links to other pages. Files written in HTML generally use an .html or .htm extension.

HTTP: HyperText Transfer Protocol. It is the main protocol used on the World Wide Web that enables linking to other Web sites. Addressing to other Web pages begins with http:// and is followed by the domain name or IP address.

Typertext: Generally, any text that contains links to other documents—words or phrases in the document that can be chosen by a reader and which cause another document to be retrieved and displayed.

Internet: A network of many networks that interconnect worldwide and use the IP.

Intranet: A network of networks that interconnects within a single widespread organization and uses the IP. The sites within an Intranet are generally closed to the Internet and are accessible to organization members only.

IP: Internet protocol.

IP Number: Internet protocol number. Sometimes called a dotted quad. A unique number consisting of four parts separated by dots, for example, 165.113.245.2. Every machine that is on the Internet has a unique IP number. If a machine does not have an IP number, it is not really on the Internet.

IP address: IP address and domain addresses are the two forms of Internet addresses in common use. IP addresses consist of four numbers between 0 and 255 separated by dots.

ISP: Internet service provider. An institution that provides access to the Internet in some form, usually for money.

Java: Java is a network oriented programming language invented by Sun Microsystems that is specifically designed for writing programs that can be safely downloaded to your computer through the Internet and immediately run without fear of viruses or other harm to your computer files.

JPG, JPEG: Joint Photographic Express Group. A common graphical format that is widely used in WWW pages and is particularly well suited to photographs and 3D images. Filenames will have a .jpeg, .jpg, or .jpe extension in their filename.

Kilobyte: A thousand bytes. Actually, usually 1024 bytes.

LAN: Local Area Network. A computer network limited to the immediate area, usually in the same building or floor of a building.

Login: The account name used to gain access to a computer system.

Megabyte: A million bytes. Actually, technically 1024 kilobytes.

MIME: Multipurpose Internet Mail Extensions. The standard for attaching non-text files to standard Internet mail messages. Non-text files include graphics, spreadsheets, formatted word-processor documents, sound files, etc. An e-mail program is said to be MIME compliant if it can both send and receive files using the MIME standard.

Modem: Modulator, demodulator. A device that you connect to your computer and to a phone line that allows the computer to talk to other computers through the phone system. Basically, modems do for computers what a telephone does for humans.

Netscape: A WWW browser and the name of a company. The Netscape browser was originally based on the Mosaic program developed at the National Center for Supercomputing Applications (NCSA). Netscape has rapidly grown in features and is widely recognized as the best and most popular Web browser. Netscape Corporation also produces Web server software.

Network: Any time you connect two or more computers together so that they can share resources, you have a computer network. Connect two or more networks together and you have an Internet.

Password: A code used to gain access to a locked system. Good passwords contain letters and non-letters and are not simple combinations.

Port: One meaning is a place where information goes into or out of a computer, or both. On the Internet, port often refers to a number that is part of a URL, appearing after a colon right after the domain name. Every service on an Internet server listens on a particular port number on that server. Most services have standard port numbers.

Server: A computer, or a software package, that provides a specific kind of service to client software running on other computers. The term can refer to a particular piece of software, such as WWW server, or to the machine on which the software is running.

Spam: An inappropriate attempt to use a mailing list or other networked communication facility as if it was a broadcast medium by sending the same message to a large number of people who did not ask for it. The term probably comes from a famous Monty Python skit that featured the word spam repeated over and over.

SQL: Structured Query Language. A specialized programming language for sending queries to databases. Most industrial-strength and many smaller database applications can be addressed using SQL.

SSL: Secure Sockets Layer. A protocol designed by Netscape Communications to enable encrypted, authenticated communications across the Internet. SSL is used mostly in communications between Web browsers and Web servers. URLs that begin with "https" indicate that an SSL connection will be used. SSL provides three important things: privacy, authentication, and message integrity.

Sysop: System Operator. Anyone responsible for the physical operations of a computer system or network resource.

T-1: A leased-line connection capable of carrying data at 1,544,000 bits-per-second. At maximum theoretical capacity, a T-1 could move a megabyte in less than 10 seconds. It is not fast enough for full-screen, full-motion video, for which you need at least 10,000,000 bits-per-second.

T-3: A leased-line connection capable of carrying data at 44,736,000 bits-per-second. This is more than enough to do full-screen, full motion video.

TCP/IP: Transmission Control Protocol/Internet Protocol. This is the suite of protocols that defines the Internet. To be truly on the Internet, your computer must have TCP/IP software.

Terabyte: 1000 gigabytes.

URL: Uniform Resource Locator. URLs specify the location or address of a web page. You can type or paste the URL into the address bar of your browser and then connect to it. For example, the IRS URL is http://www.irs.gov.

USENET: A worldwide system of discussion groups, with comments passed among hundreds of thousands of machines. Not all USENET machines are on the Internet. USENET is completely decentralized, with more than 10,000 discussion areas, called newsgroups.

VPN: Virtual Private Network. Usually refers to a network in which some of the parts are connected using the public Internet, but the data sent across the Internet are encrypted, so the entire network is virtually private.

WAN: Wide Area Network. Any Internet or network that covers an area larger than a single building or campus.

WWW Called Web: World Wide Web is an Internet protocol that makes use of the HTML hypertext and hypermedia to create pages with links to other pages. WWW pages can include graphics, audio, and video as well as text.

Appendix F
Engagement Letters

Many fraud examiners are employed by federal, state, and local agencies. These fraud examiners must adhere to their employment rules and conduct. However, some fraud examiners are retained by private companies and individuals for the specific purpose of finding fraud. These cases are mostly civil in nature; however, they can become criminal. Cases involving embezzlement or theft of assets should be worked up for criminal prosecution even if the prosecutor does not accept the case. Criminal cases should be worked up and referred to a prosecutor before any civil case is filed. It is better for the client to prosecute the fraudster. Failure to do so generally will lead to other employees committing the same fraud. It is always best for the fraud examiner to obtain an engagement letter before starting to work on a case. The engagement letter should outline the responsibilities for the fraud examiner and what the client is to provide, both internally and externally. This serves as a contract for services. The engagement letter should address the following topics.

1. The fraud examiner cannot guarantee that fraud is present. The fraud examiner can only examine books and records for fraud indicators and follow up on those fraud indicators. Fraud indicators are NOT poor accounting records and controls, mismanagement, or misplaced assets.
2. Fraud examinations and investigations can sometimes require many hours of work. The degree of work depends on the sophistication of the fraud scheme. Example: Money laundering can take many hours in tracing funds if it covers 3 or more years and entails many transactions. It also can take time to find all the ways an employee embezzled funds. Example: The fraud might involve payroll checks and withholding, paying credit card bills, personal living expenses, diversion of merchandise, padding expense reports, etc.
3. The client should provide at the start of the engagement a letter detailing why he/she suspects fraud, the type of fraud, and who may be committing the fraud. Remember, the identified person may not be the perpetrator. This can help the fraud examiner to narrow down their examination and investigation.
4. All information must be kept confidential. This is to protect the innocence of all parties in the case. A leak in a case, however small, can compromise the whole case and could lead to legal action against one or both of us. Information can only be shared to those who have a need to know.
5. During the course of the examination and investigation, evidence must be obtained, both culpatory and exculpatory.
6. The company or individual should provide all necessary records in order to conduct the examination. Note: May want to describe the books and records needed.
7. Any and all employees should be made available for interview if or when it becomes necessary to conduct an interview.

8. The fraud examiner should give details on their fees and when payments are to be made. Any retainers should be shown. The fraud examiner should provide details about reimbursement of expenses.
9. If confirmations for accounts receivables or accounts payable become necessary, then the company should prepare and mail these confirmations. The confirmations should be received by the fraud examiner unopened.
10. The fraud examiner should give status reports. These status reports should be given periodically, usually on a monthly basis. Also, the fraud examiner should give a final report. In a criminal case, the fraud examiner should prepare a report as shown in Chapter 22 of this book. This report should be signed by the fraud examiner and undersigned by the client. In civil cases, the fraud examiner should provide a report like the criminal report, but the report is addressed to the client's attorney for recovery of assets.
11. If fraud has been discovered that is material, then the client must have their tax returns amended and financial statements amended, which go to third parties, for example, lending institutions or anyone who requires them.
12. In cases involving embezzlement and skimming, a 1099 MISC should be filed with the Internal Revenue Service at year end. Failure to file a 1099 MISC may disallow a deduction for embezzled funds. The 1099 MISC should show "EMBEZZLED FUNDS."
13. The fraud examiner may wish to provide an additional letter on how to set up internal controls so the client will not suffer another loss by another employee or future employee.

The fraud examiner should sign the engagement letter after advising the client of the above terms and conditions. A copy of the engagement letter should be retained by the client. The fraud examiner should retain the original.

If the client accepts the engagement, then he/she should sign and date the engagement letter below "I ACCEPT THE TERMS AND CONDITIONS FOR THIS ENGAGEMENT." A line for his/her signature and date should be provided.

Bibliography*

Central Intelligence Agency. World Factbook, www.cia.gov/cia/publications/factbook.

Curren, Daniel L., and Claire M. Renzetti. *Theories of Crime*. Needham Heights, MA: Allyn and Bacon, 1994.

Federal Bureau of Investigation. A Parent's Guide to Internet Safety, www.fbi.gov/publlication/pguide/pgidee.htm.

Federal Civil Judicial Procedure and Rules. St. Paul, MN: West Publishing Co., 2009.

Federal Criminal Code and Rules. St. Paul, MN: West Publishing Co., 2009.

Gleim, Irvan N., and Patrick R. Delaney. *CPA Examination Review*. 11th ed., Vols. 1 and 2. New York, NY: John Wiley & Sons, 1984.

Kasish, Sanford H., ed. *Encyclopedia of Crime and Justice*, 4 vols. New York, NY: The Free Press, 1983.

Moore, James T., Commissioner, Florida Department of Law Enforcement. *Sources of Information*, Division of Criminal Investigations, Investigative Analysis Bureau, 1990.

President's Commission on Organized Crime, *The Impact: Organized Crime Today*. Washington, DC: U.S. Government Printing Office, April 1986.

Smith, John C. *Investigation and Prosecuting Network Intrusions*, Hi-Tech/Computer Crime Unit, Santa Clara County District Attorney's Office, San Jose, CA, www.eff.org/Legal/scda_cracking_investigation.paper.

Rabon, Don. *Analyzing Written Statements*, A course by the Association of Certified Fraud Examiners, The Gregor Building, 716 West Avenue, Austin, Texas 78701, 2008.

Walters, Stan B. *Principles of Kinesic Interview and Interrogation*. Boca Raton, FL: CRC Press, 1996.

Standard Federal Tax Reporter. Chicago, IL: Commerce Clearing House, 1989.

U.S. Department of the Army, *Physical Security*, Field Manual 3-19-30, Washington, DC, January 2001.

U.S. Department of Justice, Criminal Division, Asset Forfeiture and Money Laundering Section. *Financial Investigation Guide*, Washington, DC, June 1998.

U.S. Department of Justice. *Federal Guidelines for Searching and Seizing Computers*, www.usdoj.gov.

U.S. Department of Justice. *Compilation of Selected Federal Asset Forfeiture Statutes* (Rev. 7-95), Washington, DC, 1995.

U.S. Department of Justice. *Searching and Seizing Computer and Obtaining Electronic Evidence in Criminal Investigation*, July 2002, www.usdoj.gov/criminal/cybercrime/s&smanual2002.htm.

U.S. Department of the Treasury. *Special Agents Handbook, Internal Revenue Manual*, Washington, DC.

U.S. Department of the Treasury. *Tax Audit Guidelines for Revenue Examiners*, Internal Revenue Manual, Washington, DC.

U.S. Department of the Treasury, Executive Office for Asset Forfeiture, Office of Assistant Secretary (Enforcement). *Guide to Equitable Sharing for Foreign Countries and Federal, State, Local Law Enforcement Agencies*, Washington, DC, 1993.

---

* The U.S. Department of Justice, federal law enforcement agencies, and many state and local law enforcement agencies have Web sites. These Web sites provide information about indictments, prosecutions, and their outcomes on various types of crimes. Some of those press releases have been used in this book. In addition, some law enforcement agencies provide advice on how to prevent becoming a victim of crime. The most notable of these agencies are the U.S. Postal Inspection Service, the Federal Trade Commission, and the Florida Attorney General's Office.

U.S. Department of the Treasury, Internal Revenue Service. *Financial Investigations,* Publication 1714 (Rev. 6-93), Catalog 15271F. Washington, DC: U.S. Government Printing Office, 1993.

U.S. Department of the Treasury, Internal Revenue Service. *Search Warrants,* Document 9026 (Rev. 6-95), Catalog 148998S, Washington, DC, 1995.

U.S. Department of the Treasury, Internal Revenue Service. *Sources of Information from Abroad,* Document 67443 (Rev. 2-93), Catalog 45395E. Washington, DC: U.S. Government Printing Office, 1993.

U.S. Department of the Treasury, Internal Revenue Service. *Special Enforcement Training for Revenue Agents,* Training 3148-02 (Rev. 8-84), TPDS 86837, Washington, DC, 1984.

U.S. Department of the Treasury, Internal Revenue Service, Criminal Tax Division. *Forfeitures,* Document 9283 (Rev. 8-94), Catalog 20996F, Washington, DC, 1994.

U.S. Department of the Treasury, Internal Revenue Service, Criminal Tax Division. *Money Laundering from the Federal Perspective,* Document 7919 (Rev. 1-93), Catalog 14337A, Washington, DC, 1993.

U.S. Department of the Treasury, Internal Revenue Service. *Internet Primer,* Document 11318 (Rev. 8-2000), Catalog 30634A, Washington, DC, 2000.

U.S. Department of the Treasury, Internal Revenue Service. *Internet/IRS Intranet Quick User Guide,* Document 11236, Catalog 29247P, Washington, DC, April 2000.

U.S. Department of the Treasury, Financial Crimes Enforcement Network (FinCen). *The Hawala Alternative Remittance System and Its Role in Money Laundering,* Vienna, VA.

U.S. General Accounting Office. *Money Laundering Regulatory Oversight of Offshore Private Banking Activities,* GAO/GGD-98-154, Washington, DC, June 1998.

U.S. Secret Service. Best Practices for Seizing Electronic Evidence, 2002, www.secretservice.gov/electronic_evidence.shtml.

U.S. Senate, Hearings before the Committee on Judiciary, *Organized Crime in America,* Serial J-98-2. U.S. Government Printing Office, Washington, DC, 1998.

Wells, Joseph T. et al. *Fraud Examiner's Manual.* Austin, TX: Association of Certified Fraud Examiners, 1989.

Storrs, K. Larry, Foreign Affairs, Defense and Trade Division, Congressional Research Service (CRS) Report to Congress. *Mexico's Counter-Narcotics Efforts Under Fox, Dec. 2000 to Oct. 2004,* Nov. 10, 2004, Order Code RL32669, Washington, DC.

Miro', Ramon. *Organized Crime and Terrorist Activity in Mexico, 1999–2002,* Federal Research Division, Library of Congress, Washington, DC, 20540-4840, Feb. 2003.

Cook, Colleen W., Foreign Affairs, Defense, and Trade Division, Congressional Research Service, Feb. 25, 2008, *Mexico's Drug Cartels,* Order Code RL34215, Washington, DC.

National Gang Intelligence Center. *National Gang Threat Assessment,* NGIC-VA #405, Washington, DC 20535, 2009, ngic@leo.gov.

Ellen, David. *Scientific Examination of Documents.* Boca Raton, FL: Taylor & Francis Group, 2006.

Huber, R. A., and A. M. Headrick. *Handwriting Identification: Facts and Fundamentals.* Boca Raton, FL: CRC Press, 1999.

Suggested Reading and References

Barlow, Hugh D. *Introduction to Criminology.* 3rd ed. Boston, MA: Little, Brown and Co., 1984.

Carson, Carl S. The underground economy: An introduction. *Survey of Current Business* 64 (1981) 21–37.

Cook, James. The invisible enterprise. *Forbes* (September 29, 1980) 60–71.

Dirty dollars: Laundering drug cash. *The Miami Herald,* 11–14 February 1990.

Drugs in America. *The Miami Herald,* 3 September 1989.

Gugliotta, Guy, and Jeff Leen. *Kings of Cocaine.* New York, NY: Harper & Row, 1989.

Kadish, Sanford H., ed. *Encyclopedia of Crime and Justice*, Vols. 1–4. New York, NY: The Free Press, 1983.

Kleinknecht, William. *The New Ethnic Mobs*. New York, NY: The Free Press, 1996.

Nash, Jay Robert. *World Encyclopedia of Organized Crime*. New York, NY: Da Capo Press, 1993.

O'Brien, Joseph F., and Andris Kurins. *Boss of Bosses*. New York, NY: Dell, 1991.

Siegel, Larry J., *Criminology Theories, Patterns and Typologies*. 5th ed. St. Paul, MN: West Publishing Co., 1995.

Sifakis, Carl. *The Mafia Encyclopedia*. New York, NY: Facts on File, 1987.

Simon, Carl P., and Anne D. Witte. *Beating the System: The Underground Economy*. Boston, MA: Auburn House Publishing, 1982.

Spitz, Barry. *Tax Havens Encyclopedia*. London, England: Butterworths, 1986.

Ullman, John, and J. Colbert. *The Reporter's Handbook*. New York, NY: St. Martin's Press, 1991.

Index

Printed in the United States
by Baker & Taylor Publisher Services